AN ENGLISH-DAKOTA DICTIONARY

John P. Williamson

With a New Foreword by
Carolynn I. Schommer

MINNESOTA HISTORICAL SOCIETY PRESS • ST. PAUL

Borealis Books are high-quality paperback reprints of books chosen by the Minnesota Historical Society Press for their importance as enduring historical sources and their value as enjoyable accounts of life in the Upper Midwest.

Cover: front, Minnesota Historical Society Collections (E.A. Bromley); back, MHS Collections

∞ The paper used in this publication meets the minimum requirements for the American National Standard for Information Sciences – Permanence for Printed Library Materials, ANSI Z39.48 – 1984.

MINNESOTA HISTORICAL SOCIETY PRESS, St. Paul 55102

First published by the American Tract Society, New York, in 1902

International Standard Book Number 0-87351-283-9
Manufactured in the United States of America
10 9 8 7 6 5 4 3 2 1

Library of Congress Cataloging-in-Publication Data

Williamson, John Poage, 1835–1917.
An English-Dakota dictionary / John P. Williamson : with a new foreword by Carolynn I. Schommer.
p. cm. – (Borealis books)
Originally published: New York : American Tract Society, 1902.
ISBN 0-87351-283-9 (alk. paper)
1. English language – Dictionaries – Dakota. 2. Dakota language – Dictionaries – English. I. Schommer, Carolynn I. II. Title.
PM1023.W62 1992
423'.975 – dc20 92-28737

FOREWORD TO THE REPRINT EDITION

During the eighteenth century Dakota tribal groups moved south and west from the central Minnesota area that they had inhabited to the Minnesota River valley and present-day South Dakota. From that period forward the Dakota people identified themselves as belonging to the Oceti Sákowin (Seven Council Fires). The seven divisions are: Wah'petonwan (in English, Wahpeton), Dwellers among the Leaves; Mdewakantonwan (Mdewakanton), Dwellers of the Spirit Lake; Sisitonwan (Sisseton), Dwellers of the Fish Grounds; Wah'pekute (Wahpekute), Leaf Shooters; Ihanktonwan (Yankton), Dwellers at the End; Ihanktonwana (Yanktonais), Little Dwellers at the End; Titonwan (Teton), Prairie Dwellers.

This migration led to changes in the Dakota language, making it a diverse language with regional variations or dialects. Dialectic divisions in the Oceti Sákowin parallel the political divisions. The first four groups named above are called the Santee, and they speak what is called the D or Dakota dialect. This dialect is used predominantly by four communities in Minnesota in the 1990s. They are the Pejihutazizi or Pajutazee (Yellow Medicine), Upper Sioux Community, at Granite Falls; Cansayapi (Trees Marked Red), Lower Sioux Community, at Morton; Mde Maya To (Blue Bank Lake), Shakopee-Mdewakanton Community, at Prior Lake; Tinta Wita (Prairie Island), Prairie Island Community, near Red Wing.

The N or Nakota dialect is used by the Yankton and Yanktonais. It can be heard on the Sisseton (Fish Ground) Reservation in Sisseton, South Dakota. The L or Lakota dialect occurs among the Teton, who reside predominantly on the Pine Ridge,

Standing Rock, Cheyenne River, and Rosebud reservations in western South Dakota.

The Dakota language and culture are one and the same. The language is the foundation of the Dakota culture. Until the mid-nineteenth century, the Dakota language existed in oral form only. In 1834 missionaries Samuel W. and Gideon H. Pond, Stephen R. Riggs, and Dr. Thomas S. Williamson, operating in Minnesota under the auspices of the American Board of Commissioners for Foreign Missions, created a written form of Dakota and translated biblical texts into it. The missionaries wanted to teach the Dakota people to read and write in their own language first; later, after learning to speak English, the Dakota learned to read and write English.

Three Dakota speakers and one Nakota speaker cooperated closely with the missionaries on the language project, which lasted into the twentieth century. They were Michael Renville, son of fur trader Joseph Renville, Sr.; the Reverend David Grey Cloud; the Reverend James Garvie; and Walking Elk, a Yankton tribal leader.

The missionaries translated the Bible into Dakota with the help of Joseph Renville, Sr., whose father was French and mother Dakota and who was bilingual in his parents' native languages. Williamson read the Bible in French, Renville translated the verses into Dakota, and Riggs and the Pond brothers struggled to write the words down. Thereafter, various chapters of the Bible, prayer books, and hymnals were issued in the D dialect. The collection effort bore additional fruit in 1852 when the *Grammar and Dictionary of the Dakota Language*, edited by Riggs and sponsored by the Minnesota Historical Society, was published by the Smithsonian Institution. An expanded version of the dictionary, also the result of work by Riggs, appeared in 1892 as *A Dakota-English Dictionary* and is the version now reprinted.

Serious study of the Dakota language was hindered by the lack of a dictionary that translated from English to Dakota. This deficiency was finally remedied in 1902 with *An English-Dakota Dictionary* edited by John P. Williamson, son of Dr. Thomas Williamson. The younger Williamson grew up speaking both Dakota and English and also became a missionary, spending most of his career at Santee Reservation in northeastern Nebraska.

Other scholars were interested in preserving the Dakota language, a part of the Siouan linguistic family. In the early twentieth century, anthropologist Franz Boas and his colleagues in linguistics, ethnology, and anthropology were working and studying toward preservation of language and customs. Ella C. Deloria, a Yankton, a student of Boas, and a graduate of Columbia University, later became an associate and collaborator. She was proficient in the translation of older, written Dakota into English. A notable aspect of these various translation projects using the D, N, and L dialects is that they were accomplished prior to 1934. Until that year the federal government had worked vigorously to eradicate the languages and culture of the indigenous people. With passage of the Indian Reorganization Act in 1934, Congress modified its stance and allowed use of native languages.

Riggs, Williamson, and the Pond brothers were in the forefront among scholars, linguists, and anthropologists who were transforming an oral language into written form. Because many sounds in the Dakota language are not present in the English language and are not comparable, the missionaries used diacritics–modifying marks indicating the different phonetic sounds. They noted differences in sounds and compared various equivalencies between the English alphabet and Dakota. They borrowed sounds from other languages, such as the German guttural and the French "j" and nasal sound. The

Dakota language structure is much different from the English, and no literal translation can be made from either language into the other.

The reprint editions of *A Dakota-English Dictionary* and *An English-Dakota Dictionary* will be a great resource for the Dakota language courses at colleges and universities and to Indian education classes in elementary and secondary schools and community colleges. The spelling system developed by Stephen Riggs and subsequently adopted and improved by Dakota speakers works quite well in Dakota language courses, provided the instructor insists that the students acquire a speaking knowledge of Dakota expressions before they refer to the written form.

These language classes are crucial to the cultural survival of the Dakota people. The preservation of the language is the key to the revitalization of Dakota culture and traditions; it will help suppress the derogatory stereotyping to which, for generations, the Dakota have been subjected. Through the oral traditions the younger generation will gain knowledge of their culture, traditions, and self-determination.

WAH'PETONWIN (Leaf Dweller Woman)
CAROLYNN I. CAVENDER SCHOMMER

American Indian Studies Department
University of Minnesota

Bibliographic Note

Barton, Winifred W. *John P. Williamson: A Brother to the Sioux.* New York: Fleming H. Revell, 1919.

Pond, Samuel W. *The Dakota or Sioux in Minnesota as They Were in 1834.* St. Paul: Minnesota Historical Society, 1908, Borealis Books, 1986.

——. *Two Volunteer Missionaries among the Dakotas, or the Story of the Labors of Samuel W. and Gideon H. Pond.* Boston: Congregational Sunday-School and Pub. Soc., 1893.

Riggs, Stephen R. *Mary and I: Forty Years with the Sioux.* Boston: Congregational Sunday-School and Pub. Soc., 1887; Minneapolis: Ross and Haines, 1969.

List of Abbreviations

adj. = adjective

adj.red. = adjective reduplicated

adv. = adverb

adv.red. = adverb reduplicated

cont. = contraction

Ih. = Ihanktonwan (Yankton)

imp. = imperative

intj. = interjection

i.q. = *idem quod* (the same as)

n. = noun

n.dim. = noun diminutive

n.p. = noun plural

num.adj. = numeral adjective

part. = participle

prep. = preposition

pron. = pronoun

red. = reduplicated

Si. = Sisseton

T. or Ti. = Titonwan (Teton)

v. = verb

v.a. = verb active

v.col.pl. = verb collective plural

v.cont. = verb contraction

v.imperat. = verb imperative

v.n. = verb noun

v.pos. = verb possessive

v.recip. = verb reciprocal

v.red. = verb reduplicated

v.reflex. = verb reflexive

INTRODUCTION.

THE DAKOTA ALPHABET.

a (ah), sound of *a* in *far*.

b (be), same as English.

c (che), sound of *ch* in *chin*.

ç, an exploded c, not in English.

d (de), same as English.

e (e), sound of *e* in *they*.

g (ghe), sound of *g* in *give*.

ġ, a guttural, not in English.

h (he), same as English.

ḣ, sound of *ch* in German *ach*.

i (e), sound of *i* in *machine*.

k (ke), same as English.

ķ an exploded k, not in English.

l (le), same as English.

m (me), same as English.

n (ne), same as English.

ŋ (in), a nasal sound, nearly similar to *n* in *ink*. In Dakota it is only used at the end of a syllable.

o (oh), sound of *o* in *go*.

p (pe), same as English.

p̧, an exploded p, not in English.

s (see), same as English.

ṡ (she), sound of *sh* in *she*.

t (te), same as English.

ţ, an exploded t, not in English.

u (oo), sound of *oo* in *ooze*.

w (we), same as English.

y (ye), same as English.

z (ze), same as English.

ż, sound of *z* in *azure*.

A few letters are sometimes followed by a short hiatus. Such are marked thus, *s'*.

There are four dialects to the Dakota language: the *Santee*, *Yankton*, *Teton* and *Assiniboin*. Each of these dialects has slight differences, not sufficient to prevent Dakotas from understanding each other. To give these differences would require additional characters to present fully; but this has not been attempted as the differences are slight. The dictionary follows in the main the Santee dialect, with which the author is most familar. The other dialects differ from it in extent, in the order named. The number of different words used in the different dialects is small. The different words used by the Yanktons and Tetons have been mostly noted. The number of words pronounced differently is very large, especially in the Teton dialect. No attempt has been made to give all these. A few have been noted to give the student an idea of the changes. In the other three dialects the sound of *l* never occurs, but the Teton changes all the *ds* and many of the *ns* into *l;* so *Dakota* becomes **Lakota**; **nina,** *very,* becomes **lila.** In the Yankton one of the most notable changes is that *hd* of the Santee becomes *kd,* and this in the Teton becomes *gl.* Thus, **hda,** *go home,* in Yankton becomes **kda,** and in Teton **gla.**

No attempt has been made to give the peculiarities of the Assiniboin dialect, as our knowledge of it is too limited.

A fuller account of the differences in the dialects may be found in Dr. S. R. Riggs' "Dakota Grammar," and a larger number of the different words in his Dakota-English Dictionary, both of which are published by the "Smithsonian Institution," Washington, D. C.

When **a** ends a word it is often changed to **e,** principally for euphony, as **ṭa kta,** to **ṭe kta.**

TO READ DAKOTA.

The Dakota is an easy language to read if one will learn the sounds of the letters, and stick to them.

The division of the words into syllables is simple. As a rule every vowel ends a syllable. The following are the exceptions:

1. The nasal ŋ always closes a syllable; as **ka-hiŋ-ta,** *sweep;* **wo-taŋ-iŋ,** *news.*

2. A syllable, contracted by dropping the vowel, is attached to the preceding syllable, thus making it close with a consonant. Ex.: **I-piḣ-ya,** *cause to boil,* is contracted from **i-pi-ġa,** *boil,* and **ya,** *cause.*

3. The words **en,** *in,* and **iṡ,** *he, she* or *it,* and their compounds, do not close the syllable with a vowel.

Accent is very important in Dakota. A misplaced accent is as bad as a mispronounced letter. Indeed a change of accent often changes the meaning of a word; as, **ma′-ġa** means *field,* whereas **ma-ġa′** means *goose.*

Most Dakota words are accented on the second syllable; and, in this dictionary, such are not marked. Then, all words commencing with **wo** are accented on the first syllable, and such are not marked. The accent on all other words is marked, and the student should carefully note such.

FORMING SENTENCES.

1. The construction of the simple sentence, composed of the bare subject and predicate, is the same as in English. Ex.: **Zitkadaŋ dowaŋpi,** *birds sing.* **Wa skaŋ,** *snow melts.*

2. Where the subject has qualifying words they follow the word they qualify. Ex.: **Wicaṡta ksapa kiŋ ia,** *the wise man talks.* **Zitkadaŋ oŋġe dowaŋpi,** *some birds sing.*

3. When the predicate has qualifying words they immediately precede the verb. Ex.: **Jane oiyokipiya dowaŋ,** *Jane sings beautifully.*

Exceptions.—(*a*) The sign of the future, **kta,** follows the verb. Ex.: **John hi kta,** *John will come.*

(*b*) The negative, **ṡni,** follows; as, **u ṡni,** *do not come.*

(*c*) **Ḣiŋ,** *very,* and its compounds **ḣiŋca** and **ḣca,** follow the verb; as, **wayazaŋke ḣiŋ,** *is very sick.*

(*d*) Connective adverbs which imply a succeeding clause follow the verb and all other qualifiers. Ex.: **Yahi kte ṡni kiŋhaŋ, mde kta,** *if you will not come, I will go.*

4. When the verb has an object, it precedes the verb but follows the subject. Ex.: **John James apa,** *John struck James.*

5. When the object has qualifying words, they follow it. Ex.: **John taḣca cepa topa o,** *John shot four fat deer.*

6. Where a number of words qualify either subject or object, they generally follow in the inverse order of the English. Ex.: **Śuŋktaŋka cistiŋna ska waŋ caŋpahmihma wiciŋyaŋna iśta-toto oẑudaŋ yusdohaŋ,** *a little white horse drew a wagon full of blue-eyed girls.*

7. An interrogative sentence is distinguished by closing it with the word **he.** Ex.: **Hokśidaŋ waśte,** *he is a good boy.* **Hokśidaŋ waśte he,** *is he a good boy?*

8. An imperative sentence is distinguished by ending it with **wo** or **ye.** The women use **ye** and the men generally **wo.** Ex.: **Den u wo,** *come here.* **Taspaŋ waŋ maḳu ye,** *please give me an apple.*

The signs of the interrogative and imperative sentences are sometimes omitted, and the fact left to be determined by the connection or tone of voice. However, the rising inflection is never given for an interrogation, but rather the opposite.

Parts of Speech.

NOUNS.

Dakota nouns make no change of form on account of number or case, and but seldom of gender.

Number is shown by numerals or other adjectives. Ex.: **Tipi waŋẑi,** *one house.* **Tipi ota,** *many houses.*

The *Case*, whether *objective* or *nominative* is shown, by the relative position in the sentence, as already explained. The *possessive* case is shown by following the word with **tawa,** *his.* Ex.: **Tipi de John tawa,** *this is John's house.* Sometimes the pronoun **tawa** is contracted to **ta** and prefixed to the principal noun; never to the possessive. Ex.: **John tahaŋpa ḳu,** *he gave him John's moccasins.* Sometimes again the possessive case is shown only by position. Ex.: **He śuŋka pa,** *that is a dog's head.*

Gender is not distinguished in most nouns. Those referring to different classes of human beings and a very few of the animals are distinguished. Ex.: **Wicasta,** *man.* **Winohiŋca,** *woman.* **Heħaka,** *male elk.* **Upaŋ,** *female elk.* If it is desired to indicate the sex of any neuter noun, **wica** and **wiŋyaŋ** are added for human beings, and **mdoka** and **wiye** for animals. Ex.: **Hokśiyopa wica,** *a male child.* **Śuŋka mdoka,** *a male dog.* Occasionally they are compounded; as, **tamdoka,** *a male deer;* **tawiye,** *a female deer.* Female proper names very often take the termination **win** (contraction of **wiŋyaŋ**); as, **Tatedutawiŋ.** The same name, **Tateduta,** *Scarlet-Wind,* is often given to men, but **wica** (*male*) is never added to it, nor is it to any other name for men.

Simple, derivative, and *compound* nouns are all found in Dakota; but the study of the language has progressed so little that there is yet much to do before a full presentation of them can be given. We, however, state some of the most common ways in which nouns are formed.

Wo prefixed to an adjective or verb transforms it into an abstract noun. Ex.: **Waśte,** *good:* **wowaśte,** *goodness.* **Ka'ta,** *hot:* **wokata,** *heat.* **Kiciza,** *fight:* **wokicize,** *a fight.* By prefixing **wica** instead of **wo** the object is limited to man; as, **kte,** *kill:* **wokte,** *slaughter:* **wicokte,** *human slaughter.*

O prefixed to a verb makes it a verbal noun, with about the same effect as prefixing the definite article in English; as, **iyuweġa,** *cross:* **oiyuweġa,** *the crossing.* Occasionally it is prefixed to an adjective with the same force.

Wa prefixed to a transitive verb changes it into a noun, signifying the agent; as, **apa,** *strike:* **waapa,** *striker.* Sometimes the plural form of the verb is used, making the prefix **wica,** instead of **wo**; as, **yaśica,** *to slander:* **wicayaśica,** *a slanderer.*

I, prefixed to an active verb, makes a noun signifying the instrument by which the action is done; as, **kahiŋta,** *sweep:* **icahiŋte,** *broom;* **yumdu,** *to plow:* **iyumdu,** *a plow.*

The third person plural of any verb may be used as a verbal noun; as, **mani,** *walk:* **manipi,** *walking.*

Kin, after any adjective, noun or clause, shows it is used as a noun.

Daŋ (*Y.* **na**; *T.* **la**) is often suffixed to nouns, verbs and adjectives. It is a diminutive, and is generally attached to the last word in the clause, but refers to the leading noun, whether subjective or objective; as, **John śiyo waŋ ktedaŋ**, *John killed a little prairie chicken.*

Compound nouns are numerous and may be made of any part of speech. Sometimes of two nouns; as, **watapeta** (*fire boat*), *steamboat;* sometimes of a noun and adjective: as, **hasapa** (*black skin*), *negro;* sometimes of a noun and verb: as, **ḣemani** (*walks on land*), *railway train.*

PRONOUNS.

The *personal pronouns* are generally incorporated in the verb; and the objective are different from the subjective; and in incorporate pronouns the third person singular is never expressed, and only the sign of the plural for the third person plural.

The *subjective incorporate pronouns* are: **ya,** *thou;* **wa,** *I;* **ya--pi,** *you;* **un--pi,** *we.* Ex.: **Kte,** *he kills;* **yakte,** *you kill;* **wakte,** *I kill;* **ktepi,** *they kill;* **unktepi,** *we kill.*

The *objective incorporate pronouns* are: **ni,** *thee;* **ma,** *me;* **ni--pi,** *you;* **uŋ--pi,** *us.* Ex.: **Nikte,** *he kills thee;* **makte,** *he kills me;* **niktepi,** *he kills you;* **uŋktepi,** *he kills us.*

When both are incorporated they are as follows: **iċi,** *he--himself;* **ni--pi,** *he--you;* **uŋ--pi,** *he--us;* **maya,** *thou--me;* **wicaya,** *thou--them;* **uŋya--pi,** *thou--us;* **niċi,** *thou--thyself;* **miċi,** *I--myself;* **wicawa,** *I--them;* **ci--pi,** *I--you;* **iċi--pi,** *they--themselves;* **ni--pi,** *they--thee,* or *you;* **ma--pi,** *they--me;* **wica--pi,** *they them;* **uŋ--pi,** *they--us;* **niċi--pi,** *you--yourselves;* **maya--pi,** *you--me;* **wicaya--pi,** *you--them;* **uŋya--pi,** *you--us;* **uŋkici--pi,** *we--ourselves;* **uŋni--pi,** *we--thee;* **wicuŋ--pi,** *we--them;* **uŋni--pi,** *we--you.*

When we reach the verb further examples of incorporate pronouns will be given.

Separate Personal Pronouns are also found in Dakota. They are: **Miye** or **miś,** *I;* **niye** or **niś,** *thou;* **iye** or **iś,** *he* or *she;* **uŋkiyepi,** *us;* **niyepi,** *you;* **iyepi,** *them.* Ex.: **Iye, niye qa miye uŋyaŋpi kta,** *he, you and I will go.* The same pronouns are used for the objective case. Ex.: **Iye, niye qa miye kapi,** *they meant him, thee and me.*

The *Possessive Personal Pronouns* are: **Tawa,** *his;* **nitawa,** *thy* or *thine;* **mitawa,** *my* or *mine;* **tawapi,** *their* or *theirs;* **nitawapi,** *your* or *yours;* **uŋkitawapi,** *our* or *ours.* Ex.: **Tipi tawa,** *his house.* The possessive pronouns are often prefixed to the noun, in which case the syllable **wa** and often the two syllables **tawa** are stricken out. Ex.: **Siha,** *foot;* **tasiha,** *his foot;* **misiha,** *my foot;* **tasihapi,** *their feet.* **Ma'ġa,** *field;* **mita'maġa,** *my field.* Sometimes the first person singular is contracted to **ma** instead of **mi**; as, **mapa,** *my head.*

There is also a Possessive Personal Pronoun that is incorporated in the verb. It is: **ki,** *his;* **ye,** *thy;* **we,** *mine.* Ex.: **John pte kikte,** *John killed his cow.*

The *demonstrative pronouns* are **de.** *this,* and **he,** *that;* **dena,** *these,* and **hena,** *those.* Also **ka,** *that,* and **kana,** *those.* They have also a number of compounds, as: **decen,** *like this;* **deceedaŋ,** *this alone;* **denaos,** *these two;* **denakeca,** *these many.*

The *interrogative pronouns* are **tuwe,** *who;* **taku,** *what;* **tukte,** *which;* **uŋmaŋtukte,** *which* or *whether;* **tona, tonaka, tonakeca,** *how many.* The above are either *subjective or objective.* The only *possessive* is **tuwe tawa,** *whose.*

The only *definitive relative pronoun* is **he,** *that, who, which, what, whose.* Ex.: **Winoḣiŋca wayazaŋke ciḳoŋ he waŋna asni,** *the woman who was sick is now recovered.* Any of the interrogative pronouns may be used as *indefinite relative pronouns.* Ex.: **Tuwe kte kiŋ taŋyaŋ sdonyapi,** *who killed him is well known.*

The *indefinite pronouns* are nearly all the equivalents of the English, and are used much like adjectives.

VERBS.

In Dakota the pronoun is incorporated in the verb, but for the third person singular no incorporate pronoun is used. Therefore, for the *bare* form of the verb we look to the third person singular, and not to the infinitive as in English, and that is the form in the Dictionary. Thus, if you look for the verb *come* you will find **u.** That means *he comes.* Then **yau** means *you come;* **wau,** *I come;* **upi,** *they come;* **yaupi,** *you come;* **uŋkupi,** *we come* From this you see the incorporate subjective pronouns are: **ya,** *thou;* **wa,** *I;* **ya--pi,** *you;* **un--pi,** *we.* Also you will note that the sign of the plural, **pi,** is added to the third personal plural, to distinguish it from the third person singular, and that in the first person plural **k** is inserted for euphony.

If the verb is *transitive,* the *objective* pronouns are also inserted. They are: **ni,** *thee;* **ma,** *me;* **wica,** *them;* **ni--pi,** *you;* **uŋ--pi,** *us.* As an example take the verb **kte,** *kill.*

He kills him, **kte;** *he kills thee,* **nikte;** *he kills me,* **makte;** *he kills them,* **wicakte;** *he kills you,* **niktepi;** *he kills us,* **uŋktepi.** *Thou killest him,* **yakte;** *thou killest me,* **mayakte;** *thou killest them,* **wicayakte;** *thou killest us,* **uŋyaktepi.** *I kill him,* **wakte;** *I kill thee,* **cikte;** *I kill them,* **wicawakte;** *I kill you,* **ciktepi.** *They kill him,* **ktepi;** *they kill thee,* **niktepi;** *they kill me,* **maktepi;** *they kill them,* **wicaktepi;** *they kill you,* **niktepi;** *they kill us,* **uŋktepi.** *You kill him,* **yaktepi;** *you kill me,* **mayaktepi;** *you kill them,* **wicayaktepi;** *you kill us,* **uŋyaktepi.** *We kill him,* **uŋktepi;** *we kill thee,* **uŋniktepi;** *we kill them,* **wicuŋktepi;** *we kill you,* **uŋniktepi.**

Besides the *singular* and *plural* numbers given above, the Dakota has also the *dual* number. It consists of the person speaking and the person spoken to, and only in the subjective case, and is therefore equivalent to *we two.* In form it is the same as the plural without the plural ending **pi.** Thus, take the verb **waŋka,** *lie down:* **uŋwaŋkapi** is *we lie down:* and **uŋwaŋka,** *we two lie down.* Intransitive verbs like this can only take one form. Transitive verbs can take the third person plural objective pronoun. Thus, with the verb **kte,** *kill,* two dual forms may be used: **uŋkte,** *we kill him;* and **wicuŋkte,** *we kill them.* No one verb takes more than these two forms.

The *relative position* of incorporate pronouns should be noted. The objective, as a rule, precedes; as, **mayakte,** *you kill me.* There is one exception. The first person plural pronoun always precedes the second person, whether subjective or objective. Ex.: **Uŋniktepi,** *we kill you.*

The *position of the pronouns* in the verb must also be noted. So far the verbs selected have had the pronouns prefixed, and the most Dakota verbs have the pronouns prefixed. But a large number of verbs insert them after the first syllable. Ex.: **Mani,** *walk;* **mayani,** *you walk,* etc. A few verbs insert the pronouns after the second syllable. Ex.: **Ituħaŋ,** *give away;* **ituwaħaŋ,** *I give away,* etc.

The sign of the plural, **pi,** is always placed at the end of the verb. Ex.: **Yuta,** *eat;* **uŋyutapi,** *we eat.* When an adverbial particle is attached to the verb, it is placed after the sign of the plural. *Ex.:* The diminutive particle **daŋ. Hokšiyopa ceyapidaŋ,** *the little babies cry.*

Contractions resulting from the incorporation of the pronouns are quite numerous. 1. Where **wa** and **ya** come before **ki** the two syllables are contracted to **we** and **ye**; as, **wehdeġa** for **wakihdeġa,** *I overtake;* and **ayektoŋża** for **ayakiktoŋża,** *you forget.*

2. Where the pronouns come before **y** in the second person, **yay** is changed to **d,** and in the first person **way** to **md.** Ex.: **Yatkaŋ,** *drink,* becomes **datkaŋ,** *you drink;* and **mdatkaŋ,** *I drink.* **Iyotaŋka,** *sits,* becomes **idotaŋka,** *you sit;* **imdotaŋka,** *I sit.* One of the verbs of this class, **yuta,** *eat,* drops its first syllable and prefixes the pronouns without change; as, **yata,** *you eat;* **wata,** *I eat.*

SECOND CLASS.

So far we have spoken only of one class of verbs; those which have the corporate pronoun **wa,** *I,* for the first person singular subjective. We come now to speak of another class, in which the first person singular is **ma.** The class is not very numerous, being mostly intransitive verbs, and not all of them. Ex.: **Asni,** *get well;* **anisni,** *you get well;* **amasni,** *I get well;* **asnipi,** *they get well;* **anisnipi,** *you get well;* **uŋkasnipi,** *we get well.* **Ištiŋma,** *sleep;* **ništiŋma, mištiŋma,** etc. **Wayazaŋka,** *sick;* **waniyazaŋka, wamayazaŋka,** etc.

A number of verbs in this class make changes in incorporating the pronoun.

1. Simply drop the pronoun vowel. Ex.: **Un,** *use;* **nuŋ,** *thou usest;* **muŋ,** *I use.* **Ihduhomni,** *turn self around;* **miduhomni,** *I turn myself around,* etc. Most reflective verbs commencing with **ihd** take this form.

2. Some, in addition to dropping the vowel of the pronoun, drop the succeeding consonant in the verb. Ex.: **Yaŋka,** *is situated;*

maŋka, *I am situated.* **Owiŋża,** *spread to lie on;* **omiŋża,** *I spread to lie on*, etc. **Iwaŋġa,** *ask,* changes also the succeeding vowel **a** to **o**; thus, **inoŋġa,** *thou askest;* **imoŋġa,** *I ask.* In the incorporation of the objective pronoun the consonant **y** is restored; as, **imayanoŋġa,** *thou askest me.*

3. There are a few verbs which suffix the pronouns, with other changes. Ex.: **Iŋ,** *wear,* prefixes **h** and suffixes the pronouns, thus: **hiŋni,** *thou wearest;* **hiŋmi,** *I wear.* **Eciŋ,** *consider;* **ecaŋmi,** *I consider*, etc. **Ecoŋ,** *do;* **ecanoŋ,** *you do;* **ecamoŋ,** *I do.*

Eya, *say,* together with its compounds **heya** and **keya,** are alike, but still more irregular. **Eha,** *thou sayest;* **epa,** *I say.* **Ehapi,** *you say;* **uŋkeyapi,** *we say.*

THIRD CLASS.

To this class belong what are called adjective and substantive verbs, which have the same set of incorporate pronouns as the Second Class, and we speak of them separately because of the peculiarity of their formation and the great extent to which they are used. Any adjective or noun may be so used.

The construction is much the same as the use in English of the adjective and substansive verbs with the *copula.* But in Dakota the copula is omitted. Thus: *John is tall,* in Dakota is **John haŋska.** Here is a complete sentence, a definite assertion, with what appears to be only a noun and adjective. But **haŋska** is here more than an adjective, or it would not be an assertion. The two words are used to assert that *John is tall.* It is then more than an adjective. It is a complete predicate, and combines the powers of adjective and verb.

Perhaps a clearer analysis would be to say that it is predicate adjective, and that in Dakota the copula is understood with predicate adjectives and nouns.

These predicates, from the nature of the case, have no objective pronouns, and, as already stated, the subjective incorporate pronouns are of the Second Class. And, like other classes, they are incorporated between different syllables. Ex.: **Waśte,** *he is good;* **niwaśte,** *thou art good;* **mawaśte,** *I am good;* **waśtepi,** *they are good;* **niwaśtepi,** *you are good;* **uŋwaśtepi,** *we are good.* **Dakota,** *he is a Dakota;* **Damakota,** *I am a Dakota;* **Danikota,** *thou art a Dakota,* etc.

In some instances the student may be at a loss to know whether an adjective or a noun is in the predicate or not. For instance, does **John haŋska** mean *John is tall* or *tall John.* It might mean either, and so is ambiguous. But in fact one need seldom be in doubt. In this case, if the connection shows that **John haŋska** is a complete sentence, it must mean *John is tall.* Whereas if another predicate follows, and the full sentence is, **John haŋska waŋna hi,** then **haŋska** is only an adjective, and the translation is, *Tall John has come.*

TENSE.

As we have now seen, inflections in the form of the verb show very fully the *person* and *number* to which it relates. In the matter of *time* and *mode* no changes are made in the form of the verb. *Tense* and *mode* are shown by auxiliaries and not by inflection.

The time expressed in the body of the verb is *aorist*, that is, indefinite, completed time. And it is used both for the past and present. Ex.: **Waŋhiŋkpe wakaġe,** *I made an arrow.*

The definite time is often shown by circumstances. Ex.: (*Present*) **Taku yakaġa he?** *what are you making?* **Waŋhiŋkpe wakaġa,** *I am making an arrow.* Sometimes it is shown by adverbs of time. Ex.: (*Preterite*) **Ḣtanihaŋ waŋhiŋkpe wakaġa,** *yesterday I made an arrow.* (*Perfect*) **Wanna mduśtaŋ,** *I have finished it.* If the present tense is to be distinguished, **dehan** is the most definite word, though **wanna** is also used.

Future time is shown by the auxiliary **kta,** which is placed immediately after the verb. Ex.: **Wakaġe kta,** *I will make it.*

The *future perfect* has no regular form of expression. Sometimes it is not distinguished from the future. Ex.: *Do good and you will not have lived in vain,* **taku waśte econ, ḳa ituya yani kte śni.** Sometimes **waŋna** is introduced as in the present perfect. Ex.: *Will he have collected enough money?* **Mazaska iye waŋna mnaye kta he.**

MODES.

As already stated there are no changes of inflection to designate different modes. The *Indicative* is the regular form, the only one I have so far referred to.

The *Subjunctive Mode*, being one of conditional assertion, is made by adding **kinhaŋ, uŋkanś; śta, keś,** or some other conditional conjunction to the end of the clause. Ex.: **Yahi śni kiŋhaŋ, mde kte śni,** *if you do not come, I will not go.*

The Dakota is not adapted to the classification of a *Potential Mode.* The different senses of our English auxiliaries would require many more auxiliary verbs in Dakota. Ex.: *I can* (am able to) *go,* **mda owakihi.** *I can* (am permitted to) *go,* **mda iyowiŋmakiyapi.** Then again, many potential clauses are paraphrased in Dakota. Ex.: *It may be so,* **okini hecetu.** *Whatever may happen,* **toketu çeyaś.**

The *Imperative Mode* is formed by placing certain particles immediately after the bare form of the verb. The regular particles used are **wo** and **ye,** in the singular, and **po** and **pe** in the plural. **Wo** and **po** are used in command, and **ye** and **pe** in entreaty. For propriety's sake the women never use the former. Ex.: **U wo,** *come.* **U ye,** *do come* (or *please come*). These are said only to a single person.

With transitive verbs the Imperative takes the objective pronouns. Ex. When a single person is spoken to: **Ḳu wo,** *give it to him.* When more than one is spoken to: **Wicaḳu po,** *give it to them.*

Instead of **pe, miye** is sometimes used, and this again is sometimes contracted to **m.** Ex.: Instead of **Iŋyaŋka pe,** *run,* they sometimes say **iŋyaŋka miye,** and sometimes **iŋyaŋkam.**

Sometimes the sign of the Imperative is omitted.

THE INFINITIVE.

When the *Infinitive* is the object of a verb the root form is used. Ex.: **U ciŋ,** *he wants to come.*

There is no sign of the Infinitive, but the sign of the future is generally used. Ex.: **U kta ciŋ,** *he wants to come.*

The Infinitive takes the incorporate pronouns. Ex.: **Kicizapi ciŋpi,** *they want to fight.* **Wicakizapi ciŋpi,** *they want to fight them.*

When the infinitive is the subject of another verb it takes the form of the third person plural. Ex.: **Waŋyakapi he wicadapi ee,** *to see is to believe.*

THE PARTICIPLE.

The *Present Participle* takes the root form of the verb. Ex.: **Hokšidaŋ waŋ iŋyaŋka waŋmdaka,** *I saw a boy running.*

The *Past Participle* takes the form of the third personal plural. Ex.: **Wicašta nakaha ktepi iyewaya,** *I discovered a man just killed.*

The transitive participle takes an object. **Taȟca kute uŋkipi,** *we went shooting deer.*

THE PASSIVE VOICE.

The Dakota verb has no distinctive form for the Passive Voice. Instead of saying: *I was struck by John,* they say, *John struck me,* **John amapa.**

Where the form is the indefinite passive the third person plural active is always used. Ex.: *John was struck,* **John apapi**; that is, *they struck John. He was a man that was loved,* **wicašta waštedapi heca.**

OTHER VERBAL MODIFICATIONS.

The Dakota verb has some other modal changes peculiar to the language. Sometimes a syllable is repeated to indicate repetition of action. Ex.: **Apa,** *strike;* **apapa,** *strike repeatedly.* The accented syllable is generally repeated.

Then there is a set of causative incorporate verbal prefixes which show the manner of the action. They are: **ba, bo, ka, na, pa, ya** and **yu. Ba** means it is done with a sawing motion; **bo,** by a blowing, shooting or punching motion; **ka,** by a striking or sweeping motion; **na,** by kicking or bursting; **ya,** by biting; **yu,** in an indefinite manner. These prefixes are attached to verbal roots, neuter verbs and adjectives. Ex.: **Ksa** (root), *separate;* **baksa,** *separate by cutting;* **boksa,** *by blowing,* etc. **Ska** (*adj.*), *white;* **yuska,** *make white.* **Ṭa,** *die;* **kaṭa,** *cause to die by striking.*

There is also a causative suffix, **ya,** with the same meaning as the prefix **yu.** Thus: **nažiŋ,** *stand;* **yunažiŋ** and **nažiŋya,** are both used for, *cause to stand.* Some verbs take the suffix and some the prefix; rarely either may be used. The suffix can only be used with other verbs.

ADJECTIVES.

The Dakota adjective, like the noun, is not declined. There are no changes for person, number, or case.

Comparison is shown by qualifying words: **saŋpa,** *more*, and **iyotaŋ,** *most.* Ex.: *Good,* **waŝte**; *better,* **saŋpa waŝte**; *best,* **iyotaŋ waŝte.**

Another form is sometimes used. If one asks, *Which is the larger?* he says, **tukte taŋka?** And if the other replies, *This is larger than that,* he says, **de taŋka he cistiŋna.**

Reduplication of a syllable expresses much the same idea as with the verb, but as it implies the plural, it is sometimes spoken of as the plural. Ex.: **Mdo waŝteŝte,** *nice potatoes.* The true sense is doubtless, *potatoes successively nice.*

The plural ending **pi** is often attached to adjectives, but as we understand, it is a verbal termination, and is properly attached only to verbal adjectives. Ex.: **Wicaŝta waŝtepi,** *they are good men.* **Wicaŝta waŝte hipi,** *good men have come.*

ADVERBS.

Adverbs need cause the student no trouble, as there are few changes from the form found in the dictionary. As in English, they qualify verbs, adjectives and other adverbs.

Their *position* is immediately before the word they qualify. Ex.: *He did well,* **taŋyaŋ ecoŋ.** There are a few exceptions to this rule. (*a*) The negative **ŝni,** *not;* and **hiŋca,** *very,* follow the words they qualify. Ex.: **Ecamoŋ ŝni,** *I did not do it.* **Taŋka hiŋca,** *very large.* (*b*) Interrogative pronouns are the first words in the sentence. Ex.: **Tokeca niṭapi kta he.** *Why will ye die?* (*c*) **He,** which might be called an interrogative exclamation, always closes the sentence. Ex.: **Yau he.** *Are you coming?*

The number of *primitive* adverbs in Dakota is not large, but the facility of forming *derivatives* is ready and well improved. They may be formed from any part of speech, but are largely formed from adjectives, verbs, pronouns and adverbs.

1. The suffix **ya** (or **yaŋ**) attached to an adjective or verb transforms it into an adverb with much the effect as the suffix *ly* in English.

Ex.: **Śica,** *bad;* **śicaya,** *badly.* **Iyuśkiŋ,** *rejoice;* **iyuśkiŋyaŋ,** *rejoicingly.* Sometimes there is a contraction: **Oŋśika,** *poor;* **oŋśiya,** *poorly.*

2. The *demonstrative pronouns* are transformed into a large number of adverbs, mostly by suffixes.

(*a*) The suffix **en,** *in,* contracted makes **den,** *here,* and **hen,** *there;* also **tukten,** *where,* and **kan,** *yonder,* etc.

(*b*) The suffixes **ki, ci, kiya** and **ciya** make adverbs used with verbs of motion. Ex.: **Kaki,** *that way;* **deciya,** *this way.*

(*c*) The suffixes **ken** and **cen** make adverbs of manner. Ex.: **Decen,** *in this manner.* **Kaken,** *in that manner.*

(*d*) The suffixes **han** and **haŋ** form adverbs of time and locality. Each may refer to time or place, which is to be determined by the connection. **Han** conveys the idea of *at;* **haŋ** of *to.* Thus: **hehan,** *at that time,* or *at that place;* **hehaŋ,** *to that time,* or *to that place.* Ex.: **Hehan ecamoŋ kta,** *I will do it at that time* (*then*)*;* **hehan ehde kta,** *he will set it up at that place* (*there*). **Hehaŋ wani kiŋhaŋ,** *if I live to that time* (*till then*)*;* **hehaŋ wai kiŋhaŋ,** *if I go to* (*reach*) *that place.*

To form adverbs from other adverbs there are a number of suffixes used. **Tkiya** has about the same force as the English suffix *wards.* Ex.: **kun,** *down;* **kuntkiya,** *downwards.* The suffix **yaŋ** has the force of *to.* Ex.: **Hehan,** *there;* **hehaŋyaŋ,** *to there.* Sometimes they are accumulative, with only the object of holding to the idea. Ex.: **Dehan,** *now;* **dehantu,** *at now;* **dehantuya,** *about at now;* **dehantuyaken,** *somewhere at about now.*

Prepositions are sometimes transformed into adverbs by suffixing **tu, tuya, ya** and **wapa.** Ex.: **Mahenya iyotaŋka,** *he sat inside.*

PREPOSITIONS.

Prepositions have no proper inflection, but where they govern the objective pronoun the pronoun is generally incorporated in the preposition. Ex.: **Śuŋka niyahna hi,** *a dog came with you.* In the union they are often contracted. Ex.: **Micahda** (**miye icahda**) **iyotaŋka,** *sit by me.* The objective pronouns are not always incorporated. Ex.: **Miye etkiya u,** *he comes towards me.*

When the preposition governs nouns, or unincorporate pronouns, its position is not before but after the word it governs and its qualifying words. Ex.: **Tipi ska taŋka etaŋhaŋ,** *from the big white house.*

There are a number of prepositions in Dakota that are incorporated into other words.

To nouns are affixed **ta, ata** and **yata,** all meaning *at* or *to.* Ex.: **Tiyata uŋ,** *he is at the house.* **Caŋyata iyaya,** *he has gone to the woods.* **Akan, on,** is often suffixed. Ex.: **Ḣeakan,** *on the hill.* **En** is also suffixed, but generally contracted to **n.** Ex.: **Tin u,** *come in the house.*

The first four vowels are used as prepositional attachments to intransitive verbs, enabling them to take an object, and occasionally to a transitive verb, enabling it to take a second object. The prefix **a** has the force of *on.* Ex.: **Caġa amani,** *he walked on the ice.* The prefix **e** signifies *to.* Ex.: **Atkuku ekihdeġa,** *he overtook* (*reached to*) *his father.* The prefix **i** means *for, on account of.* Ex.: **Cekiya,** *pray;* **icekiya,** *pray for.* The prefix **o** means *in.* Ex.: **Kaŝtaŋ,** *pour;* **okaŝtaŋ,** *pour in.*

Prepositions are both *primitive and compound,* but neither are numerous; neither is their composition intricate. One of the most numerous classes of derivatives is formed from adverbs of place by prefixing **i.** Ex.: *Walk behind,* **hekta mani;** *walk behind the horse,* **ŝuŋktaŋka ihektam mani.**

CONJUNCTIONS.

The form and construction of conjunctions is so simple and so similar to the English that we need use no space for them here.

EXCLAMATIONS.

Exclamations are plentiful, but often local, and soon change.

The Dictionary.

The abbreviations are mostly the same as found in other dictionaries, with the following exceptions. *S.* stands for *Santee;* *Y.* for *Yankton;* and *T.* for *Teton.*

The most common definition is placed first.

English-Dakota Dictionary

A

a, *a.* Waŋ ; waŋżi.
aback, *adv.* He'kta.
abandon, *vt.* Enakiya ; eħpeya.
abandoned, *pa.* Eħpeyapi ; śi'ca.
abase, *vt.* Yuhukuya.
abash, *vt.* Inihaŋya.
abate, *vi.* Asni aya. *vt.* Asni kiya; a'okpaniya.
Abba, *n.* Ate.
abbreviate, *vt.* Yuptecedaŋ.
abdicate, *vi.* Enakiya.
abdomen, *n.* Cowohe ; paġe.
abduct, *vt.* Naħmaŋicu ; i'naħbe.
abed, *adv.* Owiŋża ohna.
abet, *vt.* O'kiya.
abeyance, *n.* Woakipe.
abhor, *vt.* Waħtedaśni.
abhorrence, *n.* Wowaħtedaśni.
abide, *vi.* Uŋ ; yaŋka ; ti ; owaŋżi uŋ. *vt.* Akipe.
ability, *n.* Wowaś'ake ; wookihi.
abject, *a.* Waciŋyeyeśni ; ihanke.
abjure, *vt.* Wakaŋtaŋka cażeyan eħpeya.
ablaze, *a.* Ide.
able, *a.* Okihi ; waokihi.
ablution, *n.* Woyużaża.
ably, *adv.* Waśagya.
aboard, *adv.* Akan ; o'pa.
abode, *n.* Ti'pi ; ouŋyaŋ.
abode, *imp.* of ABIDE.
abolish, *vt.* Enakiya.
abominable, *a.* Waħteśni.
abominate, *vt.* Waħtedaśni.
aboriginal, *a.* Otokahe.
aborigines, *n.* Ikcewicaśta.
abound, *vi.* O'ta ; żinya uŋ.
about, *prep.* 1. O'kśaŋ ; ohomni : *about the house.* 2. Ecetu : *about a dozen men.* 3. Eciyataŋhaŋ ; oŋ : *about the war.*
about, *adv.* O'kśan ; ohomni ; wi'yeya uŋ : ikiyedaŋ.
above, *prep.* Iwaŋkam ; i'saŋpa.
above, *adv.* Waŋkan ; akantu.
aboveboard, *adv.* Taŋiŋyaŋ.
abreast, *a.* I'cipatkuħ ; iyehan.
abridge, *vt.* Yuptecena.
abroad, *adv.* Tokaŋ ; taŋ'kaya ; makoce to'keca.
abrogate, *vt.* Yuecetu śni.
abrupt, *a.* Ihnuhaŋ to'keca.
abruptly, *adv.* Ihnuhaŋna.
abscess, *n.* Toŋye.
abscond, *vt.* Naħmaŋiyaye.
absence, *n.* 1. Yokaŋ uŋ : *a week's absence.* 2. Wanica : *in the absence of war.*
absent, *a.* En uŋ śni ; tokaŋ uŋ.
absent, *vt.* Ihdutokaŋ.
absentminded, *a.* Kiksuyeśni.
absolute, *a.* A'taya ; suta.
absolution, *n.* Wakażużupi.
absolve, *vt.* Kiyuśka ; ki'cicażużu.
absorb, *vt.* Yuħepa ; icu ; e'cedaŋ awaciŋ.

absorption, *n.* Oyuḣepa.
abstain, *vi.* Ihdutokaŋ.
abstinence, *n.* Ikpataŋpi.
abstract, *vt.* Icu; manoŋ. *n.* Yucoya owapi. *a.* Coyapi; maḣentu.
abstruse, *a.* Okaḣniḣśica.
absurd, *a.* Eyepicaśni; iyecetuśni; wowiḣa.
abundance, *n.* Wotaŋtoŋ; o'ta.
abundant, *a.* O'ta; otaŋtoŋ.
abuse, *vt.* Śicaya kuwa; yaśica. *n.* Śicaya kuwapi.
abusive, *a.* Śicaya wicakuwa.
abut, *vi.* Ipataŋ haŋ.
abyss, *n.* Wośbe.
academy, *n.* Wooŋspetipi ocoka.
accede, *vi.* Iyowiŋyaŋ; o'ŝtaŋ iwaŋka.
accelerate, *vt.* Yuoḣaŋko.
accent, *vt.* Ho ni'na eya; iyapa. *n.* Ho iyapapi.
accept, *vt.* Icu; iyokipi; iyowiŋyaŋ.
acceptable, *a.* Iyowicakipi.
acceptance, *n.* Icu kta eya; woiyokipi.
access, *n.* Oau.
accessible, *a.* En u'pi waŝte.
accession, *n.* Aicaġe; o'papi.
accessory, *a.* O'kiya.
accident, *n.* Wanuwoakipa.
accidental, *a.* Ecaken; wanu.
acclamation, *n.* I'yaŝ'api.
acclimate, *vt.* Makiyokipiya.
acclivity, *n.* Maya.
accommodate, *vt.* Taŋyaŋ kuwa; pikiya.
accommodating, *pa.* Wawiyowiŋyaŋ.
accompaniment, *n.* Kicica.
accompany, *vt.* Kici ya.
accomplice, *n.* Kici ecoŋ.
accomplish, *vt.* Yuŝtaŋ; ecoŋ.
accomplishment, *n.* Woyuŝtaŋ.
accord, *vt.* Ḳu. *vi.* Tawaciŋ waŋżi. *n.* O'waŋżina.
accordance, *n.* O'waŋżina uŋpi.
according to, *prep.* Ohnayaŋ.
accordingly, *adv.* He'cen; iyecen.
accost, *vt.* Ho'uya.
account, *v.* To'ketu oyaka; yawa. *n.* 1. Oicazo owapi: *you keep the account.* 2. Oyakapi: *an account of his journey.* 3. Wowiyukcaŋ: *on no account.* 4. Wowiyuŋyaŋpi: *of no account.*
accountable, *a.* Ohdake kta.
accountant, *n.* Oicazoowa.
accouter, *vt.* Koyagya.
accrue, *vt,* Aicaġa.
accumulate, *vt.* Mnayaŋ; pahi. *vi.* O'taaya; wapahi.
accumulation, *n.* Womnaye.
accuracy, *n.* Yuŝnaŝnieconpi.
accurate, *a.* Wayuŝnaŝni.
accurately, *adv.* Yuŝnaŝni.
accursed, *pa.* Yaŝicapi.
accusable, *a.* Iyaoŋpepica.
accusation, *n.* Woiyaoŋpa.
accuse, *vt.* Iyaoŋpa.
accustom, *vt.* Ecewaktakiya.
accustomed, *pa.* Ecewakta.
ache, *vi.* Yazaŋ. *n.* Woyazaŋ.
achieve, *vt.* Okihi; ohiya.
achievement, *n.* Ta'ku okihipi.
acid, *a.* Śkumna; sku'ya.
acknowledge, *vt.* Ohdaka; he'cetu keya.
acme, *n.* Iŋ'kpa.
acorn, *n.* U'ta.
acquaint with, *vt.* 1. Sdonyekiya: *acquaint him with the facts.* 2. Sdonkiya; iyekiya; *acquainted with each other.*
acquaintance, *n.* Iyekiciyapi.
acquainted, *pa.* Wasdonya.
acquiesce, *vt.* Iyowiŋkiya.
acquire, *vt.* Kamna; okini; oŋspe; mnayaŋ.
acquired, *pa.* Oŋspekiyapi.
acquisition, *n.* Wakamnapi.
acquit, *vt.* Ecoŋŝniyacopi; kiyuŝka; ihunikiya.
acquittal, *n.* Kiyuŝkapi
acre, *n.* Makaoŝpe.
acrid, *a.* Pa; ṭa'ġa.

acrimony, *n.* Woyaṭaġe; woyaśice.
across, *prep.* & *adv.* 1. O'pta; hdakiŋyaŋ: *go across; sweep across.* 2. Akasaŋpa; *I.* koakata; ako: *he lives across the river.*
act, *vt.* Ecoŋ; śka'ta; *vi.* Śkaŋ; śka'ta. *n.* Woecoŋ; wokaġe.
action, *n.* Wośkiŋciye; oḣaŋ; wicoḣaŋ; waecoŋpi.
active, *a.* Mdiheca; oḣaŋko.
activity, *n.* Womdiheca; ni'naśkaŋ.
actor, *n.* Waecon; śka'ta.
actual, *a.* Wowicake.
actually, *a.* A'wicakeya.
actuate, *vt.* I'yopaśtaka.
acute, *a.* Pe'sto; waciŋksapa.
adage, *n.* Ehaŋna wicoie.
adapt, *vt.* Kipiya ka'ġa.
add, *vt.* 1. Yuwitaya: *add two and ten.* 2. Aehnaka: *I will add my mite.*
adder, *n.* Wamduśkaśica.
addict, *vt.* Ecoŋsa; ecoŋkiya.
addition, *n.* Yuwitayapi; oŋśpa akaġapi.
additional, *a.* Saŋ'pa.
address, *vt.* 1. Wahokoŋkiya; eciya: *he addressed the people.* 2. Oz'uha akan owa: *address a letter.* 3. Kuwa. *n.* Woowohdake; oz'uha akan owapi; tuktenyeyapi; wohdakapi en opiiçiyapi; okiyapi; wowayupika.
adduce, *vt.* Cażeyata; pazo.
adept, *n.* Wayupika.
adequate, *a.* Iyenakeca; iyecetu.
adhere, *vi.* O'ha; o'skapa; opa.
adherent, *n.* O'peyauŋ.
adhesion, *n.* Wi'yaskape.
adhesive, *a.* I'kapa; a'skape.
adieu, *n.* Wakaŋtaŋka onsinida nuŋ.
adjacent, *a.* I'yokihe; ikiyena.
adjective, *n.* Wocaże o'kihe.
adjoin, *vt.* I'yokihe uŋ. *vi.* I'ciyokihe uŋ.
adjourn, *vt.* Kihnaka; aehnaka; enakiye.
adjudge, *vt.* Yuhe kta yaco.
adjudicate, *vt.* Yaco; *Y.* yasu.
adjunct, *n.* Ta'ku ikoyake.
adjure, *vt.* Wakaŋtaŋka cażeyan eciya.
adjust, *vt.* Kipiya ka'ġa.
adjustable, *a.* Piyepica.
adjustment, *n.* Piyapi.
adjutant, *n.* Akicita o'kihe itaŋcaŋ.
administer, *vt.* Ecoŋ; wicaḳu; awaŋyaka; kicaŋyaŋ.
administration, *n.* Kicaŋyaŋpi.
admirable, *a.* Waśtedapi.
admirably, *adv.* Yaŋyaŋ.
admiral, *n.* Ozuyewata itaŋcaŋ.
admiration, *n.* Śtedapi.
admire, *vt.* Śteda; inihaŋ.
admissible, *a.* O'peyepica.
admission, *n.* 1. O'pekiyapi; en ukiyapi. 2. He'cetu eyapi.
admit, *vt.* 1. En iyayeya; o'pekiya. 2. Iyowiŋyaŋ; he'cetu keya.
admittance, *n.* En ya'pi.
admonish, *vt.* Iwaktaya; wahokoŋkiya.
admonition, *n.* Wowahokoŋkiya.
ado, *n.* Owodutatoŋ.
adopt, *vt.* Ta'waye kta icu.
adoption, *n.* Ciŋcayapi icupi.
adorable, *a.* Ohodapica.
adoration, *n.* Waohodapi.
adore, *vt.* Ohoda; waśteda.
adorn, *vt.* Yuwaśte; yuwitaŋ.
adrift, *adv.* O'kaḣbog.
adroit, *a.* Wayupika; oḣaŋko.
adult, *n.* Taŋ'ka.
adulterate, *vt.* He'caśni icahiyapi.
adulterer, *n.* Wawiciḣaḣapi ecoŋ.
adultery, *n.* Wawiciḣaḣapi.
advance, *vt.* 1. Iyopteya: *advance the army.* 2. Pazo; yataŋiŋ: *advance the statement.* 3. Waŋkan yeya: *advance the price.* *vi.* Iyopta; waŋkan ya: *advance in his studies.* *a.* I'tokam: *an*

advance payment. n. Woiyopte; iyoptapi; tokahaŋpi.
advanced, *pa.* Tokahaŋ; waŋkantu.
advancement, *n.* Woiyopte.
advantage, *n.* Wookihi; wokiciwaŝte. *You have the advantage of me:* mi'kapeya wookihi duha.
advantageous, *a.* Okiciwaŝte.
advent, *n.* Hi; hi kta.
adventure, *n.* Woakipa okokipe. *vt.* Kokipe ŝni ŝkaŋ.
adventurer, *n.* Wa'kinomani.
adverb, *n.* Wawoyaka o'kihe.
adversary, *n.* To'ka.
adverse, *a.* Itkom u; wakipażiŋ.
adversely, *adv.* Kipażiŋyaŋ.
adversity, *n.* Wocanteŝica.
advert, *vi.* Cażeyata.
advertise, *vt.* Yaotaŋiŋ. *vi.* Wayaotaŋiŋ.
advertisement, *n.* Wayaotaŋiŋpi.
advice, *n.* 1. Ciŋkiyapi; ecoŋŝipi: *the advice of his friends.* 2. Woyakapi; toketu oyaka: *a letter of advice.*
advisable, *a.* Ecoŋpiiyececa.
advise, *vt.* 1. Ciŋkiya; ecoŋŝi: *advise a friend.* 2. Okiyaka: *I will advise you when I go.*
advised, *pa.* Ecoŋŝipi: *ill-advised.*
adviser, *n.* Tuwe oŋspekiya.
advocate, *vt.* Iciya. *n.* Wawiciya.
adz, *n.* Caŋicakaŋ.
aerial, *a.* Tate ohna.
aeronaut, *n.* Wicaŝtakiŋyaŋ.
afar, *adv.* Te'han.
affable, *a.* Wohdakesa.
affair, *n.* Wicoh̔aŋ; ta'ku.
affect, *vt.* Kuwa; kuwakoŋza; iyokipi; ececa.
affected, *pa.* Ta'kuiçiya; waciŋyuza.
affecting, *pa.* Cantiyowicakiŝica.
affection, *n.* Wowaciŋyuza.
affectionate, *a.* Waihakta.
affectionately, *adv.* Waihaktaya.
affiance, *vt.* Yu'ze kta yuŝtaŋpi.
affidavit, *n.* Wowicake wowapi.
affiliate, *vt.* Om ŝkaŋ; kodaya.
affinity, *n.* Woihakta.
affirm, *vt.* He'cetu eya.
affirmation, *n.* He'cetu eyapi.
affix, *vt.* Ikoyaka.
afflict, *vt.* Iyokiŝinya.
afflicted, *pa.* Iyokiŝica.
affliction, *n.* Woiyokiŝica.
afflictive, *a.* Iyokiŝinyapi.
affluence, *n.* Wowiżice.
affluent, *a.* Żica; wiżica.
afford, *vt.* 1. Iyecen wi'żica: *I can't afford to buy coffee.* 2. Okihi: *the good can well afford to die.* 3. Icah̔ya; yukaŋ: *the well affords plenty of water.*
affray, *n.* Kicizapi.
affright, *vt.* Yuŝiŋyeya.
affront, *vt.* Iŝtenya; oŝtehda.
afire, *a.* Ide.
afloat, *a.* Okapota; yukaŋ.
afoot, *adv.* Huiŋyuŋ; *Y. & T.* makaamani.
afore, *prep.* I'tokam.
aforesaid, *a.* I'tokam cażeyatapi.
afraid, *a.* Kokipa; wakokipe.
afresh, *adv.* Akta; piya.
African, *n.* Waŝicuŋsapa. *Y. & T.* Ha'sapa.
aft, *a.* Wahektapa.
after, *adv.* & *prep.* 1. Iyohakam: *after supper.* 2. Wi'cihakam: *I stood after him.* 3. Huwe; *Y.* hiyo: *go after water.* 4. Oŋ: *inquired after you. After all,* uŋ'haŋketa; he'caŝta.
afterbirth, *n.* Tamni.
afternoon, *n.* Wi'cokayasaŋpa.
afterwards, *adv.* Iyohakam.
again, *adv.* Ake; akeŝ; iŝ. *Again and again,* akihdehde.
against, *prep.* 1. Itkom; i'tkokim: *go against.* 2. Akan; kaŝeya iyam: *dashed against the rocks.* 3. Ipataŋ: *lean it against the wall.* 4. Oŋ: wi'yeya: *toys laid up against Christmas. Against each other,* ki'cipatitaŋ.—

Against the wind, tatoheya.—*Over against,* i'yotakons.
age, *n.* 1. Wicoicaġe : *ages gone by.* 2. Oicaġe : *twelve years of age.* 3. Ta'waihdawapi ; waniyetu wikcemna noŋ'pa sam waŋżi : *he is of age.* *vt.* Wicaḣca a'ya.
aged, *pa.* Wicaḣca ; waniyetu ; kaŋ ; waniyetu o'ta.
agency, *n.* 1. Ateyapi ti ; owopamni ; *Y.* Owakpamni : *Santee Agency.* 2. Woecoŋ ; wośkiŋciye : *it is an agency for good.* 3. Waecoŋśipi : *a mercantile agency.*
agent, *n.* 1. Ateyapi : *Indian agent.* 2. e'ekiya awaŋyaka. 3. Waecoŋ.
aggrandize, *vt.* Yutaŋka.
aggravate, *vt.* Akaġa ; sam yuśica; caŋzeya.
aggravation, *n.* Sam yuśica ; wocaŋze.
aggregate, *vt.* & *a.* Yuwitaya ; wi'taya. *n.* O'yuwitaya.
aggressive, *a.* Wicakuwasa.
aggressor, *n.* Tokaheya ecoŋ.
aggrieve, *vt.* Iyokiśinya.
aghast, *a.* Inihaŋ ; taŋsag ṭa.
agile, *a.* Oḣaŋko.
agility, *n.* Oḣaŋkopi.
agitate, *vt.* Yuśkaŋśkaŋ ; aia.
aglow, *a.* Śaśa ; ide.
ago, *adv.* Ehaŋtaŋhaŋ ; hekta.
agoing, *adv.* Ya ; iyopte.
agonize, *vi.* Kakiśya śkaŋ.
agony, *n.* Wokakiże.
agree, *vi.* 1. O'koŋwaŋżidan awaciŋpi : *brothers should agree.* 2. Okiciwaśte : *agree with thine adversary.* 3. He'cetu kta eya ; wicada ; keya : *all agreed to the proposition.*
agreeable, *a.* Iyowicakipi ; waśte ; ohnayaŋ.
agreeably, *adv.* Iyokipiya.
agreement, *n.* Woyuśtaŋ iapi ; o'koŋwaŋżidaŋ awaciŋpi.
agriculture, *n.* Maḣkicaŋyaŋpi.
aground, *a.* & *adv.* A'zi.
ague, *n.* Caŋcaŋpi woyazaŋ.
ah, *interj.* E ; ḣo ; ho.
aha, *interj.* Ehaŋ ; ohaŋ.
ahead, *adv.* Tokaheya ; tokata.
ahem, *interj.* Ḣo.
ahoy, *interj.* Hiwo.
aid, *vt.* O'kiya ; waśagya. *n.* Waokiyapi ; ookiye.
ail, *vt.* Iyazaŋ ; to'keca.
ailment, *n.* Woyazaŋ.
aim, *vt.* 1. Pazo ; e'pazo : *aim a gun.* 2. Hiyuya ; yapa : *His remark was aimed at me.* *n.* Ta'ku kuwa ; wapazo.
aimless, *a.* Woawaciŋ co'daŋ.
air, *n.* 1. Tate ; aŋptaniya : *breathe pure air.* 2. Dowaŋpi ho itaŋcaŋ : *you sing the air.* 3. Oḣaŋ ; oḣaŋ koŋ'zapi. *vt.* Okadusya ; yutaŋiŋ.
airtight, *a.* Tate okaduześni.
airy, *a.* Tatesa ; okaduza ; kapożedan ; wi'haha.
aisle, *n.* Ti'piwakaŋ ocaŋkuye.
ajar, *adv.* Akazamni.
akin, *a.* & *adv.* Takuya. *They are akin,* takukiciyapi.
alacrity, *a.* Womdiheca.
alarm, *vt.* Inihaŋya ; iwaktaya. *n.* Woyuśiŋyaŋ ; wowakta.
alarming, *pa.* Woyuśiŋyaŋ.
alarmingly, *adv.* Wokokipeya.
alas, *interj.* He'hehe.
albino, *n.* Ukaska.
alcohol, *n.* Miniwakaŋ ska.
alderman, *n.* Otoŋwe itaŋcaŋ.
ale, *n.* Minitaḣtoŋ haŋpi.
alert, *a.* Wakta uŋ ; oḣaŋko.
algebra, *n.* Wi'yaciŋ wayawapi.
alias, *adv.* Caże uŋmaŋ.
alibi, *n.* Tokaŋ uŋ.
alien, *n.* Oyatetokeca ; to'keca.
alienate, *vt.* Yutokeca.
alight, *vi.* Iyahaŋ.
alike, *a.* I'akidececa. *adv.* I'akidecen.

alive, *a.* Ni; ṭe'śni; mdiheca; itkoŋ; a'taya śkaŋśkaŋ.
alkali, *n.* Caȟota haŋpi.
all, *a.* 1. Owasiŋ; *T.* oyasiŋ; iyuȟpa, *T. & Y.* iyuha: *all men.* 2. Ihuniyaŋ: *all the way.* 3. A'taya: *all the nation.*
all, *adv.* A'taya. *All along,* ihuŋniyaŋ.—*All but fell,* owaṭeca hiŋȟpaye kta tka.—*At all,* ecaca.—*All for play,* śka'tapi e'cedaŋ oŋ.—*All of a sudden,* ihnuhaŋna.—*All over,* a'taya ihuni.—*All the same,* to'keca śni.—*For all that,* he'caśta.
allay, *vt.* Yuasni.
allege, *vt.* Eya; iyaoŋpa; caźeyata.
allegiance, *n.* Ihakam uŋ'pi.
allegory, *n.* Wi'yaciŋpi.
alleviate, *vt.* Yuaokpani; oŋśpa yuwaśte.
alley, *n.* Otoŋwe caŋku cis'tina.
alliance, *n.* Wodakota.
allied, *pa.* Odakonkiciyapi.
alligator, *n.* Ahdeśkataŋka.
allot, *vt.* Ḳu; ikiyuta.
allotment, *n.* Ta'ku ḳu'pi; makoce ikiciyutapi.
allow, *vt.* 1. Iyowiŋkiya: *no smoking allowed.* 2. Ḳu: *allows good wages.* 3. Keciŋ: *I allow he was drunk.*
allowable, *a.* Iyowiŋyepica.
allowance, *n.* Ḳu'pi; iyowiŋyaŋpi.
all-round, *a.* Ecaowaŋcaya.
allude, *vi.* Ka.
allure, *vt.* Iyutaŋye; ȟmuŋ'ġa
allusion, *n.* Wacaźeyatapi.
alluvium, *n.* Makikceka.
ally, *n.* Kici ti'daŋ; ookiye. *vt.* Wodakota ki'caġa.
almanac, *n.* Wiyawapiwowapi.
almighty, *a.* Iyotaŋ waśaka.
almond, *n.* Yaȟuġapiwaŋkadaŋ.
almost, *a.* Ikiyedaŋ; owaṭeca; iśnikaeś.
alms, *n.* Waȟpanica taku ḳupi.
aloft, *adv.* Waŋkaŋ.
alone, *a. & adv.* Iśnana; ecedaŋ.
along, *adv. & prep.* Iyopta; ohna. *Along by,* kahda.—*Along with,* kici; ko'ya.
alongside, *adv.* I'sakim.
aloof, *adv.* I'tehaŋ; tokaŋ.
aloud, *adv.* Taŋiŋyaŋ; ho'taŋkaya.
alphabet, *n.* Oowa; a-b-c.
already, *adv.* Waŋna; e'eś waŋna.
also, *adv. & conj.* Nakuŋ.
altar, *n.* Wa'hnawośnapi; *T.* wa'gnawauŋyaŋpi; oyaŋke.
alter, *vt.* Yutokeca; *vi.* To'keċaaya.
alteration, *n.* Yutokecapi.
alternate, *a.* Uŋmaŋ itogto: *alternate stripes.* *vi.* Uŋmaŋ itogto śkaŋ'pi: *day alternates with night.* *n.* E'ekiya ye kta.
alternately, *adv.* U'ŋmaŋ itogto.
although, *conj.* Eśta; *Y.* eśa; keyaś.
altitude, *n.* Waŋkantuya.
alto, *n.* Wiŋ'yaŋ ho o'kihe.
altogether, *adv.* Owasiŋ wi'taya: a'taya; e'cedaŋ.
alum, *n.* Peźutaźaŋźaŋ seca.
always, *adv.* Ohiŋni. *Always the same,* o'hiŋni he'cetuwaŋźica.
am, *v. 1st pers. sing.* of BE.
amass, *vt.* Pahi.
amateur, *a. & n.* Woihakta oŋ kuwa.
amaze, *vt.* Inihaŋya.
amazement, *n.* Wowinihaŋ.
amazingly, *adv.* Wowinihaŋyaŋ.
ambassador, *n.* Oyateyeśipi.
ambiguous, *a.* Ta'ku ka'pi taŋiŋ śni.
ambition, *n.* Ohiyewaciŋpi.
ambitious, *a.* Ohiyewaciŋ.
ambulance, *n.* Caŋpahmihma wayazaŋka tokśu.
ambush, *n.* Iyawicapepi.
ameliorate, *vt.* Yuwaśte.
amen, *n.* Ḥe'cetu nuŋwe.
amenable, *a.* Ihukuya uŋ.
amend, *vt.* Piya. yuwaśte.

amends, *n.* Piyapi; wokażużu.
American, *n.* Isaŋtaŋka; *Y.* Mi'na-haŋska.
amiable, *a.* Tawaciŋ waśte.
amicable, *a.* Waihakta.
amicably, *adv.* Iyokipiya.
amid, *prep.* E'hna; cokaya.
amidst, *prep.* E'hna; cokaya.
amiss, *adv.* & *a.* He'cetu śni; eciŋśniyaŋ.
amity, *n.* Wowaśtekiciyapi.
ammunition, *n.* Iożu.
among, amongst, *prep.* E'hna; *Y.* e'kna; *T.* e'gla; a'kipam; o'peya.
amorous, *a.* Wacantiheye.
amount, *n.* To'nakeca; yuwitaya-pi; to'ken ka'pi. *vi.* Iyohi; ka.
ample, *a.* Otaŋkaya; iyohiḣca; o'ta.
amply, *adv.* Taŋyeḣca.
amputate, *vt.* Baksa; hu baksa.
amuse, *vt.* Maġaġaya; iḣaya; wi'-ḣahaya.
amusement, *n.* Womaġaġa.
an, *a.* Waŋ; waŋżi.
analogous, *a.* Iyececa.
anarchy, *n.* Woope wanica.
anathema, *n.* Woyaśica.
anatomy, *n.* Wicataŋcaŋ wooŋspe.
ancestor, *n.* Huŋkake.
anchor, *n.* Ma'zaaspeyapi: wat-icaspe. *vt.* Aspeya.
ancient, *a.* Ehaŋna; wanakaża. *n.* Ehaŋna wicaśta.
and, *conj.* Ḳa; ça; *T.* na: uŋ'kaŋ; *T.* yuŋ'kaŋ; nakuŋ.
anecdote, *n.* Woyakapi.
anew *adv.* Piya; te'ca.
angel, *n.* Maḣpiyaohnihde; waho-śiyewakaŋ.
anger, *n.* Wocaŋniye; wocaŋze. *vt.* Caŋzeya.
angle, *n.* Okaḣmiŋ. *vi.* Ho'psica.
angry, *a.* Caŋniyaŋ; caŋze; wo-hitika.
anguish, *n.* Woiyokiśice.
animal, *n.* Wamakaśkaŋ; (small animals) watutka; (ruminating) woteca.
animate, *vt.* Niya; nikiya; yu-niya; mdihenya. *a.* Ni.
animated, *pa.* Ni; mdiheca.
animosity, *n.* Waḣtekicidapi śni.
animus, *n.* Co; ta'ku ka'pi.
ankle, *n.* Iśkahu.
annals, *n.* Woyakapi: o'maka oya-kapi.
annex, *vt.* Aehnaka; onśpa akaġa. *n.* Akaġapi.
annexation, *n.* Ikoyagyapi.
annihilate, *vt.* Atakuniśniya; owi-hankeya.
anniversary, *n.* Wokiksuye aŋpe-tu; o'maka iyehantu.
announce, *vt.* Yaotaŋiŋ.
announcement, *n.* Yaotaŋiŋpi.
annoy, *vt.* Naġiyeya; kiśdeya.
annoyance, *n.* Wonaġiyeya.
annual, *a.* O'maka iyohi; o'maka waŋżi.
annuity, *n.* Wopamni; o'maka iyohi ta'ku ḳu'pi.
annul, *vt.* Yucecetuśni.
anoint, *vt.* Sdakiya.
anomalous, *a.* To'keca.
anon, *adv.* Ecana; to'keśta.
anonymous, *a.* Caże wanica.
another, *a.* To'keca; waŋżi to'keca.
answer, *vt.* 1. Ayupta: *I will answer.* 2. Iyehantu; ecetu: *the house will answer.* *n.* Woayupte.
answerable, *a.* Ayuptepica; wawi-waŋġapi kta.
ant, *n.* Tażuśka.
antarctic, *a.* O'kaḣ ihaŋke.
anteater, *n.* Tażuśka yu'ta.
antecedent, *n.* Otokahe.
antelope, *n.* Tatokadaŋ.
anthem, *n.* Odowaŋ haŋ'ska.
anti-, *prefix.* Kipażiŋ.
antic, *n.* Wowiḣa oecoŋ.
anticipate, *vt.* I'tokam awaciŋ; keciŋ; kapa.
antidote, *n.* Wośica kte.
antipathy, *n.* Waḣtedaśni.

antiquated, *a.* Wicoȟaŋ ehaŋna.
antique, *a.* Ehaŋna ȟca.
antler, *n.* He'yuȟaȟa.
anvil, *n.* Ma'zaahdehe.
anxiety, *n.* Wocaŋtešica; caŋtaȟdepi; ni'na ciŋ.
anxious, *a.* Caŋtešica; ni'na ciŋ; inaȟni.
anxiously, *adv.* Caŋtešinya.
any, *a.* 1. Tu'we; tu'we kašta: *any man.* 2. Oŋġe: *any sugar.* 3. Tukte: *any damage. adv.* Oŋġe; oŋ'špa.
anybody, *pron.* Tu'we; wicašta.
anyhow, *adv.* To'ketukašta.
anyone, *pro.* Tu'wekašta.
anything, *pro.* Ta'kukašta.
anyway, *adv.* To'ketukašta.
anywhere, *adv.* Tuktentukašta.
anywise, *adv.* To'ketukašta.
apace, *adv.* Dus; oȟaŋko.
apart, *adv.* Kinukaŋ; tokaŋ; yušpušpu.
apartment, *n.* Ti'pioŋšpa.
apathy, *n.* Waawaciŋpišni.
ape, *n.* Wauŋca: *T.* heolela. *vt.* Uŋ'cu.
aperture, *n.* Oȟdoka; *T.* oȟloka.
apex, *n.* Iŋ'kpa.
apiece, *adv.* Iyohi; kinukaŋ.
apologize, *vi.* Ohdaka; iciya; icaŋtešica ohdaka.
apostate. *n.* Wowicada nu'ni.
apostle, *n.* Yešipi.
appall, *vt.* Taŋsagṭeya.
appalling, *pa.* Woyušiŋyaŋ.
apparatus, *n.* Icuwa.
apparel, *n.* Heyake; *Y.* hayake; *T.* hayapi.
apparent, *a.* Taŋiŋ; se'ca.
apparently, *adv.* Se'ececa.
apparition, *n.* Wanaġi.
appeal, *vi.* 1. Tokaŋ ye kta: *I appeal to Caesar.* 2. Da; icekiya: *I appeal for aid.* 3. Iyohiya: *the call appeals to every heart.* 4. Cażeyata: *appeal to history.*

appear, *vi.* Taŋiŋyaŋ u; taŋiŋ; taŋiŋiçiya; se'ececa.
appearance, *n.* Owaŋyake; taŋiŋ; ta'ku taŋiŋ; en hi.
appease, *vt.* Asnikiya; asniyaŋ; yuasni.
appendix, *n.* Ihaŋke ka'ġapi.
appertain, *vi.* En ikoyake; ta'waya.
appetite, *n.* Wocaŋtahde; dociŋpi.
appetizing, *pa.* Oŋ dociŋpi.
applaud, *vt.* Yataŋ; i'yakiš'a.
applause, *n.* Woyataŋ.
apple, *n.* Taspaŋ; taspaŋtaŋka. *Apple of the eye,* ištasu.
applicable, *a.* Uŋpica; en aupica.
applicant, *n.* Da; wicoȟaŋ da.
application, *n.* 1. Da; da'pi wowapi: *his application was rejected.* 1. Waehnakapi: *a soft application.* 3. Ta'ku iyoważa: *the application of the sermon.* 4. Waawaciŋpi: *close application.*
apply, applied, *vt.* Aehnaka; e'hnaka; a'ya; en yeya. *vi.* 1. Da; eciya. 2. Iyoważa; kipi; kapi.
appoint, *vt.* Kaȟniġa; ecoŋši; ka'ġa; e'hde. *vi.* Wakoŋza.
appointment, *n.* 1. Wakaȟniġa. 2. Ta'ku ecoŋ kta eyapi. 3. Icuwa; heyake.
apportion, *vt.* Pamni.
appraise, *vt.* Tohantu yawa.
appreciate, *vt.* Pida; waŋkan yawa; wi'yukcaŋ; wašteda.
apprehend, *vt.* 1. Okaȟniġa. 2. Teȟi kta eciŋ; ikopa. 3. Yu'za; *Y.* oyuspa.
apprehensive, *a.* Waawaciŋ; wi'kopa.
apprentice, *n.* Wowaši oŋspekiyapi.
apprise, *vt.* Iwaktaya.
approach, *vt.* Ikiyedaŋ u; en [illegible]; kuwa. *n.* Kiyadaŋ u; oenape.
approbation, *n.* He'cetudapi.

appropriate, *vt.* 1. Aehnaka : *appropriate money for Indians.* 2. Ikikcu ; ta′wa kta icu. *a.* Iyehantu ; okiwaśte.
approval, *n.* Iyecetu da′pi.
approve, *vt.* He′cetu da ; yutaŋiŋ ; waśte ihdutaŋiŋ.
approximate, *a.* Ikiyedaŋ. *v.* Ikiyedaŋ ye.
April, *n.* Wi′itopa ; Maġaokadawi ; Watopapiwi.
apron, *n.* Makuakaḣpe; *T.* makuagnaka.
apt, *a.* 1. Wayupika ; waciŋksapa ; oḣaŋko. 2. Ecee ; sa.
aptitude, *n.* Wookihi.
aptly, *adv.* Wayupiya.
aquatic, *a.* Mini.
arable, *a.* Wożupiwaśte.
Arapahoe, *n.* Maḣpiyato.
arbitrary, *a.* Iyetokenciŋ ecoŋ ; suta ; teḣika.
arbitrate, *vt.* Woakinica yaco.
arbor, *n.* Canwapatipi.
arc, *n.* Canhdeśka oŋśpa.
arch, *n.* Mibeya awakeyapi.
arch, *prefix.* Itaŋcaŋ.
archer, *n.* Waŋyeya.
architect, *n.* Ticaḣwiyukcaŋ.
archive, *n.* Wowapi omnaye.
arctic, *a.* Waziyata ihaŋke.
ardent, *a.* Wohitika ; ka′ta.
ardor, *n.* Womdiheca.
arduous, *a.* Teḣika ; wakitaŋ.
are, *2nd pers. sing. and plur. ind. of* Be. Uŋ.
area, *n.* Oiyute ; oyaŋke.
argue, *vt.* To′keca oyaka ; iaakinica.
argument, *n.* To′ken oŋ etaŋhaŋ he′cetu.
arid, *a.* Waicaġe śni.
aright, *adv.* Taŋyaŋ.
arise, *vi.* Hinapa ; icaġa ; inażiŋ.
aristocratic, *a.* Waḣaŋiçida.
arithmetic, *n.* Wayawapi.
ark, *n.* Noah tawata ; wa′ta ; koka wakaŋ.

arm, *n.* Isto ; adetka ; wi′pe. *v.* Wi′petoŋ ; wi′pe ku̇.
armful, *n.* Istoożudaŋ.
armless, *a.* Istowanica.
armor, *n.* Ozuye heyake.
armory, *n.* Wi′petipi.
armpit, *n.* Doksi ; a.
army, *n.* Ozuye ; akicita.
aroma, *n.* Ecamna.
around, *adv. & prep.* O′kśaŋ ; ohomni ; kohdamniyaŋ ; a′kibeya.
arouse, *vt.* Yuḣica ; i′yopaśtaka.
arraign, *vt.* Iyaoŋpa ; kaśka.
arrange, *vt.* Taŋyaŋ e′hnaka ; piya. *vi.* Wayuśtaŋ ; piiçiya.
arrangement, *n.* Oehnake.
array, *vt.* 1. E′hde ; koyagya.
arrear, *n.* Iyohiśni.
arrest, *vt.* Kaśka ; oyuspa ; anapta ; na′żiŋkiya.
arrival, *n.* Hi ; ehaŋi ; tu′we hi.
arrive, *vi.* Hi ; hihuni ; ehaŋi.
arrogant, *a.* Aokaḣyaśkaŋ ; waḣaŋiçida.
arrow, *n.* Waŋhiŋkpe ; waŋ.
arrowhead, *n.* Waŋhi.
arson, *n.* Tiideyapi.
art, *2nd pers. sing. of* Be. Uŋ.
art, *n.* Wooŋspe.
artery, *n.* We′kaŋ dus iyapa.
artesian, *a.* Minibosdi.
artichoke, *n.* Paŋġi.
article, *n.* Ocaże ; iapi ; aehnakapi iapi.
articulate, *vt.* E′napeya ; o′kihe ka′ġa.
artifice, *n.* Wowayupika.
artificial, *a.* Ka′ġapi.
artillery, *n.* Ma′zakaŋtaŋka.
artist, *n.* Wakaḣwayupika.
artless, *a.* Waḣaŋiçidaśni.
as, *adv. & conj.* 1. Iyecen : *as good as,* iyecen waśte. 2. To′ken : *as I do, so he does.* 3. He′ca : *some animals are cunning, as the fox.* 4. Icuŋhaŋ : *as we were riding home.* 5.

keyas: *bad as he is.* 6. Nakaeṡ: *as he is little, he can play. As for,* e'ḳeṡ. — *As if,* or *as though,* iyecen. — *As yet,* nahaŋhiŋ; dehaŋyaŋ.
ascend, *vt.* Waŋkan ya; adi.
ascending, *pa.* I'taŋwaŋkaŋhde; aiyakapteya.
ascension, *n.* Iyakaptapi; waŋkanyapi.
ascent, *n.* Oiyakapte; waŋkanyapi.
ascertain, *vt.* Sdonya.
ascribe, *vt.* Ki'ciyawa; ḳu.
ash, *n.* Pseh'tiŋ.
ashamed, *a.* Iṡteca.
ashes, *n. pl.* Çahota.
ashore, *adv* Hen; hutata.
ashy, *a.* Cahotase.
aside, *adv.* Icuŋom; tokaŋ.
ask, *v.* 1. Da; kida. *He asked a dime,* kaṡpapi waŋżi da. — *He asked him for a dime,* kaṡpapi waŋżi kida. 2. Iwaŋġa. *He asked him the road,* caŋku iwaŋġa. 3. Kico; uṡi: *he asked him to dinner.*
askance, *adv.* Hdakiŋyaŋ.
askew, *adv.* Ḣmiŋyaŋ.
aslant, *adv.* Nakeya.
asleep, *a.* Iṡtiŋma. *The foot asleep.* siha ṭaṭake.
asp, *n.* Wamduṡka.
aspect, *n.* Owaŋyake.
aspen, *n.* Wahciŋca.
asperity, *n.* Ohaŋksizeca.
asperse, *vt.* Yaṡihtiŋ.
aspirant, *n.* Akita; ciŋ.
aspirate, *a.* Oowa oniyaṡi'ca.
aspiration, *n.* Caŋtiheyapi.
aspire, *vi.* Akita; kuwa; ciŋ.
aspiring, *pa.* Waŋkantuwaciŋ.
ass, *n.* Ṡoŋ'ṡoŋnahca.
assail, *vt.* Iyahpaya; aia.
assassin, *n.* Tin'wicakte.
assault, *vt.* Takpe; nataŋ.
assemblage, *n.* Omniciye.
assemble, *vt.* Mni'ciya.
assembly, *n.* Omniciye.
assent, *vi.* He'cetuda eya.
assert, *vt.* Eya; kitaŋ.
assertion, *n.* Ta'ku eya; iapi.
assess, *vt.* Woyuha owa.
assessor, *n.* Owicawa.
assets, *n.* Każużu kta hna'ka.
assiduous, *a.* Wakitaŋpi.
assign, *vt.* Oŋ kahniġa; e'kicihnaka; ḳu.
assignation, *n.* Wicaḳupi.
assimilate, *vt.* Ta'waiçiya ka'ġa.
assist, *vt.* O'kiya.
assistance, *n.* Wookiye; o'kiyapi.
assistant, *n.* Ookiye.
associate, *vt.* Yuokoŋwaŋżina; kici uŋ; kodaya. *n.* Kicica.
association, *n.* Kodakiciyapi; o'kodakiciye: *Young Men's Association.*
assort, *vt.* Obe ecekcen e'hnaka.
assortment, *n.* Ocaże; ocaże ece e'hnakapi.
assuage, *vt.* Yuasni; yuhukuya. *vi.* Kun ya; asni.
assume, *vt.* Icu; he'cetu yawa; koŋ'za.
assurance, *n.* Yuwicakapi; a'wicakeya sdonyapi.
assure, *vt.* A'wicakehaŋ sdonyekiya; ecetukiya.
assuredly, *adv.* A'wicakehaŋ.
astern, *auv.* Wahektapa; he'kta.
astir, *a.* Ṡkaŋṡkaŋ.
astonish, *vt.* Yuṡiŋyeya.
astonishing, *pa.* Woyuṡiŋyaye.
astound, *vt.* Taŋsagṭeya.
astounding, *a.* Wowinihaŋ.
astray, *adv.* Onuniyaŋ; nu'ni.
astride, *adv.* Akamdaṡ.
astringent, *a.* Pa; ṭa'ġa.
astronomy, *n.* Wicaŋhpi wooŋspe.
astute, *a.* Ksa'pa; wakcaŋka.
asunder, *a.* Yukinukaŋ.
asylum, *n.* Wicaoŋṡikatipi; wowinapetipi.
at, *prep.* Ekta; iyehan. *He is at the river,* wakpa ekta uŋ. —

I will come at noon, wi'cokaya iyehan wau kta.

At all, ecaca. — *At hand,* ikiyedaŋ. — *At last,* uŋ'haŋketa. — *At least,* he'ceca ṡta; daŋ. — *At your service,* wi'yeya. *Get at,* iyohi; yu'za. — *Run at,* anataŋ.

ate, *imp.* of EAT, yu'ta.
atheist, *n.* Ta'kuwakaŋ wanica keciŋ
athirst, *a.* I'puza.
athletics, *n.* Taŋcaŋ kaoŋspepi.
athwart, *prep.* Hdakiŋyaŋ.
atlas, *n.* Makoce owapi.
atmosphere, *n.* Tate.
atom, *n.* Wokpena.
atone, *vt.* Kaẓuẓu; ecetuya.
atrocious, *a.* N'ina ṡi'ca.
attach, *vt.* Ikoyagya; a'skamya. *Attach to,* ikoyaka; iyayuḣa; ihakta.
attack, *vt.* Anataŋ; kuwa; kipaẓiŋ. *n.* Wonataŋ.
attain, *vt.* Iyohi.
attainment, *n.* Wooŋspe okihi.
attempt, *vt.* Iyuta; ecoŋuta. *n.* Ecoŋutapi.
attend, *vt.* 1. Kici ya; o'pa: *attend the king; attend the meeting.* 2. Kuwa; en e'waciŋ: *attend to your lessons.*
attendance, *n.* O'papi; en hi'pi.
attendant, *n.* Tu'we o'pa; kicica.
attention, *n.* Ṭiŋsaawaciŋpi.
attentive, *a.* Waawaciŋ.
attest, *vt.* Yuwicaka.
attic, *n.* Tice; waŋkantipi.
attire, *vt.* Koyaka; kiçuŋ. *n.* Wokoyake; hayake.
attitude, *n.* Piiçiyapi; piiçiya.
attorney, *n.* Waaiawicaṡta.
attract, *vt.* Yutitaŋ; iyutaŋye.
attraction, *n.* Woyutitaŋ.
attractive, *a.* Iyutaŋwicaya; wi'ciyokipi.
attribute, *n.* Oḣaŋ; ta'ku ta'wakiyapi; (Gram.) wi'yatokeca.
attribute, *vt.* En ai; ḳu.
attune, *vt.* Ho i'ciyokipiya.
auburn, *a.* Ṡa ġi; ṡaṡa.
auction, *n.* Paŋ'wiyopeyapi.
audacious, *a.* Ta'kudaŋohodaṡni.
audible, *a.* Taŋiŋ.
audience, *n.* Naḣoŋyaŋkapi; omniciye; wonaḣoŋ.
audit, *vt.* He'cetu keya.
auditorium, *n.* Omniciyetipi.
auger, *n.* Caŋiyumni. *T.* Caŋiyuḣloke.
aught, *n.* Ta'ku kaṡta.
augment, *vt.* Yutaŋka.
augur, *vt.* Ayata.
august, *a.* Okinihaŋ.
August, *n.* Wi'iṡahdoġaŋ; Wasutoŋwi.
aunt, *n.* Toŋwiŋ; (if mother's sister) ina.
auspices, *n. pl.* Woawaŋyake.
auspicious, *a.* Owaṡtecaka.
austere, *a.* Ḳe'za; ksizeca.
authentic, *a.* Wicaka.
authenticate, *vt.* Yuwicaka.
author, *n.* Ka'ġa; tu'we ka'ġa.
authority, *n.* Wowaṡ'ake.
authorize, *vt.* Wowaṡ'ake ku.
autobiography, *n.* Oniohdaka.
autocrat, *n.* Ta'waiçiya itaŋcaŋ.
autograph, *n.* Caẓe oiçiwa.
autonomy, *n.* Oyate iṡnaihduhapi.
autumn, *n.* Ptaŋyetu.
auxiliary, *a.* Waokiya. *n.* Ookiye.
avail, *vt.* Okiciwaṡte; kiçuŋ; iyokihi.
avail, *n.* Wi'yokihi. *Avails,* wokamna.
available, *a.* Icupica; uŋpica.
avalanche, *n.* Ca'ġa kaṡduta.
avarice, *n.* Wateḣiŋdapi.
avaricious, *a.* Woyuha caŋtahde.
avenge, *vt.* Watokiçoŋ.
avenue, *n.* Caŋku; otoŋwecaŋku.
aver, *vt.* Wowicake eya.
average, *vt.* Yuocokaya. *a.* Ocokaya; ecee. *n.* Cokaya.
averse, *a.* Iyokipiṡni.

aversion, *n.* Wowaȟtedašni.
avert, *vt.* Yutokaŋ.
aviary, *n.* Zitkadaŋtipi.
avidity, *n.* Wocaŋtahde.
avocation, *n.* Wicoȟaŋ.
avoid, *vt.* Aohomni ya; ecoŋ šni.
avouch, *vt.* Wowicake eya.
avow, *vt.* Ohdaka.
avowed, *pa.* Taŋiŋyaŋ oyakapi.
await, *vt.* Akipa.
awake, awoke, *vt.* Yuȟica. *vi.* Kikta; mdes'hiŋhda. *a.* Kikta uŋ.
awaken, *vt.* Yuȟica.
awakening, *n.* Woyuȟica.
award, *vt.* Ḳu; woohiye ḳu; *n.* Woohiye; ta'ku ḳu'pi.
aware, *a.* Sdonya; wakta.
away, *adv.* Tokaŋ; to'kiya; he'cetuwaŋżica. *Run away,* tokaŋ iyaya, nażica. — *Sing away,* dowaŋ yaŋka. — *Work away,* he'cetuwaŋżica ecoŋ. — *Away back,* ehaŋna. — *Away with,* tokaŋ a'ya. — *Do away with,* or *make away with,* ayuštaŋkiya; ihaŋgya. — *Right away,* katiŋyaŋ.
awe, *vt.* Yušiŋyeya. *n.* Woyušiŋyaye.
awestruck, *a.* Inihaŋ.
awful, *a.* Wowinihaŋ; wowitoŋpe; okokipe.
awfully, *adv.* Wowinihaŋyaŋ.
awhile, *adv.* Ki'taŋna te'han.
awkward, *a.* Waoŋspekešni; e'cipe šni; to'ketu taŋiŋ šni.
awl, *n.* Tahiŋṡpa.
awning, *n.* Miniȟuhaohaŋzi.
awoke, *imp.* of Awake.
ax, *n.* Oŋspe; mazoŋspe.
axiom, *n.* Ecawowicake.
axis, *n.* Ayuhomnipi.
axle, *n.* Huhdakiŋyaŋ.
aye, *n.* Haŋ; ho.
azure, *a.* To; maȟpiyato.

B

Baal, *n.* Aŋ'pawiwakaŋ.
babble, *vi.* Iaa: ȟmuŋȟmuŋ.
babbler, *n.* Ies'a.
babe, *n.* Hokšiyopa. *Y.* Hokšiçopa. *T.* Hokšicala.
Babel, *n.* Iapiota.
baboon, *n.* Wauŋca.
baby, *n.* Hokšiyoḳopa. *a.* Cis'tiŋna. *vt.* Hokšiyopakiya.
babyish, *a.* Hokšiyopaseca.
bachelor, *n.* To'hiŋni tawicutoŋ šni.
back, *n.* Tapete; *T.* tapetu; caŋkahu. *Lie on your back,* ituŋkam yaŋka.
back, *a.* Heyata; i'siŋyaŋ; he'kta.
back, *vt.* 1. He'kta iyayeya: *back the horse.* 2. Nakiciżiŋ: *back a candidate.* 3. Caŋkahu ki'caġa: *back a book.* 4. Akan owa: *back a letter. adv.* He'kta; icicawiŋ; ȟeyata.
backache, *n.* Caŋkahuyazaŋ.
backbite, *vt.* Naȟmana yaȟtaka.
backbone, *n.* Caŋkahu.
backdown, *n.* Enakiya.
backer, *n.* Nakiciżiŋ.
backfire, *n.* Kokam ideyapi.
background, *n.* I'siŋyaŋ; he'kta.
backhanded, *a.* He'ktaitoheya.
backing, *n.* Nakiciżiŋpi.
backset, *n.* He'kta iwaŋka.
backside, *n.* Nite; oŋze.
backslide, *vi.* He'kta iyaya.
backward, *adv.* He'kta. *a.* He'kta uŋ; huŋ'kešni.
backwater, *n.* Minitaŋmini.

backwoods, *n.* Canyata; makoskan.
bacon, *n.* Waśiŋ; kukuśecosyapi.
bad, *a.* Śi'ca; oŋspeśni.
bade, *imp.* of BID.
Bad River, *n.* Wakpaśica.
badge, *n.* Wa'petokeca; ceśkikaŋ.
badger, *n.* Ḣoka. *v.* Naġiyeya.
badly, *adv.* Śicaya; teḣiya.
Bad Hills, *n.* Ḣesapa.
baffle, *vt.* Okihiśniya.
bag, *n.* 1. Wożuha: *a big bag.* 2. Ożutoŋpi: *a bag of oats.* 3. Aze: *a cow's bag.* *vt.* Ożutoŋ; hmuŋ'ka.
baggage, *n.* Waḣpayeca; caŋ'ohnaka.
bah, *interj.* Hoḣ.
bail, *n.* 1. E'ekiya kaśkapi. 2. Ce'ġa ihupa. *vt.* 1. E'ekiya ihdaśka oŋ kiyuśkapi. 2. Kapta; mini eḣpeya.
bairn, *n.* Hokśiyopa; ciŋca.
bait, *n.* Wataŋ; wonapce. *vt.* Wataŋkicatoŋ; won'kiya.
bake, *vt.* Śpaŋyaŋ. *vi.* Śpaŋ aya; tasaka.
baker, *n.* Aġuyapiśpaŋyaŋ.
bakery, *n.* Aġuyapiowaśpaŋye.
baking-powder, *n.* Wi'napoḣye.
balance, *n.* 1. On'aspeyapi. 2. Iyaye. *vt.* Aspeya; oicazo to'ketu yawa.
bald, *a.* Śda; pe'śda.
baldly, *adv.* Ża'żaya.
bale, *n.* Wapaḣtapi; wopaḣte. *vt.* Paḣta.
baleful, *a.* Wayuśica.
balk, *vi.* Ihdonica; wicadaśni. *vt.* Kaġiya; okihiśniya.
balky, *a.* Ihdonicesa.
ball, *n.* 1. Ta'pa: *throw the ball.* 2. Ta'ku mibe: *the earth is a ball.* 3. Ma'zasu: *a riffle-ball.*
ball, *vt.* Pśuŋkakaġa. *vt.* Wa o'tkapa: *the horse's feet ball.*
ballad, *n.* Ikceodowaŋ.
ballast, *n.* Wiya'ka; ta'ku oŋ witawata yuowotaŋnapi.
balloon, *n.* Wożuhakiŋyaŋ.
ballot, *vi.* Kaŋsuiyoḣpeya. *n.* Kaŋsuiyoḣpeyapi.
ballroom, *n.* Owacitipi.
balm, *n.* Peżutawaśtemna; wiconipeżuta.
balmy, *a.* Ecamna; waśtemna.
balsam, *n.* Isdayewaśtemna.
bamboozle, *vt.* Ḣna'yaŋ.
ban, *n.* Wokaśke.
banana, *n.* Iyaġezizi.
band, *n.* 1. Iyuskite; ipaḣte; wiciśke. 2. Okodakiciye; optaye.
bandage, *n.* Miniḣuhaiyuskite. *vt.* Yuwi; yuskiskita.
bandit, *n.* Wamanoŋwicaśta.
bane, *n.* Woyuśice.
baneful, *a.* Wayuśica.
bang, *vt.* 1. Kabu. 2. Iteḣiŋbaksapi. *vi.* Bu'hiŋhda. *n.* Bu. *With a bang,* buyena.
banish, *vt.* Iyayeya; oyate to'keca ekta iyayeya.
banjo, *n.* Ha'sapatacaŋbubu.
bank, *n.* 1. Maya; paha. 2. O'huta: *the river bank.* 3. Ma'zaskatipi: *money in the bank.* *vt.* Mayakaġa; aokata; ma'zaskatipi en e'hnaka.
bankbill, *n.* Ma'zaskawowapi.
banker, *n.* Ma'zaskatipi yuha.
bankrupt, *a.* Każużu okihi śni.
banner, *n.* Wi'yokihedaŋ.
banquet, *n.* Kicicowotapi.
banter, *vt.* Ecoŋape; oŋ'śkate.
baptism, *n.* Mniakaśtaŋpi.
Baptist, *n.* Okodakiciye kihnug mniawicakaśtaŋpi.
baptize, *vt.* Mniakaśtaŋ.
bar, *n.* 1. Wi'natake, mazinatake; caŋ'inatake: *let down the bars.* 2. Wokaġi; wiyaka: *a bar in the river.* 3. Wa'kiyapioyaŋke, *the prisoner stands at the bar.* 4. Wa'hna miniwakaŋ wi'yope-

yapi. *vt.* Nataka; anapta; kaġiya: kaġo.
barb, *n.* Keze; ope; oḣci.
barbarian, *n.* Ikcewicaśta.
barbarism, *n.* Ikceouŋ.
barbarity, *n.* Wowaoŋśidaśniwicoḣaŋ.
barbarous, *a.* Ikceka; to'keca.
barbacue, *n.* Ikcewonmniciyapi.
barbed, *a.* Pepe; pe; pe'sto.
barber, *n.* Putiŋhiŋkasaŋ.
bard, *n.* Odowaŋikcekaġa.
bare, *a.* 1. Śda: *bare ground.* 2. Taŋcodaŋ: *bare feet.* 3. E'cedaŋ; napiŋyuŋ co'daŋ: *with bare hands.* *vt.* Śdaya eḣpeya.
bareback, *a.* Akiŋ co'daŋ.
barefaced, *a.* Iśteceśni.
barefoot, *a.* Sicodaŋ.
barely, *adv.* Kitaŋyaŋ; iyusoyaḣ.
bargain, *n.* Woecoŋ yuśtaŋpi; wokamna. *vt.* Yuśtaŋ: *bargain away,* wi'yopeya. *Bargain for,* opetoŋ.
barge, *n.* Wa'ta sicumdaska.
bark, *vi.* Pa'pa; pa. *n.* Pa'pi.
bark, *n.* Caŋha. *vt.* Caŋha yuḣu.
bark, *n.* Wi'tawata.
barley, *n.* Wayahotahiŋśma.
barn, *n.* Wanuyaŋpitipi.
barnyard, *n.* Wanuyaŋpionażiŋ.
barrack, *n.* Akicitatipi.
barrel, *n.* Kokapahmihma; ma'zakaŋoḣdoġeca.
barren, *a.* Waicaġeśni; ciŋca wanica.
barricade, *vt.* Nataka. *n.* Wonataka.
barrier, *n.* Coŋ'kaśke; wokaġi.
barroom, *n.* Miniwakaŋ hde'pi.
barrow, *n.* Kukuśe susu wanica.
barter, *vt.* Tokiyopeya.
barytone, *n.* Wicaho ocoka.
basal, *a.* Ku'ceyedaŋ; hu'te.
base, *n.* Hu'te; hutkaŋ; onażiŋ. *a.* Ku'ceyedaŋ; ta'kutaŋiŋśni; śi'ca.
baseball, *n.* Takapapi.
baseless, *a.* Hu'tenica; ituya.
basely, *adv.* Ituya; śicaya.
basement, *n.* Tihute.
baseness, *n.* Wowaḣteśni.
bashful, *a.* Wi'śteca.
bashfulness, *n.* Wi'śtecapi.
basin, *n.* 1. Wakśica; napożaża 2. Makoce ośkokpa.
basis, *n.* Hu'te; oahehde.
bask, *vi.* Kaniçiya.
basket, *n.* Makaŋopiye; coḣwaŋżica woknake; yaŋ'kapina.
bass, *n.* Wakadaŋhiyuzapi.
bass, or **base,** *n.* Hokuya.
bassviol, *n.* Caŋpakiŋzapitaŋka.
basswood, *n.* Hiŋ'tacaŋ.
bastard, *n.* Tuwecincataŋiŋśni; wohnaye.
baste, *vt.* 1. I'ḣad kaġeġe. 2. Wopasnoŋ iuŋ.
bastile, *n.* Coŋ'kaśke.
bat, *n.* 1. Ḣupahuwakihdakena: *a bat can fly.* 2. Takicapope: *a baseball bat.* 3. Oape: *a bat on the head.* *vt.* Apa; ta'pa apa.
batch, *n.* Okaḣwaŋżina; opahi.
bath, *n.* Ihdużażapi; niwaŋpi.
bathe, *vt.* Yużaża; spa'yeya.
baton, *n.* Caŋ'ḣpi.
battalion, *n.* Akicitaoptaye taŋka.
batten, *n.* Caŋmdaska sbu'na. *vt.* Okoaokataŋ.
batter, *n.* Aġuyapicocoyapi. *vt* Apapa; kaḣuḣuġa; bomdeca.
battery, *n.* Waapapi; ma'zakaŋ taŋka ota: wakaŋhdiokaġe.
batting, *n.* Ta'ḣcahiŋkakcapi.
battle, *n.* Okicize; akicita kicizapi. *vi.* Kiciza; kici ecoŋ.
bauble, *n.* Ta'kuśni; wi'napiśkaŋye.
bawl, *vi.* Ho'taŋkaceya; paŋ.
bay, *a.* Hiŋ'śa; *Y. & T.* Hiŋikceka. *n.* Mde'caḣmiŋ; śuŋ'kahotoŋ. *At bay,* oyaŋke i'tehaŋ.
bayonet, *n.* Ma'zakaŋhi.

bayou, *n.* Mdecaȟmiŋ.
bazaar, *n.* Mazopiyedaŋ.
be, am, is, was, *vi.* 1. Uŋ; ni. *I am,* wauŋ. — *You are,* yauŋ. — *He is,* uŋ. 2. As a copulative and auxiliary, it is not expressed. *You are fat,* nicepa. — *Be it so,* he'cetu. — *Let it be,* ayuśtaŋ.
beach, *n.* Huta; miniwaŋca huta.
beacon, *n.* Wowakta; pe'ta.
bead, *n.* Totodaŋ; śipto; wanapiŋ.
beak, *n.* Pasu; zitkapasu.
beam, *vt.* I'żaŋżaŋ; iyoyaŋpa. *n.* Iyożaŋżaŋ; caŋ'ihupa.
bean, *n.* Omnica.
bear, bore, *vt.* 1. Yuha; toŋ: *he bore it on his head; she bore twins.* 2. Icaȟya: *that tree bears apples.* 3. Ecoŋ; yuśtaŋ: *bear the expenses.* 4. Pataŋyuza: *bear down.* *vi.* Ahdaskin waŋka; pataŋyuza; iyowiŋyaŋ. *Bear a hand,* o'kiya. — *Bear off,* tokaŋ ya. — *Bear date,* wiyawapi ka'ġapi. — *Bear with,* iyowiŋyaŋ.
bear, *n.* Mato. *Black bear,* waȟaŋksica. — *Grey bear,* matoȟota; śakehaŋska.
beard, *n.* Putiŋhiŋ; ikuhiŋ. *vt.* i'tkokipa.
bearer, *n.* Yuha; a'ye.
bearing, *n.* 1. Yuhapi: *bearing of children.* 2. Oihduhe: *his bearing.* 3. Oiyahde; ta'ku iyoważa: *in all its bearings.* 4. Wowaciŋtaŋka.
beast, *n.* Wahutopa; woteca.
beastly, *a.* Wotecase; śi'ca.
beat, *vt.* 1. Apa; iyapa; kaśuśuża. 2. Kapa; kte'daŋ: *Henry beat.* *Beat a drum,* ceȟkabu. — *Beat back,* aŋapta.
beat, *n.* Oape; apapi; oomani.
beaten, *a.* Nasutapi; ke'za.
beau, beaux, *n.* Kośka wi'taŋtaŋ; kośka waśte.
beauteous, *a.* Waśte; oiyokipi.
beautiful, *a.* Waśte; taŋwaśte: owaŋyagwaśte.
beautifully, *adv.* Yupiya.
beautify, *vt.* Yuwaśte.
beauty, *n.* Wowaŋyakewaśte; tuwe owaŋyagwaśte.
beaver, *n.* Ca'pa.
becalm, *vt.* Yuamdakedaŋ.
became, *imp.* of BECOME.
because, *adv.* Nakaś; he'oŋetaŋhaŋ. *Y.* Dakaś; caŋke.
beck, *n.* Wi'kiyutapi.
beckon, *vt.* Wi'kiyuta; napekoza.
becloud, *vt.* Yuataŋiŋśni.
become, *vi.* Icaġa; a'ya; iyaya: *the boy becomes a man.* *What became of,* to'kaȟoŋ. *vt.* Ki'ciwaśte; iyokipi; iyecetu: *a becoming hat.*
bed, *n.* 1. Owiŋża; tukten iśtiŋmapi; owaŋka: *go to bed; a bed of coal.* 2. Wożupi owaŋka, *a bed of roses.* 3. Ohna waŋka; sicu; ożuha: *the bed of the river.* — *Bed-fast,* to'hiŋni na'żiŋ śni. — *Bed-fellow,* kici iśtiŋma.
bedaub, *vt.* Akastaka.
bedazzle, *vt.* Iśtośniśya.
bedbug, *n.* Wamduśka śaśa.
bedding, *n.* Owiŋża.
bedeck, *vt.* Iŋkiya.
bedew, *vt.* Acuya.
bedim, *vt.* Yuataŋiŋśni.
bedlam, *n.* Hnaśkiŋyaŋpi.
bedridden, *a.* Na'żiŋ śni uŋ.
bedroom, *n.* Iśtiŋmatipi.
bedside, *a.* Owaŋka icahda.
bestead, *n.* Ohehdepi; owaŋka.
bedtick, *n.* Owiŋżaożuha.
bedtime, *n.* Waŋ'kapi iyehantu.
bee, *n.* 1. Tuȟmaġa: *the bee makes honey.* 2. Omniciye: *a quilting bee.*
beech, *n.* Utuhu haska.
beef, beeves, *n.* Tado; tataŋka

conica: *tender beef.* *Beef cattle,* tataŋka tadoyapi kta.
beefsteak, *n.* Tado ceġuġuyapi.
beehive, *n.* Tuĥmaġatipi.
bee-line, *n.* Caŋku owotaŋna.
been, *pp.* of BE.
beer, *n.* Minitaĥtoŋ.
beeswax, *n.* Tuĥmaġa ihdi.
beet, *n.* Paŋġiśaśa.
beetle, *n.* 1. Tapopuska. 2. Caŋiyapetaŋka.
befall, *vt.* Akipa; iyahdeya.
befit, *vt.* Iyokipi; iyecetu.
befog, *vt.* Poya; waciŋhnuniya.
before, *prep.* I'tokam; i'kokam. *Before long,* ecadaŋ. — *Before night,* ĥtayetu i'tokam. *adv.* I'tokam; tokaheya.
beforehand, *adv.* I'tokam. *a.* Oiçihi; wayuha.
befriend, *vt.* Kodaya; o'kiya.
beg, *vt.* Da; kida; icekiya. *vi.* Wada; wacekiya. *I beg you,* ce'ciciya. — *Come begging,* timata hi. *To beg I am ashamed,* wadapi imaśteca.
began, *imp.* of BEGIN.
begat, *imp.* of BEGET.
beget, *vt.* Ka'ġa; icaĥya.
beggar, *n.* Wadasa; oŋ'śika.
beggarly, *a.* Oŋ'śika; ta'kuśni.
beggary, *n.* Wowaĥpanica.
begin, *vt.* Tokaheya ecoŋ; tokahaŋ; watokahaŋ. *It begins to rain,* waŋna maġażu. — *He can't begin to run as fast,* iyowaś iŋ'yaŋka okihi śni.
beginner, *n.* Nakaha ecoŋ.
beginning, *n.* Otokahe.
begone, *interj.* Iyaya; kihda.
begot, *imp.* of BEGET.
begrudge, *vt.* Koŋ.
beguile, *vt.* Hna'yaŋ; iyutaŋye.
behalf, *n.* Oŋ etaŋhaŋ.
behave, *vt.* Piiçiya; oĥaŋyaŋ.
behavior, *n.* Oĥaŋye; woecoŋ.
behead, *vt.* Pa'baksa.
behest, *n.* Oie.
behind, *prep.* Iĥeyata; ihektam; ihakam. *adv.* He'kta.
behindhand, *a.* He'ktauŋ.
behold, *vt.* Waŋyaka. *vi.* Ahitoŋwaŋ.
beholden, *a.* Yu'zapi; icazopi.
beholder, *n.* Wawaŋyaka.
behoove, *vi.* Iyececa.
being, *ppr.* of BE.
being, *n.* Ouŋ; oni.
belated, *pa.* Te'han ihuni śni.
belch, *vt.* Poĥ hiyuya.
beleager, *vt.* Aohomniya.
belfry, *n.* Ḣda'ĥdatipi.
belie, *vi.* Ecen eye śni; ecetuyeśni.
belief, *n.* Wowicada; wicadapi; to'ken keciŋpi.
believe, *vt.* Wicada; awaciŋ; keciŋ.
believer, *n.* Wicada; o'pa.
belittle, *vt.* Yatakuniśni.
bell, *n.* Ma'zaĥdaĥda; ĥda'ĥda.
belle, *n.* Wiwaśte itaŋcaŋ.
belligerent, *a.* Okicize.
bellow, *vi.* Hotoŋ; bu.
bellows, *n.* Tatekaġa.
belly, *n.* Niġe; ikpi; tezi.
belong, *vi.* Ti; oyaŋketawa.
belong to, *vi.* Ta'wa; en ikoyaka.
belonging, *n.* Ta'ku ta'wa.
beloved, *a.* Waśtedapi.
below, *prep.* Ihukuya; i'hutam. *adv.* Ku'ya; o'kaĥ.
belt, *n.* Ipiyaka.
bemoan, *vt.* Aceya.
bench, *n.* Caŋ'akaŋyakapi haŋ'ska: ahna pażipapi; wayacopi; paha hepiya omdaye.
bend, bent, *vt.* Yukśaŋ; yukśiża; yuwiŋża; yuhomni; yukśa śkaŋ; e'cedaŋ awaciŋ. *Bend the ear,* anaġoptaŋ. — *Bend the grass,* peżi kawiŋża. *vi.* Kśaŋ; kśaŋ ye. *n.* Ipakśaŋ; oyukśaŋ. *Inside the bend,* okaĥmiŋ. — *Outside the bend,* ipuśi. — *One bend,* o'ha waŋżi.

beneath, *prep.* Ihukuya. *adv.* Ku'ya; hukuya.
benediction, *n.* Woyawaŝte.
benefaction, *n.* Wowaŝte wicoḣaŋ.
beneficence, *n.* Wowaoŋŝida.
beneficent, *a.* Waoŋŝida.
beneficial, *a.* Wayuwaŝte; waŝte.
beneficiary, *n.* O'kiyapi.
benefit, *vt.* O'kiya; yuwaŝte.
benefit, *n.* Wookiye; wowaŝte.
benevolence, *n.* Taŋyaŋ waciŋkiciyuzapi; wowaoŋŝida.
benevolent, *a.* Taŋyaŋ waciŋyuza; wacantkiya.
benighted, *a.* Aokpasya uŋ.
benign, *a.* Wacaŋtkiya.
benignant, *a.* Wayuwaŝte.
bent, *imp.* of BEND.
bent, *pa.* Kŝaŋ; en ihdutitaŋ.
bent, *n.* Wocaŋteyuza.
benumb, *vt.* Kiksuyeŝniya.
bequeath, *vt.* Aiḣpekiya.
bequest, *n.* Woaiḣpeye.
bereave, bereft, *vt.* Ki; e'yaku.
bereavement, *n.* Waḣpaniyapi.
berry, *n.* Waskuyeca; su.
berth, *n.* Owaŋka.
beseech, *vt.* Ce'kiya; da.
beset, *vt.* Anażiŋ; kuwa; aohduteya; żu.
beside, *prep.* Kahda; icahda; isakim. *adv.* Ikiyedaŋ; icahda.
besides, *prep. & adv.* Iakam; icuŋom; ko'kta; ahna.
besiege, *vt.* Aonawicataka.
besmear, *vt.* Akastaka.
besom, *n.* Wi'cahiŋte.
besotted, *pa.* Itomni.
besought, *imp.* of BESEECH.
bespatter, *vt.* Akaŝtaŋŝtaŋ.
bespeak, *vt.* Iwahoya; iciya.
bespoke, *imp.* of BESPEAK.
best, *a.* Iyotaŋwaŝte. *n.* Tukte iyotaŋ waŝte. *adv.* Wakapeya; iyotaŋ; itaŋcaŋyaŋ.
bestial, *a.* Wotecase.
bestir, *vt.* Aiçiciya; mdiheiçiya.
bestow, *vt.* Ķu; e'hnaka.
bestride, *vt.* Akamdaŝ na'żiŋ.
bet, *vt.* Yekiya. *n.* Ta'ku yekiyapi; kaŝkapi.
betake, *vt.* Iyaya; inaŋpa.
bethel, *n.* Owacekiyatipi.
bethink, *vt.* Kiksuya; awaciŋ.
betide, *vt.* Ki'ciyaŋka; ayata.
betimes, *adv.* Ecadaŋ; oḣaŋko.
betoken, *vt.* Iwaktaya.
betook, *imp.* of BETAKE.
betray, *vt.* To'ka o'kiya; wi'yopeya; hna'yan; yutaŋiŋ.
betroth, *vt.* Yu'ze kta yuŝtaŋ.
better, *a.* Saŋ'pawaŝte. *vt.* Saŋ'pawaŝte ka'ġa; yuwaŝte. *adv.* Saŋ'pataŋyaŋ.
betting, *n.* Wayekiyapi.
between, *prep.* Otahedaŋ; okitahedaŋ; okookna. *adv.* Okitahedaŋ.
betwixt, *prep.* Okitahedaŋ.
bevel, *vt.* Oḣ'ya ka'ġa. *a.* Oḣ'ya.
beverage, *n.* Woyatke.
bevy, *n.* Optaye.
bewail, *vt.* Aceya.
beware, *vt.* Itoŋpa. *vi.* Wakta.
bewilder, *vt.* Waciŋhnuniya.
bewildered, *pa.* Waciŋhnuni.
bewitch, *vt.* Ḣmuŋ'ġa; yuhnaŝkiŋyaŋ; iyokipiya.
beyond, *prep.* Ako; akotaŋhaŋ; i'saŋpa; ikapeya.
bi-, *prefix.* Noŋ'pa.
bias, *a.* Oḣ'ya. *n.* Owaciŋyuze.
bib, *n.* Makuakaḣpe. *vt.* Yatkaŋ.
Bible, *n.* Wowapi Wakaŋ.
bickering, *n.* Kiciġepi.
bicycle, *n.* Caŋhdeŝkaakaŋyaŋkapi.
bid, bade, *vt.* 1. Ecoŋŝi: *he bid the boy come in.* 2. Eciya: *he bid her, good day.* 3. Ķu kta eya: *I bid a dollar.* *n.* To'ken ke ciŋ.
bide, *vt.* Akipe.
biennial, *a.* Waniyetu noŋ'pa ni.
bier, *n.* Caŋ'akiyuhapi.
big (bigger, biggest), *a.* Taŋ'ka.

To feel big, taŋ'kaiçida. — *To talk big,* itaŋka.
bigamy, *n.* Tawicu noŋpapi.
Bighorn Mountains, *n.* Heska.
bigot, *n.* Wataŋkaiçida.
Big Sioux River, *n.* Can'kasdata.
bile, *n.* Minizi; pizi.
bilious, *a.* Miniziyukaŋ; ociŋśica.
bill, *n.* 1. Oicazo wowapi; miniḣuha ma'zaska. 2. Zitkapasu. *vt.* Wowapi on yaotaŋiŋ.
billet, *n.* Wowapi ci'stiŋna; caŋksa.
billiards, *n.* Ta'pa bohmihmapi; *T.* icaslo ecoŋpi.
billow, *n.* Miniwaŋca ta'ża.
bin, *n.* Opiye; woknake.
bind, bound, *vt.* Kaśka; yuskiskita; opapoŋki'caġa; ożuhatoŋ. *Bind wheat,* aġuyapipaḣta. — *Bind books,* wowapi ożuhatoŋ.
binding, *n.* Apaḣdate; iyuskite; ożuha.
biography, *n.* Oḣaŋoyakapi.
biped, *n.* Hunoŋpa.
birch, *n.* Taŋpa caŋ.
bird, *n.* Zitkadaŋ. *Y.* Zitkana. *T.* Zitkala.
birth, *n.* Toŋ'pi; oicaġe. *Give birth to,* toŋ.
birthday, *n.* Toŋ'pi aŋpetu.
birthplace, *n.* Toŋ'pi oyaŋke.
birthright, *n.* Toŋ'pi oŋ ta'waya.
biscuit, *n.* Aġuyapi pśuŋka.
bisect, *vt.* Cokaya baksa.
bishop, *n.* Waawaŋhdake.
bishopric, *n.* Woawaŋyake.
bison, *n.* Tataŋka ikceka.
bit, *n.* 1. Oŋśpa. *a bit of paper.* 2. Ma'zaiiyuwi. *T.* Ma'zayapa. 3. Caŋiyumni hi.
bit, *imp.* of BITE.
bitch, *n.* Śuŋ'ka wi'yedaŋ.
bite, *vt.* Yaḣtaka; yapa; yaksa; yaṭiŋza. *vi.* Wayaḣtaka. *n.* Oŋśpa; woyaḣtake. *Bite to death,* yaṭa.
bitter, *a.* 1. Pa: *bitter medicine.* 2. Oteḣika; wayażipa: *bitter cold.*
bitterly, *adv.* Pe'stoya; caŋteśiŋya.
bittern, *n.* Hokadaŋ.
bitterness, *n.* Wopaza; woiyokiśica.
black, *a.* Sa'pa; ha'sapa; hiŋ'sapa; śica; śapa. *n.* Sa'pa; ha'sapa. *vt.* Samya.
blackberry, *n.* Takaŋheca taŋ'ka.
blackbird, *n.* Zitkataŋka; *Y.* Pteaḣpaye; *T.* Waḣpataŋka.
blackboard, *n.* Caŋmdaskasapa.
blacken, *vt.* Samya; śamya; aokpasya.
Blackfeet, *n.* Sihasapa.
blackguard, *vt.* Ośtehda. *a.* & *n.* Iśica; wayaśica.
blackhaws, *n.* Mna.
blacking, *n.* Wi'samye.
blackish, *a.* Sa'peca.
blackmail, *vt.* Wakokipekicaḣ ki.
blacksmith, *n.* Ma'zakaġa.
blacksnake, *n.* Wamduśkasapa.
blacktail, *n.* Sintesapedaŋ.
bladder, *n.* Odeża.
blade, *n.* 1. Ape: *a long blade of grass.* 2. Ope; oyukśiża: *a knife with two blades.*
blamable, *a.* Iyaoŋpepica.
blame, *vt.* Iyaoŋpa; ba; en ai. *n.* Woba.
blanch, *vt.* Skakaġa; yuska. *vi.* Skahiŋhda; iteska.
bland, *a.* Wa'ḣba; iyokipi.
blandly, *adv.* Iwaśtedaŋ.
blank, *a.* Ta'kuna owapi śni; ska; ecececśni.
blanket, *n.* Śina; śina ikceka. *Wear the blanket,* śinahdoiŋ. *vt.* Śina oŋ akaḣpa.
blaspheme, *vt.* Ohodaśni ia.
blast, *vt.* Bożużu; bośeca; boṭa. *n.* Tate; tateyaŋpa; yahotoŋpi.
blasted, *pa.* Bośiḣtiŋ; śica.
blat, *vt.* Oŋspekeśni eya.

blaze, *vi.* Ide : *the fire blazes.* *vt.* 1. Yaotaŋiŋ : *blaze his name abroad.* 2. Kasku : *blaze the trees.* *n.* 1. Oide ; iyoyaŋpa. 2. Kaskupi ; ska.
bleach, *vt.* Skaya. *vi.* Ska aya.
bleak, *a.* Oaŝica ; tatesa ; osni
blear, *a.* Aoġi ; mini au.
bleat, *vt.* Hotoŋ ; ta'ȟcaskahotoŋ.
bleed, bled, *vi.* We ; wewe ; we uya ; we au. *vt.* Weya ; we icu ; kakpa ; mazaska ki.
blemish, *n.* Oŋŝpa ŝi'ca.
blend, *vt.* I'cicahiya.
bless, *vt.* Yawaŝte ; canwaŝteya.
blessed, blest, *pa.* Yawaŝtepi.
blessedness, *n.* Wowaŝte.
blessing, *n.* Woyawaŝte ; wotapi ce'kiyapi.
blew, *imp.* of BLOW.
blight, *vt.* Yuŝniża ; *n.* Woŝiȟtiŋ.
blind, *a.* Iŝtaġoŋġa ; ki'taŋ taŋiŋ ; taŋiŋ ŝni. *vt.* Iŝtaġoŋġaya ; yutaŋiŋ ŝni. *n.* Iŝtaġoŋġa ; oakaȟpe ; wohnaye.
blindfold, *vt.* Iŝtapaȟta.
blindly, *adv.* Taŋiŋŝniyan.
blink, *vi.* Iŝtakakpaŋ ; waŋyakeŝni koŋża.
bliss, *n.* Wocaŋtewaŝte.
blissful, *a.* Caŋtewaŝte.
blister, *vt.* Hayuŝdoka.
blithe, *a.* Wi'haha ; wi'yuŝkiŋ.
blithesome, *a.* Wi'haha.
blizzard, *n.* Icamnataŋka.
bloat, *vt.* Napoȟya. *vi.* Napoġa.
bloated, *pa.* Napoġa ; ce'pa.
block, *n.* 1. Caŋobaksa ; caŋpŝuŋka ; iŋyaŋ omdotoŋ. 2. Otoŋwe obaŝpe. 3. Wokaŝe. *vt.* Nataka ; kaġiya ; kaomdotoŋ ; okaġe pazo.
blockade, *n.* Natakapi ; akicita con'kaŝke. *vt.* Nataka.
blockhead, *n.* Waciŋtoŋŝni.
blond, *n.* Haska.
blood, *n.* We ; wotakuye ; tuwe ọhitika.
bloodshed, *n.* We papsoŋpi.
bloodshot, *n.* We kaȟtan.
bloodthirsty, *a.* Weye kta ȟca.
bloody, *a.* We ; wewe ; weyesa.
Blood , *n.* We'wicaŝta.
bloom, *vi.* Ḣca ; ŝaiçiya. *n.* Ḣca ; iyotaŋwaŝte.
blooming, *pa.* Ḣca ; waŝte.
blossom, *n.* Waȟca ; ȟcapi. *vi.* Ḣca.
blot, *vt.* Yuŝapa ; akastaka ; ŝamya. *Blot out,* yuataŋiŋ ŝni ; pażużu. *n.* Woŝapa ; samya aŝbuyapi.
blotch, *n.* Woŝapa ; onŝpa to'keca.
blotter, *n.* Minisapa ipuspe.
blouse, *n.* O'kdeġaŋġaŋ.
blow, blew, blown, *vt.* 1. Ipoġaŋ, *blow the fire.* 2. Yahotoŋ yażo, *blow the horn.* *vi.* Ipoġaŋ ; poȟ'iyeya ; bobdu ; taŋ'kaiçidaia. *Blow away,* bohaiyeya.—*Blow down,* bowaŋka.—*Blow off,* bohiŋta.—*Blow out,* boŝni.—*Blow the nose,* poġe yużiŋca.—*Blow up a steamboat,* wa'tapeta namdasya. *The dust blows,* maka bobdu. *n.* 1. Apapi ; oape : *a blow with a stick.* 2. Woakipe teȟika : *a hard blow to the family.* 3. Tate : *a big blow last night.* 4. Honaġidan cinca : *the meat was full of blows.* 5. Taŋ'kaiçidaŝkaŋpi.
blower, *n.* Oŋ ipoġaŋpi ; ihdataŋsa.
blown, *pa.* Ḣca.
blubber, *n.* Hoġaŋ ŝiŋ. *vi.* Ce'yektakta ; ce'ya eya.
bludgeon, *n.* Caŋksa ; caŋ'ȟpi.
blue, *a.* 1. To ; maȟpiyato. *Dark blue,* to sa'pa ; to staŋ. 2. Caŋteŝica se : *I feel blue.* 3. Waciŋyepica ; suta : *he is true blue.*
bluebell, *n.* Waȟcato.
blueberry, *n.* Auŋyeyapi.
Blue Earth River, *n.* Makatooze wakpa.

bluff, *n.* Ḣe ; paha ; maya. *vt.* Kakam eḣpeya. *a.* Oḣan katiŋyaŋ ; maya.
bluing, *n.* Wi'toye.
bluish, *a.* Ki'taŋna to.
blunder, *vi.* Yuśna ; ḣicahaŋ ecoŋ. *n.* Woyuśna.
blunt, *a.* Pe'śni ; otoza ; ża'żaya eya. *vt.* Otosya.
bluntly, *adv.* Otosya ; ża'żaya.
blur, *vt.* Aoġiya.
blurt, *vt.* Poḣya oyaka.
blush, *vi.* Itenaśaḣiŋhda. *n.* Iteśa ; waŋyagiheyapi.
bluster, *vi.* Bobdu ; icapta. *n.* Ibobdu ; woḣitiya śkaŋpi.
boa, *n.* Waŋmduśkataŋka
boar, *n.* Kukuśemdoka.
board, *n.* 1. Caŋmdaska : *a wide board.* 2. Wa'hnawotapi ; wotapi. 3. Wa'ta : *come on board.* 4. Optaye. *vt.* 1. Caŋmdaska aokataŋ : *board it up.* 2. Woku : *I will board you.* 3. Wata en opa : *board the ship.* *vi.* Wota ; każużu wota : *he boards elsewhere.*
boarder, *n.* En wota.
boarding, *n.* En wotapi.
boarding-house, *n.* Owotetipi.
boast, *vi.* Ihdataŋ.
boaster, *n.* Ihdataŋs'a.
boastful, *a.* Ihdataŋs'a.
boat, *n.* Wa'ta. *A bull boat,* tahukawata.
boating, *n.* Wa'taayapi.
boatable, *a.* Wa'ta a'yepica.
boatman, *n.* Wa'tawicaśta ; watopa.
bob, *n.* Oiŋ ; ta'ku pśuŋka ; pakapsaŋpi. *vt.* 1. Kapsaŋpsaŋ ; kacegceg : *bob his head.* 2. Baksa, *bob the horse's tail.*
bobtail, *n.* Oŋżiŋca.
bob-white, *n.* Śiyośapena.
bode, *vt.* Iwaktaya.
bodily, *a.* Taŋcaŋ. *adv.* Taŋtoŋyaŋ.
body, *n.* 1. Taŋcaŋ ; ceḣpi. 2. Wicaśta ; tuwe : *she is a merry body.* 3. Optaye : *a body of soldiers.* 4. Mnayaŋpi ; yuwitayapi : *a body of laws.*
bog, *n.* Wiwi ; maka coco.
bogus, *a.* Wohnaye.
boil, *vt.* Ohaŋ ; ipiḣya. *Boil beef,* tado ohaŋ. *Boil water,* mini ipiḣya. *vi.* Ipiġa ; śkaŋśkaŋ.
boil, *n.* Śiyakao : *a boil on his hand.* 2. Ipiḣyapi.
boiler, *n.* Ohna ipiḣyapi ; wa'tapeta oipiḣya.
boiling, *n.* Ohaŋpi ; ipiḣyapi.
boisterous, *a.* Okoyaśkaŋ ; woḣitika.
bold, *a.* Ohitika ; waditaka ; okitaŋiŋ ; ta'kuohodaśni.
boldly, *adv.* Waditagya.
boldness, *n.* Wowaditake.
boll, *n.* Su'ożuha.
bolster, *n.* Ipahiŋhaŋska ; ipahiŋ. *vt.* Ipahiŋkitoŋ.
bolt, *n.* 1. Mazinatake ; tiyominatake. 2. Ma'zaoyuskite ; ma'za : *fastened with bolts.* 3. Wayeyapi. *A thunderbolt,* wakiŋyaŋ kutepi. 4. Miniḣuha opaḣte : *a bolt of calico.* 5. Wi'yucaŋ haŋ'ska. *vt.* 1. Nataka : *bolt the door.* 2. Yucaŋ, *bolt the flour.* *vi.* 1. Botoŋyaŋ ya, *he bolted into the room.* 2. Iyaya ; napa : *ten delegates bolted.* *adv.* Patiŋyaŋ : *bolt upright.*
bolter, *n.* Napapi ; tokaŋ śkaŋpi.
bomb, *n.* Ma'zasu napomyapi.
bombard, *vt.* Ma'zasu anapomyapi.
bombastic, *a.* Wayataŋkaia.
bonafide, *a.* Wowicake.
bonanza, *n.* Ma'zaskaoke.
bonbon, *n.* Caŋhaŋpisuksuta.
bond, *n.* Wokaśke ; wowapi oŋ iḣdaśkapi. *vt.* Kaśka.
bondage, *n.* Wokaśke ; kaśkapi.
bonded, *a.* Każużu kta kaśkapi.

bondman, *n*. Kaśka un; wayaka.
bone, *n*. Hu; huhu.
boneless, *a*. Huhu wanica.
bonfire, *n*. Wi'yuśkiŋ cetipi.
bonnet, *n*. Wiŋ'yaŋwapaha *Ih*. Wapośtaŋ.
bonny, *a*. Waśte; taŋwaśte.
bonus, *n*. Iakamk̦upi; sinte.
bony, *a*. Huhu ota; huhu taŋiŋ.
booby, *n*. Witkotkoka.
boodle, *n*. Wi'śi; optaye.
book, *n*. Wowapi; wowapi ożuhatoŋ. *vt*. Owa; wowapi en owa.
bookbinder, *n*. Wowapi ożuha ka'ġa.
bookcase, *n*. Wowapi opiye.
bookkeeper, *n*. Owakiyapi.
booklet, *n*. Wowapi cis'tiŋna.
bookmark, *n*. Wowapi wasaghde.
bookshop, **bookstore**, *n*. Wowapi mazopiye.
bookworm, *n*. Wowapi e'cedaŋ kuwa.
boom, *n*. Bu; ni'na śkaŋ'pi; minitaŋ; can'icoġe okaśke. *vi*. Bu; ni'ŋa śkaŋ; ni'na kuwa.
boon, *n*. Wowaśte. *a*. Waśte.
boor, *n*. Waoŋspekeśni.
boost, *vt*. Pataŋiyeya.
boot, *n*. Caŋ'haŋpahaŋska; siŋte; *vt*. Naḣtaka.
booth, *n*. Caŋwapaohaŋzi.
booty, *n*. Woyuha zuyaahdipi.
boozy, *a*. Itomni.
border, *n*. Opapuŋ; ihaŋke; huta. *vt*. Opapuŋ ka'ġa. *vi*. I'ciyokihe wanka.
bore, *vt*. 1. Oḣdogya; ka'ġa: *bore a hole* 2. Naġiyeya. *n*. Wonaġiyeya.
bore, *imp*. of BEAR.
borer, *n* Oŋ oḣdogyapi.
born, *a*. Toŋ'pi. *Still born*: itkokpe.
borne, *pp*. of BEAR.
borough, *n*. Otoŋwe.
borrow, *vt*. Odota; odonicu.
bosh, *n*. Ta'kuśni.
bosom, *n*. Maku; cuwi; omahentu.
boss, *n*. 1. Itaŋcaŋ; wowaśi itancan: *the boss comes*. 2. Ptewiye. *vt*. Awaŋyaka; ecoŋkiya.
botany, *n*. Wato wooŋspe.
botch, *vt*. Śinya ka'ġa.
both, *a*., *adv*. & *pro*. Sakim; napin: *T*. nupin.
bother, *vt*. Naġiyeya.
bots, *n*. Wamduśka skaska.
bottle, *n*. Żaŋżaŋ.
bottom, *n*. Cete: *bottom of the kettle*. 2. Maka: *touch bottom*. 3. Kun'ihaŋke: *the bottom of the class*. 4. O'smaka; ku'ya. 5. Sicu: *the bottom of a boat*.
bottomless, *a*. Cetewanica.
bough, *n*. Adetka.
bought, *imp*. of BUY.
boulder, *n*. Iŋ'yaŋ pśuŋka.
bounce, *vt*. Waŋkaniyeya; eḣpeya; ayuśtaŋkiya. *vi*. Waŋkanhiyu; ipsica.
bouncer, *n*. Tuwetaŋka.
bouncing, *a*. Taŋ'ka.
bound, *imp*. of BIND.
bound, *vi*. Ipsica: psin'iyaya: *the ball bounds*. *vt*. 1. Oicaġo ka'ġa; aohomniya: *bounded by a swamp*. 2. Opapuŋoyaka: *bound the State of Ohio*. *n*. 1. Oipsica; ipsica: *he came with a bound*. 2. Owihaŋke; opapun: *knows no bounds*. *a*. Kaśka: *bound hand and foot*. 2. Wowicake; he'cetuḣca: *bound to go*. 3. Ożuhaton: *a bound book*. 4. Ekta ya: *bound for New York*.
boundary, *n*. Oḣomnioicaġo.
boundless, *a*. Woptecaśni.
bounteous, *a*. Oḣaŋpi'.
bountiful, *a*. Oḣaŋpi'; woptecaśni.
bounty, *n*. 1. Wawicak̦u; wowaoŋśida. *God's bounty*. 2. Woohiye; wokażużu.
bouquet, *n*. Waḣcaopaḣte.

bourn, *n.* Owihaŋke.
bow, *vi.* Patuża ; pakapsaŋ, *bow to the king.* *vt.* Yukśa ; yukśiża, *bow the knee.* *n.* 1. Wopatuża, *a low bow.* 2. Ipa, *the bow of the boat.*
bow, *n.* 1. Itazipe, *the Indian's bow.* 2. Kśaŋ ; caŋ kśaŋ, *a wagon bow.* *vt.* Yukśaŋ ; yuktaŋ.
bowel, *n.* Śupe ; taŋmahen ; mahentu ; caŋte.
bower, *n.* Caŋohaŋzi.
bow=knot, *n.* Yuwosokaśkapi.
bowl, *n.* 1. Wakśica śkokpa ; wi'yatketaŋka : *a bowl of milk.* 2. Ośkokpa : *a bowl in the rock.* 3. Ta'pa bohmihmapi
bowstring, *n.* Itazipeikaŋ.
bow=wow, *vi. & n.* Pa'pi ; hotoŋ.
box, *n.* 1. Caŋ'koka ; caŋ'opiye ; koka, *a box of crackers.* 2. Apapi ; oape. *vt.* Apa ; nape mdaska apa ; koka ohnaka.
boxelder, *n.* Taśkadaŋ ; *Y.* Caŋśuśka.
boy, *n.* Hokśidaŋ ; *Y.* Hokśina ; *T.* Hokśila.
boycott, *vt.* Toghda
boyhood, *n.* Wicahokśidaŋ.
boyish, *a.* Wakaŋheża se.
brace, *vt.* Ipataŋhde ; pataŋyuza ; i'ciyakaśka. *n.* 1. Ipataŋ ; caŋ'ipataŋ. 2. I'ciyakaśkapi ; tawaŋżi, *a brace of pistols.* 3. Caŋiyumni ipataŋ.
bracelet, *n.* Istoapaȟte ; napokaśke ipaȟte : *T.* napoktaŋ.
bracing, *pa.* Waśagya ; pataŋhaŋ.
bracket, *n.* Wi'yuze.
brackish, *n.* Sku'ya ; śi'ca.
brad, *n.* Ma'zaiokataŋcistina.
brag, *vi.* Ihdataŋ.
braid, *vt.* Soŋ. *n.* Soŋ'pi.
brain, *n.* Nasu ; wowiyukcaŋ.
brake, *n.* 1. Caŋpahmihma huinakeȟye ; wokaśe. 2. Taśkoża.
bramble, *n.* Caŋpepe.
bran, *n.* Aġuyapiha .
branch, *n.* Adetka ; ożate ; ośpaye. *vi.* Ża'ta ; a'kiżan ya.
branching, *pa.* Żagżanyauya.
brand, *vt.* ·Guya ; wa'petogtoŋ. *n.* 1. Petuspa : *a fire-brand.* 2. Ma'zawiġuye. 3. Oġuye : *Mr. Smith's brand.* 4. Ocaże : *a brand of crackers.*
branded, *pa.* ·Guyapi.
brandish, *vt.* Ko'za.
brand=new, *a.* Nakahateca.
brandy, *n.* Miniwakaŋ.
brant, *n.* Maġaśekśeca.
brash, *n.* Woyazaŋ ahinapa ; *a.* Suta śni.
brass, *n.* Ma'zazi ; wi'śteceśni.
brat, *n.* Hokśiyopa.
bravado, *n.* Wohitikakon'za.
brave, *a.* Waditaka. *n.* Tu'we ohitika ; zuyawicaśta.
bravery, *n.* Wowaditake.
bravely, *adv.* Waditagya.
brawl, *n.* Woakinica. *vi.* Akinica.
brawn, *n.* Ceȟpi.
brawny, *a.* Ceȟpitaŋka.
bray, *vt.* Bopaŋ ; hotoŋ.
brazen *a.* Ma'zazi ; iśteceśni.
breach, *n.* Kicaksapi ; oȟdoka.
breachy, *a.* Paȟdokesa.
bread, *n.* Aġuyapi ; aġuyapitacaġu ; woyute.
breadstuff, *n.* Oŋ aġuyapi ka'ġapi.
breadth, *n.* Ohdakiŋyaŋ.
break, broke, *vt.* (*Root forms*) Ksa; śpa ; mdeca ; weġa ; ȟdo'ka. *Break in two,* yuksa.—*Break a piece off,* yuśpa. — *Break in pieces,* yumdeca.—*Break, but not separate,* yuweġa.—*Break a hole,* yuȟdoka.

(Other prefixes.) *Break by cutting,* baksa :—*by punching* or *shooting,* boksa :—*by striking,* kaksa:—*by pushing,* paksa: —*by biting,* yaksa :—*with the foot,* naksa. (These prefixes may be attached to either of the other four root forms.)

To break a bank, okihiśniya : *bread*, yuśpaśpa :—*a colt*, kaoŋspe :—*the fall*, yuahececa :—*glass*, kamdeca :—*the heart*, namdasya :—*the law*, kicaksa : —*the leg*, yuweġa :—*the news*, otokahe oyaka :—*prairie*, maȟteca yumdu :—*a promise*, yuwicake śni :—*silence*, enakiye :—*a string*, yupsaka :—*through*, naoksa :—*up*, nażużu ; ayuśtaŋ. *vi.* 1. Naȟdeca ; napopa ; namdaza : *the boil broke.* 2. Ihnuhaŋ hihuni ; hi ; taŋiŋ : *the storm broke; the day breaks.* 3. Każużu okihi śni : *the bank broke.* 4. Yutokeca : *the horse broke his gait.*

n. 1. Oko; oksahe; onasdeca : *a break in the ice.* 2. Wohiyu ; wonataŋ : *a break for liberty.* 3. Wokiyuśpe ; yukinukaŋpi : *a break in the tribe.* 4. Kun ya : *a break in the price of wheat.*

breakable, *a.* Yuksepica.

breakage, *n.* Woihaŋke ; wi'cażużu.

breakdown, *n.* Oiyanicapi.

breaker, *n.* Ta'ża ; wayuksa.

breakfast, *n.* Haŋȟaŋnawotapi.

breaking, *n.* Maȟteca.

breakup, *n.* Woyużużu.

breakwater, *n.* Miniokaśke.

breast, *n.* 1. Maku : *a large breast.* 2. Aze : *one breast has no milk.* 3. Cuwi : *anger hid in the breast.* *vt.* I'tkokipa.

breast=bone, *n.* Makuhu.

breastpin, *n.* Makuipasisa.

breastplate, *n.* Makuakaȟpe.

breastwork, *n.* Makaoḳapi.

breath, *n.* Oniya ; niya.

breathe, *vt.* & *vi.* Niya ; iwaśtena eya. *Breathe out*, ipoġaŋ.

breathing, *n.* Niyapi.

breathless, *a.* Niya śni ; ṭa.

breech, *n.* Ceca ; pahu. *Breech of a gun*, pahu.

breeches, *n.* Oŋzeoġe.

breed, *n.* Obe ; ośpaye. *vt.* Ciŋcatoŋkiya ; icaȟya. *vi.* Ciŋcatoŋ.

breeder, *n.* Waicaȟya.

breeze, *n.* Tate ; okaduza.

brethren, *n.* Huŋkawaŋżipi.

brevet, *a.* Yuonihaŋ.

brevity, *n.* Pte'cedaŋ.

brew, *vt.* Minitaȟtoŋkaġa ; kaȟwaciŋśkaŋ. *vi.* Icaġa.

bribe, *vt.* Naȟmaŋkicicażużu. *n.* Ta'kuḳupi ; wokażużu.

brick, *n.* Makaśpaŋ ; makakaska.

brickbat, *n.* Makaśpaŋoksahe.

brick=kiln, *n.* Makaśpaŋacetipi.

brick=layer, *n.* Makaśpaŋ ehnaka.

brick=yard, *n.* Makaśpaŋ okaġe.

bridal, *a.* Nakaha kiciyuzapi.

bride, *n.* Nakahahihnaton.

bridegroom, *n.* Nakaha tawicutoŋ.

bridesmaid, *n.* Hihnatoŋkta nakiciżiŋ.

bridge, *n.* Caŋkaȟonpapi ; ceyagtoŋpi. *vt.* Caŋkaȟtoŋ.

bridle, *n.* Śuŋgiyuwi ; ipaȟte. *vt.* Ikiyuwi ; kaśka.

bridlebits, *n.* Ma'zaiyuwi.

bridle=path, *n.* Śuŋgakancaŋku.

brief, *a.* Pte'cena ; cis'tiyena. *n.* Ptenyena oyakapi.

brier, *n.* Caŋpepe.

brig, *n.* Witawata ihupa noŋpa.

brigade, *n.* Akicita optaye kokiżu.

brigadier, *n.* Akicitataŋcaŋ.

brigand, *n.* Wamanoŋwicaśta.

bright, *a.* 1. Wiyakpa ; iyeġa ; i'żaŋżaŋ : *a bright star.* 2. Waciŋksapa ; wicimdeza : *a bright writer.* 3. Wowiyuśkiŋ ; waśte ; *bright hours.* *A bright red*, śa'ȟca.

brighten, *vt.* Pawiyakpa ; waciŋksamya ; iyoyamya ; yuteca. *vi.* Iyoyaŋpaaya.

brightly, *adv.* Mdesya ; otaŋiŋyaŋ.

brightness, *n.* Wowiyakpa.
brilliancy, *n.* Woiyeġa.
brilliant, *a.* Yeḣyeġa ; okitaŋiŋ ; waciŋksapa.
brilliantly, *adv.* Yeḣya ; inihaŋyaŋ.
brim, *n.* Tete.
brimful, *a.* Iyużimnana ; ożuna.
brimstone, *n.* Makazi ; caḣdizi.
brindled, *a.* Hdehdeza.
brine, *n.* Miniskuya mini.
bring, brought, *vt.* Au ; ahi ; ahioŋpa ; iyokihi.—*Bring about,* ecetuya.—*Bring forth,* toŋ ; uya. —*Bring on,* kohaŋ ecoŋya.— *Bring to pass,* ecetuya.—*Bring up a child,* icaḣya. — *Wheat brings fifty cents,* aġuyapisu kaśpapi za'ptaŋ iyokihi.
brink, *n.* Tete ; maya ; huta.
briny, *a.* Sku'ye.
brisk, *a.* Oḣaŋko.
brisket, *n.* Maku.
bristle, *n.* Kukuśe ḣiŋ. *vi.* Nasa. *vt.* Nasakiya.
British, *n.* Saġdaśiŋ.
brittle, *a.* Śtaśtadaŋ ; waŋ'kadaŋ.
broach, *vt.* Cażeyata.
broad, *a.* Taŋ'ka ; ohdakiŋyaŋ ṭaŋ'ka.
broadaxe, *n.* Oŋspetaŋka ; caŋicakaŋ.
broadcast, *adv.* Kadaeḣpeya.
broadcloth, *n.* Śinato.
broaden, *vt.* Yutaŋka. *vi.* Taŋ'kaaya.
broadly, *adv.* Taŋ'kaya.
brogan, *n.* Caŋ'haŋpa śo'ka.
brogue, *n.* Wayatokecapi.
broil, *vt.* Ceoŋpa ; pasnoŋ. *n.* Wopasnoŋ ; woakinica.
broke, *imp.* of BREAK.
broken, *pa.* Ksawahe. *Broken-hearted,* caŋteśica ; waciŋyeyeśni.
broker, *n.* Wiyopekiciciya.
bronchitis, *n.* Dotehbeze ḣdi.
bronze, *n.* Ḣda'ḣdamaza.

brood, *vt.* Akihnawaŋka ; caŋtohnaka. *n.* Obe ; optaye.
brook, *n.* Wakpadaŋ.
brooklet, *n.* Wakpadaŋ cistiŋna.
broom, *n.* Owaŋkicahiŋte.
broomstick, *n.* Owaŋkicaḣiŋte ihupa.
broth, *n.* Haŋpi ; wahaŋpi.
brothel, *n.* Witkowiŋtipi.
brother, *n.* Huŋkawaŋżi. *My brother,* mihuŋkawaŋżi ;—*His brother,* huŋkawaŋżitku. (The following are more endearing terms.) *A son's older brother,* ciŋye.—*A son's younger brother,* suŋka.—*A daughter's older brother,* timdo.—*A daughter's younger brother,* suŋka. A father's brother's children, and a mother's sister's children are accounted the same relation as their own children.
brotherhood, *n.* Huŋkawaŋżikiciyapi.
brother-in-law, *n.* *A man's brother-in-law,* tahaŋ. *A woman's brother-in-law,* śiçe.
brotherly, *a.* Suŋkaku iyececa.
brought, *imp* of BRING.
brow, *n.* Iśtaḣe ; ḣe ; maya.
browbeat, *vt.* Wakokipekicaġa.
brown, *n.* & *a.* ġi ; ġitka. *vt.* ġiya. *vi.* ġi aya ; ġuġu.
browse, *vt.* Caŋiŋkpa yuta.
bruin, *n.* Mato.
bruise, *vt.* Kaśuża ; kaskica. *n.* Kaśużapi.
brunette, *n.* Haġina.
brunt, *n.* Iyotaŋteḣika.
brush, *n.* 1. Caŋḣaka ; caŋadetka; oteḣi. 2. Wi'casto ; wi'cahiŋte. *Shoe brush,* can'haŋpaisamye. *Clothes' brush,* o'kdeicapowaya. —*Hair brush,* wi'casto.—*Paint brush,* oŋwikiuŋpi. 3. Wokicize ptecedaŋ. *vt.* Payeza ; pastosto ; kahiniyeya ; pakiŋta.
brushy, *a.* Oteḣi.

brusque, *a.* Ohaŋkeza.
brutal, *a.* Wamanicase.
brute, *n.* & *a.* Wamanica.
brutish, *a.* Wamanica se.
bubble, *n.* Taġetaŋka. *vt.* Taġekaġa; bomdumdu; anapšapša; ȟmuŋ.
buck, *n.* Tamdoka; koška; ho'bu. *vt.* Paȟpewaciŋ škaŋ.
bucket, *n.* Kokatodaŋ; miniyaya.
buckle, *n.* Ma'zawiyuze; *vt.* Ma'zawiyuze ikoyake.
buckler, *n.* Wahacaŋka.
buckskin, *n.* Taha.
buckwheat, *n.* Aġuyapisu omdotoŋ.
bud, *n.* Camni. *vt.* Camni uya; camni o'štaŋ.
budge, *vt.* Yuškaŋškaŋ; tokaŋ ya.
budget, *n.* Apaȟte; owapi.
buff, *n.* ·Gi; ġiži; tahazi.
buffalo, *n.* Tataŋka; pteikceka. *Buffalo robe,* ptehašina.
buffalo-berry, *n.* Maštinpute.
buffet, *vt.* Apa; kiciecoŋ.
bug, *n.* Tapopuska; wamduškana.
bugbear, bugaboo, *n.* Oŋ waȟamyapi; wanaġikaġapi.
buggy, *n.* Caŋpahmihma ci'stina.
bugle, *n.* He'yahotoŋpi.
build, built, *vt.* Ti'pi ka'ġa; ticaġa; ka'ġa; sutaya e'hde. *n.* Okaġe.
builder, *n.* Ticaġe.
building, *n.* Ti'pi; ticaġapi.
bulb, *n.* Hutkaŋ pšuŋka.
bulge, *vt.* Yutaŋka. *vi.* Po. *n.* Taŋ'ka; paha.
bulk, *n.* Taŋcaŋ; hohaŋke.
bulky, *a.* Paŋ'ġa; taŋ'ka.
bull, *n.* Tataŋkabdoka. *vt.* Pawaŋkan iyeya.
bull-boat, *n.* Tahukawata.
bulldoze, *vt.* Wakokipekicaġa.
bullfrog, *n.* Toŋtoŋtaŋka.
bullet, *n.* Ma'zasu; suwaŋži.
bulletin, *n.* Woyaotaŋiŋ.
bullock, *n.* Tataŋka susu wanica.

bully, *n.* Ohitiiçida. *vt.* Ohitiya kuwa.
bulrush, *n.* Psa; cedi.
bulwark, *n.* Makaķapi; wowinape.
bum, *vi.* As'in. *n.* Waas'in.
bumblebee, *n.* Tuȟmaġataŋka.
bump, *vt.* Iboto; iyapa. *n.* Woiyapa; pažo.
bun, *n.* Aġuyapi skuyena.
bunch, *n.* Opaȟte; omnaye; wopamna; iyaġe. *A bunch of flowers,* opaȟte.—*A bunch of weeds,* wopamna.—*A bunch of grapes,* iyaġe. *vt.* Yuwitaya; e'žu.
buncombe, *n.* Wayataŋkapi.
bundle, *n.* Wopaȟte. *vt.* Paȟta; oheyuŋ.
bung, *n.* Ioštaŋ. *Bung-hole,* koka oȟdoka.
bungle, *vt.* Wayušin ecoŋ. *n.* Woyušica.
bungler, *n.* Wayušikšica.
bunk, *n.* Owaŋka; ohekdepi. *vi.* Waŋ'ka; ištiŋma.
bunt, *vt.* Pa oŋ iboto; iboto.
bunting, *n.* Wi'yokihedaŋ.
buoy, *n.* Miniwapetokeca. *vt.* Okaponya; waŋkan yu'za.
buoyancy, *n.* Okapota.
buoyant, *a.* Kapožedaŋ; wi'haha.
bur, *n.* Same as BURR.
burden, *n.* Woķiŋ; woiyokišica; wokakiže; ta'ku ka. *vt.* Tkeya ķiŋkiya; kakišya.
burdensome, *a.* Tkedapi; teȟike.
bureau, *n.* 1. Heyakeopiye. 2. Woawaŋyake. *The Indian Bureau.*
burg, *n.* Otoŋwe.
burglar, *n.* Ti'pi kaȟdog wamanoŋ.
burial, *n.* Wicaȟapi.
burlap, *n.* Psa'ožuha.
burlesque, *vt.* Uŋ'ca. n. Wowiȟa; uŋ'capi.
burly, *a.* Taŋcaŋtaŋka.
burn, burnt, *vt.* Ȟuȟnaȟya; ġuya; aceti; ideya. *Burnt his house,*

ȟuȟnaȟya.—*Burnt his finger,* ġuya. —*Burn brick,* aceti.—*Burn oil,* ideya. *vi.* Ḣuȟnaga; ġu; ide; iyeġa; ka'ta. *Sunburnt,* maśtiśpaŋ. *n.* Oġu; ġuyapi.

burner, *n.* Ma'za oideyuza.

burning, *pa.* Ide; ka'ta; teȟika. *n.* Oide; wokata.

burnish, *vt.* Pawiyakpa.

burnt, *pa.* ·Gu.

burr, *n.* Wi'nawizidaŋ; ma'zapepe; ma'zayuhomni.

burrow, *n.* Waśuŋ; wamanica ti. *vt.* Makaoȟdogya.

burst, *vt.* Napomya; naȟdeca. *Burst an egg,* napomya.—*Burst a blood-vessel,* naȟdeca. *vi.* Po'pa; napopa; hiyu. *Burst open,* namdaya.—*Burst out,* hiyu.—*Burst out laughing,* napopa se. —*Burst to pieces,* namdeca.—*The bud burst,* namdaġa.—*The canon burst,* namdaza.

burthen, *n.* Same as BURDEN.

bury, *vt.* Ḣa; hna'ka; akaȟpa; taŋiŋśni iyeya. *He buried his wife,* ȟa.—*Bury one's talents,* naȟmaŋ.—*Bury a knife in the ox,* taŋiŋśni iyeya·-*Bury strife,* ayuśtaŋ.

bus, *n.* Wicaśtatokśu.

bush, *n.* Oteȟi; caŋwopamna.

bushel, *n.* Kokaowiyute.

bushy, *a.* Yuȟaȟa; oteȟi.

busily, *adv.* Mdihenya.

business, *n.* Woecoŋ; wowaśi; wokuwa. *It is none of your business,* ta'kuna iyoniważa śni. —*He means business,* awaciŋ kuwa.

bust, *n* Wicapa' maku ahna.

bustle, *vi.* Śkiŋ'ciya. *n.* Ni'na śkaŋ'pi; niteipahiŋ.

busy, *a.* Ta'ku ecoŋ; o'hiŋni ta'ku ecoŋ. *vt.* śkiŋ'ciya; kuwakiya.

busy-body, *n.* Iyoważaśni śkaŋ.

but, *conj* 1. Tuka: *I went, but came back.* 2. He: *there is no doubt but he will come.* *adv.* 1. Heceedaŋ; henana;-na'na. *But one day,* heceedaŋ.—*But two men,* wicaśta nom'nana.—*But now,* de'cehnana. 2. E'eśni kiŋȟaŋ, *who can do it but Adam.*

butcher, *n.* Wapate. *v.* Pa'ta; wayuśin kuwa.

butt, *vt.* Pa oŋ iboto. *n.* Hu'te; ma'za yuhomniośtaŋpi.

butte, *n.* Paha okitaŋiŋ.

butter, *n.* Asaŋpiihdi; ihdi.

butterfly, *n.* Ki'mama; kimimana; *T.* kimimala.

butternut, *n.* Tazuka.

buttock, *n.* Oŋze.

button, *n.* Taśpu; *Y.* & *T.* ceśkikaŋ. *vt.* Ikoyagya.

buttonhole, *n* Taśpuoȟdoka.

buxom, *a.* Taŋwaśte.

buy, bought, *vt.* Opetoŋ. *Buy off,* ayuśtaŋ kta każużu.—*Buy a wife,* woȟpa. *vi.* Wopetoŋ.

buyer, *n.* Wopetoŋ.

buzz, *vi.* Ḣmuŋ. *n.* Ḣmuŋ.

buzzard, *n.* Heca.

by, *prep.* 1. Icahda; ikiyedaŋ; isakim: *by the river; he stood by.* 2. Oŋ; eciyataŋhaŋ: *died by poison; walk by faith.* 3. Ohnayaŋ: *by the dozen; by rule.* 4. Iyehan; eca: *by noon; by night.* 5. Kici: *a house ten feet by twelve.* *adv.* Icahda; hiyaya; icuŋom. *By all means,* to'ketu çeyaś.—*By and by,* to'keśta.—*By the way,* cuŋ'haŋnakeś.—*Come by* (obtain), iyokihi.—*Day by day,* aŋpetu iyohi.—*One by one,* waŋżikżi.—*Set store by,* teȟiŋda.

bygone, *a.* He'kta; henana.

bylaw, *n.* Woope ikoyagyapi.

byway, *n.* Caŋku cis'tiŋna.

byword, *n.* Oweśtepi.

C

cab, *n.* Ḣemani acetipi onażin; caŋpahmihma.
cabbage, *n.* Waḣpetaŋka. *vt.* Manoŋ.
cabin, *n.* Ti'pidaŋ; wa'tapetahocoka.
cabinet, *n.* 1. Tuŋkaŋśidaŋ wi'kiyukcaŋpi. 2. Caŋ'opiye wohnake. 3. Ta'ku wowaŋyake womnaye.
cable, *n.* Wi'caśketaŋka; miniwaŋca o'pta ma'zaapapi.
caboose, *n.* Wicaśtaohnayapi.
cache, *n.* Woḣa. *vt.* Ḣa.
cackle, *vi.* Hotoŋ; paŋ'niya.
cactus, *n.* Uŋkcekcepepe.
cadet, *n.* Akicita waoŋspeiciciya.
cage, *n.* Wamaniti; ma'zatipidaŋ. *vt.* Timahen nataka.
cajole, *vt.* I'ḣad kuwa.
cake, *n.* Aġuyapiskuya; kacocokaġapi; obaśpe; oŋśpa. *vi.* Sa'ka.
calamity, *n.* Wokakiże.
calamus, *n.* Siŋkpetawote.
calculate, *vt.* Yawa; iyukcaŋ; eciŋ; se'ececa.
calculation, *n.* Woyawa; wowiyukcaŋ.
caldron, *n.* Ce'ġataŋka.
calendar, *n.* Wiyawapi.
calf, *n.* 1. Pteżicadaŋ; *T.* ptehecala. 2. Sicoġaŋ: *calf of the leg.*
calfskin, *n.* Pteżicanaha.
caliber, *n.* Oiyute.
calico, *n.* Miniḣuha owapi. *Calico pony,* śuŋkdeśka.
calk, caulk, *vt.* Opuḣdi.
calker, *n.* Wa'taopuḣdi.
call, *vt.* 1. Kipaŋ; kico: *call John.* 2. Cażeyata: *he called his son John.* *vi.* 1. Paŋ; paŋ niyaŋ: *call for help.* 2. Inaḣni waŋyag i. *n.* Paŋ'pi: wicaho; kicopi; inaḣni titokaŋ i'pi. *Call for,* da.—*Call over,* cażeyan a'ya.—*Call to order,* owaŋżi yaŋkewicaśi.—*Call to mind,* tawaciŋ kiksuyeya.
calling, *n.* Paŋ'pi; kicopi; ta'ku oŋ kicopi; wowaśi.
callous, *a.* No'ġe; iyanoġe; śo'ka.
calm, *a.* Amdakedaŋ; wa'ḣbadaŋ. *n.* Amdakedaŋ; śkaŋśkaŋśni. *vt.* Yuasni; yuamdakedaŋ.
calmly, *adv.* Waḣ'bayedaŋ.
calmness, *n.* Wowaḣbadaŋ.
calumet, *n.* Wi'yakatacaŋnoŋpa.
calumniate, *vt.* Aia.
calumny, *n.* Woaie.
calve, *vt.* Ciŋcatoŋ.
cambric, *n.* Miniḣuhaska.
came, *imp.* of COME.
camel, *n.* Caŋkahupażo.
camera, *n.* Iteowapi opiye.
camp, *n.* Owaŋka; wicoti; ozuye. *vi.* Waŋ'ka; e'ti. *A deserted camp,* otiwota.
campaign, *n.* Okicize; ozuye; wokuwa.
camphor, *n.* Wi'pakiŋteska.
campus, *n.* Wayawatipi tiokśaŋ.
can, *n.* Ma'zakokadaŋ. *vt.* Mazakoka ohnaka.
can, could, *v. aux.* Okihi. *Can but,* ecena okihi.—*Cannot but,* okihiśni śni.
canal, *n.* Wakpakaġapi.
canard, *n.* Iapi wicake śni.
canary, *n.* Zitkazi.
cancel, *vt.* Każużu.
cancer, *n.* Po'pi ohiŋni icaġa.
candid, *a.* Wicake; hna'ye śni.
candidate, *n.* Oitaŋcaŋ akita.
candidly, *adv.* Anaḣbe śni.
candle, *n.* Wasnapetiżaŋżaŋ.
candor, *n.* Iewicaka.
candy, *n.* Caŋhaŋpiśaśa.
cane, *n.* Caŋsagye; cedihu; caŋhaŋpihu. *vt.* Caŋsagye oŋ apa.

canine, *a.* Ṡuŋ'ka.
canister, *n.* Waḣpekokamaza.
canker, *vt.* Ḣdi ; kuka.
cannibal, *n.* Wicaṡtaceḣpi yuta.
cannon, *n.* Ma'zakaŋtaŋka.
cannonade, *vt.* Ma'zakaŋtaŋka ecoŋ.
cannot, *v.* Okihi ṡni.
canoe, *n.* Caŋwaŋżi w'ata. *Birch bark canoe,* taŋpawata.
canon, *n.* Woope ; yusutapi.
canyon, *n.* Imniżaisdeca.
canonize, *vt.* Cażeyawakaŋ.
canopy, *n.* Awakeyapi.
cant, *vt.* Nake ehde : *cant the tub.* *n.* Nake ; ho'ṡinya eyapi.
can't, *contr.* for CANNOT.
canted, *pa.* Nake ; naptaŋyaŋ.
canteen, *n.* Akicitaminiyaya.
canter, *vi.* Nawaŋka.
canton, *n.* Makobaṡpe.
canvas, *n.* Miniḣuhaska ; wakeya.
canvass, *v.* Wamnayaŋ; wicacaże mnayaŋ ; yawa.
cap, *n.* Wapaha ; *Y.* Wapoṡtaŋ. *Gun-cap,* waŋhiṡa.
capable, *a.* Waokihi. *Capable of,* okihi.
capacious, *a.* Okipika.
capacity, *n.* Wookihi ; wokipi ; wicoḣaŋ.
cape, *n.* 1. Ipa ; makoce ipa. 2. Hiyete akaḣpa.
caper, *vi.* Psi'psin ṡka'ta.
capital, *n.* 1. Otoŋweitaŋcaŋ. 2. Oowataŋka. 3. Woyuha ; ma'zaska. 4. Caŋwakaŋpa. *a.* 1. Itaŋcan ; tokahaŋ. 2. Oŋ ṭewicayapi. 3. Iyotaŋ ; ni'nawaṡte.
capitalist, *n.* Tu'we watoŋka.
capitally, *adv.* Ni'na taŋyaŋ.
capitol, *n.* Otoŋwe itaŋcaŋ.
capitulate, *vi.* Wokicize enakiye.
caprice, *n.* Tawaciŋ ṡke'he.
capricious, *a.* Ṡke'he.
capsize, *vt.* Naptaŋyaŋ.
capsule, *n.* Su'ożuha.
captain, *n.* Akicitataŋcaŋ ; opawiŋġe itaŋcaŋ.
caption, *n.* Iwaŋkam owapi.
captious, *a.* Waienhiyeyesa.
captivate, *vt.* Caŋte hmuŋ'ka.
captive, *n.* Wayaka. *a.* Kaṡka yuhapi.
captivity, *n.* Wokaṡke.
captor, *n.* Wayaka icu.
capture, *vt.* Icu ; ohiya. *n.* Waicupi ; woohiye.
car, *n.* Ḣemani caŋpahmihma.
caravan, *n.* Ouŋhdake ; wicota e'yaya.
carbuncle, *n.* Ṡiyaḳao ḣdi.
carcass, *n.* Taŋcaŋ.
card, *n.* Kaŋsu ; ipakca. *Play cards,* kaŋsukutepi.
cardinal, *n.* Ṡinasapa o'kihe itaŋcaŋ. *a.* Itaŋcaŋ : ṡa.
care, *vi.* 1. En e'waciŋ ; awaciŋ : *I do not care to go.* 2. Caŋtahde : *do you care if I take this.* *vt.* 1. Ihakta : *she don't care for you.* 2. Awaŋyaka : *care properly for the cow.* *n.* 1. Wacaŋtahdepi ; woawaciŋ ; waawaciŋpi : *care wearies him.* 2. Woawaŋyake : *he has the care of the cattle.* *Take care,* itoŋpa.—*Take care of,* awaŋyaka. —*With care,* itoŋpeya.
career, *n.* Oni ; woecoŋ.
careful, *a.* Itoŋpe ṡkaŋ ; waawaciŋ ; taŋyaŋ kuwawaciŋ.
careless, *a.* Itoŋpeṡni ; awaciŋṡni.
caress, *vt.* Kastosto ; kihna.
careworn, *a.* Watuka.
cargo, *n.* Watohnaka.
caricature, *n.* Wowiḣa owapi.
carmine, *n.* Wi'ṡaye.
carnage, *n.* Wokte.
carnal, *a.* Wicaceḣpi.
carnival, *n.* Ṡkan'omniciye taŋ'ka.
carol, *n.* Wowiyuṡkiŋ odowaŋ.
carouse, *vi.* Witkoṡkaŋ.
carpenter, *n.* Caŋkażipa.
carpet, *n.* Owaŋka akaḣpa.

carpetbag, *n.* Wapapšuŋka.
carriage, *n.* 1. Caŋpahmihmasapa. 2. Tokšupi. 3. Oihduhe.
carried, *imp.* of CARRY.
carrier, *n.* Watokšu.
carrion, *n.* Tado šicamna.
carry, *vt.* A'ya; yuhaya; yuha; ohiya; yuštaŋ. *Carry away,* akiyahda.—*Carry on,* kuwaškaŋ.—*Carry a bill,* yuštaŋ.—*Carry a fortress,* ohiya; icu.
cart, *n.* Caŋpahmihma hu noŋpa. *vt.* tokšu; a'ya.
cartoon, *n.* Iteowapi oȟaŋko ka'ġapi.
cartridge, *n.* Iožu apaȟtapi.
carve, *vt.* 1. Bašpašpa: *carve the turkey.* 2. Baġo: *a carved head.*
cascade, *n.* Miniiȟaȟa.
case, *n.* 1. Opiye: *a case of books.* 2. Oecoŋ; ouŋ; woakipe: *a sad case.* 3. Tuwe kiŋ: *a hard case.* *vt.* Ožuhakaġa.
case-knife, *n.* Isaŋmdaska; mipišdaye.
cash, *n.* Ma'zaska.
cashier, *n.* Ma'zaskatipiawaŋyaka.
casing, *n.* Ožuȟa.
cask, *n.* Kokapahmihma.
casket, *n.* Wopiyena; wicaṭa opiye.
cast, *vt.* 1. Kaȟoiyeya; eȟpeya; hiyuya; yuwitaya: *cast a stone.* 2. Šdoya: *cast a statue.* *vi* Waciŋyeya: *he cast about to know what to do.*
cast, *n.* Kaȟoiyeyapi; šdoyapi; okaġe; obe.
castaway, *n.* Eȟpeyapi.
caste, *n.* Obe.
castigate, *vt.* Kasaksaka.
casting, *n.* Ma'zašdoyapi.
castle, *n.* Coŋ'kašketipi.
castor oil, *n.* Wi'hdi oŋ iheyapi.
castrate, *vt.* Susu eȟpeyapi.
casual, *a.* Ecaken; inaȟni.
casuality, *n.* Woakipa teȟika.
cat, *n.* Inmušuŋka. *Y.* Ikmuŋšuŋka. *T.* Igmuŋšuŋka.
catalogue, *n.* Caže owapi.
catamount, *n.* Inmu. *T.* Igmuŋ.
cataract, *n.* Ḣaȟa; ištaaoġi.
catastrophe, *n.* Woyutakunišni.
catch, caught, *vi.* Yu'za; oyuspa; icu; kiȟdeġa. *Catch at,* yuswaciŋ.—*Catch up,* kihdeġa.—*Catch a train,* iyohi. *vi.* 1. Ikoyaka: *caught in a tree.* 2. Ide: *the wood caught.* *n.* Oicu; oyuze.
catching, *a.* I'ciyaȟpaya: *a catching disease.*
catechism, *n.* Wi'wicawaŋġapi.
catechist, *n.* Waoŋspekiya.
cater, *vi.* Ki'cicuwa.
caterpillar, *n.* Wi'ihdutena.
catfish, *n.* Howasapa.
cathartic, *n.* Iyoptaiyeyapi.
cathedral, *n.* Bishop ti'piwakaŋ.
catholic, *a.* Siŋtomni. *The Catholic church,* okodakiciye siŋṭomni.—*Roman Catholic church,* Šinasapa okodakiciye.
cattle, *n.* Ptewanuyaŋpi; *Y.* ptewaniyaŋpi; *T.* ptegleška.
Caucasian, *n.* Ska'wicaša.
caucus, *n.* Wi'yukcaŋ omniciye.
caught, *imp.* of CATCH.
cause, *vt.* Ka'ġa; -ya. *Cause to smile,* iȟaya.
cause, *n.* 1. Ka'ga; hutkaŋ: *the cause of his death.* 2. Woecoŋ: *the temperance cause.*
causeless, *a.* Oŋ ecoŋkta wanica.
caustic, *a.* Wi'ġuye; pe'sto.
caution, *n.* Wawitoŋpapi; woitoŋpe. *vt.* Iwaktaya.
cautious, *a.* Wawitoŋpe.
cautiously, *adv.* Itoŋpeya.
cavalry, *n.* Šuŋgakan akicita.
cave, *n.* Pahaoȟdoġeca. *vi.* Kaoksa: *the bank caved.*
cavern, *n.* Makoȟdoka.
cavil, *vi.* Ceṭuŋhdaia; ienhde.
cavity, *n.* Oȟdoka.

caw, *vi.* Uŋcišicahotoŋ.
cease, *vt.* & *vi.* Ayuštaŋ ; iyasni.
ceaseless, *adv.* Ayuštaŋ wanin.
cedar, *n.* Ḣaŋteša.
cede, *vt.* Ḳu ; makawiyopeya.
ceil, *vt.* Mahen okataŋ.
celebrate, *vt.* Yuonihaŋ.
celebrated, *a.* Okitaŋiŋ.
celebration, *n.* Woyuonihaŋ.
celerity, *n.* Woohaŋko.
celestial, *a.* Maḣpiya.
celibacy, *n.* Tawicutoŋpišni.
cell, *n.* Ti′pidaŋ.
cellar, *n.* Makatipi ; woḣa.
cement, *n.* Makasaŋ wi′puspe. *vt.* Puspa.
cemetery, *n.* Wicahnakapi.
censer, *n.* Owizinye.
censor, *n.* Wa′mdeza.
censurable, *a.* Bapica.
censure, *vt.* Iyopeya ; ba. *n.* Woba ; woiyopeye.
census, *n.* Owicawapi.
cent, *n.* Ma′zaša. *Five cents,* kašpapi okise ; šo′kela.—*Ten cents,* kašpapi.—*Twenty-five cents,* kašpapi nom sam okise.
centenary, *n.* Waniyetu opawiŋġe.
center, *n.* Cokaya ; caŋte.
central, *a.* Cokaya ; itaŋcaŋ.
centralize, *vt.* Yuwitaya
centrally, *adv.* Ocokaya.
century, *n.* Waniyetu opawiŋġe.
cereal, *n.* Wahuwapa.
ceremony, *n.* To′ken piiçiyapi.
certain, *a.* 1. He′cetu ; wicaka : *he is certain to come.* 2. Tukte kapi : *on a certain day.* 3. Wicakeiçida : *he is certain of it.*
certainly, *adv.* A′wicakehaŋ; a′wicakeya.
certainty, *n.* Wowicake.
certificate, *n.* Wayaotaŋiŋ wowapi.
certify, *vt.* Wicakaoyaka ; yuwicaka.
cessation, *n.* Ayuštaŋpi.
cession, *n.* Ḳu′pi.
chafe, *vt.* Ha kašdoka ; naġiyeya.
chaff, *n.* Ha ; suožuha.
chagrin, *n.* Wošihda.
chain, *n.* Ma′zaicicaḣiḣa ; wi′caške ; i′ciyaza yeye. *vt.* Kaška ; ma′zaikoyagya.
chair, *n.* Caŋ′akaŋyaŋkapi.
chairman, *n.* Omniciyeitaŋcaŋ.
chaise, *n.* Caŋpahmihma.
chalk, *n.* Makasaŋ.
challenge, *vt.* Kicieconape.
chamber, *n.* Waŋkantipi; oištiŋma.
champ, *vt.* Kiŋskiŋsyata.
champion, *n.* A′tayawakapa.
chance, *n.* 1. To′ketutaŋiŋšni : *games of chance.* 2. Wanu : *he was killed by chance.* 3. Ihnuhaŋ okiḣipi : *there is some chance.* *vt.* Iyuta. *vi.* Ihnuhaŋ akipa.
chandelier, *n.* Petižaŋžaŋ yuḣaḣa.
change, *vt.* 1. Yutokeca : *change the time.* 2. Yušpušpu : *change a dollar.* 3. Ki′ciçu ; tokiyopeya : *change places.* *n.* Yušpušpupi ; yutokecapi ; to′keca.
changeable, *a.* To′kecasa.
changeless, *a.* To′kecašni.
channel, *n.* Minitacaŋku ; caŋku.
chant, *vt.* Ahiyaya ; iahaŋdowaŋ. *n.* Woahiyaye.
chaos, *n.* Ta′kutaŋiŋšni ; woškiške.
chap, *vi.* Našdešdeca ; ḣdiḣdi.
chap, *n.* Cehupa ; tu′we.
chapel, *n.* Owacekiyetipi.
chaplain, *n.* Wicaštawakaŋ.
chapter, *n.* Wicowoyake.
char, *vt.* Guġuya ; samya.
character, *n.* Oḣaŋ; wacažeyatapi; ta′kuiçiyapi ; oowa.
characteristic, *a.* Oḣaŋ ta′wa.
characterize, *vt.* Cažeyata.
charcoal, *n.* Pe′tacaḣdi.
charge, *vt.* 1. Eciya ; wahokoŋkiya : *charge him to go.* 2. Kažužuši ; išikicaton : *he charged me a dollar.* 3. Iyaoŋpa : *he was charged with theft.* 4. Ica-

zoowa: *he charged it twice.* 5. Ożuya: *charge the gun.* 6. Kiksuyeya: *charge your mind.* 7. Anataŋ: *charge the fort.* *vi.* Wakażużuśi; nataŋ. *n.* Iożu; woawaŋyake; wokażużu; wowahokoŋkiye; woiyaoŋpa; wonataŋ.
chargeable, *a.* Enayepica.
charger, *n.* Waanataŋ.
chariot, *n.* Zuyacaŋpahmihma.
charity, *n.* Wacantkiyapi; wowaoŋśida.
charm, *vt.* Iyokipiya; yuhnaśkiŋyaŋ; ḣmuŋġa.
charming, *a.* Oiyokipi.
chart, *n.* Makoceowapi.
charter, *n.* Wayuḣekiyapiwowapi; *vt.* Odota; opetoŋ.
chase, *vt.* Kuwa; pasi. *Chase away,* ḣamya. *n.* Wakuwapi; kuwapi.
chaser, *n.* Wakuwa.
chasm, *n.* Makośkokpa; oko.
chaste, *a.* Zani; śape śni.
chasten, *vt.* Iyopeya; yuska.
chastize, *vt.* Kasaksaka.
chastisement, *n.* Iyopeyapi.
chastity, *n.* Wozani.
chat, *vi.* Iayaŋka. *n.* Wohdahdakapi.
chattel, *n.* Woyuha yuha omanipica.
chatter, *vi.* Hi'hdakaka; iaa.
chatty, *a.* Wohdakesa.
chaw, *vt.* Yata.
cheap, *a.* Waśakedaŋ.
cheapen, *vt.* Yuwaśakedaŋ.
cheat, *vt.* Hna'yaŋ; ki. *n.* Wohnaye.
cheater, *n.* Wicahnayesa.
check, *n.* 1. Woanapte; wokaġi. 2. Wowapi oŋ ma'zaska icupi. 3. Kaŋsu; wowapetokeca. 4. Ta'ku hdeze. *vt.* Kaġiya; anapta; wa'petogtoŋ.
checkered, *a.* Hdehdeze.
checkmate, *vt.* Kaġiya.
cheek, *n.* Tapoŋ; iyoḣa.
cheeky, *a.* Iśteceśni.
cheer, *vt.* I'yaś'a; caŋtewaśteya. *n.* Wocaŋtewaśte; i'yaśapi.
cheerful, *a.* Caŋtewaśte; wowiyuśkiŋ; wi'haha.
cheerily, *adv.* Wi'yuśkiŋyaŋ.
cheerless, *a.* Wowiyuśkiŋcodaŋ.
cheery, *a.* Wi'yuśkiŋ.
cheese, *n.* Asaŋpipasutapi. *T.* Asaŋpi samna.
chemistry, *n.* Wokpaŋna wooŋspe.
cherish, *vt.* Tehiŋda; caŋtohnaka; taŋyaŋ kuwa.
cherry, *n.* Caŋpa; caŋpakakaŋ.
cherub, *n.* Maḣpiyaohnihde ka'ġapi.
chest, *n.* 1. Caŋ'koka; caŋ'ohnaka; opiye. 2. Cuwi.
chestnut, *n.* Yaḣuġapi hazizipena. *a.* ·Gi; sa'peca.
chew, *vt.* Yata; yu'ta; yakpaŋ: *chew tobacco.* *n.* Oyata.
Cheyenne, *n.* Śahiyena.
Cheyenne River, *n.* Wakpawaśte.
chick, *n.* Zitkaciŋca.
chicken, *n.* Aŋpaohotoŋna; *Y.* kokoyaḣaŋna; *T.* ko'kena. *Prairie-chicken,* śiyo.
chide, *vt.* Iyopeya.
chief, *n.* Itaŋcaŋ; wicaśtayatapi. *a.* Tokapa; iyotaŋ.
child, children, *n.* 1. Hokśiyopa: *a little child.* 2. Ciŋca: *the children of Israel.* *Child's play,* woecon śni.—*With child,* ihduśake.
childhood, *n.* Hokśiyopaouŋ.
childish, *a.* Hokśiyopa iyececa.
childless, *a.* Ciŋca ni'ca.
children, *pl.* of CHILD.
chill, *n.* Caŋcaŋpi; cuwitapi. *vt.* Yusni; cuwita.
chilly, *a.* Osni; cusni. *To feel chilly,* cuwitahda.
chime, *n.* Ḣda'ḣdadowaŋkiyapi. *vt.* Dowaŋeya; okiciwaśte.
chimney, *n.* 1. Oceti: *a brick*

chimney. 2. Ihupa : *a lamp chimney*.
chin, *n*. Iku ; cehupa.
china, *n*. Kampeska.
Chinaman, *n*. Pecokahaŋska.
Chinese, *n*. Pecokahaŋska.
chink, *vt*. Oko kaoṭiŋza.
chinking, *n*. Kaoṭiŋzapi.
chip, *n*. Caŋokaħpa. *vt*. Kaṡpa.
chipmunk, *n*. Taṡnaheca.
chipper, *a*. Mdiheca.
chirp, *vi*. Żo ; kiŋs'hotoŋ.
chisel, *n*. Caŋicaħdoke.
chitchat, *n*. Takuṡniṡniiapi.
chivalrous, *a*. Wawaditake.
chivalry, *n*. Wowaditake.
chloroform, *n*. Kiksuyeyapiṡni peżuta.
chocolate, *n*. Peżutasapazi. *a*. ·Gi; ġitka.
choice, *n*. Kaħniġapi ; wokaħniġe. *a*. Kaħniħyuhapi ; waṡte.
choir, *n*. Wocekiye en dowaŋpi obe ; dowaŋpi oyaŋke.
choke, *vt*. Yuniyaṡni. *vi*. Katka; yahoteṡni.
cholera, *n*. Makoṡica nakṡecapi.
choose, chose, *vt*. Kaħniġa ; ciŋ.
chop, *vt*. Kaksa ; katkuġa ; kaṡpaṡpa. *Chop down*, kawaŋka. *Chop up*, kaksaksa. *n*. Okaṡpe; cehupa.
chord, *n*. Hoiciyokipi.
chore, *n*. Takuṡniṡni oecoŋ.
chorister, *n*. Dowaŋitaŋcaŋ.
chorus, *n*. Wicota dowaŋpi.
chose, *imp*. of CHOOSE.
chosen, *pa*. Kaħniġapi.
christen, *vt*. Baptisma ḳu ; cażeḳu.
Christendom, *n*. Christ taoyate ; Christ tawocekiye.
Christian, *n*. Jesuswaciŋyaŋ ; Jesustawa.
Christianity, *n*. Jesus tawowaciŋye.
Christianize, *vt*. Jesus awaciŋwicaya.
Christmas, *n*. Jesus toŋ'pi aŋpetu; Napekiciyuzapi.
chronic, *a*. Ecahececa.
chronicle, *vt*. Oyaka.
chrysalis, *n*. Wamniomni.
chuck, *vt*. En'iyeya.
chuck-full, *n*. Ożudaŋħca.
chuck-hole, *n*. Caŋkuoħdoka.
chuckle, *vi*. Iohmuŋsiħaħa.
chum, *n*. Kicuwa.
chunk, *n*. Caŋksa.
chunky, *a*. Hu'na ; pte'cena.
church, *n*. Okodakiciyewakaŋ; ti'piwakaŋ.
churlish, *a*. Oħaŋṡica.
churn, *n*. Asaŋpiiboco. *vt*. Bococo.
chute, *n*. Ohnaiyeyapi.
cider, *n*. Taspaŋhaŋpi.
cigar, *n*. Caŋdiyukmuŋpi.
cigarette, *n*. Miniħuhacanoŋpapi.
cinder, *n*. Ca'ta ; caŋġuġu.
cinnamon, *n*. Caŋha'ṡa.
cipher, *n*. Itkoŋsa ; ta'kuṡni. *vi*. Yawa.
circle, *n*. Caŋhdeṡkakaġapi ; ta'kumibe ; okodakiciye. *vi*. Aohomniya.
circuit, *n*. Ohomni yapi.
circuitous, *a*. Aohomni.
circuitously, *adv*. Iohdamnayaŋ ; aohomniyaŋ.
circular, *a*. Mibe ; ohomniya.
circulate, *vi*. Iyazaya. *vt*. Iyayeya ; oyaka.
circumcise, *vt*. Bakiħdaya.
circumference, *n*. Aohomni.
circumspect, *a*. Wakta un.
circumstance, *n*. To'ketu ; ta'ku ; to'ken un.
circus, *n*. Ho'cokaoṡkate.
cistern, *n*. Miniwoħa.
citadel, *n*. Coŋ'kaṡke.
cite, *n*. Cażeyate.
citizen, *n*. Ihduha ; oyate o'pa.
citron, *n*. Sa'kayutapiseca.
city, *n*. Otoŋwetaŋka.
civil, *a*. 1. Wa'ħbadaŋ ; oħaŋwaṡte : *a civil boy*. 2. Ikceka :

in civil life. 3. Oyate iye en'na: *the civil war.*
civilian, *n.* Wicaṡtaikceuŋ.
civilization, *n.* Waṡicuŋiçiyapi.
civilize, *vt.* Waṡicuŋya.
civilized, *a.* Waṡicuŋ; waoŋspeka.
civilly, *adv.* Taŋyaŋ.
clabber, *n.* Asaŋpi nini. *T.* Asaŋpi gbugbu.
clad, *imp.* of CLOTHE.
claim, *vt.* Ta'wa keya; kica; keya. *n.* Ta'wapi keyapi; makoce icupi; keye ciŋ.
clam, *n.* Tuki; tukihasaŋ.
clamber, *vi.* Adi; nape kiçuŋ adi.
clamor, *n.* Owodutatoŋ. *vi.* Wohitiya eyapi.
clamp, *n.* Maswiyużipe.
clan, *n.* Tioṡpaye.
clandestine, *a.* Naḣmaŋ.
clang, *vi.* Ka'ka.
clannish, *a.* Iṡnaiçidapi.
clap, *vt.* Apa; kaskapa. *n.* Bu se iyapa; kaskapapi.
clapper, *n.* Ḣda'ḣda icakoka.
clarify, *vt.* Yumdeza.
clash, *vt.* I'ciyapa; kaġikiciya.
clasp, *vt.* Yu'za. *Y.* Oyuspa. *n.* Ma'zawiyuzedaŋ.
class, *n.* Obe. *T.* Owe. *The Bible class.*
classify, *vt.* Obe ecekcen e'hnaka.
classmate, *n.* Kici obe waŋżidaŋ.
clatter, *vi.* Kokoka; oḳoya.
clause, *n.* Iapi o'kihe.
claw, *n.* Ṡake; nape. *vt.* Naḣdata; naḳeġa.
clay, *n.* Makaġi; makacoŋpeṡka.
clean, *a.* Ska; ṡapeṡni. *vt.* Yuska; pakiŋta.
cleanly, *a.* Ska; ska ihduha.
cleanse, *vt.* Yużaża; yuska.
cleansing, *n.* Yużażapi.
clear, *a.* Mde'za: *clear water.* 2. Kasota: *a clear sky.* 3. Kohdi: *a clear stone.* 4. Adetka wanica: *clear lumber.* 5. Iyoważaṡni: *clear of guilt.* 6. Wokaġi wanica: *a clear track. vt.* 1. Ta'ku owasiŋ yutokaŋ: *clear the table.* 2. Mdesya: *clear the water.* 3. Kiyuṡka: *clear the prisoner.* 4. Kamna; yusota iwaŋkam kamna: *I cleared a dollar.* 5 Icaḣtake ṡni iyaya: *he cleared the fence. vi.* Tokaŋ iyaya; kasota: *the clouds cleared off. Clear off the ground,* maka kakmiŋ.—*Clear out,* tokaŋ iyaya. *n.* Ta'ku to'keca wanica: *ten feet in the clear. adv.* A'taya; taŋiŋyaŋ.
clearly, *adv.* Taŋiŋyaŋ; ża'żaya.
clearness, *n.* Taŋiŋ; taŋiŋyaŋ uŋ. *With clearness,* taŋiŋyaŋ.
cleave, cleft, *vt.* Kaptuża; kaṡpa. *vi.* A'skapa; ikoyaka.
cleft, *n.* Oko; onasdeca.
clemency, *n.* Wowaḣba.
clement, *a.* Wa'ḣbaka.
clench, *vt.* Sutaya yu'za.
clergy, *n.* Wicaṡtawakaŋ.
clerical, *a.* Wowapikaġa.
clerk, *n.* Wowapikaġa; mazopiye awaŋyaka.
clever, *a.* Wayupika; waṡte.
clevis, *n.* Maziyutitaŋ ṡko'pa.
clew, *n.* Oŋ sdonyapi.
click, *vi.* & *n.* Ko'ka; kakoka.
client, *n.* O'kiya; nakiciżiŋ.
cliff, *n.* Iŋyaŋmaya.
climate, *n.* Tate; tatetokeca.
climax, *n.* Iapi sam waṡ'aka; pes dete.
climb, *vt.* Adi; waŋkan ya.
clime, *n.* Makoce.
clinch, *vt.* Yus'hiyaŋka; iŋ'kpa yukṡaŋ; suta ikoyake.
cling, *vi.* Ni'na ikoyaka.
clink, *vi.* Sna. *vt.* Kasna.
clip, *vt.* Baksa; yuksa; yuṡda.
clipper, *n.* Wi'baksa; wi'tawata du'zahaŋ.
clique, *n.* Kodakiciyapi.
cloak, *n.* Hiyeteakaḣpe. *vt.* Akaḣpa.

clock, *n*. Wi'hiyayedaŋ. *Y.* & *T.* Ma'zaškaŋškaŋ.
clod, *n*. Makatasaka. *vt.* Makatasaka oŋ kiŋiŋ.
clog, *vt.* Kaġiya. *n*. Wokaġi; haŋ'pa caŋsicu.
close, *a*. 1. Ikiyedaŋ: *close to the fire.* 2. Okaduze šni: *a close room.* 3. Wateȟiŋda: *a close trader.* 4. Ohnayaŋȟ; ecetuya: *a close copy.* 5. Oṭiŋza; teȟike: *money is close.* *vt.* 1. Ecen iyeya; nataka: *close the door.* 2. Aohdute: *the opening is closed.* 3. Ihunikiya; ayuštaŋ: *closed the speech.* *n*. Owihaŋke; ihaŋke.
closely, *adv.* Ikiyedaŋ; aoṭiŋsya.
closet, *n*. Tiokaȟmiŋ; oȟnoġa. *T.* Unhnaġa.
closeted, *pa*. Kicišnana uŋ.
clot, *vi*. Tasaksaka.
cloth, *n*. Miniȟuha šo'ka; hayakesapa.
clothe, clad, *vt.* Koyagya; heyakekicatoŋ; o'ġekitoŋ.
clothes, *n*. Heyake. *Y.* Hayake. Wokoyake.
clothes-pin, *n*. Heyake wiyuze.
clothier, *n*. Heyakewopetoŋ.
clothing, *n*. Heyake.
cloud, *n*. 1. Maȟpiya; maȟpiyašapa. 2. Maȟpiyase: *clouds of dust.* *vt.* Maȟpiya; aohaŋziya. *vi*. Amaȟpiya.
cloudless, *a*. Amaȟpiyašni.
cloudy, *a*. Amaȟpiya.
clove, *n*. Pežutayuȟaȟa. *T.* Hi'iyaṭiŋze.
cloven, *pa*. Ża'ta; sdesdeca.
clover, *n*. Pežicaŋȟdoȟu.
clown, *n*. Waoŋcakoŋza.
clownish, *a*. Waoŋcase.
club, *n*. 1. Caŋksa; caŋnaksa; caŋwibopa. *War club*, caŋ'ȟpi. 2. Ikce omniciye. *vt.* 1. Caŋksa oŋ apa. 2. Kuwa: *club together.*
cluck, *n*. I'hdaskapapi. *vi*. I'hdaskapa; ciŋca kicoco.
clue, *n*. Oŋ'odepi.
clump, *n*. Wopamna; caŋwita.
clumsy, *a*. Waoŋspekešni.
clung, *imp*. of CLING.
cluster, *n*. Iyaġe; wopamna. *vi*. Yuwitaya; wi'tayahi.
clutch, *vt.* Sutayayuza.
co-, *pref*. Kicica; kici.
coach, *n*. Caŋpahmiȟma wašte; wowapitokšu. *vt.* Oŋspekiya.
coal, *n*. Makacaȟdi; caȟdiikce. *A coal of fire*, petaġa. *vi*. Makacaȟdiicu.
coal-pit, *n*. Makacaȟdioḳe.
coalesce, *vi*. Yuwitaya.
coarse, *a*. Taŋ'ka; šo'ka; ikceka.
coast, *n*. Huta; o'huta. *vi*. Huta kahda ya; osdohaŋkiçuŋ.
coat, *n*. 1. Oŋ'ȟoȟda. *Y.* O'kde. *T.* O'gle. 2. Iuŋpi: *a coat of paint.* *vt.* Iuŋ; akaȟpa.
coating, *n*. Oakaȟpe.
coax, *vt.* Da; ciŋkiya; kihna.
cob, *n*. Huwapahu.
cobble, *vt.* Caŋ'haŋpapiya.
cobblestone, *n*. Iŋ'yankmikmaŋna.
cobbler, *n*. Caŋ'haŋpapiya.
cobweb, *n*. Uŋktomitahokata; wahiŋpeya.
cock, *n*. Aŋ'paohotoŋ mdoka; mazakaŋ noġe. *vi*. No'ġeehde.
cockade, *n*. Wa'ciŋhe.
cocktail, *n*. Miniwakaŋpa.
cocoanut, *n*. Yaȟuġapitaŋka.
cocoon, *n*. Wamniomni.
coddle, *vt.* Kihna.
code, *n*. Woope; woope opahi.
codfish, *n*. Hoġaŋcosyapisa.
codger, *n*. Wicaša oȟaŋ to'keca.
coequal, *a*. Kiciakidececa.
coerce, *vt.* I'yopaštaka.
coeval, *a*. Iyehan ni.
coexist, *vi*. Kici ni.
coffee, *n*. Pežutasapa; wakadyapi.
coffeemill, *n*. Pežutasapaiyukpaŋ.
coffeenut, *n*. Waȟnaȟna.

coffeepot, *n.* Pe żutasapawiyokaś-taŋ.
coffer, *n.* Opiyesuta.
coffin, *n.* Caŋ'ohnahnakapi.
cog, *n.* Ma'zayuhomnipi hi.
cogent, *a.* Waś'aka.
cogitate, *vt.* Awaciŋ.
cognizant, *a.* A'taya sdonya.
cohabit, *vi.* Kiciyus uŋ.
cohere, *vi.* Kiciiciyaskapa.
coil, *vt.* Kakśa. *n.* Okakśa.
coin, *n.* Ma'zaska. *vt.* Ma'zaska śdoya; ka'ġa.
coincide, *vi.* A'kidececa.
cold, *a.* Sni; osni; cuwita. *Cold iron,* ma'za sni.—*A cold day,* aŋpetu osni.—*I am cold,* macuwita.
cold-blooded, *a.* We sni; caŋtewanica.
colic, *n.* Teziyazaŋpi.
collapse, *vi.* Napopa; hiŋhpaya.
collar, *n.* Wanapiŋ; tahuska; tahuakahpe. *vt.* Wanapiŋkicatoŋ.
collar-bone, *n.* Ceśkicate; *T.* ceblohu.
collate, *vt.* Mnayaŋ.
colleague, *n.* Kicica.
collect, *vt.* Pahi; mnayaŋ. *vi.* Wi'taya.
collect, *n.* Wocekiye ptecena.
collection, *n.* Womnaye.
collective, *a.* Yuwitaya.
collector, *n.* Wamnaye.
college, *n.* Wooŋspewaŋkantu.
collide, *vi.* I'ciyapa.
collision, *n.* I'ciyapapi.
colloquial, *a.* Wi'kcekceiapi.
colonel, *n.* Kektopawinġeitaŋcaŋ.
colonize, *vt.* Ośpayetoŋ i'yotaŋka.
colony, *n.* Ośpaye ahitipi.
color, *n.* 1. Owapi; śayapi; hiŋ'tokeca. 2. *pl.* Oyate tawowapi; wi'yokihedaŋ.
colored, *pa.* Owapi.
colorless, *a.* Owapiwanica.
colossal, *a.* Ni'nataŋka.
colporteur, *n.* Wowapiwiyopeyaomani.
colt, *n.* Śuŋkciŋcana.
column, *n.* 1. Wowapi caŋkuye obosdata. 2. Caŋipa'taŋ.
Comanches, *n.* Siŋtehdawicaśa.
comb, *n.* 1. Ipakca. *A fine comb,* ipakca sbuna. 2. Tuhmaġa ihdi ożuha, *honey comb.* 3. Aŋpaohotoŋna peśa, *chicken's comb.* *vt.* Kakca. *Comb one's own,* hda'ka.
combat, *vt.* Ki'za; kiciza. *n.* Wokicize.
combatant, *n.* Wakiza.
combative, *a.* Wakizesa.
combine, *vt.* Yuokoŋwaŋżina.
combustible, *a.* Ideyepica.
come, came, *vi.* 1. (in progress) U. 2. (completed) Hi.—*I come,* wau.—*I came,* wahi.—*I will come,* wau kta, *or,* wahi kta.—*Come after* (later), ihakam u, (*come for*) huwe hi; hiyohi.—*Come off* (*as a shoe*) śdokahaŋ.—*Come to,* iyohi.—*Come up with,* kihdeġa.
comedy, *n.* Wośkate.
comely, *adv.* Owaŋyagwaśte.
comet, *n.* Wicaŋhpisiŋtetoŋ.
comfort, *vt.* Kicaŋpta; o'kiya. *n.* 1. Wokicaŋpte; woozikiye; ta'ku oŋ taŋyaŋ uŋ'pi: *live in comfort.*
comfortable, *a.* Taŋyaŋ; waśte.
comforter, *n.* Wakicaŋpte; owiŋża śo'ka.
comfortless, *a.* Oozi wanica.
comic, comical, *a.* Wawihaye.
comity, *n.* O'kiciyapi.
comma, *n.* Oehnakedaŋ.
command, *vt.* 1. Wowaś'ake oŋ eya;—śi. *He commanded him to go,* yeśi. 2. Itaŋcaŋuŋ; waecoŋ śi: *the captain commands the compauy.* 3. Iyokihi, *wheat commands a high price.* *n.* Woeye; woawaŋyake; wookihi.

commandant, commander, *n.* Itaŋcaŋ.
commandment, *n.* Woahope.
commemorate, *vt.* Kiksuya.
commemoration, *n.* Wokiksuye.
commence, *vt.* Tokaheya ecoŋ; waŋna ecoŋ.
commencement, *n.* Otokahe.
commend, *vt.* Yawaŝte; caẑeyata.
commendable, *a.* Yawaŝtepica.
commensurate, *a.* Iyehantu.
comment, *vi.* Ia; to'ketu oyaka.
commentary, *n.* To'ken ka'pi oyakapi.
commerce, *n,* Oyate wopekicatoŋpi.
commercial, *a.* Wopetoŋ.
commiserate, *vt.* Oŋ'ŝida.
commissary, *n.* Woyute awaŋyake.
commission, *vt.* Woecoŋ ḳu. *n.* 1. Waecoŋkiyapi : *a commission to try him.* 2. Ecoŋpi : *the commission of crime.* 3. Ta'ku ecoŋŝipi; wowaŝi. 4. Waecoŋŝipi wowapi.
commissioner, *n.* Awaŋyake itaŋcaŋ.
commit, *vt.* 1. Ecoŋ : *commit sin.* 2. E'hnaka : *commit to jail.* 3. En iyayeiçiya : *he committed himself to the work.*
committee, *n.* Waecoŋŝipi.
commodious, *a.* Okipika.
commodity, *n.* Woyuha.
commodore, *n.* Ozuyewataitaŋcaŋ.
common, *a.* 1. He'cecasa; yukesa : *a common event.* 2. Ikceka; ikceuŋ : *the common people.* 3. I'akidecen ta'wapi : *common property; common schools.* *n.* Makobaŝpe oyate ta'wapi.
commonly, *adv.* Ece; sa.
commonplace, *a.* He'cetuka.
commonwealth, *n.* Oyate a'taya.
commotion, *n.* Woŝkaŋŝkaŋ.
commune, *vi.* Wohdaka; wohduze icu.
communicant, *n.* Wohduze o'pa.
communicate, *vt.* Ḳu; hiyukiya; oyaka. *vi.* Woyake; i'ciyahde waŋka.
communication, *n.* Wokiciyakapi; wowapi.
communicative, *a.* Woyakesa.
communion, *n.* 1. Wohduze; ḣtayetuwotapi. 2. Odakonkiciyapi; o'kiciyapi; wokiciyakapi.
community, *n.* Oyate; wicoŝpaye; ta'ku wi'taya ta'wayapi.
commute, *vt.* Yuaokpani.
compact, *a.* Oṭiŋza; suta. *n.* Wokoŋze; woecoŋ.
companion, *n.* Kicica; kicuwa.
company, *n.* 1. Optaye; wicawitaya : *a company of believers.* 2. Tuwe kici uŋpi : *she loves company.* 3. Okodakiciye : *a dry goods company.*
comparative, *a.* I'ciwaŋyakapi.
compare, *vt.* I'ciwaŋyaka. *vi.* Iyehaŋyaŋ uŋ.
comparison, *n.* I'ciwaŋyakapi
compass, *n.* Maziwaŋyake; makiwaŋyake; woiyohiya; aohomniya. *vt.* Iyohiya.
compasses, *n.* Caŋhdeŝkawicazo.
compassion, *n.* Wowaoŋŝida.
compassionate, *a.* Waoŋŝida.
compatible, *a.* Kicicayepica.
compel, *vt.* I'yopaŝtagya; -ya; -ki'ya.
compensate, *vt.* Kaẑuẑu.
compensation, *n.* Wokaẑuẑu.
compete, *vi.* Kici ecoŋ.
competence, *n.* Wookihi; oiçihi.
competent, *a.* Okihi; iyecetu.
competition, *n.* Kiciecoŋpi.
compile, *vt.* Wi'taya e'hnaka.
complacent, *a.* Waciŋiyokipi.
complain, *vi.* Iyokipi ŝni ia.
complaint, *n.* Woaie.
complete, *a.* Yuŝtaŋpi; a'taya. *vt.* Yuŝtaŋ; ecetuya.
completely, *adv.* Taŋyeḣca.
complex, *a.* Oŝkiŝke.
complexion, *n.* Uka; ha.

compliance, *n.* Iyowiŋyaŋpi.
complicate, *vt.* Yuškiška.
complicated, *pa.* Oškiške.
complicity, *n.* Waokiyapi.
compliment, *vt.* Yaonihaŋ. *n.* Woyuonihaŋ.
comply, *vi.* Wicakicida; ecen ecoŋ.
comport, *vt.* Oȟaŋye.
compose, *vt.* 1. Ka'ġa : *compose a hymn.* 2. Yuasni : *compose yourself.* 3. Ma'zaehde.
composition, *n.* Iapi ka'ġapi.
compost, *n.* Tacesdiicahi.
composure, *n.* Wowaȟba.
compound, *vt.* Icahiya ; a'okpani yawa. *a.* Yuokoŋwaŋžipi ; yuwitaya.
comprehend, *vt.* Okaȟniġa.
comprehension, *n.* Wokaȟniġe.
compress, *vt.* Paskica.
comprise, *vt.* Ka ; o'pekiya.
compromise, *vt.* Wokiya ; tawaciŋ enakiye.
compulsion, *n.* Woiyopaštake.
compunction, *n.* Wocaŋtiyapa.
compute, *vt.* To'nakeca yawa.
comrade, *n.* Kicuwa ; kicica.
con, *vt.* Atanse awaciŋ.
concave, *a.* Ško'pa.
conceal, *vt.* Anaȟbe.
concede, *vt.* Iyowiŋyaŋ ; ḳu.
conceit, *n.* Iyotaŋiçida; woawaciŋ.
conceited, *a.* Waȟaŋiçida.
conceivable, *a.* Waciŋiyohipica.
conceive, *vt.* Waciŋehde; awaciŋ; iyukcaŋ ; ihdušaka.
concentrate, *vt.* Yuwitaya.
conception, *n.* Waawaciŋpi; ihdušakapi.
concern, *vt.* Iyowaža ; içicuwa ; en e'wacin. *n.* Woawaciŋ ; ta'ku ; okodakiciye.
concerning, *prep.* Eciyataŋhaŋ; –i.
concert, *n.* 1. Omniciye wicakidowaŋpi. 2. O'kiciyapi.
conciliate, *vt.* Okiciyuwašte.
concise, *a.* Pte'cena ; katiŋyaŋ.
conclave, *n.* Naȟmaŋomniciye.
conclude, *vt.* Iyukcaŋ ; yuštaŋ ; ihuŋniyaŋ.
conclusion, *n.* Ihaŋke ; woyuštaŋ ; wowiyukcaŋ.
conclusive, *a.* Wayuštaŋ.
concoct, *vt.* Ka'ġa.
concord, *n.* Okiciwaštepi.
concourse, *n.* O'yuwitaya.
concubine, *n.* Tawicu wakaŋyuzešŋi.
concur, *vi.* 1. He'cetuda. 2. Iakiyehantu.
condemn, *vt.* Yaco ; ši'cayawapi.
condense, *vt.* Yuciḳana.
condescend, *vi.* Ihduhukuya.
condition, *n.* Ouŋ ; to'ken uŋ.
conditional, *a.* Ta'ku ikoyake.
condole, *vt.* Caŋtekicišica.
condone, *vt.* En e'toŋwe šni.
conduce, *vi.* Waokiya.
con'duct, *n.* Oȟaŋ ; kuwapi.
conduct', *vt.* 1. Yus a'ya : *conduct the boy home.* 2. Awaŋyaka ; kuwa : *conduct the campaign.* 3. Oȟaŋyaŋ : *he conducts himself well.*
conductor, *n.* Tokahaŋ ; itaŋcaŋ.
cone, *n.* Mibeya pe'sto.
confection, *n.* Ta'ku sku'ya icahi.
confederacy, *n.* Wodakota.
confer, *vt.* Ḳu. *vi.* Wohdaka.
conference, *n.* Owohdake.
confess, *vt.* Ohdaka.
confide, *vt.* Awaŋyagkiya ; wicakeda.
confidence, *n.* Wowaciŋye ; wowicakeda.
confident, *a.* Wicakeiçida.
confidential, *a.* Waciŋyaŋ ; naȟmaŋyuha.
confine, *vt.* Aonataka.
confirm, *vt.* Yusuta ; yuwicaka.
confirmation, *n.* Wicayusutapi.
confiscate, *vt.* Ki.
conflagration, *n.* Oide.
conflict', *vi.* Kaġikiciya.
con'flict, *n*, Woakinica ; wokicize.
confluence, *n.* Mdo'te.

conform, *vi.* Iyecenecoŋ.
confound, *vt.* Waciŋhnuniya; i'cihnuniya; i'cicahiya.
confront, *vt.* I'tkokipa.
confuse, *vt.* Waciŋhnuniya; i'cicaḣiya.
confusion, *n.* To'ketu taŋiŋ śni.
confute, *vt.* Yuwicake śni.
congeal, *vt.* Tasagya. *vi.* Tasaka.
congenial, *a.* Wi'ciyokipi.
congested, *a.* Oẑudaŋ; oṭiŋza.
conglomerate, *a.* I'cicahi.
congratulate, *vt.* Ikiciyuśkiŋ.
congregate, *vi.* Mni'ciya.
congregation, *n.* Omniciye.
Congregational, *n.* — Okodakiciye wakaŋ obe. — A'tayedaŋ.
congress, *n.* Tuŋkaŋśina omniciye.
conical, *a.* Mibepesto.
conjecture, *vt.* Eciŋ; iyukcaŋ.
conjugal, *a.* Wakaŋkiciyuzapi.
conjugate, *vt.* Adetka oyaka.
conjunction, *n.* Wokaḣtake. (*Gram.*) Iyayuze.
conjure, *vt.* Wapiya; eya.
connect, *vt.* I'cikoyake; kicica.
connectedly, *adv.* Yuzunya.
connection, *n.* I'ciyahde; kicica; wotakuye.
connive, *vi.* Iyowiŋyaŋ; o'kiya.
connubial, *a.* Okiciyuze.
conquer, *vt.* Ohiya; kte'daŋ.
conquest, *n.* Ohiyapi.
conscience, *n.* Wi'ihdukcaŋ.
conscientious, *a.* Tawiihdukcaŋ ahope.
conscious, *a.* Kiksuye.
conscript, *n.* Akicita opekiyapi.
consecrate, *vt.* Yuwakaŋ; ḳu.
consecutive, *a.* I'ciyokiheya.
consent, *vi.* Iyowiŋyaŋ.
consequence, *n.* 1. Ta'ku etaŋhaŋ icaġe. 2. Wookinihaŋ.
consequential, *a.* Okinihaŋ.
consequently, *adv.* He'cen.
conservative, *a.* Tawaciŋ; ḣaŋhi.
consider, *vt.* Awaciŋ; eciŋ.
considerable, *a.* Ki'taŋna o'ta.
consideration, *n.* Woawaciŋ; wokaẑuẑu.
consign, *vt.* Ḳu; yuhekiya.
consist, *vi.* He'ca; oŋ ka'ġapi.
consistent, *a.* He'cetuwaŋẑica.
consolation, *n.* Wokicaŋpte.
console, *vt.* Kicaŋpta.
consolidate, *vt.* Yuokoŋwaŋẑina.
consonant, *n.* Oowa taŋśna śni. *a.* Kici okiciwaśte.
consort, *vi.* O'haŋhde; ihakta. *n.* Kicica.
conspicuous, *a.* Okitaŋiŋ.
conspiracy, *n.* Naḣmaŋ kuwapi.
conspire, *vt.* Kuwa.
constable, *n.* Waoyuspa.
constancy, *n.* Wowaciŋtaŋka.
constant, *a.* O'hiŋni; pa'tawaŋẑina.
consternation, *n.* Woyuśiŋyaye.
constipated, *a.* Suksuta iheya.
constituency, *n.* Tiŋs'koya ta'wayapi.
constitute, *vt.* Ka'ġa.
constitution, *n.* Wokaġewowapi; wokaġe; okaġe.
constrain, *vt.* I'yopaśtake.
construct, *vt.* Ka'ġa.
construction, *n.* Ka'ġapi.
construe, *vt.* To'ketu oyaka.
consult, *vt.* Kici iwohdaka.
consultation, *n.* Iwohdakapi.
consume, *vt.* Ihaŋgya; yusota; (*by eating*) temya; (*by fire*) ḣuḣnaġa.
consummate, *vt.* Ihunikiya. *a.* Waŋkantuya.
consumption, *n.* Ihaŋgyapi; caġuśica woyazaŋ.
contact, *n.* Icaḣtakapi.
contagious, *a.* I'ciyaḣpeyapi.
contain, *vt.* Ohnaka; en uŋ; kipi; ihduha.
contaminate, *vt.* Yuśica.
contemplate, *vt.* Awaciŋ; ka.
contemporary, *n.* Iyehan ni.
contempt, *n.* Wowaḣtedaśni.

contemptible, *a.* Wahtešni.
contend, *vt.* Akinica; kitaŋ.
content, *a.* Iyokipi. *vt.* Iyokipiya. *n.* Woiyokipi; woozi.
contention, *n.* Woakinica.
contentious, *a.* Waakinicasa.
contentment, *n.* Woozi.
contest′, *vt.* Akinica.
con′test, *n.* Woakinica.
context, *n.* Iapikicica.
contiguous, *a.* Icahtaka.
continent, *n.* Makotaŋka.
continual, *a.* O′hiŋni.
continually, *adv.* O′hiŋniyaŋ.
continuous, *a.* O′hiŋni yeya.
continue, *vt.* Saŋ′pa ya; kuwa.
contortion, *n.* Taŋcaŋ yuhmiŋpi.
contract′, *vt.* Yuptecena; natipa; yuštaŋ.
con′tract, *a.* Woyuštaŋ.
contraction, *n.* Ayucik̦api.
contractor, *n.* Waecoŋ.
contradict, *vt.* He′cetušni eya; yuwicakešni.
contrary, *a.* To′keca; kašeya.
contrast, *vt.* I′ciwaŋyag e′hde. *n.* To′kecapi.
contribute, *vt.* Womnaye en ehpeya; k̦u; kiçuŋ.
contribution, *n.* Womnaye.
contrite, *a.* Icaŋtešica.
contrive, *vt.* Iyukcaŋ; kuwa.
control, *vt.* Awaŋyaka.
controversy, *n.* Woakinica.
controvert, *vt.* Yuwicakešni kuwa.
contumacy, *n.* Wanahoŋpišni.
convalesce, *vi.* Akisni.
convene, *vt.* Mni′ciya.
convenience, *n.* Okiciwaštepi.
convenient, *a.* Uŋ′piwašte; taŋyaŋ.
convent, *n.* Šinasapawiŋyaŋ tipi.
convention, *n.* Omniciye.
converge, *vt.* I′ciyahde ye.
conversant, *a.* A′taya sdonya.
conversation, *n.* Wohdahdakapi.
con′verse, *a.* Kaicucuya.
converse′, *vi.* Wohdaka; iaa.
conversion, *n.* Ihduhomnipi.
convert′, *vt.* Yuhomni.
con′vert, *n.* Yutokecapi.
convex, *a.* Pažo; apaha.
convey, *vt.* A′ya; ai.
conveyance, *n.* Oaye; k̦u′pi.
convict′, *vt.* Yaco; kaška.
con′vict, *n.* Yacopi.
convince, *vt.* Wicadakiya.
convocation, *n.* Wicaštawakaŋ omniciye.
convoke, *vt.* Wicakico; mni′ciya.
convulse, *vt.* Yuškaŋškaŋ.
convulsion, *n.* Kaŋ′natipapi.
coo, *vi.* Zitkadowaŋ.
cook, *vt.* Ohaŋ; špaŋyaŋ. *vi.* Wohaŋ; wašpaŋyaŋ; dotihaŋ. *n.* Wohe.
cooked, *pa.* Špaŋ.
cooky, *n.* Aġuyapi sku′yena.
cool, *a.* Cusni; sni; mde′za. *vt.* Sniyaŋ; yusni; canasni.
coolly, *adv.* Ohaŋk̦esya.
coon, *n.* Wica.
coop, *n.* Ti′pidaŋ. *n.* Maheniyeya.
cooper, *n.* Kokapahmihma ka′ġa.
cooperate, *vi.* O′kiya.
coot, *n.* Caŋhpaŋ.
cope, *vi.* Kici ecoŋ.
copious, *a.* Okamdaya; o′ta.
copper, *n.* Ma′zaša.
copulate, *vt.* Kiyuha.
copy, *vt.* Iyecen owa.
copyright, *n.* Ta′wayapi.
cord, *n.* 1. Hakahmuŋpi; hahoŋta; wi′kaŋ. 2. Caŋ′iyutapi.
cordial, *a.* Caŋtewašte. *n.* Pežuta ocaže.
core, *n.* Çaŋte; co.
cork, *n.* Žaŋžaŋioštaŋ.
cormorant, *n.* Huŋ′tka; mdo′za.
corn, *n.* 1. Wamnaheza; *Y.* wakmaheza; *T.* wagmeza; wahuwapa. 2. Siyukaza anoġe.
corner, *n.* 1. Oise: *the street corner.* 2. Okahmin: *the corner of the room.* *vt.* Kahmiŋyata iyeya.
cornice, *n.* Ti′pitete.

coronation, *n.* Te'šdagkiyapi.
coroner, *n.* Wicaṭe wi'yukcaŋ.
corporal, *a.* Wicataŋcaŋ. *n.* Wicapasi.
corps, *n.* Optaye.
corpse, *n.* Wicaṭa.
corpulent, *a.* Ce'pa; taŋcaŋtaŋka.
corral, *n.* Caŋkaškapi.
correct, *a.* Owotaŋna; he'cetu. *vt.* Yuowotaŋna; iyopeya.
correction, *n.* Apiyapi; yuowotaŋnapi.
correctly, *adv.* Taŋyaŋ; zun'ya.
correspond, *vi.* 1. Kici iyececa; kicica: *corresponds with the copy.* 2. Wowapi kiciçu: *she corresponds with her mother.*
corroborate, *vt.* Yuwicaka.
corrode, *vt.* Yukuka.
corrupt, *vt.* Yušica. *a.* Ši'ca; ḣwiŋ; owotaŋnašni.
corruptible, *a.* Yušicepica.
corruption, *n.* Woyušice.
corset, *n.* Cuwiiyuskite.
cost, *vt.* Iyusote; iyopeya. *n.* Woiyopeye; wokažužu.
costive, *a.* Suksuta iheya.
costly, *a.* Teḣike.
costume, *n.* Oihduze.
cot, *n.* Owaŋka cis'tiŋna.
coteau, *n.* Ḣe.
cottage, *n.* Ti'pikuciyena.
cotton, *n* Hiŋ'ožupi; miniḣuha.
cottontail, *n.* Maštiŋcana.
cottonwood, *n.* Wa'ġacaŋ.
couch, *vi.* Pustag iwaŋka. *n.* owaŋka. *vt.* E'hnaka.
cough, *vi.* Hoḣpa. *Cough up,* kašpa. *n.* Hoḣpapi.
could, *imp.* of CAN.
council, *n.* Omniciye.
counsel, *vt.* Eciya; ecoŋši; ikiciyukcaŋ. *n.* Wowahokoŋkiye.
count, *vt.* To'nakecayawa; yawa. *n.* Woyawa; wowicada; itaŋcaŋ.
countenance, *n.* Ite; itohnake; wookiye. *vt.* Iyowiŋkiya.
counter, *n.* Wa'hna wopetoŋpi; tuweyawa. *adv.* & *pref.* Itkom; uŋmaŋ eciyataŋhaŋ; i'cipaš.
counteract, *vt.* Yuecetušniya.
counterfeit, *n.* Wohnaye. *vt.* Wohnaye ka'ġa.
countermand, *vt.* Yutokeca.
countess, *n.* Wiŋ'yaŋitaŋcaŋ.
countless, *a.* Yawapicašni.
countrified, *pa.* Wožuwicaša seca.
country, *n.* 1. Makoce: *my country.* 2. Ikcemakoce; wožutipi; *he lives in the country.* 3. Oyate: *the whole country rose in arms.*
countryman, *n.* Wožuwicaša.
county, *n,* Makobašpe.
couple, *a.* Noŋ'pa; tawaŋži. *vt.* I'ciyakaška; i'cikoyake.
coupler, *n.* Wi'koyake.
coupon, *n.* Oŋšpaikoyake.
courage, *n* Wowaditake.
courageous, *a.* Waditaka.
courier, *n.* Wahošiye.
course, *n.* 1. Woiyopte; to'ken ecoŋ: *his course was not wise.* 2. Tokiyotaŋ ya: *the ship's course.* 3. Oweciŋhaŋ ecoŋpi: *a course of lectures.* *vi.* Ya; iyopte; kuwa.
court, *vt.* Okiya; wiokiya; akita. *n.* Wayacoomniciye; ho'coka; itaŋcaŋti.
courteous, *a.* Oḣaŋwašte.
courtesy, *n.* Wokinihan.
courtier, *n.* Itaŋcaŋ taokiye.
courtly, *a.* Okinihaŋ.
courtship, *n.* Okiyapi.
courtyard, *n.* Ti'wašteokšaŋ.
cousin, *n.* (*A man's male cousin*) Tahaŋši; (*A man's female cousin*) haŋkaši; (*A woman's male cousin*) içeši; (*A woman's female cousin*) içepaŋši.
cove, *n.* Okaḣmiŋ.
covenant, *n.* Wokoŋze.
cover, *vt.* Akaḣpa; ahdeyuza. *n.* Oakaḣpe; iha.

covering, *n.* Oakaȟpe.
coverlet, *n.* Owiŋżaakaȟpe.
covert, *a.* Naȟmaŋpi.
covet, *vt.* Koŋ; as'iŋ; *T.* koŋ'la.
covetous, *a.* Wakoŋs'a.
covetousness, *n.* Wakoŋpi.
covey, *n.* Zitka optaye.
cow, *n.* Ptewiye; pte. *vt.* Iniȟaŋya.
coward, *n.* Tu'we canwaŋka.
cowardly, *a.* Canwaŋka.
cowbird, *n.* Pteaȟpaye; *T.* waȟpaȟota.
cowboy, *n.* Pteawaŋyake.
cowhide, *n.* Pteȟa; taȟado.
coworker, *n.* Kicica.
coy, *a.* Wi'steca.
coyote, *n.* Mi'ca; mi'caksica.
cozy, *a.* Wayuco; taŋyaŋ.
crab, *n.* Matuśkataŋka; taspaŋ.
crabbed, *a.* Waciŋko.
crack, *vt.* *As a nut,* kaȟuġa; kakpi. *As a plate, or a board,* yusdeca. *As ice,* otiŋ; bu. *As a joke,* wawiȟaye. *As a whip,* po'pa. *n.* Oko; onasdeca; bu; oape.
cracker, *n.* Aġuyapisaka; caȟdi napomyapi.
crackle, *vt.* Nakpakpa.
crackling, *n.* Waśiŋ oġuġu.
cradle, *n.* I'yoḳopa.
craft, *n.* 1. Woecoŋ; wowaśi: *of what craft are ye.* 2. Wa'ta.
crafty, *a.* Wicahnaye ksa'pa.
crag, *n.* Iŋ'yaŋmaya.
cragged, craggy, *a.* Heȟe.
cram, *vt.* Paoṭiŋza; akaska.
cramp, *n.* Kaŋ natipapi. *vt.* Natimya; aoṭiŋsya.
cranberry, *n.* Potpaŋka.
crane, *n.* Pehaŋ; pehaŋsaŋ.
crank, *n.* 1. Iyuhomni; ma'zakśaŋ. 2. Tawaciŋ tokecas'a.
cranky, *a.* Oȟaŋto'keca.
crape, *n.* Apaȟdate ġaŋġaŋ.
crash, *vt.* Kaȟuȟuġa. *n.* Woihaŋgye; ta'ku bu; miniȟuhapepe.
crate, *n.* Caŋyaŋkapiopiye.
crater, *n.* Ḣeide'oȟdoka.
cravat, *n.* Taȟuiyuskite.
crave, *vt.* Ni'naciŋ; icekiya.
craw, *n.* Zitkatapo.
crawfish, *n.* Matuśka.
crawl, *vi.* Sdohaŋ; wiŋ'ta.
crayon, *n.* Makasaŋ wi'yowa.
craze, *vt.* Yuhnaśkiŋyaŋ. *n.* Ihnaśkiŋyaŋpi.
crazy, *a.* Waciŋhnuni.
creak, *vi.* Kiŋ'za.
cream, *n.* Asaŋpizi; waśte.
creamery, *n.* Asaŋpi okaġe.
crease, *vt.* Yukśiża.
create, *vt.* Ka'ġa; otokaheka'ġa.
creation, *n.* Otokaheka'gapi.
creator, *n.* Tu'we ka'ġa.
creature, *n.* Ka'ġapi.
credence, *n.* Wowicada.
credentials, *n.* Ta'ku yuwicaka.
credible, *a.* Wicadapica.
credit, *n.* Oicazo; wowicada; woyuonihaŋ. *vt.* Oicazoḳu; wicakeda.
creditable, *a.* Yawaśtepica; wicadapica.
creditor, *n.* Tu'weicazo.
credulous, *a.* Kohaŋna wicada.
Cree, *n.* Maśtiŋca oyate.
creek, *n.* Wakpana.
creep, *vi.* Sdoḥaŋ; wiŋ'ta.
cremate, *vt.* Ḣuȟnaȟya.
Creole, *n.* Spaniyociŋca.
crest, *n.* Pesdete.
crevice, *n.* Oko; onasdeca.
crew, *n.* Wowaśi optaye.
crib, *n.* Wamnaheza opiye; woknake; i'yoḳopa; *T.* tioslola.
cricket, *n.* Psi'psicana sa'pa.
cried, *imp.* of CRY.
crier, *n.* E'yaŋpaha.
cries, 3d ps. of CRY.
crime, *n.* Woope kicaksapi; wośice.
criminal, *a.* Woope kicaksa.
criminate, *vt.* Woope kicaksekiya.
crimp, *vt.* Yumniża.

crimson, *a.* Ṡa; we ṡa.
cringe, *vi.* Napa; pustaka.
cripple, *vt.* Kiuŋniya. *n.* Tu'we oṡteka.
crisis, *n.* Oyuhomni.
crisp, *a.* Waŋ'kadaŋ.
critic, *n.* Wakcaŋkiyapi.
critical, *a.* Wakcaŋkcaŋka; to'-ketu taŋiŋ ṡni.
criticise, *vt.* Iiya; i'eniyeya.
croak, *vi.* Ḣdo; hotoŋ.
crock, *n.* Makaceġa.
crocodile, *n.* Ahdeṡkataŋka.
crony, *n.* Tu'weohaŋhdeya.
crook, *vt.* Yukṡaŋ. *n.* Oyukṡaŋ.
crooked, *a.* Kṡaŋ; ḣmiŋ.
crookedly, *adv.* Yukṡaŋkṡaŋ.
crop, *n.* Wożupi; ta'ku icaġe; tapo. *vt.* Basmiŋ; iŋ'kpabaksa; kaṡda; icaḣya. *vi.* Kas'iŋ-yaŋ u.
cross, *n.* Caŋicipaweġe; caŋhda-kiŋyaŋ; i'cipaweġe. *vt.* Hda-kiŋyaŋ icaġopi; i'cipaweġa; icahiya; kaġiya. *a.* 1. Waciŋ-ko; caŋksiksi: *a cross woman.* 2. Ce'yesa: *a cross baby.* 3. Ociŋsica: *a cross bull.* *adv.* Hdakiŋyaŋ; o'pta.
cross-eyed, *a.* Iṡtakṡiŋ.
cross-grained, *a.* Yuwi; ḣmiŋ.
crossing, *n.* O'pta ya'pi.
crosswise, *a.* Hdakiŋyaŋ.
crotch, *n.* Caŋżate.
crotchety, *a.* Oḣaŋtokeca.
crouch, *vi.* Pustaka.
croup, *n.* Kiŋsya niyapi.
crow, *n.* Uŋciṡicedaŋ. *vi.* Hotoŋ; taŋ'kaiçidahotoŋ.
Crow, *n.* Ḳaŋġitoka.
crowbar, *n.* Ma'zahoŋpe.
Crow Creek, *n.* (*The Agency*) Coŋ'kicakse. (*The stream*) Kaŋ-ġiokute.
crowd, *n.* Wicota; o'ta. *vt.* Pao-ṭiŋza; paoṭiŋsiyeya.
crown, *n.* Wateṡdake. *vt.* Wate-ṡdagkicatoŋ.

crucifix, *n.* Je'sus i'cipaweġa ka'-ġapi.
crucify, *vt.* I'cipaweḣ okataŋ.
crude, *a.* Ikce; ka'ġapiṡni.
cruel, *a.* Waoŋṡidaṡni; caŋtewa-nica; wakiuŋnis'a.
cruelly, *adv.* Waoŋṡidaṡniyaŋ.
cruelty, *n.* Wowaoŋṡidaṡni.
cruise, *n.* Wi'tawata omani.
crumb, *n.* Aġuyapi oṡnaṡna. *vt.* Yukpaŋkpaŋ.
crumble, *vi.* Ḣpuwahe; ptuḣaḣa. *vt.* Yuptuḣa.
crumple, *vt.* Yukṡikṡiża.
crupper, *n.* Siŋteiyutitaŋ.
crusade, *n.* Kuwapi; wotakpe.
crush, *vt.* Kaskica; kaṡuża.
crust, *n.* Ha; haakamatasaka.
crusty *a.* Ksizeca; ḳe'za.
crutch, *n.* Caŋ'huyapi.
cry, cries, *vi.* 1. Ce'ya: *the baby cries.* 2. Eya niya; paŋ'niya; e'yaŋpaha; houya: *he stood and cried.* *n.* Woceye; ce'ya-pi; hotoŋpi; eyapi. *Cry out,* eya niyaŋ.
crying, *a.* Ce'yes'a; wakitaŋ; taŋ'ka.
crystal, *a.* Kohdi; żaŋżaŋ.
cub, *n.* Waciŋca.
cube, *n.* I'akidecen omdotoŋ.
cubit, *n.* Wiciṡpa oiyute.
cucumber, *n.* Sa'kayutapi yuḣiḣi.
cud, *n.* Woyata. *Chew the cud,* wayatekoŋza.
cuddle, *vi.* Adoksohaŋ.
cudgel, *n.* Caŋksa.
cue, *n.* Pe'hiŋsoŋpi; siŋte.
cuff, *vt.* Napemdaskaapa. *n.* 1. Oape. 2. Napokaṡkeska.
culinary, *a.* Oŋwohaŋpi.
cull, *vt,* Kaḣniḣpahi. *n.* Oka-ptapi; ṡikṡica.
culminate, *vi.* Iyotaŋwaŋkan i.
culpable, *a.* Bapica.
culprit, *n.* Tu'wewaḣtani.
cultivate, *vt.* Kicaŋyaŋ; icaḣya.
cultivation, *n.* Wakicaŋyaŋpi.

culture, *n.* Kicaŋyaŋpi.
cultured, *pa.* Waoŋspeka.
culvert, *n.* Ceyagtoŋpi.
cumber, *vt.* Naġiyeya; kaġiya.
cumbersome, *a.* Okicaŋyeśica.
cunning, *a.* 1. Wayupika: *a cunning workman.* 2. Wicaśtaśni: *a cunning fox.* 3. Waśtena: *a cunning baby.*
cunningly, *adv.* Wayupiya.
cup, *n.* Wi'yatke. *vt.* We icu.
cupboard, *n.* Wakśinopiye.
cupidity, *n.* Wocaŋtahde.
cupola, *n.* Ḣda'ḣdatipi.
curable, *a.* Asniyepica.
curative, *a.* Oŋ asnipi.
curb, *vt.* Kaġiya; anapta. *n.* Iŋ'yaŋ caŋkunataka; i'iyuwiṭiŋza.
curd, *n.* Asaŋpi suksuta.
curdle, *vi.* Suksuta a'ya.
cure, *vt.* 1. Asniyaŋ: *cure the sick.* 2. Pusya: *cure hams.*
curiosity, *n.* Wasdonyewaciŋpi; wowaŋyake.
curious, *a.* Wasdonyewaciŋ; wayupika; wakaŋ.
curl, *n.* Owiŋġe; oyuḣa. *vt.* Yumnimniża; yuḣaḣaye.
curly, *a.* Yuḣaḣa.
curlew, *n.* Pasuśkopa.
currant, *n.* Captaheza.
currency, *n.* Iyaza ya; ma'zaska.
current, *a.* Hiyaya; uŋ'pi; de. *n.* Kadus ya.
curry, *vt.* Yuṣtosto; kakca.
curry-comb, *n.* Wi'cakca.
curse, *vt.* Yaśica; Wakaŋtaŋka cażeyan yaśica. *n.* Woyaśica.
cursed, *a.* Yaśicapi.
cursory, *a.* Inaḣni.
curt, *a.* Yaṭiŋzapi.
curtail, *vt.* Yuaokpaŋiya.
curtain, *n.* O'zaŋpi.
curvature, *n.* Womibe.
curve, *vt.* Yukśaŋ. *n.* Oyukśaŋ; mibe.
curved, *pa.* Kśaŋ; mibe.
cushion, *n.* Ipahiŋ.
custard, *n.* Wi'tkayużapi.
custom, *n.* 1. Woecoŋ; woope: *an Indian custom.* 2. Enkiciipi: *draws custom.* 3. Oyate wokażużu.
customary, *a.* Ecoŋpi ecee.
customer, *n.* Enkiciis'a; tu'we.
cut, *vt.* Baksa; bahoŋ. (*By striking*) Kaksa. (*By cutting* or *sawing*) Baksa. *To cut down,* kawaŋka.—*To cut off* (*as grass*), kaśda.—*To cut out* (*as clothes*), bapta; yupta.—*To cut a gash,* bahoŋ.—*To cut loose,* yuśdoka.—*Cut teeth,* hi'uya.—*Cut up* (*in pieces*), baksaksa; (*to play*), śkata.
n. 1. (*a gash*) Obahoŋ. 2. (*a stroke*) Oape. 3. (*a piece*) Obaśpe. 4. (*a drawing*) Iteowapi. 5. (*railway*) Caŋku okapi. 6. (*a short cut*) Caŋku.
pa. Baksapi; paśdutapi.
cute, *a.* Waśtena; waciŋksapa.
cutlas, *n.* Miwakaŋ.
cutlet, *n.* Obakse.
cutoff, *n.* A'kokam caŋku.
cutter, *n.* Wi'caśda; caŋwiyusdohe; wi'tawata.
cutting, *n.* Obakse; bahoŋpi.
cutworm, *n.* Wamduśkadaŋ.
cycle, *n.* Mibe; aohomni.
cyclone, *n.* Tatehomni.
cyclopedia, *n.* Wooŋspe siŋtomni oyaka.
cylinder, *n.* Mibehaŋska.
cymbal, *n.* Ma'za kasnapi.
cynical, *a.* Wawiḣa.
cypress, *n.* Ḣaŋtehaŋska.
czar, *n.* A'taya itaŋcaŋ.

D

dab, *vt.* Akastaka ; apa. *n.* oape ; wokastake.
dabble, *vi.* Mini en ška'ta ; aspayeya.
dabbler, *n.* Aškate.
dad, daddy, *n.* Ate ; atkuku.
daddy-long-legs, Uŋktomi hu haŋ'ska.
dagger, *n.* Isaŋ taŋ'ka ; *Y.* & *T.* miwakaŋ ; anoġope.
daily, *a.*, *adv.* Aŋpetu iyohi ; aŋpetu iyohi ka'ġapi.
dainty, *a.* Waštena. *n.* Ta'ku skuskuyena.
dairy, *n.* Asaŋpiihdi ka'ġapi.
daisy, *n.* Waħca cuwizizi.
Dakota, *n. pr.* Dakota.
Dakota river, *n. pr.* Caŋsaŋsaŋwakpa.
dale, *n.* Makosmaka.
dally, *vi.* Huŋ'kešni ecoŋ.
dam, *n.* 1. Huŋka wi'ye. 2. Ceyaka. *vt.* ceyagtoŋ; mininataka.
damage, *vt.* Yušica. *n.* Woyušice ; wokiuŋni.
dame, *n.* Wıŋ'yaŋ itaŋcaŋ.
damn, *vt.* Yašica ; wakaŋšicati ekta iyayeya.
damnable, *a.* Yašinpica.
damnation, *n.* Woyašice.
damp, *a.* Tkiŋ ; spa'ya ; ħpaŋ.
dampen, *vt.* Ħpaŋye ; kaġiya.
damper, *n.* Woanapte.
damsel, *n.* Wikoška.
dance, *v.* Waci ; waciƙiya. *n.* Wowaci.
dancer, *n.* Wacisa.
dandelion, *n.* Waħcazi.
dander, *n.* Pa'ġaŋġeca.
dandle, *vt.* Kihnahna ; kiškata.
dandruff, *n.* Pa'ġaŋġeca.
dandy, *n.* Tu'we wi'taŋtaŋ.
danger, *n.* Wokokipe. *In danger of,* okokipeya ; a'etopteya.
dangerous, *a.* Okokipe.
dangerously, *adv.* Okokipeya.
dangle, *vi.* Otkehaŋ ; ikoyaka.
dangles, *n. pl.* Oħciħci.
dapper, *a.* Wayuco.
dapple, *a.* Hdeška.
dare, *vi.* Tawaṭenya. *vt.* canwaŋkeda.
dare-devil, *n.* Wakaŋšica.
daring, *a.* Ta'ku kokipe šni.
dark, *a.* & *n.* 1. O'kpaza ; o'tpaza. 2. To'ketutaŋiŋšni : *a dark problem.* 3. Sa'pa ; si'ca : *a dark villain.* 4. Sa'peca ; staŋ : *dark skin.*
darken, *vt.* Aokpasya.
darkly, *adv.* Aokpasya.
darkness, *n.* O'kpaza.
darling, *n.* & *a.* Teħiŋda.
darn, *vt.* 1. Pasisakaġeġe. 2. Yašica.
dart, *vt.* Kaħo-iyeya. *vi.* Ni'naiyaya. *n.* Wi'cape.
dash, *vt.* Iyameħpeya ; kamdeca ; akaštaŋštaŋ ; oħaŋko yuštan. *vi.* Ni'na iyaya. *n.* Wonataŋ ; woiyapa ; wokaħtaka.
dash-board, *n.* Caŋpahmihmaŋ ite.
dastard, *a.* Canwaŋka.
date, *n.* Wiyawapi ; watohaŋtu. *vt.* Wiyawapi ka'ga ; o'maka yawa.
daub, *vt.* Akastaka ; apuspa.
daughter, *n.* Cuŋwiŋtku. *My daughter,* micuŋkši ; cunš. *Your daughter,* nicuŋkši.
daughter-in-law, *n.* Takoš. *Your daughter-in-law,* nitakoš. *His daughter-in-law,* takošku.
daunt, *vt.* Naṭuŋgya.
dauntless, *a.* Naṭuŋgyapicašni.
dawn, *n.* Aŋ'pao ; oicaġe. *vi.* Icaġe ; u.
day, *n.* Aŋpetu ; caŋ ; *Y.* aŋ'pa.

All day, aŋpetu ihuŋni.—*All the days*, aŋpetu owasiŋ.—*By day*, aŋpetu icuŋhan. —*Day about*, aŋpetu itogto.—*Day by day*, aŋpetu iyohi. —*To-day*, nakaha.
day-break, *n*. Aŋ'pa kamdeza.
daylight, *n*. Aŋ'pao.
day-time, *n*. Aŋ'pa icuŋhaŋ.
daze, *vt*. Waciŋhnuniya.
dazzle, *vt*. Iśtośniśya. *vi*. Iśtośniża.
deacon, *n*. Ookiye.
deaconess, *n*. Wiŋ'yaŋ ookiye.
dead, *a*. 1. Ṭa : *a dead man*. 2. Śe'ca : *a dead tree*. 3. Ṭa : *dead capital; dead faith*. 4. A'taya ; wowicake : *a dead calm; dead sleep*. *n*. Wicaṭa. *adv*. A'wicakehaŋ.
deaden, *vt*. Ṭeya.
deadfall, *n*. Oŋhmuŋ'kapi.
deadhead, *n*. Każużuśni o'pa.
deadly, *a*. Oŋṭekta ; oŋṭa'pi ; ktewaciŋ. *adv*. Ṭa se'ca ; kte kta.
deadness, *n*. Ṭa ; ececə śni.
deaf, *a*. No'ġe kpa ; kpa ; wana ḣoŋ śni.
deafen, *vt*. No'ġe kpeya.
deafness, *n*. Wonaḣon śni.
deal, *vt*. & *vi*. Ḳu ; pamni ; ecoŋ ; wi'yopeya.
deal, *n*. 1. Oiyute : *a great deal*. 2. Kiciçupi : *a land deal*.
dealer, *n*. Wopetoŋ ; wapamni.
dear, *a*. 1. Teḣika ; o'ta iyawapi : *a dear horse*. 2. Teḣiŋda. *My dear father*, ate tewaḣiŋda. *int*. Ecaḣe.
dearly, *adv*. Teḣiya ; ni'na.
dearth, *n*. Wicaakiḣaŋ ; ta'ku owasiŋ teḣike ; wanica.
death, *n*. Wicoŋṭe. *To be the death of*, ṭeya. —*To put to death*, kte ; yuṭa.—*To bite to death*, yaṭa.—*To tramp to death*, naṭa.
deathly, *a*. Ṭa se ; oaśica.
debar, *vt*. Okihiśniya.
debark, *vi*. Ḣen inażiŋ.
debase, *vt*. Yuhukuya.
debatable, *a*. Akininpica.
debate, *v*. Iaakinica ; akinica. *n*. Waakinicapi.
debater, *n*. Iaakinica.
debauch, *vt*. Yuśica. *n*. Oḣaŋ witkotkoka.
debauchery, *n*. Witkopi.
debility, *n*. Wowaśake śni.
debt, *n*. Oicazo.
debtor, *n*. Icazo.
decade, *n*. Waniyetu wikcemna.
decalogue, *n*. Woahope wikcemna.
decamp, *vi*. Tokaŋ e'ti.
decapitate, *vt*. Pa baksa.
decay, *vi*. Kukaaya ; taŋniaya ; ecetuśniaya. *n*. Woecetuśni.
decease, *n*. Naġiiyaya ; ṭa.
deceit, *n*. Wohnaye.
deceitful, *a*. Wicahnayesa ; wohnaye.
deceitfully, *a*. Hna'yaŋ.
deceitfulness, *n*. Wohnaye.
deceivable, *a*. Hna'yepica.
deceive, *vt*. Hna'yaŋ.
deceiver, *n*. Wicahnayesa.
December, *n*. Wi'iakenoŋpa.
decency, *n*. Woecetu ; woiyokipi.
decent, *a*. Ecetu ; taŋyaŋ.
decently, *adv*. Taŋyaŋ.
deception, *n*. Wohnaye.
decide, *vt*. To'ketuyuśtaŋ.
decided, *a*. Yuśtaŋpi ; suta.
decidedly, *adv*. A'wicakeya.
decimal, *a*. & *n*. Wikcemnamna woyawa.
decimate, *vt*. Iyokise ihaŋgya.
decipher, *vt*. Yawa.
decision, *n*. 1. Woyuśtaŋ; woyaco; 2. Tawaciŋ suta.
decisive, *a*. Wayuśtaŋ.
deck, *vt*. Koyagya ; śaya.
deck, *n*. Owiŋża ; kaŋsu opaḣte.
declaim, *vi*. Wohdaka ; iaa.
declamation, *n*. Woowohdake.
declaration, *n*. Yaotaŋiŋpi.

declaratory, *a.* Yaotaŋiŋ.
declare, *vt.* Yaotaŋiŋ; eya.
declension, *n.* Yuhukuyapi; (*Gram.*) iokawiŋh aya.
decline, *vi.* Kun ya; wicada ṡni. *n.* Kun ya.
declivity, *n.* A'pamahde.
decompose, *vt.* & *vi.* Yukuka; kuka.
decorate, *vt.* Yuwaṡte; ṡaya.
decorous, *a.* Iyecetu.
decoy, *n.* Hna'yan icu; hmuŋ'ka. *n.* wi'hmuŋke.
decrease, *vi.* To'nana a'ya; a'okpani a'ya. *vt.* A'okpaniya.
decree, *v.* Koŋ'za; woope ka'ga.
decrepit, *a.* Kaŋ; oṡteka.
decry, *vt.* Yaṡica; yaṡiḣtiŋ.
dedicate, *vt.* Ḳu; yuwakaŋ.
deduce, *vt.* Icu; iyukcaŋ.
deduct, *vt.* Icu; yutokaŋ.
deed, *n.* 1. Woecoŋ; wicoḣaŋ; ta'ku ecoŋpi. 2. Makocewowapi suta. *vt.* Ḳu; makocewowapi ḳu.
deem, *vt.* Yawa; eciŋ.
deep, *a.* Mahentu; (*Of water*) ṡbe; ni'na. *n.* Woṡbe; miniwaŋca.
deepen, *vt.* Yumahentuya.
deeply, *adv.* Mahentuya.
deer, *n.* Ta'ḣiŋca; ta'ḣca.
deerskin, *n.* Taha.
deface, *vt.* Yuṡica; paẓuẓu.
defalcate, *vt.* Oŋġe manoŋ.
defame, *vt.* Yaṡica.
default, *v.* & *n.* Ecoŋṡni.
defeat, *vt.* Kte'na; ohiya. *n.* Kte'pina.
defect, *n.* Oŋṡpa iyecetu ṡni.
defective, *a.* Oŋṡpa ṡi'ca.
defence, *n.* Wowinape; anaiçikṡinpi.
defend, *vt.* Nakiciẓiŋ.
defender, *n.* Waanakikṡiŋ.
defenseless, *a.* Woawaŋyake co'daŋ.
defensible, *a.* Awaŋyakapiwaṡte.
defensive, *a.* Naiçiẓiŋ.
defer, *vt.* Kihnaka. *vi.* Akipe; ohoda.
deference, *n.* Ahopapi.
defiance, *n.* Wokipaẓiŋ; wonaḣoŋ ṡni.
deficiency, *n.* Iyohi ṡni.
deficient, *a.* A'okpani; iyohi ṡni.
defile, *vt.* Yuṡapa; yuṡica. *n.* Caŋku ocistiyedaŋ.
define, *vt.* To'ketu oyaka.
definite, *a.* Taŋyaŋoyakapi; yutaŋiŋpi ḣca.
definitely, *adv.* Taŋiŋyaŋ ḣca.
definition, *n.* To'ken ka'pi oyakapi.
deform, *vt.* Yuṡica.
deformed, *pa.* Oṡteka.
defraud, *vt.* Ki; hna'yaŋ.
defray, *vt.* Kaẓuẓu.
deft, *a.* Wayupika.
defunct, *a.* Ṭa; owihaŋke.
defy, *vt.* Kipaẓiŋ; ohoda ṡni.
degenerate, *vi.* Ṡi'ca a'ya. *a.* Ṡiḣtiŋ.
degradation, *n.* Wotakuni ṡni.
degrade, *vt.* Yuhukuya.
degraded, *pa.* Kun'tuḣ uŋ'pi.
degree, *n.* 1. Ca'hde; oiyute. 2. Wacaẓeyatapi: *the degree of A. B.*
dehorn, *vt.* He kawanica.
deify, *vt.* Yuwakaŋ.
deign, *vi.* En ahiwaciŋ.
deist, *n.* Wowapi Wakaŋ ohna ṡni Wakaŋtaŋka awaciŋ.
deity, *n.* Wowakaŋ.
deject, *vt.* Caŋteṡinya.
dejected, *pa.* Caŋteṡica.
dejection, *n.* Caŋteṡicapi.
delay, *vt.* Yutehan; kaġiya.
delegate, *n.* Yeṡipi. *vt.* Yeṡi; ecoŋ kta wowaṡ'ake ḳu.
delegation, *n.* Yeṡipioptaye.
deliberate, *v.* Awaciŋ. *a.* Awaciŋ ecoŋ; ḣaŋhi.
deliberately, *adv.* Awaciŋyaŋ.
delicacy, *n.* Ta'ku waṡtena; wowaṡte.

delicate, *a.* Waśtena; wasazeca; suta śni.
delicately, *adv.* Iwaśtena; wasasyena; iyokipiya.
delicious, *a.* Waśteḣca.
deliciously, *adv.* Oiyokipiya.
delight, *n.* Wowiyuśkiŋ. *v.* Iyuśkiŋ; iyokipiya.
delightful, *a.* Oiyokipi.
delineate, *vt.* Icazo; pazo.
delinquency, *n.* Woyuśna.
delinquent, *a.* & *n.* Ecoŋśni.
delirious, *a.* Waciŋhnuni.
deliver, *vt.* 1. E'hdaku : *deliver from death.* 2. Ḳu : *deliver the letter.* 3. Oyaka : *deliver the oration.*
deliverance, *n.* Waehdakupi; oie.
deliverer, *n.* Waehdaku.
dell, *n.* O'smaka.
delude, *vt.* Nu'niya.
deluge, *n.* Minitaŋ. *v.* Amnitaŋya.
delusion, *n.* Wohnaye.
delve, *v.* Kaḣdoka; oḳa.
demagogue, *n.* Oyate hna'yaŋ.
demand, *vt.* Da; kitaŋ da. *n.* Da'pi; ciŋ'pi; wi'waŋġapi.
demean, *vt.* Oḣaŋyaŋ.
demented, *a.* Waciŋhnuni.
demi-, *pref.* Haŋke.
demise, *n.* Ṭa.
Democrat, *n. pr.* Itokaḣwicaśta.
demolish, *vt.* Yużużu.
demon, *n.* Wakaŋśica.
demonstrable, *a.* Yuwicakepica.
demonstrate, *vt.* Yuwicaka.
demoralize, *vt.* Yuśiḣtiŋ.
demur, *vi.* Kaġiya ia.
demure, *a.* Oḣaŋ sta'ka.
den, *n.* Ti'pidaŋ; wamaniti.
denial, *n.* Wicakeśnieyapi; wicadaśni.
denominate, *vt.* Cażeyata.
denomination, *n.* Cażé; ocażé.
denominator, *n.* Kiyuśpapi oyaka.
denote, *vt.* Yaotaŋiŋ; ka.
denounce, *vt.* I en iyeya; yaotaŋiŋ.
dense, *a.* Pasihicapi; śo'ka.

dent, *vt.* Paosmaka.
dentist, *n.* Hi piya.
denude, *vt.* Taŋcodaya; kakmi.
denunciation, *n.* Yaśicapi.
deny (denied), *vt.* Wicakeśni eya; he'cetuśni eya; ḳu wicadaśni; ipida.
deodorize, *vt.* Śicamna asniya.
depart, *vi.* Iyaya; tokaŋya.
department, *n.* Ośpaye.
departure, *n.* Tokaŋya'pi.
depend, *vi.* Ikoyaka; waciŋyaŋ.
dependence, *n.* I'cikoyaguŋpi; wowaciŋye.
depict, *vt.* Owa; yutaŋiŋ.
deplete, *vt.* Yusota.
deplorable, *a.* Oiyokiśica.
deplore, *vt.* Icaŋteśica.
deponent, *n.* Wayataŋiŋ.
depopulate, *vt.* Wicayusota.
deportment, *n.* Oḣaŋ.
depose, *vt.* Ayuśtaŋkiya. *vi.* Yataŋiŋ.
deposit, *vt.* E'hnaka; kihnaka. *n.* Wakihnakapi; oiheye.
depot, *n.* Ḣemanionażiŋ; owohnake.
deprave, *vi.* Yuśica.
depravity, *n.* Yuśicapi.
deprecate, *vt.* Iyokipi śni.
depreciate, *vt.* Kun yawa. *vi.* Kun iyaya.
depress, *vt.* Kun iyeya.
depressed, *pa.* Iyokiśica; yuhukuyapi.
deprivation, *n.* Waḣpaniyapi.
deprive, *vt.* Ki.
depth, *n.* Śbe; wośbe; omahentu.
derange, *vt.* Yuśkiśka.
deride, *vt.* Iḣaḣa.
derision, *n.* Wowiḣa.
derivation, *n.* Etaŋhaŋ icupi.
derive, *vt.* Etaŋhaŋ icu.
descend, *v.* Kun ya; kun iyahe; icaġe.
descendant, *n.* Etaŋhaŋ icaġe.
descent, *n.* Kun ye; wonataŋ; wicoicaġe.

describe, *vt.* Oyaka ; owa.
description, *n.* Woyake.
descriptive, *a.* Wawoyake ; iokawiŋh oyaka.
descry, *vt.* Toŋweya.
desecrate, *vt.* Yuikceka.
desert′ *vt.* Ehpeya ; nažica.
des′ert, *n.* Makoce waicaġeśni. *a.* Waicaġeśni.
desert′, *n.* Ta′ku kuwa.
deserter, *n.* Tu′we nažica.
desertion, *n.* Ehpeyapi ; nažica.
deserve, *vt.* Kamna : ķu iyececa.
design, *vt.* Iwaŋyaka ; awaciŋ. *n.* Woawaciŋ ; wowiyukcaŋ.
designate, *vt.* Ka ; kahniġa.
designer, *n.* Wi′yukcaŋ.
desirable, *a.* Ciŋpica ; waśte.
desire, *vt.* Ciŋ ; caŋtokpani. *n.* Ta′ku ciŋ′pi.
desirous, *a.* Awaciŋ ; ciŋ.
desist, *vi.* Ayuśtaŋ ; enakiye.
desk, *n.* Ahna wowapi ka′ga.
desolate, *a.* Makoskantu ; otiwota. *vt.* Ihaŋgya.
despair, *vi.* Waciŋyeśni ; eciŋśni. *n.* Waciŋyeyapiśni.
desperado, *n.* Tu′we wohitika.
desperate, *a.* 1. Wohitika : *a desperate man.* 2. Mde′ze śni ; tehika.
desperately, *adv.* Wohitiya.
despicable, *a.* Wahteśni.
despise, *vt.* Wahtedaśni.
despite, *n.* Wowahtedaśni. *prep.* Ķe′yaś ; he′caśta.
despiteful, *a.* Ociŋśica.
despitefully, *adv.* Śicaya.
despoil, *vt.* Ki ; wahpaniya.
despond, *vi.* Waciŋibośake.
despot, *n.* Itaŋcaŋsuta.
despotic, *a.* Suta ; tehika.
dessert, *n.* Sku′yawotapi.
destination, *n.* Oahuni.
destine, *vt.* Kahniġa ; yuśtaŋ.
destiny, *n.* Ta′ku ki′ciyaŋka.
destitute, *a.* Wahpanica : ni′ca.
destitution, *n.* Wowahpanica.
destroy, *vt.* Yutakuniśni.
destroyer, *n.* Wayutakuniśni.
destructible, *a.* Ihaŋgyepica.
destruction, *n.* Woyutakuniśni ; ihaŋgyapi.
destructive, *a.* Wayuśica.
desultory, *a.* Katiŋyaŋśni.
detach, *vt.* Yuśpa ; yukca.
detached, *pa.* I′cikoyakeśni.
detachment, *n.* Ośpaye.
detail, *vt.* 1. Kpaŋyena oyaka. 2. Kiyuśpa. *n.* Ośpaye ; woyake.
detain, *vt.* Kaġiya ; i′yaninya.
detect, *vt.* Yuaśdaya.
detection, *n.* Yuaśdayapi.
detective, *n.* Wayuaśdaya.
detention, *n.* I′yanicapi.
deter, *vt.* Anapta ; hamya.
deteriorate, *vi.* Śi′ca a′ya. *vt.* Yuśihtiŋ.
determinable, *a.* Sdonyepica.
determination, *n.* Waciŋyuza ; tawaciŋ ; iyaye.
determine, *vt.* Koŋ′za ; yuśtaŋ ; yaco ; *T.* yasu.
detest, *vt.* Wahtedaśni.
detestable, *a.* Wahteśni.
detestation, *n.* Wowahtedaśni.
dethrone, *vt.* Ḣeyataiyeya.
detract, *vt.* Ki ; oŋśpaicu.
detriment, *n.* Woyuśica.
detrimental, *a.* Wayuśica.
deuce, *n.* Noŋ′pa.
Deuteronomy, *n.* Woope I′takihna.
devastate, *vt.* Ihaŋgya.
develop, *vt.* Yutaŋiŋ ; icahya. *vi.* Icaġa.
development, *n.* Yutaŋiŋpi ; icahyapi.
deviate, *vi.* Icuŋom ya.
device, *n.* Wowiyukcaŋ.
Devil, *n.* Wakaŋśica.
devilish, *a.* Wakaŋśica se.
Devil's Lake, *n.* Miniwakaŋ.
deviltry, *n.* Wonaġiyeya.
devious, *n.* Ḣmiŋ.
devise, *vt.* Iyukcaŋ.
devoid, *a.* Wanica.

devolve, *vt.* Hiŋh̓paya.
devote, *vi.* Ḳu ; ituh̓aŋ.
devoted, *pa.* E′cedaŋkuwa.
devotion, *n.* Woawaciŋ ; woohoḍa ; wotaŋkadapi.
devotional, *a.* Waohoda ; wacekiya.
devour, *vt.* Napcaiyeya ; temya ; ihaŋgya.
devout, *a.* Waawaciŋ.
devoutly, *adv.* Yuonihaŋyaŋ.
dew, *n.* Cu.
dew-drop, *n.* Cumnise.
dewy, *a.* Cumni ; custaka.
dexterity, *n.* Wowayupika.
dexterous, *a.* Wayupika.
diabolic, *a.* Ni′naśica.
diadem, *n.* Teśdake.
diagonal, *a.* O′h̓ya.
diagram, *n.* Oicaġo.
dialect, *n.* Iapi ocaże.
dialogue, *n.* Akiciyupteeyapi.
diameter, *n.* Oiyute ohdakiŋyaŋ.
diamond, *n.* Iŋ′yaŋ teh̓ika.
diaper, *n.* Hokśiyopa adeża ; nitiyapehe.
diarrhea, *n.* Każopi.
diary, *n.* Aŋpetuwowapi.
dice, *n.* Huhu kaŋsukutepi.
dicker, *vi.* Wopeton.
dictate, *vt.* Eya ; owawicaśi ; ecoŋwicaśi. *n.* Ta′ku eya.
dictation, *n.* Ecoŋśipi.
dictator, *n.* Itaŋcaŋ.
diction, *n.* Woeye.
dictionary, *n.* Iapi wowapi ; ieska wowapi.
did, *imp.* of DO.
didactic, *a.* Wahokoŋkiya.
didst, *2nd p. s. imp.* of DO.
die (died), *vi.* Ṭa ; naġiiyaye ; owihaŋke.
diet, *n.* Woyute ; omniciye. *vt.* Ci′stiŋna won′kiya.
differ, *vi.* To′keca ; togye awaciŋ.
difference, *n.* Wotokeca; toghdapi. *It makes no difference,* e′taŋhaŋ to′keca.
different, *a.* To′keca.
differently, *adv.* Togye.
difficult, *a.* Teh̓ike.
difficulty, *n.* Woteh̓ika ; woakinica.
diffidence, *n.* Wi′śtecapi.
diffident, *a.* Wi′śteca.
diffuse, *vt.* Iyayeya ; yeya. *vi.* Iyaya.
diffuse, *a.* Ṭiŋ′ześni.
dig, *vt.* Ḳa ; oḳa ; pah̓doka.
digest, *vt.* Ecetuya.
digger, *n.* Oḳesa.
dignified, *pa.* Wowimnaka.
dignify, *vt.* Yuonihaŋ.
dignity, *n.* Wokinihaŋ.
digress, *vi.* Icuŋom ya.
dike, *n.* Mini makaokaśke.
dilapidated, *pa.* Żużuwahe.
dilate, *vt.* Yutaŋka. *vi.* Taŋ′kaaya.
dilatory, *a.* Haŋhi.
dilemma, *n.* To′ketu taŋiŋ śni.
diligence, *n.* Womdiheca.
diligent, *a.* Mdiheca. *T.* Bliheca.
dilute, *vt.* Miniicahi; sutaśni ka′ġa.
dim, *a.* Aokpaza ; ki′taŋna taŋiŋ.
dim, *vt.* Aoġiya.
dime, *n.* Kaśpapi.
dimension, *n.* Oiyute.
diminish, *vt.* Yucistiŋna. *vi.* Ci′stiŋna a′ya.
dimly, *adv.* Ataŋiŋśniyaŋ.
dimple, *n.* Uka osmaka.
din, *n.* Oko ; bu.
dine, *vi.* Wota ; wicokayawota. *vt.* Won′kiya.
ding, *vt.* Apapa ; kabubu.
dingy, *a.* Staŋ′ka ; śapa.
dining, *n.* Wotapi ; owote.
dinner, *n.* Wicokayawotapi.
dint, *n.* O′smaka.
diocese, *n.* Woawaŋyake.
dip, *vt.* 1. Oputkaŋ ; iyeya : *dip the pen in the ink.* 2. Kapta ; icu : *dip up some water.* *vi.* 1. Oŋṡpa o′peiċiya. *Dip into politics.* 2. Nake han

diphtheria, *n.* Doteaoġi.
diphthong, *n.* Oowaiciyakaśkapi.
diploma, *n.* Waayataŋiŋ wowapi.
diplomacy, *n.* Woitaŋcaŋ wicoḣaŋ; wowayupika.
dipper, *n.* Iyokapte.
dire, *a.* Oteḣika.
direct, *vt.* Yeya; yeśi; ecoŋśi; ecoŋkiya; ożuha owa.
direct, *a.* Katiŋyaŋ; owotaŋna.
direction, *n.* Tokiyotan; woawaŋyake; tokiyotaŋoyakapi.
directly, *adv.* Katiŋyaŋ; a'tayena; ecadaŋ.
director, *n.* Waecoŋwicakiya.
directory, *n.* Wicacażewowapi; woecoŋwowapi.
direful, *a.* Oiyokiśica.
dirge, *n.* Woceye ho.
dirk, *n.* Isaŋanogope.
dirt, *n.* Maka.
dirty, *a.* Śa'pa. *vt.* Yuśapa.
dis-, *prefix.* Śni; wowanica.
disable, *vt.* Okihiśniya.
disadvantage, *n.* Taŋyaŋśni.
disaffect, *vt.* Iyokipiśniya.
disagree, *vi.* O'koŋwaŋżinaśni; okiciwaśteśni.
disagreeable, *a.* Owaśteśni; oiyokiśica.
disagreement, *n.* To'kecapi.
disallow, *vt.* Wicadaśni.
disappear, *vi.* Taŋiŋśni.
disappoint, *vt.* Caŋteśinya; caŋḣiya.
disapprove, *vt.* Iyokipiśni.
disarm, *vt.* Wi'pe ki.
disarrange, *vt.* Yużużu.
disaster, *n.* Woakipa teḣika.
disastrous, *a* Śicaya; teḣika.
disavow, *vt.* He'cetuśni eya.
disband, *vt.* Yużużu. *vi.* Enakiye.
disbelieve, *vt.* Wicadaśni.
disburse, *vt.* Wicaku; pamni.
discard, *vt.* Eḣpeya.
discern, *vt.* Iyukcaŋ; waŋyaka.
discernible, *a.* Waŋyagpica.
discernment, *n.* Wowiyukcaŋ.
discharge, *vt.* 1. Ayuśtaŋkiya: *discharge a soldier.* 2. Kiyuśka: *discharge a prisoner.* 3. Bośdoka: *discharge a gun.* 4. Eḣpeya; każo; hiyuya: *discharge water.* 5. Każużu: *discharge a debt.*
discharge, *n.* Kiyuśkapi; iheya.
disciple, *n.* Waoŋspekiya. *vt.* Oŋśpekiya.
discipline, *vt.* Kaoŋspe. *n.* Wokaoŋspe; iyopeyapi.
disclaim, *vt.* Ta'waśni keya.
disclose, *vt.* Yuzamni.
discolor, *vt.* Yutokeca.
discomfit, *vt.* Iyokiśinya; napeya.
discomfort, *n.* Woiyokipiśni.
discommode, *vt.* Naġiyeya.
discompose, *vt.* Inihaŋya.
disconcert, *vt.* Waciŋhnuniya.
disconnect, *vi.* Yuśdoka.
disconsolate, *a.* Iyokiśica.
discontent, *n.* Woiyokipiśni.
discontented, *pa.* Caŋteśica.
discontinue, *vt.* Ayuśtaŋ.
discord, *n.* Woakinica; ho yaśniśniża.
discount, *vt.* Ihukunyawa.
discountenance, *vt.* Iyowiŋyeśni.
discourage, *vt.* Waciŋibośagya.
discouraged, *pa.* Waciŋibośake.
discouragement, *n.* Woiyokiśice.
discourse, *vi.* Ia; wohdaka. *a n.* Woowohdake.
discourteous, *a.* Śinyaoḣaŋyaŋ.
discover, *vt.* Iyeya; yutaŋiŋ.
discovery, *n.* Tokaiyeyapi.
discredit, *vt.* Wicadaśni.
discreet, *a.* Ksapa; wayupika.
discreetly, *adv.* Ksamyahaŋ.
discrepancy, *n.* To'kecapi.
discretion, *n.* Wowiyukcan.
discriminate, *vt.* Iwaŋyaka.
discuss, *vt.* Iwohdaka.
disdain, *vt.* Waḣtedaśni.
disease, *n.* Wowayazaŋ.
disembark, *vi.* Ḣen'inażin.
disengaged, *pa.* Ikoyakeśni.
disentangle, *vt.* Kiyuśka.

disfigure, *vt.* Yuśica.
disgorge, *v.* Hiyuya.
disgrace, *vt.* Iśtenya. *n.* Wowiśteca.
disgraceful, *a.* Oŋ iśtecapi.
disguise, *vt.* Ihdutokeca.
disgust, *vi.* Waḣtedaśni; hitida.
dish, *n.* Wakśica. *vt.* Wakśica ohnaka; kaśkokpa.
dishearten, *vt.* Caŋteokiçuŋniya.
disheveled, *pa.* Yuḣaḣa.
dishonest, *a.* Owotaŋnaśni.
dishonor, *vt.* Yuonihaŋśni; iśtenya.
dishonorable, *a.* Kinihaŋpicaśni.
disinclined, *pa.* Ciŋ'śni.
disinterested, *a.* Iyoważaśni.
disjoin, *vt.* Yukinuŋkaŋ.
disjoint, *vt.* O'kiheyuksa.
disk, *n.* Ma'zamdaskamibe.
dislike, *vt.* Ṡi'cedaka.
dislocate, *vt.* Papśuŋ.
dislodge, *vt.* Iyayeya.
disloyal, *a.* Wakinihaŋśni.
dismal, *a.* Oaśica.
dismay, *vt.* Yuśiŋyeya.
dismiss, *vt.* Ayuśtaŋkiya.
dismount, *vi.* Kun'iyahaŋ. *vt.* Kun eḣpeya.
disobedience, *n.* Wowanaḣoŋśni.
disobedient, *a.* Wanaḣoŋśni.
disobey, *vt.* Anaġoptaŋśni.
disobliging, *pa.* Waokiyeśni.
disorder, *n.* Wośkiśke.
disorganize, *vt.* Yużużu.
disown, *vt.* Ta'wayeśni.
disparage, *vt.* Yaśiḣtiŋ.
dispatch. See DESPATCH.
dispel, *vt.* Kaḣamiyeya.
dispensable, *a.* 1. Co'daŋuŋpica. 2. Wicaḳupica.
dispense, *vt.* Wicaḳu; pamni; kpaġaŋ.
disperse, *vt.* Iyayeya; yuomdeca. *vi.* Iyaya.
dispirited, *pa.* Waciŋyeyeśni.
displace, *vt.* Eciŋśni e'hnaka; yutokaŋ.
display, *vt.* Yutaŋiŋ; pazo. *n.* Wapazopi; wowitaŋ.
displease, *vt.* Iyokipiśniya; caŋzeya.
displeasure, *n.* Wocaŋze.
disposal, *n.* Wokuwa; tawaciŋ.
dispose, *vt.* E'hnaka; wicaḳu; awaciŋ.
disposed, *pa.* Waciŋyuza.
disposition, *n.* Tawaciŋ; wokuwa.
dispossess, *vt.* Ki.
disprove, *vt.* Yuwicakeśni.
disputable, *a.* Akininpica.
dispute, *v.* Akinica; i'eniyeya. *n.* Woakinica.
disqualify, *vt.* Okihiśniya.
disregard, *vt.* Enewaciŋśni.
disreputable, *a.* Caże śi'ca.
disrespectful, *a.* Waohodaśni.
dissatisfy, *vt.* Iyokipiśniya.
dissect, *vt.* Pa'ta; baśpa.
disseminate, *vt.* Oyaka.
dissent, *vi.* Togyeawaciŋ; wicadaśni.
dissenter, *n.* Obetokeca.
dissertation, *n.* Woyake.
dissever, *vt.* Kiyuśpa.
dissipate, *vt.* Iyayeya; yutakuniśni. *vi.* Witkoyauŋ.
dissipation, *n.* Wayutakuniśni; witkopi.
dissolve, *vt.* Skaŋyaŋ; śdoya; ihaŋkeya. *vi.* Skaŋ; śdo; ihaŋke.
dissuade, *vt.* Iyokiśni.
distance, *n.* I'citehaŋ; oiyute. *A long distance.*, tehan. *A short distance*, aśkadaŋ. *vt.* Te'han kapa.
distant, *a.* Te'hantu; i'citehaŋ.
distaste, *a.* Wowaḣtedaśni; ciŋ'-śni.
distasteful, *a.* Iyokipiśni.
distemper, *n.* Po'ġeḣdiḣdi.
distend, *vt.* Yutaŋka.
distil, *vt.* Minipoaśbuya.
distillery, *n.* Miniwakaŋokaġe.

distinct, *a.* Taŋiŋ ; i'citaŋiŋ ; to'keca.
distinction, *n.* Wotokeca ; wowapetokeca ; itokeca ; wokitaŋiŋ.
distinctly, *adv.* Taŋiŋyaŋ.
distinguish, *vt.* Kaħniġa ; iyekiya ; okitaŋiŋ ka'ġa.
distinguishable, *a.* Oiyekiyawaŝte.
distinguished, *pa.* Okitaŋiŋ.
distort, *vt.* Yuħmiŋ.
distract, *vt.* Waciŋhnuniya.
distress, *vt.* Iyokiŝinya ; kakiŝya.
distress, *n.* Wokakiże.
distribute, *vt.* Pamni ; iyayeya.
district, *n.* Makoceoiyute.
distrust, *vt.* Wicadaŝni. *n.* Waceṭuŋhdapi.
distrustful, *a.* Waceṭuŋhda.
disturb, *vt.* Naġiyeya ; yuŝkiŝka.
disturbance, *n.* Owodutatoŋ.
disunion, *n.* Wobdeca.
disuse, *n.* Uŋ'piŝni.
ditch, *n.* Minicaŋkuḳapi ; makaoḳapi.
ditto, *n.* Ake iyececa.
ditty, *n.* Odowaŋci'stiŋna.
dive, *vi.* Kihnuka ; en ya.
diverge, *vi.* A'kiżanya.
divers, *a.* O'ta.
diverse, *a.* Toktokeca.
diversify, *vt.* Yutokeca.
diversion, *n.* Woŝkate.
divert, *vt.* Tokaŋ a'ya ; maġaġaya.
divest, *vt.* Yuŝdoka ; ki.
divide, *vt.* Kiyuŝpa ; yukinukaŋ ; pamni. *vi.* Kinukaŋya. *n.* Makoce mdoya. *T.* Blowaŋżi.
dividend, *n.* Kiyuŝpapi.
divine, *vt.* Wi'yukcaŋ ; ayata. *a.* Wakaŋ. *n.* Wicaŝtawakaŋ.
divinely, *adv.* Wakaŋyaŋ.
diving, *pa.* Kihnukapi.
divisible, *a.* Kiyuŝpepica.
division, *n.* Kiyuŝpapi ; oŝpe.
divisor, *n.* Oŋ kiyuŝpapi.
divorce, *n.* Wakaŋkiciyuzapi yużużupi ; kiyuŝpa ; eħpeya.
divulge, *vt.* Yataŋiŋ.

dizzy, *a.* Itomni.
do (does, did, done), *v.* 1. Ecoŋ. *Do your work well,* wowaŝi nitawa taŋyaŋ ecoŋ. 2. Yuŝtaŋ : *he is done plowing.* 3. Iyecetu : *that will do.* 4. Uŋ : *how do you do.*
Do away with, ihaŋkeya.—*Do for,* ecakicicoŋ ; iyecetu.—*Do his best,* to'ken okihi ecoŋ.—*Do over,* akta ecoŋ.—*Do up,* paħta ; ihaŋkeya.—*Do to,* ecakicoŋ.
do, *aux. v.* (Okiyapi iapi heca). *Do we go? We do go,* uŋyaŋpi he ; uŋyaŋpi.—*Do you see? I do,* waŋdaka he ; waŋmdake.
docile, *a.* Wa'ħbana.
dock, *n.* Wataoahuni. *vt.* Oŋŝpa eħpeya.
docket, *n.* Woecoŋ owapi.
doctor, *n.* Peżutawicaŝta ; ksapotaŋcaŋ. *vt.* Peżuta oŋ kuwa ; kuwa.
doctrine, *n.* Wowicada ; wooŋspe.
document, *n.* Wayaataŋiŋ wowapi.
dodge, *vi.* Napa ; tokaŋya.
doe, *n.* Ta'ħcawiye.
doer, *n.* Waecoŋ.
does, *3rd per. s.* of DO.
doff, *vt.* Yuŝdoka.
dog, *n.* Ŝuŋ'ka. *vt.* Ŝuŋ'ka kuwakiya.
dog-days, *n.* Mdokecokaya.
dogged, *a.* Ociŋŝica.
dogma, *n.* Wooŋspesuta.
dole, *vt.* Ci'stiŋnaḳu.
doleful, *a.* Oiyokiŝica.
doll, *n.* Hokŝinkaġapi.
dollar, *n.* Ma'zaska ; kaŝpapi wikcemna.
dolorous, *a.* Oiyokiŝica.
domain, *n.* Makoce ; woawaŋyake.
dome, *n.* Tiiŋkpamibe.
domestic, *a.* Tihdepi ; tiyata ; tiawaŋyaka. *Domestic animals,* wanuyaŋpi. *n.* Tiwahe ookiye.
domesticate, *vt.* Yuwaħbadaŋ.

domicil, *n.* Ti'pi.
dominant, *a.* Iyotaŋ ; itaŋcaŋ.
dominion, *n.* Wokicoŋze.
don, *vt.* Kiçuŋ.
donate, *vt.* Ḳu ; ituħaŋ.
done, *pp.* of DO. Yuštanpi ; špaŋ.
donkey, *n.* Šoŋšoŋnaħca.
donor, *n.* Waiħpeye ; ḳu.
doom, *n.* Woyaco. *vt.* Yaco; yasu.
doomsday, *n.* Woyaco aŋpetu.
door, *n.* Tiyopa. Y. Tiyepa. *In doors*, timahen. — *Out doors*, taŋkan.
door-way, *n.* Tiyopa oħdoka.
dooryard, *n.* Tiyopa oštaŋ.
dope, *n.* Ta'ku coco.
dormant, *a.* Ištiŋmaseca.
dormitory, *n.* Oištiŋmatipi.
dose, *n.* Oyatkewaŋži. *vt.* Yatkekiya ; ḳu.
dot, *n.* Samyapi. *vt.* Samya.
dotage, *n.* Kaŋ'pi.
dotted, *pa.* Samyapi.
double, *a.* Noŋ'pa ; noŋ'paakihde ; i'takihna.
double, *vt.* Akihdekaġa; yukipaža.
doubly, *adv.* Akihde.
doubt, *vt.* Ceṭuŋhda. *vi.* Waceṭuŋhda. *n.* Ceṭuŋhdapi ; to'ketutaŋiŋšni.
doubtful, *a.* To'ketutaŋiŋšni.
doubtless, *adv.* Ceṭuŋhdapicašni ; ciŋ'to ; a'wicakehaŋ.
dough, *n.* Aġuyapi do.
doughnut, *n.* Aġuyapiwihdienšpaŋyaŋpi.
dove, *n.* Tin'wakiyena.
dower, *n.* Wiwazica tawa.
down, *adv.* Kun ; ku'ya : *fall down*. *vt.* Kun eħpeya. *Down the river*, o'kaħ ; *Ih.* hu'tam.
down, *n.* Wahiŋyažica ; tiŋ'tapaha.
downcast, *a.* Pamahenuŋ ; caŋtešica.
downfall, *n.* Hiŋħpaya ; hiŋhe.
down-hill, *a.* A'pamahde ; Y aiyoħpeya.
downright, *adv.* A'wicakehaŋ.
downward, *adv.* Kun'kiya.
downy, *a.* Žiži ; paŋpaŋna.
doxology, *n.* Woyataŋ oehde.
doze, *vi.* Ištiŋma.
dozen, *a.* Akenoŋpa.
drab, *a.* Ḣo'taka.
draft, *vt.* Owa ; o'pekiya.
draft, *n.* 1. Woyutitaŋ ; yutitaŋpi : *a cart of easy draft*. 2. Oŋ'mazaskaicupi : *a draft on New York*. 3. Okaduze ; boide : *sitting in the draft*. 4. Woyatke : *a draft of milk*. 5. Oicu : *a draft of fishes*. 6. Owapi ; tihuħaowapi.
drag, *vt.* 1. Yusdohaŋ : *drag a stone*. 2. Ayuhiŋhe : *drag the field*. *n.* Maħiyuhiŋhe ; wosdohe ; wokaše.
draggle, *vt.* Maka asdohaŋ.
dragon, *n.* Wamduška.
dragoon, *n.* Šungakanakicita.
drain, *vt.* Yuskepa ; yusota. *n.* Wiyuskepa ; minitacaŋku.
drake, *n.* Maġaksicamdoka.
dram, *n.* Miniwakaŋoyatke ; oṫkeutecistiŋna.
drama, *n.* Škan'owohdake.
drank, *imp.* of DRINK.
drape, *vt.* Miniħuha oŋ akaħpa.
draught. Same as DRAFT.
draw, drew, drawn, *vt.* 1. Yusdohaŋ : *draw the log*. 2. Iyutaŋye ; yutitaŋ : *his speaking drew great crowds*. 3. Yusduta ; yušdoka : *draw a sword*. 4. Icu ; yuwaŋkan icu : *draw a long breath ; draw water*. 5. Icaġo ; ka'ġa : *draw a picture*. 6. Owa : *draw a check*. 7. Minin waŋka : *the boat draws a foot*. 8. Boide : *the stove draws well*. *Draw off*, ehdaku.—*Draw out*, yužuŋ.—*Draw near*, ikiyedaŋ hi.—*Draw up*, natipa.
draw, *n.* Wosdohe ; yusdohaŋpi ; o'smaka ; caŋkaħoŋpapihomni.

drawback, *n.* Wokaġi.
drawer, *n.* Caŋ'opiyeyusdutapi.
drawers, *n.* Oŋzeoġemahenuŋpi.
drawing, *n.* Napeoŋiteowapi.
drawl, *vi.* Yaȟaŋhi.
drawn, *pp.* of DRAW.
dray, *n.* Hunoŋpaowatokšu.
dread, *vt.* Ikopa; kokipa.
dreadful, *a.* Woyušiŋyaŋ.
dreadfully, *adv.* Okokipeya.
dream, *vi.* Wi'haŋmna. *n.* Wowihaŋmna.
dreamer, *n.* Tu'we wihaŋmna.
drear, dreary, *a.* Oašica.
dredge, *vt.* Yukiŋca.
dregs, *n.* Wokpukpe.
drench, *vt.* A'taya spayeya.
dress, *n.* 1. Heyake; Y. hayake: *citizen's dress.* 2. Nitoške; *T.* cuwignaka: *she bought a new dress.*
dress, *vt.* 1. Heyake kiçuŋ; heyake uŋkiya; koyagya. 2. Piya: yuwašte; pa'ta. *Dress a pig,* kukuše pa'ta.—*Dress a skin,* ha kpaŋyaŋ.—*Dress a stone,* iŋyaŋ kakaŋ.—*Dress a wound,* oyazaŋ pikiya.
dressing, *n.* Oihduze; oŋ piyapi; špaŋyaŋpi opuȟdi.
dressy, *a.* Wi'taŋtaŋihduza.
drew, *imp.* of DRAW.
dribble, *vt.* Šbu'šbu.
driblet, *a.* Wokitaŋ.
dried, *pa.* Pusyapi; sa'ka.
drier, *n.* Wapusya.
drier, driest, *comp.* & *super.* of DRY.
drift, *vi.* 1. Kaȟboka; kaȟbogiyaya: *the boat drifted.* 2. Bobdu; kata iheya: *the snow drifts.*
drift, *n.* Caŋokaȟboka; caŋicoġe; woġaŋ; ta'ku bota iheya.
driftwood, *n.* Caŋicoġe.
drill, *vt.* 1. Paȟdoka; yuȟdoka. 2. Akicita kaoŋspe. 3. Hi oȟdogya ożu. *n.* Iyuȟdoka; hi'ȟdokaiożu; wokaoŋspe.
drilling, *n.* Miniȟuhakaġopi seca; oȟdogyapi.
drink, *vt.* Yatkaŋ; yaȟepa. *vi.* Wayatkaŋ; miniwakaŋ yatkaŋ. *n.* Woyatke; wayatkaŋpi.
drinkable, *a.* Yatkepica.
drinker, *n.* Wayatkesa.
drinking, *n.* Wayatkaŋpi.
drip, *vi.* Šbu; šbu'šbu.
drive, drove, *vt.* 1. Kaȟapa; iyayeya: *drive oxen.* 2. Okataŋ: *drive a nail.* *Drive away,* ȟamya.—*Let drive,* howo.
drive, *n.* Oomani; woiyopaštaka.
driver, *n.* Wakaȟapa.
driving, *pa.* Kaȟo se hiyu.
drizzle, *vi.* Minibozaŋ.
droll, *a.* Wowiȟa.
drollery, *n.* Wowiȟaoȟaŋyaŋpi.
dromedary, *n.* Caŋkahupażo.
drone, *n.* Tu'we kuża; tuȟmaġamdoka.
droop, *vi.* Kun'ya; šnišaya.
drop, *vi.* Šbu; hiŋȟpaya; taŋiŋšniiyaya. *vt.* Yušna: *John dropped the egg.* Kun eȟpeya; kun iyeya: *drop corn.* Ayuštaŋ: *drop the subject.*—Yušna se ku: *drop a line.*
drop, *n.* Ošbuye; *T.* oš'e; kun'ya; boȟpaye.
dropsy, *n.* Miniotakiyukaŋ.
dross, *n.* Giŋġiŋca.
drought, *n.* Maġażušni; wapuza.
drove, *imp.* of DRIVE.
drove, *n.* Optaye; wamakaškaŋ optaye.
drover, Pteawaŋyake.
drown, *vt.* Miniṭeya; akiktoŋšya. *vi.* Miniṭa.
drowsy, *a.* Ḣba.
drub, *vt.* Apa.
drudge, *n.* Wowidake; wowaši.
drudgery, *n.* Woȟtani; wowaši.
drug, *n.* 1. Pežuta. 2. Ehaeš ota. *vt.* Pežuta ku.
druggist, *n.* Pežutawiyopeya.
drum, *n.* Caŋ'ceġa. *vt.* Caŋ'ceġa

apa; kabu. *Drum out,* kihdeya. —*Drum up,* mnayaŋ.
drumstick, *n.* Icabu.
drunk, *pp.* of DRINK. *a.* Witko. *n.* Witkoiçiya.
drunkard, *n.* Witkosa.
drunken, *a.* Witko; witkopi.
drunkenness, *n.* Witkopi.
dry, *a.* 1. Pu′za: *dry dirt.* 2. Śe′ca: *a dry leaf.* 3. Miniwakaŋ wanica: *a dry town.* 4. Ţaţake; wi′hahaśni: *a dry speech.*
dry, *vt.* Pusya; kapuza. *vi.* Pu′za; oyaĥe.
dry-goods, *n.* Miniĥuha.
dryness, *n.* Wopuza.
dubious, *a.* To′ketutaŋiŋśni.
duck, *n.* 1. Maġaksica. 2. Maheniyeiçiyapi. 3. Miniĥuĥaśoka.
duck, *vt.* Mininiyeya. *vi.* Kihnuka.
dude, *n.* Tu′we wi′taŋtaŋ.
duds, *n.* Heyake.
due, *a.* 1. Każużupi iyehantu: *the debt is due to-morrow.* 2. Iyecetu: *due honor.* 3. Iyehantu; hi iyehantu: *due at noon.* 4. Oŋ′etaŋhaŋ he′ceca: *due to carelessness.*
due, *n.* Ta′kutawa; woicazo.
due, *adv.* Owotaŋna.
duel, *u.* Nom kicizapi.
duet, *n.* Wicaho noŋpa.
dug, *imp.* of DIG.
dug out, *n.* Caŋwaŋżiwata.
duke, *n.* Itaŋcaŋtaŋka.
dull, *a.* 1. Pe′śni; oţoza: *a dull knife.* 2. Tawaciŋ ţaţake; waciŋksape śni: *a dull boy.* 3. Oĥaŋhi; huŋ′keśni: *a dull fire; a dull trade; a dull pain.*
duly, *adv.* Iyehaŋyaŋ.
dumb, *vt.* Ieśni.
dump, *vt.* Eĥpeya.
dumpling, *n.* Aġuyapi coya śpaŋ.
dun, *a.* Hiŋ′zi.
dun, *vt.* Każużuśi.
dunce, *n.* Waciŋtoŋśni.
dung, *n.* Tacesdi.
dungeon, *n.* Wicakaśkatipi.
dupe, *vt.* Hnayaŋ. *n.* Tu′wehnayaŋpi.
duplicate, *vt.* Iyececa ka′ġa.
duplicity, *n.* Wohnaye.
durable, *a.* Te′hansuta.
duration, *n.* Tohaŋyaŋ ya.
during, *prep.* Icuŋhaŋ.
durst, *imp.* of DARE.
dusk, *n.* O′kpaza.
dusky, *a.* Owataŋiŋśni.
dust, *n.* Makamdu; wakpukpa. *vt.* Katata; pakiŋta.
dusty, *a.* Makamduota; makabobdu.
Dutch, *n.* Iaśicaĥca.
dutiful, *a.* Wanaĥoŋ.
duty, *n.* 1. Ta′kuecoŋiyececa: *it is your duty.* 2. Woecoŋ: *he is on duty.* 3. Woyuha wokażużu.
dwarf, *n.* Ecaciķana; śtuŋka. *vt.* Yuciķana.
dwell, *vt.* 1. Ti; ouŋyaŋ: *dwell in a city.* 2. Te′hanoyaka.
dweller, *n.* Oti.
dwelling, *n.* Ti′pi.
dwindle, *vi.* Ci′stiŋnaaya; hiŋĥpaya.
dye, *n.* Wi′uŋpi: *red dye.* *vt.* Wi′uŋpi akaĥtaŋ: *to dye cloth.* *Dye blue,* toya.
dying, *pa.* Waŋnaţekta; ţe kta en.
dynamite, *n.* Caĥdisuta.
dysentery, *n.* We′każopi.
dyspepsia, *n.* Woyute iśicapi.

E

each, *a.* & *pro.* Iyohi ; owasiŋ. *Each one,* iyohi.—*Each other,* ki′ci–. *Love each other,* waśtekicidapi.
eager, *a.* Ciŋ′ȟca ; oȟaŋko.
eagerly, *adv.* Inaȟni ; ciŋ′ȟca.
eagerness, *n.* Woinaȟni.
eagle, *n.* Waŋmdi ; ȟuya ; anokasaŋ.
ear, *n.* 1. No′ġe ; (*the auricle*) nakpa. 2. Wahuwapa : *an ear of corn.*
earache, *n.* No′ġeyazaŋpi.
early, *a.* 1. Otokahe : *his early writings.* 2. Ecadaŋ : *early decay.*
early, *adv.* Ecadaŋ : *rise early.*
earn, *vt.* Kamna ; ohiya.
earnest, *a.* Wakitaŋ ; wicaka. *n.* Oŋ yuwicakapi.
earning, *n.* Wokamna.
earring, *n.* Nakpa oiŋ.
earth, *n.* Maka ; maka mibe.
earthen, *a.* Maka.
earthly, *a.* Makata.
earthquake, *n.* Makacaŋcaŋ.
earthy, *a.* Maka etaŋhaŋ.
ease, *vt.* Ozikiya. *n.* Woozikiye ; ṫeȟiśni.
easily, *adv.* Teȟiśniyaŋ ; waśakayedaŋ.
easiness, *n.* Woteȟiśni.
east, *a.* & *n.* Wiyohiyaŋpa.
Easter, *n.* Woekicetuaŋpetu.
easterly, *a.* Wiyohiyaŋpata.
eastern, *a.* Wiyohiyaŋpa.
eastward, *a.* Wiyohiyaŋpata.
easy, *a.* 1. Teȟikeśni : *an easy lesson.* 2. Awaśte ; owaśte ; iwaśtena śkaŋ.
eat, ate, *vt.* Yu′ta. *Eat a hole,* yaȟdoka.—*Eat up,* temya. *vi.* Wota.
eatable, *a.* Oyunwaśte.
eaves, *n.* Ti′pitete.
ebb, *n.* Oyaȟe ; kunya.
ebony, *n.* Caŋsapa.
eccentric, *a.* Oȟaŋtokeca.
ecclesiastical, *a.* Okodakiciyewakaŋ.
echo, *vt.* Kaiyowaza.
eclectic, *a.* Kaȟniȟyuhapi.
eclipse, *n.* Wiṭa. *vt.* Aohaŋziya ; kapeya.
economical, *a.* Wakpataŋ.
economy, *n.* Wakpataŋpi ; okicaŋye.
ecstasy, *n.* Mde′ześni.
eddy, *n.* Miniomni.
edge, *n.* I ; ope ; tete ; opapuŋ. *The edge of the ax,* ope.—*The edge of the table,* tete.—*The edge of the cloth,* opapuŋ.
edgewise, *a.* Omdecaya.
edible, *a.* Yu′tapiwaśte.
edict, *n.* E′yaŋpahapi.
edifice, *n.* Ti′pitaŋka.
edify, *vt.* Yuksapa ; yuwaśte.
edit, *vt.* Iapikaȟniġa.
editor, *n.* Iapikaȟniġa.
editorial, *a.* Itaŋcaŋ toie.
educate, *vt.* Oŋspekiya ; kihiya.
education, *n.* Waoŋspewicakiyapi; wooŋspe.
educator, *n.* Waoŋspekiya.
educe, *vt.* Etaŋhaŋicu.
eel, *n.* Ho′waŋmduśka.
e'en, *contr.* EVEN.
e'er, *contr.* EVER.
efface, *vt.* Paźuźu.
effect, *vt.* Ka′ġa ; ecoŋ. *n.* 1. Ta′ku ka′ġa ; oŋ itokeca : *the effect of the storm.* 2. Wowaśake : *to speak with effect.* 3. Woyuha : *his total effects.*—*To this effect,* deciyotaŋ.
effective, *a.* Waokihi.
effectual, *a.* Wi′yokihi.

effeminate, *a.* Wiŋ'yaŋ iyececa.
effete, *a.* Taŋni ; huŋ'keṡni.
efficacious, *a.* Waokihi.
efficient, *a.* Wi'yokihi.
effigy, *n.* I'ḣad ka'ġapi.
effort, *n.* Wokuwa ; ecoŋutapi.
effulgent, *a.* Wiyakpa.
egg, *n.* Wi'tka. *vt.* Wi'tka oŋ kiŋiŋ ; i'yopaṡtaka.
eggshell, *n.* Wi'tkaha.
egotist, *n.* Ihdataŋsa.
egregious, *a.* Ihaŋketa.
egress, *n.* Oenape.
eh, *interj.* Waŋ.
eight, *a.* Ṡahdoġaŋ ; *Y.* ṡakdoġaŋ ; *T.* ṡagloġaŋ.
eighteen, *a.* Akeṡahdoġaŋ.
eightfold, *a.* Ṡahdoġaŋakihde.
eighth, *a.* 1. Iṡahdoġaŋ : *the eighth.* 2. Ṡahdoġaŋ yuṡpapi waŋżi : *one eighth.*
eighty, *a.* Wikcemna ṡahdoġaŋ.
either, *a.* 1. Uŋmaŋtukte ṡta : *give me either one.* 2. Sakim : *trees on either side.*
either, *conj.* Uŋmaŋtukte kaṡta.
ejaculate, *vt.* Ni'na eya.
eject, *vt.* Taŋkan iyayeya.
eke, *vt.* Akaġa ; okipata.
elaborate, *vt.* Ka'ġa. *a.* Oṡkiṡke ka'ġapi.
elapse, *vi.* Hiyaya ; owihaŋke.
elastic, *a.* Ziġzica. *n.* Caŋṡiŋziġzica.
elated, *pa.* Wi'yuṡkiŋ.
elbow, *n.* Iṡpaokihe ; ipakṡaŋ ; ihupa kṡaŋ. *vt.* Paoskin ya.
elder, *a.* Tokapa. *n.* 1. Huŋkayapi ; huŋka. 2. Ipapope caŋ ; caputahu.
elder-berry, *n.* Caputa.
elderly, *a.* Ehaŋna.
eldest, *a.* Tokapaḣca.
elect, *vt.* Kaḣniġa. *a.* Kaḣniġapi.
election, *n.* Kaŋsuiyoḣpeyapi; wakaḣniġapi
elector, *n.* Kaŋsuiyoḣpeya.
electric, *a.* Wakaŋhdi.
electricity, *n.* Wakaŋhdi.
electrify, *vt.* Wakaŋhdiiheya ; yuhnaṡkiŋyaŋ.
elegance, *n.* Wowaṡte.
elegant, *a.* Waṡteḣca.
elegy, *n.* Aceyapi odowaŋ.
element, *n.* 1. O'kihe : *one of the elements.* 2. Wooŋspe otokahe : *elements of arithmetic.*
elementary, *a.* Otokahe.
elephant, *n.* Putehaŋska.
elevate, *vt.* Waŋkaniyeya ; yuwaṡte.
elevated, *pa.* Yuwaŋkantu.
elevation, *n.* Waŋkantu.
eleven, *a.* Akewaŋżi.
elicit, *a.* Oyagkiya.
eligible, *a.* Kaḣniḣpica.
eliminate, *vt.* Eḣpeya.
elite, *n.* Kaḣniḣwaṡtepi.
elk, *n.* (male) Heḣaka ; (female), upaŋ.
elipses, *n.* Yuṡnapi.
elm, *n.* p̣e ; p̣ecaŋ ; (*Slippery elm*) p̣e'tu'tupa. (*Rock elm*), p̣e'itazipe.
elocution, *n.* Woowohdake wooŋspe.
elongate, *vt.* Yuhaŋska.
elope, *vi.* Naḣmaŋiyaye.
eloquent, *a.* Wohdakawayapika.
else, *adv.* 1. To'keca : *what else have you?* 2. He'cece ṡni kiŋhaŋ : *else would I die.*
elsewhere, *adv.* Tukten to'kcca.
elucidate, *vt.* Iyoyamya.
elude, *vt.* Hna'yaŋ.
emaciated, *a.* Sta'ka.
emancipate, *vt.* Kiyuṡka.
embankment, *n.* Mayakaġapi.
embark, *vi.* Wa'ta o'pa.
embarrass, *vt.* Iniḣaŋya ; kaġiya.
embellish, *vt.* Yuwaṡte.
ember, *vt.* Petaġa.
embezzle, *vt.* Ta'waṡni uŋ; manoŋ.
embitter, *vt.* Waciŋhiŋyaŋsya.
emblem, *n.* Wowapetokeca.
embody, *vt.* Ka'ġa ; taŋiŋyaŋhde.

embolden, *vt.* Yuwaditake.
embrace, *vt.* Adoksoyuza ; o'pa.
embroider, *vt.* Ipata.
embroil, *vt.* En'ikoyagya.
embryo, *n.* Su'caŋte.
emerald, *n.* Iŋ'yaŋto.
emerge, *vi.* Hinapa.
emergency, *n.* Ihnuhaŋ to'keca.
emetic, *n.* Oŋhde'papi.
emigrant, *n.* Ihdaguŋpi.
emigrate, *vi.* Ihdaka ; oyate tokeca ekta i'yotaŋka.
eminence, *n.* Paha ; wokitaŋiŋ.
eminent, *a.* Okitaŋiŋ.
eminently, *adv.* Wakapeya.
emissary, *n.* Naȟmaŋ yeṡipi.
emission, *n.* Hiyuyapi.
emit, *vt.* Hiyuya.
emolument, *n.* Wokażużu.
emotion, *n.* Canteyuṡkaŋṡkaŋ.
emotional, *a.* Wacaŋtiheyesa.
emperor, *n.* Itaŋcaŋtaŋka.
emphasis, *n.* Hoyaŋka.
emphasize, *vt.* Ni'na eya.
emphatic, *a.* Iyotaŋ.
empire, *n.* Oyate ; wokicoŋze.
employ, *vt.* Waṡi ; ecoŋṡi ; uŋ.
employee, *n.* Wowaṡi.
employer, *n.* Wawicaṡi.
employment, *n.* Ḣtanipi ; wowaṡi.
emporium, Ho'coka ; caŋte.
empower, *vt.* Wowaṡ'ake ḳu.
empress, *n.* Wiŋ'yaŋitaŋcaŋ.
emptiness, *n.* Ituuŋpi ; ta'kuṡni.
empty, *a.* Cokana ; *T.* kokala ; ta'kuna en uŋ ṡni ; ituya uŋ. *vt.* Yucokadaŋ ; okaṡtaŋ ; eȟpeya.
emulate, *vt.* Iyecen ecoŋ.
enable, *vt.* Okihiya.
enact, *vt.* Ka'ġa ; ecoŋ.
enactment, *n.* Wokaġe.
enamel, *n.* Huhuska.
enamour, *vt.* Awaṡtedaye.
encamp, *vi.* E'ti ; e'yotaŋke.
encampment, *n.* Oeti.
enchant, *vt.* Yuhnaṡkiŋyaŋ.
enchantment, *n.* Woȟmuŋġa.
encircle, *vt.* Aohomniya.
enclose, *vt.* Nataka ; apaȟta.
enclosure, *n.* Acaŋkaṡkapi.
encomium, *n.* Woyawaṡte.
encompass, *vt.* Aokibeya.
encore, *vt.* Akihdedapi.
encounter, *vt.* Akipa ; i'tkokipa. *n.* I'tkokipapi ; kicizapi.
encourage, *vt.* Waṡ'agya ; i'yopaṡtaka.
encouragement, *n.* Wookiye.
encroach, *vi.* Kiaya.
encumber, *vt.* Kaṡ'agya.
encyclopedia, *n.* Wooŋspe siŋtomni oyaka.
end, *n.* 1. Owihaŋke : *the end of the road.* 2. Wokuwa : *man's chief end.* 3. Iŋ'kpa ; ihaŋke : *odds and ends.* *On end :* bosdan. *vt.* Owihaŋkeya ; yuṡtaŋ.
endanger, *vt.* Okokipekaġa.
endear, *vt.* Waṡtedaya.
endeavor, *vt.* Ecoŋwaciŋ ; akita.
endless, *a.* Owihaŋkewanica.
endow, *vt.* Woyuha ki'cihde.
endowment, *n.* Woyuhahde.
endue, *vt.* Yuhekiya.
endurance, *n.* Wakiṡ'akapi.
endure, *vt.* Iwakiṡ'aka ; iwaciŋtaŋka. *vi.* Ecen haŋ ; uŋ.
enduring, *pa.* Te'han uŋ.
endwise, *adv.* Ohaŋskeya.
enemy, *n.* To'ka.
energetic, *a.* Ohitika ; mdiheca.
energy, *n.* Wowaṡ'ake ; woohitika.
enervate, *vt.* Waṡ'akeṡniya.
enfeeble, *vt.* Yuṡiȟtiŋ.
enforce, *vt.* Ecen ecoŋkiya.
enfranchise, *vt.* Ta'waiçiya.
engage, *vt.* Kici yuṡtaŋ ; ḳu kta yuṡtaŋ ; kici ecoŋ. *vi.* 1. Eya : *she engaged to go.* 2. Ecoŋ ; kuwa : *engage in trade.*
engaged, *pa.* 1. Yu'ze kta yuṡtaŋpi : *she is engaged.* 2. Owaŋżi uŋ ṡni ; kuwa : *he is engaged just now.*
engaging, *pa.* Wawiyutaŋye.
engender, *vt.* Ka'ġa.

engine, *n.* Icuwa; ȟemani; ma′-zayuhomni.
engineer, *n.* Ma′zayuhomni awaŋyaka. *vt.* Kuwa; kicaŋye.
English, *n.* Sagdaša; Wašicuŋ. *Do you speak English,* Wašicuŋ iyaa he.
engorge, *vt.* Akaska.
engrave, *vt.* Baġo.
engraving, *n.* Wabaġopi.
engross, *vt.* 1. Wi′taya owa: *engross the proceedings.* 2. Ecedaŋ en uŋ; ożudaŋye: *engrossed his mind.*
engulf, *vt.* Napcaiyeya.
enhance, *vt.* Saŋ′pa ka′ġa.
enigma, *n.* Wowiyukcaŋ teȟike.
enjoin, *vt.* Awaciŋši.
enjoy, *vt.* Iyuškiŋ; awašteda; oŋ taŋyaŋ uŋ.
enjoyment, *n.* Wowiyuškin; wi′yuškiŋpi.
enlarge, *vt.* Yutaŋka. *vi.* Taŋ′ka a′ya.
enlargement, *n.* Taŋ′ka a′ye.
enlighten, *vt.* Iyoyamya
enlightened, *pa.* Ksapapi.
enlist, *vt.* O′pekiya. *vi.* O′pa.
enliven, *vt.* Yuȟica; mdihenya.
enmity, *n.* Wowaȟtedašni.
ennoble, *vt.* Yuwašte.
enormity, *n.* Wotaŋka.
enormous, *a.* Taŋ′kaȟca.
enough, *a.* Iyenakeca; o′ta: *bread enough. adv.* Iyehaŋyaŋ; ni′na; ki′taŋna.
enraged, *pa.* Caŋniyaŋ.
enraptured, *pa.* Mde′zešni.
enrich, *vt.* Wi′żinya; yuwašte.
enroll, *vt.* Cażeowa.
ensign, *n.* Wa′paha.
enslave, *vt.* Wowidake ka′ġa.
ensnare, *vt.* Hmuŋka.
ensue, *vt.* Kuwaaya.
entail, *vt.* E′yaȟpeya.
entangle, *vt.* Hmuŋ′ka; kaška.
enter, *vt.* 1. En ya: *enter the house.* 2. En owa: *enter his name.*
enterprise, *n.* Wicoȟaŋ omdihecapi.
enterprising, *pa.* Mdiheca.
entertain, *vt.* 1. Maġaġaya: *entertain with stories.* 2. Woḳu; taŋyaŋ kuwa: *entertain strangers.* 3. En e′waciŋ: *entertain his proposals.*
entertaining, *pa.* Onaȟoŋwašte.
entertainment, *n.* Kicicopi.
enthrone, *vt.* Itaŋcaŋka′ġa.
enthusiast, *n.* Oȟaŋdita.
enthusiastic, *a.* Waštedaškaŋ.
entice, *vt.* Iyutaŋye.
entire, *a.* Ocowasiŋ; a′taya.
entirely, *adv.* A′taya.
entitle, *vt.* Oŋ caże ku′pi.
entomb, *vt.* Maka en e′ȟnaka.
entrails, *n.* Šupe.
en′trance, *n.* Tiyopa; oenape; en ya′pi.
entrance, *vt.* Wi′ȟaŋmnakiya.
entreat, *vt.* Ce′kiya.
entreaty, *n.* Wacekiyapi.
entrench, *vt.* Wowinape ḳa′pi.
entrenchment, *n.* Makaḳapi.
entrust, *vt.* Awaŋyagkiya.
entry, *n.* En ya; en owa; tiyopa; timahen ocaŋku.
entwine, *vt.* Yuwi.
enumerate, *vt.* To′nakecayawa.
enunciate, *vt.* Hoenapeya.
envelope, *vt.* Iyapehaŋ; akaȟpa. *n.* Wowapiożuha.
envious, *a.* Wi′nawizi.
environment, *n.* Ta′ku o′kšaŋ uŋ.
envy, *n.* Wowinawizi. *vt.* Nawizi.
epaulet, *n.* Hiyeteboȟciuŋpi.
epidemic, *n.* Woyazaŋ a′taya iyaye.
Episcopal Church, *n.* Ska′iŋ Okodakiciye; Cuwiknakeska.
episode, *n.* Woakipa.
epistle, *n.* Wowapi.
epithet, *n.* Wocaże.
epoch, *n.* Aŋpetu.
equal, *a.* 1. I′akidececapi: *of equal strength.* 2. I′akidehantu;

o'waŋżina : *equal temperature.* 3. Iyehan ; okihi : *he is equal to the task. vt.* Iyehan un ; iyehan ecoŋ : *no one can equal God. Two and two equal four,* noŋ'pa qa noŋ'pa hecen to'pa.
equality, *n.* 1. I'akidececapi : *equality of weight.* 2. Omdaye.
equalize, *vt.* I'akidecen ka'ġa.
equally, *adv.* A'kidecenya.
equanimity, *n.* Tawaciŋ mda'ya.
equator, *n.* Wi'ocaŋku.
equestrian, *a.* Šuŋgakanuŋ.
equi-, *pref.* I'akidehantu.
equilateral, *a.* Cuwiakidececa.
equinox, *n.* Aŋ'pa haŋhepi iyehantu.
equip, *n.* Koyagya ; yuwiyeya ; ta'ku yuhekiya.
equipment, *n.* Icuwa.
equitable, *a.* Owotaŋna.
equity, *n.* Woowotaŋna.
equivalent, *a.* Kici iyececa.
equivocal, *a.* To'ketu taŋiŋ šni.
era, *n.* O'maka ; woyawa.
eradicate, *vt.* Yużuŋ eḣpeya.
erase, *vt.* Pażużu.
eraser, *n.* Ipażużu.
ere, *prep.* I'tokam.
erect, *a.* Bosdan ; *T.* woslal ; atiŋyaŋ ; botiŋ. *vt.* E'hdə.
erection, *n.* E'hdepi.
erelong, *adv.* Ecadaŋ.
ermine, *n.* Hituŋkasaŋ.
err, *vi.* Yušna ; nu'ni ; waḣtani.
errand, *n.* Wahošiyapi ; ta'ku huweyapi.
erratic, *a.* Wi'cišniyaŋ ya.
erroneous, *a.* He'cetušni.
error, *n.* Woyušna ; nu'nipi.
erudite, *a.* Waoŋspeḣca.
eruption, *n.* Ahinapapi ; bobdu hiyuya ; pom'hiyu.
escape, *vi.* Iyaya ; nażica. *vt.* Etaŋhaŋ ihdušpe ; ececešni.
eschew, *vt.* Ecoŋšni.
escort, *vt.* Kiciya ; awaŋyaka.
especial, *a.* I'atayedaŋ.
espouse, *vt.* Yu'zekta yuštaŋpi.
espy, *vt.* Waŋyagiheya.
essay, *n.* Iwohdag wowapi.
essence, *n.* Co ; miniwaštemna.
essential, *a.* E'eḣca ; itaŋcaŋ.
establish, *vt.* Sutaya e'hde.
establishment, *n.* Sutaya e'hdepi ; tipi ko hde'pi.
estate, *n.* Woyuhaataya ; wicašta ţa tawoyuha ; ouŋ.
esteem, *vt.* Yawa ; -da. *I esteem him well,* taŋyaŋwada. *n.* Wowaštedapi ; yuonihaŋpi.
estimable, *a.* Yuonihaŋpica.
estimate, *vt.* Yawa ; iyukcaŋ. *n.* Wowiyukcaŋ.
estimation, *n* Wi'yukcaŋpi; woyuonihaŋ.
estrange, *vt.* Watokaye ; yutokaŋ.
eternal, *a.* O'hiŋnini.
eternity, *n.* Owihaŋke wanica.
Ethiopian, *n.* Ha'sapa.
etiquette, *n.* Yuonihaŋ wicoḣaŋ.
eucharist, *n.* Wotapiwakaŋ.
eulogize, *vt.* Yawašte.
eulogy, *n.* Woyawašte.
eunuch, *n.* Wicašta susu wanica.
euphony, *n.* Oeyewašte.
eureka, *excl.* Iyewaya.
evacuate, *vt.* Etaŋhaŋ iyaya ; iheya.
evade, *vt.* Napa; yuspicašni; icuŋom ia.
evanesce, *vi.* Ske'pa.
evangelical, *a.* Wotaŋiŋ Wašte ; Jesus oie ohna.
evangelist, *n.* Wotaŋiŋ Wašte oyaka.
evangelize, *vt.* Wotaŋiŋ Wašte oŋspekiya.
evaporate, *vi.* Ske'pa ; taŋiŋšni. *vt.* Yuskepa ; kapuza ; pusya.
evasion, *n.* Napapi ; yatokecapi.
eve, *n.* Aḣtayetu ; i'tokam ḣtayetu ; ḣtayetu.
even, *vt.* Yumdaya ; yuotkoŋza. *a.* 1. Mda'ya ; o'waŋżidaŋ. 2. O'tkoŋza : *even numbers. adv.*

1. Kaeṡ : *even he.* 2. Hehaŋyaŋ ṡta : *even to death.*
evening, *n.* Ḣtayetu.
evenly, *adv.* Mda′yena.
event, *n.* Woecoŋ; woyuṡtaŋ.
eventful, *a.* Woakipa o′ta; taŋ′ka.
eventless, *a.* Ta′ku caẑeyanpica wanica.
eventually, *adv.* Uŋ′haŋketa.
ever, *adv.* 1. To′hiŋni; ce′e : *do you ever dance.* 2. O′hiŋni : *he is ever the same.*
evergreen, *a.* O′hiŋnito.
everlasting, *a.* Owihaŋkewanica.
evermore, *a.* O′hiŋniyaŋ.
every, *a.* Iyohi; owasiŋ. *Every now and then,* iciẑehaŋ.—*Every one,* iyohi; owasiŋ.
everybody, *n.* Owasiŋ.
everything, *n.* Ta′ku owasiŋ.
everywhere, *adv.* O′waŋcaya.
evidence, *n.* Woyataŋiŋ.
evident, *a.* Okitaŋiŋ; taŋiŋ.
evidently, *adv.* Taŋiŋyaŋ.
evil, *a.* Ṡi′ca; wayuṡica : *evil deeds.* *n.* Ta′ku ṡi′ca; woṡica.
evince, *vt.* Yutaŋiŋ.
evoke, *vt.* Kico.
evolution, *n.* Yuzamnipi.
evolve, *vt.* Yuzamni.
ewe, *n.* Ta′ḣcaṡuŋka wi′ye.
ex-, *pref.* He′kta : *ex-President.*
ex, *prep.* Oŋ etaŋhaŋ.
exact, *a.* Iyecetuḣca; hehantuḣca; owotaŋnaḣca ecoŋ. *vt.* Wakitaŋicu; teḣiyakuwa.
exacting, *pa.* Wakitaŋ.
exactly, *adv.* Hecetuḣca.
exactness, *a.* Owotaŋnapi.
exaggerate, *vt.* Aokaġa.
exalt, *vt.* Yuwaŋkantuya.
exalted, *pa.* Waŋkantuya.
examination, *n.* Wi′waŋġapi.
examine, *vt.* Iwaŋġa.
example, *n.* Iwaŋyag ecoŋpi; to′keca pazopi.
exasperate, *vt.* Caŋzeya.
excavate, *vt.* Oḳa; oḣdogya.
excavation, *n.* Oḳapi; oḣdoka.
exceed, *vt.* Kapeya; i′sam ya.
exceeding, *a.* Saŋ′pa; iyotaŋ.
excel, *vt.* Kapa; sam ya.
excellence, *n.* Wakapa.
excellent, *a.* Ni′na waṡte.
except, *vt.* O′pekiyeṡni : *he excepted children.* *prep.* Tuka; tuka he o′pe ṡni : *all except one.* *conj.* Kiŋhaŋ; ehantaŋhaŋ : *except you work.*
exception, *n.* Waŋẑi to′keca.
exceptionable, *a.* Iyecetuṡni.
exceptional, *a.* To′keca.
excess, *n.* Iyecetu i′saŋpa; iyaye
exchange, *vt.* Tokiyopeya.
excitable, *a.* Kohaŋ mde′zeṡni.
excite, *vt.* Yumdezeṡni.
excitement, *n.* Mde′zapiṡni; ni′na ṡkaŋ′pi.
exciting, *pa.* Wayuḣice.
exclaim, *vt.* Ni′na eya.
exclamation, *n.* Paŋ′paŋ iapi.
exclude, *vt.* O′peṡniya.
exclusion, *n.* O′peṡniyapi.
eclusive, *a.* Iṡnaiçidapi.
excommunicate, *vt.* Ḣeyata iyeya.
excruciating, *pa.* Ni′na yazaŋpi.
exculpate, *vt.* Yaṡicapiṡni.
excursion, *n.* Ṡkan′yapi.
excusable, *a.* Iyowiŋyepica.
excuse, *vt.* Iyowiŋyaŋ. *n.* Oŋ iyowiŋyaŋpi kta iyececa.
execrable, *a.* Ni′na ṡi′ca.
execute, *vi.* Ṭeya; ecen yuṡtaŋ.
executive, *n.* Wayuṡtaŋ. *a.* Waecoŋ.
exemplary, *a.* Yuwaṡtepica.
exemplify, *vt.* Iyecen pazo.
exempt, *a.* O′pasni.
exercise, *vt.* Ṡkiŋ′çiya; içicuwa; un. *n.* Woecoŋ; uŋ′pi.
exert, *vt.* Uŋ; ka′ġa; aiçiciya.
exertion, *n.* Uŋ′pi; woecoŋ.
exhale, *vt.* Poḣ′iyeya; hiyuya.
exhaust, *vt.* Yusota; yuwaṡ′akeṡni.
exhaustless, *a.* Yusonpicaṡni.
exhibit, *vt.* Pazo. *n.* Pazopi.

exhibition, *n.* Wapazopi.
exhilarate, *vt.* Yuwihaha.
exhort, *vt.* Wahokoŋkiya; i'yapaśtaka.
exhortation, *n.* Wowahokoŋkiye.
exhorter, *n.* Wahokoŋkiya.
exhume, *vt.* Oḳa; yutaŋiŋ.
exigency, *n.* Woteḣi.
exile, *vt.* Napeya. *n.* Onażica.
exist, *vi.* Ecenuŋ; ni; yaŋka.
existence, *n.* Ni'uŋpi.
exit, *n.* Tokaŋ ya'pi.
exodus, *n.* Hdinapapi.
exonerate, *vt.* Kiyuśka.
exorbitant, *a.* Aokaġeca.
expand, *vt.* Yutaŋka; yumdaya. *vi.* Taŋ'kaaya.
expanse, *n.* Oyumdaye.
expatiate, *vi.* Taŋ'kaya ia.
expatriate, *vt.* Makoce ta'wa etaŋhaŋ napeya.
expect, *vt.* Awaciŋ uŋ; akipe.
expectorate, *vt.* Kaśpa.
expedient, *a.* Iyececa; owaśtekta. *n.* Woecoŋ.
expedite, *vt.* Inaḣniya.
expedition, *n.* Wicomani.
expeditious, *a.* Oḣaŋko.
expel, *vt.* Iyayeya.
expend, *vt.* Yusota; ḳu.
expenditure, *n.* Yusotapi.
expense, *n.* Woyusota; woyuśna.
expensive, *a.* Teḣika; ma'zaska o'ta yusota.
experience, *vt.* Sdonya. *n.* Woecoŋ oŋ sdonyapi; oḣaŋ.
experiment, *n.* Sdonyapi kta oŋ ecoŋpi.
expert', *a.* Wayupika.
ex'pert, *n.* Tu'we wayupika
expiate, *vt.* Kakiś'ya każużu.
expiration, *n.* Owihaŋke.
expire, *vi.* Niya hiyuya; ṭa; owihaŋke.
explain, *vt.* To'ketu oyaka.
explanation, *n.* Woyaka.
explode, *vt.* Napomya. *vi.* Napopa; atakuniśni.
exploit, *n.* Woecoŋ.
exploration, *n.* Waodeomanipi.
explore, *vt.* Waode.
explorer, *n.* Tu'we waode.
explosion, *n.* Wanapomyapi.
exponent, *n.* To'ketu oyaka.
export, *vt.* Yeya; makoce to'keca ekta yeya. *n.* Ta'ku yeyapi.
expose, *vt.* Yutaŋiŋ.
exposition, *n.* Wapazopi; oyakapi.
expostulate, *vi.* Iyokiśni.
expound, *vt.* Oyaka.
express, *vt.* Yataŋiŋ; yeya. *a.* Katiŋyaŋ. *n.* Owatokśu suta.
expression, *n.* Iapi.
expressive, *a.* Yaṭiŋs eyapi.
expressly, *adv.* Taŋiŋyaŋ ḣca.
expulsion, *n.* Eḣpeyapi.
expunge, *vt.* Pażużu.
expurgate, *vt.* Pakiŋta.
exquisite, *a.* Yucoya ka'ġapi.
extant, *a.* Yukaŋ.
extemporaneous, *a.* Yukseknaġ.
extend, *vt.* Yuhaŋska; yeya.
extension, *n.* Yuhaŋskapi.
extensive, *a.* Taŋ'ka.
extent, *n.* Tohaŋyaŋ yeya.
extenuate, *vt.* Yuaokpani.
exterior, *a.* Akapataŋhaŋ.
exterminate, *vt.* A'taya ihaŋgya.
external, *a.* Akantaŋhaŋ.
extinct, *a.* Śni; waŋna wanica.
extinguish, *vt.* Kasni; yużużu.
extirpate, *vt.* Yużuŋ eḣpeya.
extol, *vt.* Yawaŋkantu.
extort, *vt.* Ki; yus icu.
extortion, *n*; Wicadaśni ki'pi.
extra, *a.* Iyaye; kapeya.
extra-, *pref.* I'saŋpa.
extract', *v.* Icu.
ex'tract, *n.* Ta'ku icupi.
extraordinary, *a.* Iyotaŋ.
extravagance, *n.* Wayusotapi.
extravagant, *a.* Wayusotesa.
extreme, *a.* Ihaŋketa.
extricate, *vt.* Yusduta; icu.
exuberance, *n.* Wowiżica.

exuberant, *a.* Paŋ'ġa.
exult, *vt.* Ni'na iyuśkiŋ.
exultation, *n.* Wi'yuśkiŋpi.
eye, *n.* Iśta. *The human eye*, wiciśta.—*The needle's eye*, tahiŋśpa oḣdoka. *vt.* Waŋyaka.
eyeball, *n.* Iśtapśuŋka; iśtasu.
eyebrow, *n.* Iśtaḣehiŋ.
eyeglass, *n.* Iśtamaza; iśtażaŋżaŋ.
eyelash, *n.* Iśtaḣepehiŋ.
eyeless, *a.* Iśta wanica.
eyelet, *n.* Haḣoŋtaoḣdoka.
eyelid, *n.* Iśtożuha.
eyesight, *n.* Wi'waŋyake.
eyesore, *n.* Waŋyakapiśica.
eye-witness, *n.* Iśta oŋ waŋyaka.

F

fable, *n.* Ohuŋkakaŋ.
fabric, *n.* Wakazoŋtapi.
fabricate, *vt.* Ka'ġa.
fabulous, *a.* Kakaŋpi.
face, *n.* Ite; i'toye; omdaye. *vt.* Iteayuta; i'tkokipa; opapoŋkaġa. *Make faces*, iteśinkiya. —*The face of a moccasin*, haŋpitake.—*Face up*, ituŋkam.—*Worth its face*, owapi iyecen waśte.
facetious, *a.* Wawiḣaye.
facilitate, *vt.* Ecadaŋ okihiya.
facility, *n.* Wookihi; wayupikapi.
fact, *n.* Ta'kuhecetu; wowicake.
faction, *n.* Ośpaye.
factious, *a.* Wanaḣoŋśni.
factor, *n.* Ka'ġe waŋżi.
factory, *n.* Wokaġetipi.
faculty, *n.* Oŋ wasdonyapi; waonspekiya.
fad, *n.* Wowimdeza.
fade, *vi.* Saŋ a'ya; taŋiŋśni.
fagot, *n.* Caŋḣakaopaḣte.
fail, *vi.* Okihiśni; sni.
failure, *n.* Okihiśni; wanica.
fain, *a.* Iyowiŋyaŋ; ciŋ.
faint, *vi.* Kiksuyeśni; hu'staka. *a.* Waśakeśni; iwaśtena.
faint-hearted, *a.* Canwaŋka.
faintly, *adv.* Iwaśtedaŋ.
fair, *a.* 1. Ukaska: *fair complexion.* 2. Zi: *fair hair.* 3. Kasota; owaśtecaka: *a fair day.* 4. Ki'taŋna waśte: *fair crops.* 5. Owotaŋna: *fair in his dealings.* 6. Waśte: *a fair name.* *n.* Wapazopi.
fairly, *adv.* Ki'taŋna.
fairness, *n.* Woowotaŋna.
fairy, fairies, *n.* Wanaġi.
faith, *n.* Waciŋyaŋpi; wicadapi; wowaciŋye; wowicada.
faithful, *a.* Waciŋyepica; wicaka.
faithfully, *adv.* Taŋyaŋ; wicakeya.
faithfulness, *n.* Wowicake.
faithless, *a.* Waciŋyepicaśni.
fake, *n.* Wohnaye.
fall, fell, *vi.* Hiŋḣpaya; kun ya; waŋkahaŋ. *He fell back*, he'kta iyaya.—*Fall in with*, kici akipe. *Fall out with*, kici akinica.—*Fall through*, ohna hiŋḣpaya; ecetu śni. *n.* 1. Hiŋḣpaye: *a hard fall.* 2. Ptaŋyetu: *next fall.* 3. Minihiŋhe; ḣaḣa.
fallacious, *a.* He'cetuśni.
fallacy, *n.* Wohnaye.
fallen, *pa.* Hiŋḣpaya.
fallible, *a.* Nu'nipica.
falling, *pa.* Kun ya; hiŋḣpaya.
fallow, *a.* Ożupiśni.
false, *a.* Wohnaye; wicakeśni. *False teeth*, hi o'śtaŋpi.
falsehood, *n.* Woitoŋśni; wohnaye.
falsely, *adv.* Wicakeśniyaŋ.
falsify, *vt.* Yuwicakeśni.
falsity, *n.* Wowicakeśni.

falter, *vi.* Yaśnaśnaia; ȟicahaŋ.
fame, *n.* Wokitaŋiŋ; wacażeyatapi.
familiar, *a.* Taŋyaŋsdonya.
familiarly, *adv.* A′witukadaŋ.
familiarity, *n.* Taŋyaŋsdonyapi.
family, *n.* Tiwahe; tiohnake; wicowazi; wicobe.
famine, *n.* Wicaakiȟaŋ; wanica.
famish, *vi.* Akiȟaŋ; hu′staka.
famous, *a.* Okitaŋiŋ.
famously, *adv.* Okitaŋiŋyaŋ; ni′na taŋyaŋ.
fan, *n.* Icadu. *vt.* Kaduġa.
fanatic, *n.* Wi′yukcaŋśni śkaŋ.
fanciful, *a.* Ituyaciŋ.
fancy, fancied, *vt.* Eciŋ; wi′haŋmna. *n.* Wowiyukcaŋ; woihaŋmde. *a.* Wayuco ka′ġapi; wi′haŋmnapi se; wayupika.
fang, *n.* Hi′pesto; hiŋske.
fanning-mill, *n.* Aġuyapi icadu.
fantastic, *a.* Oȟaŋhaŋhaŋ.
far, *a.* & *adv.* 1. Te′han; te′hantu: *far distant; a far country.* 2. Ni′na: *far different. As far as,* hehaŋyaŋ.—*By far,* iyotaŋ.—*Far and wide,* taŋ′kaya.—*Far apart,* i′citehan.—*In so far as,* tohaŋyaŋ.
farce, *n.* Ta′kuśni.
fare, *n.* 1. Icażużu: *what is the fare.* 2. Ouŋ; owote: *nice fare.* *vi.* Uŋ; wota.
farewell, *a.* & *interj.* Ehakeiapi: *farewell words.*
far-famed, *a.* Taŋ′kayaotaŋiŋ.
far-fetched, *a.* Te′hanahipi.
farm, *n.* Owożumakoce. *vt.* Wożu; wożuti; kicaŋyekiya.
farmer, *n.* Wożuwicaśta.
farrow, *a.* Ihduśakeśni.
farsighted, *a.* Te′han waŋyaka.
farther, *a.* Saŋ′patehan; ako.
farthest, *a.* Iyotaŋtehan.
farthing, *n.* Ma′zaśanaokise.
fascinate, *vt.* Hna′yaŋ; yuhnaśkiŋyaŋ.
fashion, *n.* To′ken oiyokipi da′pi; wi′taŋtaŋpi. *vt.* Ka′ġa.
fashionable, *a.* Wi′taŋtaŋ.
fast, *a.* 1. Du′zahaŋ; oȟaŋko: *a fast horse.* 2. Śke′he; witkotkoka: *a fast boy.* 2. Suta; yużużupi teȟike; *a fast friend; fast colors.* *adv.* 1. Dus; oȟaŋkoya: *walk fast.* 2. Sutaya; ni′na: *fast asleep.* *vi.* Akiȟaŋiçiya; woteśni uŋ. *n.* Akiȟaŋiçiyapi.
fasten, *vt.* Ikoyagya; nataka; sutaka′ġa.
fastening, *n.* Inatake.
fastidious, *a.* Waciŋhiŋyaŋza.
fasting, *n.* Woteśniuŋpi.
fastness, *n.* Wosuta; coŋ′kaśke.
fat, *a.* Ce′pa; żi′ca. *n.* Śiŋ.
fatal, *a.* Oŋ ṭe kta; oŋ ṭa′pi.
fate, *n.* Wokoŋze; owihaŋke.
father, *n.* Atkuku; ate. *My father,* ate.—*Your father,* niyate.—*His father,* atkuku. *vt.* Ta′waya; ateya.
fatherhood, *n.* Ateyapi.
father-in-law, *n.* Tuŋkaŋ; tuŋkaŋśi. *Your father-in law,* nituŋkaŋ.—*His father-in-law,* tuŋkaŋku.
fatherland, *n.* Makoce en wicatoŋpi.
fatherless, *a.* Atkuku wanica.
fatherly, *a.* Atkuku iyececa.
fathom, *n.* Akatiŋpi. *vt.* Śbe iyuta; sicu ode.
fatigue, *vt.* Watukaye; mdo′kiṭeya. *n.* Watukapi.
fatigued, *pa.* Watuka.
fatness, *n.* Waśiŋ; wocepa.
fatten, *n.* Cemya.
fatty, *a.* Ce′pa.
fault, *n.* Woyuśna; osnaze.
faultfinder, *n.* Wayaśkiśka.
faultless, *a.* Tuktena śi′ceśni.
faulty, *a.* Oŋśpaśpa śica.
favor, *vt.* 1. O′kiya; oŋ′śida: *he favors the younger.* 2. Owaŋg-

ya: *the boy favors his mother.* *n.* Waokiyapi; wowaoŋšida; woituĥaŋ; wowapi kiciçupi. *I beg one favor,* wowaoŋšida waŋži cicida.—*Your favor of Jan. 1st is received,* Jan. 1st wowapi yakaġa iwacu.
favorable, *a.* Iyecetu; iyokipi.
favorite, *a.* Teĥiŋda; wašteda.
favoritism, *n.* Sanina o'kiyapi.
fawn, *vt.* Kihnahna. *n.* Taciŋcadaŋ.
fear, *vt.* Kokipa; ikopa. *n.* Wakokipapi; ahokipapi.
fearful, *a.* 1. Wakokipa: *a fearful rabbit.* 2. Okokipe: *a fearful storm.*
fearless, *a.* Ta'kukokipešni.
feasable, *a.* Ecoŋpica.
feast, *n.* Kicicopi. *vt.* Won'kiya; wi'piya.
feat, *n.* Woecoŋ taŋ'ka.
feather, *n.* Maġahiŋ; šuŋ; wi'yaka. *vi.* Hiŋ uya.
feathered, *a.* Hiŋ yukaŋ.
feature, *n.* Itohnake.
February, *n.* Wicatawi.
federal, *a.* Odakonkiciyapi.
fed, *imp.* of FEED.
fee, *n.* Wokažužu; wi'ši. *vt.* Kažužu; wi'ši ķu.
feeble, *a.* Waš'akešni; šiĥtiŋ.
feebly, *adv.* Iwaštena.
feed, *vt.* Woķu; yunkiya. *vi.* Wota; wiĥaŋ. *n.* Woyute; owote.
feeding, *n.* Woķu; mahen iyeya; owiĥaŋ.
feel, felt, *vt.* Yutaŋ; icaĥtaka; sdonya. *vi.* 1. Hda: *I feel cold.* 2. Ececa: *feel better.* 3. Caŋtiyapa: *feel for the oppressed. Feel like,* caŋteyuza.—*Feel sure,* taŋyaŋ sdonya.—*How do you feel,* tonikeca he.
feeler, *n.* Oŋ yutaŋpi; putehiŋ.
feeling, *pa.* Waoŋšida; waciŋiyoyaka. *n.* Caŋteoyuze.
feet, *pl.* of FOOT.
feign, *vt.* Koŋ'za.
feint, *n.* Kons ecoŋpi.
felicitous, *a.* Oiyokipi.
felicitously, *adv.* Yupiya.
felicity, *n.* Woiyokipi.
fell, *imp.* of FALL.
fell, *vt.* Kawaŋka. *a.* Ociŋšica.
fellow, *n.* Tu'we; kicica.
fellowship, *n.* Kodayapi; kicicapi. *vt.* Kodaya.
felon, *n.* 1. Woopekicaksa. 2. Napsukaza hu ekta toŋye.
felt, *imp.* of FEEL.
felt, *n.* Hiŋ i'ciyaskapa.
female, *a.* & *n.* Wiŋ'yaŋ; (*of animals*) wi'ye.
feminine, *a.* Wiŋ'yaŋ.
fen, *n.* Wiwi.
fence, *n.* Coŋ'kaške. *vt.* Acaŋkaška; nataka.
fend, *vt.* Kakamiyeya.
ferment, *vi.* Taġeicaġa; napoġaŋ; sku'ya. *n.* Hnaškiŋyaŋpise.
fern, *n.* Hiŋhaŋtoŋwaŋ.
ferocious, *a.* Wohitika.
ferret, *vt.* Kihdeġa; oyuspa. *n.* Hituŋkasaŋ.
ferriage, *n.* Iyuweĥwicayapi.
ferry, *n.* Wa'taoiyuweġa. *vi.* Iyuweġa. *vt.* Iyuweĥkiya.
fertile, *a.* Waicaĥya; wi'yukcaŋ.
fertility, *n.* Waicaġe.
fertilize, *vt.* Waicaġe ka'ġa.
fervency, *n.* Wokata.
fervent, *a.* Ka'ta; wayuĥica.
fervor, *n.* Wokata.
festal, *a.* Wi'yuškiŋ.
fester, *vi.* Toŋye; kukaaya.
festival, *n.* & *a.* Wi'yuškiŋpi; ška'tapi.
festivity, *n.* Wowiyuškiŋ.
festoon, *n.* Kaozezeyapi.
fetch, *vt.* Au; iyokihi.
fetid, *a.* Šicamna.
fetlock, *n.* Iškahuhiŋ.
fetter, *vt.* Kaška. *n.* Wi'caške; wokaġi.
feud, *n.* Woakinica.

fever, *n.* Wokata; taŋcaŋkatapi woyazaŋ.
feverish, *a.* Ka'ta.
few, *a.* To'nana; *Y.* co'nana; *T.* co'nala.
fib, *a.* Woitoŋśni.
fickle, *a.* Hahadaŋ.
fiction, *n.* Wakaŋkaŋpi.
fictitious, *a.* Wicakeśni.
fiddle, *n.* Caŋpakiŋzapi.
fidelity, *n.* Wowicake.
fidgety, *a.* Owaŋżiuŋśni.
fie, *interj.* Hoḣ.
field, *n.* Ma'ga; wożupi; owożu; ośkiŋciye.
fiend, *n.* Wakaŋśica.
fierce, *a.* Wohitika.
fiery, *a.* Idese; ka'ta.
fife, *n.* Akicita tacotaŋka.
fifteen, *a.* Akezaptaŋ.
fifth, *a.* Izaptaŋ.
fifty, *a.* Wikcemnazaptaŋ.
fig, *n.* Waskuyecasuota.
fight, fought, *vt.* Ki'za; kiciza; kici ecoŋ. *n.* Okicize.
fighter, *n.* Kicisohitika.
figurative, *a.* Wi'yaciŋpi.
figure, *vt.* Yawa; owa. *vi.* Wayawa. *n.* Owapi; wayawapi; taŋcaŋ; wi'yaciŋpi.
figured, *pa.* Owapi; hde'ġa.
filch, *vt.* Manoŋ.
file, *n.* 1. Mazipabe. 2. I'cipatkuḣ e'nażiŋ. *vt.* Pamaŋ; kihnaka; makoce akan caże owa.
filial, *a.* Wicaciŋca.
fill, *vt.* Ożuya; ożutoŋ; wi'piya; ohnaehnaka.
fillet, *n.* Ipaḣte.
filly, *n.* Śuŋġwiyedaŋ.
film, *n.* Aoġi; ha.
filter, *vt.* Puskepa.
filth, *n.* Ta'kuśica.
filthy, *a.* Śa'pa; śi'ca.
fin, *n.* Hoġaŋape.
final, *a.* Ehake.
finally, *adv.* 1. Uŋ'haŋketa: *finally I succeeded.* 2. Ehake: *finally I say.*
finance, *n.* Ma'zaskaokicaŋye.
financial, *a.* Ma'zaskaoŋ.
find, found, *vt.* Iyeya; ehaŋi; ihni; sdonya.
finding, *n.* Iyeyapi; yasupi.
fine, *a.* 1. Waśte; wayupika; owaśtecaka; oiyokipi. 2. Ci'stiŋna; sbu'na; kpaŋ'na; zizipena. *vt.* Wayuśica każużukiyapi. *n.* Wokażużu.
finely, *adv.* Oiyokipiya.
fineness, *n.* Wowaśte.
finery, *n.* Oŋitaŋpi.
finger, *n.* Napsukaza; nape. *vt.* Yutaŋtaŋ.
finger-ring, *n.* Ma'zanapcupe; *Y.* napsioḣdi; *T.* napsioḣli.
finish, *vt.* Yuśtaŋ; ihuŋni.
finite, *a.* Ihaŋkeyukaŋ.
finny, *a.* Ho'apeyukaŋ.
fir, *n.* Waziśiŋota.
fire, *n.* 1. Pe'ta; oide: *make a fire.* 2. Ma'zakaŋ utapi. *vt.* 1. Ideya: *fire the hay.* 2. Ma'zakaŋ ecoŋ: *fire the cannon.*
firearm, *n.* Ma'zakaŋ.
firebrand, *n.* Petuspa.
firecracker, *n.* Napobyapi.
firefly, *n.* Waŋyeca.
fireman, *n.* Pe'takuwa.
fireplace, *n.* Ikceoceti.
fireproof, *a.* Ideyepicaśni.
fireside, *n.* Petkahda.
firesteel, *n.* Caŋka.
firewood, *n.* Caŋ'aoŋpi.
firm, *a.* Suta; ṭiŋ'za. *n.* Woecoŋ okodakiciye.
firmament, *n.* Okotoŋyaŋ.
firmly, *adv.* Sutaya.
firmness, *n.* Wosuta.
first, *a.* & *adv.* Tokaheya; *Y.* Tokeya; tokapa.
first-begotten, *a.* Tokaheya icaġa.
first-born, *a.* Tokapa.
first-class, *a.* Iyotaŋwaśte.
first-fruit, *n.* Tokaicaġe.

first-hand, *a.* Toka-yuha.
firstling, *a.* Tokaheyatoŋpi.
firstly, *adv.* Tokaheya.
first-rate, *a.* Ni'nawaŝte.
fish, *n.* Hoġaŋ. *vt.* Hokuwa; ho'psica; kuwa. *Fish out,* yusduta; yuze.
fish-bone, Hoġaŋ hu.
fisher, *n.* Ŝkeca; hokuwa.
fisherman, *n.* Hokuwa wicaŝa.
fishery, *n.* Hokuwapi.
fish-hawk, *n.* Żożoka.
fish-hook, *n.* Cakiyuȟuġe; hoiyupsice.
fish-net, *n.* Ho; ho wi'yuze.
fishscales, *n.* Hoceŝpu.
fishy, *a.* Hoġaŋse; hmuŋ'za.
fissure, *n.* Oko; onasdeca.
fist, *n.* Napeyupŝuŋka.
fit, *a.* Iyececa; iyecetu; he'cetu. *vi.* Kipi; iyecetu: *the dress fits well.* *vt.* Kipi ka'ġa; ecetuya; iyokipiya. *n.* Hnaŝkiŋyaŋpi; kiksuyeŝni; inaȟni ni'na ececapi.
fitful, *a.* Hahayedaŋ ŝkaŋpi.
fitly, *adv.* Taŋyaŋ.
fitness, *n.* Woiyecetu.
fitting, *n.* Kipikaġa.
five, *a.* Za'ptaŋ.
fix, *vt.* 1. Piya: *fix the broken wheel.* 2. Taŋyaŋ e'hnaka: *fix the room up.* 3. E'hde; suta ka'ġa: *fix your eyes on me.* *n.* To'ketu taŋiŋ ŝni: *I'm in a fix.*
fixed, *pa.* Piyapi; sutayahaŋ.
fixings, *n.* Oŋ'piyapi.
fixture, *n.* Ta'ku ikoyaghdepi.
fizz, *vi.* Sdi.
fizzle, *vi.* Ecacaokihi ŝni.
flabby, *a.* Deȟdeġa.
flag, *n.* 1. Wi'yokihedaŋ; *Y.* & *T.* wowapi. 2. Peżiapemdaska. *vt.* Miniȟuhakoza: *flag the train.* *vi.* Huŋ'keŝni aya.
flagon, *n.* Wiyokaŝtaŋ.
flagstone, *n.* In'yaŋmdaska.
flagrant, *a.* Taŋiŋ; ni'na ŝi'ca.

flail, *vt.* Apa. *n.* Wi'bopaŋ.
flake, *n.* Wokpaŋ; waokpe.
flame, *n.* Oide; ideŝaŝa; wocaŋtaȟde.
flaming, *pa.* Ide; wohitika.
Flandreau, *n.* Wakpaipakŝaŋ.
flange, *n.* Tete.
flank, *n.* Niġute; cecuŝte; *T.* Lagute. *vt.* Aohomniya.
flannel, *n.* Powayedaŋ.
flap, *vt.* Apa; ȟupahu oŋ apa. *vi.* Ko'za. *n.* Ape.
flare, *vi.* Iyeġa.
flaring, *pa.* Wiyakpa; itaŋka.
flash, *vt.* Yuwiyakpa; kohaŋyeya. *vi.* Wiyakpa hiŋhda; dus'hiyaya. *n.* Ŝa'hiŋhda.
flashy, *a.* Kpa'kpa; iȟapise.
flask, *n.* Żaŋżaŋmdaska; caȟdiożuha.
flat, *a.* 1. Mdaska: *a flat stone.* 2. Mdaya: *a flat country.* 3. Ihukuya: *a flat note.* *vt.* Yuhukuya; yumdaya. *n.* Makomdaya; ta'ku mdaska; ti'pi owaŋka. *adv.* Mdaskaya.
Flathead, *n.* Natamdeca.
flatiron, *n.* Wi'pamdaye.
flatly, *adv.* A'wicakeya.
flatten, *vt.* Yumdaska.
flatter, *vt.* Ecayawaŝte.
flatterer, *n.* Iskuya.
flaunt, *vt.* Ko'za; ihda⁺aŋ.
flavor, *n.* Ecamna; utapi. *vt.* Waŝtemnaya; sku'yeya.
flaw, *n.* Oŋŝpa ŝi'ca; osnaze.
flax, *n.* Haȟoŋtahu.
flaxen, *a.* Zizi.
flaxseed, *n.* Haȟoŋtahusu.
flea, *n.* Ha; *T.* hala.
fled, *imp.* of FLEE.
fledged, *a.* Kihipi.
fledgling, *a.* Żiżi.
flee, fled, *vi.* Nażica.
fleece, *n.* Ta'ȟcaska hiŋ; hiŋ; hiŋ okaŝda waŋzi. *vt.* Ki.
fleet, *a.* Du'zahaŋ. *n.* Wi'tawata optaye.

fleeting, *pa.* Oĥaŋkohiyaya.
flesh, *n.* Conica; ceĥpi; tado.
fleshly, *a.* Wicaceĥpi.
fleshy, *a.* Ceĥpitaŋka; ce'pa.
flew, *imp.* of FLY.
flexible, *a.* Świŋświŋżedaŋ.
flicker, *vi.* Taŋiŋiŋ.
flier, *n.* Ta'kukiŋyaŋ.
flies, *n. pl.* of FLY, honaġidaŋ.
flies, *vi. 3d p. sing.* of FLY.
flight, *n.* Wonażice; kiŋyaŋpi.
flighty, *a.* Śke'he.
flimsy, *a.* Zigzica; ta'kuśni.
flinch, *vi.* Napa.
flinder, *n.* Wokpe.
fling, flung, *vt.* Kaĥoiyeya. *n.* Okaĥoiyeyapi.
flint, *n.* Waŋhi.
flinty, *a.* Waŋhise; ni'nasuta.
flippant, *a.* Awaciŋśni; śke'he.
flirt, *vt.* Kaĥoiyeya; kiśkata. *n.* Wiŋ'yaŋ śkatesa.
flit, *vi.* Dus hiyaye; kiŋyaŋ.
float, *vi.* O'kapota; o'kaĥboka. *vt.* O'kaponya; iyayeya.
flock, *n.* Optaye; obe. *vi.* Wi'taya hiyu; mni'ciya.
flog, *vt.* Kapsiŋpsiŋta; apa.
flogging, *n.* Kapsiŋpsiŋtapi.
flood, *n.* Minitaŋ; o'ta. *vt.* Amnitaŋ.
floor, *n.* Owaŋka; caŋmdaska owiŋża. *vt.* Owiŋżakaġa; kun eĥpeya.
flooring, *n.* Owiŋża caŋmdaska.
flop, *vt.* Kaskapa; ko'za.
florid, *a.* Śa; śaśa.
florist, *n.* Waĥcakicaŋye.
flossy, *a.* Paŋpaŋna.
flounder, *vi.* Kaĥoĥo iyeiçiya.
flour, *n.* Aġuyapi; ta'ku mdu.
flour-mill, *n.* Wokpaŋtipi.
flourish, *vi.* Taŋyaŋ icaġa; taŋyaŋ waŋka: *crops flourish.* 2. Kaĥoĥośkaŋ: *he flourished around.* *vt.* Ko'za: *he flourished his whip.* *n.* Koskosya owapi; ko'zapi.

flow, *vt.* Kaduza; uya; bomdu. *n.* Hiyupi.
flower, *n.* 1. Waĥca: *red flowers.* 2. Tona iyotaŋ waśte: *the flower of the army.* *vi.* Ḣca.
flowing, *pa.* Kaduza.
flown, *pp.* of FLY.
fluctuate, *vi.* Aketokeca; haĥadaŋ.
flue, *n.* Śo'taoĥdoka.
Floyd River, *n.* Coĥwaŋżica Wakpa.
fluent, *a.* Hdaheyaia; kaduza.
fluid, *a.* Ta'kukaduza; mini.
flung, *imp.* of FLING.
flurry, *vt.* Waciŋhnuniya. *n.* Ibobdu; to'ketu taŋiŋ śni.
flush, *vi.* Itenaśa; mini ożudaŋ. *a.* Ożudaŋ; o'citkoŋza.
flustrate, *vt.* Kiksuyeśniya.
flute, *n.* Co'yataŋka.
flutter, *vi.* Ko'za; śkaŋśkaŋ.
flux, *n.* Każopi; we'iheyapi.
fly, flew, flown, *vt.* 1. Kiŋyaŋ: *birds fly.* 2. Kiŋyaŋ se iyaye: *she flew to his aid.* *vt.* Kiŋyaŋkiya. *n.* Honaġidaŋ; kiŋyaŋpina. *The flag flies,* wi'yokihedaŋ kaĥboka.—*To fly into fragments,* kpaŋyeṇa napopa. —*Let fly,* kaĥoiyeya.
flyaway, *a.* Śke'he.
flyblow, *n.* Honaġidaŋitka.
flying, *pa.* Dus'yapi; ko'za.
flypaper, *n.* Honaġidaŋikmuŋke.
flyspecks, *n.* Honaġidaŋcesdi.
flying-squirrel, *n.* Pśiŋca.
flying-visit, *n.* Inaĥnititokaŋipi.
foal, *n.* Śuŋkciŋcana.
foam, *n.* Taġe.
focus, *n.* Okiwita.
fodder, *n.* Wanuyaŋpiwoyute.
foe, *n.* To'ka.
fog, *n.* Minipo; opo.
foggy, *a.* Opo; po.
fogy, *n.* Ehaŋnawicaśa.
foible, *n.* Woyuśna.
foil, *vt.* Okihiśniya; hna'yaŋ. *n* Omdaskazizipena.
foist, *vt.* En'iyeya.

fold, *vt.* Pehaŋ; yukipaža. *n.* 1. Opehe; oyukšiža. 2. Optaye.
folder, *n.* Wi'yukšiže.
foliage, *n.* Caŋwapa.
folk, *n.* Wicašta; tin'takuye.
follow, *vt.* 1. Ihakam ya; ihakam u; iyayuȟa. 2. Iyecenecoŋ; okipa: *follow instructions.* 3. Pasi; kuwa: *follow the deer.*
follower, *n.* Ookiye; hakamuŋ.
folly, *n.* Wowitkotkoka.
foment, *vt.* Yukata; icaȟya.
fond, *a.* 1. (with *of*) Waštedaka; teȟiŋda: *fond of playing.* 2. Waihakta; wacantkiya: *a fond mother.*
fondle, *vt.* Kihna; kicaŋpta.
fondly, *adv.* Ihaktaya.
fondness, *n.* Woihakta.
font, *n.* Miniohnakapi; miniȟdoka; mazaoowa.
food, *n.* Woyute; do.
fool, *n.* Witkotkoka; waciŋtoŋšni. *vt.* Hna'yaŋ. *vi.* Ecaecoŋ. *Fool with,* kici ška'ta.
foolhardy, *a.* Waciŋtoŋšni waditaka.
fooling, *pa.* Ṡka'ta.
foolish, *a.* Waciŋtoŋšni.
foolishness, *n.* Wowitkotkoka.
foot, feet, *n.* 1. Siha; si: *a sore foot.* 2. Sihaiyutapi: *two feet long.* 3. Kun'ihaŋke; ihukuya: *at the foot of his class.* *vi.* Makaamaniya; huiŋyuŋya. *vt.* 1. Yawa; yuwitaya: *foot up the column of figures.* 2. Kažužu: *foot the bill.*
football, *n.* Sitapa.
foothold, *n.* Oiyahe.
footing, *n.* Sihahdepi.
footprint, *n.* Owe.
footrace, *n.* Kiŋiŋyaŋkapi.
footsore, *a.* Sihayazaŋ.
footstep, *n.* Cahdepi.
footstool, *n.* Sihaahdehe.
fop, *n.* Heyakeitaŋ.
foppish, *a.* Wi'taŋtaŋ.
for, *prep.* 1. Oŋ; oŋ'etaŋhaŋ: *do it for me.* 2. Eciyataŋhaŋ: *I am for peace.* 3. Ee; he'ca: *I took you for a gentleman.* 4. Ta'wa: *this book is for you.* *As for me,* miye eḳe.—*For all he can do,* ċeyaš; he'cašta.—*For a year,* hehaŋyaŋ.—*For all the world,* a'taya.—*Go for,* oŋ ya; huweya; hiyoya; takpe ya.—*Were it not for,* e'e šni kiŋhaŋ.—*We took train for,* ekta uŋyaŋpi kta oŋ ȟemani o'uŋpapi. *conj.* Nakaeš; oŋ etaŋhaŋ; caŋkedaka: *I did not go, for it was cold.*
forage, *n.* Wanuyaŋpi woyute. *vi.* Woyute ihni.
forasmuch, *conj.* Nakaeš.
foray, *n.* Wamanoŋ ozuye.
forbad, *imp.* of FORBID.
forbear, *vt.* Pataka; ecoŋšni.
forbearance, *n.* Waciŋtaŋkapi.
forbid, *vt.* Teȟiŋda; iyokišni.
forbidden, *pa.* Teȟiŋdapi.
force, *vt.* I'yopaštaka; kitaŋyaŋ ecoŋkiya. *n.* 1. Wowaš'ake: *the force of law.* 2. Ozuye; optaye; obe: *the American forces,*
forceful, *a.* Waš'aka.
forcible, *a.* Waš'aka.
ford, *vt.* Copa; iyuweġa. *n.* Oiyuweġa.
fore-, *pref.* I'tokam.
fore, *a.* Watokahaŋ; otokahe.
forebode, *vt.* I'tokam oyaka.
forecast, *vt.* I'tokam iyukcaŋ.
forecastle, *n.* Watokapa.
foreclose, *vt.* Nakitaka.
forefather, *n.* Huŋkake.
forefoot, *n.* Si'toka.
forefront, *n.* Otokahe.
forego, *vt.* Kpaġaŋ.
foregoing, *pa.* I'tokamwaŋka.
foregone, *pa.* I'tokam yuštaŋpi.
forehanded, *a.* Kohaŋ yuštaŋ.
forehead, *n.* Ite; nasu.

foreign, *a.* Oyatetokeca; to'keca.
foreknow, *vt.* I'tokam sdonya.
forelock, *n.* Itehiŋ.
foreman, *n.* Tokahekiyapi.
foremost, *a.* Tokahaŋ.
forenoon, *n.* Wi'cokayaśni.
foreordain, *vt.* I'tokam yuśtaŋ.
forerunner, *n.* I'tokam ya.
foresee, *vt.* I'tokam sdonya.
forest, *n.* Coŋ'taŋka.
forestall, *vt.* I'tokam kaġiya.
foretaste, *n.* I'tokam utapi.
foretell, *vt.* I'tokam oyaka.
forethought, *n.* Iwaktapi.
forever, *adv.* Owihaŋkewanica.
forewarn, *vt.* Iwaktaya.
forfeit, *vt.* Yuśna.
forgat, *imp.* of FORGET.
forgave, *imp.* of FORGIVE.
forge, *vt.* Ka'ġa. *n.* Ma'zakaġa oceti.
forgery, *n.* Wowapi wohnaye ka'ġa.
forget, *vt.* Akiktoŋża.
forgetful, *a.* Waciŋktoŋża.
forgive, *vt.* Ki'cicażużu.
forgiveness, *n.* Wokażużu.
forgot, *imp.* of FORGET.
fork, *n.* 1. Wi'cape: *knives and forks.* 2. Ożate: *the fork of a tree.*
forked, *a.* Ża'te; ġa'ta.
forlorn, *a.* Oŋ'śika; oiyokiśica.
form, *n.* Oka'ġe; taŋcaŋ; ouŋ; oecoŋ. *Forms of worship,* wocekiye oecoŋ. *vt.* Ka'ġa.
formal, *a.* Woope ohnaḣca ecoŋpi.
formation, *n.* Okaġe.
former, *a.* Tokaheya; i'tokam. *n.* Tu'we ka'ġa.
formerly, *adv.* Ehaŋna.
formidable, *a.* Wowinihaŋ.
formula, *n.* Woeye.
formulate, *vt.* Woeye ka'ġa.
fornication, *n.* Wawiciḣaḣapi.
forsake, *vt.* Ayuśtaŋ; eḣpeya.
forsooth, *adv.* Ieśni.
fort, *n.* Akicitatipi; coŋ'kaśke.
Fort Berthold, *n.* Ḣewaktoktotipi.
Fort Buford, *n.* Miniśośeożate.
Fort Laramie, *n.* Kampeskawakpa Okiżate.
Fort Pierre, *n.* Wakpaśica.
Fort Snelling, *n.* Ḣaḣamdote.
Fort Sully, *n.* Huḣbożu.
Fort Totten, *n.* Miniwakaŋ.
Fort Yates, *n.* Iŋ'yaŋbosdata.
forte, *n.* Ta'ku okihi.
forth, *adv.* Tokata; taŋkan.
forthcoming, *a.* Hi kta.
forthwith, *adv.* Waŋ'cahnana.
fortification, *n.* Makaokapi.
fortify, *vt.* Ohomnikapi.
fortitude, *n.* Wowaditake.
fortnight, *n.* Aŋpetuaketopa.
fortress, *n.* Akicitacoŋkaśke.
fortuitous, *a.* Wanuwakipapi.
fortunate, *a.* Wa'pi; okiciwaśte.
fortune, *n.* Wowiżice; woakipa.
forty, *a.* Wikcemnatopa.
forward, *a.* 1. Otokahe: *the forward seat.* 2. Oḣaŋko: *a forward spring.* 3. Tokata: *a forward jump. vt.* 1. Iyopteya: *forward the work.* 2. Iyayeya: *forward my letters. adv.* Tokata: *go forward.*
fossil, *n.* Iŋ'yaŋhuhu.
foster, *vt.* Icaḣya.
foster-parent, *n.* Huŋkakeśni icaḣya.
fought, *imp.* of FIGHT.
foul, *a.* 1. Śa'pa; śi'ca. 2. Woope ohna śni; *foul play. vt.* Yuśica; yuśośa.
found, *imp.* of FIND.
found, *vt.* E'hde; otokahe ka'ġa.
foundation, *n.* Oahehde.
founder, *n.* Tu'weka'ġa. *vi.* Spa'ya; mininiyaya. *vt.* Spa'yeya.
foundry, *n.* Ma'zaśdoyatipi.
fount, fountain, *n.* Miniuya; miniḣdoka; minibobduyapi.
four, *a.* To'pa. *By fours,* tom'tom.
fourfold, *n.* To'paakihde.

fourscore, *a.* Wikcemnaśahdoġaŋ.
fourteen, *a.* Aketopa.
fourth, *a.* Itopa; to'payuśpapi.
fourthly, *adv.* Itopa.
fowl, *n.* Kokoyaḣaŋna; waḣupakoza.
fowler, *n.* Waḣupakoza kutesa.
fox, foxes, *n.* Śuŋġidaŋ.
Fox, *n.* Beśdeke.
foxy, *a.* Ksa'pa.
fraction, *n.* Oŋśpa; kibaśpapi.
fractious, *a.* Śke'he; wanaḣoŋśni.
fracture, *vt.* Yuweġa. *n.* Yuweġapi; yuksapi.
fragile, *a.* Waŋ'kadaŋ.
fragment, *n.* Oŋśpa; otutka.
fragrance, *n.* Woomna.
fragrant, *a.* Waśtemna.
frail, *a.* Sutaśni; hahadaŋ.
frame, *vt.* Ka'ġa; ti'pihuḣaka'ġa. *n.* Huḣa; waciŋoyuze.
framer, *n.* Tu'weka'ġa.
franchise, *n.* Kaŋsuiyoḣpeyapi.
frank, *a.* Anaḣbeśni. *n.* Cażekaġa.
frankly, *adv.* Anaḣbeśni.
frantic, *a.* Mde'ześni.
fraternal, *a.* Huŋkawaŋżitku.
fraternity, *n.* Huŋkawaŋżikiciyapi.
fraud, *n.* Wohnaye.
fraudulent, *a.* Wicakeśni; wohnaye.
fraught, *pa.* Ożudaŋ.
freak, *n.* Wośkateoḣanye.
freckle, *n.* Ukahdeze.
free, *a.* 1. Ta'waiçiya; ihduha; kaśkapiśni: *a free man. Set free,* kiyuśka. 2. Oḣaŋpi; kpataŋśni: *he is too free with his money: free and easy.* 3. Co'daŋ: *free from pain.* 4. Kaġiśni: *free to talk.* 5. Każużuśni: *a free dinner. Make free with,* to'ken ciŋ ecoŋ. *vt.* Yuśka; kiyuśka.
freedman, *n.* Kiyuśkapi.
freedom, *n.* Ta'waiçiyapi.
freely, *adv.* Iyuwiŋcodaŋ.
free trade, *n.* Każużuśni wopetoŋpi.
freewill, *a.* Iye tawaciŋ ohna.
freeze, *vt.* Tasagya. *vi.* Tasaka; ca'ġa. *Freeze to death,* cuwita ṭa.
freezing, *pa.* Ca'ġa.
freight, *vt.* Tokśu; watokśu.
French, *a.* Waśicuŋikceka.
frenzy, *n.* Wohnaśkiŋyaŋ.
frequency, *n.* I'cikiyedaŋ.
fre'quent, *a.* I'cikiyedaŋ.
frequent', *a.* En i'pi s'a.
frequently, *adv.* Iciżehaŋ; -s'a.
fresh, *a.* 1. Te'ca; nakaha icaġe: *fresh flowers.* 2. Nakaha kte'pi; do: *fresh meat.* 3. Watukaśni: *a fresh horse.* 4. Sku'ye śni: *fresh fish.* 5. Oŋspekeśni: *a fresh country lad.*
freshen, *vt.* Yuteca.
freshet, *n.* Minitaŋ.
freshly, *adv.* Piya; tecanien.
fret, *vt.* Iyokipiśni; ce'yektakta.
fretful, *a.* Ce'yes'a.
friction, *n.* I'cipayezapi; kicipażiŋpi.
Friday, *n.* Aŋpetu Izaptaŋ.
friend, *n.* Koda; kicuwa; ta'waśi; waśtedaka. *His friend,* takodaku.
friendless, *a.* Takodaku wanica.
friendly, *a.* Kodayapi iyececa.
friendship, *n.* Kodakiciyapi.
frigate, *n.* Ozuye wi'tawata.
fright, *n.* Woyuśiŋyaye.
frightful, *a.* Okokipe.
frigid, *a.* Sni; osni.
frill, *n.* Opapuŋ yukipaś ka'ġapi.
fringe, *n.* Opapuŋ ḣ'eḣ'e.
frisk, *vi.* Psi'psin śkaŋ.
frisky, *a.* Śka'tewaciŋ.
fritter, *vt.* Yutakuniśni. *n.* Aġuyapiġuġuna.
frivolous, *a.* Ta'kuśni.
frizzle, *vt.* Yumnimniża.
fro, *adv.* Etaŋhaŋ. *To and fro,* i'cipaś.

frock, *n.* Nitoṡke.
frog, *n.* Hna′ṡka. *Tree frog,* hna′ṡkacandidaŋ.
frolic, *n.* Ṡka′tapi; woṡkate. *vi.* ṡka′ta.
frolicsome, *a.* Ṡka′tes′a.
from, *prep.* Etaŋhaŋ. *From whence,* totaŋhaŋ.—*Where from,* to′kiyataŋhaŋ.
front, *n.* Ite: *the front of the store. In front of,* i′tokam; ikaŋye. *vi.* Itoheyahaŋ. *a.* O′tokahe.
frontier, *a.* O′tokahe; opapuŋ.
frontiersman, *n.* Tokaaḣiyotaŋke.
frost, *n.* Ḣewaŋka; wotasaka.
frosty, *n.* Caŋḣotka; sni′sni.
froth, *n.* Taġe; ta′kuṡni.
frothy, *a.* Taġeyukaŋ.
frow, *n.* Winoḣca.
froward, *a.* Pemni.
frown, *vi.* Iteakṡiŋkiya.
froze, *imp.* of FREEZE.
frozen, *pa.* Tasaka; ca′ġa.
frugal, *a.* Wakpataŋ.
frugality, *n.* Wakpataŋpi.
fruit, *n.* 1. Waskuyeca: *peaches and other fruits.* 2. Ta′ku icaġe; *the fruits of the earth.* 3. Wokażużu: *the fruit of evil deeds.*
fruitful, *a.* Waicaġa.
fruitless, *a.* Waicaġeṡni; wakamnaṡni.
frustrate, *vt.* Okihiṡniya.
fry, fried, *vt.* Ceġuġuya. *n.* Ceġuġuyapi; optaye.
frying-pan, *n.* Ceḣhupatoŋna.
fuddled, *pa.* Itomni.
fudge, *interj.* Hoḣ.
fuel, *n.* Ta′kuaoŋpi; caŋ.
fugitive, *n.* Nażicauŋ.
ful, *suffix.* Ożudaŋ: *a cupful.*
fulfill, *vt.* Ecetukiya; yuṡtaŋ.
full, *a.* 1. Ożudaŋ: *a full house.* 2. A′taya: *full pay.* 3. Tan′ka: *a full face. adv.* I′tkoŋsya; iyehaŋyaŋ.
fullness, *n.* Woożudaŋ.
fully, *adv.* A′taya; iyehaŋyaŋ.
fumble, *vt.* Yutaŋtaŋ; yuṡna.
fume, *vi.* Ṡo′ta; izita; caŋze.
fumigate, *vt.* Izinya.
fun, *n.* Woṡkate; wowiḣa. *Make fun of,* wowiḣa kuwa.
function, *n.* Wookihi; woecoŋ.
fund, *n.* Ma′zaskahnakapi; womnaye.
fundamental, *a.* O′hute.
funeral, *n.* Wicaḣnakapi.
funnel, *n.* Iokaṡtaŋ pesto.
funny, funnier, *a.* Wowiḣa.
fur, *n.* Hiŋ; wawaha.
furious, *a.* Wohitika.
furiously, *adv.* Wohitiya.
furl, *vt.* Yupehaŋ.
furlong, *n.* Cahdepi opawiŋġe noŋ′pa.
furlough, *n.* Akicita inaḣni hdi.
furnace, *n.* Oceti ka′ta.
furnish, *vt.* Ḳu; ikicaŋye ihni.
furnished, *pa.* Ikicaŋye yukeya.
furniture, *n.* Ti′pi ikicaŋye.
furor, *n.* Wicayumdezapiṡni.
furrow, *n.* Yuġopi.
further, *a.* 1. Saŋpa te′haŋ: *it is further than that.* 2. Nakuŋ: *what further.* 3. Ako; akotaŋhaŋ: *the further side. vt.* Iyopteya; o′kiya.
furthermore, *adv.* Nakuŋ.
furthermost, *a.* Akoihaŋke.
furthest, *a.* Iyotaŋ te′han.
fury, *n.* Woohitika.
fuse, *vt.* Ṡdoya; iciyaskapa. *n.* On itkoŋyapi.
fusion, *n.* Yuokoŋwaŋżidaŋ.
fuss, *vi.* Ta′kuṡni okoya.
fussy, *a.* Ta′kuṡni iyokipiṡni.
futile, *a.* Iyokihiṡni.
future, *n.* Tokata.
fuzz, *n.* Hiŋkpaŋna.

G

gab, *n*. Ta′kuśniia ; iayaŋka.
gabble, *vi*. Ta′kuśni oŋ ni′ŋa iaa.
gable, *n*. Tice.
gad, *vi*. Ituya omani un. *n*. Caŋicape.
gag, *vt*. I yuhmuŋza ; katka.
gage, *vt*. Iyuta.
gaiety, *n*. Wi′yuśkiŋpi.
gaily, *adv*. Wi′yuśkiŋyaŋ.
gain, *vt*. 1. Kamna : *gain a dollar*. 2. Ohiya ; okihi : *gain the suit*. 3. Kihdeġa; iyohi : *gain ground*. *n*. Wokamna ; ma′zaska ; aicaġe ; obaġo.
gainsay, *vt*. I en hiyeya.
gait, *n*. Omani.
gaiter, *n*. Caŋ′haŋpaiśkahutoŋ.
gale, *n*. Tateyaŋpa waś′aka.
gall, *n*. Pizi. *vt*. Ha′yuśdoka.
gallant′, *vt*. Awaŋyag a′ya.
gal′lant, *n*. Tu′we awaŋyag ya ; tu′we waditaka. *a*. Wawiyokipi.
gallantly, *adv*. Iyokipiya.
gallantry, *n*. Wowaditake.
gallery, *n*. Tihepiya owaŋka ; iteowapi ti′pi.
galley, *n*. 1. Wi′tawata mdaska ; ma′zaehdepi wohnake.
galling, *pa*. Teḣika ; ha′yuśdoka.
gallon, *n*. Ceġaŋstiŋna oiyute.
gallop, *vi*. Nawaŋka ; iŋ′yaŋka.
galloway, *n*. Ptesapahiŋśma.
gallows, *n*. Ahna wotkeyapi.
galvanism, *n*. Wakaŋhdi hde′pi.
gamble, *vt*. Wayekiya ; ecoŋna.
gambler, *n*. Ecoŋnas′a.
gambol, *vi*. Śka′ta ; psi′psinuŋ.
game, *n*. 1. Wośkate ; ecoŋpina : *a game of ball*. 2. Wamakaśkaŋ ; ta′ku ikce uŋ. *a*. Waditake.
gander, *n*. Maġa mdoka.
gang, *n*. Obe ; optaye.
gangway, *n*. Caŋkuyapi.
gantlet, *n*. Oiŋyaŋgkuwapi.
gap, *vt*. Kaḣci. *n*. Ḣci ; oko.
gape, *vi*. Iyowa ; yukawa ; *T*. iyoya. *n*. Yukawapi.
garb, *n*. Heyake ; oihduze.
garbage, *n*. Ta′kueḣpeyapi.
garble, *vt*. Oŋśpaśpa eḣpeya.
garden, *n*. Maḣcistiŋna.
gardener, *n*. Wakicaŋye.
garfish, *n*. Ho′waŋmduśka.
gargle, *vt*. Dote hdużaża.
garland, *n*. Caŋwapaokaśke.
garlic, *n*. Pśiŋ ikceka.
garment, *n*. Heyake ; o′kde.
garner, *vt*. Ohnaka. *n*. Wohnaka ; womnaye.
garnish, *vt*. Yuwaśte ; koyagya.
garret, *n*. Tice.
garrison, *n*. Akicitatipi.
garter, *n*. Huŋskicaḣe.
gas, *n*. Tateide ; tateśica.
gash, *vt*. Bahoŋ. *n*. Obahoŋ.
gasoline, *n*. Wi′hdi oŋ acetipi.
gasp, *vi*. Ki′taŋḣ niya.
gate, *n*. Coŋ′kaśketiyopa.
gateway, *n*. Tiyopa oko.
gather, *vt*. Pahi ; mnayaŋ : *gather sticks; gather fruit*. 2. Iyukcaŋ : *I gather from his remarks*. 3. Kaġe icu : *gather the skirt*. 4. Yuksa : *gather corn*. *vi*. 1. Wi′taya ; *a crowd gathered*. 2. Toŋye : *the sore gathered*.
gathering, *n*. O′yuwitaya ; omniciye ; po ; toŋye.
gaudy, *a*. Śayapiḣca.
gauge, *vt*. Iyuta.
gaunt, *a*. Sta′ka ; tamaheca.
gauze, *n*. Capoŋgokeya.
gave, *imp*. of GIVE.
gavel, *n*. Itaŋcaŋ tacaŋḣpi.
gawky, *a*. Oḣaŋoŋspekeśni.
gay, *a*. Wi′haha ; wi′yuśkiŋ.

gaze, *vi.* Opaĥtakuwa.
gazelle, *n.* Tatokadaŋ.
gazette, *n.* Wotaŋiŋwowapi.
gear, *n.* Ikaŋ; wi'yuhomni. *vt.* Ikoyagya.
gee, *vi.* Akoyuhomni.
geese, *pl.* of GOOSE.
gelatine, *n.* Tadonini.
gelding, *n.* Susuwanica.
gem, *n.* Iŋ'yaŋteĥika; ta'ku ni'na waŝte.
gender, *n.* Wica ķaiŝ wiŋ'yaŋ.
genealogy, *n.* Wicoicaġe oyakapi.
general, *n.* Akicitataŋcaŋ taŋ'ka. *a.* 1. A'taya; ecaken: *the general welfare.* 2. A'taya yuhapi; ece: *a general custom.*
generally, *adv.* Ecee; a'taya.
generate, *vt.* Ka'ġa.
generation, *n.* Wicoicaġe; ka'gapi; ciŋcakaġapi.
genesis, *n.* Wicoicage oyakapi.
genial, *a.* Okiciwaŝte.
genius, *n.* Wowayupika; wakaĥdoka.
gens, *n.* Tioŝpaye.
genteel, *a.* Oiyokipi.
gentility, *n.* Wowaĥbadaŋ.
gentle, *a.* Wa'ĥbadan; ci'stiŋna.
gentleman, *n.* Wicaŝtawaĥba.
gentleness, *n.* Wowaĥbadaŋ.
gently, *adv.* Iwaŝtedaŋ.
gentry, *n.* Wicaŝta okinihaŋ.
genuine, *a.* Wicaka.
genus, *n.* Obe.
geography, *n.* Makaoyakapi.
geology, *n.* Makamahentuoyaka.
germ, *n.* Su; caŋte.
German, *n.* Iaŝica.
germinate, *vi.* Natuuya.
gesticulate, *vi.* Wi'kiyuta.
gesture, *n.* Wi'kiyutapi. *vi.* Wi'kiyuta.
get, got, *vt.* 1. Icu; huweya; okini: *get some water.* 2. Yuha: *she has got brown hair.* 3. Kuwa; oŋspeiçiçiya: *get your lesson.* 4. Iyaya: *get out.* 5. Kiya; ecoŋkiya: *get him to work.* 6. I'yopaŝtaka; to'ketu çeyaŝ: *you have got to go. Get ahead,* iyopte.—*Get along,* iyopte.—*Get at,* iyohi.—*Get away,* tokaŋya.—*Get away with,* yusota; yuha iyaya.—*Get back,* hdi; ĥeyam inaẑiŋ.—*Get before,* i'tokam iyaye.—*Get behind,* he'kta iyaya.—*Get clear,* ihduŝdoka.—*Get drunk,* witko.—*Get forward,* iyopta.—*Get home,* tiyata ki.—*Get hurt,* ksu'weya.—*Get in,* mahen iyaya.—*Get loose,* yuŝka.—*Get off,* ipsica; kinaẑiŋ.—*Get on,* iyopte.—*Get rid off,* kiihduŝpa.—*Get out,* taŋkan iyaye.—*Get over,* sam ya; akisni.—*Get sick,* wayazaŋka.—*Get together,* wi'tayapi—*Get up,* inaẑiŋ; iyaya.—*Get wind of,* nakiĥon.
gewgaw, *n.* Ta'kuŝni.
geyser, *n.* Makoĥdoka minibosdi.
gastly, *a.* Woyuŝiŋyaye.
ghost, *n.* Wanaġi.
ghostly, *adv.* Wanaġise.
giant, *n.* Wicaŝta taŋka.
gibe, *vt.* Yaŝica.
giddy, *a.* Itomni.
gift, *n.* Ta'ku ituĥaŋpi; wicaķu; wowaoŋŝida.
gifted, *pa.* Ksa'pa; ẑinyapi.
gig, *n.* Caŋpakmiyaŋhunoŋpa.
gigantic, *a.* Taŋ'kaĥca.
giggle, *vi.* Pamahen iĥaĥa.
gild, *vt.* Ma'zaskazi apawiŋta. *n.* Okodakiciye.
gill, *n.* 1. Caka. 2. Wi'yatke ci'stiŋna oiyute.
gilt, *a.* Ma'zaskazi apawiŋtapi.
gimlet, *n.* Caŋiyumni ci'stiŋna.
gin, *n.* Miniwakaŋ waŝtemna.
ginger, *n.* Aġuyapiicahi ġi.
gingerly, *adv.* Itoŋpeya.
gingham, *n.* Miniĥuhahdeze.
gird, girt, *vt.* Ipiyagkitoŋ.
girder, *n.* Caŋiciyakaŝka.

girdle, *n.* Ipiyake.
girl, *n.* Wiciŋyaŋna. *Y.* Wiciŋcana. *T.* Wiciŋcala.
girlish, *a.* Wiciŋyaŋnase.
girth, *n.* Ipiyake.
gist, *n.* Co.
give, gave, *vt.* Ḳu; itukiḣan; eciya; okiyake; yutaŋiŋ. *Give away,* ituḣaŋ. —*Give back,* ki'çu.—*Give chase,* kuwaeyaya.—*Give in,* enakiye.—*Give out,* pamni; oyaka; okihiśni; ma'niśni.—*Give up,* i'yakiçuŋni; ḳu.—*Give way to,* kiyukaŋ. *vi.* Sutaśni; iyaya.
gizzard, *n.* Tezi; zitkātezi.
glad, *a.* 1. Iyuśkiŋ; pida: *a glad boy.* 2. Wowiyuśkiŋ: *a glad day.*
gladden, *vt.* Iyuśkiŋkiya.
gladly, *adv.* Iyuśkiŋyaŋ.
gladness, *n.* Wowiyuśkiŋ.
gladsome, *a.* Wi'yuśkiŋkiya.
glance, *vt.* Waŋyag iheya. *vi.* 1. Kaśdun iyaya: *the ball glanced.* 2. Ahitoŋwaŋ: *he glanced at me.* 3. Dus iyaye.
glanders, *n.* Ṡuŋ'kawakaŋ po'ġeḣdipi.
glare, *vi.* Wiyakpa; iyeġa.
glaring, *pa.* Iśtowicaśniża; taŋiŋḣca.
glass, *n.* 1. Żaŋżaŋ: *a piece of glass.* 2. Iśtamaza; iśtażaŋżaŋ: *eye-glasses.* 3. Żaŋżaŋwiyatke: *drinking-glass.*
glassy, *a.* Żaŋżaŋse.
glaze, *vt.* Żaŋżaŋse apawiŋtapi.
gleam, *vi.* Iyeġa; wiyakpa.
glean, *vt.* To'na okapta mnayaŋ.
glee, *n.* Wowiyuśkiŋ.
glee-club, *n.* Wi'yuśkiŋdowaŋpi obe.
glen, *n.* Kaksiza.
glib, *a.* Ṡduśduta.
glide, *vi.* A'ninidushiyaya.
glimmer, *vi.* Taŋiŋiŋ; kpa'kpa.
glimpse, *n.* Waŋyag iheyapi.
glitter, *vi.* Wiyakpakpa.
gloam, *n.* Owataŋiŋśni.
gloat, *vi.* Wośice wi'piiçiya.
globe, *n.* Makamibe.
globular, *a.* Mibe.
globule, *n.* Ta'kumibe ci'stiŋna.
gloom, *n.* Woiyokiśica; o'kpaza.
gloomy, *a.* Oiyokiśica; o'kpaza.
glorify, *vt.* Yataŋ; yawaśte.
glorious, *a.* Waśteḣca; wowinihaŋ.
glory, *n.* Wowitaŋ. *vi.* Itaŋ.
gloss, *vt.* Paśduta; pawiyakpa; to'ketu oyaka.
glossy, *a.* Wiyakpa; śduśduta.
glove, *n.* Ṇapiŋkpayuġaġa.
glow, *vi.* Ṡaśa; ka'ta.
glowing, *a.* Ka'ta; iżaŋżaŋ.
glue, *n.* Coŋ'peśka. *vt.* A'skamya.
glue-pot, *n.* Coŋ'peśka iokanye.
glum, *a.* Ininaḣuŋ.
glut, *vt.* Ożuya; wi'piyeḣca. *n.* oṭiŋswaŋka.
glutton, *n.* Wotesa; wi'piṭeiçiya.
gluttonous, *a.* Wotesa.
gluttony, *n.* Wi'piṭapi.
gnarl, *n.* Osnaze; yuwipi.
gnash, *vt.* Yakiŋskiŋza.
gnat, *n.* Hopoŋkadaŋ.
gnaw, *vi.* Yaḳeġa.
go, went, gone, *vi.* 1. Ya; iyaye: *go east.* 2. Iyopte: *the mill goes.* 3. Ohnaya; e'yuśtaŋpi: *the election went Republican.* *Go against,* i'tkokimya; iyapa. —*Go astray,* nu'ni.—*Go bail for,* iye oŋ woyuha kaśka.—*Go for,* huweya; kuwa.—*Go hard with,* teḣike kta.—*Go off,* to'ki ya; bośdoka.—*Go on,* saŋ'pa ya; śka'ta.—*Go on a journey,* i'cimani ya.—*Go it,* to'ken okihi ecoŋ.—*Go out,* taŋkanya; śni; oyakapi.—*Go through,* iyopta iyaya; yuśtaŋ; akipa. *Let go,* iyayeya; ayuśtaŋ.
goad, *vt.* Capa. *n.* Wi'cape.
goal, *n.* Oinażiŋta.

goat, *n.* He'kiŋśkayapi.
goatee, *n.* Ikuhiŋ.
gobble, *vt.* 1. Hotoŋtoŋ: *the turkey gobbles.* 2. Oħaŋko napcapca.
gobbler, *n.* Zi'cataŋka mdoka.
goblet, *n.* Żaŋżaŋwiyatkehaŋska.
go-by, *n.* Woaktaśni.
God, *n.* Wakaŋtaŋka; Ta'kuwakaŋ.
goddess, *n.* Ta'kuwakaŋ wiŋ'yaŋ.
godfather, *n.* Baptisma en atewicakiyapi.
Godhead, *n.* Wakaŋtaŋka ouŋcaġe.
godless, *a.* Wakaŋtaŋka ohodaśni.
godlike, *a.* Ta'kuwakaŋ iyececa.
godly, *a.* Wakaŋtaŋka awaciŋ.
Godsend, *n.* Wakaŋtaŋka etaŋhaŋ.
Godspeed, *n.* Wakaŋtaŋka ni'ci uŋ.
goer, *n.* Tu'we iyopte.
goes, *3d per. sing.* GO.
goggles, *n.* Iśtamaza o'ġetoŋ.
going, *n.* Woiyopte; oaye.
gold, *n.* Ma'zaskazi.
golden, *a.* 1. Ma'zaskazi: *golden spectacles.* 2. Zizi; ziyena: *golden hair.* 3. Ni'na waśte: *golden words.*
gone, *pa.* Iyaya; kihda; henana.
gong, *n.* Caŋ'ceġa sna.
good, *a.* 1. Waśte: *a good boy.* 2. Ki'taŋna: *a good deal* (kitaŋna ota). 3. Wowicake: *a good whipping.* *Good at,* taŋyaŋ okihi.—*Good for:* oŋ waśte; iwaśte. — *Good looking:* owaŋyag waśte. — *Good to:* taŋyaŋ kuwa.—*In good time:* iyehantu.
good, *n.* Ta'ku waśte; wowaśte; wokiciwaśte.
good-by, *n.* Taŋyaŋ yauŋ nuŋwe.
good-day, *n.* Aŋpetu ouiciwaśteni.
good-humored, *a.* Wawihaha.
goodly, *a.* Waśtecaka.
good-natured, *a.* Tawaciŋwaśte.
goodness, *n.* Wowaśte.
goods, *n.* Woyuha; waħpaya.

goodwill, *n.* Tawaciŋwaśte.
goose, geese, *n.* Maġa.
gooseberry, *n.* Wicahdeśka; *Y.* wicaknaśka; *T.* wicagnaśka.
gopher, *n.* Manica. *Striped gopher,* taśnaheca.
gore, *n.* 1. We; we nini. 2. Tete ħci. *vt.* Capa.
gorge, *vt.* Akaska; oṭiŋsya.
gorgeous, *a.* Wowinihaŋ.
gormandize, *vi.* Ni'nawota.
gory, *a.* Wewe.
gosling, *n.* Maġaciŋca.
gospel, *n.* Wotaŋiŋ Waśte.
gossip, *vi.* Ta'kuśniśni oyaka. *n.* 1. Ta'kukeyapi. 2. Woyakesa.
got, *imp.* of GET.
gouge, *vt.* Paħdoka; icu; ki.
gourd, *n.* Wamnuha.
gout, *n.* O'kihepopi woyazaŋ.
govern, *vt.* Awaŋyaka.
governess, *n.* Wiŋ'yaŋitaŋcaŋ.
governing, *a.* Itaŋcaŋ; tokahaŋ.
government, *n.* Woitaŋcaŋ; woawaŋyake; wokicoŋze.
governor, *n.* Itaŋcaŋ; makaitaŋcaŋ.
gown, *n.* Nitośke; saŋksanica; o'kde; *T.* cuwignake.
grab, *vt.* Yukabicu; botica.
grace, *n.* Wowaśte; wowaoŋśida. *vt.* Yuwaśte.
graceful, *a.* Owaśte; oiyokipi.
gracefully, *adv.* Oiyokipiya.
graceless, *a.* Wowaśte ni'ca.
gracious, *a.* Waoŋśida; waśte.
graciously, *adv.* Waoŋśidaya; oiyokipiya.
gradation, *n.* Kaocipten waŋka.
grade, *vt.* O'cipten e'hnaka; caŋku oḳa. *n.* Oḳapi; obe.
gradual, *a.* Iwaśtedaŋ.
graduate, *vi.* Wooŋspe ihuŋni.
graft, *vt.* Caŋ o'śtaŋ icaħya.
grain, *n.* 1. Ta'ku su; aġuyapi su: *much grain is sown.* 2. Sukaza; o'kpe: *a grain of sand.* *Against the grain,* apaħatka.

vt. Ta'ku su won'tkiya : *grain hogs.* Mduya : *grain the sugar.*
grammar, *n.* Iapi wooŋspe.
grammatical, *a.* Wooŋspe ohna.
granary, *n.* Dotopiye.
grand, *a.* Wowinihaŋ ; taŋ'ka ; okinihaŋ ; woimnaķe.
grandchild, *n.* Takożakpaku.
granddaughter, *n.* Takożakpaku wiŋ'yaŋ.
grandeur, *n.* Wowinihaŋ.
grandfather, *n.* Tuŋkaŋśidaŋ. *His grandfather,* tuŋkaŋśitku.
grandly, *adv.* Wowinihaŋyaŋ.
grandmother (grandma), *n.* Kuŋ'śi. *My grandmother,* uŋci.—*Your grandmother,* nikuŋśi.—*His grandmother,* kuŋ'śitku.
grandpa, *n.* Tuŋkaŋśidaŋ.
grandparent, *n.* Saŋ'pa huŋkake.
grandson, *n.* Takożakpa wica.
granger, *n.* Wożuwicaśta.
granite, *n.* Iŋ'yaŋȟcake.
granny, *n.* Uŋciyapi ; wakaŋka.
grant, *vt.* Ķu ; he'cetu eya. *n.* Ta'ku ķu'pi ; wicaķupi.
granulated, *a.* Sbu'na.
grape, *n.* Hastaŋhaŋka. *T.* Caŋwiyape.
grapevine, *n.* Hastaŋhaŋkahu ; caŋwiyuwi.
graphic, *a.* Taŋiŋȟca.
grapple, *vt.* Yu'za ; oyuspa.
grasp, *vt.* Sutaya yu'za.
grasping, *pa.* Wayuhektehca.
grass, *n.* Wato ; peżi kaśdapiśni.
grasshopper, *n.* Psi'pśicadaŋ. *T.* Gnugnuśka.
grassy, *a.* Peżi o'ta.
grate, *vt.* Yuķeġa : yukpaŋ. *n.* Oceti ma'zayuȟaȟa.
grateful, *a.* Pida ; iwicawaśte.
grater, *n.* Wi'yuķeġa.
gratification, *n.* 1. Wowiyuśkiŋ ; wopida : *your gift is a great gratification to me.* 2. Woiyowiŋkiye : *the gratification of appetite.*
gratify, *vt.* Iyokipiya ; iyowiŋya.
gratis, *adv.* Wokażużu co'daŋ.
gratitude, *n.* Wapidapi.
gratuitous, *a.* Iśicodaŋ.
gratuitously, *adv.* Ituya.
gratuity, *n.* Woituȟaŋ.
grave, *a.* Taŋ'ka ; oȟaŋsta'ka. *n.* Wicaȟapi ; wicaknakapi.
gravel, *n.* Iȟ'e ; isbu ; iŋ'yaŋ.
gravelly, *a.* Iȟ'e ota.
gravely, *adv.* Oȟaŋ stagya.
gravestone, *n.* Wicahnakapiiŋyaŋ.
graveyard, *n.* Wicahnakapi.
gravitate, *vt.* Ihdutitaŋ.
gravity, *n.* 1. Makawoyutitaŋ. 2. Woś'ake ; woawaciŋ.
gravy, *n.* Waśpaŋyaŋpi wi'hdi.
gray, *a.* Ḣo'ta ; ska. *A gray coat,* o'kde ȟo'ta.—*Gray-headed,* paska.
graze, *vt.* 1. Wi'ȟaŋkiya : *graze the cattle on the hill.* 2. Icaȟtaka : *the stone grazed his head.* *vi.* Wi'ȟaŋ.
grease, *n.* Wi'hdi ; sda. *vt.* Sdaya.
greasy, *a.* Sda.
great, *a.* 1. Taŋ'ka : *a great nation.* 3. Ni'na. *A great many,* ni'na o'ta.—*A great while,* ni'na te'-han.
greatly, *adv.* Ni'na.
greatness, *n.* Wotaŋka.
greed, *n.* Wayuhapi kte ȟca.
greedy, *a.* Wateȟiŋda ; wotesa.
greedily, *adv.* Ciŋ'ȟca.
green, *a.* 1. To ; ziyato ; pežito : *the trees are green.* 2. Sutoŋśni ; śtuŋka ; to : *a green plum.* 3. Te'ca ; pu'ześni : *green wood.* 4. Do : *a green hide.*
greenhorn, *n.* Tu'we oŋspeśni.
greet, *vt.* Napeyuza ; ho eya.
greeting, *n.* Kiciyuonihaŋpi.
grew, *imp.* of GROW.
greyhound, *n.* Śuŋ'kahuhaŋskaska.
griddle, *n.* Owaśpaŋye mdaska.
grief, *n.* Woiyokiśica.
grievance, *n.* Oŋ iyokiśicapi.

grieve, *vt.* Iyokiśinya. *vi.* Iyokiśica.
grievous, *a.* Woiyokiśica.
grim, *a.* Ksizeca ; suta.
grimace, *n.* Iteśinkiyapi.
grimly, *adv.* Ksizeya.
grin, *vi.* Iḣa ; hi pazo.
grind, ground, *vt.* 1. Yukpaŋ : *grind corn.* 2. Yumaŋ : *grind the ax.* 3. Kakiśya : *grind the poor.*
grindstone, *n.* Izuzataŋka.
grip, *vt.* Nape sutaya oyuspa.
gripe, *vt.* Yukśayu'za.
grizzled, *n.* Ḣo'ta.
grizzly-bear, *n.* Matoḣota.
groan, *vi.* Howaya ; ṭiŋ'ġa.
grocery, *n.* Woyute mazopiye.
grog, *n.* Miniwakaŋ.
groggy, *a.* Itomni.
groom, *vt.* Śuŋ'kawakaŋ kakca. *n.* Śuŋgawaŋyake ; tawicutoŋkta.
groove, *vt.* Bakoŋta.
grope, *vi.* Botoŋtoŋ kuwa.
gross, *a.* 1. Taŋ'ka : taŋiŋ ḣca : *gross errors.* 2. Ce'pa : *a gross woman.* 3. A'taya : *gross earnings.*
grossly, *adv.* Taŋiŋyaŋḣca.
Gros Ventres, *n.* Ḣewaktokta.
grotesque, *a.* Wowiḣa.
grotto, *n.* Makatipi waśte.
ground, *n.* 1. Maka ; makoce ; oyaŋke. 2. Oahehde ; etaŋhaŋ uya. *vt.* Sutaya e'hde. *a.* Maka ekta ; yukpaŋpi.
ground, *imp* of GRIND.
ground-cherries, *n.* Waġioġi.
ground-hog, *n.* Hakaśana.
groundless, *a.* Ituyaciŋ.
grounds, *n. pl.* Cetetahe : *coffee grounds.*
groundwork, *n.* Hu'te.
group, *n.* Optaya ; obe. *vt.* Optaye kaḣya e'żu.
grouse, *n.* Śi'yo.
grove, *n.* Caŋwita ; caŋwożupi.
grovel, *vt.* Sdohaŋ uŋ.
groveling, *a.* Oŋ'sika ; waḣteśni.
grow, *vi.* Icaġa ; a'ya ; taŋ'kaaya. *Corn grows,* wamnaheza icaġa. —*Father grows thin,* ate ci'stiŋnaaya. *vt.* Icaḣya.
growl, *vi.* Ḣdo ; ieniyeya.
growler, *n.* Ienhdesa.
grown, *pa.* Icaġa ; taŋ'ka.
growth, *n.* Oicaġe ; woicaġe.
grub, *vt.* Ḳa ; oḳa. *n.* Caŋhutkaŋ ; wamduśkadaŋ.
grudge, *vt.* Koŋ ; nawizi. *n.* Wowaḣtedaśni.
gruel, *n.* Wożapi sutaśni.
gruff, *a.* Ḳe'za ; suta.
grum, *a.* Ḳsizeca.
grumble, *vi.* Aḣdo ; iyokipiśni ia.
grunt, *vi.* Ḣdo ; ṭiŋ'ġa ; ġiŋ'ca.
guano, *n.* Zitkacesdi.
guarantee, *vt.* Yuwicaka.
guaranty, *n.* Oŋ yuwicakapi.
guard, *vt.* Awaŋyaka. *n.* Wa'waŋyake ; ikaŋ.
guarded, *pa.* Waktauŋ.
guardian, *n.* Awaŋyagkiyapi.
guerilla, *n.* Akicita naḣmaŋ uŋ.
guess, *vt.* Iyukcaŋ ; eciŋ ; ituyaeya. *n.* Wowiyukcaŋ.
guest, *n.* Tu'we titokaŋhi.
guidance, *n.* Ihakam uŋ'pi.
guide, *vt.* Caŋkuoyaka ; yusaya ; awaŋyaka ; yuhomni. *n.* Toŋweya ; caŋkupazo.
guild, *n.* Okodakiciye.
guile, *n.* Wohnaye.
guileless, *a.* Wohnaye ni'ca.
guilt, *n.* Woaḣtani.
guiltless, *a.* Woaḣtani co'daŋ.
guilty, *a.* 1. Ta'ku śi'ca ecoŋ : *he is guilty.* 2. Śi'ca : *a guilty deed.*
guise, *n.* Koŋ'za ; kaḣya.
guitar, *n.* Wi'kaŋyudowaŋpi.
gulch, *n.* O'smaka ; miniboḣya.
gulf, *n.* Miniwaŋca okaḣmiŋ.
gull, *n.* Wicataŋktaŋkadaŋ. *vt.* Hna'yaŋ.
gullet, *n.* Wi'napce.

gully, *n.* Oškokpa.
gulp, *vt.* Taŋk'taŋka napca.
gum, *n.* Caŋšiŋ ; caka.
gumbo, *n.* Makaotkapa.
gummy, *a.* O'tkapa.
gun, *n.* Ma'zakaŋ.
gunnery, *n.* Ma'zakaŋ ecoŋpi.
gunnysack, *n.* Psa'wožuha.
gunpowder, *n.* Caȟdi.
gurgle, *vi.* Miniȟmuŋ.
gush, *vi.* Ni'na hiyu.
gusher, *n.* Minibosdi.
gust, *n.* Tateȟca.
gusto, *n.* Woiyokipiȟca.
gut, *n.* Šupe. *vt.* Šupe icu.
gutter, *n.* Minicaŋkuoķapi; upšiža.
guttural, *a.* Hoȟmuŋ.
guzzle, *vt.* To'ken okihi yatkaŋ.
gymnasium, *n.* Ohnaihduzicapi.
gymnastics, *n.* Ihduzicapi.
Gypsy, *n.* Oyateomanisa.
gyrate, *vi.* Yuhomni.

H

ha, *interj.* Eca (iȟapi iapi).
habeas corpus, *n.* Auwicašipi.
habit, *n.* Oȟaŋ ; oihduze.
habitable, *a.* Otipica.
habitation, *n.* Ti ; ti'pi.
habitual, *a.* Ecahececa.
habituate, *vt.* Ecewaktakiya.
hack, *vt.* Apapa ; kaksaksa. *n.* Oape ; oȟci ; caŋpahmihma.
hackberry, *n.* Yamnumnuğapi.
had, *imp.* of HAVE.
Hades, *n.* Wanağiouŋyaŋpi.
hag, *n.* Wakaŋkašicedaŋ.
haggard, *a.* Watuka ; sta'ka.
haggle, *vt.* Kaȟciȟci.
hail, *n.* Wasu. *vi.* Wasu hiŋhe.
hail, *interj.* Ho (woyuonihaŋ iapi). *vt.* Kipaŋ : *he hailed me.*
hailstorm, *n.* Wasu hiŋhe.
hair, *n.* Hiŋ ; pahiŋ ; paha.
hair-breadth, *a.* Kitaŋyaŋ.
hairy, *a.* Hiŋ yukaŋ ; hiŋšma.
hale, *a.* Taŋcaŋsuta.
half, *a.* Haŋke : *half a day. adv.* Haŋkeya : *half understood.*
half-breed, *n.* Wašicuŋciŋca. *Y.* Dako'acinca.
half-past, *a.* Sam'haŋke.
half-way, *a.* Cokaya.
hall, *n.* 1. Titaŋka ; omniciyetipi : *city hall.* 2. Timahen ocaŋkuyapi : *hang your hat in the hall.*
halleluiah, *n.* Wakaŋtaŋkayataŋ.
halloo, *interj.* Hiwo ; ho.
hallow, *vt.* Yuwakaŋ.
hallucination, *n.* Ta'ku iċihnayaŋpi ; woihaŋmde.
halo, *n.* Wi'acetipimibe ; te'šdakeša.
halt, *vi.* Huštemani ; na'žiŋ. *a.* Hušte.
halter, *n.* Iteoğe ; iteha. *vt.* Kaška.
halve, *vt.* Cokaya kibaksa.
ham, *n.* Ceca ; kukušececa.
hame, *n.* Wanapiŋakaškapi.
hamlet, *n.* Otoŋwena.
hammer, *n.* Maziyape. *vt.* Apa.
hammock, *n.* Ho'tedaŋ owaŋka.
hamper, *vt.* Kağiya.
hamstring, *n.* Cecakaŋ.
hand, *n.* 1. Nape : *a sore hand.* 2. Ookiye; wowaši; tuwe ċeyaš : *all hands joined in the sport.* 3. Nape oŋ ka'ğapi : *he writes a nice hand. Back of the hand,* napakaha.—*From hand to hand,* i'ciyaza.—*From hand to mouth,* ta'kudaŋ iċihdešni.—*Hand in hand,* napekiciyus ; o'kiciya.—*Hands off,* yutaŋšni.—*Had a*

hand in it, en nape yekiya.—*Left hand*, catka.—*Right hand*, etapa; *Y.* onspeapataŋhaŋ.—*Inside the hand*, napcoka.—*Off hand*, katiŋyaŋ; i'tokam piiciyeśni.—*On hand*, yuha uŋ.—*On the one hand... on the other hand*, de'ciyataŋhaŋ... he'ciyataŋhaŋ.—*One hand*, napsani.—*Shake hands*, napeyuza.—*Slack hand*, huŋ'keśni.—*Change hands*, kiciçupi.—*Come to hand*, en hi; icu.—*Lend a hand*, o'kiya.—*On all hands*, o'waŋcaya. *Second hand*, waŋna uŋ'pi; tani.—*Wash the hands*, iyoważaśniiçiya. *vt.* Hiyukiya.

handbill, *n.* Wayaotaŋiŋ wowapi.

handbreadth, *n.* Wicanape oiyute.

handcuff, *n.* Napokaśke.

handful, *n.* Napeohnaka.

hand-glass, *n.* Mniokdasiŋ ci'stiŋna.

handicap, *vt.* Kaś'agya.

handiwork, *n.* Woecoŋ.

handkerchief, *n.* Itipakiŋte.

handle, *n.* Ihupa; wiyuze. *vt.* Nape en yeya; kuwa; kicaŋye.

handless, *a.* Nape wanica.

handling, *n.* Kuwapi.

handmaid, *n.* Wiŋ'yaŋookiye.

handsaw, *n.* Caŋibaksanapsani

handsome, *a.* Owaŋyagwaśte; taŋwaśte; oiyokipi; taŋ'ka.

handsomely, *adv.* Taŋyaŋ.

handspike, *n.* Hoŋ'pe; caŋ.

handwriting, *n.* Napeoŋkaġapi.

handy, *a.* Okiŋyaŋwaśte; wayupika.

hang, hung, *vt.* 1. Otkeya: *hang out the clothes.* 2. Ikoyaka; ecen ehde: *hang the scythe; hang the door.* 3. Pa'nakseya: *hang the murderer.* *vi.* 1. Otkehan: *the lamp hangs from a hook:* 2. Ikoyaka: *it hangs to him.* *n.* Otke; tokiyotaŋ.

hanging, *n.* Otkeyapi.

haphazard, *a.* To'kenciŋciŋ.

hapless, *a.* Wa'piśni.

happen, *vi.* 1. Wanu: *I happened to find.* 2. Akipa: *death happens to all alike.*

happily, *adv.* 1. Canwaśteya: *they lived happily.* 2. Wa'piya: *happily I did not fall.*

happiness, *n.* Wocaŋtewaśte.

happy, *a.* Caŋtewaśte.

harangue, *vt.* Wahokoŋkiya.

harass, *vt.* Naġiyeya.

harbinger, *n.* Wahośiye.

harbor, *n.* Wi'tawataonażiŋ; onapapi waśte. *vt.* 1. Anakikśiŋ: *harbor a thief.* 2. Awaciŋ uŋ: *harbor malice in his heart.* *vi.* Onapa; inażiŋ.

hard, *a.* 1. Suta: *hard as a stone.* 2. Tehike: *a hard lesson.* 3. Nina kuwa; wohitika: *a hard student.* *adv.* 1. Ni'na: *run hard.* 2. Tehiya: *he trots hard.* 3. Sutaya: *tie it hard.* *Hard by*, ikiyedaŋ.—*Hard up*, kakiśya.—*Hard earned*, kitaŋyaŋ kamna.

harden, *vt.* Yusuta.

hardihood, *n.* Wocaŋteţiŋza.

hardly, *adv.* Ki'taŋh; iyus'oya; iyehaŋyaŋśni; tehiya.

hardness, *n.* Wosuta.

hardship, *n.* Wotehi.

hardtack, *n.* Aġuyapisaka suta.

hardware, *n.* Ma'zaicuwa.

hardy, *a.* Suta; wakiś'aka.

hare, *n.* Maśtiŋtaŋka.

hark, *vi.* Anaġoptaŋ; a; śi.

hearken, *vi.* Anaġoptaŋ.

harlot, *n.* Witkowiŋ.

harm, *vt.* Yuśica; kiuŋniya. *n.* Wokiuŋni; woyuśice.

harmful, *a.* Wakiuŋni.

harmless, *a.* Wayuśiceśni.

harmonize, *vt.* Yuokoŋwaŋżidaŋ.

harmony, *n.* Okiciwaśtepi.

harness, *n.* Śungikaŋ; ikaŋ. *vt.* Ikaŋ ikoyagya.

harp, *n.* Wi'kaŋ yudowaŋpi. *vi.* Heyaya.
harpoon, *n.* Wahukeza.
harrow, *n.* Maħiyuhiŋhe. *vt.* Yuhiŋhe.
harsh, *a.* 1. ·Gahaŋ : *a harsh voice.* 2. Ksizeca : *harsh conduct.*
hartshorn, *n.* Wi'pakiŋteska.
harvest, *n.* Wasutoŋ ; woksapi. *vt.* Yuksa ; mnayaŋ ; kaśda.
harvester, *n.* Wi'nakse.
has, *3d p. s.* of HAVE.
hash, *n.* Tadobakpaŋpi. *vt.* Bakpaŋ.
haste, *vi.* Inaħni. *vt.* Inaħniya. *n.* Woinaħni.
hasten, *vt.* Yuinaħni ; inaħni.
hastily, *adv.* Inaħniyaŋ.
hasty, *a.* Inaħni ; oħaŋko.
hat, *n.* Wapaha. *Y. & T.* Wapośtaŋ.
hatch, *vt.* Maŋ ; pakpiya. *vi.* Pakpi ; ikpaħdoka.
hatchet, *n.* Oŋspedaŋ.
hate, *vt.* Waħtedaśni ; śi'cedaka. *n.* Wowaħtedaśni.
hateful, *a.* Waħteśni.
hatred, *n.* Wowaħtedaśni.
hatter, *n.* Wapahakaġa.
haughty, *a.* Ohitiiçida.
haul, *vt.* 1. Tokśu : *haul wood.* 2. Yusdohaŋ : *haul ten cars.* *n.* Oyusdohaŋ ; oicu.
haunt, *vt.* O'kśaŋ uŋ ; ouŋyaŋ.
haunted, *pa.* Wanaġi ouŋyaŋpi.
have, has, had, *vt.* 1. Yuha : *I have a dog.* 2. Kiya ; ya : *I had him come.* 3. Iyopaśtaka : *he had to go.* 4. *Aux.*, not expressed. *I have come,* wahi ; waŋna wahi. —*I have never seen him,* to'hiŋni waŋmdake śni.
haven, *n.* Oahuni.
haversack, *n.* Waŋeya oźuha.
havoc, *n.* Woihaŋgye.
haw, *vt.* Catkata yuhomni. *vi.* Iħaṭa ; hoħpa.
hawk, *n.* Cetaŋ ; caŋśka ; upizica ; pteġopeca. *vt.* Paŋ'wiyopeya. *vi.* Hoħpa.
hay, *n.* Peźi. *vt.* Peźi ka'ga.
haycock, *n.* Peźipśuŋkaka.
hayrack, *n.* Peźiitokśu.
haystack, *n.* Peźipaha.
hazard, *vt.* Oṭohnaka ; iyuta.
hazardous, *a.* Okokipe.
hazelnut, *n.* U'ma.
hazy, *a.* Śotoźu ; owataŋiŋśni.
he, *pro.* I'ye : *he did it.* (*Generally not expressed.*)
head, *n.* 1. Pa : *my head aches.* 2. Itaŋcaŋ ; tokahaŋ : *the head man.* 3. Sukaza : *I have ten head of cattle.* 4. O'iŋkpa : *the head of the river.* 5. Oiwaŋyake : *the heads of discourse.* *vt.* Tokahaŋ ; itoheyaya ; aohomniya ; en'tkiya pa yu'za ; paka'ġa. *a.* 1. Tokahaŋ : *head cook.* 2. Tatoheya : *We had a head wind.*
headache, *n.* Nasuyazaŋpi.
headdress, *n.* Wapaha ; teśdake.
header, *n.* Tokahaŋ; iŋ'kpaibakse.
heading, *n.* Pa ; ta'ku ka'pi.
headlong, *adv.* Botoŋyaŋ.
headmost, *a.* Tokahaŋ.
headquarters, *n.* Itaŋcaŋtoyaŋke.
headstone, *n.* Wicaħapiiŋ'yaŋ ; iŋ'yaŋ itaŋcaŋ.
headstrong, *a.* Tawaciŋ suta.
headway, *n.* Woiyopte.
heal, *vt.* Asniyaŋ ; yuasni. *vi.* Okizi.
health, *n.* 1. Wozani : *seek health.* 2. Ouŋ ; taŋcan : *bad health.*
healthful, *a.* Taŋcaŋ yuwaśte.
healthy, *a.* Zani ; waśte.
heap, *vt.* Pahi ; pahakaġa. *n.* Paha ; opahi ; o'ta.
hear, heard, *vt.* 1. Naħoŋ : *I hear you.* 2. Naħoŋyaŋka : *hear this class.* *vi.* Wanaħoŋ.
hearing, *n.* Wonaħoŋ ; no'ġe.
hearken, *vi.* Anaġoptaŋ.
hearsay, *n.* Keyapi.

hearse, *n.* Wicaṭe caŋpakmiyaŋ.
heart, *n.* Caŋte. *Break his heart,* caŋte ihaŋkeya.—*Learn by heart,* tawaciŋ oŋ kiksuye.—*Lose heart,* waciŋiboṡ'ake.—*Take heart,* caŋte kiçuŋ.—*Take to heart,* caŋte en yeya.—*Set the heart on,* ni'na ciŋ.
heartburn, *n.* Caŋteyazaŋ.
hearth, *n.* Pe'taoahe; petkahda.
hearthstone, *n.* Iŋ'yaŋpetkahda.
heartily, *adv.* Caŋwaṡteya.
heartless, *a.* Caŋtewanica.
heartrending, *a.* Caŋtiyapapa.
hearty, *a.* 1. Caŋte oŋ: *a hearty greeting.* 2. Zani; suta: *a hearty boy.* 3. Otaŋtoŋka; ciŋḣca.
heat, *vt.* Kanya. *n.* Wokata; oecoŋ.
heater, *n.* Oŋ kanyapi.
heathen, *n.* Wakaġapi ohodapi; ikcewicaṡta.
heave, *vt.* Yuwaŋkan icu; hiyuya.
heaven, *n.* Maḣpiya; maḣpiya to.
heavenly, *a.* Maḣpiyata; waṡte.
heavily, *adv.* Tkeya; ni'na.
heaviness, *n.* Tke; woiyokiṡica.
heavy, *a.* 1. Tke: *a heavy stone.* 2. Ṡo'ka: *a heavy fall of snow.* 3. Oiyokiṡica: *heavy news.*
hedge, *n.* Oteḣi coŋ'kaṡke. *vt.* Nataka; caŋkaṡka.
hedgehog, *n.* Sagdaṡiŋ pahiŋ.
heed, *vt.* Awaciŋ; anaġoptaŋ. *n.* Woanaġoptaŋ.
heedless, *a.* Waawaciŋṡni.
heedlessly, *adv.* Waawaciŋṡniyan.
heel, *n.* Siyete; ihaŋke.
heifer, *n.* Ptewiye aṡkatudaŋ.
height, *n.* Obosdatu; waŋkantu.
heighten, *vt.* Sam yuwaŋkantu.
heinous, *a.* Ni'na ṡi'ca.
heinously, *adv.* Ṡicayaḣca.
heinousness, *n.* Woṡice.
heir, *n.* Ta'wakte.
heirloom, *n.* Ehaŋna huŋkake ta'wa.
held, *imp* of HOLD.
hell, *n.* Wakaŋṡicati; wicaṭe makoce.
helm, *n.* Iyupse; woyuhomni.
helmet, *n.* Ozuye wapaha.
helmsman, *n.* Wasiŋteyuhomni.
help, *vt.* O'kiya. *I will help you,* o'ciciye kta. 2. Yutokeca; anapta: *I can't help it.* 3. Yuwaṡte, *it helps my cough. Help to,* ku. *n.* Waokiyapi; ookiye; wowaṡi.
helper, *n.* Ookiye; waṡ'agya.
helpful, *a.* Waokiya; yuwaṡte.
helpless, *a.* 1. O'kiyepicaṡni. 2. Ta'ku okihi ṡni: *a helpless babe.*
helpmate, helpmeet, *n.* Ookiye.
helterskelter, *adv.* To'ken ciŋ'yaŋ.
helve, *n.* Ihupa.
hem, *n.* Opapuŋ. *vt.* Opapuŋkaġeġe. *vi.* Wakaṡpewaciŋ.
hemi-, *pref.* Haŋke.
hemisphere, *n.* Makahaŋke.
hemlock, *n.* Wazicaŋ.
hemorrhage, *n.* Weuyapi.
hemp, *n.* Haḣoŋtahu taŋ'ka.
hen, *n.* Aŋpaohotaŋna wi'ye. *Y.* Kokoyaḣaŋna wi'ye; wi'ye.
hence, *adv.* 1. Detaŋhaŋ; tokaŋ: *go hence.* 2. Tokata: *a year hence.* 3. He'on etaŋhaŋ; hetaŋhaŋ: *hence it is.*
henceforth, *adv.* Tokata.
her, *pron.* 1. Ta'wa (wiŋyaŋ kapi): *her book.* 2. I'ye; he (*Generally not expressed in Indian*). *Call her,* kipaŋ.
herald, *n.* & *v.* E'yaŋpaha; oyaka.
herb, *n.* Wato.
herculean, *a.* Ni'na waṡaka.
herd, *n.* Optaye; obe. *vt.* Wi'taya awaŋyaka. *vi.* Wi'taya uŋ'pi.
herder, *n.* Pteawaŋyake.
here, *adv.* Den; de'ci.
hereafter, *adv.* Tokata.
hereby, *adv.* De'ciyataŋhaŋ; de'oŋ.
hereditary, *a.* Aiḣpekiciyapi.
herein, *adv.* De'en.

heresy, *n.* Wooŋspe to′keca.
heretofore, *adv.* De i′tokam.
heritage, *n.* Huŋkake etaŋhaŋ yuhapi.
hermit, *n.* Taŋśna makoskan ti.
hero, *n.* Itaŋcaŋka; ważaża.
heroic, *a.* Waditaka.
heron, *n.* Hoka.
hers, *pron.* I′ye ta′wa.
herself, *pron.* Iyeh̄ca.
hesitate, *vi.* Naṭuŋka; ecoŋkapiŋ.
hew, *vt.* Kakaŋ; kaksa.
hey, *interj.* Waŋ.
hibernate, *vi.* Waniyetu uŋ.
hickup, hiccough, *vi.* Mdokaska.
hickory, *n.* Caŋsu.
hid, *pp.* of HIDE.
hidden, *pa.* Nah̄maŋpi.
hide, hid, *vt.* Anah̄ma; nah̄maŋ. *n.* Ha; tataŋkaha; uka.
hidebound, *a.* Ukaaskapa.
hideous, *a.* Owaŋyagśica; oaśica.
hideously, *adv.* Oaśinya.
hie, *vi.* Inah̄ni.
hierarchy, *n.* Wowakaŋitaŋcaŋpi.
hieroglyph, *n.* Woiyaciŋowapi.
high, *a.* 1. Waŋkantu; tehaŋwaŋkantu: *a high hill.* 2. Taŋ′ka; iyotaŋ: *high heat.* *adv.* Waŋkantuya.
high-flown, *a.* Wah̄aŋiçida.
highly, *adv.* Ni′na.
high-road, *n.* Caŋkutaŋka.
high-spirited, *a.* Iyotaŋiçida.
high-toned, *a.* Waciŋtaŋka.
highway, *n.* Caŋkutaŋka.
highwayman, *n.* Wamanoŋwicaśa.
hilarity, *n.* Wawih̄ayapi.
hill, *n.* 1. Paha; h̄e: *the river hills.* 2. Mah̄pażu: *a hill of corn.* *vt.* Pahaya akata.
hillock, *n.* Paha ci′stiŋna.
hillside, *n.* H̄euŋnaptaŋ.
hilltop, *n.* Pahaiŋkpa.
hilly, *a.* H̄o′śki.
hilt, *n.* Ihupa; wi′yuze.
him, *pron.* I′ye (*Generally not expressed*). *Give him a book,* wowapi waŋ ḳu.
himself, *pron.* Iyeh̄ca.
hind, *n.* Tawiye. *a.* He′kta.
hinder, *vt.* Kaśeya; kaġiya.
hinder, *a.* He′kta; uŋzeta.
hinderance, *n.* Wokaśe.
hindmost, *a.* He′kta ihaŋke.
hinge, *n.* Tiyopaokihe. *vi.* En ikoyaka.
hint, *vt.* Icah̄tag eya; nah̄mana okiyake. *n.* Wowakta.
hip, *n.* Nite. *Hip-bone,* nisehu.
hipshot, *a.* Nisehu papśuŋ.
hire, *vt.* Każużu odota. *Hire out,* każużu oḳu. *n.* Wokażużu.
hireling, *n.* Ḳażużu yuha.
his, *pro.* Ta′wa; i′ye ta′wa.
hiss, *vi.* Sdi; sdi′sdi. *vt.* Asdisdi; kiśiça. *n.* Asdisdipi; sdi.
hist, *interj.* Śi. Anaġoptaŋ.
historian, *n.* Ehaŋna wicoh̄aŋ oyaka.
history, *n.* Ehaŋna woyakapi.
hit, *vt.* 1. Apa. *You hit it,* ni′ye apa. 2. Iyohi; iyecen ecoŋ. *vi.* Iyapa. *n.* Apapi; iyapa.
hitch, *vt.* Iyakaśka; ikoyagya. *n.* Ikoyagyapi; wokaġi.
hither, *adv.* De′ciya. *a.* De′ciyataŋhaŋ; *Y.* Tahena.
hitherto, *adv.* Dehaŋyaŋ.
hive, *n.* Tuh̄maġa ti′pi.
hives, *n.* Ahinapapi.
ho, *interj.* Hi′wo.
hoar, *a.* Ska; h̄o′ta.
hoard, *vt.* Kpataŋ; mnayaŋ. *n.* Womnaye; o′ta.
hoarhound, *n.* Caŋhaŋpiśaśa pa.
hoarse, *a.* Ho′ġita; ġi′ta.
hoary, *a.* Ska.
hoax, *vt.* Hna′yaŋ. *n.* Wohnaye.
hobble, *vt.* Siha pah̄ta. *vi.* Huśtemani.
hobby, *n.* E′cena kuwa.
hobby-horse, *n.* Caŋ′śuŋktaŋka.
hod, *n.* Upśiżaitokśu.
hoe, *n.* Mah̄icamna. *vt.* Akata.

hoedown, *n.* Ha'sapa tawowaci.
hoecake, *n.* Wokpaŋpi śpaŋ.
hog, *n.* Kukuśe.
hoggish, *a.* Oḣaŋśuŋkeca.
hogshead, *n.* Kokataŋka.
hoist, *vt.* Waŋkaniyeya.
hold, *vt.* 1. Yu'za; oyuspa: *hold the book.* 2. Sutaya yuza; owaŋżiyuza: *hold the train.* 3. Yuha; kuwa: *hold a meeting.* 4. Kipi; ohna yuha: *it will hold all.* 5. Awaciŋ; yawa: *hold guiltless.* *vi.* Inażiŋ; hehaŋyena ecoŋ.—*Hold forth,* yutaŋiŋ; wohdaka. —*Hold his own,* he'cehna ye.—*Hold the horse for me,* śuŋktaŋka mi'ciyuza. *n.* Oyuspa: *lost his hold.* Wokaśke: *the law has a hold on him.* Coŋ'kaśke: *a mountain hold.* Wa'tasicu: *the hold was full.*
holdback, *n.* Oŋ he'kta yu'zapi.
holder, *n.* Wi'yuze.
hole, *n.* Oḣdoka.
holiday, *n.* Wośkate aŋpetu.
holily, *adv.* Wakaŋyaŋ.
holiness, *n.* Wowakaŋ.
hollow, *a.* Śkokpa; ḣdo'ġeca; oḣdoġeca: *a hollow tree.*—*Hollow-horn,* heḣdoġeca.—*Hollow of the foot,* siḣape.—*Hollow cheeked,* tapoŋ śko'pa. *vt.* Yuśkopa: *hollow out a tree.*
hollow-hearted, *a.* Wicakeśni.
holy, *a.* Wakaŋ.
homage, *n.* Woyuonihaŋ.
home, *n.* Ti'pi; tiyata; ti. *At home,* tiyata.—*My home,* ti'pi mitawa.—*Take home,* ahda.
homeless, *a.* Ticodaŋ.
homely, *a.* 1. Okinihaŋśni; ikceka: *a homely house.* 2. Tiyata iyececa.
homesick, *a.* Tiawakiciŋ; icomni.
homestead, *n.* Makoce oicu; ti'pi.
homeward, *adv.* Tiyata.
homicide, *n.* Wicaśta kte'pi.
homily, *n.* Wowahokoŋkiya.
hominy, *n.* Paśdayapi.
homogeneous, *n.* Okaġe waŋżina.
hone, *n.* Iyohdi; izuza.
honest, *a.* Oḣaŋ owotaŋna; wowicake; zoŋ'ta.
honestly, *adv.* Owotaŋna.
honesty, *n.* Woowotaŋna.
honey, *n.* Tuḣmaġacahaŋpi; waśtena.
honey-comb, *n.* Tuḣmaġaśiŋ.
honeysuckle, *n.* Caŋwiskuye.
honor, *n.* Woyuonihaŋ. *vt.* Yuonihaŋ; ohoda.
honorable, *a.* Okinihaŋ.
honorably, *adv.* Yuoŋihaŋyaŋ.
honorary, *a.* Woyuonihaŋ.
hood, *n.* Sagdaśiŋ wapaha; wapośtaŋ.—*Hood,* ouŋ; okodakiciye.
hoodwink, *vt.* Iśtaakaḣpa; ḣna'yaŋ.
hoof, *n.* Śake; woteca śake.
hook, *n.* Ma'zayukśaŋ. *vt.* Icu; ikoyaka; manoŋ.
hoop, *n.* Caŋhdeśka; kokawiyuskite. *vt.* Yuskita. *vt.* Hotoŋ.
hoot, *vi.* Hiŋyaŋkaġa hotoŋ.
hop, *vi.* Sisani ipsica; ipsica; waci. *n.* Oipsica; waḣpeonapoḣye.
hope, *vi.* Ciŋ; waciŋyan; awaciŋ: *hope thou in God.* *n.* Ta'ku ciŋ'pi; wowaciŋye; woape.
hopeful, *a.* Waciŋyaŋ; waśte kta keciŋ; waśte kta se'ca.
hopeless, *a.* Wowaciŋye ni'ca.
hopper, *n.* 1. Tu'we ipsica. 2. Ohna ohnakapi.
horde, *n.* Wicobe.
horizon, *n.* Maḣpiya maka i'ciyahde.
horizontal, *a.* Mda'ya icazopi.
horn, *n.* He; ptehe; wayażopi.
horned, *a.* He'toŋna.
hornet, *n.* Tuḣmaġa kaḣohiyu.
horn-owl, *n.* Hiŋhaŋhetoŋna.
horrible, *a.* Ni'na śi'ca.
horribly, *adv.* Okokipeya.

horrid, *a.* Okokipe.
horrify, *vt.* Yuśiŋyeya.
horror, *n.* Woyuśiŋyaŋ.
horse, *n.* Śuŋktaŋka. *Y.* & *T.* Śuŋ'kawakaŋ. *Saw-horse*, akan caŋbaksapi.
horseback, *adv.* Śuŋgakan.
horse-dealer, *n.* Śuŋgwopetoŋ.
horsefly, *n.* Tatawaŋmduśka.
horseman, *n.* Śuŋgakanwicaśta.
horseshoe, *n.* Śakemaza.
horsewhip, *n.* Śuŋgicapsiŋte.
hose, *n.* 1. Iyahdehuŋska ; *Y.* huyakoŋ. 2. Mnibosdiikaŋ.
hospitable, *a.* Wonwicayesa; oȟaŋpi ; ti en i'pi waśte.
hospitably, *adv.* Iyokipiya.
hospital, *n.* Wayazaŋkatipi.
hospitality, *n.* Wicaśato'keca oŋśidapi.
host, *n.* 1. Wicota ; ozuye : *a host of people.* 2. Ti'pitawa.
hostage, *n.* E'ekiya kaśkapi.
hostess, *n.* Wiŋ'yaŋ ti'pitawa.
hostile, *a.* To'ka ; watoghda.
hostility, *n.* Kicizapi ; to'kakiciyapi.
hostler, *n.* Śuŋgawaŋyake.
hot, *a.* Ka'ta ; pa.
hotbed, *n.* Owaŋka ka'ta.
hotel, *n.* Owoteti'pi.
hotly, *adv.* Ni'na ; kanya.
hound, *n.* Śuŋ'ka oŋ wakuwapi.
hour, *n.* Wi'hiyaya ; oape.
hourly, *adv.* Oape iyohi.
house, *n.* 1. Ti'pi ; Waśicuŋti'pi. 2. Oyate, *the house of Judah.*
house, *vt.* Timahen e'hnaka.
housebreaker, *n.* Wabotica.
household, *n.* Tiwahe.
housekeeper, *n.* Ti'piyuha.
houseless, *a.* Ticodaŋ.
housemaid, *n.* Wiŋ'yaŋ wowaśi.
housewarming, *n.* Ti'piteca kicicopi.
housewife, *n.* Ti'piyuha tawicu.
hove, *imp.* of HEAVE.
hovel, *n.* Ti'piśicedaŋ.
hover, *vi.* O'kśaŋkiŋyaŋ uŋ.
how, *adv.* To'ken ; to'ketu. *How are you*, to'ken yauŋ he.—*How is the corn*, wamnaheza to'ketu he.—*How far ; how near*, tohaŋyaŋ he.—*How many ; how much*, to'nakeca he. — *How large ; how small*, tiŋ'skokeca he. *Excla.* Ta'ku. *How far !* ta'ku te'han.
howbeit, *conj.* He'caśta.
however, *conj.* He'caśta. *adv.* To'ken... eśta. *However good he is*, to'ken waśte eśta.
howl, *vi.* Hotoŋ ; śicahowaya.
howsoever, *adv.* To'ketu ċe'yaś.
hub, *n.* Hu pśuŋka.
hubbub, *n.* Ś'a'se śkaŋ'pi.
huckleberry, *n.* Ha'za.
huddle, *vt.* Yuwitaya. *vi.* Wi'taya.
hue, *n.* Owapi ; iuŋpi.
hug, *vt.* Po'skin yu'za.
huge, *a.* Taŋ'ka ; otaŋtoŋka.
hugely, *adv.* Ni'na ; otaŋtoŋyaŋ.
hugger, *n.* Po'skin yu'za.
hulk, *n.* Wa'ta taŋcaŋ.
hull, *n.* 1. Ha ; ożuha : *nut hulls.* 2. Wa'taśkokpa. *vt.* Ha eȟpeya; naśdaya.
hum, *vi.* Żiżidowaŋ ; a'nini dowaŋ ; ȟmuŋ. *interj.* E ; ehaŋ.
human, *a.* Wicaśta ; wica. *Human voice*, wicaho.
humane, *a.* Wicaśta iyececa ; waoŋśida.
humanely, *adv.* Waoŋśidaya.
humanity, *n.* Wicaśta.
humanize, *vi.* Wicaśta ka'ga.
humanly, *adv.* Wicaśta iwaŋyagya.
humble, *a.* Oŋ'śika ; wa'ȟbadaŋ.
humbly, *adv.* Oŋ'śiya.
humbug, *vt.* Hna'yaŋ. *n.* Wohnaye.
humdrum, *a.* Oaśica.
humerus, *n.* Hiŋtkaŋhu.
humid, *a.* Spa'ya.
humiliate, *vt.* Yuhukuya.

humility, *n.* Wicowaȟba.
humming-bird, *n.* Tanaġidaŋ.
humor, *n.* 1. Tawaciŋ : *good humor.* 2. Wowiȟatawaciŋ : *he is full of humor.* 3. Mini : *the humor of the eye,*
humorist, *n.* Wawiȟa.
humorous, *a.* Wawiȟaye.
humorously, *adv.* Wawiȟaya.
hump, *n.* Pažo.
humpback, *n.* Caŋkahupažo.
hunch, *n.* Pažo : *the camel's hunch.* *vt.* Panini.
hundred, *a.* Opawiŋġe.
hung, *imp.* of HANG.
hunger, *n.* Wotektehdapi ; ciŋ'pi. *vi.* Caŋtiheya ; ciŋ.
hungry, *a.* Wotektehda ; dociŋ.
hunt, *vt.* Ode ; ihni ; kuwa. *Hunt buffalo,* wanase.—*Hunt game for food,* wotihni.—*Hunt the horses,* śuŋgode. *n.* Wotihnipi ; odepi.
hunter, huntsman, *n.* Wotihnisa.
hurl, *vt.* Kaȟ'o iyeya.
hurly-burly, *n.* Owodutatoŋ.
hurrah, *vt.* I'yakiś'a.
hurricane, *n.* Tateohitika.
hurried, *pa.* Inaȟni.
hurriedly, *adv.* Inaȟniyaŋ.
hurry, *vt.* Inaȟniya. *n.* Woinaȟni.
hurt, *vt.* Ksu'weya ; kiuŋniya. *n.* Wokiuŋni.
hurtful, *a.* Wakiuŋniya ; śi'ca.
husband, *n.* Hihnaku ; wicaśta. *vt.* Kpataŋ ; kuwa.
husbandman, *n.* Wožuwicaśta.
husbandry, *n.* Wakicaŋyaŋpi ; wakpataŋpi.
hush, *vi.* Inina uŋ. *vt.* Yuasni.
husk, *vt.* Yuġa ; ha eȟpeya. *n.* Ha ; wahuwapa ha.
husky *a.* Ho'ġita ; ho'śica.
hustle, *vt.* Ni'na śkaŋ ; iyayeya.
hustler, *n.* Wohitika.
hut, *n.* Ti'pidaŋ.
huzza, *interj.* Wi'yuśkiŋ paŋ'pi.
hydrant, *n.* Minioicu.
hyena, *n.* Śuŋgmanituśicamna.
hymeneal, *a.* Kiciyuzapi.
hymn, *n.* Odowaŋ. *vt.* Idowaŋ.
hyperbolic, *a.* Akawiŋ.
hyphen, *n.* O'kihe icazopi.
hypnotize, *vt.* Wicaȟmuŋġa.
hypocrisy, *n.* Wohnaye.
hypocrite, *n.* Wicakeśni.
hypothesis, *n.* Woiyaciŋ.
hysterics, *n.* Hnaśkiŋyaŋpi.

I

I, *pro.* Mi'ye ; miś ; wa. *Who will go? I will go,* tu'we ye kta, mi'ye mde kta.—*I want,* waciŋ.
ice, *n.* Ca'ġa. *To break through the ice,* ca'ga naoksa.—*Running ice,* caȟhiyaya.
iceberg, *n.* Miniwaŋca caȟwita.
icebound, *a.* Caȟiyanica.
icecream, *n.* Asaŋpi acaȟyapi.
iced, *pa.* Acaȟyapi.
iceplow, *n.* Caȟ'icazopi.
icicle, *n.* Caȟ'oiŋ.
icy, *a.* Ca'ġa se ; sni.
I'd, *contr.* of *I would* or *I had.*
idea, *n.* Woawaciŋ.
ideal, *n.* Woiyaciŋ. *a.* Tawaciŋ en'tu ; ihaŋmnapi.
identical, *a.* He'eȟca.
identify, *vt.* Iyekiya ; yawicaka ; yuokoŋwaŋžidaŋ.
idiom, *n.* Iapi okaġe.
idiot, *n.* Ecawitkotkoka.
idle, *a.* 1. Ta'kudaŋ ecoŋ śni ; ku'ža : *an idle boy.* 2. Ta'kuśni ; ituya uŋ : *idle words.* *vt.* Yutakuniśni.

idleness, *n.* Wokuża.
idler, *n.* Tu'we ku'ża.
idly, *adv.* Kużiṭeya.
idol, *n.* 1. Wakaġapi ; wowakaŋ. 2. Ta'ku iyotaŋda : *he is the idol of his mother.*
idolater, *n.* Wakaġapi ohoda.
idolatry, *n.* Wakaġapi ohodapi.
idolize, *vt.* Wakaġapi yuha.
if, *conj.* 1. Kiŋhaŋ : *if you go.* 2. He'ciŋhaŋ : *she asked if you had come.* 3. Eṡta : *I will go, if it kills me.*
ignite, *vt.* Itkoŋya. *vi.* Itkoŋ.
ignoble, *a.* Ta'ku taŋiŋ ṡni.
ignominious, *a.* Waḣteṡni.
ignorance, *n.* Wasdonyeṡni.
ignorant, *a.* Ta'kuna sdonye ṡni.
ignore, *vt.* Aktaṡni.
ilium, *n.* Nisehu.
ill, *a.* Wayazaŋka : *he is ill.* 2. Ṡi'ca : *ill temper.* *adv.* Taŋyaŋṡni : *ill able.*
illbred, *a.* Taŋ'yaŋ icaḣyapiṡni.
illegal, *a.* Woope ohna ṡni.
illegitimate, *a.* Owotaŋnaṡni.
illfavored, *a.* Owaŋyagṡica.
illiberal, *a.* Waciŋtaŋkaṡni.
illicit, *a.* Woope kaṡeya.
illiteracy, *n.* Waoŋspepiṡni.
illiterate, *a.* Oŋspekeṡni.
illnatured, *a.* Tawaciŋṡica.
illness, *n.* Woyazaŋ.
ill-tempered, *a.* Tawaciŋṡica.
ill-treatment, *n.* Ṡicayakuwapi.
illuminate, *vt.* Iyoyamya.
illustrate, *vt.* Yutaŋiŋyaŋ oyaka.
illustrious, *a.* Okitaŋiŋ.
illwill, *n.* Tawaciŋṡica.
illy, *adv.* Taŋyaŋṡni.
im-, *pref.* Ṡni : *imperfect.*
I'm, *contr.* *I am.*
image, *n.* Wakaġapi ; okaġapi.
imaginable, *a.* Awaciŋpica.
imagination, *n.* Woawaciŋ.
imagine, *vt.* Awaciŋ ; keciŋ ; ituya keciŋ.
imbecile, *a.* Waṡ'akeṡni.
imbibe, *vt.* Icu ; yaḣepa.
imbue, *vt.* Awaciŋyą.
imitate, *vt.* Iyecenecoŋ ; uŋ'ca.
immaculate, *a.* Woṡapenica.
immaterial, *a.* Ṭo'kecaṡni.
immature, *a.* Ṡtuŋka.
immediately, *adv.* Waŋ'cahnana.
immemorial, *a.* Kiksuyapi i'tokam.
immense, *a.* Ni'na taŋ'ka.
immerse, *vt.* Okaspeya ; minin iyeya.
immigrant, *n.* Oyatetokeca.
imminent, *a.* Waape uŋ.
immodest, *a.* Iṡteceṡni.
immoral, *a.* Owotaŋnaṡni ; ṡi'ca.
immortal, *a.* Owihaŋkewanica.
immortality, *n.* Wicoŋṭewanica.
immovable, *a.* Yuṡkaŋpicaṡni.
immutable, *a.* Yutokecapicaṡni.
imp, *n.* Wakaŋṡica ciŋca.
impair, *vt.* Yuṡica.
impale, *vt.* Icam e'hde.
impart, *vt.* Ḳu ; okiyaka.
impartial, *a.* I'akidecen kuwa.
impassable, *a.* O'pta yepicaṡni.
impatient, *a.* Waciŋtaŋkaṡni.
impeach, *vt.* Iyaoŋpa.
impede, *vt.* Kaġiya.
impel, *vt.* Iyayeya.
impend, *vi.* Iyape haŋ.
impenetrable, *a.* En yepicaṡni.
impenitent, *a.* Iyopeiçiyeṡni.
imperative, *a.* Katiŋyaŋ.
imperceptible, *a.* Taŋiŋṡni.
imperfect, *a.* Yuṡtaŋpiṡni ; oŋṡpa waṡteṡni.
imperial, *a.* Itaŋcaŋḣca.
imperil, *vt.* Oṭoya.
imperious, *a.* Waŋkantu ; waḣaŋiçida.
imperishable, *a.* Ihaŋgyepicaṡni.
impertinent, *a.* Iyehaŋyaŋṡni ; oḣaŋwicaṡtaṡni.
impetuous, *a.* Wohitika ; oḣaŋko.
impinge, *vt.* Kaṡewaŋka.
impious, *a.* Waohodaṡni.
implant, *vt.* Ożu.
implement, *n.* Wi'kicaŋye.

implicate, *vt.* Aopekiya.
implicit, *a.* Ecaken ; a′taya.
implore, *vt.* Icekiya.
imply, *vt.* Ikoyake.
impolite, *a.* Oȟaŋeciŋŝniyaŋ.
impolitic, *a.* Wayupikeŝni.
import′, *vt.* Oyatetokeca etaŋhaŋ ahi.
im′port, *n.* 1. Ta′kuahipi. 2. To′kenkapi.
importance, *n.* Wotaŋka.
important, *a.* Ta′kuȟca.
importune, *vt.* Kitaŋyaŋ da.
impose, *vt.* Aehnaka ; ḳinkiya.
imposing, *a.* Wowinihaŋ.
imposition, *n.* 1. Ḳiŋkiya ; aokaȟya ḳiŋkiyapi. 2. Aehnakapi.
impossible, *a.* Okihipicaŝni.
impostor, *n.* Tu′we wicahnaŋ.
impotent, *a.* Wowaŝ′ake ni′ca.
impoverish, *vt.* Waȟpaniya.
impracticable, *a.* Ecoŋpicaŝni.
impregnable, *a.* Ohiyepicaŝni.
impress, *vt.* Apuspe ; awaciŋya.
impressible, *a.* Waŋ′kadaŋ.
impression, *n.* Apuspapi ; woawaciŋ.
impressive, *a.* Awaciŋwicaye.
imprint, *vt.* Owa ; sutaya ikoyake.
imprison, *vt.* Kaŝka.
improbable, *a.* Wicadapicaŝni.
impromptu, *a.* Piiçiyeŝni.
improper, *a.* He′cetuŝni.
improve, *vt.* Yuwaŝte ; taŋyaŋkiçuŋ. *vi.* Waŝteaya ; sam ecoŋ.
improvement, *n.* Yuwaŝtepi ; ta′ku oŋ yuwaŝtepi.
improvident, *a.* Wakpataŋŝni.
imprudent, *a.* Ksa′peŝni.
impudent, *a.* Iŝteceŝni.
impugn, *vt.* I′eniyeya.
impulse, *n.* Wocaŋtahde.
impulsive, *a.* Tawaciŋ oȟaŋko.
impunity, *n.* Woiyopeye co′daŋ.
impure, *a.* E′cedaŋŝni ; ŝi′ca.
impute, *vt.* Iyaoŋpa ; ki′ciyawa.
in, *prep.* En ; mahen ; ohna. *In the house,* timahen.—*In time,* iyehan.—*In turn,* i′ciyokiheya.
in-, *pref.* Ŝni.
inability, *n.* Okihiŝni.
inaccurate, *a.* He′cetuŝni.
inactive, *a.* Mdiheceŝni.
inadequate, *a.* Iyehantuŝni.
inadmissible, *a.* Icupicaŝni.
inadvertence, *n.* Awaciŋpiŝni.
inanimate, *a.* Niyaŝni.
inappropriate, *a.* Iyecetuŝni.
inasmuch, *adv.* Ehaŋtaŋhaŋŝ ; he′oŋ.
inattentive, *a.* Awaciŋŝni.
inaudible, *a.* Taŋiŋŝni.
inaugurate, *vt.* Ohnahde.
inborn, *a.* Yuhatoŋpi.
incapable, *a.* Okihiŝni.
incapacitate, *vt.* Okihiŝniya.
incarcerate, *vt.* Kaŝka.
incarnate, *a.* Wicaceȟpi.
incase, *vt.* Ohnaka.
incautious, *a.* Waawaciŋŝni.
incendiary, *n.* Tiideya.
incense, *n.* Wi′zinyapi.
incensed, *pa.* Caŋze.
incentive, *n.* Oŋ′ecoŋ.
inception, *n.* O′tokahe.
incessant, *a.* Ayuŝtaŋŝŋi.
incest, *n.* Takuya yu′za.
inch, *n.* Napsuoiyute.
incident, *n.* Woakipa ; ta′ku. *a.* Kicica ; ikoyake.
incidental, *a.* Ecaken ; wanu.
incite, *vt.* I′yopaŝtaka.
inclement, *a.* Kiȟaŋŝica.
incline, *vt.* En yeya. *vi.* Waciŋyuza ; patuża.
inclined, *pa.* Atakiŋyaŋhaŋ.
inclose, *vt.* Nataka ; aohomniya.
inclosure, *n.* Natakapi ; coŋkaŝke.
include, *vt.* O′pekiya ; en uŋ.
inclusive, *a.* Ko′ya ; o′pekiya.
incognito, *a.* Tu′we naiçiȟbe.
incoherent, *a.* I′cikoyakeŝni.
income, *n.* Wokamna.
incommode, *vt.* Naġiyeya.
incomparable, *a.* Iyececa wanica.

incompatible, *a.* Okiciwaŝteŝni.
incompetent, *a.* Waokihiŝni.
incomplete, *a.* Yuŝtaŋpiŝni.
incomprehensible, *a.* Okaȟniȟpicaŝni.
inconsiderate, *a.* Waawaciŋŝni.
inconsistent, *a.* O'citkoŋzeŝni.
inconvenient, *a.* Wowiyuŋyanpiŝica.
inconvertible, *a.* Yutokecapicaŝni.
incorrect, *a.* He'cetuŝni.
incorrigible, *a.* Yuwaŝtepicaŝni.
incorruptible, *a.* Yuŝinpicaŝni.
increase, *vt.* Yuota; yutaŋka. *vi.* O'ta a'ya; icaġa. *n.* Aicaġe.
incredible, *a.* Wicadapicaŝni.
increment, *n.* Aicaġe.
incubate, *vi.* Maŋ; akikna uŋ.
inculcate, *vt.* Iwahokoŋkiya.
incumbent, *a.* Ikoyaka.
incumbrance, *n.* Wokaġi.
incur, *vi.* Akipeiçiya; icu.
incurable, *a.* Asniyepicaŝni.
indebted, *a.* Icazo.
indecent, *a.* Wowiŝteca.
indecision, *n.* Tawaciŋsutaŝni.
indecisive, *a.* Yuŝtaŋŝni.
indecorous, *a.* Oŋspekeŝni.
indeed, *adv.* A'wicakehaŋ. *excl.* Eca; ehaŋ.
indefatigable, *a.* Ecoŋkap'iŋŝni.
indefensible, *a.* Anaẑiŋpicaŝni.
indefinite, *a.* To'ketutaŋiŋŝni.
indelible, *a.* Paẑuẑupicaŝni.
indelicate, *a.* Aŝiceca.
indemnity, *n.* Wokaẑuẑu.
indent, *vt.* Paosmaka.
indenture, *n.* Wowapi apuspapi.
independence, *n.* Ta'waiçiyapi.
independent, *a.* Ihduha; ihduhaiçida; ta'waiçiya.
indescribable, *a.* Oyagpicaŝni.
indestructible, *a.* Ihangyepicaŝni.
index, *n.* Ta'ku en uŋ oyaka.
Indian, *n.* Ikcewicaŝta.
indicate, *vt.* Pazo.
indication, *n.* Oŋ sdonyapi.
indicative, *a.* (*Gram.*) Woyaka.
indicator, *n.* Wapazo.
indict, *vt.* Iyaoŋpa.
indictment, *n.* Woiyaoŋpa.
indifferent, *a.* To'kecaŝni.
indigenous, *a.* Makoce ta'wa.
indigent, *a.* Waȟpanica.
indigestion, *n.* Won'owaŝteŝni.
indignant, *a.* Waȟtedaŝni.
indigo, *n.* Wi'toye; tosapa.
indirect, *a.* Katiŋyaŋŝni.
indirectly, *adv.* Aohomniyaŋ.
indiscernible, *a.* Sdonyepicaŝni.
indiscreet, *a.* Wi'yukcaŋŝni.
indiscriminate, *a.* To'kenciŋyaŋ.
indispensable, *a.* Co'daŋ uŋpicaŝni
indisposed, *a.* Ecetukeŝni.
indisputable, *a.* I'eniyeyepicaŝni.
indissoluble, *a.* Ŝdoyepicaŝni.
indistinct, *a.* Ohmuŋ; taŋiŋŝni.
indite, *vt.* E'ya; owa.
individual, *n.* Wicaŝta; tu'we. *a.* I'yatayedaŋ; wicitawa.
individually, *adv.* Iyohiya.
indivisible, *a.* Kiyuŝpepicaŝni.
indolent, *a.* Ku'ẑa; huŋ'keŝni.
indomitable, *a.* Kaoŋspepicaŝni.
indoor, *a.* Timahen.
indorse, *vt.* Caẑeakanowa.
indubitable, *a.* Ceṭuŋhdapicaŝni.
induce, *vt.* Ciŋkiya; iyutaŋyaŋ; ka'ġa.
inducement, *n.* Woiyutaŋye.
induct, *vt.* En au.
indulge, *vt.* Iyowiŋyaŋ.
industrial, *a.* Wokaġe.
industrious, *a.* Ta'ku ka'ġesa; mdiheca.
industry, *n.* Womdiheca.
indwell, *vt.* En oti.
inebriate, *n.* Witkos'a.
ineffective, *a.* Wawokihiŝni.
inelegant, *a.* Owaŝteŝni.
ineligible, *a.* Iyecetuŝni.
inequality, *n.* O'citkoŋzeŝni.
inert, *a.* Ŝkaŋŝkaŋ okihiŝni.
inestimable, *a.* Oyagpicaŝni; wakapeyawaŝte.
inevitable, *a.* Yuŝnapicaŝni.

inexcusable, *a.* Akaȟpepicaśni.
inexhaustible, *a.* Yusonpicaśni.
inexpedient, *a.* Iyehantuśni.
inexpressible, *a.* Oyagpicaśni.
infallible, *a.* To'hiŋni yuśnaśni.
infamous, *a.* Ni'na śi'ca.
infancy, *n.* Hokśiyopa ouŋ.
infant, *n.* Hokśiyopa.
infanticide, *n.* Hokśiyopa kte'pi.
infantry, *n.* Makaamani akicita.
infatuate, *vt.* Yuhnaśkiŋyaŋ.
infect, *vt.* Wośice kaȟtaŋ.
infectious, *a.* I'ciyaȟpaya.
infelicity, *n.* Wa'piśni.
infer, *vt.* Iyukcaŋ.
inferior, *a.* Hukuya ; ku'ya uŋ.
infernal, *a.* Wakaŋśica.
infest, *vt.* Naġiyeya ; kuwa.
infidel, *n.* Wicadaśni.
infinite, *a.* Woptecaśni ; owihaŋkewanica.
infinitive, *a.* Ecaken.
infirm, *a.* Huŋ'keśni ; śiȟtiŋ.
infirmity, *n.* Woyazaŋ.
inflame, *vt.* Ideya.
inflammatory, *a.* Waideya.
inflate, *vt.* Yupoġaŋ.
inflexible, *a.* Yutokecapicaśni.
inflict, *vt.* Ecakicoŋ ; iyopeya.
influence, *vt.* Iyutaŋye ; ecoŋkiya. *n.* Woiyutaŋye ; wowaś'ake.
influential, *n.* Oie naȟoŋpi.
influenza, *n.* I'ciyaza hoȟpapi.
influx, *n.* Oahi ; en u.
inform, *vt.* Okiyaka ; sdonyekiya.
informal, *a.* Ikceka.
informally, *adv.* Ikceya.
informant, *n.* Tu'we wokiyake.
information, *n.* Wosdonye.
informed, *pa.* Wasdonya.
informer, *n.* Tu'we okiyaka.
infraction, *n.* Kicaksapi.
infringe, *vt.* Awaȟtani.
infuse, *vt.* En okaśtaŋ ; ożuya.
ingenious, *a.* Wayupika.
ingraft, *vt.* En o'śtaŋ.
ingratitude, *n.* Pidapiśni.
ingredient, *n.* Oŋ ka'ġapi.
ingress, *n.* Eŋ ya.
inhabit, *vt.* En ti.
inhabitant, *n.* En ti'pi.
inhale, *vt.* Yahota.
inhere, *vi.* Ikoyaka.
inherit, *vt.* Huŋkake aiȟpeya.
inhospitable, *a.* Wonwicayeśni.
inhuman, *a.* Wicaśta iyececeśni
inimical, *a.* To'kaye.
inimitable, *a.* Wakapa.
iniquity, *n.* Woaȟtani.
initial, *a.* Otokahe.
initiate, *vt.* Tokaecoŋkiya.
inject, *vt.* Mahen iyeya.
injudicious, *a.* Wi'yukcaŋśni.
injure, *vt.* Yuśica.
injurious, *a.* Wayuśica.
injustice, *n.* Woowotaŋnaśni.
ink, *n.* Minisapa.
inkling, *n.* Wowakta.
inkstand, *n.* Minisapa ożuha.
inland, *a.* Ḣeyata.
inlay, *vt.* Okookaśtaŋ.
inlet, *n.* Okaȟmiŋ ; oȟdoka.
inmate, *n.* En ti.
inmost, *a.* Mahentuȟca.
inn, *n.* Owotetipi.
innate, *a.* Ecahececa.
inner, *a.* Mahentu.
innocence, *n.* Woaȟtanicodaŋ.
innocent, *a.* Waȟtaniśni ; wayu śiceśni.
innovation, *n.* Ituwayutokecapi.
innumerable, *a.* Yawapicaśni.
inoculate, *vt.* O'śtaŋ ; paȟdoka.
inoffensive, *a.* Wayuśiceśni.
inordinate, *a.* Aokaġeca.
inorganic, *a.* Okaȟcodaŋ.
inquest, *n.* Wawiwaŋȟomniciye.
inquire, *vt.* & *vi.* Iwaŋġa ; akita.
inquiring, *pa.* Wawiwaŋġa.
inquisitive, *a.* Wasdonyewaciŋ.
inroad, *n.* Caŋku.
insane, *a.* Waciŋhnuni.
insatiable, *a.* I'mnaśni.
inscribe, *vt.* Sutaya owa.
inscription, *n.* Owapi.
inscrutable, *a.* Okaȟniȟpicaśni.

insect, *n.* Watutka.
insecure, *a.* Okope.
insensible, *a.* Kiksuyeśni; taŋiŋśni.
insensibly, *adv.* Taŋiŋśniyaŋ.
inseparable, *a.* Yukinukaŋpicaśni.
insert, *vt.* En'iyeya; ośtaŋ.
inside, *prep.* Mahen. *a.* Mahentu. *n.* Mahentu; śupe.
insidious, *a.* Waape.
insight, *n.* Mahenwakita.
insignia, *n.* Wa'petokeca.
insignificant, *a.* Ta'kuśni.
insincere, *a.* Wicakeśni.
insinuate, *vt.* Naħmaŋ en i; ataŋiŋśnieya.
insipid, *a.* Takumnaśni.
insist, *vi.* Kitaŋ.
insolent, *a.* Taŋ'kaiçida.
insoluble, *a.* Ḣpaŋyaŋ picaśni.
insolvent, *a.* Każużu okihiśni.
insomuch, *adv.* Hehaŋyaŋ
inspect, *vt.* Amdeza.
inspector, *n.* Wa'mdeza.
inspiration, *n.* Woniya; ecoŋkiya.
inspire, *vt.* Oniya ku. *vi.* Niya.
instability, *n.* Tawaciŋ sutaśni.
install, *vt.* Sutaya hde.
instance, *n.* Woecoŋ; he'ceca.
instant, *a.* Waŋ'cahna; dehantu. *n.* Wowasaġhde; onażiŋ.
instantly, *adv.* Waŋ'cahnana; kitaŋyaŋ.
instead of, *prep.* E'ekiya.
instep, *n.* Siitakaha.
instigate, *vt.* Ecoŋkiya.
instill, *vt.* Oŋspekiya.
instinct, *n.* Iyeciŋkaawaciŋpi. *a.* Aiçiciya.
instinctively, *adv.* Iyeciŋka.
institute, *vt.* Hde; ka'ġa. *n.* Ta'ku hde'pi; woope; wooŋspetipi.
instruct, *vt.* Oŋspekiya.
instruction, *n.* Wooŋspe; woope; to'ken ecoŋśipi.
instructive, *a.* Oŋ oŋspepi wa'śte.
instructor, *n.* Waoŋspekiya.
instrument, *n.* Icuwa; wowapi.
instrumental, *a.* Oŋ'ecoŋpi. *Instrumental music,* caŋ'dowaŋkiyapi.
insubordinate, *a.* Wanaħoŋśni.
insufferable, *a.* Otawaṭeśica.
insufficient, *a.* Iyenakecaśni.
insulate, *vt.* Iśnaehde.
insult, *vt.* Ośtehda. *Insult a woman,* wikiśde.
insuperable, *a.* Okiħipicaśni.
insupportable, *a.* Tawaṭenyepicaśni.
insurance, *n.* Idekażużupi.
insure, *vt.* Idekażużu.
insurgent, *n.* Wakipażiŋ.
insurmountable, *a.* Adipicaśni.
insurrection, *n.* Wokipażiŋ.
intact, *a.* Zani; he'cehna.
intangible, *a.* Yutaŋpicaśni.
integer, *n.* A'taya.
integrity, *n.* Wozani.
intellect, *n.* Wasdonye; nasu.
intellectual, *a.* Waawaciŋ.
intelligence, *n.* Wasdonyapi; wosdonye.
intelligent, *a.* Wasdonya.
intemperance, *n.* Iyatahdeiçiyapi; witkopi.
intend, *vt.* Waciŋyuza; awaciŋ.
intense, *a.* To'kenokihi; wohitika.
intensely, *adv.* Ni'na.
intent, *n.* Tawaciŋ.
intention, *n.* Waciŋyuza.
intentional, *a.* Ciŋ'ecoŋpi.
intently, *adv.* Awaciŋħca.
inter', *vt.* Ḣa; hna'ka.
in'ter-, *pref.* Otahedaŋ.
intercede, *vt.* Iciya.
intercept, *vt.* Otahenaicu.
intercession, *n.* Icekiyapi.
interchange, *vt.* Kiciçu.
intercourse, *n.* Ki'ciśkaŋpi.
interdict, *vt.* Teħiŋda.
interest, *vt.* Awaciŋya; en e'waciŋ. *n.* Waawaciŋpi; iyoważapi; ma'zaska aicaġe; aicaġe; ta'wayapi.

interesting, *pa.* Onaḣoŋwaŝte; awaciŋpiwaŝte.
interfere, *vi.* En iyeiçiya; kaġiya.
interference, *n.* Wokaġi.
interim, *n.* Oko; iyozipi.
interior, *a.* Mahentu.
interject, *vt.* Maheniyeya.
interjection, *n.* Ihnuhaŋeyapi.
interline, *vt.* Otahedaŋowa.
intermarry, *vi.* Kici kiciyuza.
intermeddle, *vi.* Iyowaźaŝniŝkaŋ.
interment, *n.* Wicahnakapi.
intermingle, *vi.* Icahiya uŋ.
intermission, *n.* Oko.
intermit, *vt.* Ci'stiyedaŋ ecoŋŝni.
internal, *a.* Mahentaŋhaŋ.
international, *a.* Oyate wi'ciyotahedaŋ.
interpolate, *vt.* Iapi akaġa.
interpose, *vt.* En iyeya; en hiyuiçiya.
interpret, *vt.* Ieskaoyaka.
interpreter, *n.* Ieska.
interrogate, *vt.* Wi'waŋġa.
interrupt, *vt.* Kaġiya; anapta.
intersect, *vt.* I'cipaweġa.
intersperse, *vt.* Enana ehde.
intertwine, *vt.* Icahi yuwi.
interval, *n.* Oko; otahedaŋ.
intervene, *vi.* Otahedaŋ uŋ.
interview, *vt.* Wi'waŋġa.
intestate, *a.* Woyuha oŋ tak eyeŝni.
intestine, *a.* Mahentu.
intimate, *a.* Kici uŋ sa; ikiyena; mahentu. *vt.* Oŋŝpa yataŋiŋ.
intimidate, *vt.* Yuŝiŋyeya.
into, *prep.* Mahen; en.
intolerable, *a.* Tawaţenyepicaŝni.
intolerant, *a.* Iyowiŋyeŝni.
intoxicate, *vt.* Witkoya.
intoxicated, *a.* Witko.
intractable, *a.* Kuwapicaŝni.
intransitive, *a.* Aiḣpeyapiŝni.
intransitu, *a.* Tokŝupi en.
intrepid, *a.* Itoŋpeŝni.
intricate, *a.* Oŝkiŝke.
intrigue, *n.* Naḣmaŋ ŝkaŋ'pi.
intrinsic, *a.* A'tayedaŋ.
introduce, *vt.* En iyeya; en ahi. 2. Tuweoyaka.
introductory, *a.* Otokahe.
intrude, *vt.* Kitaŋŝkaŋ; iyecetuŝni en i.
intuition, *n.* Ecakensdonyapi.
inundate, *vt.* Amnitaŋ.
inure, *vt.* Ecewaktaya. *vi.* Ki'cihaŋ.
invade, *vi.* En i; takpei.
in'valid, *a.* Ŝiḣtiŋ.
inval'id, *a.* Ta'kuŝni.
invalidate, *vt.* Ta'kuŝniya.
invaluable, *a.* Waokiyeḣca; ni'na waŝte.
invariable, *a.* He'cetuwaŋźica.
invariably, *adv.* O'hiŋni.
invasion, *n.* Wotakpe; eni'pi.
invective, *n.* Woyaŝiḣtiŋ.
inveigh, *vi.* En ohoyeya.
invent, *vt.* Ka'ġa; tokakaġa.
inventive, *a.* Okaḣwayupika.
inventor, *n.* Tokawoḣdoka.
in'ventory, *n.* Woyuhaowapi.
inverse, *a.* Uŋmaŋ eciyataŋhaŋ.
invest, *vt.* En e'hnaka; kiçuŋ; akaḣpa; uŋkiya.
investigate, *vt.* To'ketu ode.
inveterate, *a.* Ayuŝtaŋ okihiŝni.
invidious, *a.* Waḣteŝni.
invigorate, *vt.* Waŝ'agya.
invincible, *a.* Ohiyepicaŝni.
invisible, *a.* Waŋyagpicaŝni.
invitation, *n.* Kicopi.
invite, *vt.* Kico; iyutaŋye.
invoice, *n.* Woyuhaowapi.
invoke, *vt.* Icekiya.
involuntary, *a.* Awaciŋŝni.
involve, *vt.* Aopekiya.
invulnerable, *a.* O'picaŝni.
inward, *a.* & *adv.* Mahentu.
iodine, *n.* Iuŋpizi.
iota, *n.* Ci'stiŋna.
Iowa, *np.* Ayuḣba.
ire, *n.* Wocaŋze.
Irish, *n.* Sagdaŝaiaŝica.
irksome, *a.* Wawicatuka.

iron, *n.* Ma'za ; mazasapa ; mazipamdaye. *a.* Ma'za iyececa ; suta. *vt.* Ma'za ikoyaka ; ma'za okataŋ.
ironical, *a.* I'ȟad eyapi.
irrational, *a.* Waciŋksapeśni.
irreconcilable, *a.* Yuwaśtepicaśni.
irregular, *a.* Woopeohnaśni ; katiŋyaŋśni.
irrelevant, *a.* A'etoptaśni.
irreligious, *a.* Ta'ku Wakaŋ ohodaśni.
irreparable, *a.* Piyepicaśni.
irresistible, *a.* I'tkokipepicaśni.
irresolute, *a.* Tawaciŋhahadaŋ.
irreverent, *a.* Waohodaśni.
irrigate, *vt.* Wożupi amnitaŋya.
irritable, *a.* Waciŋhiŋyaŋza.
irritate, *a.* Yucaŋze ; yazaŋya.
irruption, *n.* Ahinaŋpapi.
is, am, are, be, *vi.* 1. Uŋ ; yaŋka : *he is well.* 2. E'e : *this is the man.* 3. He'ca : *this is a horse.*
island, isle, *n.* Wi'ta.
islander, *n.* Witoti.
isolate, *vt.* Iśnana uŋkiya.
issue, *vt.* Wicaķu ; pamni : *issue clothing.* *vi.* U̇ ; hinaŋpa ; owihaŋkeya. *n.* Hiyu ; uya ; ta'ku hiyu ; ciŋca ; owihaŋke.
isthmus, *n.* Makoce skiskita.
it, *pro.* He. *It is I,* he miye. (*Generally unexpressed in Dakota.*) *It snows,* wapa.—*It is too bad,* ni'na śicaya.
Italic (*letters*), *a.* Oowa atakiŋyaŋ.
itch, *n.* Yaśpuyapi.
itchy, *a.* Yaśpuya.
item, *n.* Ptenyena oyakapi ; oiyawa.
itemize, *vt.* Kpaŋyena oyaka.
itinerate, *vi.* Iyaza omani.
its, *pron. pos.* He ta'wa.
itself, *pron.* Iyeȟca.
ivory, *n.* Pasuhaŋska hi.
ivy, *n.* Wi'yuwi ecato.

J

jab, *vt.* Capa ; capaiyeya.
jabber, *vt.* Oŋspekeśni ia.
jack, *n.* Kośka ; wica ; śoŋ'śoŋmdoka ; ma'zaicuwa ; wi'yokihedaŋ.
jackall, *n.* Śuŋgmanitu.
jackass, *n.* Śoŋ'śoŋmdoka.
jacket, *n.* Okdeoŋżiŋca
jack-knife, *n.* Mi'yukśiżapi.
jaded, *pa.* Watuka.
jag, *n.* Ḣci ; woķiŋ.
jagged, *a.* Ḣci'ḣci ; ḣe'ḣe.
jail, *n.* Owicakaśke.
jailbird, *n.* Tu'we kaśkapi.
jailer, *n.* Wokaśke awaŋyake.
jam, *vt.* Wi'tayaiyeya ; paskica ; *vi.* Kataiheya. *n.* O'cikaŋśni ; waskuyeca yużapi.
jamb, *n.* Tiyopaożuha.
jangle, *n.* Akinicapi ; yuwiwi.
janitor, *n.* Tiyopaawaŋyake.
January, *n.* Witeȟi.
jar, *vt.* Yuhuhuza. *n.* Wocaŋcaŋ ; makaceġa.
jargon, *n.* Iapiȟcaśni.
jaunt, *n.* Wi'kcekceomanipi.
javelin, *n.* Wahukezadaŋ.
jaw, *n.* Cehupa. *vt.* Aia.
jay, *n.* Zitkato.
jealous, *a.* Nawizi.
jealousy, *n.* Wowinawizi.
jeer, *vt.* Iḣa.
Jehovah, *np.* Jehowa.
jehu, *n.* Śuŋgkaȟapaohitika.
jelly, *n.* Nini.
jeopardize, *vt.* Okokipe ka'ġa.
jeopardy, *n.* Wokokipe.
jerk, *vt.* Yukabicu ; kaȟoiyeya. *Jerked meat,* pa'pa.
jest, *vi.* I'ȟad eya.

jester, *n.* Wawiħaka.
jet, *n.* Obosdi ; iŋ'yaŋsapa.
Jew, *np.* Judawicaśta. *v.* Yahukuya.
jewel, *n.* Iŋ'yaŋteħika ; oiŋ.
jibe, *vi.* O'citkoŋza.
jig, *n.* Wowaci oħaŋko.
jigjog, *adv.* Kaħoħo.
jill, *n.* Wikośkadaŋ.
jilt, *vt.* Okiya hna'yaŋ.
jingle, *vt.* Yusna. *vi.* Sna'sna.
job, *vt.* Opiye ecehna wi'yopeya. *n.* Woecoŋ.
jockey, *n.* Śuŋgkuwawicaśa. *vt.* Hna'yaŋ.
jocose, *a.* Wowiħa.
jocular, *a.* Wawihaha.
jog, *vt.* Panini. *vi.* Nacamya.
join, *vt.* 1. Yuokoŋwaŋżidaŋ ; i'cikoyagya : *join fortunes; join the ends.* 2. O'pa ; kici ya : *I will join you.* 3. Kici ecoŋ : *join battle.* *vi.* 1. I'ciyokihe uŋ : *the farms join.* 3. O'koŋwaŋżidaŋ uŋ : *let us join in our work.* *a.* Pta'ya.
joint, *n.* O'kihe ; obaśpe. *Put out of joint*, papśuŋ.
jointed, *a.* O'kihe yukaŋ.
jointly, *adv.* Wi'taya.
joist, *n.* Owaŋka cutuhu.
joke, *vt.* I'ħadeciya. *vi.* I'ħadeya. *n.* Wowiħa ; wowiħa iapi.
jollification, *n.* Wihahakiciyapi.
jolly, *a.* Wi'haha ; wowiħa.
jolt, *vt.* Kahuhuza.
jostle, *vt.* Panini ; yucaŋcaŋ.
jot, *n.* Wokpe ; ci'stiyedaŋ. *vt.* Ptenyedaŋ owa.
journal, *n.* Aŋpetuiyohi owapi ; wotaŋiŋ wowapi ; wicoħaŋ owapi.
journalist, *n.* Wotaŋiŋka'ġa.
journey, *n.* Oicimani. *vi.* I'cimani ya.
journeyman, *n.* Wowaśi ecoŋomani.
jovial, *a.* Wi'yuśkiŋ ; wi'haha.
jowl, *n.* Cehupa.
joy, *n.* Wowiyuśkiŋ.
joyful, *a.* Wi'yuśkiŋ.
joyfully, *adv.* Wi'yuśkiŋyaŋ.
joyless, *a.* Wowiyuśkiŋ co'daŋ.
joyous, *a.* Wi'yuśkiŋ.
jubilant, *a.* Wi'yuśkiŋ paŋ'paŋ.
jubilee, *n.* Wowiyuśkiŋ aŋpetu.
judge, *n.* Wayaco ; wayasu. *vt.* Yaco ; *Y.* & *T.* yasu ; yukcaŋ ; iyukcaŋ.
judgment, *n.* Woyaco ; woyasu ; wowiyukcaŋ ; wi'yukcaŋpi.
judicatory, *n.* Wi'yukcaŋ omniciye.
judicature, *n.* Wi'yukcaŋpi.
judicial, *a.* Wi'yukcaŋ.
judicious, *a.* Wowiyukcaŋ ohna ; waśte.
jug, *n.* Makażaŋżaŋ.
juggle, *vt.* Hna'yaŋ. *vi.* Wakaŋkaŋyaŋśkaŋ.
juggler, *n.* Wapiya.
jugular, *a.* Tahu.
juice, *n.* Haŋpi ; mini.
juicy, *a.* Haŋpi o'ta.
July, *n.* Mdokecokawi ; caŋpaśawi.
jumble, *vt.* To'kenciŋyaŋ eħpeya. *n.* To'ketutaŋiŋśni.
jump, *vt.* Ipsica ; waŋkankan iyeya ; ipsinkiya. *n.* Oipsica. *Jump over*, apsica.
junction, *n.* I'ciyoħpaya ; mdo'te.
juncture, *n.* Woakipa.
June, *n.* Ważuśtecaśawi.
jungle, *n.* Oteħi ; taśkożu.
junior, *a.* Hakakta ; o'kihe.
Jupiter, *n.* Wakiŋyaŋ.
jurisdiction, *n.* Woawaŋyake.
jurist, *n.* Waaiawicaśa.
juror, *n.* Wi'yukcaŋkiyapi.
jury, *n.* Wi'yukcaŋ optaye.
just, *a.* Owotaŋna ; woope yuha : *a just man.* *adv.* 1. Iyehantudaŋ ; hehantudaŋ ħca : *just noon.* 2. Ki'taŋna : *I can just see.* 3. Ħca : *just alike; just*

now. 4. He'e ȟca : *just to hurt me.*
justice, *n.* Woowotaŋna ; wowicake.
justification, *n.* Yuowotaŋnapi.
justify, *vt.* Yuowotaŋna.
justly, *adv.* Owotaŋna.
justness, *n.* Woowotaŋna.
jut, *vi.* Pażohiyu.
juvenile, *n.* Wakaŋheża.

K

Kansas, *n.* Kaŋ'ze ; Kahaŋze.
keel, *n.* Wa'ta sicu.
keen, *a.* 1. Pe : *a keen edge ; a keen breeze.* 2. Waciŋksapa : *a keen lawyer.*
keenly, *adv.* Ni'na.
keep, *vt.* Yuha ; awaŋyaka. *vi.* Uŋ ; yaŋka. *Keep at it,* ayuśtaŋ śni śkaŋ.—*Keep his bed,* owaŋka en uŋ.—*Keep cool,* mdesya ihduha.—*Keep company,* o'haŋhdeya.—*Keep down,* kun yu'za.—*Keep a feast,* omniciye ecoŋ.—*Keep for,* ki'ciyuha.—*Keep from,* ȟeyam yuha.—*Keep on,* saŋ'pa ecoŋ.—*Keep out of,* etaŋhaŋ ihduha.—*Keep still,* inina un ; owaŋżi uŋ.—*Keep the road,* caŋku ohna ya.—*Keep up,* iyehan uŋ.—*Keep warm,* cosya uŋ.—*Keep well,* zaniyaŋ uŋ.
keeper, *n.* Wa'waŋyake.
keeping, *n.* Woawaŋyake ; awaŋyake ; okiciwaśte.
keepsake, *n.* Oŋ kiksuyapi.
ken, *vt.* Sdonya.
kennel, *n.* Śuŋ'katipi.
kept, *imp.* of KEEP.
kernel, *n.* Co ; su.
kerosene, *n.* Petiżaŋżaŋ wi'hdi.
kettle, *n.* Ce'ġa.
key, *n.* 1. Iyuȟdoka ; *Y.* iyuśdoka ; *T.* iyuȟloka. 2. Iyuhomni : *watch-key.* 3. Ho oiyahe.
keyhole, *n.* Iyuśdoke oȟdoka.
key-note, *n.* Hohute.
keystone, *n.* Iŋ'yaŋawakeyapiitaŋcaŋ.
kick, *vt.* Naȟtaka ; nabagbaka. *Kick up a fuss,* wośkiśke ka'ġa. *n.* Wonaȟtake.
kid, *n.* Tatokadaŋciŋca; tatokaha.
kidnap, *vt.* Wicaśta manoŋ.
kidney, *n.* Pakśiŋ ; *Y.* ażuŋtka.
kill, *vt.* Kte ; ţeya ; eȟpeya.
killer, *n.* Wicakte.
kiln, *n.* Iŋ'yaŋ acetipi.
kin, *n.* Wotakuye.
kind, *a.* Waoŋśida ; waśte. *Kind to,* oŋ'śida. *n.* Ocaże ; obe.
kindle, *vt.* Ideya ; ka'ġa. *vi.* Ide.
kindling, *n.* Oŋ ideyapi.
kindly, *adv.* Waoŋśidaya ; caŋtewaśteya.
kindness, *n.* Wowaoŋśida.
kindred, *a.* & *n.* Takukiciyapi.
kine, *n.* Ptewiye.
king, *n.* Wicaśtayatapi.
kingdom, *n.* Wokicoŋze.
kingfisher, *n.* Kusdeca.
kink, *n.* Oyuȟa. *vt.* Yuȟaȟa.
kinky, *a.* Yumnimniża.
kinnikinic, *n.* Caŋśaśa.
kinsfolk, *n.* Wotakuye.
Kiowa, *n.* Wi'tapaha.
kip, *n.* Pteżicanaha.
kiss, *vt.* I'itputaka.
kissing, *n.* I'itputakapi.
kit, *n.* Kokana ; inmu ciŋca.
kitchen, *n.* Owohetipi.
kite, *n.* Miniȟuhakiyekiyapi ; upiżate taŋ'ka.
kitten, *n.* Inmuśuŋkana.
kitty, *n.* Inmuśuŋka cincana.
knack, *n.* Wowayupika.
knapsack, *n.* Wapapśuŋka.
knave, *n.* Wicahnayesa.

knead, *vt.* Paṭiŋza.
knee, *n.* Hupahu; śiyoto; *Y.* & *T.* caŋkpe.
kneel, knelt, *vt.* Caŋpeśkamakahde inażiŋ.
knee-pan, *n* Takaŋġi. *T.* Caŋkpehu.
knell, *n.* Paŋ'paŋpi.
knew, *imp.* of KNOW.
knicknack, *n.* Ta'kuśni.
knife, *n.* Isaŋ. *Y.* Mi'na. *T.* Mi'la. *Butcher-knife*, isaŋpesto; mi'napesto.—*Case-knife*, isaŋmdaska; mipiśda.—*Pocket-knife*, isaŋyukatiŋpi; miyukśiżapi.
knight, *n.* Wowaśte itaŋcaŋ.
knit, *vt.* Kazoŋta; ikoyaka; yuśki.
knives, *n. pl.* of KNIFE.
knob, *n.* Pśuŋka.
knock, *vt.* Apa: *knock him on the head.* 2. Kabubu; katoto: *knock at the door.* *Knock a thing away*, kakamiyeya. — *Knock down*, kawaŋka; kun eḣpeya. —*Knock a hole*, kaḣdoka.— *Knock off*, kaha iyeya.—*Knock out the eye*, iśta kakpa.—*Knock together*, i'ciyapa.—*Knock under*, kahukun iyeya.—*Knock up*, kawaŋkan iyeya. *n.* Katotopi; oape.
knoll, *n.* Pażodaŋ; paha.
knot, *n.* 1. Okaśke: *tie a knot.* *A bow-knot*, okaśke yusdutapi. 2. Adetka; osnaze: *the board was full of knots.*
knotty, *a.* Adetka o'ta; yuwi; iyukcaŋteḣika.
know, knew, *vt.* 1. Sdonya: *do you know the road.* 2. Oŋspe: *I know my lesson.* 3. Iyekiya: *I don't know you.*
knowledge, *n.* Wosdonye.
known, *pp.* of KNOW.
knuckle, *n.* Napakaha. *vi.* Patuś uŋ.
kodak, *n.* Oŋ'iteicupiciḳa.
Kootenai, *np.* Śku'tani.
Koran, *np.* Mohammed Wowapiwakaŋ.
Kwapas, *np.* Pe'śa.

L

label, *n.* Ḳaŋsu; wowasagkde.
labor, *vi.* Ḣtani. *n.* Woḣtani.
laboratory, *n.* Ośkiŋciyetipi.
labored, *a.* Oŋ ni'na ḣtanipi.
laborer, *n.* Tu'we ḣtani; wowaśi.
laborious, *a.* Ecoŋpi teḣike; tke; ni'na śkaŋ.
lace, *n.* Śinaapaḣdate ġaŋġaŋ. *vt.* Iyakaśka; yuwi.
lacerate, *vt.* Bahoŋhoŋ.
lack, *vt.* Ni'ca; iyokpaniuŋ; icakiża; iyohiśni.
laconic, *a.* Coya; pte'cena.
lacrimal, *a.* Iśtamni.
lacrosse, *n.* Takapsicapi.
lad, *n.* Kośkana.
ladder, *n.* Caŋiyadipi. *Y.* Caŋnakde.
lade, *vt.* Ḳiŋkiya; ożudaŋya. *Laden*, ożudaŋ; waḳiŋ.
ladle, *n.* Iyokapṭe.
lady, ladies, *n.* Wiŋ'yaŋ; wiŋ'yaŋ waśte.
lady's slipper, *n.* Pi'śkotahaŋpe.
lag, *vi.* He'ktauŋ; ḣaŋhi.
laggard, *n.* Ḥuŋ'keśni.
lagoon, *n.* Minikazedaŋ.
laid, *pp.* of LAY.
lair, *n.* Wamaniti.
lake, *n.* Mde.
lamb, *n.* Ta'ḣcaska ciŋca.

lame, *a.* Ḣuŝte ; ecetuŝni. *vt.* Yuecetuŝni.
lamely, *adv.* Oŋ'ŝiya.
lament, *vt.* Aceya. *vi.* Ce'ya.
lamentable, *a.* Oiyokiŝica.
lamp, *n.* Petiżaŋżaŋ.
lampblack, *n.* Wi'sapa ; ceḣnaġi.
lance, *n.* Wahukeza. *vt.* Capa.
lancet, *n.* Kaŋicakpe.
land, *n.* Maka ; makoce. *Moist land,* maka spa'ya.—*View the land,* makoce waŋyaka. *vt.* Ḣeteżu. *vi.* Ihuni ; hihuni.
landing, *n.* Oahuni ; hihuni.
landlady, *n.* Wiŋ'yaŋ tiyuha.
landlord, *n.* Owotetipiyuha.
landmark, *n.* Wowasagḣde.
land-office, *n.* Makoce owiyopeye.
landscape, *n.* Makoce owaŋyake.
landslide, *n.* Makoce kaoksa.
landwarrant, *n.* Makoce oŋ icupi.
lane, *n.* Caŋkuacaŋkaŝkapi.
language, *n.* Iapi.
languid, *a.* Aḣtate ; waecoŋkapiŋ.
languish, *vi.* Ḣaŋye.
languor, *n.* Woecoŋkapiŋ.
lank, *a.* Sta'ka ; tamaheca.
lantern, *n.* Taŋkanpetiżaŋżaŋ.
lap, *n.* Ŝiyoto ; caŋkpe. *vt.* I'takihna iyeya ; sdi'pa.
lap-dog, *n.* Ŝiyoto ŝuŋ'ka.
lapse, *vi.* Hiyaya ; ihuŋni.
larboard, *n.* Wa'tacatkata.
larceny, *n.* Womanoŋ *Grand larceny,* womanoŋ taŋ'ka.
lard, *n.* Kukuŝe ihdi.
large, *a.* Taŋ'ka ; woptecaŝni. *So large,* hiŋ'skotaŋka.
largely, *adv.* Taŋ'kaya.
lariat, *n.* Wi'kaŋ ikceka.
lark, *n.* Ŝdo'ŝdona.
larva, *n.* Wamduŝkana.
lascivious, *a.* Eciŋŝniyaŋ.
lash, *n.* Icapsiŋteikaŋ ; apapi. *vt.* Apa ; kapsiŋpsiŋta.
lass, *n.* Wikoŝka.
lasso, *vt.* Wi'kaŋkaḣ'ooyuspa. *n.* Wi'kaŋ.
last, *a.* & *adv.* Ehake : *the last cent.* Hekta : *last Summer. At last,* owihaŋke ekta ; uŋ'haŋketa. *vi.* Ecen uŋ ; te'han uŋ. *n.* Caŋ'siha.
lastly, *adv.* Ehake.
lasting, *pa.* Te'han uŋ.
latch, *n.* Inatake.
late, *adv.* Te'han. *a.* 1. Te'han hi ŝni : *a late Spring.* 2. Aŝkatudaŋ : *late news.* 3. Te'hantu ; ihaŋketa : *he was late coming. Of late,* aŝkatudaŋ.
lately, *adv.* Aŝkatudaŋ. *Y.* Decana.
latent, *a.* Taŋiŋŝni uŋ.
later, *a.* Iyohakam.
lateral, *a.* Hdakiŋyaŋ.
latest, *a.* Ehake.
lath, *n.* Caŋsbuna.
lathe, *n.* Yuhomni pażipapi.
lather, *n.* Wipażaża taġe.
latitude, *n.* Ohdakiŋyaŋ.
latterly, *adv.* Aŝkatudaŋ.
laud, *vt.* Yataŋ ; yataŋka.
laudable, *a.* Yawaŝtepica.
laudanum, *n.* Iŝtiŋma peżuta ŝbu.
laudatory, *a.* Wayataŋpi.
laugh, *vi.* Iḣa. *n.* Iḣapi.
laughable, *a.* Wowiḣa.
laughter, *n.* Iḣapi.
launch, *vt.* Mininiyeya ; iyayeya. *n.* Wa'tamdaska.
laundress, *n.* Wiŋ'yaŋ wożaża.
laundry, *n.* Wożażatipi.
lava, *n.* Iŋ'yaŋ ŝdo.
lavatory, *n.* Owożaża.
laver, *n.* Ohna wożażapi.
lavish, *a.* O'tayusota ; wayusota.
law, *n.* Woope ; wowasukiye ; woecoŋ ; wa'kiyapi.
lawful, *a.* Woopeohna ; he'cetu.
lawgiver, *n.* Woopekaġa.
lawless, *a.* Woope ahopeŝni.
lawn, *n.* Ticahda peżito ; miniḣuha.
lawsuit, *n.* Woope ekta kuwapi.
lawyer, *n.* Waaiawicaŝta.

lax, *a.* Ṭiŋ'ześni; sutaśni.
laxly, *adv.* To'kenciŋyaŋ.
lay, *vt.* 1. E'hnaka: *lay it down.* —2. Okada: *lay eggs.* —3. Eḣpeya: *lay waste the country.* —4. Yuwiyeya: *lay plans.*— 5. Kun iyeya: *lay the storm. Lay away,* kihnaka.—*Lay hold,* oyuspa. *imp* of LIE, *which see. n.* Odowaŋ; makomdaye. *a.* Itaŋcaŋ śni.
layer, *n.* Oehnake; okaġe.
layman, *n.* Itaŋcaŋśni.
lazily, *adv.* Iwahnana.
laziness, *n.* Wicokuża.
lazy, *a.* Ku'ża; huŋ'keśni; ecoŋkapin.
leach, *vt.* Ske'pa.
lead, *n.* Ma'zasu.
lead, led, *vt.* A'ya; yus a'ya: *lead your sister. vi.* 1. Tokaheya ya: *you lead.* 2 Iyahde: *leads to the river. n.* O'tokahe; oyaŋke tokaheya.
leader, *n.* Wotokahaŋ; itaŋcaŋ.
leading, *pa.* Tokahaŋ.
leaf, leaves, *n.* Ape; caŋwapa. *vi.* Ape uya.
leafless, *a.* Ape wanica.
leafy, *a.* Ape o'ta.
league, *n.* 1. Wodakota; okodakiciye. 2. Makaiyutapi ya'mni.
leak, *vt.* 1. Kuse: *the pail leaks.* 2. Ohiyu: *the roof leaks.*
leaky, *a.* Kuse.
lean, *a.* Tamaheca. *vt.* Ataoŋpa; patuża. *vi.* Icaŋhaŋ; kaoḣya haŋ.
leap, leapt, *vt.* Apsica: *leap the fence. vi.* Ipsica. *n.* Oipsica.
leap-frog, *n.* Akicipsicapi.
leap-year, *n.* Waniyetu itopa.
learn, *vt.* Oŋspeiçiciya; iyukcaŋ. *vi.* Oŋspe; okaḣniġa; naḣoŋ.
learned, *a.* Waoŋspeka.
learning, *n.* Wosdonye; woksape.
lease, *vt.* Oḳu; makoce oḳu.
least, *a.* Iyotaŋ ci's'iŋna. *adv.* Iyotaŋ.
leather, *n.* Tataŋkaha; taha.
leave, left, *vt.* 1. Eḣpeya; ayuśtaŋ; kihnaka: *leave it here.* 2. Okapta: *not a drop left.* 3. Tokaŋ ya: *I want him to leave. n.* Woiyowiŋkiya; napeyuzapi.
leaven, *n.* Wi'napoḣye. *vt.* Napoḣya.
leaves, *n. pl* of LEAF.
leavings, *n.* Okaptapi.
lecherous, *a.* Wiciŋs'a.
lecture, *vt.* Wahokoŋkiya. *n.* Wowahokoŋkiye.
led, *imp.* of LEAD.
ledge, *n.* In'yaŋ maya.
ledger, *n.* Oicazowowapi taŋ'ka.
lee, *n.* I'tahdaḣbe.
leech, *n.* Tusda.
leek, *n.* Pśiŋ.
leer, *vi.* Hdakiŋyaŋetoŋwaŋ.
left, *imp.* of LEAVE.
left, *a.* Catka; napecatka.
leg, *n.* Hu; huha; oyaya.
legacy, *n.* Waiḣpeyapi.
legal, *a.* Woope ohna.
legalize, *vt.* Woope oŋ yuecetu.
legend, *n.* Ehaŋnawoyakapi.
legged, *a.* Hu yuha.
legging, *n.* Huŋska.
legible, *a.* Yawapiwaśte.
legion, *n.* Ni'naota.
legislate, *vi.* Woopeka'ġa.
legislature, *n.* Woopekaġa omniciye.
legitimate, *a.* Woopeohna.
leisure, *n.* Oko; ta'ku ecoŋśni.
leisurely, *adv.* Inaḣniśniyaŋ.
lemon, *n.* Taspaŋżi haŋ'ska.
lemonade, *n.* Taspaŋżihaŋpi.
lend, lent, *vt.* Oḳu.
length, *n.* Ohaŋska. *At length,* uŋ'haŋketa; haŋ'skeya.
lengthen, *vt.* Yuhaŋska.
lengthwise, *adv.* Ohaŋskaya.
lengthy, *a.* Haŋ'ska.
lenient, *a.* Waoŋśida; wa'ḣba.

lenity, *n*. Wowaȟba.
lens, *n*. Iśtażaŋżaŋ żaŋżaŋ.
lent, *n*. Akiȟaŋiçiyapi haŋ'ska.
lent, *imp*. of LEND.
leopard, *n*. Inmuhdeśka.
leper, *n*. *Leprosy* ececa.
leprosy, *n*. Ukaȟdiśica woyazaŋ.
less, *a*. & *adv*. A'okpani; ihukun; ci'stiŋna. *suf*. Co'daŋ; wanica: *a fatherless child*.
lessen, *vt*. Yucistina; yuaokpani.
lesser, *a*. Ci'stiŋna.
lesson, *n*. Woope.
lest, *conj*. O'kini.
let, *vt*. 1. Iyowiŋkiya; ito. *Let alone*, ayuśtaŋ. —*Let down*, kun'iyeya.—*Let go*, ayuśtaŋ.—*Let in*, en'iyeya. 2. Oḳu; każużu oḳu: *he let his farm*.
lethargy, *n*. Wokuża.
letter, *n*. 1. Wowapi (kiciçupi he'ca): *write me a letter*. 2. Oowa: *he don't know his letters*. 3. Wowapi oŋspe: *a man of letters*. *vt*. Oowa ka'ġa.
lettuce, *n*. Waȟpeyutapi.
levee, *n*. 1. Kicicopi: *the president's levee*. 2. Wakpa o'huta.
level, *a*. Mda'ya; iyehaŋyaŋ waŋkantu. *vt*. Yumdaya. *n*. Omdaye; waŋkantu oiyute.
lever, *n*. Caŋipaptaŋye.
levity, *n*. Tke'śni; ta'kuśni.
levy, *vt*. Mnayeśi; aehnaka.
lewd, *a*. Śi'ca; wiciŋpi.
lexicon, *n*. Ieskawowapi.
liable, *a*. Ikoyake; iyececa.
liar, *n*. Itoŋśni; owewakaŋ.
libel, *n*. Woyaśica. *vt*. Yaśica.
liberal, *a*. Oȟaŋpi: *a liberal giver*; okamdaya: *a liberal education*; to'ken ciŋ'ciŋ: *a liberal thinker*. *n*. I'ye to'ken ciŋ uŋ.
liberate, *vt*. Kiyuśka.
libertine, *n*. Wi'hduheśni; wicawihomni.
liberty, *n*. Ta'waiçiyapi; woiyowiŋkiye.
librarian, *n*. Wowapiawaŋyake.
library, *n*. Wowapiopahi.
license, *vt*. Iyowiŋkiya.
licentiate, *n*. Ecoŋktaiyowiŋkiyapi.
licentious, *a*. Wawiciȟaȟas'a.
lick, *vt*. Sdi'pa. *n*. Oape; wosdipa.
lid, *n*. Iha; oakaȟpe. *Eyelid*, iśtożuha.
lie, lay, lain, *vi*. 1. Iwaŋka: *lie down and sleep*. 2. Waŋka; ȟpa'ya: *it lies east*. 3. Yaŋka: *lie hid*.
lie, lied, *vi*. Itoŋśni. *Y*. & *T*. Owewakaŋ: *he lied about it*. *n*. Woitoŋśni; owewakaŋpi.
liege, *a*. Wicaka; okinihaŋ.
lien, *n*. Wokaśke.
lieu, *n*. To'he. *In lieu of*, e'ekiya.
lieutenant, *n*. O'kiheitaŋcaŋ.
live, lives, *n*. Oni; wiconi; ni'pi.
life-estate, *n*. Woyuha ni'pi hehaŋyaŋ yuhapi.
lifeless, *a*. Ni'śni; ṭa; huŋ'keśni.
lifelike, *a*. Ni iyececa; ni se'ca.
lifelong, *a*. Tohaŋyaŋ ni.
lifetime, *n*. Aŋpetu ni.
lift, *vt*. Yuwaŋkan icu; icu.
ligament, *n*. Kaŋ.
ligature, *n*. Ikaŋ; wi'caśke.
light, *n*. Iyoyaŋpa; petiżaŋżaŋ: *bring me a light*. *vt*. Iyoyamya; ideya: *light the lamp*. *vi*. Iyahaŋ; en hi. *a*. 1. Kapożedaŋ: *light wood*. 2. Ci'stina: *a light snow*; *a light error*. 3. Ska; saŋ: *a light complexion*. 4. Iyoyaŋpa; i'żaŋzaŋ: *a light room*.
lightbread, *n*. Aġuyapitacaġu.
lighten, *vt*. 1. Yukapozedaŋ: *lighten the boat*. 2. Iyoyamya: *lighten the way*.
lightly, *adv*. Iwaśtedaŋ; kapożedaŋ; awaciŋśniyaŋ.
lightning, *n*. Wakaŋhdi.
lightning-bug, *n*. Waŋyeca.

lignite, *n.* Pe'tacaȟdi sutaśni.
like, *vt.* Iyokipi ; waśtedaka : *I like to run.* *a.* Iyececa : *like his mother.* *adv.* Iyecen : *do it like he does.* *vi.* Ikiyedaŋ; owateca : *he liked to have fallen.*
likelihood, *n.* Se'ececa.
likely, *a.* 1. Naceca. 2. Waśte.
liken, *vt.* Iyaciŋ.
likeness, *n.* Ouncaġe ; iteowapi.
likewise, *conj.* Nakuŋ ; iś'eya.
liking, *n.* Wowaśtedake.
lily, *n.* Mnaȟcaȟca.
limb, *n.* Adetka ; oyaya.
limber, *a.* Wiŋświŋżedaŋ.
lime, *n.* Iŋ'yaŋacetipi.
limit, *n.* Owihaŋke. *vt.* Hehaŋyaŋanapte.
limitation, *n.* Owihaŋkeyapi.
limited, *a.* A'okpani uŋ.
limp, *vt.* Huśtemani. *a.* Patiŋśni.
limpid, *a.* Mde'za.
line, *n.* 1. Wi'kaŋ ; haȟoŋta : *stretch the line.* 2. Oicaġo ; oicazo : *draw a line ; the north line of my place.* 3. Caŋkuye : *read four lines ; stand in line ; a line of houses.* 4. Wicoȟaŋ ; woecoŋ : *line of business.* *vt.* 1. Caŋkuye ka'ġa : *line up the men.* 2. I'takihna ka'ġa : *line a dress.*
lineage, *n.* Ouŋcaġe.
lineal, *a.* Caŋkuye owotaŋna.
linen, *n.* Miniȟuhasuta.
linger, *vi.* Ye'kapiŋ ; ye'śni uŋ.
lingering, *a.* Te'haŋuŋ.
linguist, *n.* Iapi wayupika.
liniment, *n.* Wi'pakiŋte.
lining, *n.* Apate ; imahen uŋ.
link, *n.* Oyukśa ; okaśke. *vt.* Ikoyake.
linseed, *n.* Wi'hdisu.
linsey, *n.* Ta'ȟcahiŋ icahi.
lint, *n.* Miniȟuha hiŋ.
lion, *n.* Mna'ża.
lioness, *n.* Mna'ża wi'ye.
lionize, *vt.* Yawaṫ'aka.

lip, *n.* Iha. *Sore lips,* iha ȟdi. *Upper lip,* pute. *Lower lip,* iśti. 2. Opapuŋ ; tete : *the lip of the cup.*
liquefy, *vt.* Cocokaġa.
liquid, *n.* Miniiyececa ; ta'ku kaduza ; oeyewaśte.
liquidate, *vt.* Tikticaya ; każużu.
liquor, *n.* Miniwakaŋ ; mini iyececa.
lisp, *vi.* Yasdiia.
list, *n.* 1. Owicawapi ; owapi. 2. Śinatoopapuŋ. *vt.* Owa.
listen, *vi.* Anaġoptaŋ ; naȟoŋ.
listless, *a.* Enewaciŋśni.
literal, *a.* Ohnaȟca.
literary, *a.* 1. Wowapioŋspeȟca : *a literary man.* 2. Wowapi oŋ : *a literary conversation.* 3. Wowapi.
literature, *n.* Wowapi.
lithe, *a.* Wiŋświŋżedaŋ.
litigate, *vt.* Woope en kuwa.
litter, *n.* Watuśekśeca.
little, *a.* Ci'stiŋna, *a little boy. A little while,* ci'stiyedaŋ.
Little Missouri river, *n.* Wakpacanśoka.
Little Rocky mountains, *n.* Ḣe'psuŋkaka.
Little Sioux river, *n.* Iŋ'yaŋyaŋke wakpa.
liturgy, *n.* Wocekiye owapi.
live, *vi.* Ni : *live by eating.* 2. Ti : *where do you live.*
live, *a.* Ni ; ṭe'śni ; sni'śni.
livelihood, *n.* Wokamna ; oŋ ni.
liveliness, *n.* Womdiheca.
livelong, *a.* Ihuŋniyaŋ.
lively, *a.* Mdiheca ; ni.
liver, *n.* Pi. *Beef liver,* ta-pi.
livery, *n.* 1. Śuŋ'kawakaŋ owicaḳupi : *livery stable.* 2. Oiȟduze.
livid, *a.* Staŋ.
living, *a.* Ni ; he'cetuwaŋżica. *n.* Oŋ ni.
lizard, *n.* Ahdeśka.

lo, *interj.* 1. Iho ; waŋ ; ikcewicaśta.
load, *n.* 1. Wok̇iŋ : *a heavy load.* 2. Ohnaka : *two wagon loads.* *vt.* Ohnaka ; ożuya. *Load your gun,* ma'zakaŋ okikśu.
loading, *n.* Ta'ku ohnakapi.
loaf, loaves, *n.* Opaṭiŋze : *a loaf of bread.* *vi.* Wi'kcekce uŋ ; as'iŋ ; wicaoḣa.
Loafer, *n.* Wa'kduḣe ; *T.* Wa'gluḣe.
loam, *n.* Makikceka.
loan, *vt.* Ok̇u ; inaḣni k̇u. *Please loan me a dollar.* *n.* Owicak̇upi ; odotapi.
loathe, *vt.* Hitihda ; ciŋ'śni.
loathing, *n.* Wowaḣtedaśni.
loathsome, *a.* Waḣteśni.
loaves, *pl.* of LOAF.
lobby, *vi.* Ciŋwic ıkiyapi ; kuwa.
lobster, *n.* Matuśkataŋka.
local, *a.* Hen'tu ; hen e'cedaŋ. *n.* En'tu wotaŋiŋ.
locality, *n.* Oyaŋke ; makoce.
locate, *vt.* Oyaŋke k̇u ; iyeya.
location, *n.* Oyaŋke.
lock, *n.* 1. Inatake : *a door-lock.* 2. Nawate : *a gun-lock.* 3. Aśke ; oŋśpa : *a lock of hair.* *Scalp-lock,* pecoka. 4. Oiyanicapi : *a lock of carriages.* *vt.* 1. Nataka : *lock the door.* 2. I'ciyuwi : *lock arms.*
lock-jaw, *n.* Cehupapatiŋ.
lock-up, *n.* Wokaśketipi.
locomotive, *n.* Ḣemani.
locust, *n.* Psipsicadaŋ ; heḣakacaŋteyaśniśniża.
lodge, *vt.* 1. E'hde : *lodge arms.* 2. Owaŋka k̇u : *lodge the travellers.* 3. Paḣdi iheya : *lodge an arrow in his side.* 4. Kawiŋża : *the wind lodged the oats.* *vi.* Waŋ'ka ; ti. *n.* Ohna waŋ'kapi ; wakeya.
lodging, *n.* Owaŋka ; ti'pi.
loft, *n.* Waŋkantipi.
loftily, *adv.* Waŋkantuya.
lofty, *a.* Waŋkantu.
log, *n.* Caŋkaġa ; wa'taiyopte oiyute.
log-cabin, *n.* Caŋkaġatipi.
loggerhead, *n.* Nasuwanica ; ki'zapi.
logic, *n.* Waawaciŋpi wooŋspe.
logical, *n.* Woawaciŋhecetu.
loin, *n.* Nitiyuksa ; nite.
loiter, *vi.* Ituyauŋ ; ḣaŋhi.
loll, *vi.* Temni ; ceżihiyuya ; oziiċiyauŋ.
lone, *a.* Iśnanauŋ.
loneliness, *n.* Icomnipi.
lonely, *a.* 1. Makoskantu : *a lonely place.* 2. Icomni : *I am lonely.*
lonesome, *a.* Wicaśta wanica.
long, *a.* 1. Haŋ'ska : *a long stick.* 2. Ohaŋska : *a foot long.* 3. Te'haŋ : *a long time ago.* *All day long,* aŋpetu ihuŋni.—*As long as,* tohaŋyaŋ.—*How long,* tohaŋyaŋ.—*Long live,* te'han ni.—*So long,* hehaŋyaŋ. *vi.* Caŋtokpani : *I long to see you.* *To long for,* ciŋ : *I long for some fresh meat.*
longer, *comp.* of LONG.
longest, *super.* of LONG.
longitude, *n.* Makaipiyaka oiyute.
long-sighted, *a.* Te'haŋ wa'kita.
long-suffering, *a.* Waciŋtaŋka.
long-winded, *a.* Niyahaŋska.
look, *vi.* 1. E'toŋwaŋ : *look yonder.* Ahitoŋwaŋ, *look here.* 2. Awaciŋ ; eciŋ : *I did not look to see you to-day.* 3. Koŋ'za : *look brave.* *Look about,* o'kśaŋ wa'kita.—*Look after,* awaŋyaka ; akita.—*Look at each other,* opakiciḣta.—*Look back,* hakikta.—*Look down on,* ta'kuśnikiya.— *Look for,* ode ; akita ; hi kta wakta uŋ.—*Look into,* amdeza.—*Look like,* iyececa ; se'ca ; iteka.—*Look on,* waŋyaka.—*Look out,* ode ; akita ; haŋ'ta ; wiŋ'-

świŋś.—*Look over*, aokasiŋ; amdeza.—*Look queer*, to'kecaseca.—*Look sharp*, ni'na wa'kita.—*Looks toward*, itoheya waŋka (*the house looks toward the river*). *vt. Look down*, kun e'toŋwaŋ. *n.* Wa'kitapi; iteoyuze.

looking, *n.* Wa'kitapi; owaŋyake.

looking-glass, *n.* Ihdiyomdasiŋ. *Y.* Mniokdasiŋ. *T.* Miyoglasiŋ.

lookout, *n.* Wa'kitapi; co'wahe.

loom, *n.* Wi'cazoŋte. *vi.* Hinapa.

loon, *n.* Mdo'za. *T.* Huŋ'tka.

loop, *n.* Śuŋżoyake; oiyakaśke. *vt.* Śuŋżoyakekaġa.

loop-hole, *n.* Oḣdokaoenape.

loose, *vt.* Kiyuśka; yuśka. *a.* 1. Kaśkeśni: *a loose horse.* 2. Ḣpuwahe; ikoyakeśni: *loose leaves.* 3. Oḣdaḣdadaŋ: *a loose fit; a loose bolt.* 4. To'ken ciŋ'ciŋ: *a loose way of speaking; loose ideas.* 5. Sutaśni; hohodaŋ: *a loose tooth.*

loosely, *adv.* To'ken ciŋ'yaŋ.

loosen, *vt.* Yuśka; yupaŋpaŋ.

looseness, *n.* Wosutaśni; ṭiŋ'ześni.

loot, *vt.* Tibotica.

lop, *vt.* 1. Baksa: *lop off the limbs.* 2. Kawiŋża: *lop the ears.*

lope, *vi.* Nawaŋka.

loquacious, *a.* Ies'a; i'waśicuŋ.

lord, *n.* 1. Itaŋcaŋ: *the house of lords.* 2. Jehowa. *vi.* Itaŋcaŋ śkaŋ.

lordly, *a.* Itaŋcaŋse; okinihaŋ.

lore, *n.* Wooŋspe; woksape.

lose, lost, *vt.* 1. Tok'eḣpeya: *lost his knife.* 2. Nu'ni: *lose the way.* 3. Yuśna: *he lost two days' work.* 4. Ki'ciyutakuniśni; ki'ciśica: *I lost my hay. Lose a battle*, okicize kte'pidaŋ. —*Lose ground*, he'kta iyaye.—*Lose heart*, caŋte kiçuŋni. *vi.* Okihiśni; he'kta iyaye.

loss, *n.* Akicitakuniśni; woihaŋke; to'kaḣoŋ. *At a loss*, to'ketu taŋiŋ śni.

lost, *a.* To'kaḣoŋ; taŋiŋśni: yuśnapi; nuni.

lot, *n.* Woakipa: *a hard lot.* 2. Maka obaśpe: *a church lot.* 3. Opahi: *a lot of goods.* 4. O'ta; ni'na o'ta: *lots of people.* —*Cast lots*: wayekiyapi.

loth, *a.* Ecoŋkapiŋ.

lottery, *n.* Wayekiyapi.

loud, *a.* Ho'taŋka; taŋ'kaiçida.

loudly, *adv.* Ho'taŋkakiya.

lounge, *n.* Akaŋyaŋkapi paŋpaŋna. *vi.* Oziya uŋ.

Loup River, *n.* Kuśdeca wakpa.

louse, lice, *n.* He'ya.

lousy, *a.* He'ya o'ta.

lovable, *a.* Waśtedapi; waśte.

love, *vt.* Waśtedaka; ihakta; oŋ'śida; caŋtekiya. *n.* Waihaktapi; wacantkiyapi; woihakta; wowaśtedake; tu'we waśtewada.

love-letter, *n.* Wiciŋpi wowapi.

loveliness, *n.* Wowaśte.

lovely, *a.* Waśte; iyowicakipi.

lover, *n.* Tu'we waśtedaka.

loving, *a.* Waihakta.

lovingly, *adv.* Waśtedaya.

low, *a.* 1. Ku'ceyedaŋ: *low ground.* 2. Ka'zedaŋ: *the river is low.* 3. Teḣiśni; ci'stiŋna: *wheat is low.* 4. Waoŋspekeśni: *the low class of people. adv.* 1. Ku'ceyedaŋ: *fly low.* 2. Iwaśtedaŋ: *speak low. vi.* Pte'hotoŋ; hotoŋ.

lower, *vt.* Yuhukuya. *vt.* Wakokipe ka'ġa: *the clouds lower.*

Lower Brule, *n.* Kunwicaśa.

lowliness, *n.* Ta'kuiçidaśni.

lowly, *a.* Ku'ceyedaŋ; oŋ'śika.

lowness, *n.* Kun'tuḣ uŋ'pi.

lowspirited, *a.* Caŋtehuŋkeśni.

loyal, *a.* Waohoda; wanaȟoŋ.
lubberly, *a.* Taŋcaŋ oŋspekeśni.
lubricate, *vt.* Sdaya.
lucid, *a.* I′żaŋżaŋ; mde′za.
lucifer, *n.* Aŋpaowicaŋȟpi.
luck, *n.* Woakipa. *Good luck*, wa′pipi.—*Bad luck*, woakipa śi′ca.
luckily, *adv.* Taŋ′yaŋ.
lucky, *a.* Wa′pi.
lucrative, *a.* Wakamna.
lucre, *n.* Woyuha; wokamna.
ludicrous, *a.* Wowiȟa.
lug, *vt.* Ķiŋ; yusdohaŋ.
luggage, *n.* Woķiŋ.
lukewarm, *a.* Iţeca; huŋ′keśni.
lull, *vt.* Kihna. *vi.* Kun′ya.
lullaby, *n.* Kihnapiodowaŋ.
lumber, *n.* Caŋmdaska; wokpaŋ. *vt.* Ta′kuśniśni oŋ kaġiya.
luminary, *n.* Iyoyaŋpa.
luminous, *a.* Iyożaŋżaŋ.
lump, *n.* Wotasaka; oŋśpa. *vt.* Yuwitaya; wi′taya icu.
lumpy, *a.* Tasaksaka; pśuŋkaka.
lunacy, *n.* Waciŋhnunipi.
lunatic, *n.* Waciŋhnuni.
lunch, *n.* Inaȟniwotapi.
luncheon, *n.* Otahenawotapi.
lung, *n.* Caġu.
lunge, *n.* Kaȟoiyeiçiyapi.
lurch, *vi.* Naptaŋ iyaya.
lure, *vt.* Iyutaŋye.
lurid, *a.* Okokipe.
lurk, *vi.* Iyape; naȟmaŋ uŋ.
luscious, *a.* Skuskuya.
lust, *vi.* Ciŋ; caŋtahde.
luster, *n.* Wowiyakpa.
lustrous, *a.* Wiyakpa.
lusty, *a.* Taŋcaŋtaŋka; waś′aka.
luxuriant, *a.* Paŋ′ġa.
luxuriate, *vi.* I′mnahaŋ uŋ.
luxurious, *a.* Wi′żica aokaġeca.
lyceum, *n.* Waoŋspeiçiciya ti′pi.
lye, *n.* Caȟotahaŋpi.
lying, *imp.* of LIE.
lynch, *vt.* Woope wanin kte′.
lynx, *n.* Inmu siŋteoŋżiŋca.
lyre, *n.* Pteheyudowaŋpi.
lyrical, *a.* Dowaŋpiwaśte.

M

ma, *n.* Ina.
ma'am, *contr.* of MADAM.
macerate, *vt.* Ḣpaŋye.
machination, *n.* Wokuwa.
machine, *n.* Wi′cuwa; ma′zaicuwa.
machinist, *n.* Maza′icuwa ka′ġa.
mad, *a.* Hnaśkiŋyaŋ; caŋze.
madam, *n.* Wiŋ′yaŋ yuonihaŋpi.
madden, *vt.* Yuhnaśkiŋyaŋ.
made, *imp.* of MAKE.
madly, *adv.* Witkoya.
madness, *n.* Wohnaśkiŋyaŋ.
maelstrom, *n.* Miniomni taŋ′ka.
magazine, *n.* Wopiye; wakihnagtipi; wotaŋiŋwowapi śo′ka.
maggot, *n.* Wamdudaŋ; *T.* waglula; honaġidaŋ ciŋca.
magic, *n.* Wakaŋkaŋ śkaŋ′pi.
magical, *a.* Wakaŋse.
magician, *n.* Wapiyawicaśta.
magistrate, *n.* Oyate itaŋcaŋ.
magnanimous, *a.* Waciŋtaŋka.
magnate, *n.* Itaŋcaŋ taŋ′ka.
magnet, *n.* Ma′zawiyutitaŋ.
magnetic, *a.* Wawiyutaŋ.
magnificence, *n.* Wokinihaŋ.
magnify, *vt.* Yutaŋka.
magnitude, *n.* Tiŋ′skokeca; hiŋ′skotaŋka.
magpie, *n.* Uŋkcekiȟa.
maid, *n.* Wikośka; nahaŋȟ hihnatoŋśni.
maiden, *a.* & *n.* Witaŋśna; te′ca; uŋ′piśni.

mail, *n.* 1. Wowapitokśupi; wowapi: *where is my mail.* 2. Ma'zaheyake. *vt.* Wowapi tokśu ohnaka: *mail my letters.*
mail-carrier, *n.* Wowapitokśu.
maim, *vi.* Kiuŋniya.
main, *a.* Itaŋcaŋ; taŋcaŋ.
mainly, *adv.* Iyotaŋ.
maintain, *vt.* He'cetuwaŋżicayuha uŋ; yuha uŋ; yuha; o'kiya.
maintenance, *n.* Oŋ ni; yus uŋ'pi.
maize, *n.* Wamnaheza.
majestic, *a.* Okinihaŋ.
major, *n.* Itaŋcaŋ; ateyapi. *a.* Taŋ'ka.
majority, *n.* Haŋke i'śaŋpa.
make, made, *vt.* 1. Ka'ġa: *make a shoe; God made man.* 2. Yu-; yuśica: *make bad.* 3. -kiya; -ya: *make him do it. Make him go,* iyayeya. 3. Icaġa; tokata he'ca kta: *a good boy makes a good man.* 4. Iyohi: *he can't make the shore.* 5. Kamna: *make money. Make amends,* yuecetu.—*Make free with,* ta'wa se śkaŋ.—*Make good time,* du'zahaŋ.—*Make light of,* ta'kuśnikiya.—*Make love to,* okiya.—*Make much of,* ta'kukiya; kinihaŋ.—*Makes no difference,* to'kecaśni.—*Make out,* to'ketu iyukcaŋ.—*Make use of,* uŋ.—*Make water,* de'ża.—*Make for the shore,* hutatakiya ya.—*Make at; make towards,* en hiyuiçiya.—*Make up with him,* kici okiciwaśte. *n.* Okaġe.
maker, *n.* Kaġa; tu'we ka'ġa.
makeshift, *n.* Inaȟni uŋ'pi.
mal-, *pref.* Śi'ca.
malady, *n.* Wośica; woyazaŋ.
malaria, *n.* Tate śi'ca.
malcontent, *n.* Iyowicakipiśni.
male, *n.* & *a.* Wica; mdoka.
malediction, *n.* Woyaśica.
malefactor, *n.* Wośiceka'ġa.
malevolent, *a.* Śicaya waciŋyuza.
malice, *n.* Śicawaciŋpi.
malicious, *a.* Śicawaciŋśkaŋ.
maliciously, *adv.* Śicawaciŋ.
malign, *vt.* Yaśica. *a.* Śi'ca.
malignant, *a.* Wayuśica.
mallard, *n.* Paġoŋta.
malleable, *a.* Pamdaskapica.
mallet, *n.* Caŋwiyape.
malt, *n.* Su'ȟpaŋyaŋpi.
maltreat, *vt.* Śicayakuwa.
mama, *n.* Ina.
mammal, *n.* Wamakaśkaŋ aziŋpi.
mammon, *n.* Woyuha; ma'zaska.
mammoth, *n.* Wamakaśkaŋ iyotaŋ taŋ'ka. *a.* Iyotaŋtaŋka.
man, men, *n.* Wicaśta. *Y.* & *T.* Wicaśa. *vt.* Wicaśta en uŋwicakiya.
manacle, *n.* Ma'zaicaśke.
manage, *vt.* Kuwa; yu'za.
manageable, *a.* Kuwapica.
management, *n.* Kuwapi.
manager, *n.* Kuwaitaŋcaŋ.
Mandan, *n.* Mawatani.
mandate, *n.* Itaŋcaŋ to'ie.
mane, *n.* Apeȟiŋ.
maneuver, *vi.* Śkaŋ; ośkiśke śkaŋ.
manful, *a.* Wicaśta.
manfully, *adv.* Ohitiya.
manger, *n.* Ohnawotapi.
mangle, *vt.* Kaȟdeȟdeca.
manhood, *n.* Wicaśta ouŋcaġe.
mania, *n.* Wohnaśkiŋyaŋ.
maniac, *n.* Waciŋhnuni.
manifest, *a.* Taŋiŋ. *vt.* Yutaŋiŋ.
manifesto, *n.* Yaotaŋiŋpi.
manifold, *a.* O'takiya. *vt.* O'ta ka'ġa.
manipulate, *vt.* Iyopteya.
Mankato, *n.* Makatooze.
mankind, *n.* Wicaśta.
manly, *a.* Wicaśta; wicaśtase.
manner, *n.* 1. Oȟaŋ; oecoŋ. 2. Ocaże; obe: *all manner of beasts.*
mannerly, *adv.* Oȟaŋwaśte.

man=of=war, *n.* Ozuye wi'tawata.
manse, *n.* Wicaŝtawakaŋti.
mansion, *n.* Ti'pitaŋka.
manslaughter, *n.* Wicaŝta kte'pi.
mantel, *n.* Wa'ḣnakapi.
mantle, *n.* Hiyeteakaḣpe.
manual, *a.* Napiŋyuŋ. *n.* Wowapi ci'stiŋna.
manufacture, *vt.* Ka'ġa.
manure, *vt.* Tacesdiakada. *n.* Ta'ku maka yuwaŝte; tacesdi.
manuscript, *n.* Wowapinapeoŋkaġapi.
many, *a.* O'ta. *As many as,* iyena. —*Great many,* ni'na o'ta.—*Good many,* ki'taŋna o'ta.—*How many,* to'nakeca. — *So many,* henakeca; ni'na o'ta.—*Too many,* ehaeŝ o'ta.
many=ways, *adv.* O'takiya.
map, *n.* Makoce wowapi.
maple, *n.* *Hard maple,* caŋhasaŋ. *Soft maple,* ta'ḣdohu.
mar, *vt.* Yuŝica.
marauder, *n.* Wamanoŋwicaŝta.
marble, *n.* 1. Iŋ'yaŋ pamdaskapi. 2. Iŋ'yaŋ bohmihmapi.
march, *vi.* Ma'ni; caehde. *vt.* Omaniya. *n.* Oomani; ma'nipi.
mare, *n.* Ŝuŋgwiye.
margin, *n.* Opapuŋ; o'ḣuta.
marine, *a.* Miniwaŋca. *n.* Miniwaŋca akicita.
mariner, *n.* Wi'tawata kicaŋye.
marital, *a.* Tawicutoŋpi.
mark, *vt.* Icazo; wa'petogtoŋ; amdeza. *n.* Wowapetokeca; wowasaghde; wokitaŋiŋ; iheca. *He hit the mark,* iheca en iheya.
marker, *n.* Oŋ icazopi.
market, *n.* Owiyopeye. *vt.* Wi'yopeya.
marketable, *a.* Wi'yopeyepica.
marksman, *n.* Wicaŝta waoka.
marl, *n.* Makasaŋ.
marquis, *n.* Okinihaŋ itaŋcaŋ.
marriage, *n.* Wakaŋkiciyuzapi.
married, *a.* Yu'zapi : *a married man.*
marrow, *n.* Cupe.
marry, married, *vt.* Yu'za; wakaŋyuza; wakaŋkiciyuskiya. *She is married,* hihnatoŋ.—*He is married,* tawicutoŋ.
marsh, *n.* Wiwi; makaspa'ya.
marshal, *n.* Itaŋcaŋ; waoyuspaitaŋcaŋ. *vt.* Ecoŋwicakiya.
mart, *n.* Owiyopeye.
marten, *n.* Nakpaġica.
martial, *a.* Akicita; ozuye.
martyr, *n.* Tawowicada oŋ kte'pi.
marvel, *n.* Wowapetokeca. *vi.* Inihaŋ.
marvelous, *a.* Wowinihaŋ.
masculine, *a.* 1. (*Of man*) Wica. (*Of animals*) Mdoka. 2. Wicaŝta; taŋ'ka.
mash, *vt.* Paŝuŝuża; pamdu.
mask, *n.* Itekaġapi. *vt.* Akaḣpa; itekaġapi iŋ.
mason, *n.* Iŋ'yaŋticaġe; makasaŋ apawiŋta.
masquerade, *n.* Iteakaḣpawacipi.
mass, *n.* 1. Opahi; taŋcaŋ. 2. Ŝinasapa wohduze. *vt.* Yuwitaya.
massacre, *vt.* Kte; kasota. *n.* Wicakasotapi; tinktepi.
massive, *a.* Taŋ'ka.
mast, *n.* Wi'tawata ihupa; u'ta.
master, *n.* Itaŋcaŋ; waoŋspeka. *vt.* Ohiya; kte'daŋ.
masterly, *a.* Oitaŋcaŋ.
masterpiece, *n.* Iyotaŋwaŝte.
mastery, *n.* Woohiye.
masthead. *n.* Caŋihupaiŋkpa.
masticate, *vt.* Yakpaŋkpaŋ.
mastiff, *n.* Ŝuŋ'ka cehupataŋka.
mastodon, *n.* Pasuhaŋskataŋka.
mat, *n.* Psa'owiŋża; aŝke.
match, *n.* 1. Caŋ'kaidepi; *Y.* Yuidepi; *T.* Wailepi. 2. Okiciyuze : *a love match.* 3. Kici ecoŋ; iyececa. *vt.* Iyececa aḣihnaka.
matchless, *a.* Iyececa wanica.

mate, *n.* Kicica; itaŋcaŋokihe. *vt.* Kiciyuskiya.
material, *n.* Oŋ ka'ġapi. *a.* Taŋtoŋ; woawaciŋḣca.
materialize, *vt.* Yuecetu.
maternal, *a.* Wicahuŋku.
mathematics, *n.* Wayawapi.
matin, *n.* Haŋḣaŋnacekiyapi.
matriculate, *vt.* O'pekiye.
matrimony, *n.* Kiciyuzapi.
matrix, *n.* Tamni.
matron, *n.* Inayaŋpi.
matronly, *a.* Inayapise.
matter, *n.* 1. Ta'ku taŋtoŋ; ta'ku. 2. Wicoḣaŋ; ta'ku: *bring every matter to me.* 3. Toŋ: *the sore runs matter. What is the matter,* to'ketu se.—*Nothing is the matter,* ta'ku to'ketu śni. —*No matter,* etaŋhaŋ to'ketuśni. *vi.* Toŋye.
matting, *n.* Psa'owiŋża.
mattock, *n.* Maziçe.
mattress, *n.* Owiŋżaśoka.
mature, *a.* Sutoŋ; icaġayuśtaŋ. *vt.* Sutoŋya. *vi.* Iyehantu.
maul, *n.* Caŋiyapetaŋka.
maw, *n.* Tapo.
maxim, *n.* Woopeptecena.
maximum, *n.* Waŋkanihaŋke.
may, might, *v.* (Waokiyapi iapi) 1. Iyowiŋkiya: *may I go.* 2. O'kini; naceca: *he may come, I don't know.* 3. Kta: *I go that you may come.* 4. Nuŋwe; nuŋ: *may you always be happy.*
May, *n.* Wożupiwi.
may-be, *adv.* O'kini.
mayor, *n.* Otoŋweitaŋcaŋ.
maze, *n.* Wośkiśke.
me, *pro.* Mi'ye; ma-. *Give me,* maku.
meadow, *n.* Pėżiokaśda.
meadow-lark, *n.* Śdo'śdona.
meager, *a.* Iyohiśni; oŋ'śika.
meal, *n.* 1. Wokpaŋpi: *corn-meal.* 2. Wotapi; waŋ'cadaŋwotapi.
meal-time, *n.* Wotapi iyehantu.

mealy, *a.* Mdu.
mean, *a.* 1. Śi'ca; oḣaŋśica: *a mean man.* 2. Ocokaya; i'yotahedaŋ: *the mean distance. vt.* (*Mean, meant.*) Ka; awaciŋ: *what do you mean.*
meander, *vi.* Kśaŋkśaŋ ya.
meaning, *n.* Ta'ku ka'pi.
meanly, *adv.* Śicaya.
meanness, *n.* Śi'ca; wośice.
means, *n. pl.* Oŋ wi'yokihipi; woyuha; ma'zaska.
meant, *imp.* of MEAN.
meanwhile, *adv.* Icuŋhaŋ.
measles, *n.* Śayaahinapapi.
measurable, *a.* Iyutepica; iyuteya.
measure, *vt.* Iyuta. *n.* Oiyute.
meat, *n.* Tado; woyute. *Dried meat,* waconica; pa'pa.
mechanic, *n.* Wakaġa wayupika.
medal, *n.* Ma'zaskawanapiŋ.
meddle, *vi.* Iyoważaśni śkaŋ.
meddlesome, *a.* Iyoważaśni śkaŋ.
mediate, *vi.* Wi'ciyotahedaŋuŋ.
mediator, *n.* Wawiciya.
medical, *a.* Pėżuta.
medicate, *vt.* Pėżuta icahi.
medicine, *n.* Pėżuta.
medieval, *a.* Makaoicaġe ocoka.
meditate, *vt.* Awaciŋ.
meditative, *a.* Waawaciŋs'a.
medium, *n.* 1. Oyaŋke ocoka: *the true medium.* 2. Oŋ wi'yokihipi; wi'yotahedaŋ uŋ. *a.* Ocokaya: *medium size.*
medley, *n.* I'cicaḣikaġapi.
meed, *n.* Wokażużu.
meek, *a.* Wa'ḣbadan; oŋ'śiḣaŋ.
meekly, *adv.* Wa'ḣbayedaŋ.
meekness, *n.* Wicowaḣbadaŋ.
meet, met, *vt.* Akipa; waŋyaka. *vi.* Wi'tayapi; mniciyapi: *when does Congress meet. a.* Iyecetu: *meet for war.*
meeting, *n.* 1. Omniciye: *a full meeting.* 2. Waŋkiciyag hi'pi: *a meeting of friends.*

meeting-house, *n.* Ti′piwakaŋ.
melancholy, *a.* Waciŋiyokiśica.
mellow, *a.* Paŋpaŋna; mdu; waśte.
melodeon, *n.* Caŋ′nahotoŋpi.
melodious, *a.* Ho′waśte.
melody, *n.* Odowaŋ ho.
melon, *n.* Sa′kayutapi; *Y. & T.* śpaŋ′śniyutapi.
melt, *vt.* Ṡdunya; skaŋya; śdoya. *vi.* 1. Skaŋ: *snow melts.* 2. Ṡdo: *iron melts.*
member, *n.* 1. O′kihe: *members of the body.* 2. O′pa: *a member of the church.*
memento, *n.* Wokiksuye.
memoir, *n.* Oḣaŋoyakapi.
memorable, *a.* Wokiksuye.
memorandum, *n.* Oŋ′kiksuyapi.
memorial, *a.* Wakiksuya: *memorial services.* *n.* Icekiyapi wowapi: *a memorial to Congress.*
memorialize, *vt.* Icekiya.
memorize, *vt.* Kiksuyeiçiya.
memory, *n.* Wokiksuye; tawaciŋ.
men, *n. pl.* of MAN.
menace, *vt.* Wakokipekaġa.
menagerie, *n.* Wamakaśkaŋwapazopi.
mend, *vt.* Piya. *vi.* Waśteaya.
mendicant, *n.* Wadauŋ.
menial, *a.* Oŋ′śika; oaśica.
menses, *n.* Iśnatipi.
mental, *a.* Tawaciŋ.
mention, *vt.* Cażeyata.
mercantile, *a.* Wopetoŋpi.
mercenary, *a.* Ma′zaskaiyotaŋda.
merchandise, *n.* Wopetoŋpi; ma′-za.
merchant, *n.* Wopetoŋ.
merchantable, *a.* Wi′yopeyepica.
merciful, *a.* Waoŋśida.
merciless, *a.* Waoŋśidaśni.
mercury, *n.* Ma′zanini.
mercy, *n.* Wowaoŋśida.
mere, *a.* He′cehnana.
merely, *adv.* He′cehnana.
merge, *vt.* En iyeya; aopekiya.
meridian, *n.* Wi′cokaya oicaġo.
merit, *n.* Woohiye; wowaśte. *vt.* Kamna; ohiya; aiyahdeya.
meritorious, *a.* Ohiya iyececa.
merrily, *adv.* Wi′yuśkiŋyaŋ.
merriment, *n.* Wowiyuśkiŋ.
merry, *a.* Wi′yuśkiŋ; wi′haha.
mess, *n.* 1. Wi′tayawotapi; obe. 2. Wośkiśke. *vi.* Wota.
message, *n.* Iapiyeyapi.
messenger, *n.* Iapiaya; wahośiya.
met, *imp.* of MEET.
metal, *n.* Ma′za.
metaphor, *n.* Woiyaciŋ iapi.
metaphysics, *n.* Wicotawaciŋwooŋspe.
mete, *vt.* Ikiyuta; ḳu. *a.* Iyecetu.
meteor, *n.* Wakaŋwoḣpa.
meteorology, *n.* Tatewooŋspe.
meter, *n.* Oiyute; odowaŋ ho.
methinks, *vi.* Kepca; se′ca.
method, Woawaciŋ.
methodical, *a.* Awaciŋecoŋpi.
metrical, *a.* Iyutakaġapi; odowaŋse ka′gapi.
metropolis, *n.* Otoŋweitaŋcaŋ.
mettle, *n.* Okaġe; caŋte.
mew, *vi.* Inmuśuŋkahotoŋ.
Mexican, *n.* Spaniowicaśta.
mice, *pl.* of MOUSE.
microbe, *n.* Wamdudaŋ.
microscope, *n.* Maziwaŋyake.
microscopic, *a.* Ni′na ci′stiŋna.
mid, *a.* Cokaya; hepiya.
midday, *a.* Aŋpecokaya.
middle, *a.* Cokaya; ocokaya.
middle-man, *n.* Wi′ciyotahedan uŋ.
middling, *a.* Ocokaya.
midnight, *n.* Haŋcokaya.
midst, *n.* Cokaya.
midsummer, *n.* Mdokecokaya.
midway, *n.* Cokaya.
midwife, *n.* Ciŋcatoŋwicakiyewiŋ.
mien, *n.* Oihduhe.
might, *n.* Wowaś′ake: *with all my might.* *v. imp.* of MAY.
mightily, *adv.* Was′agya; ni′na.
mightiness, *n.* Wicaohitika.

mighty, *a.* Waś'aka ; ohitika ; ni'-na ; oteḣika.
migrate, *vi.* Tokaŋ ya ; ihdaka.
migration, *n.* Ihdagomanipi.
milch, *a.* Asaŋpiyuha.
mild, *a.* Wa'ḣbadaŋ ; *T.* wa'ḣwala ; waśtecaka.
mildew, *n.* Aa ; waanunu.
mildly, *adv.* Aḣbayena.
mildness, *n.* Wicowaḣbadaŋ.
mile, *n.* Caŋkuoiyute.
mileage, *n.* Omanipi wokażużu.
militant, *a.* Akicita.
military, *a.* Akicita ; ozuye.
militate, *vi.* Wakaġiya.
militia, *n.* Inaḣniakicita.
milk, *n.* Asaŋpi. *vt.* Yuskica. *Y.* Yusdi. *T.* Yusli.
milky-way, *n.* Wanaġitacaŋku.
mill, *n.* 1. Wokaġetipi. *Grist-mill,* wokpaŋtipi. *Saw-mill,* caŋnasdeca. 2. Kaśpapicistiŋna.
millenium, *n.* Wowaśte waniyetu kektopawiŋġe.
miller, *n.* Wokpaŋawaŋyaka.
millet, *n.* Pezioźupi obe.
milliner, *n.* Wiŋ'yaŋtawapaha ka'ġa.
million, *n.* Woyawataŋ'ka.
millionaire, *n.* Ma'zaska woyawataŋka yuha.
mimic, *vt.* Uŋ'ca.
mince, *vt.* Bakpaŋ ; wayatokeca. *vi.* Waśtekoŋza.
mind, *vt.* Awaciŋ ; naḣoŋ ; awaŋyaka. *n.* Tawaciŋ.
mindful, *a.* Kiksuya ; awaciŋ.
mine, *a.* Mitawa ; mi'yemitawa. *n.* Ma'zaoḳe ; oḳe. *vt.* Ḳa ; oḳa.
mineral, *n.* Ma'za.
mineralogy, *n.* Ma'zawooŋspe.
mingle, *vt.* I'cicaḣiya.
miniature, *a.* Ci'stiŋna.
minimum, *n.* Ihaŋkeci'stiŋna.
minion, *n.* Ookiyedaŋ.
minister, *n.* Ookiye ; wicaśtawakaŋ. *vt.* O'kiya ; ḳu.
ministerial, *a.* Wawokiya.
ministration, *n.* Wawokiyapi.
ministry, *n.* Wookiye.
mink, *n.* Dokśiŋca.
Minnesota River, *n.* Wakpaminisota.
minnow, *n.* Hoġaŋstiŋna ; *T.* hoġaŋscila.
minor, *a.* Ci'stiŋna ; ta'kuśni. *n.* Ta'waiçiyeśni.
minority, *n.* 1. Waniyetu iyenakecaśni. 2. Haŋkeśni.
minstrel, *n.* Dowaŋomani.
mint, *n.* 1. Ma'zaskaokaġe. 2. Ceyakata ; ceyaka.
minuend, *n.* Etaŋhaŋicupi.
minus, *a.* A'okpani ; wanica.
minute', *a.* Ci'stiŋna.
min'ute, *n.* Oapecistiŋna.
minutely, *adv.* Kpaŋyena.
minuteness, *n.* Ecaataya.
miracle, *n.* Wowapetokeca ; oḣaŋwakaŋ.
miraculous, *a.* Wakaŋ.
mirage, *n.* Amaśtenaptapta.
mire, *n.* Upśiża. *vi.* Kaḣdi.
mirror, *n.* Ihdiyomdasiŋ. *Y.* Mniokdasiŋ. *T.* Miyoglasiŋ.
mirth, *n.* Wi'yuśkiŋpi.
mirthful, *a.* Wi'yuśkiŋ.
miry, *a.* Ḣdiḣdidaŋ.
mis-, *pref.* Śi'ca ; eciŋśniyaŋ.
misanthropist, *n.* Ecawicawaḣtedaśni.
misbehave, *vi.* Śínyaoḣaŋyaŋ.
miscalculate, *vt.* Eciŋśniyaŋ iyukcaŋ.
miscarry, *vi.* Eciŋśniyan iyaya.
miscegenation, *n.* Oyatetokeca kiciyuzapi.
miscellaneous, *a.* Enanakiya.
mischief, *n.* Woyuśica
mischievous, *a.* Wicaśtaśni.
miscon'duct, *n.* Oḣaŋeciŋśniyaŋ.
misconduct', *vt.* Eciŋśniyaŋ ecoŋ.
misdirect, *vt.* Eciŋśniiyayeya.
miser, *n.* Wateḣiŋda.
miserable, *a.* Oŋ'śika ; śi'ca.
miserably, *adv.* Oŋ'śiya ; śicaya.

miserly, *a.* Watehiŋda.
misery, *n.* Wokakiże.
misfit, *n.* Iyekicihantuśni.
misfortune, *n.* Śicawakipa.
misgiving, *n.* Wacetuŋhda.
mishap, *n.* Tehiwakipapi.
misjudge, *vt.* Eciŋśni iyukcaŋ.
mislay, *vt.* Eciŋśni e'hnaka.
misrule, *vt.* Eciŋśni awaŋyaka.
miss, *vt.* Yuśna; kaśna; bośna. Hemani yuśna: *He missed the train.*—*He shot at two deer but missed both,* ta'hca nom kute, tuka sakim bośna.—*He lost his knife, but did not miss it,* isaŋ tok ehpekiya tka sdonye śni. *n.* Wikośka nahaŋh taŋśna uŋ.
missile, *n.* Wi'pe; ta'ku yeyapi.
missing, *a.* Taŋiŋśni; to'kahoŋ.
mission, *n.* 1. Wicomani; yewicaśipi: *a mission is coming.* 2. Wotaŋiŋ Waśte a'yapi: *the Episcopal Mission.* 3. Oŋ yeśipi: *what is your mission.*
missionary, *n.* Wotaŋiŋ Waśte aya; wicaśtawakaŋ; yeśipi.
Mississippi River, *n.* Hahawakpa.
Missouri River, *n.* Miniśośe.
missive, *a.* Yeyapi.
misspell, *vt.* Oowayuśna.
misstate, *vt.* Eciŋśni oyaka.
mist, *n.* Minibozaŋ; miniwozela.
mistake, mistook, *vt.* Yuśna; i'cihnuni. *n.* Woyuśna.
mistaken, *pa.* Yuśna; nu'ni.
mister, Mr., *n.* Wicaśta.
mistress, Mrs., *n.* Win'yaŋ hihnatoŋ; wiŋ'yaŋ; wiŋ'yaŋ itaŋcaŋ.
mistrust, *vt.* Cetuŋhda.
misty, *a.* Miniboza; owataŋiŋśni.
misunderstand, *vt.* Okahniġeśni.
misuse, *vt.* Eciŋśniyaŋ uŋ.
mite, *n.* Ta'ku ci'stiŋna; wokpe; wamdudaŋ; ma'zaska ci'stiŋna.
miter, *n.* Itaŋcaŋ tawapaha; o'hya baksapi.
mitigate, *vt.* Yuaokpani.
mitt, *n.* Napiŋkpadaŋ.
mitten, *n.* Napiŋkpa otoza.
mix, *vt.* I'cicahiya; *T.* yużena; o'peya uŋ.
mixed, *a.* I'cicahi.
mixture, *n.* Ta'ku i'cicahi.
mnemonics, *n.* Kiksuyapi.
moan, *vi.* Howaya.
mob, *v.* & *n.* Hnaśkiŋyaŋkuwapi.
mobile, *a.* Kohaŋtokeca.
mobilize, *vt.* Yuwiyeya.
moccasin, *n.* Haŋpikceka.
mock, *vt.* Uŋ'ca; ihaha.
mockery, *n.* Wohnaye.
mode, *n.* Ouŋ; ohaŋ; to'ketu.
model, *n.* Iwaŋyagkaġapi; iyececa.
model, *vt.* Okaġe.
moderate, *a.* Ki'taŋna. *v.* Yuahececa.
moderately, *adv.* Iwaśtena.
moderation, *n.* Wowahbadaŋ.
moderator, *n.* Omniciyeitaŋcaŋ.
modern, *n.* Aśkatudaŋ.
modest, *a.* Wawiśteca; wa'hba.
modesty, *n.* Wowahba.
modify, *vt.* Apiya.
modulate, *vt.* Ohna ka'ġa.
moist, *a.* Spaya; hpaŋ.
moisten, *vt.* Hpaŋye.
moisture, *n.* Wospaye.
molasses, *n.* Caŋhaŋpitiktica; tuhmaġa.
mold, mould, *n.* 1. Aa; makamdu. 2. Wi'śdoye; okaġe. *vt.* Ka'ġa.
moldy, mouldy, *a.* Aa.
mole, *n.* Napeheyatahedaŋ.
molecule, *n.* Wokpe.
molest, *vt.* Naġiyeya; kuwa.
mollify, *vt.* Yuahececa.
molt, moult, *vi.* Śoŋpa.
molten, *a.* Śdo.
moment, *n.* 1 Wihiyayeokpe; ci'stiyedaŋ. 2. Woawaciŋ.
momentary, *a.* Ci'stiyedaŋ.
momentous, *a.* Otaŋtoŋka.
momentum, *n.* Woiyopte.
monarch, *n.* Itaŋcaŋsuta.
monastery, *n.* Śinasapa woozitipi

Monday, *n.* Aŋpetutokaheya.
monetary, *a.* Ma'zaska.
money, *n.* Ma'zaska.
monger, *n.* Wopetoŋ.
mongrel, *a.* I'cicahi.
monitor, *n.* Wahokoŋkiya.
monk, *n.* Śinasapa wowaśi.
monkey, *n.* Waoŋca.
monopolize, *vt.* A'taya anica.
monopoly, *n.* A'tayaanicapi.
monotone, *n.* Ho'waŋżidaŋ.
monster, *n.* Wowinihaŋ.
monstrous, *a.* Taŋ'kaḣca.
month, *n.* Wi; wiyawapi.
monthly, *a.* Wi'iyohi.
monument, *n.* Wokiksuye.
mood, *n.* Tawaciŋ; ouŋ.
moody, *a.* Tawaciŋ to'kecas'a.
moon, *n.* Haŋyetuwi; haŋwi. *Dark of the moon,* wi yaśpapi. —*Full moon,* wi miŋbe.
moonlight, *n.* Haŋwiyaŋpa.
moonshine, *n.* Wiiżaŋżaŋ; ta'kuśni.
moor, *n.* Tıŋ'ta. *vt.* Wa'taiyakaśka.
moose, *n.* Ta.
moot, *vt.* Cażeyata.
mop, *n.* Owaŋkaipakiŋte.
mope, *vi.* Oḣaŋstaka.
moral, *a.* Oḣaŋowotaŋna. *n.* Oḣaŋ; wooŋspe.
morality, *n.* Wicoḣaŋ.
moralize, *vt.* Oḣaŋ iwohdaka.
morally, *adv* Woowotaŋna oŋ.
morass, *n.* Makaspaya; wiwi.
morbid, *a.* Aśiḣtiŋ.
more, *a.* & *adv.* Saŋ'pa; nakuŋ; o'ta; ehake. *More than,* i'saŋpa.—*No more,* henana.—*One more,* ehake waŋżi.
moreover, *adv.* Ko'kta; nakuŋ.
morn, *n.* O'haŋḣaŋna; hiŋ'haŋna.
morning, *n.* Haŋḣaŋna; *Y.* & *T.* hiŋ'haŋna.—*In the morning,* haŋḣaŋna. — *This morning,* naŋ'ka haŋḣaŋna. — *The next morning,* i'haŋḣaŋna.
morning-star, *n.* Aŋpaowicaŋḣpi.
morocco, *n.* Tatokaha.
morose, *a.* Tawaciŋśica.
morphine, *n.* Iśtiŋma peżuta.
morrow, *n.* I'haŋḣaŋna.
morsel, *n.* Onapce waŋżi.
mortal, *a.* Ṭe kta; oŋ ṭe kta.
mortality, *n.* Wicoŋṭe.
mortally, *adv.* Oŋṭekta; ni'na.
mortar, *n.* Tiisaŋyecoco; wi'bope.
mortgage, *n.* Woyuhakaśkapi.
mortification, *n.* Wocaŋteśica.
mortify, *v.* Caŋteśinya; kuka.
mortise, *n.* Caŋoḣdogyapi.
mosque, *n.* Ti'piwakaŋ.
mosquito, *n.* Capoŋka.
mosquito-bar, *n.* Capoŋgicuwa.
mosquito-hawk, *n.* Susbeca.
moss, *n.* Zitkanaipatapi; waanunu. *Water moss,* mniwaticoġe; hiŋtkaŋḣaka.
most, *a.* O'ta; owasiŋkinin. *adv.* Iyotaŋ.
mostly, *adv.* O'hiŋnise; ecee.
mote, *n.* Wokpe.
moth, *n.* Wamdudaŋkiŋyaŋ.
mother, *n.* Huŋ'ku; inayaŋpi. *My mother,* ina.—*Your mother,* nihuŋ.—*His* (or *her*) *mother,* huŋ'ku.
mother-in-law, *n.* Kuŋ'ku. *My mother-in-law,* kuŋ'śi; uŋciśi. *Your mother-in-law,* nikuŋ.—*His* (or *her*) *mother-in-law,* kuŋ'ku.
motherless, *a.* Huŋ'kucodaŋ.
motherly, *a.* Huŋ'ku seca.
mothy, *a.* Waŋmdudaŋ yukaŋ.
motion, *n.* 1. Wośkaŋśkaŋ; woiyopte, *the motion of the earth.* 2. Wi'kiyutapi, *he made motions for me to come.* 3. Omniciye wowiyukcaŋ, *I second the motion.* *vt.* Wi'kiyuta.
motive, *n.* Oŋ'ecoŋ; woyutitaŋ.
motley, *a.* Ocażeota.
motor, *n.* Woyutitaŋ.
mottle, *a.* Hdeśka.

motto, *n.* Iapi coya.
mould, *n.* Waanunu.
mouldy, *a.* Aa.
mound, *n.* Paha; pazo; makabohpa.
mount, *n.* Paha; ḣe. *vt.* Adi; iyakapta. *Mount a horse,* akan iyeiçiya.—*Mount cavalry,* akaŋyaŋgkiya.—*Mount a map,* waŋkan e'hde.
mountain, *n.* Ḣe; pahataŋka.
mountaineer, *n.* Ḣe'oti.
mountainous, *a.* Ḣe; ḣo'ŝki.
mountainside, *n.* Ḣeunaptaŋ.
mountebank, *n.* Wicahnayaŋ.
mounted, *a.* Akaŋyaŋka.
mourn, *vi.* Caŋteŝica; waŝihda. *vt.* Icaŋteŝica.
mournful, *a.* Oiyokiŝica.
mouse, *n.* Hituŋkadaŋ.
mouser, *n.* Hituŋkadaŋkuwa.
mousetrap, *n.* Hituŋkadaŋihmuŋke.
mouth, *n.* I. *My mouth,* mii. *The mouth of the river,* iyoḣdoke; mdote.
mouthful, *n.* Iohnaka.
mouthpiece, *n.* Oyape; i.
movable, *a.* Yutokaŋpica.
move, *vt.* Tokaŋ a'ya; yutokaŋ; yuŝkaŋŝkaŋ. *vi.* Tokaŋya; iyopte; ihdaka; ŝkaŋŝkaŋ.
movement, *n.* Woŝkaŋŝkaŋ; woiyopte; woecoŋ.
mow, *vt.* Kaŝda; peżikaŝda.
mow, *n.* Peżitipi.
mower, mowing machine, *n.* Peżiicaŝda.
Mr., Mister, *n.* Wicaŝta.
much, *a.* O'ta; utkaŋna. *T.* Yutkaŋla. *As much as,* iyenakeca.—*How much,* to'nakeca.—*So much,* henakeca.—*Too much,* ni'na o'ta. *n.* Wotaŋka; o'ta. *adv.* Ni'na: *much used.*
mucilage, *a.* Wiiyaskape.
muck, *n.* Peżihutkaŋ.
mucus, *n.* Paḣdi; toŋ.
mud, *n.* Upŝiża; maka coco.
muddle, *n.* To'ketutaŋiŋŝni. *vt.* Yuŝkiŝka.
muddy, *a.* 1. Upŝiża: *muddy shoes.* 2. Ŝoŝe: *muddy water.* *vt.* Akastaka; yuŝoŝe.
muff, *n.* Napeohnaiyeyapi.
muffle, *vt.* Apaḣta; yuhmuŋza.
muffler, *n.* Nakpiyutake.
mug, *n.* Kampeska wi'yatke.
mulatto, *n.* Ha'sapaciŋca.
mulberry, *n.* Caŋska; caŋska waskuyeca.
mulch, *n.* Wokpaŋka. *vt.* Caŋhuteakaḣpe.
mule, *n.* Ŝoŋ'ŝoŋna.
muley, *a.* He'wanica.
mulish, *a.* Okicaŋyeŝica.
mult-, *pref.* O'ta.
multiform, *a.* Okaḣota.
multiple, *a.* To'naakihde.
multiplication, *a.* Yuotapi.
multiplicity, *n.* Ni'na o'ta.
multiplier, *n.* Oŋ yuotapi.
multiply, *vt.* Yuota.
multitude, *n.* Wicota.
multitudinous, *a.* O'takiya.
mum, *a.* Ininauŋ.
mumble, *vt.* Iohmunsia.
mummery, *n.* I'ḣadecoŋpi.
mummy, *n.* Sagya wicahnakapi.
mumps, *n.* Cehupapopi.
munch, *vt.* Yamnumnuġa.
mundane, *a.* Makata.
municipal, *a.* Otoŋwe.
munificence, *n.* Wooḣaŋpi.
munificent, *a.* Oḣaŋpi.
munition, *n.* Oŋ kicizapi.
murder, *vt.* Tinkte. *n.* Tinktepi.
murderous, *a.* Tinktes'a; ŝi'ca.
murmur, *vi.* Ḣmuŋ; ażiżi; ba; wi'hnu.
muscle, *n.* 1. Conica pŝuŋka. 2. Tuki. *Muscle shell,* tukihasaŋ.
muscular, *a.* Taŋcaŋtaŋka; waŝ'aka.
muse, *vi.* Awaciŋ uŋ. *n.* Waawaciŋ; odowaŋ ka'ġa.

museum, *n.* Wowaŋyakehdepi.
mush, *n.* Yużapi ; wożapi.
mushy, *a.* Coco.
music, *n.* Dowaŋpi.
musical, *a.* Dowaŋs'a; dowaŋpise; oŋ dowaŋpi.
musician, *n.* Dowaŋwayupika.
musing, *pa.* Waawaciŋ.
musk, *n.* Siŋkpeoŋzimna.
musket, *n.* Akicitatamazakaŋ.
muskmelon, *n.* Sa'kayutapizi.
muskrat, *n.* Siŋkpe.
muslin, *n.* Miniȟuhaska.
musquito, *n.* Capoŋka.
muss, *vt.* Yuśkiśka. *n.* Wośkiśke.
mussel, *n.* Tukihasaŋ.
must, *v. aux.* A'wicakehaŋ ; to'ketu çeyaś ; he'cena iyecetu.
mustache, *n.* Putiŋhiŋ.
mustang, *n.* Śuŋgmaninuŋ.
mustard, *n.* Wa'ȟnakapizi'.
muster, *vt.* Yuwitaya ; mnayaŋ.
musty, *a.* Aamna ; aa.
mutable, *a.* Yutokecapica.
mute, *a.* Iapiokihiśni ; ieśni.
mutilate, *vt.* Yuśica ; baśpa.
mutilated, *pa.* Śpa ; ksa.
mutinous, *n.* Wakipażiŋ.
mutiny, *vi.* Itaŋcaŋkipażiŋ. *n.* Wokipażiŋ.
mutter, *vt.* Ȟdo'ȟdoeya.
mutton, *n.* Ta'ȟcaskatado.
mutual, *a.* Anog ; sakim.
muzzle, *n.* I ; i'paȟte. *vt.* I' paȟta.
my, *a.* Mitawa.
myriad, *n.* Ni'na o'ta.
myrrh, *n.* Caŋśiŋwaśtemna.
myself, *pron.* Miyeȟca.
mysterious, *a.* Okaȟniȟpicaśni ; wakaŋ.
mystery, *n.* Wonaȟbe.
mystical, *a.* Wakaŋkaŋ.
mystify, *vt.* Yuśkiśka.
myth, *n.* Ehaŋnawoyakapi ; hituŋkakaŋpi.
mythical, *a.* Kakaŋpi.
mythology, *n.* Wakakaŋpi.

N

nab, *vt.* Oyuspa.
nabob, *n.* Żinyaihduha.
nag, *n.* Śuŋghuna. *vt.* Yażimkuwa.
nail, *n.* Ma'zaiyokataŋ ; śake. *Finger-nail,* napsukaza śake. *vt.* Okataŋ.
naive, *a.* Katiŋyaŋ.
naked, *a.* Taŋcodaŋ ; e'cedaŋ.
namable, *a.* Cażeyanpica.
name, *n.* Caże ; wicacaże. *vt.* Cażeyata ; eciya. *What is your name,* to'ken eniciyapi he.—*He named him John,* John cażeyata.—*Call names,* ośtehda.
nameless, *a.* Cażewanica.
namely, *adv.* De'e ; dena e'e.
namesake, *n.* Cażeyuha.
nap, *n.* Woiśtiŋmacika ; hiŋkpina.
nape, *n.* Tahu.
napkin, *n.* I'ipakiŋte.
narcotic, *n.* Iśtiŋma peżuta.
narrate, *vt.* Oyaka.
narration, *n.* Oyakapi.
narrative, *n.* Woyake ; woyakapi.
narrow, *a.* Ci'stiŋna ; hdakiŋyaŋ ci'stiŋna ; oṭiŋza. *vt.* Yucikadaŋ.
narrowly, *adv.* Ci'stiyedaŋ ; kitaŋyaŋ ; aoṭiŋsya.
nasal, *a.* Po'ġe ; po'ġe etaŋhaŋ.
nasty, *a.* Śa'pa ; śi'ca.
natal, *a.* Toŋ'pi.
nation, *n.* Oyate.
national, *a.* Oyatetawa.
nationalize, *vt.* Oyatekaġa.
native, *a.* En toŋ'pi. *n.* Ikcewicaśta.

natural, *a.* Iyecinka; wicitawa; to'kecaśni.
naturalist, *n.* Ta'ku iyecinka icaġa onspeiçiciya.
naturalize, *vt.* Oyate o'pekiya.
natured, *a.* Tawacin.
naught, *n.* Ta'kudanśni.
naughty, *a.* Śi'ca; ohanśica.
nausea, *n.* Hitihdapi.
nautical, *a.* Miniwanca.
naval, *a.* Wi'tawata.
navel, *n.* Cekpaȟdoka.
navigable, *a.* Wa'takipi.
navigate, *vt.* Wa'ta on omani.
navy, *n.* Wi'tawata optaye.
nay, *n.* Hiya.
near, *a.* Ikiyedan; kiyedan; *T.* kanyela. *Near falling,* owateca hinȟpaye kta.—*Near together,* i'cikiyedan. *vt.* Ikiyedan ya.
nearly, *adv.* Ikiyedan.
neat, *a.* Wayuco; ska.
neatly, *adv.* Ayucoya.
nebulous, *a.* ·Po se.
necessary, *a.* Heceedan; heceedan econpica.
necessitate, *vt.* Togye econpicaśni.
necessity, *n.* Wokaśke.
neck, *n.* Tahu. *Neck of land,* izo.
necklace, *n.* Wanapin.
necktie, *n.* Tahuskaicaśke.
neckyoke, *n.* Tahuicaśke.
necrology, *n.* Wicaṭa owapi.
need, *vt.* Yuha iyececa; icakiża; on kuwapi iyececa. *vi.* Śta he'cetu: *you need not come.* *n.* Wokakiże.
needful, *a.* Cokaunpicaśni.
needle, *n.* Tahinśpaciḳadan.
needless, *a.* Śni śta hecetu; iyecetuśni; ituya.
needlework, *n.* Wokaġeġe.
needs, *n. pl.* Ta'ku yuha iyececa. *adv.* Iyececa.
needy, *a.* Kakiża.
ne'er, *adv. contr.* To'hinni śni.
nefarious, *a.* Ni'na śi'ca.
negation, *n.* He'cetuśni eyapi.
negative, *n.* He'cetuśni; hiya.
neglect, *vt.* Aktaśni. *n.* Waaktaśni.
neglectful, *a.* Waaktaśni.
negligence, *n.* Woaktaśni.
negligent, *a.* Waaktaśni.
negotiable, *a.* Wi'yopeyepica.
negotiate, *vi.* Woyuśtan ka'ġa.
negro, *n.* Waśicunsapa; ha'sapa.
neigh, *vi.* Śun'kawakanhoton.
neighbor, *n.* Ikiyenati.
neighborly, *a.* Kiciunpiwaśte.
neither, *a.* Unmannaśni.
nephew, *n.* Tonśka; mitonśka; nitonśka; tonśkaku.
nepotism, *n.* Takuya on o'kiya.
nerve, *vt.* On waś'agya. *n.* Kan.
nervous, *a.* Kan ececeśni; cancan; wakaȟtakeca; wasazeca.
nest, *n.* Hoȟpi; wahoȟpi.
nestle, *vt.* Adokso; kihna.
Nestor, *n.* Itancan.
net, *vt.* Hmun'ka; kamna. *n.* Wi'hmunke. *a.* Wayusota iwankam. *Fish-net,* ho-icuwa.
nether, *a.* Ku'ya.
netting, *n.* Miniȟuhaġanġan.
nettle, *vt.* Pażipa. *n.* Haśbe.
network, *n.* I'ciyuzontapi.
neuter, *a.* Unmannaśni.
neutral, *a.* Unmanna o'peśni.
never, *adv.* To'hinniśni.
nevertheless, *adv.* He'caśta.
new, *a.* Te'ca; nakaha.
newly, *adv.* Nakaha.
newness, *n.* Te'ca; wicateca.
news, *n.* Wotanin.
newspaper, *n.* Wotaninwowapi.
newt, *n.* Ahdeśka.
New-year, *n.* O'makateca.
next, *a.* I'yokihe; o'kihe.
Nez Percés, *n.* Po'ġeȟdoka.
nibble, *vt.* Yaśpaśpa.
nice, *a.* 1. Waśte: *a nice girl.* 2. Oiyokipi: *a nice time.* 3. Iwanyag teȟike: *a nice question.*
nicely, *adv.* Tan'yan.

nicety, *n.* Wowaŝte.
niche, *n.* Oko ; okaȟmiŋ.
nick, *n.* Oȟci ; oko. *vt.* Kaȟci.
nickel, *n.* Kaŝpapiokise. *Y.* Ŝo′kena. *T.* Ŝo′kela.
nickname, *n.* O′haŋhaŋ caže.
niece, *n.* Tožaŋ.
niggard, niggardly, *a.* Oȟaŋŝica ; wateȟiŋda.
nigger, *n.* Ha′sapa.
nigh, *a.* Ikiyedaŋ ; i′tato.
night, *n.* Haŋyetu. *Y.* & *T.* Haŋhepi. *Last night,* hiŋ′haŋ ; hehaŋpi. *To-night,* haŋyetu de ; haŋhepi de.
nightcap, *n.* Haŋhepi wapoŝtaŋ.
night-fall, *n.* Ḣtayetu.
nighthawk, *n.* Pi′ŝko.
nightly, *adv.* Haŋyetu iyohi.
nightmare, *n.* Iŝtiŋma iksuyapi.
nihilist, *n.* Waceṭuŋhda.
nimble, *a.* Oȟaŋko.
nine, *a.* Napciwaŋka.
ninefold, *a.* Napciwaŋka akihde.
nineteen, *a.* Akenapciwaŋka.
ninety, *a.* Wikcemnanapciwaŋka.
ninny, *n.* Witkotkoka.
ninth, *a.* Inapciwaŋka.
nip, *vt.* Yaksa ; yaŝpa ; ŝniŝya.
nippers, *n.* Mazwiyužipe.
nipple, *n.* Azeiŋkpa ; iŋ′kpa.
nit, *n.* He′ya ciŋca ; hemniŝakadaŋ.
nix, *n.* Wanica.
no, *adv.* Hiya : *no sir;* ŝni ; wanica.
nobby, *a.* Waŝtecaka.
nobility, *n.* Wokinihaŋ.
noble, *a.* Okinihaŋ ; waŝte.
nobleman, *n.* Itaŋcaŋ.
nobleness, *n.* Wokinihaŋ.
nobly, *adv.* Okinihaŋyaŋ.
nobody, *n.* Tuwedaŋŝni. *Nobody came,* tuwedaŋ hi ŝni.
nocturnal, *a.* Haŋhepi.
nod, *vi.* Pakapsaŋ ; oġiŋġiŋ.
noise, *n.* Ta′ku bu ; ho ; oḳo.
noiseless, *a.* Oḳo wanica.
noisome, *a.* Otaŋtoŋka.
noisy, *a.* Hobuŝkaŋ.
nomadic, *a.* Ihdaguŋpi.
nominal, *a.* Iapieceedaŋ.
nominate, *vt.* Cažepazo.
nominee, *n.* Cažepazopi.
non-, *pre.* Ŝni ; wanica.
none, *pro.* 1. Tuwedaŋŝni : *none spoke.* 2. Ta′kudaŋŝni : *none left. There is none,* wanica.
nonplus, *vt.* Waciŋhnuniya.
nonsense, *n.* Woawaciŋŝni.
nook, *n.* Okaȟmiŋ.
noon, *n.* Wi′cokaya ; wiyotaŋhaŋ; aŋpecokaya.
noonday, *a.* Wi′cokaya.
nooning, *n.* Wi′cokaya enakiyapi.
noontide, *n.* Wiiyotaŋ.
noose, *n.* Ŝuŋžoyake.
nor, *adv.* Ḳaiŝ... ŝni. *He did not speak nor move,* ie ŝni, ḳaiŝ ŝkaŋŝkaŋ ŝni.—*Neither... nor,* ḳaiŝ.. uŋmaŋna... ŝni.—*He can neither see nor hear,* wawaŋyaka ḳaiŝ wanaȟoŋ uŋmaŋna okihi ŝni.
normal, *a.* Wahehantu ; wooŋspe.
north, *n.* Waziyata.
northeast, *a.* Wiyohiyaŋpa waziyata.
northerly, *a.* Waziyatataŋhaŋ.
northern, *a.* Waziyata.
North Platte (river), *n.* Kampeska.
northward, *a.* Waziyatakiya.
northwest, *a.* Wiyoȟpeyata waziyata.
nose, *n.* Po′ġe ; pasu.
nosebleed, *n.* Po′gewewe.
nosegay, *n.* Waȟcaopaȟte
nostril, *n.* Po′ġeoȟdoka.
not, *adv.* Ŝni : *not good.*
notable, *a.* Okitaŋiŋ.
notary, *n.* Wowapi ma′zaapuspa.
notation, *n.* Oyawa owapi.
notch, *n.* Oȟci ; oȟi. *vt.* Baȟci.
note, *vt.* 1. Owa : *I noted it in my book.* 2. Amdeza : *I noted the spot.* *n.* 1. Wowapi ci′stiŋna :

I received your note. 2. Każużupi kta wowapi : *he gave his note for ten dollars.* 3. To'ketu oyakapi : *notes on Romans.* 4. Wokitaŋiŋ : *a man of note.* 5. Dowaŋpi ho owapi : *I want a note-book.*
noted, *a.* Okitaŋiŋ.
noteworthy, *a.* En e'waciŋpica.
nothing, *n.* 1. Ta'kudaŋ... śni. *He has nothing,* ta'kudaŋ yuhe śni. 2. Ta'kuśni : *it grew from nothing to be a great city.*
notice, *vt.* Amdeza ; en e'toŋwaŋ ; waŋyaka. *n.* Woyakapi ; wowakta ; woamdeza.
noticeable, *a.* Taŋin ; okitaŋin ; en e'toŋwepica.
notification, *n.* Iwaktayapi.
notify, *vt.* Iwaktaya ; okiyaka.
notion, *n.* Wowiyukcaŋ ; woawaciŋ.
notional, *a.* Tawaciŋ hahadaŋ.
notoriety, *n.* Ni'na oyakapi.
notorious, *a.* A'taya otaŋiŋ.
notwithstanding, *adv., prep., conj.* He'caśta ; he'cecaśta ; śta.
noun, *n.* Wocaże.
nourish, *vt.* Icaĥya ; woku.
nourishment, *n.* Oŋ icaġapi ; woyute.
novel, *a.* Te'ca ; to'keca : *a novel idea.* *n.* Kakaŋpi wowapi.
novelist, *n.* Wakakaŋ.
novelty, *n.* Ta'ku te'ca.
November, *n.* Tahecapśuŋwi.
novice, *n.* Nakaha ecoŋ.
now, *adv.* 1. Waŋna ; dehan : *do it now.* 2. Dehan : *it is cold now.* 3. Nakahaś : *I saw him just now.*
nowadays, *adv.* Dehan
noway, *adv.* To'ketuśta.
nowhere, *adv.* Tuktedaŋśni.
nowise, *adv.* To'ketuśta.
noxious, *a.* Woĥaka ; śi'ca.
nozzle, *n.* Ma'zaĥdoġeca i.
nucleous, *n.* Hu'te.
nude, *a.* Taŋcodaŋ.
nudge, *vt.* Panini.
nugatory, *a.* Wi'yokihiśni.
nugget, *n.* Oŋśpa.
nuisance, *n.* Wonaġiyeya.
null, *a.* Ta'kuśni.
nullify, *vt.* Yutakuniśni.
nullity, *n.* Ta'kuśni.
numb, *a.* Tasaka.
number, *vt.* Ya'wa. *n.* Woyawa ; wayawapi ; to'nakeca.
numerable, *a.* Yawapica.
numeral, *n.* Oŋ wayawapi.
numerate, *vt.* Yawa.
numerator, *n.* Okaśpe to'nakeca.
numerical, *a.* To'nakeca.
numerous, *a.* O'ta ; wicota.
numskull, *n.* Witkotkoka.
nun, *n.* Ṡinasapawiŋyaŋ.
nunnery, *n.* Ṡinasapawiŋyaŋ ti'pi.
nuptial, *a.* Wakaŋkiciyuzapi.
nurse, *n.* Hokśiyopa awaŋyaka ; wayazaŋka awaŋyaka. *vt.* Awaŋyaka ; aziŋkiya.
nursery, *n.* 1. Ohna hokśiyopa awaŋyakapi. 2. Caŋ'ożupi oicaĥye ; oicaĥye.
nurture, *n.* Icaĥya ; woku. 2. Woicaġe ; wooŋspe ; woyute.
nut, *n.* Yuĥuġapi ; ma'zaayuho mnipi.
nutmeg, *n.* Caŋsuukaseca.
nutriment, *n.* Oŋ waśakapi.
nutritious, *a.* Waś'agwicaya.
nutshell, *n.* Yaĥuġapiha.
nymph, *n.* Wiŋ'yaŋ wanaġi.

O

o, *interj.* Ho; howo; ye; e; waŋ; u. *O God! hear,* Wakaŋtaŋka naȟoŋ ye.—*O for a drop,* ośbuye waŋżidaŋ mduha ni. —*O dear!* ecaȟe.

oak, *n.* Utuhu; ituhu; uskuyeca. *An oak tree,* utuhu caŋ.

oaken, *a.* Utuhu.

oakum, *n.* Wa'ta opuȟdi.

oar, *n.* Wamnaheca; i'watopekiya; wadihupa.

oarsman, *n.* Watopa.

oasis, *n.* Makawaśte: makopuze ekta oŋśpa waśte.

oats, *n.* Wayahota.

oath, *n.* Wakaŋtaŋka cażeyatapi. *He was taking the oath,* Wakaŋtanka cażeyankiyapi.—*On his oath,* Wakaŋtaŋka cażeyan. —*Profane oaths,* Wakaŋtaŋka iȟad cażeyatapi.

oatmeal, *n.* Wayahota yukpaŋpi.

obduracy, *n.* Caŋtesutapi.

obdurate, *a.* Caŋtesuta; teȟika.

obdurately, *adv.* Okihipicaśniyaŋ.

obedience, *n.* Waanaġoptaŋ; wanaȟoŋpi.

obedient, *a.* Wanaȟoŋ; waanaġoptaŋ; wawiyowiŋkiya.

obediently, *adv.* Waanaġoptaŋyaŋ; iyowiŋyaŋ.

obeisance, *n.* Wapatużapi; woohoda.

obelisk, *n.* Iŋ'yaŋ omdotoŋ pasdatapi.

obey, *vt.* Anaġoptaŋ; naȟoŋ; ecen ecoŋ. *Obey your mother,* nihuŋ anaġoptaŋ. *vi.* Waanagoptaŋ.

obituary, *n.* Wicaṭe; wicaṭa oyakapi.

object', *vi.* Wicadaśni; ienhiyeya. *He objects to going,* ye kta wicadaśni.

ob'ject, *n.* 1. Ta'ku; ta'ku waŋżi. *All objects,* ta'ku owasiŋ. 2. Ta'ku oŋ etaŋhaŋ. *Man does nothing without an object,* wicaśta ta'ku oŋ etaŋhaŋśni ta'kudaŋ ecoŋśni. 3. (*Gram.*) Wi'koyake; iapi ikoyake.

objection, *n.* Wowicadaśni; wokaśe; oŋ wicadaśni.

objectionable, *a.* I'enhiyeyepica.

objective, *a.* 1. Ta'ku; i'ye taŋ'taŋhaŋ; ta'ku taŋiŋ. 2. (*Gram.*) Ikoyag uŋ.

objectively, *adv.* Taŋiŋyaŋ.

objector, *n.* I'enhiyeyes'a.

oblation, *n.* Wośnapi; *Y.* waiȟpeyapi; *T.* wauŋyaŋpi.

obligate, *vt.* Ecoŋkiya; en kaśka yu'za.

obligation, *n.* Wokaśke; wi'yuze; ta'ku ecoŋ iyececa. *The son is under obligations to his father.* Ciŋhiŋtku kin atkuku ta'ku ecakicoŋ iyececa.

obligatory, *a.* Sutayaikoyake.

oblige, *vt.* 1. Ecoŋkiya; -kiya; i'yopaśtag ecoŋkiya: *they obliged him to go.* 2. Pidakiya; o'kiya. *I am obliged to you,* pidamayakiya.—*I obliged him,* pidawakiya.

obliging, *a.* Wawapidakiye.

oblique, *a.* Atakiŋyaŋ; oȟ'ya.

obliquely, *adv.* Ipaweȟya; oh'ya.

obliquity, *n.* Woaȟtani; woyuśna.

obliterate, *vt.* Yutaŋiŋśni; yużużu.

obliteration, *n.* Wayutaŋiŋśni.

oblivion, *n.* Wokiksuyeśni.

obloquy, *n.* Wowaȟtedaśni.

obnoxious, *a.* Wayuśica; waȟtedapiśni.

obscene, *a.* Wowiśteca; śa'pa.

obscenity, *n.* Wowiśteca iapi.

obscuration, *n.* Akaȟpapi.

obscure, *vt.* Akaȟpa; yutaŋinšni. *a.* 1. Taŋiŋšni; kitaŋyaŋ taŋiŋ: *an obscure expression.* 2. Tu'we taŋiŋšni: *an obscure man.* 3. Naȟmana uŋ; tuwedaŋ se waŋyakešni: *an obscure bird.* 4. To'ken ka'pi taŋiŋšni; okaȟniȟ teȟike: *an obscure order.*
obscurely, *adv.* Taŋiŋšniyaŋ.
obscurement, *n.* Woyutaŋiŋšni.
obscureness, *n.* Otaŋiŋšni.
obscurity, *n.* Wonaȟbe; to'ketu taŋiŋšni.
obsequious, *a.* Ituya wayataŋ; waasdohaŋ.
obsequies, *n.* Wicaṭa okuwa.
observable, *a.* Waŋyagpica; kiksuyepica; opepica.
observance, *n.* Ahopapi; wooho-da; ohodapi; woahope. *The observance of the Sabbath,* Aŋpetuwakaŋ ahopapi. *Catholic observancies,* Šinasapa woahope.
observant, *a.* 1. Wa'mdeza; wa'kite: *an observant boy.* 2. Ahope; en e'toŋwe: *observant of the rules.*
observantly, *adv.* Wa'mdesya.
observation, *n.* 1. Woiwaŋyake; woamdeza; iwaŋyakapi; wi'waŋyakapi. *I know by observation.* 2. Woawaciŋ; wowiyukcaŋ; iapi: *a wise observation.* 3. Woiyute; wicaŋȟpi iyute.
observatory, *n.* Wicaŋȟpi iwaŋyakapi ti'pi; toŋweya co'wahe.
observe, *vt.* 1. Ahope; kiksuye; pataŋ; en ewaciŋ; pakaŋ: *observe the Sabbath.* 2. Iwaŋyaka; amdeza: *observe the man's actions.* 3. Oyaka; e'ya.
observe, *vi.* Wa'mdeza; woyaka.
observer, *n.* Wa'mdeza; waohoda; wawoyaka.
observing, *a.* Wa'mdeza.

obsolete, *a.* Waŋna uŋ'pi šni: *obsolete customs.*
obstacle, *n.* Wokaġi; wokaše.
obstetrics, *n.* Ciŋcatoŋwicakiyapi wooŋspe.
obstinacy, *n.* 1. Tawaciŋ sutapi; wonaȟoŋ nicapi. *Obstinacy in a pupil is dreadful.* 2. Piyepicašni.
obstinate, *a.* Wakitaŋ; wanaȟoŋšni; okihipicašni.
obstinately, *adv.* Wakitaŋyaŋ; wanaȟoŋšniyaŋ.
obstruct, *vt.* Kaġiya; anica. *Obstruct the workmen,* ȟtanipi kiŋ kaġiwicaya.—*It obstructs the flow of water,* mini kaduze cin anica.
obstructer, *n.* Wakaġiya.
obstruction, *n.* Wokaġi; woanica; kaġiyapi.
obtain, *vt.* Okini; icu; kihdeġa. *I have now obtained the money,* waŋna ma'zaska owakini.—*He did not obtain what he earned,* ta'ku kamna kiŋ icu šni.—*At last he obtained renown,* uŋ'haŋketa wokitaŋiŋ kihdeġa.
obtainable, *a.* Icupica; okihipica.
obtainer, *n.* Tu'we icu kiŋ.
obtrude, *vt.* En hiyuiçiye ȟca *He obtruded himself,* kicopišni en hiyuiçiya.
obtuse, *a.* 1. Taŋ'ka; pe'sto šni: *obtuse angle.* 2. Ȟaŋhi; waciŋksapešni.
obverse, *a.* Ite ituŋkam.
obviate, *vt.* Kakamiyeya.
obvious, *a.* Taŋiŋ; taŋiŋyan waŋka; okitaŋiŋ: *the meaning is obvious.*
obviously, *adv.* Taŋiŋyaŋ; okitaŋiŋyaŋ.
occasion, *n.* Oeyuȟpa; aŋpetu; ta'ku oŋ ciŋ'pi; ouŋ; ka'ġa. *vt.* Ka'ġa.
occasional, *a.* Wan'waŋcadaŋ; enanakiya.

occasionally, *adv.* Tuktekten.
occident, *n.* Wiyoḣpeyata.
occult, *a.* Waŋyagpicaṡni; anaḣbeya uŋ.
occupancy, *n.* Hduhapi; otipi.
occupant, *n.* Oti; yuha.
occupation, *n.* 1. Yuha uŋ'pi; otipi; en ti'pi. 2. Wicoḣaŋ; woṡkiŋciye. *Our occupation is farming,* wicoḣaŋ uŋkitawapi wożupi he'e.
occupy, *vt.* 1. Oti; ohna un: *I occupy this house.* 2. Ożudaŋya; akan uŋ: *his buildings occupy half an acre.* 3. Kuwakiya; waṡi: *Ten carpenters were occupied.* 4. Yuha; yusota. *He occupied my time ten days,* aŋpetu wikcema makiyusota.
occur, *vi.* 1. Yukaŋ; akipa; icaġa. *What has occurred at the Agency. If opportunity occurs,* oko yukaŋ kiŋhaŋ. 2. Woawaciŋ hi; kiksuya. *It occurred to me just in time,* iyehantudaŋḣiŋ we'ksuya.
occurrence, *n.* Woakipa; woyutokeca: *daily occurrences.*
ocean, *n.* Miniwaŋca; ta'ku iyotaŋ taŋ'ka.
oceanic, *a.* Miniwaŋcata.
ocher, *n.* Makaṡa.
octagon, *n.* Cuwi ṡahdoġaŋ.
octave, *n.* Ho ṡahdoġaŋ.
October, *n.* Wi iwikcemna; ważupi-wi.
octoroon, *n.* Okaṡpe iṡahdoġaŋ ha'sapa.
ocular, *a.* Iṡta oŋ waŋyakapi.
oculist, *n.* Iṡtakuwa.
odd, *a.* 1. To'keca; oḣaŋtokeca; wowiḣa: *an odd boy.* 2. Sani; sani wanica. *A lot of odd shoes.* 3. Iyaye; ta'kudaŋ kicica ṡni: *odd pieces of calico.*
oddity, *n.* To'keca; wowiḣa.
oddly, *adv.* Togye; wowiḣaya.
oddness, *n.* Wotokeca; wowiḣa.
odds, *n.* Wowiyukcaŋ.
ode, *n.* Odowaŋ okinihaŋ.
odious, *a.* Waḣteṡni; waḣtedapiṡni.
odiously, *adv.* Waḣtedaṡniyaŋ.
odium, *n.* Wowaḣteṡni.
odometer, *n.* Caŋkuiyute (caŋpahmihma hu ikoyake).
odor, *n.* Woomna; omnapi. *A sweet odor,* waṡtemna.
odorless, *a.* Takumnaṡni.
odorous, *a.* Ecamna; waṡtemna.
of, *prep.* 1. (Denoting source) Etaŋhaŋ. *I received it of my father,* ate etaŋhaŋ mduha.—*Give of your substance,* woyuha nitawa etaŋhaŋ ku.—*Within a step of the river,* wakpa etaŋhaŋ cahdepi waŋżi. 2. Oŋ; oŋ etaŋhaŋ. *Of his own will,* iye tawaciŋ oŋ. 3. (Possessory) Ta'wa; ta-; yuha. *The house of the king,* itaŋcaŋ ti'pi ta'wa.—*The strength of the lion,* mnaża to'waṡ'ake. —*The shoe of a woman,* wiŋ'yaŋ tahaŋpa.—*A man of strength,* wicaṡta wowaṡ'ake yuha. 4. (With a qualifying noun the force of the proposition is often expressed by juxtaposition.) *A boat of bark,* caŋhawata.—*The city of Omaha,* Omaha otoŋwe.—*The love of God is everlasting,* Wakaŋtaŋka to'waṡtedake owihaŋke wanica.
off, *adv.* 1. Tokaŋ; to'kiya; tokaŋyaŋ; iyog. *Don't look off,* tokaŋ e'toŋwe ṡni.—*He is gone off,* to'kiya iyaye.—*The cover is off,* iha kiŋ iyog uŋ. 2. I'tokaŋ; i'citehaŋ. *The river is a mile off,* wakpa kiŋ iyutapi waŋżi i'tokaŋ uŋ.—*Off and on,* enanakiya.—*The concert will come off,* dowaŋpi kiŋ ecoŋpi kta.—*To get off a speech,* woo-

wohdake ecoŋ.—*To get off from trial,* woyaco etaŋhaŋ tokaŋ iyaye.—*Tell off the names,* wicacaże oy.g a'ya.—*He is well off,* taŋyaŋ uŋ.—*Off hand,* waŋ'cahnana.—*Off side,* uŋmaŋ eciyataŋhaŋ.—*Cut off,* baṡpa.

off, *interj.* Tokaŋ ya; kihda.

off, *a.* 1. Akotaŋhaŋ; uŋmaŋeciyataŋhaŋ: *the off ox.* 2. Aiecetuṡni: *an off year.*

offal, *n.* 1. Ta'ku eḣpeyapi. *The offal covered the streets,* ta'ku eḣpeyapi kiŋ caŋku ożudaŋ. 2. Taṡupe; wopate to'na yu'zapi ṡni.

offend, *vi.* Iyokipiṡniya; ṡihdaya. *He was offended,* iyokipiṡniyapi.

offend, *vi.* Waḣtani; woope kicakse.

offender, *n.* Waḣtanis'a.

offense, *n.* Woaḣtaní; woiyokipi ṡni; woṡihda.

offensive, *a.* 1. Iyowicakipiṡni; woṡihda: *offensive words.* 2. I'ye wicakuwa.

offer, *vt.* 1. Ḳu kta eya; kipazo; iwaŋyagṡi: *he offered me his horse.* 2. Waiḣpeya; woṡna.

offer, *n.* 1. Woecoŋ; ecoŋ kta eyapi. *He made a kind offer,* taŋyaŋ ecoŋ kta eya. 2. Ta'ku ḳu'pi; to'nakeca oŋ ecoŋpi kta. 3. Woiyuta: *he made no offer to run.*

offering, *n.* 1. Woṡnapi; waiḣpeyapi; womnaye wakaŋ. *The missionary offering,* wotaŋiŋwaṡte womnaye. 2. Ta'ku ecoŋpi kta eyapi.

offhand, *a.* Ihnuhaŋ; i'tokam awaciŋ ṡni: *an offhand speech.*

office, *n.* 1. Ti'pi; ti; ohna ṡkiŋ'ciye: *agent's office.* 2. Woecoŋ; woitaŋcaŋ: *an office in the church.*

office-holder, *n.* Woitaŋcaŋyuha; wicoḣaŋyuha.

officer, *n.* Itaŋcaŋ: *a military officer.* *vt.* Itaŋcaŋ wicakaġa.

official, *a.* Woitaŋcaŋ; woecoŋ.

officially, *adv.* Itaŋcaŋ eciyataŋhaŋ.

officiate, *vt.* Ecoŋ; woitaŋcaŋ wicoḣaŋ ecoŋ.

officious, *a.* Itaŋcaŋ kte ḣca.

officiously, *adv.* Itaŋcaŋiçidase.

offscouring, *n.* Ta'ku eḣpeyapi.

offset, *n.* Adetka; wokażużu.

offshoot, *n.* Adetka.

offspring, *n.* Ciŋca.

oft, *adv.* See OFTEN.

often, *adv.* S'a; iżehaŋ; iciżehaŋ; akihde; o'ta. *He comes here often,* den hi s'a. *How often,* tona.

oftentimes, *adv.* Iciżehaŋ; o'takiya.

Ogalalla, *n.* *T.* Oglala; *Y.* Okdada.

oh, *interj.* E; waŋ; yu.

oil, *n.* Wi'hdi; *Y.* wi'kdi; *T.* wi'ġli; sda; wi'hdi tiktica. *Castor-oil,* wi'hdi iyoptaiyeyapi. *vt.* Sdaya.

oilcloth, *n.* Miniḣuha ṡduṡduta.

oiled, *a.* Sdayapi; sda.

oiler, *n.* Isdaye.

oilstone, *n.* Wiohdisda.

oily, *a.* Sda; ṡduṡduta.

ointment, *n.* Wi'sdaye; ihepi.

Ojibway, *n.* Ḣaḣatoŋwaŋ.

old, *a.* 1. Ehaŋna; wanakaża; o'ta. *An old man,* wicaṡta ehaŋna; wicaḣca.—*Old age,* waniyetu o'ta. 2. Icaġa; uŋ; aouŋye; (often unexpressed.) *A babe a few days old,* hokṡiyopa aŋpotu to'nana.—*How old are you,* waniyetu nitonakeca he.—*I am ten years old,* waniyetu mawikcemna. 3. Ehaŋtaŋhaŋ; ehaŋnataŋhaŋ. *An old ball player,* ehaŋnataŋhaŋ

takapas'a. 4. Ehaŋna uŋ'pi; waŋna śi'ca; kaŋ: *an old coat.*
olden, *a.* Ehaŋna.
older, *a. comp.* Tokapa.
oldish, *a.* Ki'taŋna ehaŋna.
old-fashioned, *a.* Okaġe ehaŋna.
old-man, *n.* Wicaḣca.
old-woman, *n.* Wakaŋka; *Y.* winoḣca; *T.* winoḣcala.
oleomargarine, *n.* Asaŋpi ihdi wasna oŋ ka'ġapi.
olfactory, *a.* Oŋ womnapi.
olive, *a.* To'sapa.
Omaha, *n.* Omaha.
omega, *n.* Ehake; oowa ehake.
omelet, *n.* Wi'tka kacoco śpaŋyaŋpi.
omen, *n.* Wohdece; wowakta.
omen, *vt.* Kihdeca; wakcaŋ.
ominous, *a.* Wowakta; wakihdecapi.
omission, *n.* Ecoŋpi śni; aktoŋżapi; yuśnapi.
omit, *vt.* Yuśna; ecoŋ śni.
omnibus, *n.* Caŋpahmihma anokataŋhaŋ i'yotaŋkapi; o'ta kipi.
omnipotent, *a.* Iyotaŋ waś'aka.
omnipresent, *a.* O'waŋcaya uŋ.
omniscient, *a.* Ta'ku owasiŋ sdonya.
omnium-gatherum, *n.* Wokpahi.
omnivorous, *a.* Ta'ku owasiŋ yu'ta.
on, *prep.* 1. Akan; a-: *on the table.*—*The board fell on me,* caŋmdaska amahiŋḣpaye. 2. En; icuŋhaŋ. 3. Iyehan; eca; ehan. *On the breaking out of the war,* okicize icaġa ehan. 4. I'takihna; akan. *Stones upon stones,* iŋ'yaŋ i'takihnahna. 5. Oŋ; cażeyan. *On his oath,* Wakaŋtaŋka cażeyan. 6. En; ekta. *On the public works,* oyate ta'wicoḣaŋ en.—*He bet on the little horse,* śuŋ'kawakaŋ ci'stiŋna en iyakaśka. 7. Etaŋhaŋ; ekta. *On the committee,* committee etaŋhaŋ.—*On the one hand,* de'ciyataŋhaŋ.—*Come on,* mi'hakam u; howo.—*Put your dress on,* nitośke kiçuŋ.—*Depend on,* waciŋyaŋ. *House on fire,* ti'pi ide.—*On the way,* tahepi.—*On the wing,* auŋyaŋ; owaŋżi uŋ śni.—*Placed on high,* waŋkan e'hnaka.—*Play on the violin,* caŋpakiŋzapi dowaŋkiya.—*Walk on,* amani.
on, *adv.* Saŋ'pa; iyoopta. *Go on,* saŋ'pa ya.
once, *adv.* 1. Waŋ'cadaŋ. *Do it once,* waŋ'cadaŋ ecoŋ. 2. To'hiŋni; ehaŋna: *once there was an earthquake. All at once I heard it,* ihnuhaŋna nawaḣoŋ.—*All at once, heave,* owasiŋ o'koŋwanżidaŋ, yutitaŋ.—*Do it at once,* waŋ'cahnana ecoŋ.—*Once and again,* akihdehde.—*Once more,* ehake.—*Once started,* to'hiŋni iyaye ciŋhaŋ.—*Once upon a time,* to'hiŋni aŋpetu waŋ en.—*This once,* deceedaŋ.
one, *a.* Waŋżi; waŋżidaŋ; waŋżina; waŋ'ca; sani.—*All one,* to'keca śni.—*One day,* aŋpetu waŋżi; to'hiŋni.—*One foot,* sisani.—*One hand,* napsani.—*One or the other,* de'e ķaiś he'e; uŋmaŋtukte waŋ'zi.—*The enemies are at one,* to'kakiciyapi kiŋ waŋna okowaŋżipidaŋ.
one, *n.* 1. Waŋżi. "*He will hate the one and love the other.*" 2. Oŋġe; to'na; waŋżikżi. *The big ones,* to'na taŋkiŋkiŋyaŋ.—*The little ones,* cikcistiŋpidaŋ; wakaŋheża.—*One by one,* waŋżikżi.
one, *pron.* Tu'we; tu'wekaśta. *One another,* kici.—*They embraced one another,* po'skin kiciyuzapi.
oneness, *n.* Wowaŋżidaŋ.

onerous, *a.* Tke.
one-sided, *a.* Sanina; sanito'keca.
one's self, *pron.* Iye'hca; iye i'yatayedaŋ.
ongoings, *n.* Woecoŋ; woiyopte.
onion, *n.* Pśiŋ.
only, *a.* 1. Heceedaŋ. *The only survivor,* heceedaŋ ni. 2. Iśnana; -na'na. *I only,* miśnana.—*You only,* niśnana.—*He only,* iśnana.—*The man only,* wicaśta iśnana.—*Only one,* waŋżidaŋ. —*Only two,* nom'nana.
onset, *n.* Wonataŋ; takpeyapi.
onslaught, *n.* Wonataŋ; ki'ciyaḣpayapi.
onto, *prep.* Akan.
onward, *a.* Iyopta; saŋ'pa ya: *the onward march.*
onward, *adv.* Saŋ'pa; iyopteya.
ooze, *vi.* Naśdi; śdi'śdi; ske'pa.
opaque, *a.* Kohdiśni; taŋiŋśni.
open, *a.* Yuġaŋ haŋ; kazamni haŋ; natakeśni; ca'ġaśni; taŋiŋyaŋ uŋ; akaḣpeśni. *An open account,* oicazo wowapi yuśtaŋpiśni.—*An open basket,* makaŋopiye akaḣpapiśni.—*An open door,* tiyopa yuġaŋ haŋ.—*Open air,* taŋkan tate.—*Open countenance,* waanakiḣbeśni ite.—*Open flowers,* waḣca kazamnipi. —*Open for an engagement,* ta'ku ecoŋkiyapi kta wi'yeya uŋ. —*Open guilt,* woaḣtani taŋiŋyaŋ uŋ.—*Open house,* ti'pi yuḣdog haŋ.—*Open road,* caŋku natakapiśni.—*Open shed,* ti'pi ahaŋke oḣdoka o'ta.—*Open to attack,* iyaḣpayapi waśte.—*Open winter,* waniyetu wa wanica.
open, *vt.* Yuġaŋ; yuzamni; yuḣdoka; yukawa; yutaŋin; tokaheya ecoŋ. *Opened his plans,* to'ken ecoŋ kta yutaŋiŋ.—*Open one's mouth,* i hdukawa.—*Open the box,* koka yuḣdoka.—*Open the door,* tiyopa yuġaŋ.—*Open the hand,* nape yumdaya.—*Open the letter,* wowapi yuḣdoka.—*They opened fire,* iye tokaheya ma'zakaŋ utapi. *vi.* Kazamni iyaye.
opener, *n.* Oŋ yuḣdokapi; yuḣdoke.
open-handed, *a.* Waiḣpeyes'a; oḣaŋpi.
open-hearted, *a.* Waanaḣbeśni; canwihaha.
opening, *n.* 1. Oḣdoka; oyugaŋ; oko: *there was an opening in the roof.* 2. Yuḣdokapi; wotokahe; tokaheya ecoŋpi. *I saw him at the opening of the Conference.* 3. Oko; oḣna yaŋka waśte. *An opening for a doctor.* 4. Caŋwehna oko; caŋhdehde.
openly, *adv.* Taŋiŋyaŋ; anaḣbeśni.
open-mouthed, *a.* Icam; oḣaŋśuŋkeca.
opera, *n.* Dowaŋśka'tapi; wośkateti'pi.
operate, *vt.* Ecoŋ; kuwa; ka'ġa. *Operate a sewing-machine,* oŋ wakaġeġepi ecoŋ. *vi.* Śkaŋ; waecoŋ; iheyekiya; kuwa.
operation, *n.* Wokuwa; wicoḣaŋ; woecoŋ; kuwapi.
operative, *a.* Kuwa okihi; wi'yokihi. *n.* Kuwa wayupikapi.
operator, *n.* Tu'we kuwa kiŋ.
opiate, *n.* Iśtiŋbekiyapi peżuta; ożiwicayapi.
opine, *vt.* Eciŋ; iyukcaŋ.
opinion, *n.* Woawaciŋ; wowiyukcaŋ; waciŋyuzapi. *The opinion is prevalent,* woawaciŋ kiŋ taŋ'kaya uŋ.—*The good opinion of my friends,* mitakada taŋyaŋ ecaŋmakiŋpi.
opium, *n.* Peżuta oŋ iśtiŋmapi.
opossum, *n.* Siŋteśdataŋka.
opponent, *n.* Kici ecoŋ; to'ka;

i'tkokim na'żiŋ ; kuwa ; wicada śni.
opportune, *a.* Waiyehantu.
opportunity, *n.* Ohna oecoŋ waśte ; oko ; iyehantu.
oppose, *vt.* I'tkokipa ; kipażiŋ ; wicada śni ; ecetu kte śni ; kuwa ; anapta. *I did not oppose him,* i'tkowakipe śni.—*He opposed her going,* ye kta wicada śni.—*They opposed the Government,* woitaŋcaŋ kiŋ kipażiŋpi. —*They opposed the prohibition law,* miniwakan anaptapi woope ecetu kte śni kuwapi.
opposer, *n.* Wakipażiŋ; waanapte.
opposite, *a.* Uŋmaŋ eciyataŋhaŋ ; akasaŋpa ; koakata ; uŋmaŋ ; to'keca ; itkom uŋ. *The opposite leaves,* ape i'tkokicipa.—*The opposite party,* ośpaye uŋmaŋ. *The opposite side of the street,* caŋku uŋmaŋ eciyataŋhaŋ.
oppositely, *adv.* I'citkokim.
opposition, *n.* 1. Wowicadaśni ; wokipażiŋ ; kipażiŋpi ; kaġiyapi. *Their opposition is vain,* wicadapi śni kiŋ ta'kudaŋ iyokihi śni. 2. Wakipażiŋpi ; i'tkokikapi ; uŋmaŋpi ; ośpaye uŋmaŋ. *The opposition killed the bill,* ośpaye uŋmaŋ woope kiŋ yutakunipi śni.
oppress, *vt.* Kakiśya ; tkeya ķiŋkiya.
oppression, *n.* Wakakiśyapi ; wokakiże ; iyahdaskin uŋ.
oppressive, *a.* Tke ; wakakiśya ; iyahdaskica.
oppressively, *adv.* Tkeya ; wakakiśya.
oppresssor, *n.* Wakakiśya ; śicaya wicakuwa.
opprobrious, *a.* Wowiśteca ; wahteśni.
opprobrium, *n.* Wowahteśni.
optative, *a.* Ciŋ'pi.
optic, *a.* Iśta ; oŋ toŋwaŋpi.
optical, *a.* Iśta.
optics, *n.* Wi'yożaŋżaŋ wooŋspe ; wiciśta wooŋspe.
optimist, *n.* Tu'we ta'ku owasiŋ icaŋtewaśte uŋ.
optimistic, *a.* O'hiŋni waśte kta keciŋ.
option, *n.* Wokahniġe ; wakahniġapi ; ciŋ'pi ; tohan ciŋpi.
optional, *a.* Ciŋ'pi kiŋhaŋ ecoŋpi kta : *optional studies.*
opulence, *a.* Woyuha ; wowiżice.
opulent, *a.* Watoŋka ; wi'żica.
or, *conj,* Ķaiś ; *T.* naiś.
oracle, *n.* Ta'kuwakaŋ oie ; ta'kuwakaŋ ; wakaŋdapi.
oracular, *a.* Wakaŋ.
oral, *a.* Ieyahaŋ yuhapi ; owapi śni.
orally, *adv.* Ieyahaŋ.
orange, *n.* Taspaŋġi.
orange, *a.* Zi'ġi.
orang-outang, *n.* Wauŋca istohaŋska.
oration, *n.* Owohdake ; woowohdake.
orator, *n.* Ieksapa ; wohdaka.
oratorical, *a.* Ieksapa.
oratory, *n.* Wayapiya wohdakapi.
orb, *n.* Ta'ku mima ; wi ; wicaŋhpi.
orbit, *n.* Oahomni ; ocaŋku.
orchard, *n.* Waskuyeca caŋwożupi.
orchestra, *n.* Caŋpakiŋzapi optaye.
ordain, *vt.* Ka'ġa ; wicaśtawakaŋ ka'ġa ; kahniġa.
ordained, *p.* Ka'ġapi ; yuśtaŋpi.
ordeal, *n.* Oecoŋ ; wowawiyutaŋye.
order, *n.* 1. Waecoŋśipi ; woope. *An order to sell no whisky,* miniwakaŋ wi'yopeyapi kte śni woope.—*Our orders were not to stop,* na'żiŋ śni uŋśipi. 2. To'ken o'weciŋhaŋ waŋka ecee ; owotaŋna. *Bring them in reg-*

ular order. 3. Ta'ku da'pi wowapi; ta'ku ecoŋwicaśipi; ķuwicaśipi wowapi. *I sent an order for goods*, ma'za da'pi wowapi yewaya.—*Please give me an order for beef*, tado ķuwicaśipi wowapi maķu ye. 4. Ocaże; obe: *order of talent*. 5. Okodakiciyε: *the order of Odd Fellwos*. 6. Woecon. *The old order of things*, ehaŋna woecoŋ kiŋ.—*Give orders*, ecoŋwicaśi.—*In order to*, oŋ etaŋhaŋ.—*Keep order*, owaŋżi yaŋka; ecen yaŋka.—*Money order*, oŋ ma'zaska icupi wowapi — *Order book*, ta'ku da'pi wowapi.—*Order of battle*, okicize oecoŋ.—*Put the house in order*, ti'pi kiŋ taŋyaŋ piyapi.—*Standing orders*, eca oecoŋ.—*The order of words in English*, Waśicuŋ iapi woeye to'ken o'wėciŋhaŋ waŋka.

order, *vt.* 1. Ecoŋśi; -śi. *He ordered me out of the house*, taŋkan yemaśi. 2. Da; auwicaśi: *he ordered some water*. 3. E'hnaka; kuwa.

orderly, *a.* 1. Ta'ku owasiŋ taŋyaŋ waŋka: *an orderly town*. Wanaħoŋpi; owaŋżi uŋ'pi.

ordinance, *n.* Woope.

ordinarily, *adv.* Ecee.

ordinary, *a.* He'cetuka; to'ken yuhapi ecee.

ordination, *n.* Wicaśtawakaŋ ka'ġapi; wokaġe.

ordnance, *n.* Ma'zakaŋtaŋka.

ore, *n.* Ma'za oķapi ecehna.

organ, *n.* 1. Caŋ'dowaŋkiyapi. *A cabinet organ*, caŋdowaŋkiyapi koka omdotoŋ se.—*A pipe organ*, caŋdowaŋkiyapi mazaħdoġeca. 2. Adetka; oŋśpa etaŋhaŋ; huha.

organic, *a.* Huha yukeya; o'kihe yukaŋ.

organism, *n.* Ta'ku huha yukaŋ.

organization, *n.* Ta'ku taŋcaŋ huha ko ka'ġapi; okodakiciye.

organize, *vt.* Ośkiŋciye kta iyecen ka'ġa; wicoħaŋ ecekcen itaŋcaŋ wicakaġa; itaŋcaŋ wicakaġa; ecekcen waecoŋwicakiya.

organizer, *n.* Waecoŋwicakiya.

orgies, *n.* Śka'tapi.

orient, *n.* Wi'hinaŋpa; wiyohiyaŋpa.

oriental, *a.* Wiyohiyaŋpata.

orifice, *n.* Oħdoka.

origin, *n.* Otokahe; ohinaŋpe.

original, *a.* Otokahe; tokaheya ka'ġapi; naħaŋħ uŋ'pi śni.

originality, *n.* Tokaheya wi'yukcaŋpi.

originally, *adv.* Otokaheya; iyeciŋka.

originate, *vt.* Tokaheya ka'ġa; ka'ġa. *vi.* Tokaheya icaġa.

ornament, *n.* Woyuwaśte; wowitaŋ. *vt.* Yuwaśte; wi'pata.

ornamental, *a.* Wayuwaśte.

ornamentally, *adv.* Yuwaśteya.

ornamentation, *n.* Wayuwaśtepi; wi'patapi; oiŋkitoŋpi.

ornamenter, *n.* Wayuwawaśte.

ornate, *a.* Yuwaśtepi; yucoya ka'ġapi; waśte.

ornithology, *n.* Waħupakoza wooŋspe; zitkadaŋ oyakapi.

orphan, *n.* Wamdenica.

orphanage, *n.* 1. Wamdenicatipi. 2. Wowamdenica.

orthodox, *a.* Owotaŋna; woope ohnayaŋ.

orthography, *n.* Iapi oowa taŋyaŋ e'hnakapi; oowa eyapi.

Osage (Indians), *n.* Ważaża.

oscillate, *vi.* Kazezeya.

oscillating, *a.* Kaozeze.

oscillation, *n.* Wokaze.

ossify, *vi.* Hu icaġa.

ostensible, *a.* Pazopi.

ostensibly, *adv.* Se ececa; keya.

ostentation, *n.* Wi'hdutaŋpi.
ostentatious, *a.* Wi'taŋtaŋpi.
ostracise, *vt.* Napeya; oyate ta'wa etaŋhaŋ kihdeya.
ostrich, *n.* Waȟupakozataŋ'ka.
other, *a.* Uŋmaŋ; to'keca. *Give to others,* tokaŋ wicaḳu.—*No other but,* tu'we to'heca.—*Some... other,* oŋġe... oŋġe.—*The other day,* aŋpetu he'kta; decana.—*The other side,* uŋmaŋ eciyataŋhaŋ.
otherwise, *adv.* 1. Togye. *He thought otherwise,* i'ye togye awaciŋ. 2. He'cetuśni kiŋhaŋ; togye uŋ'kaŋś.
Otoe (Indians), *n.* Oyatenoŋpa.
Ottawa (Indians), *n.* Hotawe.
otter, *n.* Ptaŋ.
Ottoman (*Turk*), *n.* Wicaśta.
ought, *v. aux.* Iyececa; he'cetu. *You ought to go,* de kta iyececa.
ounce, *n.* Otkeute ci'stiŋna.
our, *pron.* Unkitawapi; uŋki-. *Our country,* uŋkitamakoce.—*Belongs to you and me* (dual), uŋkitawa.
ours, *pron. poss.* Uŋkitawapi.
ourselves, *pron.* Uŋkiyepi ȟca. *We ourselves,* uŋkiyepiiyatayedaŋ.
oust, *vt.* Yutokaŋiyeya; iyayeya.
out, *adv.* Taŋkan. *Cried out,* ni'na eya.—*Day in and day out,* aŋpetu ad'ataya.—*Fell out of the wagon,* caŋpahmihma etaŋhaŋ hiŋȟpaya.—*Fell out about who should ride,* tu'we akaŋyotaŋke kta akinicapi.—*Find out,* iyeya.—*Fire went out,* pe'ta sni.—*Hear the speech out,* owohdake ihuŋniyaŋ naȟoŋ.—*He laughed out,* taŋiŋyaŋ iȟa.—*Out and out,* a'taya; taŋataya.—*Out at the knees,* caŋkpeȟdoka.—*Out in his calculations,* iyawa ekta yuśna; yuśna.—*Out in the field,* taŋkan ma'ga ekta; maġata.—*Out of,* etaŋhaŋ taŋkan; i'taŋkan.—*Out of breath,* niyaśni.—*Out of business,* wicoȟaŋ ni'ca.—*Out of conceit with,* iyokipi śni.—*Out of date,* aŋpetu i'saŋpa; iyehantuśni.—*Out of joint,* o'kihe papśuŋ; papśuŋ.—*Out of his mind,* tawaciŋ en uŋ śni; akiktoŋża; waciŋhnuni.—*Out of one's head,* waciŋhnuni.—*Out of order,* śicaya uŋ; yuśicapi.—*Out of pocket,* ma'zaska oŋġe kiyusota.—*Out of print,* yusotapi.—*Out of the question,* en e'waciŋpicaśni.—*Out of reach,* iyohiyepicaśni—*Out of season,* o'maka iyehantuśni.—*Out of sight,* taŋiŋśni; waŋyagpicaśni.—*Out of sorts,* caniyokipiśni.—*Out of sugar,* caŋhaŋpiyusota.—*Out of temper,* waciŋko.—*Out of the way,* caŋku icuŋom; icuŋom.—*Out West,* wiyoȟpeyata.—*Put out of the way,* icuŋom iyeya; ktepi.—*Put the lights out,* petiżaŋżaŋ bosni.—*The secret is out,* ta'ku naȟmaŋpi kiu otaŋiŋ.—*The wine is out,* miniśa kiŋ henana.—*You put me out by your noise,* oḳo kiŋ oŋ yuśnamayaya.
out, *vt.* Taŋkaŋ u; taŋiŋ. *Truth will out,* wowicake taŋiŋ kta.
out, *interj.* Taŋkaŋ iyaya; iyaya.
out-, *pref.* I'saŋpa; kapeya; kte'daŋ.
outargue, *vt.* I'akapeya.
outbalance, *vt.* I'saŋpa tke.
outbeg, *vt.* Wadapi kte'daŋ.
outbreak, *n.* Bośdokapi; wośice.
outburst, *n.* Bomdazapi.
outcast, *a.* Taŋkan eȟpeyapi.
outcome, *n.* Etaŋhaŋ ta'ku icaġe.
outcry, *n.* Owodutatoŋ; i'eniyeyapi.
outdo, *vt.* Ikapeya ecoŋ.

outdoor, *a.* Taŋkan.
outer, *a.* Haakamya ; taŋkan.
outermost, *a.* Taŋkanihaŋke.
outfit, *n.* Oŋ ihduwiyeyapi ; wi'kicaŋye.
outflank, *vt.* Aohomniya.
outgo, *vt.* Wayusotapi ; kapeya.
outgoing, *n.* Oenape.
outgrow, *vt.* I'akamicaġa ; taŋ'kaicaġa.
outhouse, *n.* Taŋkantipi.
outing, *n.* Enanakiya uŋ'pi ; tokaŋ uŋ'pi.
outlandish, *a.* To'keca ; ṡi'ca.
outlast, *vt.* I'sam te'han waṡte kta.
outlaw, *n.* Woope inażica uŋ ; woope ohoda ṡni. *vt.* Woope itaŋkan iyeya.
outlay, *n.* Ma'zaska yusotapi ; wokażużu.
outlet, *n.* Iyoḣdoke ; oenape.
outline, *n.* Ohomni icazopi ; owohdake ocaŋkuye. *vt.* Icazo ; ptenyedaŋ oyaka.
outlive, *vt.* I'saŋpa ni.
outlook, *n.* Owaŋyake ; iteka ; woiwaŋyake.
outlying, *a.* I'hdukṡaŋ ; opapuŋ.
outmost, *a.* Ihaŋke.
outnumber, *vt.* I'akam o'ta.
out-of-door, *a.* Taŋkan.
out-of-the-way, *a.* Makoskan.
outpost, *n.* Icuŋomti'pi ; wooŋspe icuŋoŋpa.
output, *n.* To'nakeca icupi ; ka'ġapi.
outrage, *n.* Ta'ku ṡi'ca ; woṡice.
outrage, *vt.* Ṡicayakuwa ; iyaḣpaya.
outrageous, *a.* Ni'na ṡi'ca ; wohitika.
outrageously, *adv.* Ni'na ṡicaya.
outrank, *vt.* I'waŋkam itaŋcaŋ
outright, *adv.* He'ceḣ.
outroom, *n.* Icuŋomtipi.
outrun, *vt.* Kapeya iŋ'yaŋka ; kapa.
outset, *n.* Otokahe.
outshine, *vt.* Ikapeya wiyakpa ; kape.
outside, *a.* Taŋkan ; ihaŋke.
outside, *n.* Akapataŋhaŋ ; taŋkantaŋhaŋ.
outsider, *n.* Taŋkan uŋ.
outskirt, *n.* Opapuŋ.
outspoken, *a.* Taŋiŋyaŋ eya ; anaḣbeṡni.
outstanding, *a.* Ecenhaŋ ; każużupiṡni.
outstrip, *vt.* Kapa.
outtravel, *vt.* Kapeyaicimani.
outwalk, *vt.* Ma'nipikapa.
outward, *adv.* Taŋkantkiya. *a.* Taŋkantaŋhaŋ ; taŋkantkiya ; haakamya.
outwardly, *adv.* Akanya.
outwear, *vt.* Te'han suta ; i'saŋpa te'han suta kta.
outweigh, *vt* I'saŋpa tke.
outwit, *vt.* I'saŋpa ksa'pa.
oval, *a.* Wi'tkamibe.
ovation, *n.* Yuonihaŋpi ; yuonihaŋpi omniciye.
oven, *n.* Owaṡpaŋye.
over, *prep.* 1. Iwaŋkam. *Hold it over your head,* pa kin iwaŋkam yu'za. 2. O'pta ; akasaŋpa ; a-. *Throw over,* o'pta eḣpeya.—*Go over the river,* akasaŋpa ya ; *T.* koakata ya.—*Jump over,* apsica. 3. Ihuŋni ; icuŋhaŋ. *Take care of it over winter.* waniyetu ihuŋni awaŋyaka.—*Stay over night,* haŋyetu uŋ.—*Have the advantage over,* iwaŋkam wookihi yuha.—*Over four dollars,* ma'zaska to'pa iwaŋkam.—*Run over and killed,* adipi ķa ţeyapi.—*The river ran over the banks,* wakpa maya apaṡboka.
over, *adv.* 1. O'pta ; hdakiŋyaŋ : *come over.* 2. Ihuŋniyaŋ ; amdesya : *go over the accounts.* 3. I'saŋpa ; akaḣya. *Over-*

zealous, aokaȟya mdiheca. 4. Ahdapśiŋyaŋ; yuptaŋyaŋ: *turn over the board*. 5. Ihuŋni; henana: *dinner was over*.—*All over*, o'waŋcaya; henana.—*All over with the sick man*, wicaśta wayazaŋka waŋna ihuŋni.—*Over again*, akihde.—*Over against*, iyotakoŋs.—*Over and above*, iyaye; okitaŋiŋyaŋ—*Over and over*, akihdehde.—*To do over*, akihde ecoŋ.

over, *a*. 1. Aokaġa; ehaeś ni'na ecoŋpi: *over-work*. 2. Akan; akanuŋpi: *over coat*.

overalls, *n*. Oŋzeogeakanuŋpi.

overanxious, *a*. Ehaeś ni'na awaciŋ.

overawe, *vt*. Inihaŋya.

overbalance, *vt*. Iwaŋkam tke.

overbearing, *a*. Ksizeca; ohitiiçida.

overboard, *adv*. Minin; wa'ta etaŋhaŋ mini en.

overcareful, *a*. Ehaeś ni'na awaŋyake.

overcast, *vt*. Akaȟpa.

overcharge, *vt*. O'ta kaźuźukiya; o'ta ohnaka.

overcoat, *n*. Akanokde; uŋ'ȟoȟda akan uŋ'pi.

overcome, *vt*. Oȟiya; kte'daŋ.

overconfident, *a*. Ehaeś ni'na awaciŋ.

overcount, *vt*. Iwaŋkam yawa.

overdo, *vt*. Ehaeś ni'na ecoŋ.

overdose, *n*. Ehaeśotaķu.

overdraw, *vt*. Iwaŋkam icu; a'kam iyaye; oźudaŋya; apaśboka.

overflow, *vt*. Amnitaŋ; o'waŋcaya iyaya. *Overflowed the field*, ma'ġa amnitaŋ. — *Foreigners overflowed the country*, oyatetokeca makoce o'waŋca iyayapi.

overflow, *vi*. Apaśboka; a'kam iyaye: *the river overflowed*.

overgrown, *a*. Ehaeś taŋ'ka.

overhaul, *vt*. Yuźuźu waŋyaka kihdeġa.

overhead, *adv*. Waŋkan.

overhear, *vt*. Naȟmaŋnaȟoŋ.

overheated, *pa*. Ni'na ka'ta.

overhung, *a*. Akeyapi.

overissue, *n*. Iwaŋkam wicaķupi.

overjoyed, *a*. Ni'na iyuśkiŋ.

overland, *a*. Makaamaui; makaadiya.

overlap, *n*. I'ciyakaȟpapi.

overlay, *vt*. Akaȟpa; źu; ahdaskica.

overload, *vt*. O'ta ohnaka.

overlook, *vt*. 1. Waŋyag haŋ; iwaŋkam uŋ: *the fort overlooks the town*. 2. Iwaŋkam e'toŋwaŋ; awaŋyaka. 3. Aktaśni e'toŋwaŋ; en e'toŋweśni.

overly, *adv*. Iwaŋkam; ni'na.

overlying, *a*. Iwaŋkam yaŋka.

overmatch, *n*. Iwaŋkam waś'aka.

overmodest, *a*. Ehaeś wi'śteca.

overnight, *adv*. Haŋyetu icuŋhaŋ; haŋyetu ihuŋni.

overpass, *vt*. I'sam ya.

overpay, *vt*. I'akam kaźuźu.

overpeople, *vt*. Ehaeś oyate oţiŋsya.

overplus, *n*. Iyaye.

overpower, *vt*. Wowaś'ake oŋ ecoŋkiya; kte'daŋ.

overproduction, *n*. Ehaeś o'ta icaġa.

overrate, *vt*. Waŋkantuyaȟ yawa.

overreach, *vt*. Iwaŋkam iyohiya; hna'yaŋ.

override, *vt*. 1. Adi: *he overrode all obstacles*. 2. Ehaeś te'han akaŋyotaŋka: *he overrode the horse*.

overrighteous, *a*. Waśte koŋzapi.

overripe, *a*. Ni'na sutoŋ.

overrule, *vt*. Iwaŋkam yuśtaŋ; yutokeca.

overrun, *vt*. 1. Adi; a'taya iyaye; o'ta. *The vine overran the fence*, wi'yuwi coŋ'kaśke adi.—*The*

weeds overran the farm, caŋhdoȟu makoce a'taya iyaya. 2. I'sam iyaya; kapa.
overscrupulous, *a.* Ehaeś woope ohoda ȟca.
oversee, *vt.* Awaŋyaka.
overseer, *n.* Waawaŋyake; awaŋyaka.
overshot, *a.* Iwaŋkam yeya.
oversight, *n.* 1. Woawaŋyake. *He has the oversight of the mill.* 2. Waŋyake śni.
overskirt, *n.* Nitiyapehe akanuŋpi.
oversleep, *vi.* Te'haniśtiŋma.
overspread, *vt.* A'tayaiyaye.
overstate, *vt.* Akaȟoyaka.
overstay, *vt.* Te'hanyaŋka.
overstep, *vt.* I'samcaehde.
overstock, *vt.* Ehaeś o'ta ahipi.
overstrain, *vi.* Ś'agya.
oversure, *a.* Ehaeś wicakeiçida.
overt, *a.* Taŋiŋyaŋ uŋ.
overtake, *vt.* Kihdeġa; e'hdeġa.
overtax, *vt.* Ehaeś tkeya ķiŋkiyapi.
overthrow, *vt.* 1. Yuptaŋ eȟpeya; kaptaŋyaŋ: *overthrew the table.* 2. Każużu; ihaŋgya.
overthrow, *n.* Woihaŋgye.
overtop, *vt.* Ikapeya waŋkantuya.
overture, *n.* 1. Wowiyukcaŋ. 2. Otokahe dowaŋpi.
overturn, *vt.* Yuptaŋyaŋ; kawaŋka.
overweight, *n.* Iwaŋkam tke.
overwhelm, *vt.* Akaȟpa; iyahdaskica.
overwhelming, *a.* Taŋ'ka; wośuŋgye.
overwork, *vt.* Ni'na tkeya ecoŋkiya; yuś'aka.
overwork, *vi.* Ś'agiçiya.
overwork, *n.* A'kam ȟtanipi.
owe, *vt.* 1. Ikicazo; icazo. *I owe*, iwakazo.—*I owe him*, iwecazo. —*You owe*, iyakazo.—*You owe him*, iyecazo.—*He owes*, icazo. —*He owes him*, ikicazo. 2. Etaŋhaŋ yuha; okihiya: *he owed it to his father.* 3. Ķu iyececa; icazo.
owing, *pa.* 1. Icazo; ikicazo. 2. (with *to*) Oŋ etaŋhaŋ; oŋ etaŋhaŋ he'ceca. *Owing to his sickness*, wayażaŋka oŋ etaŋhaŋ.
owl, *n.* Hiŋhaŋkaġa; hiŋyaŋkaġa.
own, *vt.* 1. Yuha; ta'waya; ta'wa. *Who owns that house*, ti'pi he tu'we ta'wa.—*I own it*, mi'ye mduha. 2. He'cetu eya; ohdaka.
own, *a.* Ta'wa. *My own*, mi'ye mitawa.—*Your own*, ni'ye nitawa.—*To hold one's own*, he'cehnana uŋ.
owner, *n.* Ta'waya.
ownerless, *a.* Tuwena ta'wa śni.
ownership, *n.* Ta'wayapi.
ox, *n.* (*pl.* **oxen.**) Tataŋka; tataŋka wosdohaŋ.
oxbow, *n.* Wanapiŋ oyukśaŋ.
oxgoad, *n.* Tataŋgicape.
oxhide, *n.* Tataŋkaha.
oyster, *n.* Tukihasaŋ.

P

pace, *n.* Caehdepi. *vi.* Caehde; ma'ni; naś'oś'o ma'ni.
pacer, *n.* Śuŋgonaś'o; naś'oś'o.
pacific, *a.* Amdakedaŋ; waȟbadaŋ; wawiciya.
pacification, *n.* Wicayuwaȟbapi; wicayuwaśtepi.
pacify, *vt.* Yuwaȟba; yuwaśte.
pack, *vt.* 1. Koka ohnaka; paȟta; he'yuŋ: *pack your goods.* 2. Naȟmaŋ ohnaka; naȟmaŋ kuwa: *pack a jury.* 3. Ożuya; oţiŋs ka'ġa: *pack a joint of the pipe.* *n.* Wapaȟtapi; wo-

heyuŋ ; wopaȟta ; optaye ; woyuṭiŋża.

package, *n.* Wopaȟte ; opaȟte ; oheyuŋ ; wapaȟtapi.

packer, *n.* Wapaȟta ; wapata.

packet, *n.* 1. Wapaȟtapidaŋ : *a packet of letters.* 2. Pe'tawata wowapitokšu.

pack-horse, *n.* Šuŋktaŋka waḳiŋkiyapi.

pack-house, *n.* Ti'piwakihnakapi ; tado okicaŋye.

packing, *n.* Waohnakapi ; paoṭiŋs hna'kapi.

pack-saddle, *n.* Šuŋgaḳiŋ oŋ waḳiŋkiyapi.

pad, *n.* 1. Miuŋpi : *put a pad under the collar.* 2. Wowapiska apaṭiŋzapi. 3. Wamanoŋ omani.

padding, *n.* Iyopuȟdi.

paddle, *n.* Wamnaheca ; *Y.* iwatopekiya ; wadihupa. *vi.* Watopa ; *Y.* ko'za. *vt.* Iyopteya ; wamnaheca kiçuŋ.

paddler, *n.* Watopa.

Paddy, *n.* *Irish* iašica.

padlock, *n.* Tiyominatake pšuŋka.

pagan, *n.* Wakaġapi ohoda ; ikcewicašta.

paganism, *n.* Wakaġapi ohodapi.

page, *n.* 1. Yumdapi ; wowapi oyumda : *the second page.* 2. Hokšidaŋwowaši. *vt.* Yumdapi ka'ġa.

pageant, *n.* Wowaŋyake ; wapazopi.

pageantry, *n.* Waihdataŋpi.

pagoda, *n.* Wakaġapi ti'pitaŋka.

pail, *n.* Ce'ġa ; kokadaŋ ; miniyaya : *that pail leaks.*—*A small pail,* ceġastiŋna.—*A wooden pail,* kokatodaŋ.

pailful, *n.* Ce'ġa ohnaka ; ce'ġa ożudaŋ.

pain, *n.* Woyazaŋ ; yazaŋpi ; wakakišyapi ; woteȟi : *a pain in the head.*—*Take pains,* awaciŋȟca ecoŋ.—*Under pain of,* kokipe.—*With pains,* kakišya ; awaciŋya. *vt.* Yazaŋya ; ksu'weya ; kakišya.

painful, *a.* 1. Iyazaŋ ; yazan : *his foot is painful.* 2. Teȟike : *a painful task.*

painfully, *adv.* Icakišva ; teȟiya.

painfulness, *n.* Woyazaŋ ; woteȟi.

painless, *a.* Yazaŋšnt.

painstaker, *n.* Taŋ/yaŋ ecoŋwaciŋ.

paint, *n.* Wı'saŋye ; wi'uŋpi. *vt.* 1. Owa ; iuŋ ; saŋyaŋ : *paint the house.* 2. Wi'uŋpi oŋ iteowa ; wowa. 3. Oyaka ; waŋyakapi se'ca oyaka.

painter, *n.* Ti'pisaŋyaŋ ; iteowapi ka'ġa.

painting, *n.* 1. Saŋyaŋpi ; iuŋpi : *the house needs painting.* 2. Iteowapi : *a painting hung on the wall.*

pair, *n.* Noŋ'paakicaška ; tawaŋżi : *he gave me a pair.* *vi.* Kicica ; nom'nom ya'pi. *vt.* Ki'cicaya ; kici iyayeya.

palace, *n.* Ti'piitaŋcaŋ ; ti'pitaŋka.

palatable, *a.* Oyunwašte.

palate, *n.* Caka ; u'tapi.

palatial, *a.* Ti'pitaŋka ; wašteȟca.

palaver, *n.* Owohdake. *vi.* Wohdaka ; iayaŋka.

pale, *a.* 1. Ska ; saŋ ; ececešni.—*Pale blue,* to'saŋ ; maȟpiyato.—*His face turned pale,* ite ececešni. 2. Iwaštedaŋ : *pale red.*

paleness, *n.* Woececešni.

paling, *n.* Caŋmdaska sbu'na ; coŋkaške pe'sto.

palisade, *n.* Coŋ'kaške.

pall, *vi.* Waš'akešni.

pall-bearer, *n.* Wicahnakapi akiyuhapi.

pallet, *n.* Owiŋżašicedaŋ.

palliate, *vt.* Ikiya ; to'kecašni keya.

pallid, *a.* Ececašni ; saŋ.

palm, *n.* 1. Napcoka ; napemda-

ska. 2. Caŋwapaicadu; caŋwapaicadu caŋ. *vt.* Hna'yaŋ ḳu.
palmetto, *n.* Caŋwapaicadu.
palpable, *a.* Taŋtoŋ; taŋiŋyaŋ uŋ.
palpably, *adv.* Taŋiŋyaŋ.
palpitate, *vi.* Apapa; iyapa.
palpitation, *n.* Iyapapi.
palsy, *n.* Taŋcaŋ ṭaṭake.
paltry, *a.* Ta'kuśni; ci'stiŋna; waḣteśni.
pamper, *vt.* Woḳu; iyowiŋya.
pamphlet, *n.* Wowapi ożuhaśoka waninya.
pan, *n.* Ceḣska wakśica.—*Hardpan,* maka ḳeza.
panacea, *n.* Peżuta woyazaŋ owasiŋ okihi.
pancake, *n.* Aġuyapiokaśtaŋśpaŋyaŋpi.
pander, *vi.* Ta'ku iyecetuśni iyowiŋyaŋ.
pane, *n.* O'żaŋżaŋhdepi; omdaye.
panegyric, *n.* Wayaonihaŋpi.
panful, *n.* Wakśica ohnaka.
pang, *n.* Woyazaŋicapapiseca.
panic, *n.* Iksuyapi.
panic-stricken, *a.* Iksuyapi.
panoply, *n.* Ozuye oihduze.
panorama, *n.* Wowaŋyake yuhomni ayapi.
pansy, *n.* Waḣcato.
pant, *vi.* 1. Temni; oḣaŋkoya niya; niyaśniṭa nuŋse: *how the baby pants.* 2. Ni'na ciŋ: *pant for glory.*
pantalet, *n.* Oŋzeoġedaŋ; huŋska.
pantaloon, *n.* Oŋzeoġe.
pantheism, *n.* Ta'ku siŋtomni wakaŋdapi.
panther, *n.* Inmutaŋka; *Y.* ikmuŋtaŋka; *T.* igmuŋtaŋka.
pantomime, *n.* Wowaŋyake ieśni oyakapi; ieśni woyakapi.
pantry, *n.* Waśpaŋkakihnagtipi.
pants, *n.* Oŋzeoġe.
pap, *n.* Azeiŋkpa; woyute.
papa, *n.* Aṭe; atkuku.
papacy, *n.* Śinasapa woitaŋcaŋ.
papal, *a.* Śinasapa ateyapi ta'wa.
paper, *n.* 1. Wowapiska; miniḣuhaska: *two sheets of paper.* 2. Wowapi: *he signed the paper.* 3. Wotaŋiŋ wowapi: *the morning paper.*—*Paper money,* miniḣuha ma'zaska.—*Waste paper,* wowapi eḣpeyapi. *vt.* Wowapi tiaskamya: *paper the room.*
papist, *n.* Śinasapa; okdesapa.
papoose, *n.* Hokśiyopa.
par, *n.* A'kidecece.
parable, *n.* Wi'yaciŋpi.
parabolically, *adv.* Wi'yaciŋyaŋ.
parade, *n.* Ikpazo omanipi. *vt.* Ikpazo omani; itutu omani.
paradise, *n.* 1. Wowiyuśkiŋ makoce: *what a paradise you live in.* 2. E'den caŋwożupi. 3. Maḣpiya.
paradox, *n.* Wohnaye se'ca tka wicake.
paragon, *n.* Woiyotaŋ.
paragraph, *n.* Iapi oonażin; optapi.
parallel, *a.* 1. I'akicitehan; a'kiyehan waŋka: *a parallel river.* 2. A'kidececa; iyececa: *a parallel story.*
parallelism, *n.* Ta'ku iyececa.
paralysis, *n.* Taŋcaŋ ṭaṭapike.
paralyze, *vt.* Kiksuyeśniya.
paramount, *a.* Iyotaŋ; iwaŋkam uŋ.
paramour, *n.* Naḣmaŋ waśtekicidapi; naḣmaŋ kiciyuzapi.
parapet, *n.* Akicita makaḳapi.
paraphrase, *n.* Akta taŋ'yaŋ oyakapi.
parasite, *n.* Waas'iŋ; ta'ku tokaŋ ta'wapi oŋ ni.
parasitic, *a.* Wakipi oŋ ni.
parasol, *n.* O'haŋzihdepi ci'stiŋna.
parboil, *vt.* Ipiḣya.
parcel, *n.* Wapaḣtapi; oŋġe.
parch, *vt.* 1. Papaḣya: *parch corn.*

2. Ṡpaŋye; atasagye: *the ground is parched.*
parchment, *n.* Tahasaka.
pardon, *vt.* Ki'cicażużu; kiyuṡka. *n.* Wokażużu; woyuska.
pardonable, *a.* Każużupica.
pardoning, *a.* Ki'cicażużupi.
pare, *vt.* Basku; baḣdaya; ha eḣpeya: *pare an apple.*
paregoric, *n.* Każopi anapte.
parent, *n.* Huŋkake; etaŋhaŋ icaġe. *His parents are dead.*
parentage, *n.* Wicahuŋkake.
parental, *a.* Huŋkake ta'wa.
parenthesis, *n.* Natakapi.
parhelion, *n.* Wi acetipi.
paring, *n.* Ha; ha baskupi.
parish, *n.* Woawaŋyake; wicaṡtawakaŋ to'awaŋyake; okcdakiciye.
parishioner, *n.* Okodakiciye o'pa.
parity, *n.* Woakidececa.
park, *n.* Caŋwożupi; woṡkate makoce.
parlance, *n.* Iapi.
parley, *vi.* Wohdaka.
parliament, *n.* Sagdaṡiŋ omniciye taŋ'ka.
parliamentary, *a.* Omniciye woecoŋ.
parlor, *n.* Tioyaŋke waṡte.
parochial, *n.* Okodakiciye.
parody, *n.* Wayutokecapi.
paroxysm, *n.* Kaŋ'natipapi; to'kecapi.
parricide, *n.* Huŋkake kte.
parrot, *n.* Zitkadaŋia.
parry, *vt.* Kakam iyeya.
parse, *vt.* O'kihe oyaka.
parsimonious, *a.* Wateḣiŋda.
parsimony, *n.* Wateḣiŋdapi.
parsnip, *n.* Paŋġiżiżi.
parson, *n.* Wicaṡtawakaŋ.
parsonage, *n.* Wicaṡtawakaŋoti.
part, *n.* 1. Oŋṡpa; okise: *a part of the field.* 2. Oŋġe: *a part of the flour.* 3. O'kihe: *the different parts of the body.* 4. Wawokihi; woksape: *a man of parts.* 5. Oyaŋke; makoce: *there never was a school in these parts.* 6. Wopamni; wobaṡpe: *my part of the goods.* 7. (*Mus.*) Wicaho: *what part do you sing.* 8. (*Gram.*) Wocaże: *the verb is the most difficult part of speech.*—*For my part,* miyeḳe. —*For the most part,* ecee. —*In good part,* canwaṡteya.— *Take part in,* oŋṡpa ecoŋ.— *Your part,* oŋṡpa nitawa. *vt.* Kinukaŋ iyeya; yukinukaŋ; yuksa; pamni: *they parted the children. vi.* Tokaŋ iyaye: *he parted from his wife.*—*To part with,* kpaġaŋ.
partake, *vi.* 1. Oŋġe icu; etaŋhaŋ icu: *partook of the wine.* 2. Oŋṡpa iyececa: *He partakes of the nature of God and man.*
partaker, *n.* Kicica; kodaya; o'pa: *partaker in the punishment.*
parted, *a.* Ṡpahaŋ; kinukaŋ uŋ'pi.
partial, *a.* 1. Iyokise; oŋṡpa: *a partial good.* 2. Sanina o'kiya; iyotaŋda: *Jacob was partial to Joseph.*
partiality, *n.* Sanina o'kiyapi; i'akidecen ecoŋpi ṡni.
partially, *adv.* Okiseya: *partially true.*
participant, *n.* O'pa.
participate, *vi.* O'pa.
participation, *n.* O'papi.
participle, *n.* (*Gram.*) Aehnake wawoyake.
particle, *n.* 1. Oŋṡpa ci'stiŋna; ta'ku ci'stiŋna; sukaza. 2. (*Gram.*) Wicoiedaŋ.
particular, *a.* 1. I'atayedaŋ; ka'pi e'eḣca; waŋżidaŋ: *on a particular day.* 2. Okitaŋiŋ; oyagpica: *no particular news.* 3. Ḳezeca; iyokipiyapi teḣike. *She is particular about her food. n.* O'kihe; adetka; wokpaŋka:

ta'kuśniśni : *give all the particulars.*
particularize, *vi.* Taŋ'yaŋ oyaka.
particularly, *adv.* Iohdamnayaŋ; taŋ'yeȟca.
parting, *n.* Yukinukaŋpi; oksahe.
partisan, *n.* Ta'wa e'cedaŋ o'kiya. *a.* Sanina.
partition, *n.* Ti'pi cokaya natakapi; o'zaŋpi; kiyuśpapi.
partly, *adv.* Okiseya.
partner, *n.* Kicica; o'pa.
partnership, *n.* O'kiciyapi; okodakiciyepi.
partook, *imp.* of PARTAKE.
partridge, *n.* Zi'ca.
parturition, *n.* Cincatoŋpi.
party, *n.* 1. Ośpaye : *the Democrat party.* 2. Kicicopi : *a tea party.* 3. Optaye; wicaśta oŋġe : *a party of hunters.* 4. Waŋżi ee; kicica : *he was a party to the murder.* 5. Tu'we; wicaśta : *the party accused.*
paschal, *a.* Woacakśiŋ.
pasha, *n.* *Turk* oyate itaŋcaŋ.
pass, *vi.* 1. Hiyaya; iyaya : *two men passed* 2. Yu'zapi; icupi : *the money would not pass.* 3. Iyecen waciŋkiyuzapi : *he passed for a wise man.* 4. Kihda; hihuni; ihaŋke : *the day passed.* —*His anger passed away,* wocaŋniye apaspa.—*Let it pass,* he'cehnanakte. *vt.* 1. I'sam iyaye; i'sam hiyu : *he passed the bridge.* 2. Ihunikiya yuśtaŋ : *he passed his life in ease.* 3. Aktaśni iyaya : *he passed me by.* 4. Kapa iyaya : *his horse passed all the others.* 5. He'cetudapi; yuśtaŋpi : *the bill passed both houses.* 6. Iyayeya : *pass the books along.* 7. I'ciyaza oyaka : *pass the word along.* 8. Yeya; hiyuya : *pass the bread.* 9. Wicaḳu : *he passed counterfeit money.* 10. O'pekiya; ye kta iyowiŋyaŋ : *he passed him on the train.* *n.* 1. Ohna ya'pi; ocaŋku; oko ohna ocaŋku : *a mountain pass.* 2. Oŋ każużuśni omanipi : *a pass on the railroad.* 3. Oape; wacape : *he made a pass to knock me down.* 4. Woakipe; wicoȟaŋ : *to what a pass have we come.*—*Bring to pass,* ecetuya.—*Come to pass,* iyecetu; kaketu.
passable, *a.* 1. Iyoopta yepica; ohna yepica : *the bridge is not passable.* 2. Icupi kta iyececa; yu'zapi : *the money is passable.* 3. Ki'taŋna waśte; ahececa : *the bread is passable.*
passably, *adv.* Taŋ'yaŋken; ahecenya.
passage, *n.* 1. Ohiyaye; ohna iyaye; hiyaye : *the passage of a ship through the canal.* 2. Yekta oŋ; ohnakapi : *he took passage on a steamboat.* 3. Ocaŋku; ocaŋkuyapi; ohna timahen ya'pi : *don't stand in the passage.* 4. Iapi; oeye; oehde : *a passage in the Bible.* 5. Iyoopta iyaye; yuśtaŋpi : *the passage of the law.* 6. Iheyapi : *a passage of the bowels.*
passenger, *n.* En o'pa; i'cimani; wicaśta o'papi.
passenger-car, *n.* Ḣemani wicaśta tokśu.
passer-by, *n.* Tu'we hiyaye; i'cimani.
passing, *adv.* Ikapeya; wakapeya.
passion, *n.* 1. Wocaŋteptaŋye; wocaŋniye; wośiŋhda : *he left in a great passion.* 2. Caŋtiheyapi; wocaŋtiheya : *a passion for war.* 3. Wokakiże : *the passion of Christ.*
passionate, *a.* 1. Waciŋko; caŋteptaŋyes'a : *a passionate boy.*

2. Wacaŋtahde : *a passionate lover.*

passionately, *adv.* Wohitiya ; ni'-na.

passive, *a.* Ataŋse uŋ ; waecoŋ-kiyapi e'cedaŋ škaŋ.

passover, *n.* Woacakšiŋ.

passport, *n.* Oyatetokeca ekta oi-cimani wowapi.

past, *pa.* He'kta ; ehaŋna : *the past year. prep.* Saŋ'pa ; i'saŋ-pa : *half past one. adv.* Ica-hda ; iyoopta : *he ran past.*

paste, *n.* Coŋ'peška ; wožapi ; co-coyapi ; wi'puspe : *mix the paste. vt.* A'skamya : *paste this in your book.*

pasteboard, *n.* Minihuhašoka.

pastern, *n.* Šuŋ'kawakaŋ iškahu.

pastime, *n.* Wowimaġaġa.

pastor, *n.* Waawaŋyake ; wicašta-wakaŋ ; wonwicaye.

pastoral, *a.* Waawaŋyake

pastorate, *n.* Woawaŋyake.

pastorless, *a.* Waawaŋyake co'-daŋ.

pastry, *n.* Aġuyapi zizipedaŋ.

pasturable, *a.* Owihaŋyewašte.

pasturage, *n.* Owihaŋye ; wi'haŋ-wicakiyapi : *good pasturage.*

pasture, *n.* Wato ; owihaŋye : *a large pasture. vt.* Wi'haŋwica-kiya : *pasture the sheep on the hills. vi.* Wi'haŋ.

pat, *adv.* Coyena ; yupiya. *n.* Oape : *he gave him a pat on the shoulder. vt.* Apapa : *pat him on the cheek. n. Irish* wi-cašta.

patch, *vt.* Okipata ; akihdagtoŋ : *patch a quilt ; patch his pants.*

patchwork, *n.* Minihuha okipa-tapi.

pate, *n.* Pa ; pesdete.

patent, *a.* 1. Taŋiŋyaŋ uŋ : *patent to all eyes.* 2. Okaġe anicapi ; wakaŋ : *patent medicine. n.* Waanicapi wowapi. *He has a patent on the churn. vt.* Waa-nicapi wowapi icu.

patent-office, *n.* Okaġe anicapi ti'pi.

paternal, *a.* Atkuku.

paternity, *n.* Wicaatkuku.

paternoster, *n.* Itaŋcaŋ tawoce-kiye.

path, *n.* Caŋku ; caŋku ci'stiŋna

pathetic, *a.* Iyokišicapi ; aceye wicayapi se'ca : *a pathetic story.*

pathless, *a.* Caŋkuwanica.

pathos, *n.* Woiyokišica ; waaw-ciŋwicayapi.

pathway, *n.* Makaamani caŋku.

patience, *n.* Wowaciŋtaŋka.

patient, *a.* Waciŋtaŋka : *a patient boy. n.* Tu'we pežuta ku'pi ; wayazaŋka : *his patient is getting better.*

patiently, *adv.* Waciŋtaŋkaya.

patness, *n.* Woecetu.

patriarch, *n.* Huŋkakeyapi ; atey-api : *the patriarch Noah.*

patrician, *n.* Wicašta itaŋcan : tu'we okinihaŋ.

patricide, *n.* Atkuku kte.

patrimony, *n.* Woyuha atkuku etaŋhaŋ yuha ; okodakiciye ta-womnaye ; aihpekiyapi.

patriot, *n.* Tamakoce waštedaka.

patriotism, *n.* Tamakoce tehiŋ-dapi.

patrol, *vi.* Iyaza omani. *n.* Oma-nipi.

patron, *n.* Awaŋyake ; kicica.

patronage, *n.* Waokiyapi ; waš'a-gyapi.

patronize, *vt.* O'kiya ; kici škaŋ.

patter, *vi.* Šbu'šbu ; apapa.

pattern, *n.* Iyecen ka'ġapi kta ; okaġe. *vt.* Iyecen ka'ġa.

paucity, *n.* To'nana ; wokitaŋ.

paunch, *n.* Niġe.

pauper, *n.* Wahpanica ; oŋ'çi-kpani.

pauperism, *n.* Oŋ'çikpanipi.

pauperization, *n.* Oŋ'çikpaniwicayapi.
pauperize, *vt.* Oŋ'çikpaniya.
pause, *vi.* Inażiŋ; ataŋse yaŋka; ci'stiyedaŋ ayuśtaŋ. *n.* Oenażiŋ; enakiyapi: *a pause in the work.* 2. Ochnakedaŋ: *notice the pauses in reading.*
pave, *vt* 1. Caŋku akaȟpa; caŋku kśu: *the streets are paved with rock.* 2. Caŋku ki'caġa; oŋspekiya: *he paved the way for them.*
pavement, *n.* Caŋku ażupi.
pavilion, *n.* Awakeyapi; o'haŋzihdepi.
paw, *n.* Nape; wamanica nape; śake. *vt.* Natica; naȟdata.
pawn, *vt.* Woyuha kaśka; icazo kta oŋ woyuha kaśka. *John pawned his watch for one dollar.*
Pawnee, *n.* Sci'li; Itokaȟ Padani.
pay, *vt.* Każużu; ku; ki'cicażużu: *always pay at once for what you get.* *n.* Wokażużu; iyuwiŋ; *Y.* wiśi.
pay-day, *n.* Wakażużupi aŋpetu.
pay-master, *n.* Wicakicicażużu.
payment, *n.* 1. Wicakicicażużupi: *the payment is next week.* 2. Wokażużu: *a large payment.*
pay-roll, *n.* Wicakicicażużupi kta owicawapi.
pea, *n.* Omnica hmiyaŋyaŋ.
peace, *n.* Wookiye.
peaceable, *a.* Waȟbadaŋ; kicizapi awaciŋ śni.
peaceably, *adv.* Wa'ȟbayedaŋ; caŋtewaśteya; wawokiya.
peaceful, *a.* Wokicize wanica; wookiye.
peacefully, *adv.* Kiswaciŋśni.
peacefulness, *n.* Wowaȟbana; wookiye.
peacemaker, *n.* Wookiye ka'ġa.
peach, *n.* Kaŋ'tahiŋśma.
peacock, *n.* Zizicasiŋtewaśte.
peafowl, *n.* Zizicasiŋtewaśte.
peak, *n.* Paha; pażodaŋ; ipa.
peaked, *a.* Pe'sto; pażo.
peal, *n.* Bu; sna; ȟdaȟdaopamna.
peanut, *n.* Yaȟuġapihawaŋkadaŋ.
pear, *n.* Taspaŋȟdaȟdaseca.
pearl, *n.* Iŋ'yaŋteȟika; ta'ku teȟika.
pearly, *a.* Iŋ'yaŋteȟika ażupi; ta'ku ni'na waśte.
peart, *a.* Mdiheca.
peasant, *n.* Wożuwicaśta.
peasantry, *n.* Makoskantipi.
peat, *n.* Hutkaŋ aoŋpi.
pebble, *n.* Isbu; iŋ'yaŋcistiŋna.
pecan, *n.* Yaȟuġapihaŋska.
peck, *n.* 1. Kokatodaŋ oiyute: *I want a peck of potatoes.* 2. Capapi; pasuoŋcapapi. *vt.* Capa; pasu oŋ capa; paȟdoka; kuwa: *the chick pecked it.*—*Peck away,* kuwa yaŋka.
pectoral, *n.* Cuwiyazaŋpipeżuta.
peculate, *vi.* Wamanoŋ.
peculiar, *a.* 1. To'keca; oȟaŋtokeca: *he is a peculiar man.* 2. I'ye i'yatayedaŋ.
peculiarity, *n.* Oȟaŋtokecapi.
pecuniary, *a.* Ma'zaska: *a pecuniary loss,* ma'zaska ki'citakuniśni.
pedagogic, *n.* Waoŋspewicakiyapi wooŋspe.
pedagogue, *n.* Waoŋspekiya.
pedal, *n.* Siinataŋ; caŋdowaŋkiyapi siinataŋ.
pedantic, *a.* Waoŋspekiyaoȟaŋȟaŋ.
peddle, *vt.* Tiiyaza wopetoŋ.
peddler, *n.* Tu'we wopetoŋ omani.
pedestal, *n.* Hu'te.
pedestrian, *n.* Makaamani uŋ; huwakiś'ake.
pedigree, *n.* Ehaŋnataŋhaŋ huŋkake oyag aupi.
pedobaptism, *n.* Hokśiyop̄a ko mniakaśtaŋpi he'cetudapi.
peek, *vi.* Oȟdatetaŋhaŋ waŋyaka.
peel, *vt.* Kaȟu; yaȟu; basku;

ṡdaya eḣpeya.—*Peel bark,* caŋha kaḣu.—*Peel potatoes,* mdo baskusku. *n.* Ha.

peeling, *n.* Ha : *potato peelings.*

peep, *vi.* 1. Hotoŋ ; zitka ciŋca hotoŋ : *the chicks peeped in the shell.* 2. Aokasiŋ ; kasiŋyaŋ ḣinaŋpa : *peeped over the hill.* *n.* 1. Zitka ciŋca hotoŋpi. 2. Aokasiŋpi : *Can I get a peep.* 3. Tokahinaŋpa : *peep of day.*

peer, *n.* Iyecen okihi ; kicica ; woitaŋcaŋ o'pa. *vi.* En e'toŋwaŋ.

peerless, *a.* Iyotaŋ ; kapepicaṡni.

peevish, *a.* Ce'yes'a ; waciŋko.

peevishness, *n.* Wawiyokipipiṡni.

peg, *n.* Caŋ'iyokataŋna ; wi'hutipaspe. *vt.* Okataŋ : *peg the shoe.*

Pegassus, *n.* Ṡuŋ'kawakaŋkiŋyaŋ.

pelican, *n.* Mde'ġa.

pellet, *n.* Ta'ku su se'kse ; peżutahmiyaŋyaŋ.

pell-mell, *adv.* Omdecahaŋ ; to'ken ciŋ'ciŋ.

pelucid, *a.* Kohdi.

pelt, *n.* Ha ; wawaha : *a trader with his pelts.* *vt.* Apa ; kiŋiŋ ; *pelt him with eggs.*

peltry, *n.* Wawaha.

pelvis, *n.* Co'wohe ; nite.

pemmican, *n.* Wakapaŋpi.

pen, *n.* 1. Wowapi icaġe ; wi'yowa ; wi'cazo ; minisapa icaġe : *dip your pen in the ink.* 2. Ti'pidaŋ ; coŋ'kaṡke : *the pig is in his pen.* *vt.* 1. Ka'ġa ; wowapi ka'ġa : *I will pen you a few words.* 2. Mahen iyeya ; nataka.

penal, *a.* Woiyopeye ikoyake.

penalty, *n.* Woiyopeye ; iyopeyapi ; wokażużu.

penance, *n.* Kakiṡiçiyapi.

pencase, *n.* Wi'cazo ożuha.

pence, *n. pl.* of PENNY.

pencil, *n.* Caŋ'wiyowa ; hiŋ'wiyowa. *vt.* Owa ; iuŋ.

pencilled, *pa.* Owapi ; iuŋpi.

pendant, *n.* Ta'ku otke haŋ ; wi'yokihedaŋ haŋ'ska ; oiŋ.

pending, *pa.* Kuwapi ; yuṡtaŋpi ṡni ; apeuŋpi.

Pend-Oreille, *n.* Po'geḣdoka.

pendulous, *a.* Otke ; ozezewaŋka.

pendulum, *n.* Wi'hiyayedaŋ ma'zahotedaŋ ; ma'zakaozeze.

penetrable, *a.* Kaḣdogpica ; kaḣtaŋpica.

penetrate, *vt.* 1. Kaḣdoka ; paḣdoka ; mahen ya ; kaḣtaŋ : *the spear penetrated the fish's head.* 2. Tawaciŋ on kaḣdoka : *too deep for his mind to penetrate.*

penetrating, *a.* Wakaḣdoka ; wakaḣtaka.

pen-holder, *n.* Ma'zaicaġe ihupa.

peninsula, *n.* Izo ; ipa ; makahutiyahde.

penis, *n.* Deże.

penitence, *n.* Iyopeiçiyapi.

penitent, *a.* Iyopeiçiya ; iyokiṡica. *n.* Tu'we iyopeiçiya.

penitential, *a.* Iyopeiçiyapi.

penitentiary, *n.* Wokaṡketipi.

penitently, *adv.* Caŋteṡinya ; iyopeiçiya.

penknife, *n.* Isaŋyukṡiżapidaŋ : *Y.* miyuksiżapina.

penman, *n.* Wowapikaġa.

penmanship, *n.* Owapi ; napeoŋkaġapi.

pennant, *n.* Wi'yokihedaŋ haŋ'ska.

penniless, *a.* Ma'zaska ni'ca ; waḣpanica.

penny, *n.* Sagdaṡiŋ ma'zaṡadaŋ ; ma'zaṡadaŋ.

pennywise, *a.* Wateḣiŋda ; ta'ku ci'stiŋna teḣiŋda.

pennyworth, *n.* Ma'zaṡadaŋiyawa ; wokitaŋ.

penrack, *n.* Wi'cazo ahnakapi.

pension, *n.* Akicita enakiya Tuŋkaŋṡina o'wicakiya.

pensioner, *n.* Tuŋkaŋśina o'kiya.
pensive, *a.* Wacaŋtahde uŋ; awaciŋ uŋ; iyokiśica.
pensively, *adv.* Icaŋteśinya.
pensiveness, *n.* Wocaŋteśica.
pent, *a.* Natakapi; natagunŋ.
pentagon, *n.* Za'ptaŋ oisetoŋ.
Pentateuch, *n.* Moses tawowapi za'ptaŋ.
Pentacost, *n.* Aŋpetuiwikcemnazaptaŋ.
Pentacostal, *a.* Wicayuḣicapi.
penurious, *a.* Wateḣiŋda; ma'zaśadaŋiyotaŋda.
penuriously, *adv.* Wateḣiŋdaya.
penuriousness, *n.* Wateḣiŋdapi.
penury, *n.* Ma'żaśadaŋ icakiżapi; wowaḣpanica.
peony, *n.* Waḣcataŋka.
people, *n.* Wicaśta; oyate: *there are a great many good people in town.* *vt.* Otiwicaya; wicaśta en uŋwicakiya.
pepper, *n.* Sucikcikana seca; *Y.* yamnumnuġapi su.
peppermint, *n.* Tatedaŋseca.
per, *prep.* 1. Oŋ; eciyataŋhaŋ: *per bearer.* 2. Iyohi: *per annum.*
peradventure, *adv.* O'kini.—*Without peradventure,* yuśnaśni.
perambulate, *vt.* O'pta omani.
perceivable, *a.* Okaḣnipica; waŋyagpica.
perceive, *vt.* Sdonya; waŋyaka; iyukcaŋ.
percentage, *n.* Opawiŋġe to'ken iyawapi.
perceptibility, *n.* Wasdonyepica.
perceptible, *a.* Sdonyepica; taŋiŋ.
perceptibly, *adv.* Taŋiŋyaŋ.
perception, *n.* Wowiyukcaŋ.
perceptive, *a.* Oŋ wasdonya.
perch, *n.* 1. (*A fish.*) Ho'zizi; wakadaŋhiyuzapi. 2. Caŋ; caŋhaŋska; sihaiyutapi 16½. 3. Zitkanaowaŋka. *vi.* Akan iyahaŋ; inażiŋ.
perchance, *adv.* O'kini; naceca.
percussion, *n.* I'ciyapapi.
perdition, *n.* Wicotakuniśni.
peregrinate, *vi.* Makoce to'keca ekta omani.
peremptorily, *adv.* A'wicakeya; he'cetuwaŋżica.
peremptory, *a.* Ayuptepicaśni; ḳe'za.
perennial, *a.* Waniyetu ihuŋni; te'han; o'hiŋni: *perennial fountain.* *n.* Wato waniyetu ṭe śni.
perennially, *adv.* O'hiŋniyaŋ.
perfect, *a.* A'taya waśte; yuśtaŋpi; ecetu; owotaŋna. *vt.* Yuśtaŋ.
perfectible, *a.* A'taya yuwaśtepica.
perfection, *n.* A'taya waśte; wowaśte a'taya; a'taya yuśtaŋpi.
perfectly, *adv.* A'taya; a'tayedaŋ; ocowasiŋ; ta'kudaŋ yuśnaśni.
perfectness, *n.* Woowotaŋna.
perfidious, *a.* Wicakeśni; wicahnayaŋ.
perfidy, *n.* Wohnaye.
perforate, *vt.* Yuḣdoka; paḣdoka.
perform, *vt.* Ecoŋ; yuśtaŋ.
performable, *a.* Ecoŋpica.
performance, *n.* Woecoŋ; ecoŋpi; yuśtaŋpi.
performer, *n.* Waecoŋ; ta'ku ecoŋpi o'pa.
perfume, *n.* Ta'ku waśtemna. *vt.* Waśtemnaya.
perfunctory, *a.* Awaciŋśni.
perhaps, *adv.* Naceca; o'kini.
peri, *prefix.* Ohomni.
pericardium, *n.* Caŋtoġe.
peril, *n.* Wokokipe. *vt.* Oṭohnaka.
perilous, *a.* Okokipe; wokokipe.
perilously, *adv.* Okokipeya.
perilousness, *n.* Wokokipe.
perimeter, *n.* Aohomni.
period, *n.* 1. Aŋpetu; waniyetu: *a long period.* 2. (*Gram.*) Oehnake taŋ'ka; woeye.
periodic, *a.* Ake iyehantu.

periodical, *a.* 1. Ake iyehantu eca: *periodical storms.* 2. Wotaŋiŋ wowapi : *periodical literature.* *n.* Wotaŋiŋ wowapi.
periodically, *adv.* Iyehaŋhaŋyaŋ.
perish, *vi.* Atakuniśni ; ṭa.
perishable, *a.* Waŋ'kadaŋ ; atakuniśni waś'akadaŋ.
perjure, *vt.* Ta'kuwakaŋ icażeyan eciŋśniyaŋ oyaka.
perjury, *n.* Ta'ku Wakaŋ hna'yaŋpi.
permanence, *n.* He'cetuwaŋżica uŋ'pi.
permanent, *a.* He'cetuwaŋżica ; yutokecapicaśni.
permanently, *adv.* He'cetuwaŋżica ; sutaya. *To settle permanently,* eca i'yotaŋka.
permeable, *a.* Mahen yepica ; kaḣtaŋpica.
permeate, *vt.* Mahen ya ; kaḣtaŋ.
permissible, *a.* Iyowiŋyepica ; he'cetu.
permission, *n.* Woiyowiŋkiye ; iyowiŋkiyapi.
permit, *vt.* Iyowiŋkiya. *n.* Woiyowiŋkiye ; iyowiŋkiyapi wowapi ; omanipi wowapi.
pernicious, *a.* Waihaŋgye ; wayuśica.
perniciously, *adv.* Wayuśinya.
peroration, *n.* Ehake eyapi.
perpendicular, *a.* Bosdata : *a perpendicular line.* *n.* Obosdata.
perpetrate, *vt.* Ecoŋ ; śicaya ecoŋ.
perpetration, *n.* Woecoŋ.
perpetual, *a.* O'hiŋniyaŋ uŋ ; owihaŋke wanica.
perpetually, *adv.* O'hiŋniyaŋ.
perpetuate, *vt.* Sam iyayeya ; niyaŋ.
perpetuated, *pa.* Niyaŋpi.
perpetuity, *n.* Wosuta ; owihaŋkeśni.
perplex, *vt.* Yuśkiśka ; naġiyeya ; waciŋhnuniya.
perplexedly, *adv.* Waciŋhnuniyaŋ.
perplexity, *n.* Wośkiśke ; waciŋhnunipi ; to'ketutaŋiŋśni.
perquisite, *n.* Siŋte ; i'akam ta'ku yuhapi.
persecute, *vt.* Śicaya kuwa ; wocekiye oŋ śicaya kuwa.
persecution, *n.* Śicayawicakuwapi.
persecutor, *n.* Śicaya wicakuwa.
perseverance, *n.* Wakitaŋpi ; wowaciŋtaŋka.
persevere, *vi.* Kitaŋ ; ayuśtaŋwaciŋśni.
persevering, *pa.* Wakitaŋ : *a persevering boy.*
perseveringly, *adv.* Kitaŋyaŋ.
Persian, *n.* *Persia* wicaśta.
persimmon, *n.* Kaŋ'ta pa'za.
persist, *vi.* Kitaŋ ; ayuśtaŋśni kuwa.
persistence, *n.* Wowaciŋtaŋka ; wakitaŋpi.
persistency, *n.* Wakitaŋpi.
persistent, *a.* Wakitaŋ ; wohitika : *a persistent beggar.*
persistently, *adv.* Kitaŋyaŋ ; wohitiya.
persisting, *pa.* Wakitaŋs'a.
person, *n.* 1. Wicaśta ; wicanaġi : *how many persons came.* 2. Tu'we ; taŋcaŋ : *what a nice person.* 3. Ouŋ ; oihdawa : *three persons in one Godhead.* 4. Koŋ'za ; keiçiya : *he came in the person of a robber.* 5. (*Gram.*) Tu'we ka'pi.
personage, *n.* Tu'we kiŋ : *a renowned personage.*
personal, *n.* I'ye i'yatayedaŋ ; i'ye i'yateyedaŋ ka'pi : *personal property.*
personally, *adv.* I'ye i'yatayedaŋ
personate, *vt.* I'çiya ; keiçiya ; koŋ'za : *personate a doctor.*
personification, *n.* Wicaśtakaġapi.
personify, *vt.* Wicaśtaka'ġa.
perspective, *n.* Iśtaiciyopteyauŋ.
perspicuity *n.* Wa'mdezeca ; taŋ'-

yaŋ amdespica; taŋ'yaŋ waŋyagpica.
perspicuous, *a.* Mde'za; okaȟniȟwaŝte.
perspicuously, *adv.* Okitaŋiŋyaŋ.
perspiration, *n.* Temni; itemni.
perspire, *vi.* Temni.
persuade, *vt.* Ciŋkiya; wicadakiya; ecoŋkiya: *we will persuade him.*
persuasible, *a.* Ciŋkiyepica.
persuasion, *n.* 1. Ciŋwicakiyapi: *his power of persuasion.* 2. Obe; okodakiciye: *they belong to the same persuasion.*
persuasive, *a.* Wicayuhomni.
pert, *a.* Itoŋ'peŝni; wi'ŝteceŝni; mdiheca.
pertain, *vi.* Iyoważa; ta'wa.
pertinacious, *a.* Kitaŋȟiŋca; wakitaŋ.
pertinaciously, *adv.* Kitaŋyaŋ.
pertinacity, *n.* Wakitaŋpi; tawaciŋ ķe'zapi.
pertinency, *n.* Woiyecetu; coyapi.
pertinent, *a.* Iyehantu; iyoważa.
pertinently, *adv.* Iyowaŝya; coyena.
pertly, *adv.* Wayupiya; yupiya.
pertness, *n.* Womdiheca; wowayupika.
perturb, *vt.* Yuŝkaŋŝkaŋ.
perturbation, *n.* Yuŝkaŋŝkaŋpi.
perusal, *n.* Yawapi.
peruse, *vt.* Yawa; wowapi yawa.
pervade, *vt.* Mahen iyaye; kaȟtaŋ.
perverse, *a.* Owotaŋnaŝni; ŝkopa; pemni; wanaȟoŋŝni; caŋteeciŋŝni.
perversely, *adv.* Eciŋŝniyaŋ.
perverseness, *n.* Wowanaȟoŋŝni; woowotaŋnaŝni.
perversion, *n.* Yupemnipi; yaeciŋŝniyapi.
perversity, *n.* Woeciŋŝniyaŋ; woecetuŝni.
pervert, *vt.* Yutokeca; yuŝica.
perverter, *n.* Wayuŝica.
pesky, *a.* Wanaġiyeya.
pessimist, *n.* Eca wawiyokipiŝni.
pest, *n.* 1. Makoŝica. 2. Woyuŝica; wonaġiyeya.
pester, *vt.* Naġiyeya.
pesterer, *n.* Wanaġiyeya.
pest-house, *n.* Makoŝica ti'pi.
pestiferous, *a.* Woŝice ka'ġa; ŝi'ca.
pestilence, *n.* Makoŝice; woyuŝice.
pestilent, *a.* Wayuŝica.
pestilential, *a.* Wayuŝica; ŝi'ca.
pestle, *n.* Wi'bope. *vt.* Bopaŋ.
pet, *a.* & *n.* 1. Ihaktapidaŋ; kihnapidaŋ: *my pet lamb.* 2. Wocaŋze; wocaŋteptaŋye: *the boy was in a pet.* *vt.* Kihna; kihnahna: *the mother pets her child.*
petal, *n.* Waȟca ape.
petit, *a.* Ci'stiŋna; ihukuya.
petition, *n.* Wadapi; ociŋpi; wocekiye; wadapi wowapi.
petitioner, *n.* Wada.
petitioning, *n.* Wadapi.
petrel, *n.* Miniwaŋca wicataŋktaŋka.
petrifaction, *n.* Iŋ'yaŋ icaġa.
petrify, *vi.* Iŋ'yaŋ icaġa.
petroleum, *n.* Makaihdi; petiżaŋżaŋ ikceka.
petticoat, *n.* Saŋksaŋnica; nitiyapehe.
pettifog, *vi.* Ta'kuŝniŝni; ki'cicuwa.
pettifogger, *n.* Waaiawicaŝta ta'kuŝniŝni wicakicicuwa.
pettish, *a.* Iyokipiŝni; caŋksiksi.
petty, *a.* Ci'stiŋna; ta'kuŝniŝni.
petulance, *n.* Wowaciŋko.
petulant, *a.* Waciŋko; caŋksiksi; ce'yekteȟca.
petulantly, *adv.* Caŋksiksiya.
pew, *n.* Caŋ'akaŋyakapi haŋ'ska.
pewter, *n.* Ma'zawiŝdoye.
phaeton, *n.* Caŋpahmihma nahuhuzapi haŋ'ska.

phalanx, *n.* Akicita optaye; akicita omdotoŋyaŋ na'żiŋpi.
phantasm, *n.* Kiktahaŋ wi'haŋmnapi; wanaġi waŋyakapi.
phantom. *n.* Wowaŋyake; wanaġi waŋyakapi; wanaġi.
phase, *n.* Waŋyakapi; wowaŋyake; owaŋyake.
pheasant, *n.* Żi'ca; ticabuna.
phenomenal, *a.* Wowaŋyake; to'keca.
phenomenon, (*pl.* **phenomena**), *n.* Wowaŋyake; ta'ku taŋiŋ.
philanthropic, *a.* Waoŋśida.
philanthropist, *n.* Oyate oŋ'śiwicada.
philanthropy, *n.* Oyate waoŋśidapi; wicaśta owaśiŋ waśtedapi.
philippic, *n.* Iapi woyaȟtake.
philology, *n.* Iapi wooŋspe.
philopena, *n.* Yaȟuġapi su cekpa.
philosopher, *n.* Wicaśta wi'yukcaŋ; ksapotaŋcaŋ.
philosophize, *vi.* Woksape iwohdaka.
philosophy, *n.* Woksape wooŋspe.
phiz, *n.* Ite.
phlegm, *n.* Taġe.
phlegmatic, *a.* Huŋ'keśni; ȟaŋhi.
phonetic, *a.* Ho kiŋ ohnayaŋ eyapi.
phonography, *n.* Nape oŋ oȟaŋko owapi.
phosphorous, *n.* Yuidepi caŋśiŋ.
photograph, *n.* Iteicupi; wiiyożaŋżaŋ oŋ ite icupi.
phrase, *n.* Woeye; woeye o'kihe.
phrenology, *n.* Wicapahu wooŋspe.
phthisic, *n.* Oniyaśicapi woyazaŋ.
physic, *n.* 1. Iyoptaiyeyapi: *give him a physic.* 2. Pezuta wooŋspe: *study physic.*
physics, *n.* Ta'kutaŋtoŋ wooŋspe.
physical, *a.* Wicataŋcaŋ; wicaceȟpi; ta'ku taŋtoŋ.
physically, *adv.* Wicataŋcaŋ eciyataŋhaŋ.
physician, *n.* Peżutawicaśta.
physiognomy, *n.* Ite owaŋyake.
physiology, *n.* Wicataŋcaŋ wooŋspe.
piano, *n.* Mazikaŋ dowaŋkiyapi.
piazza, *n.* O'haŋzihdepi.
picayune, *n.* Kaśpapi okise.
pick, *vt.* 1. Icu; yuwaŋkan icu: *pick up the book.* 2. Pahi; yuśpi: *pick plums.* 3. Capa; capapa: *pick a hole.* 4. Kaȟniȟ icu; icu: *he picked his men.*—*Pick at,* kuwa.—*Pick a bone,* ȟuhu yasmi. — *Pick a bird,* Zitkadaŋ yuśda. — *Pick off,* yuȟpa; boȟpa. — *Pick out,* icu; yuśdoka; kaȟniġa.—*Pick a pocket,* sicaŋopiye napiśtaŋyaŋ.—*Pick a quarrel,* ki'ze kta kuwa.—*Pick up a living,* oŋ ni kta pahi. *n.* Içe; makiçe pe'sto: *dig it with a pick.* 2. Kahniġapi; iyotaŋ waśte: *he was the pick of the family.*
pickax, *n.* Wi'çe; hokapasu.
pickerel, *n.* Tamahe.
picket, *n.* 1. Caŋpasdatapi; mazipasdate: *the horse pulled up the picket.* 2. Caŋmdaska pespesto: *the picket fence.* 3. (*Mil.*) Akicita toŋwe na'żiŋ; akicita na'żiŋ. *vt.* 1. Śuŋkawakaŋ okataŋ: *picket the horses.* 2. Acaŋkaśka; pasdata.
picking, *n.* Wośpipi.
pickle, *n.* Śkumnayaŋpi; miniskuya icahi ka'ġapi. *vt.* Sku'yeya; miniskuya icahiya.
picnic, *n.* Manin owośkate; manin śkatapi.
pictorial, *a.* Iteowapi ka'ġapi.
picture, *n.* Iteowapi; wowaŋyake. *vt.* Iteowa; taŋiŋyaŋ oyaka.
picture=frame, *n.* Iteowapi ożuha.
picture=gallery, *n.* Iteowapi ti'pi.

picturesque, *a.* Wa'petokeca; owapi waśte he'ca.

pie, *n.* 1. Opemnikaġapi: *do you eat pie?* 2. Ma'zaehdepi żużuwahe.

piece, *n.* 1. Oŋśpa: *a piece of bread.* 2. Ta'ku waŋżi; ta'ku kin; o'śpe waŋżi; waŋżi. *A fowling piece,* ta'ku oŋ wakutepi. *vt.* Okipata; akihdagtoŋ; oŋśpa akaġeġe: *piece his pants.*

piecemeal, *adv.* Oŋśpaśpa.

piecework, *n.* Okipatapi.

pieplant, *n.* Apetaŋka opemnikaġapi.

pier, *n.* 1. Caŋkaȟoŋpapi ahdehe. 2. Mini ekta iŋ'yaŋcoŋkaśke.

pierce, *vt.* Paȟdoka; capa; mahen-iyaye.

pierceable, *a.* Paȟdogpica.

Pierre, *n.* Wakpaśicaotoŋwe.

piety, *n.* Ta'ku Wakaŋ ohodapi.

pig, *n.* 1. Kukuśe ciŋca; kukuśe: *the pig is fat.* 2. Mazaśdoyapi.

pigeon, *n.* Wakiyedaŋ.

pigeon-toed, *n.* Siha naokśiŋ.

pignut, *n.* Caŋsu.

pigtail, *n.* Kukuśesiŋte; kisoŋpi.

pike, *n.* Tamahe; ho'wakaŋ; *he caught a pike.*

pile, *n.* 1. Paha; opahi; e'żupi: *a pile of stones.* 2. Caŋkaġa pasdatapi: *pounding in the piles.* *vt.* E'żu; wi'taya e'hde: *pile them up.*

piles, *n.* Uŋze oȟdoka po'pi.

pilfer, *vt.* Manoŋ. *vi.* Wamanoŋ.

pilferer, *n.* Wamanoŋs'a.

pilgrim, *n.* I'cimani; i'cimani uŋ; ohnihde uŋ; oicimani.

pilgrimage, *n.* Oicimani.

piling, *n.* Caŋ'pasdatapi.

pill, *n.* Peżutapśuŋka; peżuta hmiyaŋyaŋna.

pillage, *n.* Woyuha ozuye ekta wicakipi; taku manoŋ ahdipi. *vt.* Manoŋ; ozuye ekta manoŋ.

pillager, *n.* Wamanoŋs'a.

pillar, *n.* Ipataŋhdepi; ti'piipataŋ; wabosdata. *A pillar of cloud,* maȟpiya bosdata.

pillow, *n.* Ipahiŋ.

pilot, *n.* Iyupseyuza; wasiŋteyuhomni; makoce sdonya.

pimple, *n.* Śaśaahinaŋpa; oyuȟi.

pimpled, *a.* Yuȟiȟi.

pin, *n.* Hi'paśkudaŋ; wi'pasise. *A paper of pins.* —*Tent pins,* wihutipaspe. *vt.* Pasisa; ipasise.—*Pin the handkerchiefs together,* itipakiŋte i'cipasisa.—*Pin the tent down,* wakeya ipaspa.

pinafore, *n.* Makuakaȟpedaŋ.

pincase, *n.* Hi'paśkudaŋ wohnake.

pinch, *vt.* Yużipa; pażipa; kakiśya; paskica; oṭinsyuza. *n.* Woyużipa; yużim icupi.

pinchers, *n.* Wiyużipe.

pincushion, *n.* Hipaśkudaŋ ipaȟdi.

pine, *n.* Ważicaŋ; wazi. *vi.* Icaŋteśica; tamaheca a'ya.

pine-apple, *n.* Makataspaŋ.

pine-clad, *a.* Waziożu.

pinery, *n.* Waziokakse.

pinion, *n.* Wi'yaka; hiŋ; ȟupaȟu.

pink, *a.* Śa; śasaŋ: *a pink dress.* *n.* Waȟcaśaśa.

pinnacle, *n.* Ipasotka; iŋ'kpa.

pint, *n.* Ceȟskawiyatke oiyute: *half a pint.*

pioneer, *n.* Watokahaŋ; tokaheya hi'yotaŋke. *vi.* Caŋkukaġa.

pious, *a.* Ta'ku Wakaŋ ohoda; waciŋyaŋ: *a pious family.*

piously, *adv.* Waohodaya.

pious-minded, *a.* Wocekiye awaciŋ.

pipe, *n.* 1. Caŋduhupa; caŋnoŋpa: *he filled his pipe.*—*The pipe head,* canduhupa pahu.—*The pipe stem,* caŋduhupasuŋta.—*Fill the pipe,* opaġi.—*Smoke the pipe,* caŋnoŋpa. 2. Ma'zaoȟdoġeca. *Water-pipes,* ma'zaoȟdoġeca miniyaya.—

Stove-pipe, ma'zaoceti ihupa. 3. Co'yataŋka : *blow your pipes.* —*A pipe organ*, caŋhdoġeca dowaŋkiyapi. *vi.* Yażo ; żo.
piper, *n.* Wayażo.
pipestone, *n.* Caŋnoŋpa iŋ'yaŋ.
Pipestone Quarry, *n.* Caŋnomoke.
piping, *pa.* Yapiŋza ; piŋ'za.
piquant, *a.* Yażimżipa ; wayażimżipa.
piquantly, *adv.* Pe'stoya.
pique, *n.* Woyażipe ; wocaŋze. *vt.* Pażipa ; caŋzeya.
piracy, *n.* Wi'tawata wamanoŋpi ; wamanoŋpi.
pirate, *n.* Wamanoŋwicaśta ; wi'tawata wamanoŋ.
piratical, *a.* Wamanoŋ.
pish, *interj.* Hiŋte ; wahteśni.
piss, *vi.* De'ża ; miniiheya.
pistol, *n.* Ma'zakaŋptecedaŋ.
pit, *n.* 1. Makohdoka ; ohdoka. 2. Su. *Cherry pits*, caŋpa su. —*The arm-pit*, a.—*The pit of the stomach*, pi'mnumnuġe.—*Pitted face*, itehdohdoka. *vt.* Ohdohdogya ; su ehpeya ; kici ecoŋkiya.
pitapat, *adv.* Kabubupise.
pitch, *vt.* 1. Kah'oiyeya ; ehpeya : *pitch hay.* 2. E'hde ; ka'ġa : *pitch a tent.*—*Pitch camp*, owaŋka ka'ġa. 3. (*Mus.*) Waŋkan iyeya ; ahiyaya : *pitch the tune.* *vi.* Ticaġa ; e'ti : *they pitched in the plain.* 2. Hiŋhpaya : *he pitched head first down the bank.* 3. Kah'oh'o iyaye : *the boat pitched about all night.* *n.* 1. Maya ; oipa ; o'sinaka : *the lowest pitch of poverty.* 2. (*Mus.*) Ho'icupi. 3. Wokaho : *the pitch of the boat.* 4. Onaptaŋye : *the pitch of the roof.* 5. Caŋśiŋ : *he covered the cracks with pitch.*
pitch-black, *n.* A'wicakehaŋ sa'pa.
pitch-dark, *n.* A'wicakehaŋ o'kpaza.
pitcher, *n.* 1. Miniiokaśtaŋ : *he broke the pitcher.* 2. Wakah'oiyeya.
pitchfork, *n.* Peżiicape.
pitching, *a.* A'pamahde ; nake.
pitchpine, *n.* Wazi śiŋota.
pitchy, *n.* Caŋśiŋ yukeya ; wi'yaskape ; sa'pa ; owotaŋiŋśni.
piteous, *a.* Oiyokiśica ; oŋ'śika ; wahpaniṭa.
piteously, *adv.* Oŋ'śiya.
pitfall, *n.* Makohdoka wi'hmuŋke.
pith, *n.* 1. Coġiŋ : *punch out the pith.* 2. Co ; ta'ku ka'pi hca : *the pith of his remarks.*
pithily, *adv.* Yucoya.
pithy, *a.* 1. Yucoka ; a'taya ; yaṭiŋzapi : *pithy remarks.* 2. Popopa ; coġiŋse.
pitiable, *a.* Oŋ'śidapi iyececa ; oŋ'śika : *a pitiable company.*
pitiful, *a.* 1. Waoŋśida : *the Lord is pitiful.* 2. Oŋ'śika : *a pitiful face.* 3. Wahteśni.
pitifully, *adv.* Oŋ'śiya ; oŋśidaya.
pitifulness, *n.* Waoŋśidapi ; wowahteśni.
pitiless, *a.* Wowaoŋśida ni'ca.
pitilessly, *adv.* Waoŋśidaśni.
pittance, *n.* 1. Wokpaŋka ; ci'ṡtiŋna : *he lived on a pittance.* 2. Ta'ku oŋ'śika wicakupi.
pity, *n.* Icaŋtekiciśicapi ; wowaoŋśida ; woiyokiśica : *he has no pity.*—*What a pity*, ta'ku woiyokiśica ; ecaheś. *vt.* Oŋ'śida : *he pitied me.* *vi.* Waoŋśida.
pivot, *n.* Ahdeyuhomni.
pivotal, *a.* En yuhomnipi.
placard, *n.* Tiaskamya yaotaŋiŋpi.
place, *n.* Oyaŋke ; makoce ; otoŋwe ; wicohaŋ : *a good place to live.*—*A country place*, wożupi oyaŋke.—*Give place for the ladies*, wiŋ'yaŋ wicakiciyukaŋ po.—*He wants a place in the carpenter shop*, caŋkażipa ti'pi

en wicohaŋ ciŋ.—*In place of*, **e'**ekiya. *vt.* E'hnaka; e'hde; e'oŋpa.
placid, *a.* Amdakedaŋ; owaŋżi uŋ.
placidly, *adv.* Amdakayena.
plagiarize, *vt.* Iapi manoŋ; tu'we to'keca to'ie ta'waya.
plague, *n.* Makośica; woiyokiśica; wonaġiyeya. *vt.* Naġiyeya.
plaguer, *n.* Wanaġiyeya.
plaid, *n.* Śinahdehdeġa; hdehdeġa.
plain, *a.* 1. Taŋiŋyaŋ waŋ'ka; okaȟniȟ waśte: *he made it plain.* 2. Mda'ya; mdaska: *a plain country.* 3. Yuwaśtepiśni; sku'yeśni; ośkiśkeśni: *a plain dress; plain food.* 4. Ikceka; katiŋyaŋ: *plain people.*—*Plain cloth,* miniȟuha owapiśni.—*Plain food,* woyute sku'yeśni.—*A plain tune,* ho ośkiśkeśni. *n.* Makomdaye: *the plains of South Dakota.*
plain-dealing, *a.* Oȟaŋ owotaŋnapi.
plainly, *adv.* Taŋiŋyaŋ.
plainness, *n.* Woanaȟbeśni.
plain-speaking, *n.* Owohdake katiŋyaŋ.
plaint, *n.* Odowaŋ aceyapi.
plaintiff, *n.* (*Law.*) Tu'we kuwa.
plaintive, *a.* 1. Ce'yapi; oiyokiśica: *a plaintive song.*
plaintively, *adv.* Ce'yaya.
plait, *n.* Kisoŋpi; yuśkipi. *vt.* Soŋ; kisoŋ; yuśki: *plait your hair.*
plan, *n.* 1. Icaġopi; okaġe: *the plan of your house.* 2. Owowiyukcaŋ; wowiyukcaŋ: *what is your plan for the campaign.* 3. Huȟa ka'ġapi; iapi itaŋcaŋ: *the plan of a sermon.* *vt.* Iyukcaŋ; owa; ka'ġa.
plane, *a.* Mda'ya. *n.* Caŋicażipe; *sharpen the plane.* *vt.* Pażipa; **kamdaya**: *plane the boards.*
planet, *n.* Wicaŋȟpi omani.
plank, *n.* Caŋmdaska śo'ka.
planless, *n.* Wowiyukcaŋ ni'ca.
planner, *n.* Wawiyukcaŋ.
plant, *n.* 1. Wato; maka etaŋhaŋ ta'ku icaġa: *some plants have beautiful flowers.* 2. Okaġe; icuwa: *an electric plant.* *vt.* 1. Ożu: *plant corn.* 2. Huhde: *plant trees.* 3. Ahihnaka; makoce en i'yotaŋgwicakiya: *plant colonies.* 4. Oŋspekiya; ożu: *plant Christianity among the heathen.* 5. E'hde: *to plant cannon.*
plaintain, *n.* Caŋȟdoȟu apemdaska.
plantation, *n.* Owożu; wożupi makoce.
planter, *n.* Wożuti; taŋ'kaya wożu: *the planters of the South.* 2. Iożu: *a corn-planter.*
plaster, *n.* 1. Wi'puspe; tiisaŋye: *the plaster is falling off.* 2. (*Med.*) Peżuta iyaskamyapi: *put a plaster on the sore.* *vt.* Apuspa; a'skamya: *plaster this room next.*
plasterer, *n.* Ti'piapuspa.
plastering, *n.* Wi'puspe; tiipuspe.
plastic, *a.* Dodo; okaȟwaśte.
plat, *vt.* Kazoŋta; owa. *n.* 1. Soŋ'pi; wakazoŋtapi. 2. Makoce owapi; makobaśpe; owapi: *a plat of the town.*
plate, *n.* 1. Wakśicamdaska; kampeska: *pass your plate for some meat.* 2. Ma'zamdaska: *a roof of tin plate.* 3. Wowapi ma'zaahdiheyapi; iteowapi ahdiheyapi: *the dictionary plates.* *vt.* Ma'zaaskamya.
plateau, *n.* Makomdaye; mdamdate.
plateful, *n.* Wakśica ożudaŋ.
platform, *n.* 1. Oanażiŋ; owaŋka: *the minister's platform; the platform for the cannon.* 2.

Wicoie ahdehekiyapi : *the Democratic platform.*
platform-car, *n.* Ḣemanimdaska.
plating, *n.* Ma'zaiaskamyapi.
platinum, *n.* Ma'zaskatke.
Platte River, *n.* Kampeskawakpa.
platter, *n.* Wakšicamdaska taŋ'ka.
platting, *n.* Soŋ'pi ; owapi.
plaudit, *n.* Wayawaštepi ; idowaŋpi.
plausibility, *n.* Woiyecetu.
plausible, *a.* He'cetu se'ca ; wašte se'ca.
plausibly, *adv.* Wicaka se'ca.
play, *vt.* 1. Ṡka'ta : *he played ball.* 2. Dowaŋkiya ; yažokiya : hotoŋkiya : *play the organ.—Play cards,* kaŋsukute.—*Play a trick,* hnayaŋ kuwa. *n.* Woškate ; ška'tapi ; wapazopi woškate ; woškaŋškaŋ ; woiyowiŋkiye.—*A ball-play,* takapsicapi.—*Give full play,* woiyowiŋkiye ḳu.—*Rough play,* woškate ksizeca. *Shakespeare's plays, Shakespeare* wapazopi woškate.—*The play of the wheel,* hu'caŋhdeška icuŋom ayuhomni.
play-day, *n.* Ṡka'tapi aŋpetu.
player, *n.* Ṡka'ta ; waikpazo.
playfellow, *n.* Kiciškata ; kicica.
playful, *a.* Ṡka'tes'a.
playfully, *adv.* Ṡkanya ; ška'ta.
playfulness, *n.* Ṡka'tapi waštedakapi.
playhouse, *n.* Woškate tí'pi ; ohna ška'tapi.
playmate, *n.* Kiciškata.
plaything, *n.* Wi'napiškaŋye ; oŋ ška'tapi ; wi'škate : *the children's playthings.*
plea, *n.* 1. Iapi ; to'ken oŋ e'ya : *the lawyer's plea.* 2. Wocekiye ; ta'ku da'pi.
plead, *vi.* E'ya ; iciya ; icekiya ; oŋ etaŋhaŋ e'ya : *he plead for the boy. vt.* Cažeyata ; oŋ etaŋhaŋ da : *he plead poverty.*
pleadable, *a.* Cažeyanpica.
pleader, *n.* Wawiciya ; ki'cicuwa.
pleadingly, *adv.* Ce'kiya se.
pleasant, *a.* Wi'ciyokipi ; oiyokipi ; owaštecaka ; wi'haha.—*A pleasant family,* tiwaḣe wi'ciyokipi.—*It is pleasant,* oiyokipi. —*A pleasant day,* aŋpetu owaštecake.—*A pleasant fellow,* tu'we wi'haha.
pleasantly, *adv.* Iyokipiya ; canwašteya.
pleasantness, *n.* Woiyokipi ; iyowicakipi.
pleasantry, *n.* Iyokipiwicayapi ; wawiḣahayapi.
please, *vt.* Canwašteya ; iyokipiya : *he pleased his father.—The boy pleased me very much,* hokšidaŋ iyokipimayaŋḣiŋca. —*He is pleased,* iyokipi. *vi.* Ye ; iyonicipi ye ; ce'ciciye.—*Please come,* u ye ; yau kta iyonicipi ye.
pleaser, *n.* Iyokipiwicaya.
pleasing, *a.* Wawiyokipi ; wi'cimdeza.
pleasingly, *adv.* Iyokipiya.
pleasurable, *a.* Owicawašte.
pleasure, *n.* Woiyokipi ; wowiyuškiŋ ; tawaciŋ ; iyokipiiçiyapi. —*Use your pleasure,* ni'ye nitawaciŋ ye'çuŋ kta.—*Lovers of pleasure,* iyokipiiçiyapi ; waštedapi.
pleasure-boat, *n.* Wa'ta oŋ ška'tapi.
pled, *imp.* of PLEAD.
pledge, *n.* Oŋ yuwicakapi ; ma'zaska odotapi oŋ kaškapi. *vt.* Kaška ; oŋ yuwicakapi e'hde : *I pledge you my horse.*
Pleiades, *n.* (*Astron.*) Tawamnipa.
plenary, *a.* A'taya.
plenteous, *a.* O'ta ; ožudaŋ.
plenteously, *adv.* O'ta ; iyakicuya.
plentiful, *a.* 1. Otaŋtoŋka ; paŋ'ġa ; ni'na o'ta : *a plentiful sup-*

ply. 2. Waicaġa; o'ta icaġa: *a plentiful year*.
plenty, *n*. O'ta; woożudaŋ; wowiżice.—*Peace and plenty*, wookiye ḳa woożudaŋ. *a*. O'ta; utkaŋna: *plenty of corn*.
plethoric, *a*. Iyakiçu; i'saŋpa; ehaeṡ; o'ta.
pliable, *a*. Zigzica; paŋpaŋna.
pliancy, *n*. Wopaṭiŋṡni; ṭiŋ'zeṡni.
pliant, *a*. Okuwawaṡte; ṡwiŋṡwiŋżedaŋ; waŋ'kadaŋ.
pliantly, *adv*. Iyowiŋyaŋ.
plied, *imp*. of PLY.
plight, *n*. 1. Ouŋ; to'ken uŋ'pi: *in good plight*. 2. Waehnakapi; wocaże.
plod, *vi*. Ḣaŋhiya ya; ḣaŋhi ḣtani.
ploddingly, *adv*. Ḣaŋhiya.
plot, *n*. 1. Wokuwa; naḣmaŋ kuwapi: *a plot to kill the boy*. 2. Makoce ci'stiŋna: *a plot of ground*. 3. Makoce oiyute. *vt*. 1. Kuwa; naḣmaŋ kuwa: *he plotted destruction*. 2. Makoce owa.
plover, *n*. Zitkadaŋ hu'toto.
plow, *vt*. Yumdu; yupta; paġo; ihaŋgya: *plow the ground*. *n*. Maḣiyumdu; maḣiçe: *hitch the horses to the plow*.
plowable, *a*. Yumdupica; yumdupiwaṡte.
plowboy, *n*. Maḣyumdu hokṡidaŋ.
plower, *n*. Maḣyumdu.
plowland, *n*. Makoceyumdupiwaṡte.
plowman, *n*. Maḣyumduwicaṡta.
plowshare, *n*. Maḣiyumducuwi.
pluck, *n*. Wowaditake: *a man of pluck*. *vt*. Yuṡpi; yuksa; yuṡda: *pluck flowers*.
pluckily, *adv*. Waditagya.
plucky, *a*. Waditaka; caŋteṭiŋza.
plug, *n*. 1. Ioṡtaŋ: *put the plug in the hole*. 2. Oŋṡpa; obakse: *a plug of tobacco*. 3. Wapahasapa. 4. Ṡuŋ'kawakaŋhunoġe. *vt*. O'ṡtaŋ; yuoṭiŋza.
plum, *n*. Kaŋ'ta: *a plum tree*, kaŋtuhu.
plumage, *n*. Hiŋ; zitkadaŋhiŋ: *beautiful plumage*.
plumb, *n*. Oŋ bosdata iyutapi. *a*. Bosdata. *vt*. Yubosdata.
plumbago, *n*. Caŋwicazo coġiŋ.
plumber, *n*. Ma'zaḣdoġecaminiyaya apiya.
plumbing, *n*. Miniyaya apiyapi.
plumb-line, *n*. Wi'yutapi ikaŋ.
plum-cake, *n*. Aġuyapi kaŋ'ta icahi.
plume, *n*. Wa'ciŋhe; wi'yaka. *vt*. 1. Wa'ciŋhekiçuŋ; wa'ciŋhekitoŋ: *a plumed Indian*. 2. Okihiiçida; iwaḣaŋiçida: *he plumed himself on his strength*.
plumeless, *a*. Wi'yakacodaŋ.
plummet, *n*. Ma'zasu oŋ ṡbe iyutapi; bosdata owiyute.
plump, *a*. 1. Ce'pa; taŋ'ka: *how plump the baby is*. 2. A'taya; ocowasiŋ: *a plump lie*. *adv*. Bu se; ihnuhaŋ.
plunder, *n*. 1. Ta'ku manoŋpi. 2. Woyuha; waḣpaya. *vt*. Manoŋ; woyuha ki.
plunderer, *n*. Wawicaki; wamanoŋ.
plunge, *vt*. Mahen iyeya: *he plunged it in the water*. *vt*. Kaḣo iyeiçiya: *the horse plunged into the river*. *n*. Kaḣoiyeyapi; maheniyeyapi.
plunging, *a*. Kaḣoiyaya.
pluperfect, *a*. (*Gram*.) O'ta; waŋżiisaŋpa.
plurality, *n*. 1. Waŋżiisaŋpa; o'ta: *plurality of wives*. 2. O'ta; iṡnana o'ta: *he received a plurality of votes*.
plus, *prep*. Saŋ'pa; ḳa.
ply, *vt*. Kuwa; ecoŋ: *ply his trade*. *vi*. O'hiŋni ya; omani; ṡkaŋ: *the boat plies between*

Sioux City and Omaha. n. Oyukšiza; opehe: *two plies.*

pneumatics, *n.* Tate wooŋspe.

poach, *vt.* 1. Miniakaštaŋštaŋ špaŋyaŋpi: *poach eggs.* 2. Manoŋ; naȟmaŋ akiyahda: *he poached a cap.*

pocket, *n.* Sicaŋopiye; wożuha; oȟdoka: *put it in your pocket; a pocket in the rock. vt.* Mahen iyeya; icu.

pocket=book, *n.* Ma'zaska ożuha.

pocketful, *n.* Sicaŋopiye ożudaŋ.

pocket=knife, *n.* Isaŋyukatiŋpi; *Y.* Miyukšiżapi.

pod, *n.* Su'ożuha; ha: *a pod of beans.*

poem, *n.* Iapi odowaŋ kaȟya; odowaŋ.

poesy, *n.* Odowaŋ ka'ġapi.

poet, *n.* Odowaŋka'ġa.

poetess, *n.* Wiŋ'yaŋ odowaŋkaġa.

poetic, *a.* Odowaŋkaġa he'ca; odowaŋ se'ca.

poetry, *n.* Odowaŋ iapi; iapi waci se'ca.

poignancy, *n.* Woyaȟtake.

poignant, *a.* Wayaȟtake; pa'za.

point, *n.* 1. Iŋ'kpa; o'iŋkpa; ope: *the point of the needle.* 2. Oipa; ihaŋke: *a point of land.* 3. Oŋ okitaŋiŋ; wokitaŋiŋ; to'keca; wasaghdepi: *his good points.* 4. Wocażeyate; iapi okitaŋiŋ: *the first point in his speech.* 5. Oehnake; samyapidaŋ: *in reading notice the points.* 6. Oyaŋke; hehantu: *the freezing point.* —*In point of view,* iwaŋyakapi eciyataŋhaŋ. — *Points of the compass,* makiyutapi oepazo.— *Gain a point,* oyaŋke ohiya; waŋżi ohiya.—*Score a point,* woohiye waŋżi okiciwapi. — *Strain a point,* i'sam iyaye. *vt.* 1. E'pazo; ekta e'pazo: *point the gun at the wolf.* 2 Pazo; waŋyagši: *he pointed me to Solomon.* 3. Kapesto: *point the pickets.* 4. Samyapidaŋ e'hnaka: *point your writings.* 5. Makasaŋ apuspe: *the walls are not pointed yet.*

point=blank, *a.* Katiŋyaŋ.

pointed, *a.* 1. Kapestopi; pe'sto: *a pointed stick.* 2. Pe'sto; capapi se: *his pointed remarks.*

pointedly, *adv.* Pe'stoya.

pointer, *n.* 1. Šuŋ'ka šiyo pazo: *a brown pointer.* 2. Wapazo; wi'pazo: *that word is the pointer.*

pointing, *n.* Wowapi samyapidaŋ; ti'pi apuspapi.

pointless, *a.* Pe'stošni; ta'ku ka taŋiŋšni.

poise, *n.* Obosdan haŋ; aspeyetoŋpi. *vi.* Ze'zeya e'hnaka; aspeyetoŋ.

poison, *n.* Peżutašica; woȟaka; peżuta oŋ wicaṭa; wošica. *vt.* 1. Peżutašica ḳu; peżuta oŋ kte: *poison wolves.* 2. Yušica. 3. Peżutašica aehnaka: *poison the meat.*

poisonous, *a.* Wayušica; ši'ca; oȟaka; *poisonous roots.*

poke, *vt.* Pażipa; capa. *To poke fun at,* iȟaȟa kuwa. *n.* 1. Pażipapi; wocapa: *an iron poke.* 2. Tu'we huŋ'kešni; ku'ża: *that boy is a poke.* 3. Ptewiye caŋ'wanapiŋ.

poker, *n.* 1. Pe'ta icuwa; ma'za pe'sto. 2. Kaŋsukutepi (ocażo).

pokerish, *a.* Okokipe.

polar, *a.* Waziyata ihaŋke; itokaȟ ihaŋke. *Polar bear,* matoska.

pole, *n.* Tošu; caŋhaŋska. *A bean-pole,* omnica caŋkipasdatapi. — *A boat-pole,* ipamna. —*Liberty-pole,* caŋwakaŋ.—*A pole long,* ohaŋske sihaiyutapi 16½.—*A tent pole,* tošu.—*A wagon pole,* caŋpahmihma ihupa. *n.* Waziyata ihaŋke; ma-

kapesdete ; itokaȟ ihaŋke. *vt.* Ipamnakitoŋ.
polecat, *n.* Maŋka ; dokśiŋca.
polemic, *a.* Iaakinica.
pole=star, *n.* Waziyata wicaŋȟpi ; maȟpiyapesdete wicaŋȟpi.
police, *n.* Akicitawawaŋyake ; wawaŋyake ; caŋnakseyuha. — *Police station,* wa'waŋyake onażiŋ.
policeman, *n.* Wawaŋyake.
policy, *n.* 1. Oecoŋ ; wowiyukcaŋ ; wowayupika : *the policy of our government.* 2. Waihaŋgyapi ki'cicażużupi kta wowapi.
polish, *vt.* 1. Pawiyakpa ; payeza ; paśduta : *polish boots.* 2. Yuwaśte ; waciŋksamya : *polish his manners.* *n.* Oŋ paśdutapi ; wopaśduta ; wowiyakpa ; yuwaśtepi.
polishable, *a.* Paśdutepica.
polite, *a.* Oȟaŋ waśte ; wawiyokipi.
polite, *a.* Oȟaŋwaśte ; wawiyokipi.
politely, *adv.* Wawiyokipiya.
politeness, *n.* Woiyokipi ; oȟaŋwaśtepi.
politic, *a.* A'etopte ; ksa'pa.
political, *a.* Oyate ; oyate oihduhe.
politically, *adv.* Oyate oihduhe eciyataŋhaŋ.
politician, *n.* Oyate oihduhe wicoȟaŋ kuwa ; wa'kiia wicaśta.
politics, *n.* Woitaŋcaŋ wicoȟaŋ ; wa'kiiapi ; oyate oyuha wicoȟaŋ.
polity, *n.* Woope ; okodakiciye huȟa.
polka, *n.* Tawaŋżi wacipi.
poll, *n.* 1. Pesdete ; pa : *his poll is bare.* 2. Wicayawapi ; wicapa yawapi : *the poll made a hundred.* 3. Kaŋsu iyoȟpeyapi ; itaŋcaŋ kaȟniġapi : *go to the polls and vote honestly.* *vt.* 1. Pa kaśda ; iŋ'kpa baksa. 2. Wicacaże owa.
poll=book, *n.* Wowapi wicacaże owapi.
polled, *a.* Baksapi ; he wanica.
poll=evil, *n.* Śuŋ'kawakaŋpeȟdipi.
polliwig, *n.* Hośupeśde.
poll=tax, *n.* Wicaśta iyohi każużupi.
pollute, *vt.* Yuśapa ; yuśica ; aśamya.
polluted, *pa.* Aśamyapi.
polluter, *n.* Aśamya ; wayuśica.
pollution, *n.* Wośape ; waaśapapi.
poltroon, *n.* Canwaŋka ; ta'kutaŋiŋśni.
poly=, *prefix.* O'ta.
polygamist, *n.* Tawicuota.
polygamy, *n.* Tawicuotapi.
polyglot, *a.* Wicaceżiota ka'ġapi : *a polyglot Bible.*
polygon, *n.* Okaȟmiŋ o'ta.
Polynesia, *n.* Wi'taota.
polysyllable, *n.* Iapiokiheota.
polytheist, *n.* Ta'kuwakaŋotayuha.
pomade, *n.* Isdaye waśtemna ; ihepi.
pommel, *n.* Pśuŋka ; papśuŋka ; pa. *vt.* Apapa.
pony, *n.* Śuŋghuna ; Śuŋg Dakota. *Pony-engine,* ȟemani hu'na.
poodle, *n.* Śuŋ'kana ; śuŋkaecacistiŋna hiŋśma.
pooh, *interj.* Hoȟ.
pool, *n.* 1. Miniośkokpa ; mdedaŋ : *the pool is deep.* 2. Wayekiyapi ; ta'ku kaśkapi.
poor, *a.* 1. Tamaheca. *A poor cow,* pte tamaheca. 2. Waȟpanica : *a poor widow.* 3. Oŋ'śika : *a poor sick baby.* 4. Waśteśni ; ośteka : *a poor composition.*—*Poor clothes,* heyake waśte śni.—*A poor excuse,* iapi ta'ku śni.—*Poor fellow,* tuwe oŋ'śika.—*Poor health,* zani śni. —*Poor potatoes,* mdo śikśica.

—*Poor scholar*, wayawa oŋspekeśni.—*Poor soil*, maka waicaġe śni.—*A poor speaker*, wohdaka oŋspekeśni.
poor-house, *n.* Waḣpanica ti'pi; tukten waḣpanica awaŋyakapi.
poorly, *adv.* 1. Waḣpaniya; oŋśiya; icakiśya: *he lived poorly*. 2. Kitaŋyaŋ; wokitaŋyaŋ; ci'stiyena: *he succeeded poorly*. 3. Okihiśniyaŋ; taŋyaŋśni.
pomp, *n.* Wowitaŋ; wokitaŋiŋ.
pomposity, *n.* Wataŋkaiçidapi.
pompous, *a.* Taŋ'kaiçida; hiŋ'skotaŋka.
pompously, *adv.* Taŋ'kaiçidaya.
Ponca, *n.* (*A tribe of Indians.*) Paŋ'ka; Oya'eyamni.
pond, *n.* Miniośkokpa; mde'daŋ.
ponder, *vt.* Awaciŋ; iwaŋyaka.
ponderer, *n.* Waawaciŋ.
ponderous. *a.* Tke; taŋ'ka.
ponderously, *adv.* Tkeya.
pone, *n.* Wokpaŋpitacaġu.
pontiff, *n.* Śinasapa itaŋcaŋ; wośnaitaŋcaŋ.
pontifical, *a.* Wośnaitaŋcaŋtawa.
pontificate, *n.* Śinasapa woitaŋcaŋ.
pontoon, *n.* Wa'ta oŋ caŋkaḣoŋpapi.
pop, *n.* 1. Po'pa; pom'hiŋhda. 2. Minitaġa. *vt.* 1. Papaḣya; napomya: *pop corn*. 2. Ihnuhaŋ ecoŋ; ihnuhaŋ hiyu: *pop the question*.
pop-corn, *n.* Wamnaheza popopa.
pope, *n.* Śinasapa itaŋcaŋ.
popedom, *n.* Śinasapa wokicoŋze.
popgun, *n.* Wi'papopa.
popish, *a.* Śinasapa.
poplar, *n.* Waḣciŋca; waḣpesto.
Poplar River, *n.* Waḣciŋca wakpa.
popple, *n.* Waḣciŋca.
populace, *n.* Oyate; wicaśta.
popular, *a.* 1. Oyate waśtedapi; a'taya iyokipipi: *a popular Agent*. 2. A'taya iyoważapi; oyate ta'wa: *a popular election*. 3. A'taya okaḣniḣwicayapi; okahniḣ waśte: *popular instruction*.
popularity, *n.* A'taya waśtedapi.
popularly, *adv.* Oyate ekta; waśtedaya.
populate, *vt.* Oyate kaḣya uŋ'pi.
population, *n.* 1. Wicaśta; oyate; wicayawapi: *a small population*. 2. Oyata kaġapi; wicayuotapi.
populous, *a.* Wicaśta ożudaŋ; wicaśta o'ta.
porcelain, *n.* Kampeska.
porch, *n.* Tiyopa aohaŋziyapi.
porcupine, *n.* Pahiŋ.
pore, *n.* Uka oḣdoka; ohna temni hiyu. *vi.* Ataŋse kuwa.
pork, *n.* Kukuśe; waśiŋ. *Fresh pork*, kukuśe do.—*Salt pork*, kukuśe sku'yeyapi.—*Smoked pork*, kukuśe cosyapi.
porker, *n.* Kukuśe (ni uŋ).
porosity, *n.* Oḣdoḣdoka.
porousness, *n.* Wooḣdoḣdoka.
porridge, *n.* Wożapi. *Rice porridge*, psiŋ wożapi.
port, *n.* Wi'tawata oinażiŋ; oihuni; wi'tawatamazakaŋtaŋka ioḣdogyapi.
portable, *a.* Tokśupica; oyuhawaśte; tokśupiwaśte.
portage, *n.* Watoha.
portal, *n.* Tiyopa; oenape.
portend, *vt.* Iwaktaya; wakokipekicaġa.
portentious, *a.* Wa'petokeca.
porter, *n.* 1. Tiyopaawaŋyake: *the porter told me to come in*. 2. Caŋ'ohnaka ķiŋkiyapi. 3. Miniwakaŋ sa'pa.
portfolio, *n.* 1. Wowapiska okihnake. 2. Oecoŋ wowapi; woawaŋyake. *The portfolio of war*, akicita woawaŋyake.
portico, *n.* Tiyopa aohaŋzi.
portion, *n.* Wopamni; oŋġe; oŋ-

ṡpa. *vt.* Kiyuṡpeya wicaḳu; pamni; oŋġeġe wicaḳu.

portionless, *a.* Oŋġedaŋ yuheṡni.

portly *a.* Taŋ'ka; okinihaŋ; niġetaŋka: *a portly old gentleman.*

portmanteau, *n.* Wizipaŋ.

portrait, *n.* Iteowapi; wiciteka-ġapi: *my father's portrait.*

portray, *vt.* 1. Owa; iteowa: *portray a landscape.* 2. Oyaka; to'keca oyaka: *hear Gough portray a drunkard.*

Portuguese, *n.* PORTUGAL wicaṡta.

pose, *vt.* Na'żiŋkiya; anażiŋ.

poser, Waanażiŋ; wanaġiyeya.

position, *n.* Oyaŋke; oiḣduhe; onażiŋ.

positive, *a.* Wicaka; wowicake; waṡ'aka; wicakeiçida. *A positive benefit,* woyuwaṡte wicaka. —*Positive electricity,* wakaŋhdi waṡ'aka. —*A positive woman,* wiŋ'yaŋ wicakeiçida. *n.* Ouŋ wowicake.

positively, *adv.* A'wicakehaŋ; i'ya-tayedaŋ; yaṭiŋsya.

posse, *n.* Wicaṡta; wicota.

possess, *vt.* Yuha; toŋ; yuhekiya: *I possess nothing.*

possession, *n.* Woyuha; ta'ku yuhapi; ta'ku ta'wa.

possessive, *a.* Ta'wayapi.

possessor, *n.* Ta'waya; wayuha.

possibility, *n.* Okihipica; naceca.

possible, *a.* Okihipica; (in composition) -pica. *It is not possible to go,* yepicaṡni.

possibly, *adv.* 1. Naceca; o'kini: *possibly it will rain.* 2. To'ken okihi; to'ketu çeyaṡ; wokitaŋ ḳeyaṡ.

post, *n.* 1. Caŋ'ipasdate: *dig holes for the posts.* 2. Onażiŋ; owaŋka; ti'pi: *a military post.* 3. Wicaṡta wowapi tokṡu. *vt.* 1. Iyoḣpaya: *post my letter.* 2. Tiaskamya; okataŋ: *post the notice on the barn.* 3. Na'-żiŋkiya; e'hde: *post a sentinel.* 4. (*Book-keeping*) Oicazo yuwitaya. 5. Sdonyekiya; oŋspekiya: *I am not posted.* 6. Dus ya. *a.* Oḣaŋko: *post haste.*

postage, *n.* Wokażużu; wowapi-tokṡu wokażużu.

postage-stamp, *n.* Wiciteaskape.

postal, *a.* Wowapi oatokṡu.

post-boy, *n.* Hokṡidaŋ wowapito-kṡu.

poster, *n.* 1. Woyaotaŋiŋ tiaskam-yapi: *see the poster on the wall.* 2. Tu'we inaḣni ya.

posterior, *a.* Iyohakam; ehake.

posterity, *n.* Wicoicaġe; wica-ciŋca.

post-haste, *adv.* Inaḣni.

post-horse, *n.* Ṡuŋ'ktaŋka wowa-pitokṡu.

posthumous, *a.* Ṭa iyohakam taŋ-iŋ. *Posthumous child,* hokṡiyo-pa atkuku ṭa iyohakam toŋ'pi.

postman, *n.* Wowapitokṡu.

postmark, *n.* Wowapitokṡu apu-spapi.

postmaster, *n.* Wowapi oyużużu awaŋyaka.

post-office, *n.* Wowapioyużużu. *Post-office order,* oŋ ma'zaska icupi.

post-paid, *vt.* Każużupi; askam-yapi.

postpone, *vt.* Kihnaka; i'hakam e'hnaka.

post-road, *n.* Wowapitokṡu caŋku.

postscript, *n.* Ehake owa.

posture, *n.* To'ken waŋka; waŋ-ka; na'żiŋ: *his posture is bad.*

posy, *n.* Waḣca; odowaŋna.

pot, *n.* Ce'ġa; ce'ġa ṡo'ka. *vt.* Ce'ġa ohnaka.

potash, *n.* Caḣota haŋpi.

potatoe, *n.* Mdo; bdo; blo. *Sweet potatoe,* mdo sku'ya.

pot-bellied, *a.* Niġetaŋka.

potency, *n.* Wookihi.

potent, *a.* Waš'aka : waokihi.
potentate, *n.* Tu'we waš'aka ; itaŋcaŋ ; wicaštayatapi.
potential, *a.* Wookihi yuha.
potentially, *adv.* Waokihiya ; naceca.
potently, *adv.* Waš'agya.
pothook, *n.* Ceȟwiyuze.
potion, *n.* Woyatke.
potpourri, *n.* Icahiohaŋpi.
potsherd, *n.* Ceȟuȟuġa.
pottage, *n.* Tadoyužapi ; wožapi.
Pottawatomie, *n.* Putewata.
potter, *n.* Makaceġakaġa. *vi.* Ta'ku ecoŋ taŋiŋšni škaŋ.
pottery, *n.* Makaceġa.
pouch, *n.* Wožuha ; wozuhadaŋ. *Tobacco-pouch*, caŋdožuha. — *Shot-pouch*, tasusuožuha.—*Pelican's pouch*, mde'ġa tapo.
poultice, *n.* Ta'kucoco aehnakapi.
poultry, *n.* Waȟupakoza wanuyaŋpi.
pounce, *vt.* Iȟpaya. *Pounce on*, iyaȟpaya.
pound, *n.* 1. Tkeutapi ; otkeute : *ten pounds of sugar*. 2. Ma'zaska Sagdašiŋ ta'wa : *it cost ten pounds*. *vt.* 1. Apa ; kašušuza : *he pounds me with a club*. 2. Bopaŋ ; kapaŋ ; kamdu : *the woman was pounding corn*. *n.* Ptewanuyaŋpi okaške : *he locked the cow in the pound*.
pour, *vt.* Kaštaŋ ; kada ; papson ; okada. *Pour on water*, mini okaštaŋ.—*Pour out water*, mini kaštaŋ.—*Pour in water*, mini okaštaŋ.—*The wheat is pouring out*, aġuyapisu kadada. *vi.* Ni'na hiyu ; dus ya.
pout, *vi.* Iyokipišni uŋ ; pute šinkiya.
poverty, *n.* Wowaȟpanica ; wicawaȟpanica ; kakižapi.
powder, *n.* 1. Caȟdi : *powder and shot*. 2. Ta'ku mdu : *grind it to powder*. 3. Pežuta apaȟtapidaŋ : *take a powder every night*. *vt.* 1. Pamdu ; mduya : *powdered alum*. 2. Akadada : *powder the hair*.
powder-box, *n.* Caȟdiopiye.
powder-flask, *n.* Caȟdiožuha.
powder-magazine, *n.* Caȟdi woȟa.
powder-mill, *n.* Caȟdiokaġe.
power, *n.* Wowaš'ake ; wookihi : *the power of steam*.
powerful, *a.* Waš'aka ; otaŋtoŋ ; wohitika.
powerfully, *adv.* Ohitiya ; waš'agya.
powerless, *a.* Waš'akešni ; wowaš'ake ni'ca.
powwow, *n.* Dowaŋpi ; wapiya dowaŋpi ; Ikcewicašta owoȟdake.
pox, *n.* Oȟdi; iteȟdoȟdoka. *Small-pox*, makošice iteȟdoȟdoka.
practicable, *a.* Ecoŋpica ; uŋpica.
practical, *a.* Oecoŋ wašte ; akiȟo ; ecoŋpica.
practically, *adv.* Oecoŋ ekta.
practice, *n.* Woecoŋ ; wicoȟaŋ ; oȟaŋ. *Difficult in practice*, oecoŋ ekta teȟike. — *Practice makes perfect*, woecoŋ wowayupika ka'ġa.—*The practice of medicine*, pežutawicašta woecoŋ. *vt.* 1. Ecoŋ ; ecoŋ ecee. —*To practice fraud*, wohnaye ecoŋ ecee. 2. Kuwa ; ecoŋ.—*To practice law*, wa'kiyapi wicoȟaŋ kuwa. 3. Oŋspeiçiciya ; ecewaktaiçiya : *to practice music*.
practician, *n.* Tu'we ecoŋ ecee.
practitioner, *n.* Woecoŋ.
prairie, *n.* Tiŋ'ta.
prairie-dog, *n.* Piŋspiŋza.
prairie-chicken, *n.* Šiyo.
praise, *n.* Wowitaŋ ; woyataŋ. *His praise*, to'witaŋ. *vt.* 1. Yataŋ ; yaonihaŋ ; yawašte. — *Praise God*, Wakaŋtaŋka yataŋ.—*Praise the child*, hokšiyo-

ṡpa yawaṡte. 2. (*Of things*) Yawaṡte : *he praised the country*.
praiseworthy, *a.* Yawaṡtepica.
prance, *vi.* Psi'psin ma'ni.
prank, *n.* Woṡkate ; wowiḣa ṡkaŋ.
prate, *vi.* Ta'ku ka taŋiŋṡni ia.
prattle, *vi.* Hokṡiyopa se ia.
prattler, *n.* Ie s'a.
pray, *vi.* 1. Ce'kiya ; wocekiye eya ; wacekiya. 2. Ye ; ce'kiya. —*Pray, don't do it,* ce'ciciya, ecoŋṡni.
prayer, *n.* Wocekiye ; wakaŋcekiyapi ; a'wicakehaŋ da'pi.
prayer-book, *n.* Wocekiye wowapi.
prayerful, *a.* Wacekiya ; wocekiye waṡteda.
prayerfully, *adv.* Wacekiyes'a.
prayer-meeting, *n.* Wocekiyeomniciye.
praying, *pa.* Wacekiya ; wacekiyes'a.
pre-, *prefix.* I'tokam.
preach, *vi.* Wohdaka ; Wakaŋtaŋka oie oyaka ; wahokoŋwicakiya. *vt.* Oyaka ; wahokoŋkiya.—*Preach the Gospel,* Wotaŋiŋwaṡte oyaka.—*Preach a sermon,* wowahokoŋkiye eya.
preacher, *n.* Wahokoŋwicakiya ; wacekiyewicaṡta.
preaching, *n.* Wowahokoŋkiye.
preamble, *n.* Kaitokam eyapi.
precarious, *a.* To'ketu taŋiŋṡni ; kitaŋyaŋ.
precaution, *n.* Wawitoŋpapi ; woitoŋpe.
precede, *vt.* I'tokam ya ; tokahaŋ.
precedence, *n.* Wotokahe.
precedent, *n.* Wotokahe ; caŋkukaġa. *a.* I'tokam ya.
precentor, *n.* Dowaŋitaŋcaŋ.
precept, *n.* Woope ; wowahokoŋkiye.
preceptor, *n* Waoŋspekiya.
precinct, *n.* Makobaṡpe.
precious, *a.* O'tayawapi ; teḣike.
preciousness, *n.* Teḣike ; wowaṡte.
precipice, *n.* Maya.
precipitable, *a.* Cetete eḣpeyepica.
precipitant, *n.* Inaḣni ; to'ken okihi.
precipitate, *vt.* Kun eḣpeya ; inaḣniya ; kaḣoiyeya.
precipitately, *adv.* Inaḣniyaŋ.
precipitation, *n.* Woinaḣni ; ohiŋhe ; mini hiŋhe.
precipitous, *a.* Maya ; a'pamahde ; inaḣni.
precipitously, *adv.* Inaḣniyaŋ.
precise, *a.* Basmipi ; iyehantu ecoŋ ; tkoŋ'zedaŋ.
precisely, *adv.* Hehantudaŋḣiŋ ; iyehantudaŋḣin ; ohnaḣca.
precision, *n.* Woecetu.
preclude, *vt.* Anapta ; nataka.
precocious, *a.* Oicaḣkokedaŋ ; kohaŋna waciŋksapa.
precocity, *n.* Wokokedaŋ ; woksape oḣanko.
preconceive, *vt.* I'tokam iyukcaŋ.
preconcert, *vt.* I'tokam kici yuṡtaŋ.
preconcerted, *pa.* I'tokam kici eya.
precursor, *n.* I'tokam ya ; wowakta.
predatory, *a.* Wamanoŋ ; wawiyaḣpaye.
predecessor, *n.* Watokahe ; wi'citokam ya.
predestinate, *vt.* Wakicoŋza ; i'tokam yuṡtaŋ.
predestine, *vt.* I'tokam yuṡtaŋ.
predetermine, *vt.* I'tokam wakicoŋza.
predicable, *a.* Eyepica.
predicament, *n.* Ouŋ ; oyaŋke.
predicate, *vt.* Icażeyate ; oyaka. *n.* (*Gram.*) To'ken icażeyatapi.
predict, *vt.* I'tokam oyaka ; ayate.
prediction, *n.* Woayate.

predispose, *vt.* I'tokam awaciŋya; i'tokam caŋku ki'caġa.
predominate, *vi.* I'waŋkam uŋ; kapeya; wowidagya.
preeminence, *n.* Wotokahe.
preeminent, *a.* Iyotaŋ; tokahaŋ.
preeminently, *adv.* Iyotaŋyaŋ; iyotaŋ.
preempt, *vt.* Makoce icu; tokaheya icu; anica.
preengage, *vt.* I'tokam icu kta eya.
preexist, *vi.* I'tokam ni.
preexistence, *n.* I'tokam ni'pi.
preface, *n.* Otokahe iapi; i'tokam yaotaŋiŋpi. *vt.* I'tokam eya.
prefect, *n.* Wa'waŋyake.
prefer, *vt.* I'waŋkam e'hnaka; kaȟniġa; ciŋ; iyokipi.
preferable, *a.* Kaȟniȟpica.
preference, *n.* Kaȟniġapi; tukte ciŋ'pi.
preferment, *n.* Waŋkan e'hnakapi.
prefigure, *vt.* Wi'yaciŋyaŋ ayata.
prefix, *vt.* I'tokam e'hnaka.
pregnancy, *n.* Ciŋcaikpihnakapi.
pregnant, *a.* Ihduśaka; ta'ku o'ta ikoyake; tke.
prehistoric, *a.* Hehaŋyaŋ woyakapi wanica; wanakaża.
prejudge, *vt.* I'tokam yaco; taŋyaŋnaȟoŋśni yaco.
prejudice, *n.* Wowiyukcaŋ ȟmiŋ; woyuśice. *vt.* Sanina wi'yukcaŋkiya; tawaciŋ yutokeca.
prejudicial, *a.* Wayutokeca; wayuśica.
prelacy, *n.* Woitaŋcaŋ; wicaśta wakaŋ itaŋcaŋpi.
prelate, *n.* Wicaśtawakaŋtaŋka.
preliminary, *a.* I'tokam waŋka; i'tokam; otokaheya. *n.* O'tokaheya wicoȟaŋ.
prelude, *n.* I'tokam ecoŋpi.
premature, *a.* Iyehantuśni; iyehantuśni sutoŋ; kohaŋna.
prematurely, *adv.* I'tokam; kohaŋ; nahaŋȟ iyehantuśni.
premeditate, *vt.* Kohaŋ awaciŋ.
premeditation, *n.* I'tokam awaciŋpi.
premier, *n.* Tokaheyaitaŋcaŋ.
premise, *vt.* Iapi oaehde ka'ġa.
premium, *n.* 1. Ta'ku ohiyapi: *what is the premium.* 2. Ma'zaska odotapi wokażużu.
premonition, *n.* Wowakta.
preoccupancy, *n.* Tokaheya yuhapi.
preoccupy, *vt.* I'tokam yuha.
preparation, *n.* Yuwiyeyapi; piiçiyapi; piyapi.
preparatory, *a.* Oŋ yuwiyeyapi; en piwicayapi.
prepare, *vt.* Yuwiyeya; piya e'hnaka; piya. *vi.* Yuwiyeya; piiçiya.
prepay, *vt.* I'tokam każużu.
prepayment, *n.* I'tokam każużupi.
preponderance, *n.* I'akam tke.
preposition, *n.* Iapi i'tokam uŋ; o'takuye iapi.
prepossess, *vt.* I'tokam awaciŋya; i'tokam yuha; woawaciŋ ożudaŋya.
preposterous, *a.* Yuiciŋśniyaŋ; iyecetuśni.
prerogative, *n.* Wicoȟaŋ.
presage, *vt.* I'tokam oyaka.
presbyter, *n.* Huŋkayapi.
Presbyterian, *n.* Okodakiciyewakaŋ obe waŋżi; Huŋkaitaŋcaŋpi.
presbytery, *n.* *Presbyterian* wicaśtawakaŋ omniciye.
prescience, *n.* I'tokam sdonyapi.
prescribe, *vt.* Ecoŋśi; wowíyukcaŋ ķu.
prescription, *n.* Woecoŋ; wowiyukcaŋ.
presence, *n.* En uŋ'pi; itohnake. —*In the presence of,* i'tokam. —*Presence of mind,* tawaciŋ mde'za.
pres'ent, *a.* 1. En uŋ; o'peya uŋ. —*I am present,* en wauŋ. 2.

De ; dehan ; dehantu. —*The present age,* wicoicaġe de. 3. (*Gram.*) Dehantu. *n.* 1. Ta'ku kiciçupi ; woituħaŋ : *I send you a present.* 2. Wowapi : *know all men by these presents.*

present', *vt.* Ķu ; itukiħaŋ.—*He presented me this book,* wowapi de maķu. 2. Pazo ; i'tokam e'hde : *he presented himself.*—*Present arms,* wi'pe kipazo.—*Present the name,* cażeyata ; caże pazo.

presentable, *a.* Pazopica ; ķupica.

presentation, *n.* Pazopi ; yutaŋiŋpi.

presentiment, *n.* I'tokam wasdonyapi ; wakihdecapi.

presently, *adv.* Ecadaŋ ; to'keśta.

presentment, *n.* Kipazopi; keciŋpi.

preservation, *n.* Taŋ'yaŋ yuhapi ; niyaŋpi.

preservative, *n.* Oŋ waniyaŋpi.

preserve, *vt.* Taŋyaŋ yuha ; nikiya ; ħwiŋ'kteśni yuha : *preserve the king.*—*Preserve fruit,* waskuyeca ħwiŋ'śni hna'kapi. *Laws to preserve game,* wamakaśkaŋ so'te kte śni woope.

preserves, *n.* Waskuyeca kuke kte śni yużapi.

preside, *vi.* Itaŋcaŋ i'yotaŋka ; awaŋyaka.

presidency, *n.* Woitaŋcaŋ ; wowaŋyake.

president, *n.* Itaŋcaŋ ; omniciye yuha ; Tuŋkaŋśidaŋ.

presidential, *a.* Itaŋcaŋ ta'wa.

press, *vt.* 1. Paskica ; yuskica ; kaskica ; iyahdaskica : *press out the juice.* 2. Pataŋ ecoŋkiya ; i'yopaśtake : *he pressed me to go.* 3. Ni'na kuwa ; ni'na ciŋkiya : *he pressed him with the truth.* *vi.* Wakitaŋ ; wawiyopaśtaka : *press on to glory.* *n.* 1. Wi'caśkice ; wi'pataŋ.—*A hay-press,* peżi-icaśkica. 2. Wowapi ahdiħpeyapi : *a small printing press.* 3. Wotaŋiŋwowapi : *the press is mighter than the sword.* 4. Wokiħnake : *a clothes press.* 5. Woiyopaśtake : *in the press of business.* 6. Wicota ; kicipatitaŋpi.

pressing, *pa.* Wawiyopaśtake; wainaħni.

pressingly, *adv.* Ni'na.

pressman, *n.* Wowapiahdiħpeye.

pressure, *n.* Wokaskice ; woiyopaśtake ; tke ; wopatitaŋ.

presswork, *n.* Wowapi ahdiħpeyapi ; wowapi puspapi.

prestige, *n.* Wowiyutaŋye ; wowaś'ake.

presto, *adv.* Oħaŋko ; inaħni.

presumable, *a.* Eciŋpica.

presumably, *adv.* Iyecetuka.

presume, *vi.* 1. Eciŋ ; keciŋ.—*I presume,* kepca.—*You presume,* kecaŋi. 2. Sdonyekoŋza ; tawaţenya.

presumption, *n.* 1. Eciŋpi ; keciŋpi ; wowiyukcaŋ. 2. Wowitkotkoka ; wi'yukcaŋśni.

presumptive, *a.* Wi'yukcaŋpica.

presumptively, *adv.* Wi'yukcaŋyaŋ ; eciŋpi iyececa.

presumptuous, *a.* Ecoŋkteħca ; wohitika ; sdonya ecoŋ.

presuppose, *vt.* I'tokam eciŋ.

presupposition, *n.* I'tokam eciŋpi

pretend *vt.* Koŋ'za ; ecaecoŋ ; wicakeśni śkaŋ : *he pretended to be sick.*

pretender, *n.* Wicahnayaŋ.

pretense, *n.* Koŋ'zapi ; wicahmuŋkapi ; wohnaye ; ecaecoŋpi.

pretension, *n.* Ta'wa koŋ'zapi ; waħaŋiçida.

pretentious, *a.* Ta'kuiçida.

preterit, *a.* (*Gram.*) He'kta ; yuśtaŋpi.

preternatural, *a.* To'keca ; wakaŋse.

preternaturally, *adv.* Togye ; ni'na.

pretext, *n.* Wokoŋze; woakaȟpe.
prettily, *adv.* Waśteya; yupiya; oiyokipiya.
prettiest, *a. sup.* Iyotaŋwaśte.
prettiness, *n.* Wowaśte; woiyokipi.
pretty, *a.* Waśte; waśteka; owaŋyagwaśte: *what a pretty flower. adv.* Ki'taŋna; ahecenya: *pretty good.*
prevail, *vi.* 1. Ohiya: *Israel prevailed.* 2. I'yakapeya; ohiya: *he prevailed in the council.* 3. Ecoŋkiya; cin'śni ecoŋkiya: *they prevailed on him to go.* 4. Yuha; ecoŋ: *the custom prevails in India.*
prevailing, *pa.* 1. Waś'aka; ohiya: *prevailing prayer.* 2. O'hiŋni kinin he'ceca; iyotaŋ o'ta: *the prevailing winds.*
prevalence, *n.* Waŋkan uŋ; waś'agya uŋ; ni'na ececa.
prevalent, *a.* Ni'na ececapi; taŋ'kaya uŋ; waś'aka.
prevaricate, *vi.* Eciŋśni oyaka; yatokeca.
prevarication, *n.* Wayatokecapi; woyatokeca.
prevaricator, *n.* Eciŋśni oyaka.
prevent, *vt.* Kaġiya; kaśeya; okihiśniya; anapta.
preventable, *a.* Anaptepica.
prevention, *n.* Anaptapi; waanaptapi.
preventive, *n.* Woanapte.
previous, *a.* I'tokam; tokaheya.
previously, *adv.* I'tokam.
prey, *n.* Ta'wa; waahdipi; wakipi. *vi.* Wabotica; wamanoŋ.
price, *n.* Wokażużu; iyawapi; iyuwiŋ; *Y.* wi'śi: *the price of toil.—Without price,* iyuwiŋ codaŋ.—*What is the price,* token iyawapi he.
priceless, *a.* Yawapicaśni.
prick, *n.* 1. Wi'cape; ta'ku pe; ta'ku pe'sto: *kick the pricks.* 2. Capapi; capapa; wocapa. *vt.* Capa; icam e'hde.—*He pricked me,* camapa.—*Prick a knife into the ground,* maka en isaŋ icam hde.—*Pricked to the heart,* caŋte icapa.—*Pricked up his ears,* nakpa kabosdata.
pricker, *n.* Wi'cape.
pricking, *n.* Capapa.
prickle, *n.* Wi'cape; iŋ'kpa.
prickly, *a.* Pepe; pespesto.—*Prickly-pear,* uŋkcekceka.
pricky, *a.* Pepe.
pride, *n.* 1. Wowaȟaŋiçida; waȟaŋiçidapi; wamnaiçidapi; wataŋkaiçidapi: *pride goeth before destruction.* 2. Wowiyuśkiŋ; woiwiŋkta: *James takes pride in keeping fat horses.* 3. Wowiŋkta; wowaȟaŋiçida: *the pride of his father. vt.* (With the reflexive pronoun.) Iwiŋkta; iwaȟaŋiçida.
prier, *n.* Wa'kites'a; waaśdaye.
priest, *n.* Wawayuśna; wicaśtawakaŋ; *T.* wakaŋcekiya; (*Rom. Cath.*) śinasapa; cuwignakesapa.
prim, *a.* Wayuco; stosto. *vt.* Ayuco ka'ġa; pastosto.
primacy, *n.* O'tokahe; woitaŋcaŋ.
prima-donna, *n.* Wiŋ'yaŋ dowaŋitaŋcaŋ.
prima facie, *a.* Taŋiŋyaŋ uŋ; ite akan uŋ.
primary, *a.* O'tokahe; tokahaŋ: *primary schools.—A matter of primary importance,* ta'ku kiŋ woawaciŋ o'tokahe ȟca.
primate, *n.* Tokaheya itaŋcaŋ.
prime, *a.* Tokahaŋ; iyotaŋ; itaŋcaŋ; itaŋcaŋ.—*Prime mover,* iyotaŋ kuwa.—*Prime number,* wayawapi kiyuśpepicaśni. *n.* O'tokahe; iyotaŋ waśte; hehan waśtepi; hehaŋyaŋ waś'aka.—*He died in his prime,* iyotaŋ waś'aka hehan ṭa. *vt.* 1. Caȟdi

no'ġe akada : *prime a gun.* 2. Tokaheya iuŋ : *prime the house with oil.* 3. Oŋspekiya ; ożuya.

primer, *n.* 1. Wowapi tokaheya ; A-B-C wowapi. 2. Ma'zaahdiḣpeyapi ocaże.

primeval, *a.* O'tokahe.

priming, *n.* 1. No'ġe iyopuḣdi ; no'ġe iokadapi : *the priming of the gun.* 2. Tokaheya iuŋpi.

primitive, *a.* O'tokahe ; ehaŋna : *a primitive church.*—*A primitive style of dress,* heyake okaġe ehaŋna.

primitively, *adv.* O'tokaheya.

primly, *adv.* Yucoya ; yupiya.

primness, *n.* Wayuco.

primp, *vt.* Heyake hduwitaŋ.

prince, *n.* Itaŋcaŋ ; itaŋcaŋciŋca.

princely, *a.* Itaŋcaŋse ; itaŋcaŋ iyecen.

princess, *n.* Wiŋ'yaŋ itaŋcaŋ ; itaŋcaŋciŋca wiŋ'yaŋ.

principal, *n.* Tokahekiyapi ; iyotaŋ. *a.* Tokahaŋ.

principality, *n.* Woitaŋcaŋ ; woawaŋyake.

principally, *adv.* Iyotaŋyaŋ.

principle, *n.* O'tokaheya wooŋspe ; o'hutkaŋ ; woawaciŋ.

print, *vt.* Ma'zaoŋowa ; oweka'ġa. *n.* Owapi ; owe ; oŋ owapi ; icaḣtake. *Small print,* oowa ci'stiŋna.—*The print of his foot,* siha owe kiŋ.

printer, *n.* Ma'zaehde ; ma'zaahdiḣpeye ; ma'za oŋ wowapi ka'ġa.

printing, *n.* Ma'za oŋ wowapi ka'ġapi.—*Printing office,* wowapi okaġe.—*Printing press,* ma'zaahdiḣpeyapi.

prior, *a.* I'tokam ; tokaheya.

priority, *n.* Wotokahe.

prison, *n.* Wokaŝketipi ; owicakaŝke.

prisoner, *n.* Tu'we kaŝkapi ; kaŝkapi.

pristine, *a.* O'tokahe ; ehaŋna.

privacy, *n.* Wonaḣbe.

private, *a.* 1. Iŝnana ta'wa ; wicitawa.—*Private property,* woyuha wicitawa.—*Private secretary,* wowapikaġa i'atayedaŋ ta'wa. Naḣmaŋpi ; tuwedaŋ en i ŝni : *a private room.* 3. Ikceya uŋ ; ikceka ; itaŋcaŋŝni : *a private soldier.* 4. Tuwedaŋ sdonye ŝni ; naḣmana ecoŋpi. 5. I'yatayedaŋ : *his private property.* *n.* Akicita ikceka ; ta'ku naḣmaŋpi.

privately, *adv.* 1. Naḣmaŋna : *he did it privately.* 2. I'yatayedaŋ : *he was privately benefited.*

privateness, *n.* Wonaḣbe ; wicitawa.

privation, *n.* Wokakiże ; kakiŝyapi ; wakipi ; wicawanica.

privilege, *n.* Ta'ku ta'wa ; towiyuŝkiŋ ; wookihi ; ecatawapi.—*It is my privilege to call him father,* ate ewakiye kta he mitowiyuŝkiŋ.

privileged, *a.* Woiyowiŋkiye yuhapi.

privily, *a.* Naḣmaŋna.

privy, *n.* Taŋkantipi. *a.* 1. Sdonya. 2. Iŝnana ta'wa : *a privy purse.* 3. Tuwedaŋ en i ŝni ; naḣmaŋpi : *a privy chamber.*

prize, *n.* Ta'ku ohiyapi ; okipe ; woohiye ; wakipi ; ta'ku teḣika.—*A prize medal,* wanapiŋ ohiyapi. *Prize money,* ma'zaska ohiyapi. *vt.* 1. Teḣiŋda.—*I prize the book highly,* wowapi ni'na ṭewaḣiŋda.

probability, *n.* Woiyecetu ; se'ececa.

probable, *a.* Iyececa ; he'cetu kta se'ca ; se'ececa.

probably, *adv.* Naceca ; iteka ; se'ececa.

probate, *n.* Yuwicakapi. *Probate court,* waiḣpeyapi woyasu.

probation, *n.* Iwicayutapi ; iyuteya ecoŋwicakiyapi.
probationary, *a.* Iyutekiyapi.
probe, *vt.* Ma'za ohnahna iyeya ; pakota. *n.* Wi'pakote.
probity, *n.* Woowotaŋna ; wowaŝte yuwicakapi.
problem, *n.* Wowiyukcaŋ ; woecoŋ ; woiwaŋġe.
problematic, *a.* Iyukcaŋpica ; to'-ketu taŋiŋŝni.
proboscis, *n.* Pasu.
procedure, *n.* Oaye ; ocaŋku ; wokuwa.
proceed, *vi.* 1. Iyaye ; iyoopta ya : *he proceeded on his journey.* 2. Hiyu ; hinaŋpa.
proceeding, *pa.* Iyaya ; iyopte. *He is proceeding,* iyopte. *n.* Woecoŋ ; wicoȟaŋ.—*Read the proceedings of the meeting,* omniciye woecoŋ yawa.—*An illegal proceeding,* wicoȟaŋ woope ohna ŝni.
proceeds, *n.* Wokamna ; woicaġe.
process, *n.* 1. Woecoŋ ; wokuwa : *the process of making bread.* 2. Oiyopte ; yeye.—*In the process of time,* uŋ'haŋketa.
procession, *n.* 1. I'ciyaza omanipi.—*A funeral procession,* wicahnag ya'pi. 2. Woiyopte ; ohiyaye.
proclaim, *vt.* E'yaŋpaha ; oyaka ; yaotaŋiŋ : *proclaim war.*
proclamation, *n* Eyaŋpahapi ; woyakapi : *thanksgiving proclamation.*
proclivity, *n.* Woiyutaŋye ; wowayupika.
procrastinate, *vt.* Yutehaŋ ; kihnakes'a.
procrastination, *n.* Yutehaŋpi.
procurable, *a.* Iyeyepica ; icupica.
procure, *vt.* Okini ; icu ; kamna : *he procured three doctors.*
procurer, *n.* Wawihni ; ki'cicuwa.
prod, *vt.* Paẑipa ; paẑim kuwa.
prodigal, *a.* Wayusota ; waihaŋgya : *the prodigal son.*
prodigality, *n.* Wayusotapi ; wawihaŋgyapi.
prodigious, *a.* Taŋ'ka ; hiŋ'skotaŋka ; wa'petokeca ; *a prodigious ox.*
prodigiously, *adv.* Wowinihaŋyaŋ ; nina: *he grew prodigiously.*—*He laughed prodigiously,* ni'na iȟa.
prodigy, *n.* Wowapetokeca.
produce', *vt.* 1. Icaȟya ; aicaȟya : *this ground produces corn well.* 2. Yutaŋiŋ ; pazo ; hiyuya : *produce the evidence.* 3. Ka'ġa : *vice produces misery.*
prod'uce, *n.* Ta'ku icaȟyapi ; woicaġe ; wokaġe.
producer, *n.* Waicaȟye ; tu'we ta'ku ka'ġe ; wakamna.
product, *n.* 1. Woicaġe ; wokaġe ; ta'ku ka'ġe ; ta'ku icaġe. 2. (*Math.*) O'yuwitaya.
production, *n.* 1. Ka'ġapi ; yutaŋiŋpi : *the production of tin.* 2. Ta'kukaġapi ; ta'kuicaȟya : *the productions of the earth.* 3. Yuhaŋskapi.
profanation, *n.* Ohodapiŝni ; ta'kuŝnikiyapi.
profane, *a.* 1. Ikceka ; ikce : *a profane author.* 2. Waohodaŝni. *vt.* Ta'ku Wakaŋ ohodaŝni ; ohodaŝni : *profane the Sabbath.*
profanely, *adv.* Ohodaŝniyaŋ.
profaneness, *n.* Waohodapiŝni.
profaner, *n.* Waohodaŝni.
profanity, *n.* Waohodapiŝni.
profess, *vt.* Ohdaka ; en ihdutaŋiŋ ; he'ca keiçiya.
professed, *a.* Ihdaotaŋiŋ ; taŋiŋyaŋ uŋ.
professedly, *adv.* I'ye ohdaka.
profession, *n.* 1. Oihdakapi ; ihdutaŋiŋpi ; keiçiyapi. 2. Wic(ȟaŋ ; woŝkiŋçiye : *the professio.*

of a doctor. 3. Okodakiciye; oṡkiŋciye.

professional, *a.* Woṡkiŋciye ta′-wa; wowayupika; he′ca.

professionally, *adv.* Oṡkiŋciye eciyataŋhaŋ.

professor, *n.* 1. Wooŋspewaŋkantu waoŋspekiya: *the professor of Greek.* 2. Je′sus o′pa; wakaŋcekiya.

professorship, *n.* Waoŋs ekiya wicoḣaŋ.

proffer, *vt.* Hiyukiya; ḳu kta keya.

proficiency, *n.* Wookihi; wowayupika; wosdonye.

proficient, *a.* Wayupika; waakiḣo.

proficiently, *adv.* Wayupiya.

profile, *n.* Ohomni owapi; wicite hdakiŋyaŋ owapi.

profit, *n.* 1. Wokamna; aicaġe: *the profit is ten dollars.* 2. Iwicawaṡtepi; woiyokihi; wokamna: *there is profit in exercise.* *vt.* Okiciwaṡte; kamna: *it profited him ten dollars.* *vi.* Iwaṡte; wi′yokihi.

profitable, *a.* Wakamna; wi′yokihi; wayuwaṡte.

profitably, *adv.* Yuwaṡteya; taŋ′-yaŋ.

profitless, *a.* Wokamna co′daŋ.

profligacy, *n.* Woyuṡice.

profligate, *n.* Ṡinya oḣaŋye; waihaŋgya.

profound, *a.* Mahentu; wicaka.

profoundly, *adv.* Mahentuya.

profoundness, *n.* Omahentu.

profuse, *a.* Iyakicu; paŋ′ġa; oḣaŋpi; aokaġeca.

profusely, *adv.* Iyakiçuya.

profuseness, *n.* Wokaġeca.

profusion, *n.* Woptecaṡni; o′ta.

progenitor, *n.* Huŋkake.

progeny, *n.* Ciŋca.

prognosticate, *vt.* Oyaka; ayata.

program, programme, *n.* Woecoŋoyaka; omniciye wowapi.

pro′gress, *n.* Woiyopte; iyoptapi.

progress′, *vi.* Iyopte; sam ya.

progression, *n.* Woiyopte; woicaġe.

progressive, *a.* Iyopte; wakitaŋ; sam okihiwaciŋ.

prohibit, *vt.* Anapta; teḣiŋda: *prohibit the sale of liquor.*

prohibition, *n.* Wateḣiŋdapi; waanaptapi; miniwakaŋ anaptapi.

prohibitive, *a.* Waanapta.

prohibitory, *a.* Waanapta.

pro′ject, *n.* Wowiyukcaŋ; woecoŋ.

project′, *vt.* 1. Pasdohaŋ iyeya; hiyuya; eḣpeya.—*He projected the roof,* awakeya sam hiyuya. 2. Iyukcaŋ: *project a plan.* 3. Icazo; sam owa: *project the lines.* *vi.* Hiyu; sam hiyu: *it projects a foot.*

projectile, *n.* Ta′ku yeyapi; wayeyapi; waŋhiŋkpe; ma′zasu.

projector, *n.* Ka′ġa; wi′yukcaŋ.

prolific, *a.* Waicaḣya; ta′ku o′ta icaḣya; ciŋcota.

prolix, *a.* Haŋ′ska; ehaeṡ haŋ′-ska; aokaġa; iapi ecewiŋota.

prologue, *n.* Owohdake otokahe.

prolong, *vt.* Yuhaŋska.

promenade, *vi.* Iḣduzin omani.

prominence, *n.* Wookitaŋiŋ; wowaŋkantuya; paha.

prominent, *a.* Okitaŋiŋ.

prominently, *adv.* Okitaŋiŋyaŋ.

promiscuous, *a.* I′cicahi; tokenciŋyaŋ.

promiscuously, *adv.* I′cicahiya.

promise, *n.* 1. Wahoyapi; wowahoye: *the promise of God.* 2. Wowaciŋye; waṡte kta iyecen uŋpi. *vt.* Wahoya; iwahoya; keya; ḳu kta eya; se′ca: *the Agent promised me a wagon.—The clouds promise rain.*

promising, *a.* Waṡte kta se′ca.

promissory, *a.* Ecoŋ kta oyaka.

promontory, *n.* Ipa; makoce ipa.

promote, *vt.* 1. Icaȟya ; o'kiya ; i'yopaśtake : *promote education.* 2. Yuwaŋkantuya ; waŋkan e'hnaka : *promoted to the next class.*

promoter, *n.* Waicaȟya ; waokiya.

promotion, *n.* Yuwaŋkantuyapi.

promotive, *a.* Waokiya.

prompt, *a.* Iyehan ecoŋ ; oȟaŋko ; katiŋyaŋ.—*Prompt attendance,* iyehan hi'pi. — *Prompt obedience,* katiŋyaŋ anaġoptaŋpi. —*Prompt orders,* ecoŋwicakiyapi oȟaŋko. *vt.* Ecoŋkiya ; okiyaka : *prompt him to go.*

prompter, *n.* Tu'we ecoŋkiya ; tu'-we okiyaka.

promptly, *adv.* Oȟaŋkoya ; kohaŋna ; iyehaŋyaŋ. — *Answer promptly,* kohaŋna ayupta.— *Ring the bell promptly,* iyehaŋyaŋ woȟda.

promptness, *n.* Iyehan ecoŋpi ; woiyehantu ; owicaȟaŋkopi.

prong, *n.* O'iŋkpa ; oadetka ; oȟaka.

pronged, *a.* Oȟaka ; ġanġata.

pronoun, *n.* (*Gram.*) Wocaże e'ekiya.

pronounce, *vt.* E'ya ; e'napeya ; ecen e'ya : *pronounce distinctly.* —*I can't pronounce it,* ecen epa owakihiśni. — *He pronounced the dollar a counterfeit,* ma'zaska he wohnaye keya.

pronounceable, *a.* Ecen eyepica.

pronounced, *a.* Okitaŋiŋ ; wowicake.

pronouncer, *n.* To'ken eyapi oyaka.

pronunciation, *n.* E'napeyapi ; oenape ; iapi oenape.

proof, *n.* Oŋ yuwicakapi ; woiyute ; oŋ to'ketu sdonyapi : *he gave no proof of his sincerity.* *a.* 1. Oŋ yuwicakapi : *a proof sheet; a proof text.* 2. Okihipicaśni ; wakaȟdokeśni : *bullet proof.*

proofless, *a.* Yuwicakapi wanica.

prop, *vt.* Ipataŋ e'hde. *n.* Ipataŋ ; ipatake.

propagate, *vt.* 1. Icaȟya : *propagate religion.* 2. Sam icaȟya ; ciŋcatoŋkiya : *propagate buffalo.*

propagation, *n.* Waicaȟyapi.

propel, *vt.* Iyayeya ; iyopteya : *powder propels the balls.*—*The boat is propelled by steam,* wata kiŋ minipo kiŋ oŋ iyopte.

propeller, *n.* Waiyopteya ; wa'tayusdohaŋ.

propensity, *n.* Woiyutaŋye.

proper, *a.* 1. Wahehantu ; owotaŋna : *proper conduct.* 2. Wicitawa ; iyecetu : *water is the proper place for a fish.* 3. (*Gram*). I'yatayedaŋ ; iśnana ta'wa.

properly, *adv.* Taŋyaŋ ; yucoya.

property, *n.* 1. Woyuha : *that horse is my property.* 2. Wotokeca ; oŋ wasdonyapi : *sweetness is a property of sugar.*

prophecy, *n.* Wokcaŋpi ; woayate.

prophesy, *vt.* Ayata ; iyukcaŋ : *prophesies the destruction of Jerusalem.* *vi.* Woyaka : *John prophesied.*

prophet, *n.* Waayate ; wicaśtawokcaŋ.

prophetess, *n.* Wiŋ'yaŋ waayate.

prophetic, *a.* Waayate ; wakcaŋka.

prophetically, *adv.* Wakcaŋyaŋ.

propitiate, *vt.* Canwaśteya ; yuwaśte ; awaciŋkiya ; ta'ku ķu.

propitiation, *n.* Wokażużu ; yuwaśtepi.

propitiator, *n.* Wakażużu ; wayuwaśte.

propitiatory, *a.* Wakażużupi.

propitious, *a.* Owaśteca ; waśte kta iteka ; wayuwaśte.

proportion, *n.* Oiyute ; iyekicetu.

proportional, *a.* Iyekicetu ; i'cidehantu.
proportionally, *adv.* I'ciwaŋyagya.
proposal, *n.* Woiwaŋyake ; wawiwaŋġapi ; to'ken ecoŋ kta oyakapi.—*Proposals for building a house,* ti'pi to'ken ka'ġe kta oyaka.—*He made proposals of marriage,* wakaŋyuze kta keciya.
propose, *vt.* 1. Iwaŋyagśi ; caźeyata : *he proposed to Mr. Jones to come.* 2. Iwaŋyaka ; awaciŋ. *I propose to tell you. vi.* 1. Wi'yukcaŋ ; ecoŋwaciŋ : *man proposes, God disposes.* 2. Wakaŋyuze kta eciya : *Mr. Jones proposed to Miss Smith.*
proposer, *n.* Wawiwaŋġa.
proposition, *n.* 1. Woiwaŋġa ; iapi iwaŋyagwicaśipi : *propositions of peace.* 2. Wowicada ; iapi ihduotaŋiŋpi : *the propositions of Calvin.* 3. Woeye ; iapi iwohdakapi : *the proposition is, if liquor is injurious, it ought to be prohibited.*
propound, *vt.* Iapi e'hnaka ; iwaŋyagśi ; e'hnaka.
proprietary, *a.* Woyuha ta'wa ; ta'wa.
proprietor, *n.* Ta'wa ; yuhe ciŋ.
propriety, *n.* Woiyokipi : *observe the proprieties of society.*
pro rata, *adv.* Iyawa ; i'akidecen.
prorogue, *vt.* Enakiyewicaya.
prosaic, *a.* Tke ; wawihahaśni.
proscribe, *vt.* Ehpeya ; yutokaŋ ; he'cetuśni eya ; ṭe kta yacopi.
proscription, *n.* Ehpeyapi ; ṭe kta owapi.
prose, *n.* Iapi ikceka ; iapi katiŋyaŋ.
prosecute, *vt.* 1. Kuwa : *prosecuting his studies.* 2. Kuwa ; aia : *he is prosecuted for murder.*
prosecution, *n.* Kuwapi ; aiapi.
prosecutor, *n.* Kuwa ; aia.
proselyte, *vt.* Iwicacu ; okodakiciye to'keca etaŋhaŋ iwicacu ; titokaŋ wicaki. *n.* Nakaha titokaŋ ki'pi.
proselytism, *n.* Titokaŋ awicayapi.
pro-slavery, *a.* Wayaka yuhapi he'cetu da'pi.
prospect, *n.* 1. Wowaŋyake ; makoce owaŋyake ; e'toŋwaŋpi. 2. Makoce iteowapi : *the prospect from the hill-top.* 3. Iteka : *a prospect of rain.* 4. Tokata to'ketu kta ; tokata owaŋyake : *his prospects are good. vt.* Ode ; iwaŋyaka : *prospect the hills for gold. vi.* Waode.
prospective, *a.* Tokata iwaŋyakapi.
prosper, *vt.* O'kiya ; yuwaśte. *vi.* Taŋyaŋ uŋ ; wa'pi.
prosperity, *n.* Wotaŋyaŋ ; wa'pipi.
prosperous, *a.* Taŋ'yaŋ iyopte ; wa'pi.
prosperously, *adv.* Taŋ'yaŋ.
prostitute, *vt.* Ta'ku śi'ca en ku : *prostitute his talents. n.* Witkowiŋ.
prostitution, *n.* Wiŋ'yaŋ wi'yopeiçiyapi ; ta'ku śi'ca en içicupi.
prostrate, *a.* Waŋkahaŋ ; makata. —Makata waŋka, *lies prostrate. vt.* Makata ehpeya ; yuwaŋka ; yutakuniśni.
prostrated, *a.* Waŋkahaŋ.
prostration, *n.* Yuwaŋkapi ; wotakuniśni.
prosy, *a.* Tke ; iapi oṭoza.
protect, *vt.* Anakikśiŋ ; akahpa ; awaŋyaka : *protect your children.* — *Protect yourself from cold,* osni etaŋhaŋ aihdahpa.
protectingly, *adv.* Awaŋyagya.
protection, *n.* Woawaŋyake ; wowinape ; woakahpe ; o'kiyapi.
protector, *n.* Waawaŋyake.
protest', *vi.* Awicakehaŋ i'eniyeya.

pro'test, *n.* I'eniyeyapi; a'wicakehaŋ eyapi; wicadapiśni.
Protestant, *n.* Śinasapa Ateyapi, Pope, he itaŋcaŋ yuha wicada śni.
protract, *vt.* Yuhaŋska; yutehan: *protract the meeting.* — *Protracted meeting,* aŋpetu iyohi wacekiyapi.
protrude, *vt.* Inapeya. *vi.* Hinapa; hiyu: *his tongue protrudes.*
protuberance, *n.* Po; pażowaŋka.
protuberant, *a.* Pażowaŋka.
proud, *a.* 1. Wahaŋiçida: *a proud race.* 2. Iwiŋkta; iyuśkiŋ: *proud of his horse.* 3. Wowitaŋ; taŋ'ka; ohitika: *proud titles.*
proudly, *adv.* Wahaŋiçidaya; wowitaŋya.
prove, *vt.* 1. Yuwicaka: *prove what you say.* 2. Iyuta: *prove the strength of the wagon.* *vi.* Taŋiŋ.
proven, *a.* Yuwicakapi.
provender, *n.* Wanuyaŋpi tawoyute; peżi; woyute.
proverb, *n.* Woksape wicoie; wicoiewakaŋ; wi'yaciŋpi.
proverbial, *a.* Wicoie eyapis'a; eyapi cee.
proverbially, *adv.* A'taya sdonyapi; eca.
provide, *vt.* Kamna; kuwa; wi'yeya e'hnaka; ihni.—*Provide for his children,* ciŋca wicakicicamna.
provided, *conj.* Ehantaŋhaŋ; kiŋhaŋ.
providence, *n.* 1. Woawaŋyake; woihni: *he has no providence for his family.* 2. *n. pr.* Wakaŋtaŋka.
provident, *a.* Wawihni; wi'yeya hna'ka; wakpataŋ: *a provident husband.*
providential, *a.* Ta'kuwakaŋ etaŋhaŋ.
providentially, *adv.* Ta'kuwakaŋ oŋ; taŋyaŋ; wa'piya.
providently, *adv.* Wakpataŋyaŋ; ksamyahaŋ.
provider, *n.* Wakamna.
province, *n.* 1. Woawaŋyake; wicohaŋ: *it is not my province to act as judge.* 2. Makoce; makobaśpe: *the provinces of Canada.* 3. Tohaŋyaŋ śkaŋ; ta'ku iyoważa: *the province of poetry.*
provincial, *a.* Makobaśpe; a'tayaśni; iśnana ta'wapi.
provincialism, *n.* Iapi tiośpaye waŋżidaŋ uŋ'pi; iapihceśni.
provision, *n.* 1. Yuwiyeyapi; woihni: *make provision for a big crowd.* 2. Woyute; waŋeya: *provisions for the journey.* *vt.* Woyute ku: *provision the soldiers.*
provisional, *a.* Inahnikaġapi.
proviso, *n.* Wokaśe.
provocation, *n.* Wonaġiyeya; woiyopaśtake.
provoke, *vt.* Naġiyeya; caŋzeya; waciŋkoya; i'yopaśtake.
provoked, *pa.* Śiŋhda.
provoker, *n.* Wawiyopaśtake.
provoking, *a.* Wacaŋzeka; waciŋ iyowicakiśice.
prow, *n.* Wa'taipa; watokapa.
prowess, *n.* Wowaditake; woohitika.
prowl, *vt.* Nahmaŋ omani; nahmaŋ ode.
prowler, *n.* Nahmaŋ omani.
proximate, *a.* Ikiyedaŋ; o'kihe.
proximity, *n.* Kiyedaŋ.
proxy, *n.* E'ekiya woecoŋ.
prudence, *n.* Woksape; wopakaŋ.
prudent, *a.* Ksa'pa; wawitoŋpe; wakpataŋ. *A prudent king.*—*A prudent driver,* wakahapa wawitoŋpe.—*A prudent expenditure,* owopetoŋ wakpataŋ.
prudential, *a.* Waitoŋpapi; wi'yukcaŋ.

prudentially, *adv.* Wi'yukcaŋyaŋ; wakptaŋyaŋ.
prudently, *adv.* Ksamyahaŋ.
prune, *vt.* Iŋ'kpa baśimśipa; oŋśpaśpa eḣpeye. *n.* Kaŋ'tasapa.
pry, *n.* Iyukiŋ; iyuptaŋye. *vt.* Yuptaŋyaŋ; yuptaŋyewaciŋ; yukiŋ.
psalm, *n.* Odowaŋwakaŋ.
pshaw, *interj.* Hoḣ; hiŋte.
psychology, *n.* Wotawaciŋ wooŋspe.
puberty, *n.* Ciŋcatoŋ okihipi.
public, *a.* 1. Oyatetawa: *public property.* 2. Otaŋiŋ; o'waŋca sdonyapi: *the discovery is made public.* 3. Tu'we ċeyaś ta'wa; siŋtomni ta'wapi: *a public road.* *n.* Oyate; wicaśta a'taya. —*In public:* wicaśta i'tokam; taŋiŋyaŋ.
publican, *n.* Ro'ma wamnayaŋ.
publication, *n.* 1. Yaotaŋiŋpi; ka'ġapi; wowapi ma'za oŋ ka'ġapi: *he gathers the news for publication.* 2. Wotaŋiŋ wowapi: *a daily publication.*
publicity, *n.* A'taya otaŋiŋ.
publicly, *adv.* Taŋiŋyaŋ.
public-spirited, *a.* Oyate en waciŋyuza; wawaciŋktayuzataŋka.
publish, *vt.* 1. Yaotaŋiŋ; oyaka: *the herald publishes the victory.* 2. Wotaŋiŋwowapi oyaka; wowapi ka'ġa.
publisher, *n.* Wowapi ma'za oŋ ka'ġa.
pucker, *vt.* Yuḣaḣa; yuśke.
pudding, *n.* Cocoya waśpaŋyaŋpi.
puddle, *n.* Miniośkokpa.
pueblo, *n.* Otoŋwe. *Pueblo Indians,* Susoni wicaśa.
puerile, *a.* Wakaŋheża.
puff, *n.* 1. Ipoġaŋ: *a puff of wind.* 2. Iapi oŋ apoġaŋpi; ċażeyatapi: *a puff in the paper.* *vt.* 1. Apoġaŋ; ipoġaŋ. 2. Yutaŋka; tate oŋ ożuya: *puffed up with pride.* 3. Yawaśte; yaonihaŋ: *he puffed the doctor.*
puffing, *a.* Poḣpoḣ; niyaśni ţa nuŋ se.
pugh, *interj.* Ecaḣe; waŋ.
pugilist, *n.* Waapaśkata.
pugnacious, *a.* Wakizes'a.
puke, *vi.* Hde'pa; hiyuya.
pull, *vt.* 1. Yutitaŋ: *pull down the rope.* 2. Yusdohaŋ: *the horse can't pull it.*—*Pull down,* kun eḣpeya, yużużu.—*Pull fruit,* waskuyeca yuśpi.—*Pull in,* mahen icu.—*Pull off,* yuśdoka.—*Pull out,* yupśuŋ.—*Pull a tooth,* hi yupśuŋ.—*Pull to pieces,* yuksaksa.—*Pull up,* yużuŋ.—*Pulled up at his father's,* atkuku ti ekta hinażiŋ.
pullet, *n.* Aŋ'paohotoŋna wi'ye maka waŋżina.
pulley, *n.* Caŋayuhomnipi.
pulmonary, *a.* Caġu.
pulp, *n.* Co; nini.
pulpit, *n.* Wicaśtawakaŋ onażiŋ.
pulpy, *a.* Coco.
pulsation, *n.* Iyapa: oiyapa.
pulse, *n.* 1. Kaŋ'iyapa: *a rapid pulse.* 2. Omnica.
pulverize, *vt.* Pamdumdu; mdu ka'ġa; yupaŋpaŋ; bopaŋ.
pump, *n.* Miniicu; caŋḣdoġeca ohna mini icupi. *vt.* 1. Mini icu; icu. 2. E'ya kuwa; iwaŋġa.
pumpkin, *n.* Wamnu; *Y.* wakmu; *T.* wagmu.
pun, *n.* Iapi wawiḣaḣa.
punch, *n.* 1. Miniwakaŋ icahi: *he drank a glass of punch.* 2. Ma'zaicaḣdoke: *strike the punch hard.* *vt.* Panini; paḣdoka.
punctual, *a.* Iyehan ecoŋ; iyehantu: *a punctual payment.*
punctually, *adv.* Iyehaŋyaŋ.
punctuate, *vt.* Samyapidaŋ e'hnaka.

punctuation, *n.* Samyapidaŋ; ho'-anażiŋ.
puncture, *vt.* Paȟdoka; capa. *n.* oȟdoka; opaȟdoka.
pungent, *a.* 1. Paza; pa: *a pungent turnip.* 2. Pe'sto; wayaȟtaka: *pungent remarks.*
pungently, *adv.* Pe'stoya.
punish, *vt.* Iyopeya; kakiśya: *punish the child.*
punishable, *a.* Iyopeyepica.
punishment, *n.* Woiyopeye; iyopeyapi; kakiśyapi.
punk, *n.* Caŋkaġica.
puny, *a.* Ci'stina; sta'ka; huŋ'keśni: *a puny girl.*
pup, *n.* Śuŋȟpadan.
pupil, *n.* 1. Wayawa; waoŋspekiyapi; śiceca. *The Boarding-School pupils,* ti'pitaŋka waoŋspewicakiyapi.—*He was a pupil at Santee Training School.* 2. Iśtasusapa; iśtasu.
puppet, *n.* Wicaśtakaġapidaŋ.
puppy, *n.* Śuŋȟpadaŋ.
purr, *vi.* Ḣdo: *the cat purrs.*
purchasable, *a.* Opetoŋpica.
purchase, *vt.* Opetoŋ: *purchase a house.*—*Purchase with* (or *for*), iyopeya.—*Buy of,* opekitoŋ. *n.* 1. Owopetoŋ; wopetoŋ: *a bad purchase.* 2. Iyukiŋ; wi'yuze: *raise it with a purchase.*
purchaser, *n.* Tu'we wopetoŋ.
pure, *a.* 1. E'cedaŋ; *Y.* e'cena; *T.* e'cela; ta'kudaŋ icahiśni: *pure gold.* 2. Ska; wa'kaśoteśni; woaȟtani ni'ca: *a pure man.*
purely, *adv.* E'cedaŋ.
pureness, *n.* Woecedaŋ; e'cedaŋ.
purgative, *a.* & *n.* Oŋ iheyapi.
purgatory, *n.* Wicanaġi woyużaża.
purge, *vt.* 1. Iheyekiya: *the medicine purged him.* 2. Yużaża; yuska: *purge me from sin.* *n.* Iyoptaiyeyapi; oŋ iheyapi.
purification, *n.* Wayuskapi.
purifier, *n.* Wayuska; wayuecedaŋ.
purify, *vt.* Yuska; yuecedaŋ; kaśoteśni; yuwaśte.
purity, *n.* Woecedaŋ; wowakaśoteśni.
purloin, *vt.* Manoŋ; napiśtaŋyaŋ. *vi.* Wamanoŋ.
purple, *n.* Staŋ; śastaŋ; śa.
purport, *n.* To'ken ka'pi; wokuwa. *vt.* Ka; yutaŋiŋ.
purpose, *n.* Ta'ku kuwapi; wokuwa; tawaciŋ; ta'ku ciŋ'pi: *what is their purpose in coming.* —*On purpose,* ciŋ. *vt.* Awaciŋ; waciŋyuza: *he purposed well.*
purposeless, *a.* Tawaciŋ wanica.
purr, *vi.* Ḣdo; ḣdodowaŋ.
purse, *n.* 1. Ma'zaska ożuha; wożuha: *an empty purse.* 2. Mazaskayekiyapi: *he won the purse.*
pursuable, *a.* Kuwapica.
pursuance, *n.* Wokuwa. *In pursuance of,* a'etopta; ohnayaŋ.
pursuant, *a.* Ecen. *Pursuant to,* ecetuya.
pursue, *vt.* Kuwa; pasi; kuwa a'ya; ya; iyaya.—*Pursue the enemy,* to'ka kiŋ kuwa.—*Pursuing rabbits,* maśtiŋca pasi.
pursuer, *n.* Wakuwa.
pursuit, *n.* Kuwapi; wokuwa. *The pursuit of pleasure,* womaġaġa kuwapi.
purvey, *vt.* Ihni; okini.
pus, *n.* Toŋ. *Discharge pus,* toŋ hiyu; toŋye.
push, *vt.* 1. Pataŋ; pataŋiyeya; patitaŋ: *push the sled.*—*Push the box this way,* koka den'tkiya pasdohaŋ.—*Push hard,* ni'na patitaŋ. 2. I'yopaśtag ku'wa; ni'na ku'wa.—*He is pushing me for pay,* wokażużu oŋ ni'na makuwa.—*Push aside,* pakam iyeya.—*Push down,* kun iyeya.

—*Push off*, paȟpa.—*Push open*, paȟdoka; paġaŋ.—*Push over*, pawaŋka.—*Push up*, pawaŋkan iyeya. *n.* Wopatitaŋ; patitaŋpi womdiheca; wakitaŋpi.

pushing, *a.* Mdiheca; wakitaŋ.

pusillanimous, *a.* Caŋte huŋ'kešni.

puss, *n.* Inmušuŋka; *Y.* ikmušuŋka; *T.* igmu.

put, *vt.* E'hnaka; *Y.* e'knaka; *T.* e'gnaka.—*Put a case to the jury*, wi'yukcaŋpi oecoŋ owicakiyake.—*Put away*, tokaŋ e'hnaka; eȟpeya.—*Put about*, yuhomni.—*Put back*, he'kta iyaye.—*Put down*, kun e'hnaka; yusni.—*Put down a name*, caże owa.—*Put forth the hand*, nape yekiya.—*Put forth leaves*, ape uya.—*Put forth strength*, wowaš'ake kiçuŋ.—*Put forward*, tokata e'hnaka.—*Put in a bottle*, żaŋżaŋ ohnaka.—*Put into a harbor*, oahuni en iyaye. —*Put it off on*, ķiŋkiya; ķu.—*Put off doing*, kihnaka.—*Put off a robe*, šina yušdoka.—*Put off without anything*, coka iyaya.—*Put on a coat*, o'kde kiçuŋ. —*Put on more horses*, šuŋ'kawakaŋ nakuŋ aopekiya.—*Put on more wood*, caŋ nakuŋ aoŋ. —*Put out the lamp*, petiżaŋżaŋ, bosni.—*Put out money*, ma'zaska owicaķu.—*Put out the tongue*, ceżi hiyuya.—*Put out the thief*, wamanus'a taŋkan iyayeya.—*Put out of joint*, o'kihe papšuŋ.—*Put out (in play)*, ayuštaŋkiya.—*Put over till*, hehaŋyaŋ kihnaka.—*Put over the river*, akasam e'yaȟpeya.—*Put through*, ihunikiya; yuštaŋ.—*Put to bed*, iwaŋgkiya; ištiŋbekiya.—*Put to death*, kte.—*Put together*, wi'taya e'hnaka; i'cikoyagya.—*Put to rights*, taŋ'yaŋ e'hnaka; ecen e'hnaka.—*Put to the sword*, miwakaŋ oŋ kte.—*Put to trial*, yacopi kta ķu.—*Put trust in*, waciŋkiya.—*Put up fruit*, waskuyeca doya hna'ka.—*Put up the playthings*, wi'napiškaŋya kihnaka. —*Put up to do it*, ecoŋkiya.—*Put up a teepee*, ti'pi e'hde. —*Put up the job*, wicoȟaŋ ka'ġa. *vi.* Iyaye: *the ship put to sea*.—*Put about*, namni.—*Put back*, he'kta iyaya.—*Put in for*, da; kuwa.—*To put off*, to'ki iyaye.—*Put up with abuse*, oštehdapi en e'waciŋšni.—*At what house do you put up*, ti'pi tukte en nuŋ'ka he.

putrefaction, *n.* Kuka a'ye.

putrefy, *vt.* Kukaya; yušica; yukuka. *vi.* Kuka a'ya; ȟwiŋ.

putrid, *a.* Ḣwiŋ; kuka. *It is now putrid*, waŋna ȟwiŋ.—*A putrid smell*, ȟwiŋ'mna.

putter, *vi.* Ta'ku ecoŋ taŋiŋšni škaŋ.

putty, *n.* Mniokdasiŋ wi'puspe. *vt.* Apuspa.

puzzle, *vt.* Waciŋhnuniya; okihišniya. *vi.* Waciŋhnuni; to'ketu taŋiŋšni. *n.* Owiyukcaŋšica; to'ketu taŋiŋšni.

pyramid, *n.* Woomdotoŋ pe'sto.

pyrite, *n.* Ma'zaikceka wiyakpa.

pyrotechnic, *n.* Pe'ta okiŋyaŋpi.

Q

quack, *vi.* Hotoŋ : *the ducks quack.* *n.* 1. Hotoŋpi. 2. Oŋspekiyapiśni ecoŋ ; wicahnayaŋ ; wamnaiçida : *the doctor is a quack.*
quackery, *n.* Wamnaiçidapi.
quadrangle, *n.* Oisetopa.
quadrant, *n.* 1. Caŋhdeśka to'pabaśpapi. 2. Otakiŋyaŋ oiyute.
quadrennial, *a.* Waniyetu to'pa ; waniyetu i'topa.
quadrilateral, *n.* Cuwitopa.
quadroon, *n.* Iyokise ya'mni haska ķa iyokise wanżi hasapa.
quadruple, *a.* To'paakihde. *vt.* To'paakihde ka'ġa.
quaff, *vt.* Ni'na yatkaŋ ; yaħem iyeya.
quagmire, *a.* Hihi ; coco ; wiwi. *n.* Wiwi ; makaħdiħdi.
quail, *n.* Zi'caśapeŋa. *vi.* Naţuŋka ; napa ; kokipa.
quaint, *a.* To'keca ; heyoka se ; wowiħa.
quaintly, *adv.* Wowiħa.
quake, *vi.* Caŋcaŋ ; huhuzahaŋ ; kokipa. *n.* Caŋcaŋpi.
quaker, *n.* Wacaŋcaŋ ; caŋcaŋpi. *n. pr.* Wapahataŋka wicaśta.
quakingly, *adv.* Caŋcaŋyaŋ.
quaky, *a.* Sutaśni ; hohodaŋ.
qualification, *n.* Woyaataŋiŋ ; to'keca oyaka ; woiyecetu.
qualified, *pa.* Iyecetu ; okihi ; yuştaŋpi ; oŋśpaya.
qualify, *vt.* 1. Piiçiya ; oŋspeiçiciya : *he qualified himself to teach.* 2. Oŋśpa yatokeca ; oahececa ka'ġa ; saŋ'pa yataŋiŋ. 3. (*Gram.*) Yataŋiŋ. *vi.* Oŋ içicoŋze.
quality, *n.* Itokeca kiŋ ; oħaŋ; obe; okaġe ; ośpaye.
qualm, *n.* Wohnaśkiŋye ; wokakiże ; to'keca.
qualmish, *a.* Hde'pekteħca.
quandary, *n.* To'ketutaŋiŋśni.
quantity, *n.* To'nakeca ; oiyute ; woyawa ; o'ta.
Quapaws, *n. pr.* Pe'śa.
quarantine, *n.* Wi'tawata wokaśke ; makośica wokaśke. *vt.* Makośica oŋ kaśkapi.
quarrel, *n.* Woakinica ; wokicize ; akinicapi. *vt.* Kiciza ; akinica.
quarrelsome, *a.* Waakinices'a.
quarry, *n.* Iŋ'yaŋ oķapi. *n.* Oķe.
quart, *n.* Mniyatketaŋka oiyute.
quarter, *n.* 1. To'pakibaśpapi waŋżi. 2. Kaśpapi nom sam okise ; *Y.* kaŋġikaġapi : *I paid him a quarter.* 3. Wi ya'mni : *we are paid quarterly.* 4. Oyaŋke ; ti'pi : *miserable quarters.*—*Head-quarters,* akicitataŋcaŋ ti.—*Show no quarters,* oŋśidaśni. *vt.* 1. To'pa kibaśpa. 2. Oyaŋke ķu ; yuhekiya : *they quartered the soldiers in the church.* *vi.* Ti ; yaŋka.
quarterly, *a.* Waniyetu waŋżi to'pakibaśpapi ; wi ya'mni : *quarterly payments.*
quartermaster, *n.* Akicita tiawaŋyake ; heyake awaŋyake.
quartette, *n.* Hotopa dowaŋpi ; to'papi.
quarto, *n.* Wowapiożuhatoŋ taŋ'ka.
quartz, *n.* Iŋ'yaŋ (ocaże).
quash, *vt.* Kaśuśuża ; ihaŋgya ; yutakuniśni; yuecetuśni. *Quash an indictment,* woiyaoŋpa yutakuniśni.
quasi, *a.* Se'ececa.
quaternary, *a.* To'pa ; itopa. *n.* (*Geol.*) Icitopa.
quaver, *vi.* Ho yucaŋcaŋ ; hoħnaġica dowaŋ. *n.* Ho'yacaŋcaŋpi.
quay, *n.* Wa'taoahuni ka'ġapi.

queen, *n.* Wicaśtayatapiwiŋ; wicaśtayatapi tawicu; wiŋ'yaŋitaŋcaŋ: *the queen of England.* —*Queen-bee*, tuḣmaġa itaŋcaŋ.
queenly, *a.* Itaŋcaŋwiŋyaŋ se'ca; okinihaŋ.
queer, *a.* To'keca; wowiḣa.
queerly, *adv.* Wowiḣaya.
quell, *vt.* Yuasni: *quell the riot.*
quench, *vt.* Yusni: *quench the flames.*
quenchable, *a.* Yusnipica.
querulous, *a.* Iyokipiśni ies'a; aśicaḣdo.
querry, *n.* Woiwaŋġa. *vt.* Wi'waŋġa; ceṭuŋhda.
quest, *n.* Waodepi; wi'hnipi.
question, *n.* Woiwaŋġa; wi'waŋġapi. *vt.* Wi'waŋġa; ceṭuŋhda: *question his motives. vi.* Wawiwaŋġa.
questionable, *a.* To'ketutaŋiŋśni; waceṭuŋhdapica: *it is questionable whether he can read.*
questioner, *n.* Wawiwaŋġa.
quibble, *n.* Ecaiapi; wawiḣapi; waceṭuŋhdapi. *vi.* Heciyotaŋśni ia; ceṭuŋhda.
quick, *a.* 1. Oḣaŋko: *quick motion.* 2. Ni; ni uŋ. *adv.* Oḣaŋkoya; kohaŋna: *do it quick.* —*Be quick*, inaḣni. *n.* Oyazaŋ; tukte ni.
quicken, *vt.* Yuinaḣni; o'cim oḣaŋko ecoŋ. *vi.* Ni; śkaŋśkaŋ.
quickening, *n.* Wicayuḣicapi; woyuḣica.
quickly, *adv.* Oḣaŋkoya; inaḣni.
quickness, *n.* Wooḣaŋko.
quicksand, *n.* Wiyaka coco; wiyaka ḣdiḣdidaŋ.
quicksilver, *n.* Ma'zaska nini.
quickstep, *n.* Akicitatadowaŋ oḣaŋko.
quickwitted, *a.* Waciŋksapa.
quid, *n.* Woyata; yatapi.
quiescent, *a.* Owaŋżiuŋ; taŋiŋśni waŋka.
quiet, *a.* Owaŋżiuŋ; ataŋse uŋ; wa'ḣbadaŋ. *vt.* Kihna; yuinina. *n.* Woamdakedaŋ; woskaŋśkaŋ wanica.
quietly, *adv.* A'inina; ataŋsena: *the bird sat quietly.*
quietness, *n.* Woamdakena; woinina.
quietness, *n.* Woasni; woayuśtaŋ.
quill, *n.* Wi'yaka; wowapiicaġe. *Porcupine quills*, pahiŋ.
quill-driver, *n.* Wowapikaġa.
quilt, *n.* Śinaokipatapi; owiŋżaakaḣpe. *vt.* Wakaġeġe.
quilting, *n.* Owiŋzaakaḣpe wakaġeġepi.
quince, *n.* Taspaŋ (ocaże).
quinine, *n.* Caŋcaŋpi peżuta.
quinsy, *n.* Wi'napcepopi woyazaŋ.
quintessence, *n.* Iyotaŋwaśte; woitaŋcaŋ.
quintette, *n.* Hozaptaŋ dowaŋpi.
quire, *n.* Wowapiska wikcemna nom sam to'pa.
quirk, *n.* Wonabaka; woyukśize.
quirkish, *a.* Śkiśka; oḣaŋtokeca.
quit, *vt.* 1. Ayuśtaŋ; enakiye: *quit crying.* 2. Ihunikiya; econ: *quit you like men.*
quitclaim, *n.* Ta'waihdawa enakiye.
quite, *adv.* 1. Taŋ'yaŋ; ocowasiŋ; ni'na: *the work is quite done.* 2. Ki'taŋna: *quite sick.*
quiver, *n.* Waŋ'zu. *vi.* Caŋcaŋ.
quiveringly, *adv.* Caŋcaŋyaŋ.
quiz, *vt.* Wi'waŋġa; wi'waŋḣ kuwa. *n.* 1. Woiwaŋġa; wowiyukcaŋ: *they gave him a quiz.* 2. Tu'we wawiḣaḣa.
quizzer, *n.* Wawiwaŋġes'a.
quoit, *n.* Ma'zaokaḣ'o.
quorum, *n.* Omniciye iyenakeca.
quota, *n.* I'ye to'na ecoŋśipi.
quotation, *n.* Oie oyakapi. *Quotation marks*, to'ie wa'petokeca.
quote, *vt.* Cażeyata; oie oyaka.
quoth, *vi.* E'ya.
quotient, *n.* To'nakiya yuśpapi; to'nakeca ohna iyaye.

R

rabbet, *vt.* Tete kaśkokpa.
rabbi, *n.* Itaŋcaŋ.
rabbit, *n.* Maśtiŋca.
rabble, *n.* Tu'wepi taŋiŋśni ; wicota.
rabid, *a.* Ociŋśica ; hnaśkiŋyaŋ.
rabidly, *adv.* Wohitiya ; mde'ześni.
raccoon, *n.* Wica.
race, *n.* 1. Obe ; wicobe ; oyate. *The White race,* oyate ska. 2. Oiŋyaŋke ; kiiŋyaŋkapi : *let us run a race.* 3. Mnicaduze : *a mill race.* *vt.* Kiiŋyaŋke : *I will race with you.*
race-course, *n.* Oiŋyaŋke.
race-horse, *n.* Śuŋgiŋyaŋgkiyapi.
racer, *n.* 1. Kiŋiŋyaŋkes'a ; du'zahaŋ. 2. Waŋmduśkasapa.
racily, *adv.* Yażimżimya ; pe'stoya.
rack, *vt.* 1. Kaśkopa ; kahoho ; yuś'aka. 2. Kakiśya ; kacaŋcaŋ : *he racked his brain.* *n.* 1. Oŋ wakakiśyapi. 2. Ahnakapi : *a hay-rack.* 3. Onaś'iŋ : *a slow rack.* *vi.* Onaś'iŋ : *can your horse rack.*
racket, *n.* 1. Takicapsica : *a ball and racket.* 2. Owodutatoŋ ; oḳoyapi.
racking, *a.* Wakakiśya ; teḣika.
racy, *a.* Wayażimżipa ; wayuḣitḣica ; pe'sto.
radial, *a.* Caŋhdeśka woyuġate.
radiance, *n.* Wowiyakpa.
radiant, *a.* Wiyakpa ; wi'yeġa.
radiantly, *adv.* Wiyakpaya.
radiate, *vt.* 1. Iyeġa : *radiate heat.* 2. A'kiżanżan iyayeya ; o'waŋcaya iyayeya. *a.* A'kiżanżate ; wicaŋḣpiseca.
radiation, *n.* Waiyaḣpeya ; o'waŋcayaiyaye.
radical, *n.* 1. O'hutkaŋ ; o'tokahe. 2. Hu'tedaŋ ; wayażużu.
radically, *adv.* Hutkaŋ etaŋhaŋ ; a'taya.
radish, *n.* Paŋġiśaśa.
radius, *n.* 1. Caŋteiyohiya ; oyuġa. 2. Iśpahu : *the radius of the left arm.*
raffle, *vi.* Ecoŋna.
raft, *n.* Caŋyuwipi ; caŋiyakaśkapi. *vt.* O'kaḣbogya.
rafter, *n.* Awakeyapi huḣa.
rag, *n.* Miniḣuha oḣdecahe.
ragamuffin, *n.* Miniḣuha wicaśta.
rage, *vi.* Wohitiyaśkaŋ ; kaḣ'oḣ'o iyeiçiya. *n.* Wocaŋniye.
ragged, *a.* Ḣdeḣdecahaŋ ; ḣeḣe ; pepe.
ragman, *n.* Heyake tani opetoŋ.
raid, *n.* Wicomani ; ozuye.
rail, *n.* 1. Maḣinatake ; caŋhaŋska. 2. Ḣemanimaza : *laying the rails.—He came by rail,* ḣemani ohna hi. *vi.* Ośtehda.
railer, *n.* Wicakiġes'a ; wayaśica.
railing, *a.* Wayaśicapi. *n.* Acaŋkaśkapi.
railery, *n.* Waośteśtepi.
railroad, railway, *n.* Ma'zacaŋku.
raiment, *n.* Heyake ; *Y.* hayake ; wokoyake.
rain, *vi.* Maġażu ; hiŋhaŋ ; hiŋhe. —*Rain on,* ahiŋhe. *vt.* Maġażu ; hiŋhaŋ. *n.* Maġażu ; maġażumni ; womaġażu.
rainbow, *n.* Wihmuŋke.
rainfall, *n.* Womaġażu.
raingage, *n.* Maġażu iyute
raininess, *n.* Maġażus'a.
rainless, *a.* Maġażuśni.
rainwater, *n.* Maġażumni.
rainy, *a.* Maġażus'a.
raisable, *a.* Yuwaŋkan icupica.

raise, *vt.* Yuwaŋkan icu; waŋkan e'hde; na'żiŋkiya; icaḣya; ka'ġa.—*Raise bread,* aġuyapi napoḣya.—*Raise corn,* wamnaheza icaḣya.—*Raise the dead,* wicaṭe ciŋ ekicetuya.—*Raise the false report,* iapi wohnaye ka'ġa.—*Raise the fallen,* waŋkahaŋ na'żiŋkiya. — *Raise a flagpole,* caŋwakaŋ e'hde. — *Raise money,* ma'zaska okini. —*Raise the price,* i'waŋkam yawa.—*Raise out of sleep,* yuḣica. — *Raise troops,* akicita mnaye.

raisin, *n.* Hastaŋhaŋka pusyapi.

raising, *n.* Waŋkan yeyapi; bosdan e'hdepi.

rake, *n.* 1. Ma'zaiyuhinte; maḣiyuhiŋte. 2. Wicawihomni. *vt.* Yuhiŋta; kahiŋta; kahin eyaya; kahin e'żu.

raking, *n.* Wakahiŋtapi; wokahiŋte.

rally, *vt.* 1. Piya na'żiŋwicakiya: *he rallied his men.* 2. Ikiḣaḣa.

ram, *n.* 1. Ta'ḣcaska mdoka: *the ram has big horns.* 2. Wi'bobdeca. *vt.* Boskica; bopaŋ: *ram it down.*

ramble, *vi.* Wi'kcekce omani; to'ken ciŋ'ciŋ omani. *n.* Omanipi.

rambler, *n.* Omanis'a.

ramification, *n.* Oyuġaġa.

ramified, *pa.* Yuḣaḣa; adetka o'ta.

rammer, *n.* Iboskica; wi'bopaŋ.

rampage, *n.* Wohitiya ṡkaŋ'pi.

rampant, *a.* Wohitika; bosdata.

rampart, *n.* Wowinape; coŋ'kaṡke; makaoḳapi.

ramrod, *n.* Ma'zakaŋiyopuskice; ioṡtaŋ.

ran, *imp.* of RUN.

rancid, *a.* Hmuŋ'za.

rancor, *n.* Wowaḣtedaṡni.

rancorous, *a.* Wowaḣtedaṡni.

random, *n.* Otuyaciŋ.

rang, *imp.* of RING.

range, *vt.* Caŋkuyetoŋ e'hnaka; okamdaḣ e'hde; okawiŋḣ ya. *n.* 1. Caŋkuye: *a range of mountains.* 2. Owaṡpaŋyetaŋka: *a range in the kitchen.* 3. Wohiyohi; waciŋoaye: *his mind has a small range.* 4. Okute; wayeya: *a gun of small range.* 5. Makoce ouŋyaŋpi; owiḣaŋye: *the feed on the range.* 6. Bosdata oicazo taŋ'ka.

ranger, *n.* 1. Akicita nataŋtaŋ omani. 2. Ṡuŋ'ka womna.

rank, *n.* 1. Caŋkuye; o'cimdaḣ na'żiŋpi. 2. Woitaŋcaŋ obe: *of the rank of captain.* 3. O'he; oyaŋke: *a man of high rank.* *vt.* 1. O'cimdaḣ e'hde. 2. O'peya yawa; ko'ya e'hnaka. 3. Iwaŋkam yawapi. *a* 1. Haŋ'ska; otaŋtoŋka: *rank weeds.* 2. Iyotaŋ; wakapeya: *rank nonsense.* 3. Ṡicamna; ḣwiŋ'mna: *rank meat.*

rankle, *vi.* Icaḣ a'ya; sam ṡi'ca a'ya.

rankly, *adv.* Otaŋtoŋyaŋ.

rankness, *n.* Wotaŋtoŋ; woohitika.

ransack, *vt.* Ode; a'taya ode; napiṡtaŋyaŋ.

ransom, *n.* Wokażużu; oŋ kiyuṡkapi kta: *he paid the ransom.* *vt.* Ki'cicażużu; opekitoŋ: *he ransomed the prisoner.*

rant, *vi.* Wohitiya ia; tamya: *the preacher ranted.* *n.* Ituya ho'taŋkapi.

ranter, *n.* Ituya ho'taŋka.

rap, *vt.* Katoto; apa. *n.* Katotopi.

rapacious, *a.* Wabotica.

rapaciously, *adv.* Wohitiya.

rapaciousness, *n.* Waihaŋgya.

rapacity, *n* Woohitika.

rape, *n* Wiŋ'yaŋ iyaḣpayapi; wicadaśni tawiŋyaŋpi ; wikikśaŋpi.

rapid, *a.* 1. Oḣaŋko ; du'zahaŋ : *a rapid writer.* 2. Ni'na kaduza : *rapid waters.* 3. Kaduza ; dus ya : *a rapid current.*

rapidity, *n.* Wooḣaŋko.

rapidly, *adv.* O'ḣaŋkoya ; kohaŋna.

rapine, *n.* Waboticapi.

rapper, *n.* Icabu.

rapture, *n.* Wowiyuśkiŋ taŋ'ka.

raptured, *pa.* Wowiyuśkiŋ ożudaŋ ; hnaśkiŋyaŋ.

rare, *a.* 1. Teḣika ; wan'waŋcadaŋ yuhapi : *a rare book.* 2. Kap̣ożedaŋ : *rare atmosphere.* 3. Śpaŋ'śni ; ki'taŋna śpaŋ : *rare steak.*

rarify, *vt.* Kap̣ożedaŋ ka'ġa.

rarely, *adv.* Wan'waŋcadaŋ.

rareness, *n.* 1. Wowanica : *the rareness of the plant.* 2. Wokap̣ożedaŋ. 3. Śpaŋ'śni.

rarity, *n.* Woteḣi ; ecawanica.

rascal, *n.* Tu'we waḣteśni.

rascality, *n.* Wowaḣteśni.

rascally, *a.* Waḣteśni.

rase, *vi.* Kawaŋka.

rash, *a.* Waciŋko ; oḣaŋko ; waawaciŋśni : *rash conduct.* *n.* Ahinaŋpapi : *a rash on his face.*

rashly, *adv.* Waawaciŋśniyaŋ.

rashness, *n.* Woawaciŋśni.

rasp, *n.* Caŋipabe.

raspberry, *n.* Takaŋheca.

rat, *n.* Siŋteśda ; *Y.* hituŋktaŋka. *Rat-trap,* siŋteśdaiḣmuŋke.

ratched, *n.* Wi'yuhomnisuta.

rate, *n.* Oiyawa ; oiyute ; wokażużu : *the rate on grain is too high.—First rate,* ni'na taŋ'yaŋ. *vt.* Yawa ; iyawa ; i'enhiyeya.

rather, *adv.* 1. E'eś ; iyotaŋ ; tokaheya : *rather grew worse.* 2. Ki'taŋna : *rather cold.*

ratification, *n.* Yuecetupi ; yusutapi.

ratifier, *n.* Wayuecetu.

ratify, *vt.* Yuecetu ; yusuta.

ratio, *n.* 1. Kici oiyute iwaŋyakapi. 2. Tona iwaŋyakapi ; oiyute wi'yokihi.

ration, *n.* Wowicak̇upi ; aŋpetu iyawa wowicak̇upi ; wokpamni.

rational, *a.* Wi'yukcaŋ ; mde'zeca ; ksa'pa.

rationalism, *n.* Wi'yukcaŋiçidapi.

rationally, *adv.* Waciŋksamya.

rattle, *vt.* Ḣda ; sna ; ko'ka. *I heard the snake rattle.* *vt.* 1. Yuḣda ; kaḣda ; kasna, *etc.* 2. Yuecece śni ; waciŋksapeśniya. *n.* 1. Icakoka ; wamnuha : *the conjurer's rattle.* 2. Oyaḣnaḣna : *a rattle in the baby's throat.*

rattlesnake, *n.* Sinteḣda.

ravage, *vt.* Ihaŋgya ; sinya kuwa. *n.* Woihaŋgye : *the ravages of war.*

ravager, *n.* Waihaŋgye.

rave, *vi.* Hnaśkiŋyaŋ ; wohitiya śkaŋ.

ravel, *vt.* Yusba ; yusna. *vi.* Sbahaŋ ; snahaŋ.

raveling, *n.* Yusnapi ; osbahe.

raven, *n.* Kaŋġi. *a.* Kaŋġise.

ravening, *pa.* Wat̤eyes'a ; wohitika.

ravenous, *a.* Wohitika ; ni'na docin.

ravenously, *adv.* Wohitiya.

ravine, *n.* O'smaka ; kaksiza.

ravingly, *adv.* Hnaśkiŋyaŋse.

ravish, *vt.* 1. Wabotica ; wamanoŋ : *ravish the country.* 2. Iyuśkiŋkiya ; iḣaḣaya : *the sight ravished me.* 3. Wikikśaŋ ; yustawiŋyaŋ : *the tramp ravished the girl.*

ravisher, *n.* Wi'iyaḣpayes'a ; wi'yuśkiŋwicaye.

ravishing, *pa.* Wowiyuśkiŋ ożudaŋ.
ravishment, *n.* Wamanoŋpi; wowiyuśkiŋ.
raw, *a.* 1. Śpaŋ'śni; do; sa'ka: *raw meat.* 2. Ikceka; ecehna: *raw material.* 3. Ha wanica: *a raw sore.* 4. Oŋspeśni; nakaha ecoŋpi: *raw troops.* 5. Osni; wicacuwita.
raw=bone, *a.* Tamaheca; huħase.
rawhide, *n.* Tahasaka; tahasaka icapsiŋte.
rawness, *n.* Wosaka; waoŋspeśni; wosni.
ray, *n.* Iyożaŋżaŋ; wiiżaŋżaŋ.
rayless, *a.* Iyożaŋżaŋ wanica; o'kpaza.
raze, *vt.* Pażużu; ihaŋgya.
razor, *n.* Putiŋhiŋicasaŋ.
razor=strop, *n.* Putiŋhiŋicasaŋiyohdi.
re=, *prefix.* Ake.
re, *n.* (*Mus.*) Hoinoŋpa.
reach, *vt.* 1. Iyohiya: *I can't reach it.* 2. Hiyuya: *reach hither thy hand.* 3. Iyohi: *the line don't reach.* *n.* Caŋpahmihma; caŋkahu: *lengthen the reach.*
react, *vt.* Akihde ecoŋ: *react the play.* *vi.* Itkom hiyu: *the blow reacted.*
read, *vt.* 1. Yawa: *read the letter for me.* 2. Iyukcaŋ: *read the signs of the times.* *vi.* Wowapi yawa: *can you read.* *a.* W..oŋspeka; wowapi wayupika: *a well read man.*
readable, *a.* Yawapica; yawapi waśte.
reader, *n.* 1. Wowapi yawa: *Jane is a good reader.* 2. Wayawa; wayawa wowapi: *Second Reader.*
readily, *adv.* Katiŋyaŋ; kaġiśniyaŋ.
readiness, *n.* Ihduwiyeyapi; wokaġi wanica; wokatiŋyaŋ; woinaħni.—*In readiness,* wi'yeya.
reading, *pa.* Wowapiyawa; wayawa.
reading=book, *n.* Yawapi-wowapi.
reading=room, *n.* Wotaŋiŋwowapi oyawatipi.
readjust, *vt.* Apiya.
readmit, *vt.* Akihde en hiyuya.
ready, *a.* 1. Wi'yeya: *I am ready.* 2. Oħaŋko: *ready writer.* 3. Ki'nica; ikiyedaŋ: *ready to break.*
ready=made, *a.* Kaħ'yuśtaŋpi.
reaffirm, *vt.* Akihde e'ya; o'staŋ e'ya.
real, *a.* He'caħca; wowicake; ħca. *A real Indian,* Ikcewicaśtaħca.—*Real estate,* makoce. *adv.* Ḣca. *n.* Spaniyo kaśpapi.
realty, *n.* Wowicake.
realize, *vt.* 1. En e'waciŋ; okaħniġa; wowicake keciŋ: *he did not realize the danger.* 2. Etaŋhaŋ kamna; okini.
really, *adv.* A'wicakehaŋ.
realm, *n.* Wokicoŋze; woouŋye.
ream, *n.* Wowapiska opaħte.
reanimate, *vt.* Kiniya; yuniya.
reap, *vt.* 1. Kaśda; aġuyapi kaśda; baksa. 2. Mnaye; icu: *reap the benefit of his labor.* *vi.* Wamnayaŋ; wakaśda.
reaper, *n.* 1. Inakse; icaśda: *he broke his reaper.* 2. Wamnaye; wakaśda; *he is a good reaper.*
reappear, *vi.* Ake taŋiŋ.
reappoint, *vt.* Akihde ecoŋśi.
rear, *n.* Wahektapa; ihaŋke: *he went to the rear.* *vt.* Icaħya: *rear children.* *a.* Ihaŋke; ehake: *rear-guard.*
reascend, *vt.* Akihde e'hde.
reason, *n.* 1. Wowiyukcaŋ; to'keca he'ceca: *his reason is bad.* 2. Wotawacin; tawaciŋ: *he has lost his reason.*—*By reason of,*

on etaŋhaŋ.—*In all reason,* to'ketu çeyaś. *vi.* 1. Wi'yukcaŋ: *I reasoned thus.* 2. Wowiyukcaŋ oyaka: *he reasoned before the jury.* *vt.* Toketu oyaka; ciŋkiya.
reasonable, *a.* 1. Iyecetu; hehaŋtuka: *a reasonable request.* 2. Wi'yukcaŋ okihi: *man is a reasonable being.* 3. Wowiyukcaŋ ohna: *a reasonable answer.* 4. Ki'taŋna; waheh aŋtu: *a reasonable good crop.*
reasonableness, *n.* Woecetu.
reasonably, *adv.* Waheh aŋtuya.
reasoner, *n.* Wowiyukcaŋ oyaka.
reasoning, *n.* Wowiyukcaŋ. *a.* Wi'yukcaŋ.
reasonless, *a.* Wowiyukcaŋ ni'ca.
reassemble, *vt.* Akemniciyapi.
reassert, *vt.* Akihde e'ya.
reassure, *vt.* Piyawicadaya; kiwiditakaya.
reattain, *vt.* Ake iyohiya.
reattempt, *vt.* Piyaiyute.
rebaptism, *n.* Akta mniakaśtaŋpi.
rebaptize, *vt.* Akta mniakaśtaŋ.
rebate, *vt.* Oŋśpa kicu. *n.* Kicupi; ta'ku kicupi.
rebel, *n.* Wakipażiŋ; itaŋcaŋ ta'wa kipażiŋ. *vi.* Kipażiŋ.
rebellion, *n.* Wokipażiŋ okicize.
rebellious, *a.* Wakipażiŋs'a; wawakipażiŋ.
rebound, *vi.* Itkom hiyu.
rebuff, *n.* Kaitkokipapi. *vt.* Itkom eħpeya; anapta.
rebuild, *vt.* Aktaticaġe; aktakaġa.
rebuke, *vt.* Iyopeya. *n.* Woiyopeye.
rebut, *vt.* I'tkokipa; itkom e'hnaka.
recall, *vt.* I'cicawiŋ kuśi; kiksuya: *recall the words.*
recant, *vi.* Ihduptaŋ ia. *vt.* Iapi e'hdaku; he'cetuśni e'ya.
recapitulate, *vt.* To'ie akta yawa.
recapture, *n.* Aktaicu; aktayuza.
recast, *vt.* Aktakaġa; aktaśdoya.
recede, *vi.* 1. Oyaħe: *the waters recede.* 2. Enakiya; he'kta iyaya: *he receded from his proposition.*
receipt, *n.* 1. Icupi: *on the receipt of the goods.* 2. Icupi wowapi: *give me a receipt for the money.* *vt.* Icupiwowapi yutaŋ.
receipts, *n.* Ta'kuicupi; ta'kukamnapi.
receivable, *a.* Icupica.
receive, *vt.* 1. Icupi: *I received your letter.* 2. Tiŋ hiyuya; i'tkokipa: *he received us pleasantly.* 3. Akipa: *she received no harm.*
receiver, *n.* 1. Tu'we icu kiŋ; wokażużu icu: *the receiver of the Land Office.* 2. Ohnahnakapi.
recent, *a.* Aśkatudaŋ; *Y.* decana.
recently, *adv.* Aśkatudan; *Y.* decana.
receptacle, *n.* Wohnake.
reception, *n.* 1. Oicu; ohnakapi: *difficulty of reception.* 2. Kicicopi: *the president's reception.*
receptive, *a.* Icuokihi; okipika.
recess, *n.* 1. Ci'stiyedaŋ ecoŋpi śni; inaħni kihnakapi; oko: *they took recess till after dinner.* 2. Tiokaħmiŋ; oŋśpa omahentu.
recession, *n.* Kicupi; he'ktayapi.
recipe, *n.* To'ketu oyakapi; woecoŋ owapi; to'ken icahipi oyakapi.
recipient, *n.* Ķu'pi; ecakicoŋpi; tu'we icu.
reciprocal, *a.* Anokataŋhaŋ; anokataŋhaŋ ecakicoŋpi.
reciprocrate, *vt.* Itkom ecoŋ.
reciprocity, *n.* Anokataŋhaŋ kicicuwapi.
recital, *n.* 1. Oyakapi; ohdakapi: *the recital of the testimony.* 2. Iyuta ecoŋpi; i'tokam eyapi.

recitation, *n.* Eyewicakiyapi; obe waŋ'żi oŋspewicakiyapi; wicota en eyapi.
recite, *vt.* E'ya; oyaka: *recite your lesson.*
reckless, *a.* Waawaciŋśni; to'ken ciŋ'ciŋ śkaŋ.
recklessly, *adv.* Waawaciŋśniyaŋ.
recklessness, *n.* Woawaciŋśni.
reckon, *vt.* 1. Yawa; ma'zaska yawa: *he reckoned the cost.* 2. Yawa; e'hnaka: *he was reckoned among the transgressors. vi.* 1. Yawa; wayawa: *he can't reckon.* 2. Keciŋ; eciŋ: *I reckon so.*
reckoner, *n.* Wayawa; wi'yukcaŋ.
reckoning, *n.* Yawapi; oicazo yawapi; wakażużukiyapi.
reclaim, *vt.* 1. Kiyuwaśte; hduwaśte; hdu'za: *reclaim the desert.* 2. E'hdaku; ikikcu; kica: *he reclaimed his lost child.*
reclaimable, *a.* Yuwaśtepica; ikikcupica.
reclamation, *n.* Ikikcupi; yuwaśtepi.
recline, *vi.* Kun iwaŋka; oziiçiya waŋka.
recluse, *a.* Tu'wedaŋ waŋyake śni.
recognition, *n.* Iyekiyapi; wokiksuye.
recognizance, *n.* Woiyekiya; oiyekiye; oŋ sdonyapikta wowapi.
recognize, *vt.* Iyekiya; kiksuya eya.
recoil, *vi.* Hdukśa; itkom hiyu.
recoin, *vt.* Akta śdoya: *recoin silver.*
recollect, *vt.* Kiksuya.
re-collect, *nt.* Akta mnayaŋ.
recollection, *n.* Wokiksuye; waciŋkiksuya; ta'ku kiksuya.
recommence, *vt.* Akta ecoŋ.
recommend, *vt.* Yawaśte; ohaŋ kiciyaotaŋiŋ; ciŋkiya: *I recommend the horse.—The doctor recommended his taking exercise,* peżutawicaśta taŋçaŋ hduśkaŋśkan waśte keya.—*I want you to recommend me to the Agent for a teacher,* Ateyapi en waoŋspekiyapi owakihi miyecidaotaŋiŋ waciŋ.
recommendation, *n.* Woyawaśte; woyaotaŋiŋ; ciŋkiyapi wowapi.
recommission, *vt.* Akta ecoŋkiya.
recommit, *vt.* Ake en e'hnaka; kicu; ake iyukcaŋśi.
recompense, *vt.* Każużu; ki'cicażużu. *n.* Wokażużu; wi'śi.
recompose, *vt.* 1. Ake ka'ġa; piya e'hnaka: *recompose the song.* 2. Yuasnikiya.
reconcilable, *a.* 1. Iyokipikiciya; yuwaśtepica. 2. Yuokoŋwaŋżipica.
reconcile, *vt.* 1. Okiciyuwaśte; kiciyuwaśte; yuokoŋwaŋżidaŋ: *he reconciled the father and son.* 2. Iyowiŋyaŋ: *I could not reconcile myself to it.*
reconciliation, *n.* Okiciyuwaśtepi; okiciciyewicayapi.
recondite, *a.* Mahentu; okaħniħ teħika.
reconnoisance, *n.* Iwaŋyag omanipi.
reconnoiter, *vt.* Iwaŋyag omani.
reconquer, *vt.* Inoŋpa ohiya; inoŋpa e'hdaku.
reconsecrate, *vt.* Akta yuwakaŋ.
reconsider, *vt.* Akta iwaŋyaka.
reconsideration, *n.* Piya awaciŋpi.
reconstruct, *vt.* Piya ka'ġa.
reconvene, *vt.* Ake mniciya.
record', *vt.* Owa; wowapi en owa.
rec'ord, *n.* Ohaŋ owapi; wokiksuye wowapi. *Church records,* Okodakiciye ohaŋowapi. — *A Court of Record,* Omniciye wokiksuye wowapi yuhapi.
recorder, *n.* Wokiksuyewowapi yuha.
recount, *vt.* Akta yawa.
recourse, *n.* Wowaciŋye; ake en i'pi ece.

recover, *vt.* 1. Ikikcu ; ake yuha : *he recovered his property.* 2. Ake akaȟpa ; piya akaȟpa : *recover the cushions.* *vi.* Akisni : *the sick boy recovered.*
recoverable, *a.* Ikikcupica.
recovering, *pa* Akisni a'ya.
recovery, *n.* 1. Akisnipi ; akisnikteciŋ : *recovery from sickness.* 2. Ikikcupi ; hduhapi : *the recovery of property.*
recreant, *a.* Wicakeśni ; canwaŋka.
recreate, *vt.* 1. Ake ka'ga : *recreate the earth.* 2. Oziiçiya ; mdesiçiya ; śka'ta : *let the children recreate.*
recreation, *n.* Oziiçiyapi ; wośkate ; womaġaġa.
recruit, *vt.* 1. Piya ka'ġa ; ecetuya ; yuteca : *recruit his strength.* 2. O'pekiya ; o'śtaŋ o'pekiya. 3. Akicita nakaha o'pa.
rectangle, *n.* Cuwitopaokaȟmiŋowotaŋna.
rectify, *vt.* Yuowotaŋna ; yuecetu.
rectitude, *n.* Woowotaŋna.
rector, *n.* 1. Waawaŋhdake ; itaŋcaŋ. 2. (*Epis.*) Wicaśtawakaŋ okodakiciye awaŋyaka.
rectory, *n.* Wicaśtawakaŋ ti ; wicaśtawakaŋ tawoawaŋyake.
recumbent, *a.* Ipataŋwaŋka : kun waŋkapi.
recur, *vi.* Ake hi ; ake ececa ; ake en i.
recurrence, *n.* Ake ececapi.
red, *a.* Śa ; du'ta : *a red bird.*
redbreast, *n.* Śiśoka ; makuśaśa.
Redcoat, *n.* O'kdeśa ; Sagdaśa akicita.
redden, *vt.* Śaya ; dunya. *vi.* Ite naśa hiŋhda.
reddish, *a.* Ki'taŋna śa ; śamna.
redeem, *vt.* Opekitoŋ ; każużu.
redeemable, *a.* Każużupica ; opekitoŋpica.
redeemer, *n.* Opewicakitoŋ ; wakażużu.
Redeemer, *n.* Wanikiya ; Je'sus.
redemption, *n.* Wopekitoŋpi ; wakażużupi.
red-hand, *a.* Napewewe.
red-head, *n.* Pa'śaśa.
red-hot, *a.* Śakata ; ni'naka'ta.
red-letter, *a.* Śa ; waśte ; wa'pi.
redolent, *a.* Ecamna.
redouble, *vt.* Piyaecoŋ ; sam aiçiciya.
redoubt, *n.* Akicita makaokapi.
redound, *vi.* Aicaȟya.
redress, *vt.* Każużu ; yuecetu. *n.* Wokażużu ; woyuecetu.
red-tape, *a.* Iyuskiteśa ; oȟaŋȟaŋȟcakapi.
red-top, *n.* Pėżiiŋkpaśa.
reduce, *vt.* 1. Yuhukuya : *reduce the soldiers to the ranks.* 2. A'okpaniya : *reduce his pay.* 3 To'ken owapi kta yuśtaŋ ; owa ka'ġa : *reduce the language to writing.* 4. Oiyute to'keca ka'ġa.
reduction, *n.* Yuhukuyapi ; tona na kaġapi : *reduction of expenses.*
redundant, *a.* I'yakamtu ; ituya uŋ ; ehaeś o'ta.
reduplicate, *vt.* Akihde ka'ġa.
reecho, *vt.* Ake naiyowasya. *n.* Ake naiyowaza.
reed, *n.* 1. Cedi ; peżihaŋska. 2. (*Mus.*) Mazayażopi ceżi.
reel, *n.* 1. Caŋhdeśka oŋ wapahmuŋpi. 2. Odowaŋ oȟaŋko : *he played a reel.* 3. Wi'yapehe. *vi.* Kacegcegmani ; paptaŋptaŋ ya.
reelect, *vt.* Akihde kaȟniġa.
reembark, *vi.* Ake wata o'pa.
reenact, *vt.* Ake yuśtaŋ.
reenforce, *vt.* O'kiya ; akicita nakuŋ en yeyapi.
reenforcement, *n.* Akicita nakiciżiŋpi.

reenlist, *vi.* Ake akicita o'pa.
reenter, *vt.* Ake en ya.
refasten, *vt.* Ake iyakaśka.
refer, *vt.* 1. Iwaŋyagśi; yeya: *refer it to a committee.* 2. Ekta e'pazo; ekta yeśi: *he referred me to the preacher.* *vi.* Ka; cażeyata: *he referred to the quarrel.*
referable, *a.* En a'yepica.
referee, *n.* Yukcaŋśipi; yasukiyapi.
reference, *n.* Iwaŋyagśipi; iwaŋḣśipi; ka'pi; waŋyagśipi.—*A Reference Bible,* Wowapi Wakaŋ oŋ Odepi.—*In reference to,* eciyataŋhaŋ.
refine, *vt.* Yuecedaŋ; yuecetu.
refined, *pa.* Yuwaśtepi; waśte.
refinement, *n.* Woyuwaśte.
refiner, *n.* Waśdoye; wayuwaśte.
refinery, *n.* Waśdoye ti'pi; ma'zayuwaśtepi.
refit, *vt.* Piyakaġa.
reflect, *vi.* Awaciŋ; awaiçiciŋ; wawiśtenya: *he reflected on his past life.* *vt.* I'cicawiŋ eḣpeya; eḣpeya: *the mirror reflects the light.*
reflection, *n.* 1. Waawaciŋpi; woawaciŋ; iapi: *a severe reflection.* 2. Itkom u; i'cicawiŋ hiyu.
reflector, *n.* Iyoyaŋpa eḣpeya; mniokdasiŋ.
reflex, *a.* I'cicawiŋ u.
reform, *vt.* P'iya ka'ġa; yuwaśte: *he reformed the whole community.* *vi.* Ihduwaśte; waśte a'ya: *the drunkard reformed.* *n.* Wayuwaśtepi.
reformation, *n.* Wicayuecetupi.
reformed, *a.* Yuecetupi.
reformer, *n.* Wayuecetu.
refortify, *vt.* Piyaacaŋkaśka.
refract, *vt.* Yuktaŋ.
refractory, *a.* Ociŋśica; tawaciŋśica; ociŋśica.
refrain, *vi.* Iyowiŋyeśni; ihdutitaŋ; ipida.—*Refrain one's self,* waipiiçida.
refresh, *vt.* Yuteca; oziya; maġaġaya.
refreshing, *pa.* Wayuwaśte.
refreshingly, *a.* Oiyokipiya.
refreshment, *n.* Waś'agiçiyapi; oziiçiyapi; oŋ waś'akapi; woyute.
refrigerator, *n.* Ca'ġa opiye.
refuge, *n.* Wowinape.—*To take refuge in,* inapa.
refugee, *n.* Napapi; nażicapi.
refulgent, *a.* Wiyakpa; śaśa.
refund, *vt.* Kicu; każużu.
refurnish, *vt.* Piya koyagya; ta'ku icuwa te'ca cee e'hnaka.
refusable, *a.* Wicadaśnipica.
refusal, *n.* 1. Wowicadaśni; wicadaśni. 2. Anicapi wookihi: *he has the refusal of the horse for two days.*
refuse, *vt.* 1. Wicadaśni; *he refused to go.* 2. Icu wicadaśni: *he refused the beef.* *a.* Eḣpeyapi; śi'ca; uŋpicaśni: *refuse matter.* *n.* Ta'ku eḣpeyapi: *the refuse of the town.*
refutable, *a.* Yuḣpepica; ayuptapica.
refutal, *n.* Woayupte.
refutation, *n.* Yuwicakapiśni; yuaśdayapi; woayupte.
refute, *vt.* Yutakuniśni; yuwicakeśni; yuḣpa.
regain, *vt.* Ake iyohi; ake kamna; e'hdaku.
regal, *a.* Wicaśtayatapi ta'wa; itaŋcaŋ ta'wa.
regale, *vt.* Taŋ'yaŋ kuwa; maġaġaya; won'kiya.
regard, *vt.* Iweceya; en e'toŋwaŋ; awaciŋ; iḣakta. *n.* Woiḣakta; woawaciŋ; woayute: *I send my regards.*—*In regard to,* eciyataŋhaŋ.

regardful, *a.* Ni'na en e'waciŋ; ni'na we'ceya.
regardless, *a.* Awaciŋśni.
regardlessly, *adv.* Awaciŋśniyaŋ.
regency, *n.* Woitaŋcaŋ e'ekiya uŋ
regenerate, *a.* Te'ca; tecanientoŋpi. *vt.* Tecanienkaġa.
regeneration, *n.* Te'cawicatoŋpi.
regent, *n.* E'ekiya itaŋcaŋ; wa'waŋyake; awaŋyagkiyapi.
regiment, *n.* Akicita optaye taŋ'ka; kektopawiŋġe optaye.
region, *n.* Makoce.
register, *vt.* Owa: *register your name.* *vi.* Caże owa: *he registered at the hotel.* *n.* 1. Caże oiçiwapi wowapi: *the hotel register.* 2. Okata wi'yute. 3. Waehnake.
registry, *n.* Owicawapi.
regress, *n.* He'ktakiya iyaye.
regret, *vt.* Icaŋteśica; waciŋyokiśica; içiba.
regretfully, *adv.* Iyokiśinya.
regular, *a.* 1. He'cetu; owotaŋna: *a regular physician.* 2. Iyehantu ca; kahantu ca: *regular services.*
regularity, *n.* He'cetuwaŋżica.
regularly, *adv.* Iyehaŋhaŋyaŋ.
regulate, *vt.* Yuowotaŋna; awaŋyaka; katiŋyaŋ ecoŋkiya.
regulation, *n.* Woope; woawaŋyake.
regulator, *n.* Wa'waŋyake; ma'zaawaŋyake.
rehash, *vt.* Piyakaksaksa.
rehear, *n.* Piya naħoŋ; akta naħoŋ.
rehearsal, *n.* Ihdaoŋspepi; i'tokam iyuteya ecoŋpi; oyakapi.
rehearse, *vt.* Oyaka; akihde oyaka; e'ya.
reign, *vi.* Itaŋcaŋ uŋ; wawidake; ouŋyaŋ. *n.* Wowidake: *in the reign of Queen Victoria.*
reimburse, *vt.* Iyena kicu.
rein, *n.* Ikaŋ; śuŋgiyuwiikaŋ.—*Give the reins to,* iyowiŋyaŋ.—*Take the reins,* wicakaħapa. *vt.* Ikaŋ yuṭiŋs iyeya.
reindeer, *n.* Waziyata ta'ħca.
reins, *n.* Wicapakśiŋ.
reinstate, *vt.* Ake ohna e'hde.
reinsure, *vt.* Ake waħuħnaħyapi ki'cicażużupi o'pekiya.
reinvest, *vt.* Ake ma'zaska kiçuŋ.
reinvigorate, *vt.* Piya mdihenya.
reissue, *vt.* Ake iyececa ka'ġa.
reiterate, *vt.* Akihdehde e'ya.
reject, *vt.* Eħpeya; aktaśni.
rejoice, *vi.* Iyuśkiŋ; caŋtewaśte. *vt.* Iyuśkiŋkiya: *you rejoice me.*
rejoicing, *n.* Wowiyuśkiŋ.
rejoin, *vt.* 1. Ake o'pa; ekta ki: *rejoin his regiment.* 2. Ake i'cikoyake: *rejoin the pieces.* *vi.* Itkom e'ya; ayupta.
rejoinder, *n.* Woayupte.
rejuvenate, *vt.* Piya kośka ka'ġa.
rekindle, *vt.* Piya ceti.
reland, *vt.* Ake ihuni.
relapse, *vi.* I'cicawiŋ kiwaŋka.
relate, *vt.* Oyaka: *he related his adventures.* *vi.* Ka; iyoważa: *it relates to others.*
related, *pa.* I'ciyoważapi; takuyapi.
relation, *n.* 1. Takuya.—*Too many relations,* takuya ehaeś o'ta. 2. O'takuye: *the relation of brother and sister.* 3. Woyakapi; wicowoyake; woyake. 4. To'ken i'ciyoważapi: *the relation of the different parts of the body.*
relationship, *n.* Wotakuye.
relative, *n.* Takuya; wotakuye: *he is a near relative to me.* *a.* Iyoważa; to'keca etaŋhaŋ; waŋna ka'pi.
relator, *n.* Woyake; oyake.
relax, *vt.* Pataka; oziya; yuśka; yuzigzica: *he relaxed his running.*—*Relax the ropes,* haħoŋta yuśka.

relaxation, *n.* Oziiçiyapi.
relay, *n.* Wi'yeya hde'pi : *the relay is waiting.* *vt.* Ake aehnaka.
releasable, *a.* Kiyuśkapica.
release, *vt.* Kiyuśka ; ayuśtaŋ. *n.* Kiyuśkapi ; oziyapi.
relent, *vt.* Iyopeiçiya ; enakiye.
relentless, *a.* Caŋteyuwiŋȟpicaśni.
relet, *vt.* Ake owicaḳu.
relevant, *a.* Iyoważa.
reliable, *a.* Waciŋyepica ; wicaka.
reliance, *n.* Wowaciŋye.
relic, *n.* Ehaŋna wokiksuye ; ta'ku ehaŋna yuhapi.
relict, *n.* Wiwazica.
relief, *n.* Waokiyapi ; wookiye ; niyaŋpi.
relieve, *vt.* Asniyaŋ ; o'kiya ; kiyuśka.
relieved, *pa.* O'kiyapi ; yuśkapi.
religion, *n.* Wocekiye ; wowakaŋ ; woohoda ; wowaciŋye.
religious, *a.* 1. Wakaŋtaŋka waciŋyaŋ ; waohoda : *a religious man.* 2. Wocekiye wowapi : *religious books.* 3. Wocekiye oŋ : *religious wars.*
religiously, *adv.* Waohodaya.
relinquish, *vt.* 1. Ayuśtaŋ ; enakiye : *relinquish his claim.* 2. Kicu ; eȟpeya : *relinquish the debt.*
relinquishment, *n.* Enakiyapi.
relish, *vt.* Iyokipi ; waśtedaka : *he relished his dinner.* *n.* 1. Woiyokipi ; wocaŋtahde ; dociŋpi. 2. Oŋ dociŋpi ; icahiyutapi.
relishable, *a.* Ciŋpica ; iyowicakipi.
reload, *vt.* Ake okikśu.
reloan, *vt.* Piya oḳu.
relocate, *vt.* Piya i'yotaŋke.
reluctancy, *n.* Ecoŋkap'iŋpi.
reluctant, *a.* Ecoŋkap'iŋ.
reluctantly, *adv.* Ecoŋkap'iŋseca.
rely, *vi.* Waciŋyaŋ ; hakam uŋ.
remain, *vi.* Uŋ ; yaŋke : he'cehna uŋ : *Noah only remained.*
remainder, *n.* Okaptapi ; iyaye.
remains, *n.* 1. Ta'ku iyaye ; wokapte. 2. Wicaṭa ; taŋcaŋ : *they buried the remains.*
remake, *vt.* Piya ka'ġa ; ake ka'ġa.
remand, *vt.* I'cicawiŋ iyayeya.
remark, *vi.* 1. E'ya ; cażeyata : *he remarked on the beauty of the scenery.* *n.* Woeye ; iapi.
remarkable, *a.* Okitaŋiŋ ; wa'petokeca : *a remarkable man.*
remarkably, *adv.* Wa'petogya.
remarry, *vi.* Aketawicutoŋ.
remasticate, *vt.* Akihde yata.
remeasure, *vt.* Akihde iyuta.
remedial, *a.* Waasniyaŋ ; wayuwaśte.
remedy, *n.* Ta'ku iwaśte ; peżuta. *vt.* Yuwaśte ; asniyaŋ.
remelt, *vt.* Akta śdoya.
remember, *vt.* Kiksuya.—*Remember me,* mi'ksuya. *vi.* Wakiksuya : *he can't remember.*
remembrance, *n.* Wokiksuye.
remembrancer, *n.* Oŋ kiksuyapi.
remind, *vt.* Kiksuyeya.
reminder, *n.* Wowakta.
reminiscence, *n.* Wakiksuyapi ; ehaŋna woyakapi.
remiss, *a.* Waawaciŋśni ; ku'ża.
remission, *n.* Ki'ciyawapiśni.
remissly, *adv.* Waaktaśniyaŋ.
remissness, *n.* Woaktaśni.
remit, *vt.* 1. Yeya ; ḳu.—*Remit money,* ma'żaska yeya. 2. A'okpaniya ; eȟpeya : *remit part of the punishment.* 3. Każużu : *remit sins.*
remittal, *n.* Wicaḳupi ; yeyapi.
remittance, *n.* Ma'zaskayeyapi.
remittent, *a.* Akeececa ecee.
remnant, *n.* Oŋġeiyaye ; o'pte.
remodel, *vt.* Piyakaġa.
remonstrance, *n.* Teȟiŋdapi ; he'cetuśni eyapi.

remonstrate, *vi.* Teȟiŋda ; iyokiśni.
remorse, *n.* Woiçiba ; wocaŋteśica.
remorseless, *a.* Içibaśni.
remote, *a.* I'tehaŋ ; te'han.
remotely, *adv.* I'tehaŋyaŋ.
remoteness, *n.* Otehaŋ ; wotehaŋ.
remount, *vt.* Ake akan iyeiçiya.
removable, *a.* Tokaŋ a'yepica.
removal, *n.* Tokaŋ a'yapi.
remove, *vt.* Tokaŋ a'ya ; yutokaŋ. *vi.* Tokaŋ ya ; tokaŋ i'yotaŋka ; ihdaka ; iyaye : *he removed to the country.*
remunerable, *a.* Każużupica.
remunerate, *vt.* Każużu.
remuneration, *n.* Wokażużu.
remunerative, *a.* Wokażużu yukaŋ ; *Y.* iśitoŋ.
rencounter, *n.* I'tkokicipapi ; okicize ; wokicize.
rend, *vt.* Yuȟdeca ; (*with the teeth*) yaȟdeca ; (*with a missile*) boȟdeca ; (*by cutting*) baȟdeca ; (*by striking*) kaȟdeca ; (*with the foot*) naȟdeca ; (*one's own*) hduȟdeca.
render, *n.* Ta'ku kaȟdeca. *vt.* Kicu ; ķu ; ecakicoŋ ; ka'ġa ; oyaka.—*Render accounts,* oicazo oyaka.—*Render strong,* suta ka'ġa ; ni'na ecoŋ. —*Render into English,* Isaŋtaŋka iapi en ka'ġa. —*Render good service,* wowaśi taŋ'yaŋ ecoŋ.—*Render the Church Service,* wocekiye ka'ġapi e'ya.—*Render a song,* odowaŋ ahiyaya.—*Render tallow,* wasnaihdi ceġuġuya.—*Render vengeance,* watokiçoŋpi ecakicoŋ.
rendering, *n.* Oecoŋ ; okaġe.
rendezvous, *n.* O'yuwitaya ; omniciye. *vt.* Mni'ciya.
renegade, *n.* Wicakeśni ; nażicauŋ.
renew, *vt.* Yuteca ; piya ecoŋ ; piya ka'ġa ; ake icu.
renewable, *a.* Piya kaȟpica.
renewal, *n.* Piya ka'ġapi ; ake icupi.
renewedly, *adv.* Pipiya ; ake.
rennet, *n.* Pteżicedaŋ niġe śkumnayapi.
renounce, *vt.* Eȟpeya ; ayuśtaŋ.
renovate, *vt.* Piyakaġa ; yuteca.
renovation, *n.* Yutecapi.
renovator, *n.* Oŋ wayutecapi.
renown, *n.* Wokitaŋiŋ.
renowned, *a.* Okitaŋiŋ.
rent, *n.* 1 Makoce odotapi wokażużu ; wokażużu. 2. Oyuȟdeca ; oko. *vt.* Oķu ; odota. *v. imp. of* REND. Yuȟdeca : *the flag was rent in twain.*
renter, *n.* Waodota.
renunciation, *n.* Woenakiye ; enakiyapi ; eȟpeyapi.
reoccupy, *vt.* Ake yuha.
reopen, *vt.* Ake yuȟdoka.
reorganize, *vt.* Piyakaġa.
repaint, *vt.* Piyasaŋyaŋ.
repair, *vt.* Piya ; piyakaġa ; ecetuya. *n.* Piyakaġapi. *vi.* Iyaya.
repairable, *a.* Piyepica.
repairer, *n.* Wapiya.
reparation, *n.* Piyapi ; yuecetupi.
repartee, *n.* Woayupte.
repass, *vt.* Ake hiyaye.
repast, *n.* Wotapi.
repay, *vt.* Kicu ; ki'cicażużu.
repeal, *vt.* Ecetuśniya ; yużużu.
repealable, *a.* Yutokecapica.
repeat, *vt.* Akihdeeya ; akeeya ; akeecoŋ. *n.* Akihdeecoŋpi.
repeatedly, *adv.* Akihdehde.
repeater, *n.* Akihdeecoŋ ; ma'zakaŋ o'taiyaye.
repeating, *pa.* Akihdehde ecoŋ.
repel, *vt.* Iyayeya ; i'tkokipa ; itkom eȟpeya.
repent, *vi.* Iyopeiçiya ; woaȟtanı etaŋhaŋ ihduhomni.

repentance, *n.* Iyopeiçiya ; woiyopeiçiye.
repentant, *a.* 1. Iyopeiçiya : *he repentant stands.* 2. Iyopeiçiyapi : *repentant tears.*
repeople, *vt.* Ake oyate en ouŋyewicaya.
repetition, *n.* Akihde ecoŋpi ; akihde eyapi.
repine, *vi.* Iyokiśica.
replace, *vt.* E'kihnaka ; iyena e'hnaka ; iyececa e'hnaka.
replant, *vt.* Akta ożu.
replenish, *vt.* Ake ożuya.
replete, *a.* Ożudaŋ.
replevin, *n* Ikikcupi wowapi.
reply, *vt.* Ayupta. *n.* Woayupte.
report, *vt.* Oyaka ; ecen owa. *vi.* Wawoyaka ; ohdaka. *n.* 1. Owohdake ; wawoyake : *he made his report.* 2. Cażeyatapi : *of good report.* 3. Bu : *the report of a gun.*
reporter, *n.* Woyaka ; wotaŋiŋ ka'ġa ; iapi owakiyapi.
repose, *vi.* Waŋka ; iozi waŋka. *vt.* Owaŋżi e'hnaka. *n.* Woozi.
repository, *n.* Womnaye ; omnaye.
repossess, *vt.* Ake hduha.
reprehend, *vt.* Iyopeya.
reprehensive, *a.* Iyopeyapi.
represent, *vt.* 1. Pazo ; oyaka : *as he represented it.* 2. E'ekiya na'żiŋ : *he represented South Dakota in the Senate.*
representation, *n.* Woyake ; tu'we ki'cinażiŋ.
representative, *n.* E'ekiya na'żin ; oyate kaħniħ yeśipi. *a.* Waheħantupi ; oyate iyececa.
repress, *vt.* Yuhukun iyeya ; yutitaŋ yu'za ; yuasni.
repression, *n.* Yusnipi.
reprieve, *vt.* Woiyopeye ki'cicażużu.
reprimand, *vt.* Iyopeya ; wahokoŋkiya.
reprint, *vt.* Akta ma'zaehde. *n.* Akta ka'ġapi.
reproach, *vt.* Ba ; iyopeya. *n.* 1. Woba ; woyaśica. 2. Wowiśteca ; ośtehdapi.
reproachable, *a.* Bapica.
reproachful, *a.* 1. Wabapi ; woyaśica : *a reproachful speech.* 2. Waħteśni ; woiyaoŋpa.
reprobate, *a.* Yuwaśtepicaśni ; śi'ca.
reproduce, *vt.* Ake icaħya ; ake ecen ka'ġa.
reproof, *n.* Woiyopeya ; wowahokoŋkiya ; woba.
reprovable, *a.* Iyopeyepica.
reproval, *n.* Iyopeyapi.
reprove, *vt.* Iyopeya ; wahokoŋkiya.
reprover, *n.* Wawiyopeya.
reprovingly, *adv.* Iyopeya.
reptile, *n.* Wamduśka ; ta'ku maka asdohaŋ.
republic, *n.* Oyate itaŋcaŋ i'ye ihdaħniġapi.
Republican, *n.* 1. Ważiyatawicaśta. 2. Itaŋcaŋ i'ye ihdaħniġapi.
republication, *n.* Aktayaotaŋiŋpi ; wowapi akta ka'ġapi.
republish, *vt.* Wowapi akta ka'ġa ; akta ka'ġa.
repudiate, *vt.* Eħpeye ; ta'wayeśni.
repugnant, *a.* Teħika ; waħteśni ; śi'cedapi.
repulse, *vt.* Iyayeya ; napeya. *n.* Iyayapi ; wonażica.
repulsive, *a.* Waħtedapiśni ; woiyokıpiśni.
repurchase, *vt.* Ake opetoŋ.
reputable, *a.* Okinihaŋ ; yuonihaŋpi.
reputation, *n.* Waciŋkiyuzapi ; wookitaŋiŋ ; cażе.
repute, *vt.* Otaŋiŋ ; keyapi ; eciŋ. *n.* Woyaotaŋiŋ ; woyuonihaŋ.
reputed, *pa.* Oyakapi ; otaŋiŋ.

request, *vt.* Da; kida; okicicin; ce'kiya; eciya. *n.* 1. Wadapi; wokicinpi: *what is your request.* 2. Ta'ku da'pi: *he gave them their request.*
requiem, *n.* Wicahnakapi odowan.
require, *vt.* 1. Econsi; econkiya; kica; kida. *He requires two long lessons.* 2. Cin; e'cedan on okihi kta.
requirement, *n.* Waeconwicakiyapi; woecon.
requisite, *a.* Cin'pi; cin'pi iyececa; ka'pi; ka'pi iyenakeca. *n.* Yucokapicaśni.
requisition, *n.* Wadapi; wadapi wowapi.
requital, *n.* Wakażużupi; watokiçonpi.
requite, *vt.* Itkom ecakicon; każużu; tokiçon.
rescind, *vt.* Yutokeca; baśpa; eḣpeya.
rescue, *vt.* E'hdaku; nikiya; kiyuśka: *he rescued his brother.* —*Rescue from the grave,* wicahnakapi etanhan e'hdaku; nikiya. *n.* Waehdakupi; niyanpi.
rescuer, *n.* Waehdaku; wanikiya.
research, *n.* Waawacinpi; wa'kitapi; akta odepi.
reseize, *vt.* Akta oyuspa.
resell, *vt.* Akihde wi'yopeya.
resemblance, *n.* Woakidececa; wowanka.
resemble, *vt.* Iyececa; kinma: *he resembles Washington.* —*John resembles his father,* John atkuku kinma.
resent, *vt.* Śihda; to'kiçon.
resentful, *a.* Watokiçons'a.
resentment, *n.* Wośihda; watokiçonpi.
reservation, *n.* Onśpa ohdaptapi; makoce onśpa hduhapi.—*Mental reservation,* tawacin onśpa naḣmanpi.
reserve, *vt.* Kihnaka; patan; okapta: *he reserved a few of the best.* *n.* 1. Kihnakapi: *a reserve of oil.* 2. Waanaḣmanpi; wi'śtecapi.—*Throw off reserve,* wi'śtecapi eḣpeya. 3. Akicita ośpaye ḣeyam kihnakapi: *bring up the reserves.*
reserved, *pa.* Wi'śteca; inina un.
reservoir, *n.* Mini omnaye; mdekaġapi.
reset, *vt.* Piya e'hde; piya ma'zaehde.
resettle, *vt.* Piya ahiyotanka.
reship, *vt.* Piya iyayeya; iyoopta tokśuwicakiya.
reside, *vi.* Ti; wanka.
residence, *n.* Ti'pi; ohna ti.
resident, *n.* Oti; en ti.
residuary, *a.* To'na iyaye.
residue, *n.* Iyaye; okapta.
residuum, *n.* Ta'ku ihe.
resign, *vt.* Enakiya; kicu.
resignation, *n.* 1. Enakiyapi; woenakiye; ayuśtan kta eyapi: *his resignation was accepted.* 2. Woiyowinkiye; wowicada: *the spirit of resignation.*
resignedly, *adv.* Iyowinyan.
resin, *n.* Canśin.
resinous, *a.* Canśinśin.
resist, *vt.* I'tkokipa: kipażin; itkom inazin.
resistance, *n.* Wokipażin; wopatan; i'tkokipapi.
resistible, *a.* I'tkokipepica.
resistless, *a.* I'tkokipepicaśni.
resolute, *a.* Cantetinza; tawacin suta.
resolutely, *adv.* Inihanśniyan; a'wicakehan.
resolution, *n.* 1. Wocantetinza: wowacintanka: *he acted with resolution.* 2. Woyaco; yacopi; yukcanpi: *the resolution of the difficulty.* 3. Woyaotanin: *the meeting adopted resolutions.*
resolve, *vt.* 1. Yaco; yasu; yuśtan: *resolve a riddle.* 2. Ya-

ŝtaŋ ; yaotaŋiŋ : *it was resolved by the Synod.* *vi.* Koŋ'za ; içicoŋza : *I resolved to quit drinking.* *n.* Woiçicoŋza.
resonance, *n.* Sna ; wosna ; bu.
resonant, *a.* Sna'sna ; bu'bu.
resort, *vi.* Ya ; inapa ; akita. *n.* Tukten ni'na ai ; o'yuwitaya : *a summer resort.*
resound, *vt.* Yaotaŋiŋ ; kaiyowaza : *the cliffs resound the lay.* *vi.* Otaŋiŋ ; ho'taŋiŋ ; bu.
resource, *n.* 1. Wowaciŋye ; wowinape : *his last resource.* 2. (*pl.*) Woyuha ; wokihnake ; wowiżice.
resow, *vt.* Akihde ożu.
respect, *vt.* 1. Ohoda ; ahopa ; kinihaŋ : *respect old age.* 2. En e'towaŋ. *n.* Woohoda ; woyuonihaŋ ; wowaŝtedake : *give him my respects.*
respectability, *n.* Wokinihaŋ.
respectable, *a.* 1. Okinihaŋ waŝte : *a respectable man.* 2. Wahehaŋtu ; taŋ'yaŋ : *a respectable congregation.*
respectably, *adv.* Okinihaŋyaŋ.
respectful, *a.* Waohoda ; wapakaŋ.
respectfully, *adv.* Yuonihaŋyaŋ.
respecting, *prep.* Eciyataŋhaŋ.
respective, *a.* Iyohi : *their respective places.*
respectively, *adv.* Iyohiya.
respell, *vt.* Akta e'ya ; akta oowa cażeyata.
respirable, *a.* Yahotapica ; niyapiwaŝte.
respiration, *n.* Oniya ; niyapi.
respire, *vi.* Niya ; yahota ; temni asniiçiya.
respite, *n.* Woenakiye ; oziiçiyapi.
resplendence, *n.* Wowiyakpa.
resplendent, *a.* Wiyakpa.
resplendently, *adv.* Wiyakpaya.
respond, *vi.* Ayupta ; ecakicoŋ.
respondent, *n.* Waayupta.
response, *n.* Woayupte : *the responses of the service.*
responsibility, *n.* 1. Iyowaŝiçidapi ; waawaciŋpi : *a sense of responsibility.* 2. Woawaŋyake ; ta'ku ecoŋkiyapi : *he has many responsibilities.* 3. Wookihi ; ta'ku okihi : *a man of responsibility.*
responsible, *a.* Waciŋyepica ; waokihi.
responsive, *a.* Akiciyupta.
responsively, *adv.* Akiciyupteya ; uŋmaŋitogto.
rest, *n.* 1. Woozi ; ozikiyapi : *give him rest.* 2. Ipataŋ ; oahehde : *put a rest to the beam.* 3. (*Mus.*) Ho'oziyapi ; ho'enakiyapi : *the bass has a rest.* 4. Uŋmaŋpi ; en uŋ'pi ŝni : *the rest of the family.* 5. To'na iyaye : *I sold half and kept the rest.* *vt.* 1. Oziya ; ozikiya : *he rested the animals.* 2. E'hde ; e'hnaka : *he rested the foot on the ground.* *vi.* 1. Owaŋżi uŋ ; okiȟpa ; oziiçiya : *he rested on the Sabbath.* 2. Haŋ ; waŋka.
restate, *vt.* Akihde e'ya.
restaurant, *n.* Iŋaȟni wotapi ti'pi.
restful, *a.* Oziyapi ; en ozikiyapi waŝte.
restitution, *n.* Wokażużu ; wicakicupi.
restive, *a.* Iyowiŋyeŝni ; ŝke'he.
restiveness, *n.* Woŝkehe.
restless, *a.* 1. To'ken iyokipi taŋiŋ ŝni ; owaŋżi uŋ ŝni : *the sick boy was restless.* 2. Ayuŝtaŋ ŝni ; ohiŋni ŝkaŋŝkaŋ : *the restless waves.*
restlessly, *adv.* Iyokipiŝniyaŋ ; enakiya okihiŝni.
restorable, *a.* Asniyepica ; ekicetuyepica.
restoration, *n.* Ekicetuyapi ; kicupi ; ake ecoŋkiyapi.

restorative, *a.* Ekicetuya ; wayuwaŝte. *n.* Oŋ ekicetuyapi.
restore, *vt.* 1. Ekicetuya : *restore his health.* 2. Kicu : *restore the stolen money.* 3. Ake ohnaka.
restorer, *n.* Waekicetuya.
restrain, *vt.* Yutitaŋ yu'za ; kaġiya ; anapta.
restrainable, *a.* Yuspica ; anaptepica.
restraint, *n.* Wokaġi woanapte.
restrict, *vt.* Henana iyowiŋyaŋ ; hehaŋyena iyowiŋyaŋ ; kaŝka.
restriction, *n.* Wokaġi ; woanapte ; woope.
restrictive, *adv.* Wakaġiya.
resubjection, *n.* Ake wowidagyapi.
result, *n.* 1. Owihaŋke ; oicaġe ; to'ketu ; woyuŝtaŋ : *what is the result.* *vi.* (*with* IN) Aicaġe ; etaŋhaŋ icaġe ; icaġa.
resultant, *n.* Woicaġe.
resultless, *a.* Ituya ; ta'kudaŋ icaġeŝni.
resumable, *a.* Ake okihi.
resume, *vt.* Ake ecoŋ ; ikikcu ; ake a'ya. *n.* O'yuwitaya.
resummon, *vt.* Ake kico.
resumption, *n.* Ake ecoŋpi.
resupply, *vt.* Ake ku.
resurrection, *n.* Woekicetu.
resurvey, *vt.* Akta iyuta (makoce ka'pi).
resuscitate, *vt.* Ake niyakiya.
retail, *vt.* Yuksaksa wi'yopeya ; oŋŝpaŝpa wiyopeya.
retain, *vt.* Hduha ; anica ; ecehna hduha.
retainable, *a.* Hduhepica.
retainer, *n.* 1. Wahduhe ; yuha uŋ : *the retainer of the goods.* 2. Wokažužu ; wi'ŝi : *the lawyer wants a retainer of five dollars.*
retake, *vt.* Ake icu ; hdu'ze.
retaliate, *vt.* To'kiçoŋ ; watokiçoŋ.
retaliation, *n.* Watokiçoŋpi.
retard, *vt.* Kaġiya ; yutehaŋ.
retch, *vi.* Hde'pekteḣca.
retention, *n.* Wahduhapi ; te'haŋ hdu'zapi ; waciŋtaŋkapi ; kiksuyapi ; anicapi.
retentive, *a.* Wahduhaha.
reticence, *n.* I'ihdonicapi ; inina uŋ'pi.
reticent, *a.* Inina uŋ.
reticule, *n.* Paŋbotka ; uŋ'kŝuna.
retina, *n.* Iŝtacatku.
retinue, *n.* Itaŋcaŋ taoptaye.
retire, *vi.* Ḣeyata iyeya ; ihduḣeyapa ; enakiya ; waŋka.—*He retired from the battle,* okicize etaŋhaŋ ihduḣeyapa.—*Retiring pension,* enakiyapi ehan o'kiyapi. *vt.* Ayuŝtaŋkiya ; pažužu.
retirement, *n.* Enakiyapi : wonaḣbe.
retiring, *pa.* 1. Wi'steca ; manin uŋ : *of retiring habit.* 2. Enakiya.
retort, *vt.* Itkom e'ya ; itkom iyeya. *vi.* I'tkokipa ; ayupta. *n.* Woayupte; akiciyuptapi; itkom eyapi.
retrace, *vt.* I'cicawiŋ ya ; i'cipaŝ ya.
retract, *vt.* E'hdaku ; iapi e'hdaku. *vi.* Waehdaku ; enakiye.
retraction, *n.* Waehdakupi ; natipapi.
retranslate, *vt.* Akihde ieskakiya.
retreat, *vi.* I'cicawaŋ u ; he'kta hdicu : *the army retreated.* *n.* i'cicawiŋ hdicupi ; napapi.
retrench, *vt.* Yuaokpaniya ; ma'zaska to'nana yusota. *vi.* Wakpataŋ.
retrenchment, *n.* Wakpataŋpi ; yuaokpaniyapi ; maka okapi.
retribution, *n.* Wakažužupi ; woiyopeye.
retrieve, *vt.* Yuasni ; ekicetuya.
retrograde, *vi.* He'kta iyaya ; kun ya ; huŋ'keŝni a'ya.

retrospect, *n.* Piyaiwaŋyakapi; he'kta e'toŋwaŋpi.
retrospection, *n.* He'kta e'toŋwaŋpi.
return, *vi.* 1. Ake ku; hdi; ake hi; ihduhomni: *I returned today.* *vt.* Kicu; ki'cicahdi: *he returned the book.* 2. Ḳu: okiyaka: *to return answer.* *n.* 1. Hdi; ake hi: *they rejoiced at his return.* 2. Kicupi; każużupi: *a return for services.* 3. Wicoh̄aŋ owapi; owicawapi: *he has completed his returns.*—*At the return of the year*, o'maka iyehantu kiŋhaŋ.—*In return*, itkom.—*Cause to return*, hdicuya.
returnable, *a.* Kicupica; hdicupica.
reunion, *n.* 1. Hdiwitayapi; mni'ciyapi: *a soldier's reunion.* 2. Ake icikoyagyapi.
reunite, *vt.* Ake icikoyagya; ake yuwitaya.
Rev. *abbreviation for* REVEREND.
revaluation, *n.* Akta iyawapi.
reveal, *vt.* 1. Yuzamni; yutaŋiŋ: *he revealed the hidden wealth.* 2. Yaotaŋiŋ; oyaka.
reveille, *n.* Aŋ'pao wakabupi.
revel, *vi.* Witkoya wota; witkokoŋs śkata.
revelation, *n.* 1. Wayuotaŋiŋ: *the Revelation of St. John.* 2. Ta'ku yuzamnipi; woŋah̄be oyakapi: *it was a revelation to me.*
reveler, *n.* Witkos'a.
revelry, *n.* Witko śkaŋ'pi; witkodowaŋpi.
revenge, *vt.* Tokiçoŋ; watokiçoŋ. *n.* Watokiçoŋpi.
revengeful, *a.* Watokiçoŋs'a.
revenger, *n.* Watokiçoŋ.
revenue, *n.* 1. Wokamna; wokażużu: *the revenue of the government.*
revenue-cutter, *n.* Wa'ta womnaye awaŋyake.
reverberate, *vi.* Kaiyowaze; bu; kawiŋh̄wiŋh̄ iyaye.
reverberation, *n.* Wokawiŋġe; huhuzahaŋ.
revere, *vt.* Ohoda; kinihaŋ.
reverence, *n.* 1. Woohoda; wokinihaŋ.—*They treated him with reverence*, wokinihaŋ oŋ kuwapi. 2. Kinihaŋpi; tu'we kinihaŋpi; itaŋcaŋ: *his reverence is sick.* *vt.* Kinihaŋ; yuonihaŋ: *reverence your teachers.*
Reverend, *a.* Wicaśtawakaŋ.
reverend, *a.* Okinihaŋ.
reverent, *a.* Wokinihaŋ; waohoda.
reverently, *adv.* Kinihaŋyaŋ.
revery, reverie, *n.* Iśtiŋbeśni ihaŋmnapi.
reversal, *n.* Yutokecapi.
reverse, *vt.* Yutokeca; yuhomni; uŋmaŋ eciyataŋhaŋ iyeya: *reversed the decision.* *n.* Uŋmaŋ eciyataŋhaŋ; woyuhomni; yuhomnipi: *the reverse is whiet.* *a.* To'keca; uŋmaŋ.
reversed, *pa.* Yuhomnipi; uŋmaŋ eciyataŋhaŋ iyeyapi.
reversible, *a.* Yutokecapica.
reversion, *n.* Yuhomnipi; i'cicawiŋ hdi.
revert, *vt.* Yuhomni; i'cicawiŋ yeya: *revert the current.* *vi.* 1. I'cicawiŋ ki; hdi: *the property reverted.* 2. Ekta waciŋyeya; cażeyata: *he reverted to the incident.*
review, *vt.* Iwaŋyaka; amdeza; akta iwaŋyaka; amdesya yawa. *n.* 1. Akta iwaŋyakapi: *a review of the lesson.* 2. (*Mil.*) Akicita ikpazowicayapi. 3. Wowapi amdezapi. 4. Wowapi tak eyapi oyakapi.
reviewer, *n.* Wa'mdeża.
revile, *vt.* Yaśica; ośtehda.
reviler, *n.* Wayaśica.

revisal, *n.* Apiyapi.
revise, *vt.* Piya ; piya owa ; piya ka'ga.
reviser, *n.* Piyakaġa.
revision, *n.* Piyakaġapi.
revisit, *vt.* Ake waŋyagi.
revival, *n.* Piyaecoŋpi ; wicayuḣicapi : nikiyapi.
revivalist, *n.* Wicayuḣica.
revive, *vt.* Kiniya ; mdesya ; yuḣica ; mdihenya ; ikikcu.—*Revive learning,* wooŋspe yuḣica. —*Revive the story,* woyakapi ake nikiya.—*Revive my thoughts,* mitawacin mdesya. *vi.* Kini ; kimdiheca.
revivify, *vt.* Nikiya ; mdeskiya.
revocable, *a.* Yatokecapica.
revocation, *n.* Yatokecapi.
revoke, *vt.* Yatokeca ; yatakuniśni : *revoke a law.*
revolt, *vi.* Ayuśtaŋ ; itaŋcaŋ eḣpeya ; kipażiŋ ; itkom inażiŋ. *n.* Wokipażiŋ ; ayuśtaŋpi.
revolter, *n.* Wakipażiŋ.
revolution, *n.* 1. Oyuhomni ; yuhomnipi : *two revolutions of the wheel.* 2. Itaŋcaŋ yutokecapi ; wokipażiŋ ; wośkiśke : *a national revolution.*
revolutionary, *a.* Oyate yutokecapi ; wawakipażiŋpi : *a revolutionary soldier.*
revolutionist, *n.* Wayutokeca.
revolutionize, *vt.* Yutokeca ; te'ca ka'ga.
revolve, *vi.* Yuhomni ; pahmiḣma. *vt.* 1. Yuhomni : *revolve the wheel.* 2. Awaciŋ ; yuptaŋptaŋ : *he revolved the subject in his mind.*
revolver, *n.* Ma'zakaŋptecedaŋ ; o'taiyaye.
revulsion, *n.* Wowaḣtedaśni ; wowicadaśni.
reward, *vt.* Itkom ecakicoŋ ; ki'cicażużu ; ḳu. *n.* Wokażużu ; wi'śi.
rewarder, *n.* Wicakicicażużu.
rewardless, *a.* Wokażużu co'daŋ.
rewrite, *vt.* Akta owa.
reynard, *n.* Śuŋġidaŋ ; śuŋġi.
rhapsody, *n.* Odowaŋ kaġapi.
rhetoric, *n.* Iapi wakaḣniġapi.
rhetorician, *n.* Iapi wakaḣniġeca ; iapi oŋspewicakiya.
rheumatism, *n.* Ceḣpi yażaŋpi ; o'kihe yazaŋpi.
rhinoceros, *n.* Pasuhetoŋ.
rhomb, *n.* To'pa icaġopi atakiŋyaŋ cuwi a'kidehaŋkeca.
rhomboid, *n.* To'pa icaġopi atakiŋyaŋ.
rhubarb, *n.* Iyoptaiyeyapizi ; caŋḣdoḣuhu opemni ka'ġapi.
rhyme, *n.* Ho'waŋżidaŋ hiŋḣpaya. *vi.* Odowaŋ ka'ġa ; caŋkuye ihaŋke ho waŋżina ka'ġa.
rhymeless, *a.* Ho akidececa śni.
rhymer, *n.* Odowaŋ ka'ġa.
rhythm, *n.* Odowaŋ ca'ḣde ; ho'iyape.
rib, *n.* Cutuhu.—*Short rib,* cucuśte.
ribald, *n.* Tu'we ia waḣteśni.
ribaldry, *n.* Iapi śikśica.
ribbon, *n.* Śinaapaḣdate.
rice, *n.* Psiŋ.—*Wild rice,* psiŋ.—*Tame rice,* psiŋska.
rich, *a.* 1. Wi'żica ; watoŋka : *a rich man.* 2. Napiŋ : *rich food.* 3. Waicaḣya ; waśte : *a rich soil.* 4. Wi'ciyokipi ; naġi wi'piya : *rich music.* 5. O'ta iyawapi ; teḣika : *a rich dress.* 6. Mde'ze ; okitaŋiŋ : *rich colors.*
riches, *n.* Wowiżice.
richly, *adv.* 1. Wi'żinya : *richly dressed.* 2. Oḣaŋpiya ; o'ta : *richly paid.* 3. A'wicakehaŋ : *he richly deserved a whipping.*
richness, *n.* Owiżica ; wi'wicażice.
rick, *n.* Pahahaŋska.
rickets, *n.* Taŋcaŋ ośteka.
rickety, *a.* Ośteka ; ptaŋptaŋna.

rid, *vt.* Eḣpeya ; etaŋhaŋ ihduṡpe.
riddance, *n.* Wiihduṡpapi ; ihdutokaŋpi.
ridden, *pp.* of RIDE.
riddle, *n.* 1. Wi′yucaŋtaŋka : *the riddle don't shake.* 2. Wowiyukcaŋ ; wi′yukcaŋ teḣika : *he spake in riddles. vt.* 1. Yucaŋcaŋ : *riddle the wheat.* 2. Boḣdoḣdoka : *riddled with balls.*
ride, *vt.* Akaŋyotaŋka ; hiyaya ; iyaya ; ya : *ride the colt.*—*Ride easy,* iwaṡtedaŋ ya.—*Ride on,* iyoopta ya. *n.* Omanipi ; ṡuŋgakan omanipi ; caŋpahmihma ohna omanipi ; akaŋyaŋg ya.
rider, *n.* 1. Akaŋyaŋka : *the horse and his rider.* 2. Wowapi oŋ′ṡpa ehake ka′ġapi : *the Appropriation Bill had too many riders.*
riderless, *a.* Tu′wedaŋ akaŋyaŋkeṡni.
ridge, *n.* Ḣe ; paha ; mdamdate ; blo : *climb the ridge.*—*The ridge of the house,* ticeṡka. *vt.* Paha ka′ġa ; akata.
ridgy, *a.* Pahaha yeya ; pahaha.
ridicule, *n.* Wawiḣaḣapi. *vt.* Iḣaḣa.
ridiculous, *a.* Wowiḣaḣa.
ridiculously, *adv.* Wowiḣaya.
riding, *a.* Akaŋyaŋkapi.
riding-school, *n.* Ṡuŋgakaŋyaŋkapi oŋspewicakiyapi.
rife, *a.* Ni′na yukaŋ ; o′ta.
rifle, *n.* Ma′zakaŋ suwaŋżi ; sdayaożupi. *vt.* Bo′tica ; manoŋ.
rifleman, *n.* Wakutewicaṡta ; akicita.
rifle-pit, *n.* Akicita makaoḳapi.
rift, *n.* Onasdeca.
rig, *n.* Heyake ; ta′ku ikoyake. *vt.* Ikoyagya ; ikoyaka.—*Rig a ship,* wi′tawata ṡina ikoyagya.
rigging, *n.* Wi′tawata ikaŋ.
right, *a.* 1. Owotaŋna ; he′cetu.—*What is right,* ta′ku owataŋ na.—*That is right,* he′cetu.—*A right line,* icazopi owotaŋna. 2. E′e ; he′e : *that is the right book.* 3. Wicaka : *you are right.* 4. Waṡte ; taŋyaŋ ; hehantu : *disappointed on the right side.* 5. Etapa ; *Y.* oŋspeapataŋhan : *the right hand.* 6. Akapataŋhaŋ : *the right side.* 7. (*Math.*) Bosdatu ; owotaŋna ; itaŋcaŋ.—*A right angle,* okaḣmiŋ owotaŋna. *adv.* 1. Owotaŋna : *do right.* 2. Katiŋyaŋ : *go right along.* 3. Ḣiŋ ; *Y.* ḣtiŋ ; ḣca ; ḣciŋ : *right well.*—*l ight away ; right off,* katiŋyaŋ ; hdaheya. *n.* Woowotaŋna : *he was in the right.* 2. Wicitawa ; ta′ku ta′wa ; wowaṡake : *an Indian has no rights under the law. vt.* Yuowotaŋna ; yuwaṡte.
righten, *vt.* Yuowotaŋna.
righteous, *a.* Owotaŋna.
righteously, *adv.* Owotaŋna ; taŋ′yaŋ.
righteousness, *n.* Woowotaŋna.
rightful, *a.* Owotaŋna ; iyecetu ; wicaka.
rightfully, *adv.* Taŋ′yaŋ ; owotaŋna.
rightfulness, *n.* Woowotaŋna.
right-handed, *a.* Nape-etapa.
rightly, *a.* Owotaŋna ; taŋ′yaŋ.
rightminded, *a.* Tawaciŋ owotaŋna.
rightness, *n.* Woowotaŋna.
rigid, *a.* 1. Patiŋ ; sa′ka : *rigid limbs.* 2. Suta ; ḳe′za ; teḣika : *a rigid teacher.*
rigidly, *adv.* Sutaya ; teḣiya.
rigmarole, *n.* Ituyaciŋ iapi.
rigor, *n.* Wosuta ; woteḣi.
rigorous, *a.* Teḣika ; suta ; yutoke capicaṡni.
rigorously, *adv.* Teḣiya ; a′wica keya.
rile, *vt.* 1. Yuṡoṡe : *rile the water*

2. Caŋzeya : *the pupils riled the teacher.—To be riled,* caŋze.

rill, *n.* Wakpadaŋ ; *T.* wakpala.

rim, *n.* Tete ; ce'ġa tete.

rimple, *n.* Oyukśiża ; ta'żana. *vt.* Yukśikśiża.

rind, *n.* Ha ; ożuha.

rindless, *a.* Hawanica.

ring, *n.* 1. Ta'ku mima ; ta'ku mibe ; caŋhdeśka ; ma'żacaŋhdeśka : *a ring round the moon.* 2. Ma'zanapcupe ; *Y.* maziyoȟdi ; *T.* napsioȟli : *he put a ring on his finger.—The rings on a cow's horn,* oyuȟi. *vt.* Yuȟda ; *T.* yuȟla ; yusna ; kakoka : *ring the bells.—To ring by striking,* kaȟda.—*To ring with the hand,* yuȟda. *vi.* 1. Ȟda : *the church bell rang.* 2. Sna ; snasna : *it rang in my ear.* 3. Bu ; bu'bu ; ko'ka : *the house rang with the music.*

ringed, *a.* Mibebe ; hdeśkaśka.

ringer, *n.* Wakaȟda.

ringleader, *n.* Tokahaŋ ; itaŋcaŋ.

ringlet, *n.* Paha oyumniża.

ringstreaked, *a.* Hdeśkaśka ; hdehdeze.

ringworm, *n.* Yumniahinapa.

rinse, *vt.* Ehake yużaża.

riot, *n.* Owodutatoŋ. *vi.* Owodutatoŋ ka'ġa : wicayuhnaśkiŋyaŋ.

rioter, *n.* Wahnaśkiŋyaŋ.

riotous, *a.* Śiŋyaoȟaŋyaŋ ; wayuśkiśka.

rip, *vi.* Yumna ; yumdaza ; basdeca.—*Rip a seam,* yumna.—*Rip the hide,* ha yumdaza.—*Rip open a sack,* -wożuha yusdeca. *Rip up the floor,* owaŋka yuśdoka.—*Rip a board,* caŋmdaska basdeca. *n.* Oyumna ; oyuȟdeca.

ripe, *a.* 1. Sutoŋ ; waŋna waśte : *the wheat is ripe.* 2. Toŋ'ye : *a ripe tumor.* 3. Waŋna ihuŋni ; waokihi ; ksa'pa : *a ripe scholar.* 4. Wi'yeya uŋ : *ripe for war.*

ripen, *vi.* 1. Sutoŋ a'ya ; ġi a'ya : *the fruit ripens.* 2. Iyecetu a'ya ; ihduwiyeya ; piiçiya : *ripen for glory. vt.* Sutoŋye ; yuśtaŋ ; ksamya.

ripeness, *n.* Wosutoŋ ; woksape okihi.

ripper, *n.* Wayumna ; wabamdaza.

ripping, *n.* Wayumnapi ; wabamdazapi.

ripple, *n.* Mnitaża ; mnitata. *vi.* Taśtaża ; taża a'ya.

rip-saw, *n.* Caŋibaksa oŋ basdecapi.

rise, rose, *vi.* 1. Waŋkan ya ; waŋkan u : *smoke rises.* 2. Waŋkankan ya ; waŋkan yeya ; waŋkan waŋka. 3. Na'żiŋ ; inażiŋ ; na'żiŋhaŋ na'żiŋ : *the boys all rose.* 4. Kikta ; inażiŋ : *I rise at five o'clock.—I rise early,* haŋwekta.—*You rise early,* haŋyekta.—*He rises early,* kaŋkikta. 4. Waŋkan u ; minitaŋ : *the river rises.* 6 Hinaŋpa : *the sun rises.* 7. Ahinaŋpa : *an eruption arose on his back.* 8. Icaġa ; toka uya : *the river rises in Canada.* 9. Saŋ'pa taŋ'ka a'ya : *his fame rose.* 10. Ececa ; icaġa : *the fever rose.* 11. Kini : *Christ rose from the dead.* 12. I'taŋwaŋkaŋhde ya : *as he rose the hill.* 13. I'taŋwaŋkaŋhde waŋka : *rising ground.* 14. Waŋkan yawapi : *wheat rose. n.* 1. Waŋkan ya ; minitaŋ : *a rise of ten feet.* 2. Oicaġe : *takes its rise in the mountains.*

riser, *n.* Wakikta.—*Early riser,* haŋkikta.

risible, *a.* Wowiȟa ; wawiȟaye.

rising, *n.* 1. Ohinape ; inażiŋpi. 2. Po ; waŋkan u. *pa.* Icaġa ; waŋkan u.

risk, *n.* Wokokipe ; woţohnake ;

oṭohnakapi. *vt.* Oṭohnake; okokipeya e'hnaka; iyowiŋyaŋ; iyuta.
risky, *a.* Okokipe.
rite, *n.* Wocekiye opiiçiyapi wicoh̄aŋ; oŝkiŋciyapi.
ritual, *a.* Woope opiiçiyapi; wocekiye oŝkiŋciye wowapi.
ritualist, *n.* Opiiçiyapi wakitaŋ.
rival, *n.* Kici ecoŋ; kici akinica. *a.* Kicipatitaŋ: *rival societies* *vt.* Kapewaciŋ; uŋmaŋtukte tokahaŋ taŋiŋ ŝni.
rivalry, *n.* Waakinicapi.
rive, *vt.* Kasdeca; pasdeca.
riven, *pa.* Basdecapi.
river, *n.* Wakpa; watpa: *Missouri river.*—*Across* (or *over*) *the river,* akasaŋpa.—*By the river,* wakpicahda.—*Down the river,* o'kah̄; *Y.* & *T.* hu'tam.—*Up the river,* tatowam; *Y.* & *T.* iŋ'kpata.
rivet, *n.* Ma'zaiyokataŋ; ioŝtaŋ. *vt.* Okataŋ; i'ciyokataŋ.
rivulet, *n.* Wakpadaŋ; wakpa ci'stiŋna.
road, *n.* Caŋku; ocaŋku.
road-bed, *n.* Ḣemani caŋku.
roadster, *n.* Oicimani ŝuŋk'taŋka.
roam, *vi.* Ituomani; to'ken ciŋ'ciŋ omani. *n.* Wi'kcekce omanipi.
roan, *a.* Hiŋ'h̄ota.
roar, *vi.* 1. Hotoŋ; ho'taŋka hotoŋ: *the lion roared.* 2. S'a; bu; oṭiŋ: *the waves roared.* 3. Ih̄aṭaṭa: *the boys roared.* 4. Owodutatoŋ: *they made things roar.* *n.* Hotoŋpi; bu; s'a.
roarer, *n.* Hotoŋs'a; wohitika.
roast, *vt.* 1. Ceoŋpa: *roast the meat.* 2. Papah̄ya: *roast the corn.*—*Roast on a stick,* pasnoŋ. *n.* Ceoŋpapi; waceoŋpa.
rob, *vt.* Ki; makiŋoŋ.
robber, *n.* Wamanoŋwicaŝta.
robbery, *n.* Wamanoŋpi; wawicakipi.
robe, *n.* Ŝina; saŋksaŋnica.—*Buffalo-robe,* ptehaŝina; ŝinahiŋŝma; taġicaha. *vt.* Koyagya; akah̄pa: *the fields are robed in green.*
robin, *n.* Ŝiŝoka.
robust, *a.* Waŝ'aka; suta.
robustly, *adv.* Waŝ'agya.
rock, *n.* Imniża; iŋ'yaŋtaŋka; iŋ'yaŋ. *vt.* Nahuhuza; paptaŋ iyeya.
rocker, *n.* Ohna ikpahuhuzapi; wikpahuhuze; wikpahuhuze sicu.
rocket, *n.* Petiżaŋżaŋ wi'cute.
rocking-chair, *n.* Çaŋ'ikpahuhuze.
rocking-horse, *n.* Ŝuŋgakan ikpahuhuze.
Rock Island, *n. pr.* Wi'tawakaŋ.
rock-moss, *n.* Iŋ'yaŋ waanunu.
rock-salt, *n.* Miniŝkuya sa'ka.
rocky, *n.* Iŋ'yaŋ o'ta; iŋ'yaŋ.
rod, *n.* 1. Caŋsakadaŋ; caŋhaŋskedaŋ; ho'psicapi ihupa. 2. Owiyute sihaiyutapi akeŝakpe sam haŋke.
rode, *imp.* of RIDE.
rodent, *n.* Hituŋkadaŋ; wayah̄dokapi.
roe, *n.* Tawiyedaŋ; ta'h̄ca.
roebuck, *n.* Tamdoka; ta'h̄ca.
rogue, *n.* Tu'we oh̄aŋwicaŝtaŝni.
roguery, *n.* Wowicaŝtaŝni.
roguish, *a.* Wicaŝtaŝni.
roguishly, *adv.* Wicaŝtaŝniyaŋ; wowih̄a.
roil, *vt.* Yuŝoŝa; caŋzeya.
roily, *a.* Caŋzeya.
role, *n.* Koŋ'za oh̄aŋyaŋ.
roll, *n.* 1. Ta'ku pehaŋpi; opehe; wowapi pehaŋpi: *a roll of paper.*—*A wall roll,* opehe ti'obosdata en otkehe. 2. Wicacaże owapi: *call the roll.* 3. Paptaŋptaŋ iyaya; kah̄oh̄o iyaya: *the roll of the ship.* 4. Aki-

cita owotaŋna kabupi; nataŋpi kta kabupi. *vt.* 1. Pahmihma; pahmihma iyeya: *roll the hoop.* 2. Pehaŋ; yupehaŋ: *roll the paper.* 3. Ayuhomni; yuṭiŋza: *roll the ground.* 4. Pawaŋkankan iyeya: *the wind rolls the waves.* 5. Yuptaŋptaŋ.—*Roll one's self,* ihduptaŋptaŋ: *he rolled all night.* 6. Oṭiŋ; bu: *the thunder rolls.* 7. Ayuhmihma: *the mud rolls up on the wheels.*

rollable, *a.* Pahmihmapica.

roller, *n.* Maka ayuhmihmapi; hu'pahmihma.

roller-mill, *n.* Ma'zapahmima oŋ wokpaŋpi.

rolling, *pa.* Onaptaŋptaŋ; iwaśtedaŋ ḣo'śki: *rolling prairie.* 2. Paḣmihma ya: *the rolling carriages.*

Roman, *a.* Ro'ma wicaśta; Ro'ma ta'wa.

romance, *n.* Odowaŋ ohuŋkakaŋ.

Romanish, *a.* Ro'ma ta'wa.

romantic, *a.* Wakakaŋpi se; wi'haŋmnapi se; waakaġapi; akaḣkaġapi: *a romantic story.*

romp, *n.* 1. Śkates'a: *the girl is a romp.* 2. Wośkate: *the children are having a romp.* *vi.* Śka'ta.

roof, *n.* Awakeyapi; tiakaḣpe; waŋkantaŋhaŋ: *a flat roof.*—*the roof of the mouth,* caka. *vt.* Awakeya; akeya; akaḣpa.

roofing, *n.* Awakeyapi; tiakaḣpe.

roofless, *a.* Awakeyapi wanica; ticodaŋ.

rookery, *n.* Tiśica o'cikaŋśni.

room, *n.* 1. Oyaŋke; owaŋka.—*There is room,* okaŋ. 2. Timahen ti'pi; tiobaśpe; tioyaŋke: *the house has three rooms.*—*In the room of,* e'ekiya.—*Make room,* kiyukaŋ. *vt.* Oyaŋke yuha; waŋka.

roomful, *n.* Tiożudaŋ.

roomy, *a.* Otaŋkaya; okipika.

roost, *n.* Waḣupakoza owaŋka. *vi.* Waŋ'ka.

rooster, *n.* Aŋ'paohotaŋna mdoka.

root, *n.* 1. Hutkaŋ: *the roots of a tree.* 2. Woyute maka mahen icaġa; mdo; paŋġi: *put the roots in the cellar.* 3. Hutkaŋ; huŋkake: *they sprang from one root.* *vi.* 1. Hutkaŋ yeya: *the weeds root deep.* 2. Hutkaŋ ode; pamdumdu: *the hog roots in the field.* *vt.* 1. Huhde; hutkaŋ sutaya ehde: *well rooted.* 2. Yużuŋ; yużuŋ eḣpeya: *root them out.*

rootless, *a.* Hutkaŋ wanica.

rootlet, *n.* Hutkaŋ ci'stiŋna.

rooty, *a.* Hutkaŋ o'ta.

rope, *n.* Hakahmuŋpi; wi'kaŋ; haḣoŋta: *tie him with a rope.* *vt.* Haḣoŋta ikoyake; haḣoŋta oŋ icu: *rope the calf.*

rope-maker, *n.* Hakahmuŋpi ka'ġa.

ropy, *a.* Tiktica; o'tkapa.

rosary, *n.* 1. Oŋżiŋżiŋtka owożu: *he planted a rosary.* 2. Wocekiye śipto oŋ yawapi; Śinasapa tawocekiye.

rose, *n.* Oŋżiŋżiŋtka; śa.

rose, *imp.* of RISE.

roseate, *a.* Śaśa.

rosebush, *n.* Oŋżiŋżiŋtka hu.

rose-color, *n.* Śa; oŋżiŋżiŋtka śa.

rose-colored, *a.* 1. Śa; śaśa: *rose-colored paper.* 2. Śayapi; akaġapi: *a rose-colored story.*

rosery, *n.* Oŋżiŋżiŋtka owożu.

rosewater, *n.* Oŋżiŋżiŋtka mini.

rosewood, *n.* Caŋśa.

rosin, *n.* Caŋśiŋ sa'ka.

roster, *n.* Wicacaże wowapi.

rostrum, *a.* Oanażiŋ; akan wohdakapi; pasu.

rosy, *a.* Śaśa: *rosy-cheeked.*

rot, *vi.* Kuka; kuka a'ya; poŋpoŋ. *vt.* Kukeya; poŋpoŋya. *n.* Wokuka.

rotary, *a.* Yuhomni; itogto.

rotate, *vi.* 1. Yuhomni: *the wheel rotates.* 2. Uŋmaŋ itogto ecoŋ.

rotation, *n.* 1. Woyuhomhi. 2. Itogto ecoŋpi. 3. Su ocaže itogto ożupi.

rote, *n.* Okaȟniġeśni eyapi.

rotgut, *n.* Miniwakaŋ kuka.

rotten, *a.* 1. Kuka: *a rotten apple.* 2. Poŋpoŋ: *rotten wood.*

rottenness, *n.* Wokuka; wośice.

rotund, *a.* Mibe.

rotunda, *a.* Ti'pi mibe.

rouge, *n.* Wase; waśeśa.

rough, *a.* Mdaye śni; pespesto; pepe; taŋ'yaŋ kaoŋspepi śni. —*A rough board,* caŋmdaska każipapiśni.—*Rough cloth,* miniȟuha pepe.—*A rough country,* makoce ȟo'śki.—*A rough day,* aŋpetu kiȟaŋśica; aŋpetu oiyokiśica.—*A rough man,* wicaśta teȟika.—*A rough road,* caŋku paȟaȟa; caŋku śi'ca.—*A rough sea,* mini taȟtaġa; ta'ża waŋkantuya.—*A rough tone,* ho ġahaŋ; ho ġaheca; ho żahaŋ.—*In the rough,* ka'ġapi śni; yuwaśtepi śni. *n.* Wakizes'a. *vt.* Paȟaȟa.—*To rough it,* ikceya uŋ.

rough-cast, *n.* Iyuteya ka'ġapi; iwaŋyag ka'ġapi.

roughen, *vt.* Yuġoġo; yuȟaȟa.

rough-hew, *vt.* Ikce ka'ga.

roughish, *a.* Oŋspeśni.

roughly, *adv.* Ikceya; żaheya; teȟiya; pe'stoya; wohitiya.

roughness, *n.* Pahaha; mda'yeśni; wośkiśke; woohitika.

rough-shod, *a.* Śakemaza pepe; wohitika.

round, *n.* 1. Mibe; mima; hmiyaŋyaŋ; ta'pase. 2. I'ożudaŋ; o'ta; tkoŋ'za: *a good round sum.* *n.* Ta'ku hmiyaŋyaŋ; woohomni; kahomni wacipi; aohomnipi; i'ciyaza ecoŋpi.—*A round of beef,* tado cecaobaksa.—*The round of a ladder.* caŋiyamanipi sihdepi.—*They sang a round,* kicipasipi odowaŋ ahiyayapi. *adv.* Ohomni; o'kśaŋ; i'hdukśaŋ; okawinȟ: *he went round the field.*—*The wheel turns round,* caŋhdeśka yuhomni.—*All round,* o'waŋcaya. *prep.* Ohomni: *wrap it round the tree.* *vt.* Mibe ka'ġa; yupsoŋpsoŋ; yuwaśte: *round the edges.*—*Round up the cattle,* pte kiŋ yuwitaya.

roundabout, *a.* Aohomni; katiŋyaŋśni: *a roundabout road.*

roundhouse, *n.* Tihmiŋyaŋna.

roundly, *adv.* Aohomniyaŋ; a'wicakehaŋ.

roundness, *n.* Womibe; woożudaŋ; wowicake.

round-shouldered, *a.* Tapete pako.

rouse, *vt.* Yuȟica: *rouse the people.* *vi.* Kikta; ihduȟica.

rouser, *n.* Wicayuȟica; wohitika.

rousing, *a.* 1. Wayuȟica. 2. Taŋ'ka; otaŋtoŋka: *a rousing fire.*

rousingly, *adv.* Wohitiya; yumdesya.

rout, *n.* Wonażica; owodutatoŋ. *vt.* Iyayeya; napeya: *he routed the enemy.*

route, *n.* Caŋku; ocaŋku.

routine, *n.* Wicoȟaŋ o'weciŋhaŋ; to'ken ocaŋkuyapi.

rove, *vi.* Okawiŋȟ uŋ; itomni.

rover, *n.* Omanis'a.

row, *vt.* 1. Watopa: *row the boat.* 2. Wa'ta ohna a'ya: *row the lady over the river.* *vi.* Watopa: *I like to row.* *n.* 1. Watom omanipi: *take a row.* 2. Ocaŋkuye; i'cipatkuȟ waŋkapi: *a row of houses.*

rowdy, *n.* Ho'bu; owodutoŋ ka'ġa.

rowdyish, *a.* Oȟaŋwicaštašni.
rower, *n.* Watopa.
rowlock, *n.* Iwatopekiya wi'yuze.
royal, *a.* Itaŋcaŋ ; wašte : *a royal family.* *n.* Itaŋcaŋ ; wowapi ska taŋ'ka.
royalist, *n.* Wicaštayatapi taobe.
royally, *adv.* Itaŋcaŋ iyececa.
royalty, *n.* Itaŋcaŋ ; itaŋcaŋ ta'wa : itaŋcaŋ tawomnaye ; wokažužu.
rub, *vt.* Payeza ; pakiŋta ; yuȟdata ; pažaža.—*Rub the clothes hard,* heyake ni'na pažaža.—*Rub off,* pakiŋta.—*Rub on,* iuŋ ; apawiŋta.—*Rub out,* pataŋiŋsni ; pakiŋta.—*Rub up,* pašduta ; pakiŋta ; pawiyakpa. *vi.* Kašeya ya ; icaȟtaġ ya : *you rubbed on the wheel.* *n.* Wokaše ; wokaȟtake ; wopanini ; wokašušuža : *a hard rub.*
rubadub, *n.* Kabupi.
rubber, *n.* 1. Caŋšiŋ : *it is made of rubber.* 2. Wi'payeza ; ipažužu : *a pencil with a rubber head.* 3. Caŋšiŋ haŋ'pa : *buy a pair of rubbers.* 4. Ehakena ecoŋpi : *play the rubber.*
rubbish, *n.* Wokpukpaŋ ; ta'ku eȟpeyapi.
rubric, *n.* Woope ; wocekiye woope.
ruby, *n.* Iŋ'yaŋ teȟike ša.
rudder, *n.* Iyupse ; wa'taiyuhomni.
ruddiness, *n.* Šaša ; woša.
ruddy, *a.* Šaša.
rude, *a.* 1. Wicaštašni : *the rude boy.* 2. Waoŋspekešni ; ikceka : *our rude forefathers.* 3. Taŋ'yaŋ ka'ġapišni : *his rude plow.*
rudely, *adv.* Ikceya ; oŋspešni.
rudeness, *n.* Oŋwicaspešni.
rudiment, *n.* O'tokaheya wooŋspe ; o'hute.
rudimentary, *a.* O'tokahe ; štuŋka.
rue, *vt.* Icaŋtešica ; iyopeçiya.
ruefully, *adv.* Oiyokišinya.
ruff, *n.* Yumnimnižapi ; tahu yumnimnižapi.
ruffian, *n.* Tu'we ociŋšica.
ruffle, *vt.* Yutaštaža ; yumnimniža ; yucaŋze ; yuȟdata. *n.* Yumnimnižapi ; wocaŋze.
ruffled, *a.* Caŋze ; taštaža.
rug, *n.* Owiŋžadaŋ.
rugged, *a.* 1. Kaġoġopi ; ȟeȟe ; ȟoškiški : *the rugged mountains.* 2. Suta ; wakiš'aka ; ķe'ža : *a rugged boy.*
ruggedly, *adv.* Wakiš'agya.
ruggedness, *n.* Wowakiš'aka ; woškiške ; woteȟi.
ruin, *n.* Woyutakunišni ; woihaŋke. *vt.* Yutakunišni ; ihaŋgya.
ruination, *n.* Woihaŋgye.
ruinous, *a.* Wayušica ; waihaŋgye.
rulable, *a.* Wicoȟaŋ oȟna ; woope oȟna ; heciyotaŋ.
rule, *n.* 1. Woope : *I will read the rules of the school.* 2. Aȟna icazopi ; owiyute oŋ icazopi : *your rule is crooked.* 3. Wawidake : *under the rule of kings.* *vt.* 1. Icazo ; owotaŋna icazo : *I want you to rule this paper.* 2. Idake : *she ruled her husband.* 3. Woope oyaka : *he ruled the case out.* *vi.* Wawidake ; waawaŋyake ; woope ka'ġa.
ruler, *n.* 1. Wawidake ; itaŋcaŋ : *the ruler of England.* 2. Aȟna icazopi.
ruling, *n.* 1. Icazopi : *the ruling is too close.* 2. Woyaco ; waeyaštaŋ : *the judge's ruling.* *pa.* Itaŋcaŋ ; itaŋcaŋ uŋ ; iyotaŋ.
rum, *n.* Miniwakaŋ.
rumble, *vi.* Ḣmun ; bu ; ko'ka.
rumblingly, *adv.* Kokogya.
ruminant, *n.* Ta'ku wayatekoŋza ; ta'ȟca ; tataŋka ; ta.

ruminate, *vi.* 1. Wayatekoŋza. 2. Awaciŋ uŋ; wi'yukcan.

rummage, *vt.* Ode; mahentu ode.

rumor, *n.* Woyakapi; tu'we he'ya taŋiŋ śni e'yapi. *vt.* Oyaka.

rump, *n.* Nite; siŋte hu'te.

rumple, *vi.* Yukśikśiża.

rumpus, *n.* Oķoyapi; owodutatoŋ.

run, *vi.* 1. Iŋ'yaŋka: *the boy runs.* 2. Kaduza: *the water runs.* 3. Iyaye; iyopte: *the clock runs.* 4. Awaciŋ uŋ; okawiŋh uŋ: *his mind runs on it.*—*Run after,* kuwa iyaye.—*Run away,* nażica; naħmaŋhda.—*Run away with,* yuha iyaya.—*Run for,* oħaŋko huweiyaya; kuwa.—*Run for Congress,* Tuŋkaŋśina omniciye o'pe kta kuwa.—*Run in debt,* oicazo ka'ġa.—*Run in with,* akipa.—*Run on,* adi.—*The debt ran on,* oicazo każużuśni yaŋka.—*Run out,* henana; ihaŋke.—*Run over,* apaśboka; adi ya: *run over a child.* —*Run over a paper,* wowapi inaħni waŋyaka.—*Run up an account,* oicazo haŋ'ska ka'ġa. *vt.* 1. In'yaŋgkiya; kiiŋyaŋgkiya: *ran the horse a mile.* 2. Iyayeya: *run the rope through the hole.* 3. Kaġeġe; i'cipasisa: *run a seam.*—*Run down,* e'tapa; kihdeġa.—*Run a line,* iyute.—*Run out,* taŋkan iyayeya.—*Run a risk,* okihi kte śni se'ca ecoŋ.—*Run through,* ipaħdan iyeya.—*Run through a fortune,* woyuhataŋka yusota.—*Run up the figures.* wayawapi yuwitaya. *n.* 1. Oiŋyaŋke; kiiŋyaŋkapi: *a long run.* 2. Minicaduza; wakpadaŋ: *he drank at the run.*—*A good run for cattle,* ptewanuyaŋpi owiħaŋye waśte.—*A run of stones,* iŋ'yaŋ wi'yukpaŋ tawaŋżi.—*A run on the bank,* ma'zaskatipi ma'zaska e'ħdakupi kta anataŋpi —*The common run,* ikceka; owasiŋ iyececa.—*The run of mankind,* wicaśta iyuha se; ecaowaŋca.—*In the long run,* te'haŋtu kiŋhaŋ; owihaŋketa.

runaway, *a.* Napes'a; nażices'a.

rung, *imp.* of RING.

rung, *n.* Caŋ'oiyadi.

runner, *n.* 1. Iŋ'yaŋkes'a; iŋ'yaŋka du'zahe: *runners preparing for the race.* 2. Wahośiye: *a runner from the battle.* 3. Wopetoŋ omani: *a runner from Chicago.* 4. Hu'sdohaŋpi: *strawberry vines have runners.*

running, *a.* 1. Kiiŋyaŋgkiyapi: *a running horse.* 2. I'ciyokiheya: *two days running.* 3. Toŋ'ye; toŋ'au: *a running sore.*—*Running down to,* iyohiya. *n.* Iŋyaŋkapi; wokaduza.

runt, *n.* Ecacikana; ośteka.

rupture, *n.* 1. Kaħdecapi; wokaħdeca: *a rupture in the wall.* 2. Wokicize; woakinica: *a rupture in the king's family.* 3. Tezi naħden hiyu. *vt.* Yuħdeca: *rupture a blood vessel.*

rural, *a.* Wożupi makoce; wożupi.

ruse, *n.* Wohnaye.

rush, *vi.* 1. Nataŋ; dus ya: *all rushed to the fire.*—*Rush at,* anataŋ. 2. Ni'na hiyu; ni'na hiyaya: *the water rushed out.* 3. Mde'ześni kuwa: *don't rush into business.* *n.* 1. Wonataŋ: *see the rush of people.* 2. Waŋyeca: *rub it with rushes.* 3. Psa: *a rush mat.*

rusher, *n.* Waanataŋ; ohitika.

rusk, *n.* Aġuyapi sku'yena.

russet, *n.* Taspaŋtaŋka ha'ġi.

rust, *n.* ·Giġi; ma'zaaġi. *vi.* ·Gi a'ya; ġiġi; śin a'ya.

rustic, *a.* Wożuwicaŝta ta'wa; ikce se ka'ġapi.

rusticate, *vi.* Makoskan ti; wi'-kcekce uŋ.

rustle, *vi.* 1. Ḣamḣapa; ḣa'pa: *the leaves rustled.* 2. Ḣmuŋ se ŝkaŋ; mdiheiçiya ŝkaŋ: *rustle for yourself.*

rustler, *n.* Tu'we wohitiya ŝkaŋ.

rusty, *a.* ·Gi; ġiġi: *a rusty plow.*

rut, *n.* Oŝkokpa; caŋpahmihma hu naoŝkokpa: *keep out of the ruts.* *vi.* Takiyuḣa.

rutabago, *n.* Ti'psinażiżi.

ruthless, *a.* Waoŋŝidaŝni.

ruthlessly, *adv.* Waoŋŝidaŝniyaŋ.

rutty, *a.* Oŝkokpakpa.

rye, *n.* Aġuyapisapa.

S

Sabbath, *n. pr.* Aŋpetuwakaŋ.

Sabbath-breaker, *n.* Aŋpetuwakaŋ kicaksa.

Sabbatical, *a.* Aŋpetuwakaŋ iyececa. *Sabbatical year,* waniyetu iŝakowiŋ.

saber, *n.* Isaŋtaŋka; miwakaŋ. *vt.* Miwakaŋ oŋ apa.

sable, *n.* Nakpaġica. *a.* Sa'pa.

Sac, *n. pr.* Za'ke.

sacharine, *a.* Sku'ya; caŋhaŋpise.

sacerdotal, *a.* Wawayuŝna.

sack, *n.* 1. Wożuha; ożuha. *A sackful,* wożuha ożudaŋ. 2. Uŋ'ḣoḣda; o'kdeoŋżiŋca. *vt.* 1. Ożutoŋ; okŝu: *sack the potatoes.* 2. Ihaŋgya: *the soldiers sacked the town.*

sackcloth, *n.* Miniḣuhaŝica; wożuha.

sackful, *n.* Ożutoŋpi.

sacrament, *n.* Wohduze; wowakaŋ wicoḣaŋ (Ḣtayetuwotapi ḳa mniakaŝtaŋpi hena kapi).

sacred, *a.* Wakaŋ; ohodapi.

sacredly, *adv.* Wakaŋyaŋ.

sacredness, *n.* Wowakaŋ.

sacrifice, *n.* 1. Woŝnapi; waiḣpeyapi. 2. Woihaŋgye; wokpaġaŋ. *vt.* 1. Woŝna; waiḣpeya. 2. Eḣpeya; kpaġaŋ.

sacrilege, *n.* Wowakaŋ yuikcekapi.

sacrum, *n.* Nisehu.

sad, *a.* 1. Caŋteŝica; iyokiŝin uŋ: *a sad woman.* 2. Oiyokiŝica: *a sad day.*

sadden, *vt.* Iyokiŝinya.

sadder, *a. comp.* Saŋ'pa caŋteŝica.

saddest, *a. sup.* Iyotaŋ caŋteŝica; iyotaŋ oiyokiŝica

saddle, *n.* Awaḳiŋ; ŝungaḳin. *A saddle of meat,* napco. *vt.* Aḳiŋkitoŋ.

saddle-girth, *n.* Makuiyutitaŋ.

saddle-horse, *n.* Ŝuŋgakaŋyaŋkapi.

saddle-tree, *n.* Awaḳiŋ caŋ.

sadly, *adv.* Caŋteŝinya; oiyokiŝinya; teḣiya.

sadness, *n.* Woiyokiŝica; iyokiŝicapi.

safe, *a.* Okopeŝni; kokipepicaŝni; taŋyaŋ; waŝte. *A safe bridge,* caŋkaḣoŋpapi kokipepicaŝni. *n.* Opiye suta; ma'zaska aonatake.

safeguard, *n.* Oŋ okope ŝni.

safekeeping, *n.* Woawaŋyake waŝte.

safely, *adv.* Taŋ'yaŋ; okokipeŝniyaŋ; wakiuŋniyeŝni.

safeness, *n.* Wokokipeŝni; wozani.

safety-lamp, *n.* Petiżaŋżaŋ okopeŝni.

saffron, *a.* Zi; waḣcazi.

sag, *vi.* Kawiŋża; kawinś iyaye. *n.* Okawiŋże.
sagacious, *a.* Kesa'pa; wi'yukcaŋ.
sage, *n.* 1. Wahpehota. 2. Ksapotaŋcaŋ; wicaśtaksapa. *a.* Ksa'pa; waśte.
sagely, *adv.* Ksamyahaŋ.
sagging, *n.* Okawiŋża.
sago, *n.* Woyute yużapi (ocaże).
said, *imp.* of SAY.
sail, *n.* Śina (oŋ watopekiyapi); śinawatopekiyapi ohna omanipi.—*Strike sail,* śina puhpapi. —Śina kiçuŋ. *vi.* 1. Śina oŋ watopa: *our boat sails well.* 2. Śinawata oŋ omani; wi'tawata ohna ya. 3. Kiŋyaŋ ya; kahoya ya; nawiŋ uŋ: *the buzzard sails high.* *vt.* 1. Śina oŋ watopekiya: *sail his boat.* 2. Akiŋyaŋ: *sails aerial space.*
sailable, *a.* Śinawatopekiyepica.
sail-cloth, *n.* Wa'taśina oŋ ka'ġapi.
sailer, *n.* Śinawatopekiya.
sailing, *n.* Śinaoŋwatopapi.
sailless, *a.* Śina wanica.
sailmaker, *n.* Wa'taśina ka'ġa.
sailor, *n.* Śinawata kicaŋyaŋ.
saint, *n.* Wakaŋ; wanaġiwakaŋ.
Saint Louis, *n. pr.* Miniśośeiyohdoke otoŋwe.
Saint Paul, *n. pr.* Imnizaskadaŋ.
Saint Peter (Minn.) *n. pr.* Oiyuweġa.
sainted, *a.* Yawakaŋpi.
saintly, *a.* Wanaġi waśte.
sake, *n.* Woihakta; wokiksuye. —*For the sake of,* oŋ etaŋhaŋ. —*For his sake,* iye on etaŋhaŋ.
salable, *a.* Wi'yopeyepica.
salad, *n.* Wahpe baksaksa yu'tapi.
salary, *n.* Wokażużu; wi'śi; waniyetu waŋżi wokażużu.
sale, *n.* 1. Wi'yopeyapi: *The sale is completed.* 2. Owiyopeye; paŋ wi'yopeyapi.—*For sale,* wi'yopeyapi haŋ.
saleratus, *n.* Aġuyapi inapohye.
salesman, *n.* Wopetoŋ wicaśta; wi'yopeya śkan.
salient, *a.* 1. Okitaŋiŋ; cażeyanpica. 2. Pażoya hiyu.
saliva, *n.* Taġe; taġośa.
sallow, *a.* Uka to'keca; ukazi.
sally, *n.* Wonataŋ; iapi to'keca. *vi.* Nataŋ; kuwa e'yaya.
salmon, *n.* Hoġaŋzi; ho'wicaśtaśni.
saloon, *n.* Miniwakaŋ ti'pi.
salt, *n.* 1. Miniskuya. 2. Tu'we miniwaŋca omanis'a. *vt.* Sku'yeya. *a.* Sku'ya.
salt-cellar, *n.* Miniskuya wohnake.
salting, *n.* Miniskuya icahiyapi.
saltish, *a.* Ki'taŋna sku'ya.
saltmine, *n.* Miniskuya oķe.
saltness, *n.* Woskuye.
saltpeter, *n.* Miniskuyaśa.
salt-rheum, *n.* Ikceahinapapi.
salts, *n.* Miniskuyaseca.
salty, *a.* Sku'ya.
salubrious, *a.* Oniyawaśte.
salutary, *a.* Wayuwaśte.
salutation, *n.* Wozani ekiciyapi.
salute, *vt.* Wozani ekiciya. *n.* Akiciyutapi; ho ekiciyapi.
salvation, *n.* Wiconi; waniwicayapi; woehdaku.
salve, *n.* Sda wi'kiuŋpi.
Samaritan, *n.* *Samaria* wicaśta.
Sambo, *n.* Waśicuŋsapa.
same, *a.* He'e; o'koŋwaŋżidaŋ; waŋżidaŋ.—*Much the same,* a'kidecenya se.—*Of the same length,* a'kidehaŋkeca.—*Of the same size,* a'kiniskokeca.—*Of the same sort,* obewaŋżidaŋ.—*Of the same age,* waniyetu a'kidenakeca.—*The same day,* aŋpetu waŋżidaŋ.—*The same direction,* iś eya heciyotaŋ.—*The same man,* wicaśta waŋżidaŋ.—*The same number,* i'aki-

denakeca.—*The same time*, iyehaŋyaŋ.
sameness, *n.* O'waŋżidaŋ ; he'cetuwaŋżica.
sample, *n.* Oŋ sdonyapi kta ; oŋśpa. *vt.* Oŋśpaśpa iyuta.
sanitary, *a.* Oŋ wicazani kta.
sanctification, *n.* Wicayuecepidaŋ; wicayuwakaŋpi.
sanctify, *vt.* Yuwakaŋ ; yuecedaŋ.
sanctimonious, *a.* Wakaŋkaŋ : wakaŋkoŋza.
sanction, *n.* Woyusuta ; waokiyapi. *vt.* He'cetu keya.
sanctify, *n.* Wowakaŋ ; wocekiye.
sanctuary, *n.* Ti'piwakaŋ.
sanctum, *n.* Oyaŋkewakaŋ.
sand, *n.* Wiyaka ; casmu. *vt.* Wiyaka akada.
sandal, *n.* Haŋpsicu haŋ'pa.
sand-bag, *n.* Wiyaka ożutoŋpi.
sand-fly, *n.* Honaġidaŋ hdeśka.
sandpaper, *n.* Miniḣuhapepe.
sandstone, *n.* Wiyakaiŋyaŋ ; izuza.
sandstorm, *n.* Wiyakaibobdu.
sandwich, *n.* Aġuyapi waśiŋapaskica.
sandy, *a.* 1. Wiyaka : *a sandy road.* 2. Saŋ ; żi : *sandy hair.*
sane, *a.* 1. Mde'ze ; waciŋhnuniśni. 2. Zani : *a sound body.*
sang, *imp.* of SING.
sang-froid, *n.* Inihaŋśni.
sanguinary, *a.* Weyapi ; we o'ta : *a sanguinary war.*
sanguine, *a.* 1. We o'ta ; ka'ta ; oḣaŋko ; mdiheca : *a sanguine temperament.* 2. Okihiiçida : *sanguine of success.* 3. Śa ; we.
Sanhedrim, *n. pr.* Juda Omniciye Waŋkantu.
sanitary, *a.* Oŋ wicazani.
sanity, *n.* Waciŋhnuniśni ; wozani.
sank, *imp.* of SINK.
Sans Arc, *n. pr.* Itazipco.
Santee, *n. pr.* Isaŋyati.
Sanskrit, *n. pr.* Otakahe oyate waŋżi.
sap, *n.* 1. Caŋ haŋpi. 2. Caŋ ha ihukuya. *vt.* Hu'te oḳa.
sap-head, *n.* Tu'we waciŋtoŋśni.
sapient, *a.* Ksa'pa ; ksapaiçida.
sapless, *a.* Pu'za ; śi'ca.
sapling, *n.* Caŋ ci'stiŋna ; tośu.
sapphire, *n.* Iŋ'yaŋ teḣika to.
sappy, *a.* Miniota ; śtuŋka.
sarcasm, *n.* Iapi woyaḣtake.
sarcastic, *a.* Wayaḣtake ; pe.
sardine, *n.* Hoġaŋstiŋna wi'hdi opuskicapi.
sarsaparilla, *n.* Peżiḣutazi.
sash, *n.* 1. Ipiyaka haŋ'ska ; icaśke. 2. O'żaŋżaŋkdepi caŋ.
Saskatchewan, *n. pr.* Miniduza.
sassafras, *n.* Caŋzi ocaże.
sat, *imp.* of SIT.
Satan, *n. pr.* Wakaŋśica.
satanic, *a.* Wakaŋśica se.
satchel, *n.* Paŋbotka ; wizipaŋ.
sate, *vt.* Wi'piya ; i'mnaya.
satellite, *n.* Wicaŋḣpi o'kihe ; o'kihe.
satiate, *vt.* Wi'piya ; hitihdaya.
satiety, *n.* Wi'pipi.
satin, *n.* Miniḣuha śtośto.
satinet, *n.* 1. Miniḣuha sani stostona. 2. Onzeoġe ka'ġapiśni.
satire, *n.* I en iyeyapi owohdake ; wawiyokipi śni.
satisfaction, *n.* Woiyokipi ; wokażużu.
satisfactory, *a.* Wawiyokipi ; taŋ'yaŋ.
satisfy, *vt.* Iyokipiya ; wi'piya ; sdonyekiya ; każużu.
satisfying, *pa.* Wi'piya ; napiŋ.
saturate, *vt.* Ḣpaŋyaŋ.
Saturday, *n. pr.* Owaŋkayużażapi.
sauce, *n.* Ta'ku sku'ya. *vt.* Iapi pe'sto ḳu ; i'eniyeya.
saucebox, *n.* Tu'we wicaśtaśni.
saucepan, *n.* Waskuyaikanye.
saucer, *n.* Cetetehedaŋ.
saucily, *adv.* Wicaśtaśniyaŋ.

sauciness, *n.* Woohodaśni.
saucy, *a.* Waohodaśni; wi'śtece-śni.
saunter, *vi.* Wi'kcekce omani.
sausage, *n.* Tadoopaskicapi.
savage, *n.* Ikcewicaśta. *a.* 1. Ikce; ikce uŋ: *in savage life.* 2. Wohitika; oteħika; okokipe: *a savage dog.*
save, *vt.* 1. Nikiya: *Lord save me.* 2. Kihnaka; kpataŋ: *I will save this for you.* 3. Yuasni; yutokaŋ: *save trouble. prep.* A'okpani.
saver, *n.* Wakpataŋs'a; nikiya.
saving, *pa.* Wapataŋ. 2. Wapataŋpi.
savingly, *adv.* Kpataŋyaŋ.
savings-bank, *n.* Wakpataŋpitipi.
Savior, *n. pr.* Wanikiya; *Jesus Christ.*
savor, *n.* Woomna; iteka. *vi.* Ecamna; u'ta; se'ececa.
savorless, *a.* Takumaśni
savory, *a.* Waśtemna; oyunwaśte.
saw, *imp.* of SEE.
saw, *n.* Caŋibaksa. *vt.* Baksa.
sawdust, *n.* Caŋbakpaŋpi.
sawer, sawyer, *n.* Caŋbaksa; caŋba. 2. Caŋmnicazo.
sawmill, *n.* Caŋnasdetipi.
say, said, *vt.* E'ya; he'ya; keya. —*I say,* epa.—*You say,* eha.—*They say,* keyapi.
sayer, *n.* E'ya.
saying, *n.* Woeye. *par.* E'ya.
scab, *n.* Oħdi ce'spu; hakte.
scabbard, *n.* Isaŋożuha; miożuha; ma'zasagye ożuha.
scaffold, *n.* Co'wahe.
scaffolding, *n.* Oŋ co'wahe ka'-gapi.
scald, *vt.* Minikata aġuye.
scale, *n.* 1. Ho'ceśpu; ceśpu: *fish with scales.* 2. Oŋ aspeyetoŋpi: *hay scales.* 3. Ho'iyadipi: *sing the scale.* 4. Owiyute: *decimal scale. vt.* 1. Adi: *scale the rock.* 2. Yuħdaya; kakiŋca.
scalp, *n.* Wicapaha; paha. *vt.* Paha yu'za.
scalp-dance, *n.* Iwakicipi.
scalpel, *n.* Isaŋ; mi'na.
scaly, *a.* Ceśpuota; hakte.
scamp, *n.* Wicaśtaśni.
scamper, *vi.* Iŋ'yaŋka; tokaŋ ya.
scan, *vt.* Iwaŋyaka; ca'hdeyawa.
scandel, *n.* Woaie.
scandalize, *vt.* Woaie ki'caġe.
scandalous, *a.* Yaśicapi; waħteśni.
scandalously, *adv.* Śinya; śicaya.
scant, *a.* Iyohiśni se; ki'tanħ iyohi; a'okpani. *vt.* Yuaokpani.
scantily, *adv.* A'okpani; icakiśya.
scantling, *n.* Caŋmdaska omdotoŋ.
scanty, *a.* Iyokpani; to'nana.
scape-grace, *n.* Caŋtewanica.
scapula, *n.* Amdohu.
scar, *n.* Osnaze. *vt.* Kaħdeca.
scarce, *a.* To'nana; co'nana; wanica; teħika
scarcely, *adv.* Ki'taŋħ; ki'taŋseħ.
scarceness, *n.* Wanica; wokitaŋ.
scarcity, *n.* Wanica; oteħika.
scare, *vt.* 1. Yuśiŋyeya. 2. Ḣamya: *scare off the birds.*
scarecrow, *n.* Waħamya hde'pi.
scarf, *n.* Nakpiyutake.
scarify, *vt.* Bahoŋhoŋ; we icu.
scarless, *a.* Osnaze wanica.
scarlet, *a.* Du'ta; śa'żi.
scarry, *a.* Osnaze o'ta.
scat, *interj.* Śi'śi; huŋktiya.
scathe, *vt.* Ihaŋgya.
scathing, *pa.* Waihaŋgye; okokipe.
scatter, *vt.* 1. Kadada; kada eħpeya: *scatter seeds.* 2. Yumdeca; enana iyayewicaya: *scatter the enemy.* 3. Enana eħpeya; ihaŋgya: *scatter my hopes. vi.* Enana yapi; omdecahaŋpi.

scattered, *pa.* Obdecahaŋ ; a'bekiya.
scattering, *pa.* Enanakiya ; i'cikdekdeġa.
scatteringly, *adv.* Enanakiya.
scavenger, *n.* Ta'kušica e'yaȟpeya.
scene, *n.* Wowaŋyake ; wopazo.
scenery, *n.* Owaŋyake.
scent, *vt.* O'mna. *n.* Womna.—*Keen scented,* womnaka.
scepter, *n.* Caŋ'ȟpi ; itaŋcaŋ tacaŋȟpi ; sagye.
schedule, *n.* I'ciyazaowapi.
scheme, *n.* 1. Wowiyukcaŋ : *to form a scheme.* 2. Caŋkuyetoŋ owapi. *vt.* Wi'yukcaŋ ; naȟmaŋ kuwa.
schemer, *n.* Wakcaŋka.
scheming, *pa.* Wakcaŋka ; kuwas'a.
schism, *n.* Womdeca.
schismatic, *a.* Wayumdeca.
scholar, *n.* 1. Wayawa ; waoŋspekiyapi : *how many scholars.* 2. Tu'we wowapi wayupika : *our minister is a fine scholar.*
scholarly, *a.* Ksa'pa ; waoŋspeka.
scholarship, *n.* 1. Taku onspe : *a man of great scholarship.* 2. Wayawa ki'cicažužupi.
school, *n.* Wayawapi ; wayawapi optaye : wooŋspe ocaže. *n.* Hoġaŋ optaye. *vt.* Oŋspekiya.
school-boy, *n.* Wayawa hokšidaŋ.
school-dame, *n.* Waoŋspekiya wiŋ'yaŋ.
school-days, *n. pl.* Wayawa aŋpetu.
school-district, *n.* Makoce tiŋ'skoya oyawatipi waŋži yuhapi.
school-fellow, *n.* Kici wayawa.
school-girl, *n.* Wayawa wiciŋcana.
school-hour, *n.* Wayawa ehantu.
school-house, *n.* Wayawatipi.
schooling, *n.* Waoŋspekiyapi.
school-master, *n.* Waoŋspekiya.
school-mate, *n.* Kici wayawa.
school-mistress, school-ma'm, *n.* Wayawa wiŋ'yaŋ.
school-teacher, *n.* Waoŋspekiya.
school-teaching, *n.* Waoŋspekiyapi.
schooner, *n.* Wi'tawata.
schottish, *n.* Wacipi ho.
science, *n.* Wooŋspe ; wosdonye.
scientific, *a.* Wasdonye ; ksa'pa.
scientifically, *adv.* Okiksamya.
scimiter, *n.* Ma'zasagye.
scintillate, *vi.* Pe'ta kpa'kpa.
scion, *n.* Obaksa ; ciŋca.
scissors, *n.* Wiyušda ; iyušda ci'stiŋna.
scoff, *vi.* Iȟaȟa. *n.* Wawiȟaȟapi.
scoffer, *n.* Wawiȟaȟa.
scoffingly, *adv.* Wawiȟaȟaya.
scold, *vt.* Ki'ġe ; iyopeya. *n.* Wakiġes'a.
scoop, *vt.* Icu ; kapta ; kakam icu ; yuškopa. *n.* Wi'captetaŋka.
scope, *n.* Ta'ku kapi ; okiciyukaŋpi.
scorch, *vt.* ·Guya ; adosya. *To be scorched,* ġu.
scorching, *pa.* Ka'ta ; ġuġuya.
score, *n.* 1. Obaġo ; oicazo. 2. Wikcemna noŋpa. *vt.* Baġo ; icaġo ; icazo.
scorn, *n.* Wowaȟtedašni ; wowiȟa. *vt.* Waȟtedašni ; aktašni.
scorner, *n.* Wawiȟaȟa ; waaktašni.
scornful, *a.* Waȟtedašni.
scornfully, *adv.* Waȟtedašniyaŋ.
scorpion, *n.* 1. Waŋmduška. 2. Icapsiŋte pespesto.
Scotch, *n. pr.* Waziyata Sagdaša.
scoundrel, *n.* Waȟtešni.
scour, *vt.* 1. Payeza ; pašdušduta : *scour knives.* 2. O'waŋcaya ode ; omani. *vi.* 1. Wapašduta ; wakažo.
scourge, *n.* 1. Icapsiŋte : *he made a scourge.* 2. Wokakiže.
scout, *n.* Toŋweya. *vt.* Iȟaȟa.
scowl, *vi.* Itešinkiya.

scrabble, *vi.* Wahutopamani; naȟdaȟdanmani.
scragged, *a.* Ḣ'eȟ'e; pepe.
scraggy, *a.* Ḣ'eȟ'e.
scramble, *vi.* Wahutopa ma'ni.
scranch, *vt.* Yuḳeȟḳeġa; yuȟuȟuġa.
scrap, *n.* Wopte; oyupte; obapte; wokaptapi; oġu. *Scraps of food,* woyaptapi.
scrap-book, *n.* Wotaŋiŋ oyupte okpahi.
scrape, *vt.* Kakiŋca; nakiŋca; yukiŋca; pakiŋta; paḳoġa; paḳeġa; paḳeza; patica, etc. *To scrape (as a turnip),* yuḳoġa.—*To scrape (as mud),* pakiŋta.—*To scrape (as snow from the walk),* katica.—*To scrape (as the feet on the floor),* nakiŋca.—*To scrape (as the hair from a hide),* kakiŋca.—*To scrape (with a grating sound),* yuḳeġa.—*To scrape together,* pahi.
scraper, *n.* Wi'kakiŋce; wi'patica, etc.
scraping, *n.* Wakakiŋca.
scratch, *vt.* Yuȟdata; yuśpuya; yuḳoga; yuġo, etc.—*To scratch (as furniture)* yuġoġo; *(as a ticket)* pażużu; icaġo; *(as a letter)* oȟaŋko owa; *(with the paws)* yuȟdata; naġoġo; *(when itchy)* yuśpuya; yuȟdata.
scrawl, *vt.* Oŋspeśni owa. *n.* Śinya owapi.
scrawler, *n.* Ṭu'we śi'kśin owa.
scrawny, *a.* Śiȟtiŋ; śi'ca.
scream, *vi.* Ṭehowaya; ce'ya; hotoŋ; śicahowaya. *The child screams,* hokśiyopa ce'ya.—*The owl screams,* hiŋyaŋkaġa hotoŋ.—*To scream from fear,* ṭehowaya. *n.* Hotoŋpi; ce'yapi.
screech, *vi.* Ho'piŋza hotoŋ.
screech-owl, *n.* Popotka.
screechy, *a.* Piŋ'za; kiŋ'za.
screen, *n.* 1. O'zaŋpi; kokam hde'pi. 2. Wiyaka iyucaŋ; wi'yucaŋ.—*Screen-door,* capoŋgokeya tiyopa. *vt.* 1. Kokam nakiciżiŋ; akaȟpa; naȟmaŋ. 2. Yucaŋcaŋ.
screenings, *n. pl.* Yucaŋ eȟpeyapi.
screw, *n.* Ma'zayuhbezapi; yuhbezapi; yuhbesoṡtaŋpi. *vt.* Yuhbesokataŋ; yuhomni; yukśiża.
screw-driver, *n.* Oŋ yuhbesoṡtaŋpi.
scribble, *vt.* Tokenciŋciŋ owa.
scribbler, *n.* Tu'we oŋspeśni owa.
scribe, *n.* Wowapikaġa. *vi.* Icazo; owa.
scrimmage, *n.* Okicize.
scrimp, *vt.* Yuptecedaŋ.
scrip, *n.* 1. Wowapi oŋ wayuhapi; makocewowapi. 2. Paŋbotka.
script, *n.* Napeoŋkaġapi iyecen ma'zaebdepi.
Scriptures, *n. pl.* Wowapi Wakaŋ.
scrofula, *n.* Tahupopi woyazaŋ.
scroll, *n.* Wowapi opehe.
scrub, *vt.* Yużaża; owaŋka yużaża. *n.* Ecaciḳana; hu'na.
scrubby, *a.* Icaġeceśni; śi'ca.
scruple, *n.* 1. Woohoda; waceṭuŋhdapi. 2. Otkeute ci'stiŋna. *vi.* He'cetuśnida.
scrupulous, *a.* 1. He'cetuśni eciŋs'a. 2. Owotaŋna; taŋ'yaŋ awaciŋ.
scrupulously, *adv.* Ohodaya.
scrutinize, *vt.* Amdeza.
scrutinizer, *n.* Waamdeza.
scud, *vi.* Hiyaya.
scuffle, *vi.* Kiciyusecoŋ.
scull, *vt.* Uŋzeta watopa.
sculptor, *n.* Iŋ'yaŋ wapaġo.
sculptress, *n.* Wiŋ'yaŋ wapaġo.
sculpture, *n.* Wapaġopi.
scum, *n.* 1. Taġe: *the scum rises.* 2. Ta'kuśni; tuwetaŋiŋśni.

scurf, *n.* ·Gaŋġeca.
scurrilous, *a.* Śi'ca ; iśica.
scurvy, *n.* Taŋcaŋ po'pi.
scuttle, *n.* 1. Makacaḣdi woknake : wakiśkokpa. 2. Awakeyapi oḣdoka.
scythe, *n.* Peżiicaśda (napiŋyuŋ).
sea, *n.* Miniwaŋca. *At sea,* miniwanca ekta uŋ ; nu'ni.
sea-beach, *n.* Miniwaŋca huta.
sea-board, *n.* Miniwaŋca kahda.
sea-breeze, *n.* Miniwaŋca tate.
sea-captain, *n.* Wi'tawata itaŋcaŋ.
sea-chart, *n.* Miniwaŋca owapi.
sea-coast, *n.* Miniwaŋca opapuŋ.
sea-faring, *a.* Miniwaŋca omanis'a.
sea-girt, *a.* Miniwaŋca aohomni.
seal, *vt.* Apuspe ; nataka ; yuśtaŋ. *n.* 1. Wi'puspe : *the king's seal.* 2. Miniwaŋca wawaha.
sealing-wax, *n.* Wowapi wi'puspe.
seam, *n.* Okaġeġe ; o'kibe.
seaman, *n.* Wi'tawata wicaśta.
seamless, *n.* Okaġeġe wanica.
seamstress, *n.* Wakaġeġe wiŋ'yaŋ.
sea-otter, *n.* Miniwaŋca ptaŋ.
sear, *vt.* ·Guya ; śniś'ya.
seared, *pa.* ·Gu ; śniża.
search, *vt.* Akita ; ode ; en ode : amdeza. *The sheriff searched the house,* waoyuspa tiode. *n.* Waodepi.
searchable, *a.* Odepica.
searcher, *n.* Waode ; oŋ waodepi.
searching, *pa.* Anaḣbepicaśni ; pe'sto ; wasdonya.
search-warrant, *n.* Waodepi wowapi.
sea-room, *n.* Ocaŋnata ; okatoŋyaŋ.
sea-sickness, *n.* Paŋtaŋptaŋ iwayazaŋpi.
season, *n.* O'maka ; makoŋcaġe ; maka ; aŋpetu to'na ; tohaŋyaŋ. —*A wet season,* omaka maġażus'a.—*In season,* iyehan.—*Out of season,* iyehantuśni. *vt.* 1. Wa'payeton ; icahiya : *season food.* 2. Pusya ; yuwiyeya : *season lumber.*
seasonable, *a.* Iyehantu ; i'yaciŋyaŋ.
seasonably, *adv.* Iyehaŋyaŋ.
seasoned, *pa.* Pu'za ; yusutapi.
seat, *n.* Caŋakaŋyakapi ; oiyotaŋke ; oyaŋke. *Church seats,* ti'piwakaŋ caŋ'akaŋyaŋkapi. —*A country seat,* wożupi oyaŋke. *vt.* 1. I'yotaŋgkiya : *seat the people.* 2. Akaŋyaŋkapi ka'ġa : *seat the church.*
sea-worthy, *a.* Miniwaŋca en yepica.
secede, *vi.* Tokaŋ ya.
secession, *n.* Ihdutokaŋpi.
seclude, *vt.* Naḣmaŋ ; nataka.
seclusion, *n.* Wonaḣbe.
second, *a.* Inoŋpa ; icinoŋpa ; i'yokihe. *The second floor,* owaŋka icinoŋpa. *n.* 1. Okoka ; wi'hiyayedaŋ ko'ka. 2. I'yokihe na'żiŋ. 3. (*Mus.*) Ho o'kihe. *vt.* O'kiya. *Second the motion,* iapi o'kiya.
secondarily, *adv.* I'yokiheya ; ko'ya.
secondary, *a.* O'kihe ; icinoŋpa.
second-hand, *a.* 1. Taŋni ; waŋna uŋ'pi ; *second-hand clothing.* 2. I'yokihe ; a'tayedaŋśni.
secondly, *adv.* Inoŋpa.
second-rate, *a.* I'yokihe waśte.
secrecy, *n.* Wonaḣbe.
secret, *a.* Naḣmaŋpi ; naḣmaŋ sdonyapi. *n.* Wonaḣbe ; iśnana sdonyapi.
secretary, *n.* Wowapi kaḣkiyapi. 2. O'kihe itaŋcaŋ : *secretary of war.* 3. Wowapi ahna ka'ġapi.
secrete, *vt.* 1. Naḣmaŋ ; anaḣmaŋ. 2. Ka'ġa : *secrete bile.*
secretion, *n.* Toŋyaŋ ; toŋ ka'ġa.
secretive, *a.* Naḣbes'a.
secretiveness, *n.* Waanaḣmaŋpi.

secretly, *adv.* Naḣmana; anaḣbeya.
secretness, *n.* Wonaḣbe; naḣmaŋpi.
sect, *n.* Okodakiciye oṡpaye.
sectarian, *a.* Oṡpaye ta'wa iyotaŋda.
sectarianism, *n.* Iṡnaiçidapi.
section, *n.* 1. Obaṡpe; obapte; oŋṡpa; oyuksa; iyokise. 2. (*Gram.*) Woeye; optapi. 3. (*Surv.*) Obaṡpe; makaiyutapi 640.
sectional, *a.* Oŋṡpana en e'waciŋ.
secular, *a.* Ikce; wocekiye wicoḣaŋṡni. *Secular music,* ikceodowaŋ.
secularize, *vt.* Yuikceka; ikce ka'ġa.
secure, *a.* Okopeṡni; wi'kopeṡni. *vt.* 1. Sutaya hna'ka; sutaya yu'za; kaṡka: *secure the prisoner.* 2. Suta ikoyaka: *secured by mortgage.* 3. Icu; ta'waya; oyuspa.
securely, *adv.* Okopeṡniyaŋ.
security, *n.* 1. Wokokipeṡni: *dwell in security.* 2. Woyusuta; woyuha kaṡkapi; wokaṡke: *on security.* 3. Kici wowapi oŋ ihdaṡkapi. 4. Woyuha kaṡkapi wowapi.
sedan, *n.* Caŋ'akaŋyaŋkapi akiyuhapi.
sedate, *a.* Inina uŋ; waawaciŋ.
sedentary, *a.* O'hiŋni i'yotaŋka uŋ.
sediment, *n.* Maka cetetahaŋ.
sedition, *n.* Wakipażiŋpi.
seditious, *a.* Wakipażiŋs'a; oyate wayuṡkiṡkapi.
seduce, *vt.* Ta'ku ṡi'ca en iyutaŋye; hmuŋ'ka. hna'yaŋ; i'naḣmaŋ.
seducer, *n.* Wiinaḣbe.
seduction, *n.* Wawiyutaŋ; wiinaḣmaŋpi.
seductive, *a.* Iyutaŋye.
sedulous, *a.* O'hiŋni ecoŋ; mdiheca.
see, saw, seen, *vt.* 1. Waŋyaka; iṡta oŋ waŋyaka: *I see a house.* 2. Iyukcaŋ, sdonya; tawaciŋ oŋ waŋyaka; okaḣniġa: *I can't see what he wants.* *vt.* Toŋwaŋ; wawaŋyaka. *See into; see through,* okaḣniġa.—*See to; see about,* en e'toŋwaŋ. *n.* Woawaŋyake; wokicoŋze.
seed, *n.* 1. Su: *apple seed.* 2. Ciŋca: *the seed of Abraham.* 3. Wożupi; su ożupi. *vi.* Sutoŋ; su icaġa. *vt.* Ożu; kadada.
seed-corn, *n.* Wamnaheza ożupi kta.
seeder, *n.* Oŋ aġuyapisu ożupi.
seed-time, *n.* Wożupi iyehantu.
seedy, *a.* 1. Su o'ta. 2. Taŋni ḣ'eḣ'e.
seeing, *conj.* He'cen; he'oŋ.
seek, sought, *vt.* Akita; ode; ihni; ciŋ. *Seek after, seek for,* akita.
seeker, *n.* Waode; wi'hni.
seem, *vi.* Se'ca; se'ececa; iteka.
seeming, *pa.* Se'ca; akapataŋhaŋ.
seemingly, *adv.* Se'ececa; taŋiŋyaŋ.
seemly, *adv.* Iyecenya; iyokipiya. *a.* Iyececa; taŋ'yaŋ.
seen, *pp.* of SEE.
seer, *n.* Wakcaŋka; waayate.
seersucker, *n.* Miniḣuha hdeze.
seesaw, *n.* Oŋ nakicihuhuzapi. *vi.* Nawaŋkankaniyeiçiya.
seethe, *vt.* Ohaŋ. *vi.* Ipiġa.
segment, *n.* Oŋṡpa; obakse.
seine, *n.* Ho; oŋ hoġaŋ yuzepi.
seizable, *a.* Iyaḣpayepica.
seize, *vt.* Yu'za; iyaḣpaya.
seizing, *n.* Iyaḣpayapi; yu'zapi.
seizure, *n.* Icupi; iyaḣpayapi.
seldom, *adv.* Wan'waŋcadaŋ; enana.

select, *a.* Kaȟniġapi; waŝte pahipi. *vt.* Kaȟniġa; kaȟniȟ icu.
selection, *n.* Wakaȟniġapi; pahipi.
self, *a.* Iyeȟca; iye i'yatayedaŋ; -ȟca; -iç̣i-; -hd-; waŝteiç̣idapı. *A man's self,* wicaŝta iye a'tayedaŋ. — *Myself,* miyeȟca. — *Yourself,* niyeȟca. — *Self-support,* ihduhapi.—*Self-love,* waŝteiç̣idapi.
self-abased,*a.* Iḥduhukuya.
self-abused, *a.* Ŝicaya ecaiç̣icoŋ.
self-action, *a.* Iyeciŋka ecoŋ.
self-begotten, *a.* Iye iç̣icaġa.
self-conceited, *a.* Ksapeiç̣ida.
self-condemnation, *n.* Ihdacopi.
self-confidence, *n.* Okihiiç̣idapi.
self-conscious, *a.* Sdoniç̣ida; kiksuya.
self-contradiction, *n.* Wicakeŝniiç̣iyapi.
self-control, *n.* Caŋte ihduhapi.
self-convicted, *a.* Ihdaco.
self-culture, *a.* Waoŋspeiç̣iciyapi.
self-deceit, *n.* Iç̣ihnayaŋpi.
self-defense, *n.* Anaicikŝiŋpi.
self-denial, *n.* Waipiiç̣idapi.
self-destruction, *n.* Ihaŋgiç̣iyapi.
self-discipline, *n.* Ihdaoŋspepi.
self-distrust, *n.* Waciŋiç̣iyeŝni.
self-educated, *a.* I'ye ihdaoŋspe.
self-esteem, *n.* Wamnaiç̣idapi.
self-evident, *a.* Iyeciŋka taŋiŋ.
self-examination, *n.* Aiç̣imdezapi.
self-government, *n.* Oyateihduhapi.
self-indulgence, *n.* Iyowiŋiç̣iyapi.
self-interest, *n.* I'ye awaiç̣iciŋ.
selfish, *a.* Iŝnana awaiç̣iciŋ.
selfishness, *n.* Oȟaŋŝicapi.
self-made, *a.* I'ye okihiiç̣iya.
self-murder, *n.* Iç̣iktepi.
self-possessed, *n.* Tawaciŋ hduha; inihaŋŝni.
self-praise. *n.* Iḥdataŋpi.
self-preservation, *n.* Niiç̣iyapi.
self-reliant, *a.* I'ye waciŋiç̣iya.
self-reproach, *n.* Iç̣ibapi.
self-respect, *n.* Taŋyaŋuŋwaciŋpi.
self-righteous, *a.* Owotaŋna iç̣ida.
self-same, *a.* Heeȟca.
self-satisfied, *a.* Iyokipiiç̣iya.
self-sufficient, *a.* Okihiiç̣ida.
self-taught, *a.* Iye oŋspeiç̣ici ya.
self-torture, *n.* Kakiŝiç̣iyapi.
self-willed, *a.* Tawaciŋ suta.
sell, sold, *vt.* 1. Wi'yopeya; wicaḳu. *I sold my land,* makoce mitawa wi'yopewaya. 2. Hna'yaŋ. *n.* Wohnaye.
seller, *n.* Wi'yopeya.
selvage, *n.* Opapuŋ.
selves, *pl.* of SELF.
semblance, *n.* Iyececa.
semi-, *prefix.* Haŋke; haŋkeya.
semi-annual, *n.* Waniyetu haŋke.
semi-barbarous, *a.* Iyokise ikceuŋpi.
semicolon, *n.* Oehnake haŋke.
semifluid, *a.* Tiktica.
seminary, *n.* Woonspe waŋkantu.
semi-savage, *a.* Ḣaŋke watoghda.
semitone, *n.* Hoiyadapi haŋke.
senate, *n.* Wicaȟca omniciye.
senator, *n.* Wicaȟca omniciye o'pa.
send, sent, *vt.* 1. Yeŝi: *send George.* 2. Yeya: *send a letter.* 3. Ḳu; hiyuya: *God sent a rain.* 4. Iyayeya: *send them out.*—*Send for,* wahoya.
sender, *n.* Hiyuya; uŝi.
senior, *n.* 1. Tokapa; ehaŋna ecoŋ. 2. Wooŋspe Waŋkantu waniyetu ehake yawapi.
sensation, *n.* 1. Kiksuyapi; osdonyapi: *a sensation of cold.* 2. Woyuȟica; woawaciŋ: *the sensation caused by his speech.*
sensational, *a.* Wayuȟica; wahnaŝkiŋyaŋ.
sense, *n.* Wowiyukcaŋ; woawaciŋ; wosdonye; ka'pi; oŋ wasdonyapi.—*Common sense,* eca wasdonyapi.—*Moral sense,* wowaŝte sdonyapi.—*No sense of*

the kindness, ta'ku waŝte ecakicoŋpi wasdonyapiŝni.— *The five senses are seeing, hearing, smelling, tasting, feeling :* oŋ wasdonyapi za'ptaŋ kiŋ de'na ee, wawaŋyakapi, wanaȟoŋpi, waomnapi, wautapi ḳa wayutaŋpi.

senseless, *a.* 1. Kiksuyeŝni. *He fell senseless,* kiksuyeŝni hiŋȟpaya. 2. Waciŋtoŋŝni : *a senseless driver.* 3. Witkotkoka ; ksapeŝni.

senselessly, *adv.* Witkotkoya.

sensibility, *n.* 1. Wokiksuye : *the arm loses its sensibility.* 2. Wawiciyapi ; wasdonkiciyapi. 3. Wokaȟtake.

sensible, *a.* 1. Waciŋtoŋ ; ksa'pa : *a sensible woman.* 2. Sdonya ; wakaȟtaka.

sensibly, *adv.* Waciŋksamya; taŋ'yaŋ ; taŋiŋyaŋ.

sensitive, *a.* Wakaȟtakeca ; wopanica ; canwaŋka.

sensual, *a.* Wicaceȟpi ; wicaceȟpi wocaŋtiheye ; wiciŋs'a.

sensuous, *a.* Wicaceȟpi iyutaŋye.

sent, *imp.* SEND.

sentence, *n.* 1. Wowiyukcaŋ ; tawaciŋ ; oie : *my sentence is for war.* 2. (*Gram.*) Woeye : *a complete sentence.* 3. (*Law*) Woyaco ; woyasu. *vt.* Yaco ; yasu : *the judge sentenced him to death.*

sentiment, *n.* Tawaciŋ ; wicotawaciŋ ; woawaciŋ ; wowiyukcaŋ.

sentimental, *a.* Waawaciŋ ; waaceya.

sentimentally, *adv.* Awaciŋyaŋ.

sentinal, *n.* Akicitanaẑiŋ ; awaŋyagnaẑiŋ.

sentry, *n.* Akicitanaẑiŋ.

separable, *a.* Yuŝpepica.

separate, *vt.* Yukinukaŋ ; yutokaŋ ; yuŝpa ; tokaŋ e'hde. *vi.* A'kipamiyaya ; ksa. *a.* Kinukaŋ ; i'ciyowaẑaŝni ; i'cikoyakeŝni.

separately, *adv.* Kinukaŋkiya ; waŋẑikŝi ; hdakeya.

separation, *n.* Yukinukaŋ uŋ'pi.

separator, *n.* Wayukinukaŋ ; wayucaŋ ; wayueci.

September, *n. pr.* Wi'inapciŋwaŋka ; Psiŋ'hnaketuwi.

sepulcher, *n.* Wicaȟapi ; wicahnakapi.

sepulchral, *a.* Wicaȟapi.

sequel, *n.* Ta'ku ihaŋke yaŋke.

sequence, *n.* Ta'ku ikoyake.

seraph, *n.* Maȟpiyaohnihde.

seraphic, *a.* Maȟpiyatase ; waŝteȟca.

sere, *a.* Ŝni'ẑa.

serenade, *n.* Haŋyen kidowaŋpi. *vt.* Adowaŋ.

serene, *a.* Amdakedaŋ.

serenely, *adv.* Amdagyena.

serenity, *n.* Woamdakena.

serf, *n.* Wayaka ; wicaŝta maka ikoyag ta'wayapi.

serge, *n.* Miniȟuhahbeze.

sergeant, *n.* Akicitawicapasi.

sergeant-at-arms, *n.* Akicita tiawaŋyagkiyapi.

serial, *n.* Oŋŝpaŝpa oyakapi.

series, *n.* I'ciyokihe.

serious, *a.* 1. Ḳe'za ; iȟaŝni uŋ. *Of serious manner,* oȟaŋ ḳe'za. 2. Wowicake ; woawaciŋ. 3. Teȟike ; okokipe ; iȟapicaŝni : *a serious illness.*

seriously, *adv.* Teȟiya ; okokipeya ; wicakeya.

seriousness, *n.* Woawaciŋ ; woohoda.

sermon, *n.* Wowahokoŋkiye ; wicaŝtawakaŋ tawowahokoŋkiye.

sermonize, *vi.* Wowahokoŋkiye ka'ġa.

serpent, Waŋmduŝka.

serpentine, *n.* Waŋmduŝka se. *n.* Iŋ'yaŋsda.

servant, *n.* Wowidake; *Y.* wowaśi.
servant-girl, *n.* Wiŋ'yaŋ ookiye.
serve, *vt.* 1. Ḣtani; ḣtakini; o'kiye: *serve two masters.* 2. Woḳu; woyute iyaza a'ya: *serve the meat.* 3. Uŋ'piwaśte: *this will serve for a seat.* 4. Ecakicoŋ; kuwa: *he served me well.* —*To cause to serve,* wowidagya. —*To serve a writ,* waoyuspa wowapi ki'ciyawa. *vi.* Wowidake uŋ; uŋpiwaśte.
service, *n.* 1. Woḣtani; wowaśi; wowidake: *God requires your service.* 2. Woecoŋ; wocekiye: *the burial service.* 3. Wawokiyapi: *of great service.* 4. Icuwa: *a communion service.*
servile, *a.* Wowidakese; wowidake; iye tawaciŋ uŋ'śni.
servitude, *n.* Wowidake.
session, *n.* 1. Omniciye waŋżi; oeyotaŋke. *The session of Congress,* wa'kiyapi oeyotaŋka de. 2. Omniciye. 3. (*Presbyterian Church*) Huŋkayapi omniciye.
sess-pool, *n.* Makoḣdoka (oḣna miniśica eḣpeyapi).
set, *vt.* 1. E'hde; e'ḣnaka; hde: *I do set my bow in the cloud.* 2. Ecoŋkiya; -ki'ya. *Set him to thinking,* awaciŋkiya.—*Set him to work,* ḣtanikiya. 3. Sutaya e'hde; śkaŋśkaŋśni e'hde: *set the posts.* 4. Cażeyata; ka; kaḣniġa: *set a price.* 5. Ecen e'hde: *set the clock.* *n.* Żu. *Set with jewels,* iŋ'yaŋ teḣika żu'pi.

To set about it, kuwa.—*To set against,* ipataŋ e'hde; śi'cedaka.—*To set a-going,* iyopteya.—*To set a hen,* wakiknakiya.—*To set apart,* iyog e'hde. —*To set a saw,* caŋibaksa hi yukśaŋyaŋ.—*To set aside,* icuŋom e'hde; eḣpeya.—*To set at ease,* kiḣna.—*To set at naught,* ta'kuśnikiya.—*To set a trap,* ma'zaḣtakiyapi e'oŋpa; hmuŋ'ka.—*To set at work,* ḣtanikiya. —*To set by,* teḣiŋda; icuŋom e'hde.—*To set eyes on,* waŋyaka.—*To set forth,* taŋiŋyaŋ e'hde; oyaka; yaotaŋiŋ.—*To set forward,* iyaya; iyopteya.—*To set free,* kiyuśka.—*To set in order,* pikiya; wi'yeya e'ḣnaka. —*To set off a part,* oŋśpa icuŋom e'ḣnaka.—*To set off against,* en ki'ciyawapi kta.—*To set on* (*as a dog*), kuwakiya.—*To set the mind on,* awaciŋ.—*To set one's cap for,* hmuŋ'ka; yu'ze kta kuwa.—*To set on fire,* ideya; yuḣnaśkiŋyaŋ.—*To set on foot,* ecoŋwicakiya; ka'ġa.—*To set out* (*as food*), e'hde.—*To set out* (*as a tree*), huhde.—*To set out to go to,* ekta iyaya. —*To set right,* yuwotaŋna.—*To set the fashion,* oihduże ka'ġa.—*To set the teeth on edge,* hi manaŋka.—*To set the time,* tohantu kaḣniġa.—*To set up a factory,* wokaġetipi ka'ġapi.—*To set up* (*to exalt*), yuwaŋkantu.—*To set up* (*as a mark*), e'hde.—*To set up* (*as a post*), bosdan e'hde.—*To set up type,* ma'zaehde.—*To set up in trade,* wopetoŋpi okihiya.
set, *vi.* 1. Iyaya. *The sun is set,* wi iyaye. 2. Patiŋ; sag a'ya: *wait till the glue sets.* 3. Iyaya; kaduza: *the current sets to the other shore.* 4. Waanażiŋ.—*When the dog sets,* tohan śuŋ'ka waanażiŋ.—*To set about,* kuwa; waŋna ecoŋ.—*To set off,* iyaya.—*To set out for London, London* ekta iyaya.—*To set out in business,* woiçicuwa en iyeiçiya.—*To set to,* en iyeiçiya; ecoŋ.—*To set up* (*one's self*), en

e'içihde; iyayeiçiya. *pa.* 1. Sutaya hde'pi; suta; yuhomnipi teħike: *set in his ways.* 2. I'tokam iwaŋyakapi; kaħ'yuśtaŋpi: *set forms of papers.* *n.* 1. Optaye; obe: *another set of people.* 2. Tawaŋżi; okaħtoŋ: *a set of chairs.*

set-down, *n.* Pamahen iyeyapi.

settee, *n.* Akaŋyakapi haŋ'ska.

setter, *n.* Śuŋ'ka śiyo anażiŋ.

setting, *n.* E'hdepi; żu'pi; hiyaya.

settle, *vt.* 1. En i'yotaŋke; e'ti; ti; makoce icu: *the French settled Canada.* 2. Każużu: *settle your account.* 3. Yumdesya: *settle the water.* 4. Owaŋżi yaŋkekiya; yuwaśte: *settle the minds of the people.* 5. Yuśtaŋ; yaco: *he settled the quarrel.* 6. Sutaya yaŋkekiya; yuhekiya: *settle a minister.* *vi.* 1. I'yotaŋka; owaŋżi i'yotaŋka; tihde: *he settled in the West.* 2. Waciŋtaŋka; he'cetuwaŋżica yaŋka. 3. Iyahe; kun iyahe: *the bees settled.* 4. Kaskin iyaye; kun iwaŋka: *the hay settled.* 5. Amdakedaŋ iwaŋka; asni: *the storm settled.*

settlement, *n.* 1. Wicoti; oyate ti'pi; ti'pi: *the Indian settlement.* 2. Yuśtaŋpi; woyuśtaŋ: *the settlement of the controversy.* 3. Oeyotaŋke.

settler, *n.* 1. Ihdaka ahiyotaŋka; ahiti; woyuśtaŋ; owihaŋke.

settling, *n.* 1. Oeyotaŋke: *the settling of the country.* 2. Kun iwaŋke: *the settling of the house.* 3. Yuśtaŋpi; yuecetupi. 4. Cetete haŋ; maka oiyahe.

seven, *a.* Śakowiŋ.

sevenfold, *a.* Śakowiŋ akihde.

seventeen, *a.* Akeśakowiŋ.

seventeenth, *a.* I'akeśakowiŋ; akeśakowiŋ yuśpapi waŋżi.

seventh, *a.* Iśakowiŋ; śakowiŋ yuśpapi waŋżi.

seventhly, *adv.* Iśakowiŋ.

seventy, *a.* Wikcemna śakowiŋ.

sever, *vt.* Kiyuśpa; yuśpa; yukinukaŋ; yutokaŋ.

several, *a.* 1. Waŋżikśi; to'nana; to'nakeca: *several persons.* 2. To'keca; iyohi: *four several armies.*

severalty, *n.* Taŋ'iyohi; kiyuśpa.

severe, *a.* Teħika; ś'a'keca; ksizeca.

severely, *adv.* Teħiya; tkeya; ni'na.

severity, *n.* Wotcħi; woiyokiśica.

sew, *vt.* Kaġeġe; pasisa. *Sew up,* akaġeġe.

sewer, *n.* 1. Tu'we wakaġeġe. 2. Miniśica woħdoġeca.

sewerage, *n.* Miniśica oyuskepa.

sewing, *n.* Wakaġeġepi; wokaġeġe.

sewing-machine, *n.* Oŋ wakaġeġepi.

sex, *n.* Wica ḳaiś wiŋ'yaŋ.

sexless, *a.* Wiŋ'kta.

sexton, *n.* Ti'piwakaŋ awaŋyaka.

sexual, *a.* Kicicinpi; wica ḳaiś wiŋ'yaŋ okicicuwapi.

shabbily, *adv.* Oŋ'śiħaŋyaŋ; oŋ'śiya.

shabby, *a.* Ḣ'eħ'e; śicaya ihduza; waħteśni.

shack, *n.* Tiśica.

shackle, *vt.* Kaśka; ma'zaikoyake; kaġiya. *n.* Ma'zaicaśke; iśkahumaza.

shad, *n.* Miniwaŋca hoġaŋska.

shade, *n.* 1. O'haŋzi; caŋohaŋzi: *come and sit in the shade.* 2. Samya ka'ġapi (iteowapi ekta). 3. Icahi: *painted a different shade.* 4. Ki'taŋna; ci'stiyedaŋ: *wheat sells a shade higher.* 5. O'zaŋpi: *window shades.* 6. Wanaġi otipi: *shades of the dead.* 7. Ki'taŋna to'keca:

shade of opinion. vt. 1. O'haŋziya ; aohaŋziya : *it shades the garden.* 2. Oŋśpa samya owa : *shade the picture.*

shadeless, *a.* O'haŋzi wanica.

shading, *n.* Samsamya owapi.

shadow, *n.* O'haŋzi ; o'haŋzi hiŋȟpaya ; naġi. *vt.* Aohaŋziya ; o'haŋzi ka'ġa ; o'haŋzi iyecen ihakam uŋ ; kuwa.

shadowy, *a.* O'haŋzi se ; wohnaye.

shady, *a.* O'haŋzi ; aohaŋziyapi.

shaft, *n.* Ihupa ; hucaŋ.

shag, *n.* Hiŋśma.

shagged, *a.* Gaŋġaŋ ; ȟ'eȟ'e.

shaggy, *a.* Hiŋśma ; ȟ eȟ'e.

shake, *vt.* Yucaŋcaŋ ; yuhuhuza ; kacaŋcaŋ ; kahuhuza ; *etc.*—*Shake hands,* napeyuza —*Shake the head,* po'mnamna ; po'ptaŋptaŋ.—*Shake off* (*as dirt from a blanket*), katata.—*Shake off* (*as fruit from trees*), kahna ; kasna.—*Shake the tail,* sicupsaŋpsaŋ *vi.* Caŋcaŋ : *he shook all over. n.* 1. Wocaŋcaŋ ; caŋcaŋpi ; woyuhuhuza : *he had a big shake.* 2. Onasdeca : *a shake in the board.*

shaker, *n.* Oŋ yucaŋcaŋpi.

shaking, *n.* Wocaŋcaŋ.

shaky, *a.* 1. Caŋcaŋ : *shaky hands.* 2. Sdecahaŋ : *a shaky board.*

shale, *n.* Ha ; iŋ'yaŋ ha.

shall, *v. aux.* Kta iyececa ; kte do ; kta.

shallow, *a.* 1. Śbeśni ; pu'zedaŋ ; *Y.* ka'zena : *a shallow stream.* 2. Iwaśtedaŋ śko'pa ; mdaska ; mahentu śni : *a shallow dish.* 3. Haakamyedan ; mahentu śni ; wakaȟdokeśni.

shallow-brained, *a.* Nasuna haakamyedaŋ ; ksapeśni.

shallowness, *n.* Mahentuśni.

shalt, *2d person* of SHALL.

sham, *n.* Wohnaye ; ecaecoŋpi. *a.* Wicakeśni. *vt.* Hna'yaŋ ; koŋ'za ; uŋ'ca.

shame, *n.* Wowiśteca ; iśtecapi ; taŋcaŋ oŋśpa naȟmaŋpi. *vt.* Iśtenya.

shamefaced, *a.* Wi'śteca.

shamefacedly, *adv.* Wi'śtenya.

shamefacedness, *n.* Wi'stecapi.

shameful, *a.* Oŋ iśtecapi iyececa ; wowiśteca ; śi'ca.

shamefully, *adv.* Wi'stenya.

shameless, *a.* Iśteceśni.

shamelessly, *adv.* Iśteceśniyaŋ.

shank, *n.* Humdo ; hu.

shan't, *eq.* to SHALL NOT.

shanty, *n.* Ti'pidaŋ ; ti'pi inaȟni ka'ġapi.

shape, *n.* 1. Okaġe ; kaġopi ; icaġopi : *I don't like the shape.* 2. Oehnake ; e'hnakapi : *he left things in bad shape. vt.* Ka'ġa ; kaskica ; wi'yukcaŋ.

shapeless, *a.* Okaġe wanica ; ka'ġapiśni.

shapely, *a.* Taŋ'yaŋ ka'ġapi.

share, *n.* 1. Oŋśpa ; wopamni ; oyuspe : *give him his share.* 2. Maȟiyumdu hi. *vt.* Oŋśpa ķu ; pamni ; kiyuśpa ; kici yuha.

share-holder, *n.* Oŋśpa ta'waya.

sharer, *n.* Oŋśpayuha ; kici ta'wa.

shark, *n.* Hoġaŋ wicaśa yu'ta ; tu'we wicaśaśni.

sharp, *a.* Pe ; pe'sto ; waciŋksapa ; ksa'pa. — *Sharp contest,* woakinica wohitika. — *Sharp eye,* iśtamdeza.—*Sharp pain,* woyazan icamye.—*Sharp roof,* awakeyapi pe'sto.—*Sharp sand,* wiyaka pepe.—*Sharp tone,* ho waŋkantu ; ho piŋ'za.—*Sharp trader,* wopetoŋ wicaśtaśni.—*Sharp voice,* ho piŋ'za.—*Sharp words,* iapi pe'sto. *n.* Ho'yawaŋkantupi.

sharpen, *vt.* Kapesto ; peya ; yumaŋ; pamaŋ; mdesya. *Sharpen an ax,* oŋspe pamaŋ.—*Sharpen* *a stick*, caŋ kapesto.—*Sharpen the intellect*, tawaciŋ mdesya.

sharper, *n*. Wicaštašni; wicahnayes'a.

sharply, *adv*. Pe'stoya.

sharpness, *n*. Ope; opesto.

sharpshooter, *n*. Waoka.

sharpsighted, *a*. Ištamdeza.

sharpwitted, *a*. Waciŋksapa.

shatter, *vt*. Kamdeca; kamdemdeca. *n*. Wokpaŋka.

shattery, *adv*. Waŋkadaŋ.

shave, *vt*. 1. Kaśda; każipa; kasaŋ; basmi; basku.—*Shave the beard*, putiŋhiŋ kasaŋ.—*Shave off* (*as hair from a hide*) baśda.—*Shave off* (*as the tail of a horse*), basmi.—*Shave off* (*as shavings*), każipa. 2. Haŋke ki; manoŋ. *vi*. Hdasaŋ; *T*. iglaśla. *n*. Wakasaŋ; wakaślapi; wokażipa; wakipi; icażipe.

shaver, *n*. Wakasaŋ; wakis'a; wabotica; hokšidaŋ.

shaving, *n*. Wokażipa; wakażipapi.

shawl, *n*. Iteakaḣpeśina; śina.

Shawnees, *n*. Śawani; *T*. Shawala.

she, *pron*. I'ye (wiŋ'yaŋ ka'pi). *Not generally expressed except for emphasis.*

sheaf, sheaves, *n*. Opaḣte (aġuyapi kaśdapi ka'pi).

shear, *vt*. Yuśda; baśda: *shear the sheep*. *n*. Wi'yuśda.

shearer, *n*. Wakaśda.

shearing, *n*. Wakaśdapi.

sheath, *n*. Isaŋożuha; *T*. mi'naożuha; ożuha.

sheathe, *vt*. Ożuha en iyeya.

sheathed, *pa*. Ożuhatoŋ.

sheathing, *n*. Ożuha; caŋmdaska toka okataŋpi.

shed, *vt*. Yuśna; eḣpeya.—*Shed blood*, we papsoŋ.—*Shed feathers*, śuŋpa.—*Shed horns*, he kapśuŋ.—*Shed leaves*, ape kasna.—*Shed teeth*, hi yapśuŋ.—*Shed water*, mini ohiyuśni. *n*. Awakeyapi; o'haŋzihdepi.—*Cattle sheds*, wanuyaŋpi awakeyapi.

shedding, *n*. Wayuśdapi; śuŋpapi; hiŋ hiŋḣpaya.

sheen, *n*. Wowiyakpa.

sheep, *n*. Ta'ḣiŋcawanuyaŋpi; ta'ḣcaska; ta'ḣcaśuŋka.

sheep-cot, *n*. Ta'ḣcaska acaŋkaśkapi.

sheepfold, *n*. Ta'ḣcaska ti'pi.

sheepish, *a*. Wi'šteca; canwaŋka.

sheep-shearing, *n*. Ta'ḣcahiŋ yuśdapi.

sheep-sorrel, *n*. Waḣpeskuya.

sheer, *a*. Ecaca. *n*. Napapi.

sheet, *n*. 1. Owiŋża ska; miniḣuhaska: *sheets and pillow-slips*. 2. Wowapiska; ape.—*Give me a sheet of paper*, wowapi ska waŋżi maḳu. 3. Omdaska; o'hiye: *a sheet of iron*.

sheeting, *n*. Miniḣuhaska; wakeya; owiŋżaska.

sheik, *n*. Wicaḣca; itaŋcaŋ.

shekel, *n*. Juda tamazaska; ma'zaśa 62½.

shelf, shelves, *n*. Caŋmdaska waahnakapi; caŋmdaska.

shell, *n*. 1. Ha; yaḣuġapiha. 2. Tukiha: *oyster shells*. 3. Ma'zasubomdasyapi; napomyapi. 4. Haakamya; ożuha; opiye. *vt*. 1. Ha eḣpeya: *shell nuts*. 2. Yuśku: *shell corn*. 3. Onapomya: *shell the town*.—*Shell out*, hiyuya. *vi*. Kaŋhe; hbahaŋ: *the wheat shells*.

shell-fish, *n*. Tuki.

shelter, *n*. Waakaḣpe; woinape; o'haŋżi; ti'pi. *Take shelter*, inapa; onapa. *vi*. Akaḣpa; naḣmaŋ. *vi*. Aihdaḣpa.

shelterless, *a*. Ticodaŋ; akaḣpecodaŋ.

shelve, *vt.* Kihnaka; caŋmdaska akan e'hnaka.
shepherd, *n.* Ta'ȟcaskaawaŋyake; waawaŋyake.
shepherdess, *n.* Wiŋ'yaŋ wa'waŋyake.
shepherds-crook, *n.* Wa'waŋyake tasagye.
sheriff, *n.* Wokaśke awaŋyake; waoyuspa.
sherry, *n.* Miniśa (ocaże).
shield, *n.* Wahacaŋka; wowinape. *vt.* Akaȟpa; akaȟpetoŋ.
shift, *vt.* Yutokeca; tokaŋ e'hnaka; yutokaŋ. *vi.* Tokaŋ iyaya; piiçiya. *n.* 1. Yutokaŋpi; opiiçiyapi. 2. Mahenuŋpi.
shiftless, *a.* Oihduha oŋspeśni; wahdusota.
shiftlessness, *n.* Wakpataŋpiśni.
shifty, *a.* Wi'ihduha; mdiheca.
shillalah, *n.* Caŋnaksa.
shilling, *n.* Kaśpapi nom sam okise.
shin, *n.* Husdi.
shine, *vi.* Iyeġa; i'żaŋżaŋ; wiyakpa; okitaŋiŋ. —*Fire shines,* pe'ta i'żaŋżaŋ. —*Fish-scales shine,* hoceśpu wiyakpa.—*Shine in company,* wicota en okitaŋiŋ. *n.* Wowiyakpa; wiiżaŋżaŋ; caŋ'haŋpa pawiyakpapi.
shingle, *n.* Caŋokaȟpa; caŋbakpaŋpi; *Y.* caŋ'naȟpapa. *vt.* 1. Caŋokaȟpa okataŋ. 2. Paha kaśda; basmiŋ.
shingling, *n.* Awakeyapi.
shining, *a.* Iyożaŋżaŋ; wiyakpa; śduśduta; okitaŋiŋ.
shiny, *a.* Wiyakpa.
ship, *n.* Wi'tawata; miniwaŋcawata caŋwakaŋ ya'mni. *vt.* Wa'ta ohna yeya; yeya; hiyuya. *Ship goods,* woyuha yeya.
ship-board, *adv.* Wa'taakan.
ship-master, *n.* Wi'tawata itaŋcaŋ.
shipment, *n.* 1. Iyayeyapi: *the shipment of grain.* 2. Ta'ku iyayeyapi: *a large shipment.*
shipper, *n.* Iyayeya; watohnaka.
ship-shape, *adv.* Taŋ'yaŋ.
shipwreck, *vt.* Wa'takamdeca. *n.* Watihaŋgyapi; wotakuniśni.
shirk, *vt.* Naȟmaŋozikiya.
shirt, *n.* Oŋ'ȟdoȟda; wicauŋpi; *Y.* o'kde; o'kdemahenuŋpi; *T.* oŋ'gloġe.
shirting, *n.* Miniȟuhaska.
shirtless, *a.* O'kdecodaŋ.
shiver, *n.* 1. Wocaŋcaŋ; caŋcaŋpi: *he was in a shiver.* 2. Wokaśdeca; wokpaŋ. *vi.* 1. Caŋcaŋ: *the poor dog shivered.* 2. Mdecahaŋ. *vt.* Kamdeca; yucaŋcaŋ.
shivering, *pa.* Caŋcaŋ.
shiveringly, *adv.* Caŋcaŋyaŋ.
shivery, *a.* Caŋcaŋ; sdesdecahaŋ.
shoal, *a.* Ka'zedaŋ: *shoal water.* *n.* 1. Minikazedaŋ: *the boat stuck on the shoals.* 2. O'ta; akipśapśa hiyeye.
shoaly, *a.* Śbe'śni; ka'zedaŋ.
shoat, *n.* Kukuśedaŋ.
shock, *n.* 1. Woyuś'iŋyaye; taŋ sagṭeyapi. 2. Aġuyapi ópahi *vt.* 1. Yuś'iŋyeya; inihaŋya *you shock me.* 2. Pśuŋka e'hde
shocking, *a.* Woyuś'iŋyaŋ; wowaȟtedaśni.
shockingly, *adv.* Okokipeya; te ȟiya.
shod, *imp.* of SHOE.
shoddy, *n.* Miniȟuha akta ka'gapi; miniȟuha sutaśni.
shoe, *n.* 1. Can'haŋpa: *a fine shoe.* 2. Śakemaza: *a horse shoe.* 3. Ma'zasicu: *a sleigh shoe.* *vt.* Śakeokataŋ; sicuokataŋ.
shoe-black, *n.* Caŋ'haŋpasamya.
shoeblacking, *n.* Caŋ'haŋpaisamya.
shoeless, *a.* Caŋ'haŋpa ni'ca.
shoe-maker, *n.* Caŋ'haŋpakaġa.

shoer, *n.* Ṡakemazaokataŋ.
shone, *imp.* of SHINE.
shoo, *interj.* Ṡi; ṡ.
shook, *imp.* of SHAKE.
shoot. *vt.* 1. Kute; yeya: *shoot an arrow; shoot a gun.* 2. O; en iyeya: *he shot a bear.* 3. Uya; yeya. *Shoot out a bud,* caŋmni waŋ uya.—*Shoot at,* kute.—*Shoot off a gun,* ma'zakaŋ boṡdoka.—*He was shot at,* kutepi.—*He was shot,* o'pi.—*Shoot down,* bowaŋka. *vi.* 1. Ma'zakaŋ ecoŋ; kute; uta: *I heard some one shoot.* 2. Hinaŋpa; uya; icaġa: *the grain shot up.* 3. Dus hiyaya. *The train shot by,* ḣemani dus hiyaya. *n.* 1. Kutepi; okute. 2. Caŋ'uya; caŋadetka: *green shoots.* 3. Ohna yeyapi: *grain shoot.*
shooter, *n.* Wakute; oŋ kutepi.
shooting, *n.* Ma'zakaŋ ecoŋpi; waŋhiŋkpe yeyapi; wakutepi.
shooting=star, *n.* Wicaŋḣpiokiŋyaŋ.
shop, *n.* 1. Ohna wowaṡi ecoŋpi; wokaġetipi. 2. Mazopiye (ohna takuṡniṡni wiyopeyapi) *vi.* Wopetoŋ: *she has gone shopping.*
shop=boy, *n.* Wowaṡihokṡidaŋ; wopetoŋhokṡidan.
shop=keeper, *n.* Mazopiyeyuha.
shop=lifter, *n.* Mazopiye etaŋhaŋ wamanoŋ.
shore, *n.* O'huta; huta; minikahda. *On shore,* hutata.—*Out from shore,* caŋnan.
shorn, *pp.* of SHEAR.
short, *a.* 1. Pte'cedaŋ: *a short stick.* 2. Ci'stiyedaŋ; aṡkayedaŋ: *a short time.* 3. Iyohiṡni; a'okpani.—*Short of provisions,* woyute iyohiṡni. 4. I'tato; itahena; a'okpani.—*Nothing short of killing will do,* kte'pi a'okpani ta'kudaŋ iyecetukteṡni. 5. Oḣaŋko; waciŋko: *a short answer.* 6. (*Cookery*) Napin; waŋ'kadaŋ.—*At short notice,* kohaŋna —*Cut short his speech,* wohdaka yaptecedaŋ. *n.* Pte'cedaŋ. *adv.* Ptenyedaŋ; i'tkoṅsya.
short=breathed, *a.* Niyaptecedaŋ.
short=cake, *n.* Aġuyapi sda'icahiyapi.
short=coming, *n.* Ecenecoŋṡni.
shorten, *vt.* Yuptecedaŋ; yuaokpani. *vi.* Pte'cedaŋ icaġa.
shortening, *n.* 1. Sda; wi'hdi: *no shortening in the cake.* 2. Pte'cedaŋ ka'ġapi: *the shortening of the road.*
short=hand, *n.* Oḣaŋkoowapi.
short=lived, *a.* Ptenyedaŋ ni'pi.
shorty, *adv.* 1. Ecadaŋ: *I will come shortly.* 2. Ptenyedaŋ: *he spoke shortly.*
shortness, *n.* Pte'cedaŋ.
shorts, *n. pl.* Aġuyapiha mdu.
short=sighted, *a.* 1. Ikiyedaŋ ayuta: *short-sighted eyes.* 2. Wi'yukcaŋṡni: *to cheat is short-sighted.*
short=waisted, *a.* Makuptecedaŋ.
shortwinded, *a.* Oniyaptecedaŋ.
Shoshones, *n. pr.* Su'suni; So'soŋna.
shot, *imp.* of SHOOT.
shot, *n.* 1. Sukpaŋna; sucikciḳadaŋ: *load your gun with shot.* 2 Wokute: *he fired twenty shot.* 3. Wakute; kutepi: *a fine shot.*
shot=pouch, *n.* Tasusuoẓuha.
should, *imp.* of SHALL. (Dakota iapi iyececa wanica, qa ieskayapiṡni ecee, tuka wanwaŋcadaŋ ieskapica.) 1. Iyececa. *Should I do it,* ecamoŋ iyececa he. 2. He'cetu. *I should like to go,* mda waciŋ he'cetu. 3. Kiŋhaŋ. *Should it turn cold,* osni hiŋhda kiŋhaŋ.

shoulder, *n.* Hiyete; tapete; amdo. *Put in your shoulder,* hiyeteoŋpa.—*A shoulder of pork,* kukuśe isto. *vt.* Hiyeteoŋpa; ķin.
shoulder-blade, *n.* Amdohu.
shoulder-strap, *n.* Hiyeteaskape.
shout, *vi.* Paŋ; aś'a; ho'taŋiŋ. *Shout at,* kipaŋ. *vt.* Ho'taŋka eya; paŋ'niya. *n.* Paŋ'pi.
shouter, *n.* Paŋ's'a.
shove, *vi.* Pataŋ iyeya; pasdohaŋ iyeya: *shove it away.*
shovel, *n.* Ma'zamdaska. *Fire-shovel,* caḣota oŋ icupi.
show, *vt.* Pazo; yuotaŋiŋ; yuzamni. *Show forth,* yuotaŋiŋ.—*Show him in,* timahen ukiya.—*Show off,* ikpazo. *n.* Wapazopi; wopazo; pazopi; yuotaŋiŋpi.
show-bill, *n.* Tiaskamya yaotaŋiŋpi.
show-case, *n.* Żaŋżaŋ oakaḣpe.
shower, *n.* Wapazo.
shower, *n.* Maġażu; inaḣni maġażu; ḣiŋhe; ohiŋhe. *A shower of meteors,* wicaŋḣpi ohiŋhe. *vt.* Ahiŋheya: *he showered dirt on us.* *vi.* Maġażu; hiŋhaŋ.
shower-bath, *n.* Mniahiŋheyapi.
showerless, *a.* Maġażuwanica.
showery, *a.* Maġażus'a.
show-glass, *n.* Mniomdasiŋ.
showily, *adv.* Wi'taŋtaŋyaŋ.
show-man, *n.* Wapazowicaśta.
showy, *a.* Wowaŋyake; owaŋyagwaśte; wi'taŋtaŋ.
shred, *n.* Miniḣuhaoḣdecahe.
shrew, *n.* Wakiġes'a.
shrewd, *a.* Ksa'pa; wayupika.
shrewdly, *adv.* Wayupiya.
shrewdness, *n.* Wowayupika.
shriek, *vi.* Śicahowaya; ţehowaya: *he shrieked for fear.*
shrieker, *n.* Śicahowayas'a.
shrill, *a.* Piŋ'za; ho'piŋza. *vt.* Yapiŋża. *vi.* Piŋs'hotoŋ.
shrillness, *n.* Wopiŋza.
shrimp, *n.* Ta'ku ma'nina; wicaśta ecacistiŋna.
shrine, *n.* Owacekiye; wopiyewakaŋ.
shrink, *vi.* 1. Natipa; namniġa; ci'stiŋna a'ya: *my moccasins shrank.* 1. (*with a prep.*) Naţuŋka; kokipa; ecoŋkap'iŋ: *he shrunk from speaking.* *vt.* Namniḣya.
shrinkage, *n.* To'ken aokpani.
shrinking, *pa.* Ci'stiŋnaaya; kokipa.
shrinkingly, *adv.* Kokipeya.
shrivel, *vi.* Śni'ża; natipa; sna'ze.
shriveled, *pa.* Śniśniża; pinśpiŋża
shroud, *n.* Śina; oŋ iyapehaŋpi owiŋża. *vt.* Iyapemni; akaḣpa; aoḣaŋziya.
shrub, *n.* Caŋ ci'stiŋna; oteḣi.
shrubbery, *n.* Caŋ cikcistiŋna; waskuyeca hu.
shrubby, *a.* Caŋwopamna; oteḣi.
shrug, *vt.* Taŋnapakiya.
shrunk, *imp.* of SHRINK.
shuck, *n.* Ha; ożuha.
shudder, *vi.* Caŋcaŋ; inihaŋ. *n.* Wocaŋcaŋ; caŋcaŋpi.
shuffle, *vt.* Yuicicahi; yuśkaŋśkaŋ. *vi.* Śkaŋśkaŋ.
shumac, *n.* Caŋżi.
shun, *vt.* Aohomniya; okamna; napa: *shun bad company.*
shut, *vt.* Eceniyeya; ecenicu; nataka. *Shut in,* aonataka; nataka.—*Shut his mouth,* i nataka.
shutter, *n.* 1. Oakpaḣpe; i'ha: *a window shutter.* 2. Tu'we waakaḣpa.
shuttle, *n.* Haḣoŋta ożuha.
shy, *a.* Watoghda; wi'kopa. *To be shy of,* kokipa. *vi.* Napa. *n.* Wonape; okaḣ'oiyeya.
shyly, *adv.* Watoghdaya; wi'śtenya.
shyness, *n.* Wowatoghda.
Siamese, *n.* Si'amwicaśta.

Siberian, *n.* Siberiawicaŝta.
sibilant, *a.* Hosdi.
sibyl, *n.* Wiŋ'yaŋ wa'yate.
Sicilian, *n.* Si'cilywicaŝta.
sick, *a.* Wayazaŋka ; yazaŋ. *Sick of,* hitihda ; ŝi'ceda.
sicken, *vt.* Oyazaŋya. *vi.* Wayazaŋhiŋhda ; hiŋhpaya.
sicker, *a. comp.* Saŋ'pa wayazaŋka.
sickish, *a.* Wayazaŋka se'ca.
sickle, *n.* Isaŋŝkopa ; mi'naŝkopa ; peżiinaksehi.
sickly, *n.* Wayazaŋs'a ; sta'keca.
sickness, *n.* Wowayazaŋ.
side, *n.* 1. Cuwi ; cute. *My side aches,* cuwi mayazaŋ 2. O'huta ; opapuŋ ; cuwi ; obaŝpe.—*On the south side,* itokaġa eciyataŋhaŋ. 3. Eciyataŋhaŋ. *God is on our side.*—*Both sides.* anokataŋhaŋ.—*By the side of,* icahda.—*Chose sides,* anokataŋhan kicicahniġapi. — *On one side,* sanina.—*Side by side,* i'ciyokiheya ; icicahtag. — *Take sides,* o'kiciyapi. —*The other side,* uŋmaŋ eciyataŋhaŋ — *This side,* de'ciyataŋhaŋ.—*The side of a hill,* pahaonaptaŋ.—*Lie on the side* ,taŋmdas waŋka. *a.* Hdakiŋyaŋ ; cuwi eciyataŋhaŋ.—*A side wind,* hdakiŋyaŋ tate. *vi.* Ti'daŋ. *Side with,* kici ti'daŋ.
side=board, *n.* Caŋmdaska wa'hnakapi.
side=glance, *n.* Hdakiŋyaŋ e'toŋwaŋpi.
side=hill, *n.* Ḣuŋ'naptaŋ.
sideling, *a.* Oŋnaptaŋ.
side=saddle, *n.* Wiŋ'yaŋ ŝuŋgawakiŋ.
side=table, *n.* Wa'hnawotapi adehaŋ.
side=view, *n.* Hdakiŋyaŋ waŋyakapi.
sidewalk, *n.* Kahda ocaŋku.
sideways, *adv.* Hdakiŋyaŋ.
sidewind, *n.* Hdakiŋyaŋ tate.
sidewise, *adv.* Hdakiŋyaŋ ; nakeya.
siding, *n.* Ḣemani icuŋom caŋku.
siege, *n.* Onawicatakapi (okicize ekta otoŋwe aohomniyapi ka'-pi) ; ohomni kuwapi.
sieve, *n.* Wi'yucaŋ.
sift, *vt.* Yucaŋ ; yukcaŋ.
sifter, *vt.* Wayucaŋ.
sigh, *vi.* Howaya ; taŋmahen niya. *n.* Howayapi ; ohowaya.
sight, *n.* 1. Wowaŋyake ; *a wonderful sight.* 2. Wawaŋyakapi : *a cloud received him out of their sight; loss of sight.* 3. Iŝta ; wowaŋyake : *in his sight.* 4. Wi'waŋyake : *the gun-sight.* 5. O'ta ; ni'na o'ta. *He made a sight of money,* ma'zaska ni'na o'ta kamna.—*In sight,* taŋiŋyaŋ.—*In sight of,* o'taŋiŋyaŋ. —*Out of sight,* taŋiŋŝni ; i'siŋyaŋ.—*Take sight,* e'pazo. *vt.* Waŋyaka ; taŋiŋyan hi.
sighted, *a.* Wawaŋyake. *Long-sighted,* te'han wawaŋyaka.
sightless, *a.* Wawaŋyakeŝni.
sightly, *a.* Owaŝteca ; okitaŋiŋ.
sight=seeing, *n.* Wawaŋyag omanipi.
sign, *n.* 1. Wa'petokeca ; wowakta ; owe ; wasagkdepi. 2. Wi'-kiyutapi : *talk by signs.* 3. (*Algebra*) Icazopi ; wa'petokeca. *vt.* 1. Owa : *sign your name.* 2. Wi'yuta ; wi'kiyuta.
signal, *n.* Waktakiciyapi ; wowakta. *a.* Okitaŋiŋ : *a signal victory.* *vt.* Iwaktaya ; wi'kiyuta : *he signaled the boat.*
signalize, *vt.* Wa'petogtoŋ ; yutaŋiŋ.
signally, *adv.* O'taŋiŋyaŋ.
signature, *n.* 1. Cażeeiçihnakapi : *I want your signature.* 2. (*Mus.*) Ho wa'petogtoŋpi.

sign-board, *n.* Caŋmdaska caże owapi; caŋmdaska wasaghdepi.
signer, *n.* Cażeoiçiwa.
signet, *n.* Wi'puspe.
signet-ring, *n.* Ma'zanapcupe oŋ apuspapi.
significancy, *n.* Ta'kukapi; wowaś'ake.
significant, *a.* 1. Okitaŋiŋ; wa'petokeca: *a significant look.* 2. Taŋ'ka; waś'aka.
significantly, *adv.* Wapetogya.
signification, *n.* 1. To'ken ka'pi: *the signification of the word.* 2. Yutaŋiŋpi: *repress the signification of joy.*
signify, *vt.* 1. Sdonyekiya; oyaka: *he signified his desire.* 2. Ka; yutaŋiŋ: *it signifies nothing.*
sign-post, *n.* Caŋpasdatapi wowakta.
silence, *n.* Ininauŋpi; woyakeśni uŋ'pi. *interj.* Inina uŋkiya; ayaśtaŋkiya.
silent, *a.* Ininauŋ; inina; owaŋżiuŋ; taŋiŋśni uŋ: *a silent man.*—*A silent letter,* oowa taŋiŋśni uŋ.
silently, *adv.* Inina; a'inina.
silentness, *n.* Woinina.
silk, *n.* 1. Waŋmduśkahiŋ miniḣuha; waŋmduśkahiŋ. 2. Natu; waŋmduśkahiŋ iyececa.
silken, *a.* Stosto; śduśduta.
silkiness, *n.* Wośduśduta; wowiyakpa.
silk-worm, *n.* Waŋmduśka hiŋ ka'ġa.
silky, *a.* Waŋmduśkahiŋ se'ca; wiyakpa; paŋpaŋna.
siliness, *n.* Wowitkotkoka.
silly, *a.* Waciŋtoŋśni; witkotko.
silvan, *a.* Caŋ; pa'ta.
silver, *n.* Ma'zaska; ma'zaska ma'za. *a.* Ma'zaska; ma'zaska iyececa; wiyakpa; ska. *vt.* Ma'zaska apawiŋta; pawiyakpa; ska ka'ġa.
silver-gray, *a.* Ska ḣota.
silver-leaf, *n.* Ma'zaska miniḣuha.
silversmith, *n.* Ma'zaska ma'zakaġa.
silvery, *a.* Ma'zaska iyececa.
similar, *a.* Iyececa; i'akidececa: *a similar house.*—*Similar houses,* ti'pi i'akidececa.
similarity, *n.* Woakidececa.
similarly, *adv.* Iyecen; a'kidecen.
similitude, *n.* Iyecece; woiyecece; wi'yaciŋpi.
simmer, *vi.* Nas'a.
simoon, *n.* Tate ka'ta.
simper, *vt.* Żiżiya iḣa.
simple, *a.* 1. E'cedaŋ: *a simple idea.* 2. Waciŋtoŋśni; ksa'peśni. 3. Wicaḣnayewaciŋśni: *the simple child.*
simple-hearted, *a.* Caŋte e'cedaŋ; waḣtaniwaciŋśni.
simple-minded, *a.* Waawaciŋśni; ksa'pesni.
simpleton, *n.* Waciŋtoŋsni; witkotkoka.
simplicity, *n.* Ośkiśkeśni; waciŋtoŋpiśni.
simplify, *vt.* Yuteḣiśni; yuecedaŋ.
simulate, *vt.* Koŋ'za.
simulation, *n.* Hna'yaŋpi; koŋ'zapi.
simultaneous, *a.* Iyehan.
simultaneously, *adv.* Iyehaŋyaŋ.
simultaneousness, *n.* Woiyehantu.
sin, *n.* Woaḣtani. *vi.* Waḣtani.
since, *adv.* Ehantaŋhaŋ; itahena; iyohakam. *prep.* Ehantaŋhaŋ; hetaŋhaŋ. *conj.* 1. Ehantaŋhaŋ: *since the world began.* 2. He'on etaŋhaŋ; nakaeś; he'oŋ.—*Since love is vain,* ihakiciktapi kiŋ he ta'kuśni kiŋ he'on.
sincere, *a.* 1. Wowicake: *a sincere intention.* 2. E'cedaŋ; wi-

caka; wohnaye ni'ca: *a sincere man.*
sincerely, *adv.* A'wicakehaŋ; awi'cakeya; wicakeya.
sincereness, *n.* Wicakapi; wicahnayaŋpiśni.
sincerity, *n.* Wowicake; wohnaye wanica.
sinecure, *n.* Makoskan wokażużu yuha; ḣtaniśni kicicażużupi.
sinew, *n.* Kaŋ; wi'cuwa; takaŋ.
sinewless, *a.* Kaŋwanica.
sinewy, *a.* Kaŋota; kaŋtaŋka.
sinful, *a.* 1. Waḣtanis'a; waḣtani: *sinful man.* 2. Śi'ca; woaḣtani: *sinful words.*
sinfully, *adv.* Śicaya.
sinfulness, *n.* Śi'ce; wośice; woaḣtani.
sing, *vi.* Dowaŋ; hotoŋ; ḣmuŋ. *vt.* 1. Ahiyaya: *sing a hymn.* 2. Yataŋ; idowaŋ: *sing his deeds.*
singe, *vt.* Hihnu; ġuya.
singer, *n.* Dowaŋwayupika; dowaŋpi.
singing-book, *n.* Wowapi odowaŋ ho ka'ġapi.
singing-man, *n.* Dowaŋ wicaśta.
singing-master, *n.* Dowaŋpi oŋspewicakiya.
singing-school, *n.* Dowaŋpi oŋspewicakiyapi.
singing-woman, *n.* Wiŋ'yaŋ dowaŋs'a.
single, *a.* 1. Waŋżidaŋ: *a single star.* 2. Iśnana: *he single stood.* 3. Iśnana uŋ: *a single man.* *vt.* Kaḣniġa; waŋżi icu.
single-handed, *a.* Napsani; iśnana; taŋśnana.
single-hearted, *a.* Caŋtewaŋżidaŋ; wohnayecodaŋ.
single-minded, *a.* Tawaciŋwaŋżidaŋ.
singleness, *n.* Wowaŋżidaŋ; woiśnana; he'cetuwaŋżica.
singletree, *n.* Caŋwiyutitaŋ.
singly, *adv.* Waŋżikśi; iśnana.
sing-song, *n.* Dowaŋse.
singular, *a.* 1. (*Gram.*) Waŋżidaŋ ka'pi; wiciśnana: *the singular number.* 2. To'keca; wa'petokeca: *of singular appearance.* 3. Iśnana; iyotaŋ; wakapeya.
singularity, *n.* Wowapetokeca; wiciśnana.
singularly, *adv.* Togye; wa'petogya.
einister, *a.* Catkata; eciŋśni.
sink, *vi.* Kun iyaye; mahen iyaye; spaya: *the boat sank.* *vt.* Kun iyayeya; spa'yeya: *sink a ship.*—*Sink a debt,* oicazo yuaokpani.—*Sink a hole,* oḣdoka mahen a'ya.—*Sink money,* ma'zaska awihnuniya.—*Sink the price,* wokażużu a'okpani ka'ġa. *n.* Oṡkokpa; miniṡica tukten eḣpeyapi.
sinker, *n.* Oŋ spayeyapi.
sink-hole, *n.* Miniṡica oṡkokpa.
sinless, *a.* Woaḣtani ni'ca.
sinlessly, *adv.* Woaḣtani waninya.
sinlessness, *n.* Woaḣtani ecawanica.
sinner, *n.* Waḣtanis'a; tu'we śi'ca.
sin-offering, *n.* Woaḣtani wośnapi.
Sioux, *n. pr.* Dakota. *The Sioux nation,* Dakota oyate.
Sioux City, *n. pr.* Otoŋwe Ci'stiŋna; Caŋ'kasdate Iyoḣdoke.
Sioux Falls, *n. pr.* Caŋ'kasdate Ḣaḣa; Ḣaḣe.
sip, *vt.* Yatkaŋ; yazoka; iyoziyatkaŋ. *vi.* Wayatkaŋ. *n.* Woyatke; wonapce.
siphon, *n.* Wi'yuskepa.
sir, *n.* Wicaśta (woyuonihaŋ iapi).
sire, *n.* Atkuku; tu'we ka'ġa. *vt.* Ka'ġa (śuŋgmdoka kapi ece).
siren, *n.* Wiŋ'yaŋ wicaḣmuŋġa; wiŋ'yaŋ wawiyutaŋye.
sirloin, *n.* Tataŋka ce'ca.
sirname, *n.* Wicowazi caże.

sirocco, *n.* Tate ka'ta.
sirup, *n.* Caŋhaŋpitiktica ; haŋpiskuya ; *Y.* tuḣmaġa haŋpi.
sister, *n.* 1. Ta'winoḣtiŋ. *A man's older sister,* taŋkeku.—*My sister,* taŋke ; mitaŋke.—*A man's younger sister,* taŋkśitku.—*My younger sister,* taŋkśi ; mitaŋkśi.—*A woman's older sister,* cuŋ'ku ; cuŋweku.—*My older sister,* micuŋ ; cuŋwe.—*A woman's younger sister,* taŋkaku ; taŋ'ku.—*My younger sister,* taŋka ; mitaŋka.—*They are sisters,* taŋkakiciyapi. 2. Śinasapa wiŋ'yaŋ ookiye ; wiŋ'yaŋ ookiye.
sisterhood, *n.* Wiŋ'yanookiye okodakiciye.
sister-in-law, *n.* (*A man's*), Haŋka ; (*a woman's*), icepaŋ ; (*a woman's husband's brother's wife*), icepaŋśi.
sisterly, *a.* Ta'winoḣtiŋ iyececa ; waoŋśida.
sit, sat, *vi.* 1. I'yotaŋka ; yaŋka. *Sit down,* i'yotaŋka.—*Sit on the log,* caŋkaġa akan yaŋka. 2. Amaŋ ; akikna yaŋka : *the hen sits.* 3. Kipi ; waŋka : *the coat sits well.* 4. Mni'ciya ; hi'yotaŋka. 5. Haŋkikta : *sit up with a sick man.*
site, *n.* Oyaŋke ; ticaġapi makoce.
sitter, *n.* I'yotaŋkes'a ; wakikna yaŋka.
sitting, *pa.* I'yotaŋkahaŋ uŋ. *n.* Oiyotaŋke ; omniciye ; nażiŋśni.
situate, *a.* Yaŋka.
situated, *a.* Yaŋka ; e'hdepi.
situation, *n.* Oyaŋke ; onażiŋ ; ouŋ ; wowaśi ; woḣtani.
six, *a.* Śa'kpe.
sixfold, *a.* Śa'kpe akihde.
sixpence, *n.* (Sagdaśiŋ iapi) Ma'śadaŋ akenom.
six-shooter, *n.* Śa'kpeutapi.
sixteen, *a.* Akeśakpe.
sixteenth, *a.* 1. I'akeśakpe. 2. Akeśakpe yuśpapi waŋżi.
sixth, *a.* 1. Iśakpe : *the sixth pie.* 2. Śa'kpeyuśpapi : *one sixth of a pie.*
sixthly, *adv.* Iśakpe.
sixty, *a.* Wikcemnaśakpe.
sizable, *a.* Ki'taŋna taŋ'ka.
size, *n.* 1. Tiŋ'skokeca ; oiyute. 2. Coŋ'peśka. *vt.* 1. Coŋ'peśka iuŋ. 2. Oiyute ecekcen e'hnaka.
sized, *a.* Oiyute : *large sized.*
sizing, *n.* Coŋ'peśka.
sizy, *a.* Tiktica ; tka'pa.
sizzle, *vi.* Sdi ; sdi'sdi.
sizzling, *n.* Wosdisdi.
skate, *n.* Ma'zaokazekiçuŋpi. *vi.* Okazekiçuŋ.
skater, *n.* Tu'we okazekiçun.
skedaddle, *vi.* Nażica ; mde'ześni napa.
skein, *n.* (Haḣoŋta) Okakśa.
skeleton, *n.* 1. Huḣa : *the skeleton of a man.* 2. Owohdake iapi huḣa.
skeptic, *n.* Waceṭuŋhda ; Wowapiwakaŋ wicadaśni.
skeptical, *a.* Waceṭuŋhda.
skepticism, *n.* Waceṭuŋhdapi.
sketch, *vt.* Inaḣni owa ; inaḣni icazo ; ptenyedaŋ oyaka. *n.* Inaḣni owapi.
skew, *a.* Ḣmiŋ ; nake. *vt.* Yuḣmiŋ.
skid, *n.* Caŋ'apasdohaŋpi.
skiff, *n.* Caŋmdaskawatadaŋ.
skilful, *a.* Wayupika ; wakiḣoka.
skilfully, *adv.* Wayupiya.
skilfulness, *n.* Wowayupika.
skill, *n.* Wowayupika ; wokaḣniġe.
skilled, *a.* Waoŋspeka ; wayupika.
skillet, *a.* Ce'ġamdaska.
skim, *vt.* Kaġe ; wihdi icu. *vi.* Kaśduśdun iyaye.
skimmer, *n.* Wi'caġe.

skim-milk, *n.* Asaŋpiwihdiicupi.
skimmings, *n.* Taġe; wakaġepi.
skin, *n.* Ha; uka: *a dog skin.* *vt.* Ha yu′za; baġapa; ha basku. *Skin a hog,* kukuśe ha yu′za.—*Skin potatoes,* mdo ha basku.
skin-deep, *a.* Haakamyedaŋ.
skinless, *a.* Hacodaŋ.
skinny, *a.* Ha cee.
skip, *vi.* Psi′psin ya; ipsica. *Skip over,* apsica. *vt.* Yuśna; auŋyaŋiyaye; ecoŋśni. *n.* Oipsica; waŋkan iyeiçiyapi.
skipper, *n.* 1. Ipsices′a; wacis′a. 2. Wamdudaŋ psi′psica.
skipping, *pa.* Psi′psin ya; psi′psica.
skipping-rope, *n.* Haħoŋtawiyupsice.
skirmish, *n.* Toŋweya kicizapi. *vi.* Toŋweya kicis śkaŋ.
skirmisher, *n.* Toŋweya akicita.
skirt, *n.* Saŋksanica: *she wore a blue skirt.* 2. Opapuŋ: *in the skirts of town.* *vt.* Opapuŋ ka′ġa; aohomniya. *vi.* Ohomni uŋ.
skittish, *a.* Śke′he; watogkda.
skittishly, *adv.* Śkeheya.
skulk, *vi.* Naiciħmaŋ uŋ; ihdonica.
skulker, *n.* Naiçiħbesa; ku′ża.
skull, *n.* Pahu.
skull-cap, *n,* Wapośtaŋoŋżiŋca.
skunk, *n.* Maŋka.
sky, *n.* Maħpiyato; maħpiya.
sky-blue, *a.* Maħpiyato.
sky-high, *adv.* Maħpiya hehaŋwaŋkantu.
skylight, *n.* O′żaŋżaŋhdepi awakeyapi ekta.
sky-rocket, *n.* Caħdi waŋkankan bopomyapi.
skyward, *a.* Maħpiya ektakiya.
slab, *n.* Caŋmdaska ha; iŋ′yaŋ mdaska.
slabber, *vi.* I′mnitaġa; i′mniśtaŋ.
slab-sided, *a.* Niġemdaska.
slack, *a.* Ţiŋ′ześni; iwaśtedaŋ; ħaŋhi. *adv.* Ţiŋsayaśni; to′ken ciŋ′yaŋ. *n.* Ţiŋ′ześni hehaŋyaŋ.
slacken, *vi.* Yuţiŋześniaya: *the rope slackens.* 2. Kun ya; huŋ′keśniaya. 3. Mduwahe: *lime slackens.* *vt.* 1. Yuţiŋześni: *slacken the rope.* 2. O′cim iwaśtedaŋ ya: *he slackens his pace.* 3. Mduya: *slack the lime.*
slackly, *adv.* Ţiŋ′ześniyaŋ; to′ken ciŋyaŋ.
slackness, *n.* Woţiŋześni; woawaciŋsni.
slag, *n.* .Giŋġiŋca; iŋ′yaŋśdo.
slake, *vt.* Yusni; yuasni. *vi.* Sniaya; sni.
slam, *vt.* Ni′naiyeya. *vi.* Ninaiyaya; bu.
slander, *n.* Waaiapi; woaie. *vt.* Aia; ituya aia.
slanderer, *n.* Waaies′a.
slanderous, *a.* Waaiapi; waaies′a.
slanderously, *adv.* Waaia.
slang, *n.* Iapiśni; oweśtepi.
slant, *a.* Takiŋyaŋ; a′pamahde. *vt.* Takiŋyaŋ e′hde. *vi.* Takiŋyaŋ waŋka. *n.* Onaptaŋye.
slanting, *a.* Atakiŋyaŋ; nake.
slantingly, *adv.* Atakiŋyaŋ.
slantwise, *adv.* Atakiŋyaŋ.
slap, *vt.* Napemdaska apa. *n.* Skamyena apapi.
slapjack, *n.* Aġuyapi zizipedaŋ.
slash, *vt.* Capapi; bahoŋhoŋ. *n.* Obahoŋ; oape.
slashed, *pa.* Bahoŋpi.
slat, *n.* Caŋmdaska sbu′na.
slate, *n.* Iŋ′yaŋ sa′pa; iŋ′yaŋ mdaskaska.
slattern, *n.* Wiŋ′yaŋ śamya ihduha. *a.* Śamya uŋ.
slatternly, *adv.* Śamyena.
slaty, *a.* Iŋ′yaŋmdaska se′ca.
slaughter, *n.* Wokte; wopata. *vt.* Kte; pa′ta.

slaughterer, *n.* Wicakte ; wapata.
slaughter-house, *n.* Owokte.
slave, *n.* Wayaka ; wowidake ; ta'-waiçiyeśni.
slave-born, *a.* Wayakatoŋpi.
slave-catcher, *n.* Wayakaoyuspa.
slave-driver, *n.* Wayakawicakaȟapa.
slaveholder, *n.* Wayakayuha.
slaveholding, *n.* Wayakayuhapi.
slavehunt, *n.* Wayakanażicaodepi.
sla'ver, *n.* 1. Wayaka wopetoŋ. 2. Wi'tawata wayakatokśu.
slav'er, *n.* I'mnitaġa ; i'mnicaśtaŋ. *vi.* I'mniśtaŋ.
slavery, *n.* Wayakatoŋpi.
slave-ship, *n.* Wi'tawatawayakatokśu.
slave-trade, *n.* Wayakawopetoŋpi.
slavish, *a.* Wayaka iyececa ; teȟike.
slay, *vt.* Kaśtaka ; kte.
slayer, *n.* Wakaśtaka ; tin'wicakte.
sled, *n.* Caŋwiyusdohe ; *Y.* caŋwosdohe.
sledding, *n.* Osdohaŋpi.
sledge, *n.* 1. Maziyapetaŋka. 2. Caŋwiyusdohe.
sleek, *a.* Sto ; stosto ; śduśduta ; wiyakpa. *vt.* Kastosto. *adv.* Yupiya.
sleekly, *adv.* Stostoya ; wiyakpaya.
sleep, *vi.* Iśtiŋma ; iśtiŋbe ; ataŋseun. *n.* Woiśtiŋma.
sleeper, *n.* 1. Tu'we iśtiŋma ; iśtiŋmapi. 2. Ohna iśtiŋmapi.
sleepily, *adv.* Iśtiŋmase ; ȟbayena.
sleepiness, *n.* Wicaȟbapi.
sleeping, *pa.* Wiciśtiŋma ; oiśtiŋma. *n.* Woiśtiŋma.
sleepless, *a.* Iśtiŋmeśni.
sleeplessly, *adv.* Iśtiŋmeśniyaŋ.
sleeplesness, *n.* Woiśtiŋmeśni.
sleepy, *a.* Ȟba ; *T.* ȟwa ; ku'za.
sleet, *n.* Watutupa. *vi.* Watutumya hiŋhe.
sleety, *a.* Acaȟcaġa.
sleeve, *n.* Isto ; oŋ'ȟdoȟdaisto. *Laugh in his sleeve,* naȟmana iȟa.
sleeveless, *a.* Istowanica.
sleigh, *n.* Caŋwiyusdohe kapożedaŋ.
sleighing, *n.* Wosdohaŋpi.
sleight, *n.* 1. Woaktaśni ; woyuśna : *it was a sleight.* 2. Wooȟaŋko ; wowayupika : *sleight of hand.*
slender, *a.* 1. Ci'stiŋna ; ci'stiŋnahaŋska : *slender but strong.* 2. Waŋ'kadaŋ ; sutaśni : *a slender constitution.*
slenderly, *adv.* Cistiyedaŋ ; kpataŋyaŋ.
slept, *imp.* of SLEEP.
slew, *imp.* of SLAY.
slice, *vt.* Baksaksa ; bamda ; kamda : *slice bread ; slice beef. n.* Obaśpe.
slick, *a.* Śduśduta ; stosto. *vt.* Paśduta ; kastosto.
slid, *imp.* of SLIDE.
slide, slid, slidden, *vi.* 1. Kaśdun iyaya : *he slid by.* 2. Osdohaŋ kiçuŋ : *slide down the hill.* 3. Hiyaya ; naȟmaŋ iyaya : *he slid out of sight. vt.* 1. Kaśduŋ iyeya ; naȟmaŋ hiyuya. *n.* Osdohaŋkiçuŋpi ; wokaśduta.
slider, *n.* Wakaśduta ; kaśdutapi.
slight, *a.* Ci'stiŋna ; iwaśtedaŋ : *a slight effort. vt.* 1. Aktaśni ; we'ceyeśni : *she slighted me.* 2. Taŋ'yaŋ ecoŋ śni : *slight his work. n.* Woaktaśni ; wowaȟtedaśni.
slightingly, *adv.* Aktaśniyaŋ.
slightly, *adv.* Iwaśtedaŋ ; kitaŋeciŋyaŋ ; haakamyedaŋ.
slightness, *n.* Woteȟiśni.
slim, *a.* Ci'stinahaŋska ; ta'kuśni.
slime, *n.* Upśiża ; makacoco.
slimsy, *a.* Zigzica.
slimy, *a.* Tutupa ; hmuŋ'za.
sling, *n.* Iyuȟmuŋ ; iŋ'yaniyu-

ḣmuŋ; wi'otke. *n.* Miniwakaŋicahi. *vt.* Kaḣ'oiyeya; otkeya.

slink, *vi.* Nasdankiḣda. *vt.* Okaśkaŋtoŋ.

slip, *vi.* 1. Naśduta; kaśduniyaya: *his foot slipped.* 2. Icuŋom iyaya; kaśdun iyaya: *it slipped out.* 3. Naśdun iyaya; naḣmaŋ iyaya: *he slipped away.* 4. Naśna; yuśna. *vt.* Kaśdun iyeya; kohaŋ iyeya: *slip in the pin.—Slip on a coat,* okde kohaŋ kiçuŋ. *n.* Wonaśduta; wonaśna; woyuśna: *a slip of the foot: he made a slip.* 2. Obaksa; caŋiŋkpa obakse: *currant slips.* 3. Oŋśpa; obakse haŋ'ska: *a slip of paper.* 4. Akanuŋpi; nitośke. 5. Wa'ta onażiŋ. 6. Caŋ'akaŋyaŋkapi haŋ'ska.

slipper, *n.* Caŋ'haŋpaoŋżiŋca. 2. Kaśdutesa.

slippery, *a.* Śduśduta; waciŋyepicaśni; to'ketutaŋiŋśni.

slipshod, *a.* To'kenciŋyaŋ.

slit, *vt.* Bahoŋ; baḣdoka; basdeca. *n.* Obahoŋ; oko; oḣci.

sliver, *n.* Caŋ'osdeca; wokasdate. *vt.* Kasdesdeca.

slobber, *vi.* I'mniśtaŋ.

sloop, *n.* Wi'tawata ihupa waŋżina.

slop, *n.* Miniśica; minieḣpeyapi. *vt.* Miniśica apapsoŋ.

slope, *n.* Ḣuŋ'naptaŋ; o'ḣya icaġopi. *vt.* O'ḣya ka'ġa; a'pamahde ka'ġa. *vi.* Napa.

sloping, *a.* Onaptaŋyaŋ; o'ḣya.

slopingly, *adv.* O'ḣya.

sloppy, *a.* Upśiża; coco.

slosh, *n.* Coco; makacoco.

sloshy, *a.* Coco; ḣaŋḣi.

slot, *n.* Caŋhdakiŋyaŋ; o'smaka.

sloth, *n.* 1. Wokuża: *live in sloth.* 2. (*Zool.*) Ku'ża; (Wahutopa waŋ inmu hiŋ'skokeca).

slothful, *a.* Ku'ża; huŋ'keśni; kużiṭa.

slothfully, *adv.* Kużiṭeya; huŋ'keśniyaŋ.

slothfulness, *n.* Wokuża.

slouch, *n.* Tu'we ḣcoka; coġeca. *vt.* Ḣdoheya ecoŋ.

slough, *n.* Wiwi; oḣdiḣdi. *v.* Naḣdaya; hiŋḣpaya.

sloven, *u.* Coġeca.

slovenliness, *n.* Woḣnahaŋ.

slovenly, *a.* Ḣnahaŋ; coġeca.

slow, *a.* Ḣaŋhi; huŋ'keśni; he'kta uŋ; oḣaŋsdata.

slowly, *adv.* Ḣaŋhiya; asasyena; iwaśtedaŋ.

slowness, *n.* Woḣaŋhi.

slue, *vi.* Kahomni; kaśduniyaya; *vt.* Kahomni iyeya.

slug, *n.* Ma'zasuhaŋska; ma'zacehdiḣpeyapi siha. *vt.* Ma'zasu oŋ apa.

sluggard, *n.* Ku'za.

sluggish, *a.* Huŋ'keśni; ḣaŋhi; ecoŋkapiŋ.

sluggishly, *adv.* Kużiteyena.

sluggishness, *n.* Wokuża.

slugs, *n.* Ma'zaaġuġu; kaśpuśpupi.

sluice, *n.* Minicaŋkukaġapi; minitiyopayapi.

slum, *n.* Waḣteśniotipi.

slumber, *vi.* Oġoŋġa; iśtiŋma; iwaśtedaŋ iśtiŋma.

slumberer, *n.* Iśtiŋbes'a.

slumberless, *a.* Iśtiŋbeśni.

slung, *imp.* of SLING.

slung-shot, *n.* Ma'zasu caŋ'ḣpi.

slunk, *imp.* of SLINK.

slur, *vt.* 1. Ta'kuśica ikoyagya; iśtenya: *he slurred me.* 2. Anaḣma: *slur a fact.* 3. (*Mus.*) Ikoyaka. *n.* Wi'koyake; woiyaoŋpe.

slush, *n.* Upśiża; ta'kucoco.

slushy, *a.* Coco.

slut, *n.* Śuŋkawiye.

sluttish, *a.* Ḣnahaŋ; coġeca.

sly, *a.* Naȟmaŋ śkaŋ; sda'ta; ksa'pa; wicaśtaśni.
slyly, *adv.* Naȟmana; anaȟbeya.
slyness, *n.* Naȟmana śkaŋ'pi.
smack, *vt.* Yuskapa; po'pa. *n.* 1. Ta'kupo'pa; yaskapapi. 2. U'tapi; wokitaŋ. 3. Oape; apapi. *vi.* Kaȟtaŋ; oŋ'śpa en uŋ.
smacking, *pa.* Yaskaskapa; itaŋcaŋka.
small, *a.* Ci'stiŋna; ci'ķana; kpana. *Small potatoes,* mdo cikcistiŋna.
small-arms, *n.* Ma'zakaŋikceka.
smallish, *a.* Ki'taŋna ci'stiŋna.
smallness, *n.* Wocistiŋna.
small-pox, *n.* Itewicaȟdoȟdokapi.
smart, *a.* Waciŋksapa: *a smart boy.* 2. Pe'sto; pa'za: *a smart rebuke.* 3. Mdiheca; oȟaŋko: *smart to get around.* 4. Ni'na hiyu; ni'na: *a smart breeze.* 5. O'ta; taŋ'yaŋ: *a smart crop of grass.* 6. Wi'taŋtaŋ; ksa'pa: *most too smart.*
smartly, *adv.* Waciŋksamya; pe'stoya; wi'taŋtaŋyaŋ.
smartness, *n.* Wowaciŋksape; woohitike.
smash, *vt.* Kamdeca; kaśuśuża. *Smashed to pieces,* kpaŋyena kamdeca. *n.* Kamdecapi; wotakuniśni.
smasher, *n.* Wakamdeca; wohitika.
smatter, *vi.* Sdonyeśniia.
smatterer, *n.* Wasdonyeśni iaa.
smattering, *n.* Wosdonye haakamyena.
smear, *vt.* Akastaka; sdaya; aśamya. *n.* Akastakapi.
smell, *vt.* 1. O'mna: *smell the rose.* 2. Iyukcaŋ: *he smelled out the answer.* *vi.* Mna; o'mna: *I can't smell.* *n.* O'mnapi; woomna.
smeller, *n.* Oŋ o'mnapi; po'ġe; waomna.
smelling, *n.* Waomnapi.
smelling-bottle, *n.* Żaŋżaŋ o'mnapi.
smelt, *vi.* Śdoya.
smelter, *n.* Waśdoya.
smicker, *vi.* Iȟaȟa.
smile, *vi.* Iȟa; iyokipi; ahitoŋwaŋ; wi'yuśkiŋ. *Mother smiled,* ina iȟa.—*May heaven smile,* tokiŋ maȟpiya iyokipi ahitoŋwaŋ.—*Smiling spring,* we'tu wi'yuśkiŋ. *n.* Iȟapi; woiȟa; woihakta.
smiler, *n.* Iȟas'a.
smilingly, *adv.* Wi'hahaya; canwaśteya.
smirch, *vt.* Aśamya.
smirk, *vi.* Iȟakoŋza.
smite, *vt.* *Apa.* Apa; kaśtaka; ȟmuŋġa. *Smite off,* kaspa.
smith, *n.* Ma'zakaġa. *Silver-smith,* ma'żaskakaġa.
smitten, *pp.* of SMITE. Apapi; wiciŋpi yuhnaśkiŋyaŋ.
smock, *n.* Wiŋ'yaŋ mahenuŋpi.
smoke, *n.* Śo'ta: *I see smoke.* *vi.* 1. Śo'ta; izita; śo'takaġa: *the stove smokes.* 2. Caŋoŋpa: *do you smoke.* *vt.* 1. Izinya; śo'taya. 2. Oŋ'pa; caŋnoŋpa.
smokeless, *a.* Śo'ta wanica.
smoker, *n.* Caŋnoŋpas'a.
smoky, *a.* 1. Śo'ta; śo'tes'a: *a smoky house.* 2. Śotożu: *a smoky day.* 3. Śotkazi: *a smoky ceiling.*—*A smoky teepee,* wizi.
smolder, *vi.* Izita; itkoŋyahe.
smooth, *a.* Śduśduta; mda'ya; stosto; amdakedaŋ.—*Smooth glass,* żaŋżaŋ śduśduta.—*Smooth hair,* hiŋ stosto.—*Smooth road,* caŋku mda'ya.—*Smooth words,* iapi sku'ya. *vt.* Pastosto; kamdaya; yuasni.
smooth-faced, *a.* Hiŋ wanica.
smoothing-iron, *n.* Wi'pamdaye.
smoothing-plane, *n.* Wi'cażipeptecedaŋ.

smoothly, *adv.* Stostoya; iyokipiya.
smoothness, *n.* Womdaye.
smooth-spoken, *a.* I'waśicuŋ; i'skuya.
smooth-tongued, *a.* Cežiskuya.
smitten, *pp.* of SMITE.
smother, *vt.* Yuniyaśni; yusni.—*Smother the babe,* hokśiyopa yuniyaśni.—*Smother fire,* pe'ta yusni.—*Smother anger,* wocaŋniye apaspa.
smudge, *n.* Śo'ta; wi'zinyapi.
smuggle, *vt.* Naȟmaŋ ahi: *smuggle goods into the country.*
smuggler, *n.* Naȟmaŋwatokśu.
smut, *n.* Aġuyapisusapa; ceȟnaġi.
smutty, *a.* 1. Ceȟnaġi aśamya. 2. Aa: *smutty corn.* 3. Wowiśteca: *smutty talk.*
snag, *n.* Caŋmnicažo; caŋ; caŋhutkaŋ: *the boat ran on a snag.* *vi.* Caŋ'naoȟdoka.
snail, *n.* Wamnuȟadaŋ; tu'we hun'kedaŋśni.
snake, *n.* Wamduśka; zuzuhecedaŋ; *T.* zuzeca; waŋ.—*Rattlesnake,* siŋteȟda. *vt.* Yusďohaŋ; sdohaŋ: *snake a log.*
Snake, *n. pr.* Siŋteȟdawicaśa.
snakish, *a.* Wamduśkase.
snap, *vt.* 1. Kapsaka; yupsaka: *snapped the bars.* 2. Yupopa; kapopa: *snap the fingers.* 3. Yakoka: *the dog snapped his teeth.* *vi.* 1. Psa'ka; kapsaka: *the pole snapped.* 2. Boķeġa: *the gun snapped.* *n.* 1. Papsakapi; wopapsaka: *broke with a snap.* 2. Woakipa: *a cold snap.* 3. Ma'zawiyuze: *a bridle snap.* 4. Aġuyapi zizina: *ginger snaps.*
snappish, *a.* Wayaȟtakes'a.
snappishly, *adv.* Ksizeya.
snare, *n.* Wi'hmuŋke; wowawiyutaŋye. *vt.* Hmuŋ'ka.
snarl, *vi.* Ḣdo; *T.* ȟlo. *vt.* Yuwiwi; i'ciyakaśka. *n.* Yuwiwi; woyuśkiśke.
snatch, *vt.* Kohaŋ icu; yukam icu. *n.* Wokitaŋ.
snatcher, *n.* Yukamicus'a.
snath, *n.* Pežiicaśdaihupa.
sneak, *vi.* Pamahdedaŋ ya; iśteca se śkaŋ. *n.* Naȟmaŋśkaŋ.
sneaking, *a.* Waanaȟbe.
sneer, *vi.* Iȟaȟa. *n.* Wowiȟa.
sneerer, *n.* Wawiȟaȟa.
sneeringly, *adv.* Wawiȟaȟaya.
sneeze, *vi.* Pśa.
snicker, *vi.* Żižiya iȟa.
sniff, *vt.* O'mna; po'ġaŋ.
sniffle, *vi.* Ḣnaȟna niya; ţiŋ'ġa.
snipe, *n.* Hu'totona.
snivel, *vi.* Ţiŋ'ġa; paȟdi au.
sniveler, *n.* Ce'yakenuŋ.
snob, *n.* Waȟaŋiçida.
snooze, *vi.* Iśtiŋma; inaȟni iśtiŋma.
snore, *vi.* ·Go'pa.
snorer, *n.* ·Go'pes'a.
snort, *vi.* Po'ġaŋ; ȟnaȟna.
snot, *n.* Paȟdi.
snout, *n.* Pute; pasu: *the hog's snout.*
snow, *n.* Wa. *The snow flies,* wa bomdu; icamna. *vi.* Wapa; wa hiŋhe.
snow-ball, *n.* Wakaska. *vi.* Wakiciiŋpi.
snow-bird, *n.* Wa'kasaŋsaŋ.
snowblind, *a.* Wa'iśtaiowicaśniže.
snowdrift, *n.* Wo'ġaŋ; *T.* wawotiheye.
snowflake, *n.* 1. Wa'sukaza. 2. Waȟcaska (ocaže).
snow-plow, *n.* Wa'icatice.
snow-shoe, *n.* Pse; taŋmda.
snow-storm, *n.* Waibomdu.
snow-white, *a.* Wa'seska.
snowy, *a.* 1. Wa'se; wa'kaśoteśni. 2. Wa'akaȟpa.
snub, *vt.* Anaptakuwa; okihiśniya.

snuff, *vt.* Po'żaŋżaŋ; yażiŋca; o'mna: *the dog snuffed the breeze.* *n.* 1. Caŋdi bakpaŋpi. 2. Petiżaŋżaŋiyaġu.
snuff-box, *n.* Caŋdiyażiŋcapi opiye.
snuffer, *n.* 1. Wayażiŋca. 2. Petiżaŋżaŋ iyukse.
snuffle, *vi.* Oyaħnaħna; pożaŋżaŋ.
snug, *a.* Ayuco; taŋ'yaŋ.
snuggle, *vi.* A'skamya iwaŋka.
snugly, *adv.* Kipiya; ayucoya.
so, *adv.* 1. He'cen: *God made me so.* 2. Ni'na; he'ceħ: *I am so tired.*—*So long,* hehaŋkeca.—*He stayed so long,* ni'na te'han yaŋka.—*So far,* hehaŋyaŋ; ni'na te'han.—*So forth,* saŋ'pa he'cekcen.—*So large,* hiŋ'skotaŋka; ni'na taŋ'ka.—*So much,* henakeca; ni'na o'ta.—*So small,* hiŋ'śkoyedaŋ; ni'na ci'stiŋna.—*So so,* he'cetu; he'cetuka. *conj.* Ehantaŋhanś; kiŋhaŋ.
soak, *vt.* Ḣpaŋyaŋ; spa'yeya. *vi.* Akaħtaŋ.
soaked, *pa.* Ḣpaŋ; spa'ya.
soaking, *pa.* Kaħtaŋyaŋ.
soap, *n.* Wi'pażaża; *Y. & T.* ha'ipażaża. *vt.* Wi'pażaża iuŋ.
soap-bubble, *n.* Taġebotaŋkapi.
soap-stone, *n.* Iŋ'yaŋsaŋ.
soap-suds, *n.* Miniwipażażaota.
soapy, *a.* Wipażaża yukaŋ.
soar, *vi.* Waŋkan kiŋyaŋ; nawiŋ. *Soar away,* auŋyaŋ iyaye.
sob, *vi.* Ce'yaya; ce'yektakta. *n.* Ce'yapiho; mdokaska.
sober, *a.* 1. Mdeze; witkośni: *the man is sober.* 2. Oħaŋtaŋka; wi'hahaśni; wicaka: *a very sober boy.* *vt.* Kamdeza.
soberly, *adv.* Mdesya; a'wicakeya.
sober-minded, *a.* Tawaciŋ mde'ze.
soberness, *n.* Womdeze; wowicake.
sobriety, *n.* Wi'wicamdeza.
sobriquet, *n.* I'ħadcaże.
so-called, *a.* He'cen eciyapi.
sociable, *a.* Wohdakes'a; wawihaha; wawimaġaġa.
sociableness, *n.* Wi'cihaktapi.
sociably, *adv.* Imaġaġaya.
social, *a.* Okiciya.
socialist, *n.* Okiciyapi okodakiciye.
socially, *adv.* Okiciya.
society, *n.* Wicaśtaikicitukapi; okiciyapi; i'cikiyedaŋ ti'pi; omniciye; waŋkiciyakapi.
sock, *n.* Iyahdehuŋska; *Y. & T.* huŋyakoŋ.
socket, *n.* Oħdoka; ośkokpa.
sod, *n.* Peżihutkaŋ; peżi. *vt.* Peżi hutkaŋ ażu.
soda, *n.* Aġuyapiinapoħye suta.
soda-water, *n.* Miniipiġa yatkaŋpi.
sodomite, *n.* Iwicahusa.
sofa, *n.* Akaŋyaŋkapi haŋ'ska paŋpaŋna.
soft, *a.* 1. Paŋpaŋna; paŋśpaŋżedaŋ; hihi: *a soft bed; soft cloth; soft earth.* 2. Waŋ'kadaŋ: *soft iron.* 3. Owaśteca: *soft air.* 4. Iwaśtedaŋ: *soft whispers.* 5. Coco: *soft mud.*—*Soft water,* mini sutaśni; maġażu mini.
soften, *vt.* Kapaŋpaŋ; yupaŋpaŋ; kacoco; yuasni. *vi.* Iwaśtedaŋ aya; waŋkadaŋ a'ya; śdo.
soft-headed, *a.* Waciŋksapeśni.
soft-hearted, *a.* Canwaŋka.
softly, *adv.* Iwaśtedaŋ; iwahnana; wa'ħbayena.
softness, *n.* Wopaŋpaŋna; wowaħba.
soggy, *a.* Spa'ya; dodo se'ca.
soil, *n.* Makikceka; maka: *the soil is good.* *vt.* Yuśapa; aśamya; *don't soil your clothes.*
sojourn, *vi.* Inaħniti; ohnihde uŋ. *n.* Ouŋyaŋpi
sojourner, *n.* Ohnihdeuŋ; inaħniuŋ.

sojournment, *n.* Ouŋyaŋpi.
sol, *n.* (*Mus.*) Ho'izaptaŋ.
solace, *vt.* Waciŋtoŋhnagya; kicaŋpta. *n.* Wokicaŋpte.
solar, *a.* Aŋpawi; aŋpawi etaŋhaŋ.
sold, *imp.* of SELL.
solder, *n.* Wiśdoye. *vt.* Ceḣska apuspa.
soldier, *n.* Akicita.
soldiering, *n.* Akicitauŋpi.
soldierly, *a.* Akicita iyececa; waditaka.
sole, *n,* Sicu; sicuha: *the sole of my shoe. vt.* Sicu okataŋ.
sole, *a.* Heceedaŋ; iśnana.
solecism, *n.* Iapi eciŋśniyaŋ; wicoḣaŋ eciŋśniyaŋ.
solely, *adv.* Heceedaŋ; he'cehnana.
solemn, *a.* Wakaŋ; wakaŋse; wowicake.
solemnity, *n.* Wowakaŋ; wowicake; wowinihaŋ.
solemnization, *n.* Yuwakaŋpi.
solemnize, *vt.* Yuwakaŋ; ahopewicaya; yuśtaŋ.
solemnly, *adv.* Wakaŋyaŋ; a'wicakeya.
solicit, *vt.* Kida; da; icekiya.
solicitation, *n.* Wadapi; ociŋpi. *At the solicitation of his father,* atkuku okiciciŋ kiŋ oŋ.
solicitor, *n.* 1. Wadauŋ; waociŋ. 2. Ki'cicuwa; każużuwicakiya.
solicitous, *a.* Ciŋ'ḣca; awaciŋḣca; icaŋteśica.
solicitously, *adv.* Icaŋteśinya.
solicitude, *n.* Waawaciŋḣca.
solid, *a.* 1. Suta; ķe'za: *solid ground.* 2. Ḣdoġecaśni: *a solid ball.* 3. Omdotoŋ: *a solid foot.* 4. Tke; suta: *solid food. n.* 1. Ta'ku taŋtoŋ. 2. (*Gram.*) Ta'ku omdotoŋ.
solidify, *vt.* Yusuta. *vi.* Suta a'ya.
solidity, *n.* 1. Wosuta; hohośni. 2. Caŋteţiŋzapi; wotaŋka; wowicake.
solidly, *adv.* Sutaya; a'taya.
solidness, *n.* Wosuta; a'taya.
soliloquize, *vi.* I'ciwohdaka.
soliloquy, *n.* I'ciwohdakapi.
solitarily, *adv.* Iśnana.
solitariness, *n.* Wiciśnana uŋ'pi.
solitary, *a.* Iśnana uŋ; waŋżidaŋ; makoskan un'pi.
solitude, *n.* Makoskantu; wiciśnana uŋ'pi.
solo, *n.* Wiciśnana dowaŋpi.
solstice, *n.* Aŋ'pawi namni.
soluble, *a.* Ḣpaŋyepica; skaŋyepica; kaḣdogpica; okaḣniḣpica.
solution, *n.* 1. Ḣpuwahe; ḣpaŋyaŋhaŋ; mduwahe. 2. Kaḣdokapi; to'ketu oyakapi: *the solution of the question.* 3. (*Chem.*) Skaŋyaŋpi: *a solution of soda.* 4. Woyużużu: owihaŋke.
solvable, *a.* Oyagpica; yasupica.
solve, *vt.* Yukcaŋ; yasu; yuzamni; oyaka.
solvency, *n.* Wawokihika.
solvent, *a.* 1. Każużu okihi. 2. Skaŋyepica; waskaŋkiya.
sombre, *a.* Sa'peca; ġiġi; otaŋiŋkeśni; aokpaza.
some, *a.* 1. Oŋġe: *some water; some flour.* 2. Waŋżikśi: *some girls; some horses.* 3. Waŋżi; tu'we kaśta: *some man will do it.* 4. Ki'taŋ'na; oŋśpa. 5. Ce'tu: *some ten miles.* 6. Ki'taŋna o'ta: *it will be some days before he will come.*
somebody, *n.* Tu'we; wicaśta waŋżi.
somehow, *adv.* 1. To'ketu kacen: *somehow he fell.* 2. To'ketu kaśta: *it must be done somehow.*
somersault, somerset, *n.* Kahomni eḣpeiçiyapi.
something, *n.* 1. Ta'ku; ta'ku waŋżi. 2. Oŋśpa; iyokise.

sometime, *adv.* Tohantu kiŋhaŋ ; tohantu ṡta : *sometime come and see me.* 2. To'hiŋni.
sometimes, *adv.* Tuktentu.
somewhat, *n.* Ki'taŋna ; oŋṡpa ; ta'ku ; haŋke. *adv.* Ki'taŋna.
somewhere, *adv.* Tukteŋ ; to'kiya.
somerset, *n.* See SOMERSAULT.
somnambulist, *n.* Iṡtiŋma omani.
son, *n.* Ciŋhiŋtku ; ciŋca. *My son,* miciŋkṡi.—*Your son,* niciŋkṡi.—*His son,* ciŋhiŋtku.—*Son,* ciŋṡ.—*Sons of Jacob, Jacob* ciŋca.
song, *n.* Odowaŋ ; odowaŋ ikceka.
songful, *a.* Dowaŋs'a.
songless, *a.* Dowaŋ okihiṡni.
songster, *n.* Dowaŋs'a.
soniferous, *a.* Ḣo'kaġa.
son-in-law, *n.* Takoṡku.—*My son-in-law,* mitakoṡ ; takoṡwaya.
sonless, *a.* Ciŋhiŋtku wanica.
sonnet, *n.* Odowaŋ (ocaże).
sonorous, *a.* Ho'yukaŋ ; ho'taŋ'ka ; ho'waṡte.
sonship, *n.* Ciŋhiŋtkuyapi.
soon, *adv.* Ecadaŋ ; kohaŋna ; to'keṡta. *Sooner,* tokaheya.—*Soonest,* tokaheyaḣca.—*As soon as,* tohan.—*No sooner,* he'cehnana ; i'ecadaŋ.
soot, *n.* Ceḣnaġi ; ṡonnagi. *vt.* Ceḣnaġi akaḣpa.
sooth, *n.* Wowicake.
soothe, *vt.* Kihna ; iyokipiya.
soothingly, *adv.* Kihnaya.
soothsay, *vi.* Ayata.
soothsayer, *n.* Waayate.
sooty, *a.* Ceḣnaġi o'ta ; ṡa'pa.
sop, *vt.* Ḣpaŋye ; kaḣtaŋ ; oputkaŋ. *n.* Ḣpaŋyaŋpi ; oŋ kihnapi.
sophism, *n.* Woksape wohnaye.
sophist, *n.* Woksape iwicahnaye.
sophistical, *a.* Wicahnaye.
sophistry, *n.* Woksape wohnaye.
sophomore, *n.* Wooŋspe waŋkantu waniyetu inoŋpa.
sorcerer, *n.* Wapiyes'a ; wicaḣmuŋġa.
sorcery, *n.* Woḣmuŋġe ; wawiyutaŋye.
sordid, *a.* Ṡa'pa ; ṡi'ca.
sordidly, *adv.* Ṡicaya.
sore, *a.* Yazaŋ ; ḣdi : *my sore hand.* 2. Ni'na ṡi'ca ; teḣika : *a sore disease,* *n.* Ḣdi ; yazaŋ. *adv.* Ṡicaya ; ni'na.
sorely, *adv.* Teḣiya ; ni'na.
soreness, *n.* Oyazaŋ.
sorghum, *n.* Caŋhaŋpihu.
sorrel, *n.* Waḣpeskuya. *a.* Hiŋṡa.
sorrily, *adv.* Oiyokiṡinya.
sorrow, *n.* Woiyokiṡica ; wocaŋteṡica. *vi.* Icaŋteṡica ; iyokiṡica.
sorrowful, *a.* Iyokiṡica ; oiyokiṡica ; woiyokiṡica.
sorrowfully, *adv.* Oiyokiṡinya.
sorry, *a.* 1. Caŋteṡica : *I am sorry.* 2. Oiyokiṡica : *a sorry sight.* 3. Iyecetuṡni : *a sorry excuse.*
sort, *n.* Obe ; ocaże : *what sort of wood.*—*In some sort,* to'ketuyaka.—*Out of sorts,* ecetukeṡni. *vt.* 1. Obe ecekcen e'hnaka : *sort potatoes.* 2. Kaḣniġa ; kaḣniḣ icu. *Ill-sorted words,* iapi taŋ'yaŋ kaḣniġapiṡni. *vi.* Kicica ; kici iyokipi.
sortable, *a.* Pta'pta e'hnagpica.
so-so, *a.* Ahececa.
sot, *n.* Witkosa.
sottish, *a.* Miniwakaŋ akaska.
sottishness, *n.* Witkopis'a.
soul, *n.* 1. Naġi ; wicanaġi : *Christ came to save souls.* 2. Oni ; caŋte ; wowaṡ'ake : *no soul left within him.* 3. Wicaṡta ; tu'we : *ten souls in the boat.*
soulless, *a.* Caŋtewanica.
sound, *a.* 1. Zani ; a'taya waṡte : *a sound apple.* 2. Wicaka ; he'cetu : *a sound argument.* 3. Wowicake ; a'wicake : *a sound threshing.* 4. Suta ; ni'na :

sound sleep. *n.* 1. Ho; ta'ku bu: *I heard a sound.* 2. Mini wakpaseyeye: *go boating on the sound.* *vt.* 1. Śbe iyuta; iyuta; yukcaŋ: *sound the waters.* 2. Kahotoŋ; yahotoŋ: *sound the trumpet.* *vi.* Hotoŋ; ho'taŋiŋ; sna; bu: *the wind sounds cold.*
sounding, *pa.* Ho'taŋiŋ; ho'taŋka. *n.* Śbe iyutapi.
sounding-line, *n.* Haȟoŋta on śbeiyutapi.
soundless, *a.* Ho wanica.
soundly, *adv.* A'wicakeya.
soundness, *n.* Wozani; wowicake.
soup, *n.* Waḣaŋpi; haŋpi.
sour, *n.* 1. Śkumna; skuya: *sour milk; sour apples.* 2. Hiŋyaŋza; wociŋko: *a sour temper.* 3. Oȟaŋśica; osnaze. *vt.* Skuyeya; yuśica. *vi.* Śkumna; śica.
source, *n.* Oenape; o'iŋkpa: *the source of the river.*
sourish, *a.* Ki'taŋna śkumna.
sour-krout, *n.* Waȟpetaŋka śkumnayaŋpi.
sourly, *adv.* Śkumnayaŋ; iyokipiśniyaŋ.
sourness, *n.* Wośkumna; wocaŋze.
south, *n.* O'kaġa; itokaġa. *a.* Itokaȟ. *adv.* O'kaȟ.
south-east, *a.* Wiyohiyaŋpa itokaȟ.
southerly, *a.* Itokaȟ.
southern, *a.* Itokaġa.
southerner, *n.* Itokaȟwicaśta.
southernmost, *a.* Itokaȟ ihaŋke.
southing, *n.* Itokaȟ ye.
southward, *adv.* Itokaȟ.
southwest, *n.* Wiyohiyaŋpa itokaȟ.
souvenir, *n.* Wokiksuye.
sovereign, *n.* 1. Itaŋcaŋ; wicaśtayatapi taŋ'ka: *the sovereign of the land.* 2. Sagdaśiŋ ma'zaskazi; ma'zaska $4.84. *a.* Tokahaŋ; iyotaŋ; ihduha.

sow, *vt.* Ożu; kada; wożu; kadada. *n.* Kukuśewiye: *the sow had six pigs.*
sower, *n.* Tu'we wożu.
sown, *pp.* of sow.
space, *n.* 1. Oyaŋke; okaŋ; oko; ituocoka. 2. (*Print.*) Oowa wanica; oko. 3. (*Mus.*) Oko. *vt.* Oko ka'ġa.
spacious, *a.* Taŋ'ka; otaŋkaya; okipi. *A spacious house,* ti'pi otaŋkaya.
spade, *n.* 1. Makinaśpe; ma'zamdaska. 2. Kaŋsukutepi ocaże. *vt.* Makinaśpe oŋ oḳa; oḳa.
spadeful, *n.* Makinaśpe ożudaŋ.
spade-handle, *n.* Makinaśpe ihupa.
spake, *imp.* of SPEAK.
span, *n.* 1. Napapasdecapi: *a span long.* 2. Oiyute ci'stiŋna: *life is but a span.* 3. O'hiyohiye: *a bridge of two span.* 4. Akicaśka: *a span of horses.* *vt.* 1. Napapaśdecapi oŋ wiyuta. 2. O'pta ya; iyute.
spangle, *vt.* Yuhdeśka; kahdeśka.
Spaniard, *n. pr.* Spaniyowicaśa.
spaniel, *n.* Śuŋ'kanakpataŋka.
Spanish, *a.* Spaniyotawa.
spank, *vt.* Napemdaska apa.
spanking, *n.* Napemdaskaapapi.
span-new, *a.* Te'ca; nakaha te'ca.
spar, *n.* Wa'taipamnataŋka.
spare, *vt.* 1. Kpaġaŋ; iyakicuhnaka: *I have none to spare.* 2. Kpataŋ; itoŋpeya kuwa: *he did not spare his horse.* 3. E'hdaku; niyaŋ; kpataŋ: *spare us, good Lord.* *vi.* Wakpataŋ; kpataŋyaŋ ni; kpataŋyaŋ ecoŋ; wawitoŋpe. *a.* 1. Iyakicu: *a spare horse,* śuŋ'kawakaŋ iyakicu. 2. Iyohiśni; kpataŋyaŋ yuha. 3. Tamaheca; ce'peśni: *a spare looking boy.*
spare-rib, *n.* Cutuhu bazapapi.
sparing, *a.* 1. Wakpataŋ; wateȟiŋda: *sparing of her flour.* 2.

To'nana ; kpataŋyaŋecoŋpi : *a sparing supply.*
sparingly, *adv.* Kpataŋyaŋ ; itoŋpeya.
spark, *n.* Peśniża ; ta'ku wiyakpa.
sparking, *n.* Wiokiyapi.
sparkle, *vi.* Wiyakpa ; kpa'kpa ; piȟpiġa. *n.* Wowiyakpa.
sparkling, *pa.* Wiyakpakpa ; piȟpiġa : *sparkling eyes.*
sparrow, *n.* Zitkadaŋ ; wa'kasaŋsaŋ.
sparse, *a.* To'nana ; enana.
spasm, *a.* Kaŋ'natipapi ; ocistiyedaŋ.
spasmodic, *a.* Natiptipapi ; inaȟniececapi.
spat, *imp.* of SPIT.
spatter, *vt.* Akastastaka ; amnimni : *spatter your dress.*
spavin, *n.* Huhu anoġe.
spawn, *n.* Hoġaŋitka. *vt.* Hoġaŋ itka okada.
speak, *vt.* E'ya ; oyaka ; yaotaŋiŋ ; ia.—*To speak to,* eciya.—*Do you speak Sioux,* Dakota iyaa he. *vi.* Ia ; woyaka ; wohdaka. *Speak for,* ekiciya ; ki'ciia.—*Speak in public,* wicota en wohdaka.—*Speak, Lord,* ia wo, Itaŋcaŋ.—*Speak of,* cażeyata.
speakable, *a.* Eyepica.
speaker, *n.* Iekiyapi ; tu'we wohdaka ; omniciye itaŋcaŋ.
speaking, *n.* Iapi ; wohdakapi.
spear, *n.* 1. Wahukeza. *A rat-spear,* huȟaka. 2. Ape : *a spear of grass.* *vt.* Capa ; wahukeza oŋ capa.
spear-grass, *n.* Mi'capeca ; wi'capeca.
spear-man, *n.* Wahukeza yuha.
special, *a.* I'yatayedaŋ ; heceedaŋ ka'pi ; iyotaŋ ; to'keca.
specialist, *n.* Heceedaŋ kuwa.
speciality, *n.* Wicoȟaŋ wicitawa.
specially, *adv.* Iyotaŋyaŋ ; ta'ku waŋżi oŋ.
specialty, *n.* Iyotaŋ kuwa.
specie, *n.* Ma'zaska ma'za.
species, *n.* Ocaże ; obe ; ośpaye.
specific, *a.* I'atayedaŋ ; ta'wa ; wi'yokihi.
specifically, *adv.* I'atayedaŋ ; a'wicakehaŋ.
specification, *n.* Wacażeyatapi.
specify, *vt.* I'atayedaŋ cażeyata.
specimen, *n.* Oŋśpa etaŋhaŋ.
specious, *a.* Wicaka se'ca.
speciously, *adv.* Wicakeya.
speciousness, *n.* Wowicake se'ca.
speck, *n.* Oŋśpa ci'stiŋna ; ta'ku ci'stiŋ'na. *vt.* Yusapsapa.
speckle, *vt.* Yuhdehdeġa ; hdeśka ka'ġa.
speckled, *pa.* Hdehdeġa ; hdeśkaśka.
spectacle, *n.* Wowaŋyake.
spectacles, *n.* Ma'zaiśta ; iśtamaza.
spectator, *n.* Wawaŋyaguŋ.
specter, *n.* Wanaġi ; naġi.
speculate, *vi.* 1. Awaciŋ ; iyukcan : *speculate on his conduct.* 2. Wakamna kta opetoŋ : *speculate on wheat.*
speculation, *n.* Wi'yukcaŋ wopetoŋpi.
speculative, *a.* Wi'yukcaŋka.
speculatively, *adv.* Wi'yukcaŋyaŋ.
speculator, *n.* Wi'yukcaŋ wopetoŋ ; wi'yukcaŋ.
speculum, *n.* Ihdiyomdasiŋ.
sped, *imp.* of SPEED.
speech, *n.* 1. Iapi : *the gift of speech.* 2. Owohdake : *he made a speech.*
speechless, *a.* Iapi okihiśni.
speech-maker, *n.* Wohdakes'a.
speed, *vi.* Dus ya ; to'ken okihi ecoŋ. *vt.* Dus yekiya. *n.* Woduzahaŋ ; wooȟaŋko.
speedily, *adv.* Oȟaŋkoya ; inaȟniyaŋ ; kohaŋna.
speedy, *a.* Oȟaŋko ; du'zahaŋ.

spell, *vt.* Oowa e'ya; oowa cażeyata. *n.* Woecoŋ; itogto ecoŋpi; wohmuŋġa. *vt.* Kici itogto ecoŋ; o'kiya.
spell-bound, *a.* Ḣmuŋ'ġapi.
speller, *n.* 1. Oowa cażeyata. 2. Oowa wowapi.
spelling, *n.* Oowa e'hnakapi.
spelt, *imp.* of SPELL.
spend, *vt.* 1. Iyopeya; ku: *spend money for an education.* 2. Yusota; yutakuniśni: *spent all his father's money.* 3. Uŋ; en yaŋka: *spend the day with us.—I come to spend the night,* awaŋg wahi.—*A spent ball,* ma'zasu sniyaŋ ya.—*Spend on,* ayusota. *vi.* Wayusota; taŋiŋ śni iyaya.
spender, *n.* Tu'we wayusota.
spendthrift, *n.* Wahdusotes'a; wakpataŋśni.
spent, *imp.* of SPEND.
sperm-oil, *n.* Hoġaŋihdi petiżaŋżaŋyapi.
spew, *vt.* Hde'pa; hiyuya.
spewer, *n.* Tu'we hde'pa.
sphere, *n.* 1. Ta'pase; ta'ku mima: *the earth is a sphere.* 2. Ouŋ; ouŋye; obe: *out of his sphere.*
spherical, *a.* Mibe; hmiyaŋna.
spice, *n.* Ta'kuicahiyutapi.
spicy, *a.* 1. Ta'kuicahi o'ta. 2. Pe'stosto; ksamyahaŋ: *he made a spicy talk.*
spider, *n.* Uŋktomi.
spider-web, *n.* Uŋktomi tahokata.
spied, *imp.* of SPY. Waŋyaka.
spigot, *n.* Iośtaŋ.
spike, *n.* Ma'zaiokataŋ taŋ'ka; ma'za pe'sto. *vt.* Okataŋ; ma'żakaŋtaŋka no'ge aokataŋ.
spiky, *a.* Pespesto.
spill, *vt.* 1. Papsoŋ: *spill water.* 2. Kada; kakada: *spill corn.*
spin, *vt.* 1. Pahmuŋ; kahmuŋ: *spin wool.* 2. Pahomni; kahomni: *spin a top.* 3. Yutehan; ayucikayedaŋ: *spin out the day.*—*Spin a story,* wakakaŋ. *vi.* Wapahmuŋ; homnimni.
spinal, *n.* Caŋkahu.—*Spinal column,* caŋkahu a'taya.—*Spinal marrow,* caŋkasuŋta; *T.* caŋkaslute.
spindle, *n.* Ma'zaiyuhmuŋ.
spindle-legs, *a.* Hucistiŋnahaŋska.
spine, *n.* 1. Caŋkahu; caŋhahake: *his spine is diseased.* 2. Hoape; caŋpepe.
spinner, *n.* Tu'we wapahmuŋ; uŋktomi.
spinning-wheel, *n.* Caŋhdeśkaipahmuŋ.
spinster, *n.* Wiŋ'yaŋ wapahmuŋ.
spiny, *a.* Pespesto; tehika.
spiral, *a.* Homni ka'ġapi; ma'zaicuse; yuhbeżapi; oiyadi.
spirally, *adv.* Hbesyedaŋ; homniyaŋ; homniyaŋ oiyadi.
spire, *n.* 1. Ti'piipasotka; iŋ'kpa. 2. Peżi hucaŋ; ape.
spirit, *n.* 1. Woniya; naġi; oniya; wicaniya; wicanaġi. 2. Womdiheca: *full of spirit.* 3. Caŋte; tawaciŋ: *in good spirits.* 4. Miniwoniya; miniwakaŋ: *he drinks too much spirits.* 5. Iapi caŋte; co; to'ken ka'pi; caŋteoyuze: *his talk showed a bad spirit.* *vt.* Nahmaŋ e'yaya: *he spirited the child away.*
spirited, *a.* 1. Mdiheca; śke'he: *a spirited horse.* 2. Tawaciŋ; caŋte: *low spirited.*
spiritedly, *adv.* Mdihenya.
spiritedness, *n.* Womdiheca.
spirit-lamp, *n.* Miniwakaŋ petiżaŋżaŋ.
spiritless, *a.* 1. Tawaciŋ wanica; huŋ'keśni. 2. Ku'ża; tase.
spirit-rapper, *n.* Wapiya; wakaŋkaŋśkaŋ.
spiritual, *a.* 1. Taŋtoŋśni; cehpi wanica: *a spiritual substance.* 2. Wakaŋ; woniya.

spiritualism, *n.* Wakaŋiçidapi.
spiritualist, *n.* Wakaŋiçidapi o'pa.
spirituality, *n.* Wowaciŋye; woohoda.
spiritualize, *vt.* Yuwakaŋ; ohodakiya; taŋtoŋśnikiya.
spiritually, *adv.* Wakaŋyaŋ; taŋtoŋśniyaŋ; ohodaya.
spirituous, *a.* 1. Taŋtoŋśni; woniya. 2. Miniwakaŋicahi.
spit, *vi.* Taġośa. *Spit on*, ataġośa. *vt.* Itaġośa: *spit blood.* *n.* Caŋwipasnoŋ.
spit-box, *n.* Ohna ataġośapi.
spite, *n.* Wowaȟtedaśni; wocaŋze. *In spite of*, to'ketu çeyaś. *vt.* Caŋzeya; waȟtedaśni; sicaya kuwa.
spiteful, *a.* Waȟteśni; ociŋśica.
spitefully, *adv.* Śicaya.
spitefulness, *n.* Wowaȟtedaśni.
spitter, *n.* Ataġośas'a.
spittle, *n.* Taġe; ímnitaġośa.
spittoon, *n.* Ohna taġośapi.
splash, *vt.* Miniapapsoŋpsoŋ. *vi.* Mininaġaġa; minibosdi.
splasher, *n.* Wanaġaġa.
spleen, *n.* Piśniże; wocaŋze.
splendid, *a.* Waśteȟiŋca; wowinihaŋ.
splendidly, *adv.* Ni'na taŋ'yaŋ.
splendidness, *n.* Wowinihaŋ.
splendor, *n.* Wowiyakpa; wowitaŋ.
splice, *vt.* I'ciyakaśka; i'cikoyagya. *n.* I'ciyakaśkapi.
splint, *n.* Hu'weġahaŋ caŋiciyakaśkapi.
splinter, *n.* Wokasdatedaŋ. *vt.* Kasdeca; boptuża.
splintery, *a.* Wokasdata o'ta.
split, *vt.* Kaptuża; yaptuża; kasdeca; yusdeca. *n.* Onasdeca; kiihduśpapi. *pa.* Ptużahaŋ; sdecahaŋ; kasdecapi.
splurge, *n.* Wohitiyaśkaŋ; bobduyaśkaŋ.
splutter, *n.* Naġaġaśkaŋ. *vi.* Oȟaŋko ia.
spoil, *vt.* Yuśica; napiśtaŋyaŋ. *vi.* Śi'ca a'ya. *n.* Woyuha zuya ahdipi; womanoŋ; ta'ku ohiyapi; wawicakipi.
spoilable, *a.* Yuśinpica.
spoiler, *n.* Wawicakis'a; wayuśices'a.
spoke, *imp.* of SPEAK.
spoke, *n.* Caŋpahmihma huyuȟaȟa.
spoken, *pp.* of SPEAK.
spokesman, Iekiyapi.
spoliate, *vt.* Wicaki.
spoliation, *n.* Wawicakipi.
sponge, *n.* 1. Iyuȟepe; ġuġecase: *wipe it with the sponge.* 2. Aġuyapi cocoya napoġe. *vt.* Pakiŋta; paspaya. *vi.* Wayuȟepa; titokaŋ ce'e wota.
sponge-cake, *n.* Aġuyapisku'ya ġuġeca.
spongy, *a.* ·Guġeca; wayuȟepe.
sponsor, *n.* Waekiyapi.
spontaneous, *a.* Iyeciŋkahaŋ.
spontaneously, *adv.* Iyeciŋka.
spool, *n.* Haȟonta oiyapehe.
spoon, *n.* Tukiha; ma'zatukiha; *Y.* & *T.* kiŋśka.
spoonful, *n.* Tukiha ohnaka.
sport, *n.* Wośkate; wicośkate.—*Make sport of*, iȟaȟa.—*In sport*, iȟa kta oŋ; eca ecoŋpi. *vi.* Śka'ta; wakute. *n.* Śka'tes'a.
sporter, *n.* Wakutes'a; śka'tes'a.
sportful, *a.* Śka'tes'a; wowiȟa.
sportfully, *adv.* I'ȟadya.
sporting, *pa.* Śka'tapi.
sportingly, *adv.* I'ȟad.
sportive, *a.* Śka'tekteȟca.
sportively, *adv.* Śka'tekta oŋ.
sportsman, *n.* Wakutewicaśta.
spot, *n.* 1. Oŋśpa; oŋśpatokeca: *a black spot.* 2. Tukte śa'pa; wośape: *without a spot.* 3. Oyaŋke; tuktentu: *a building spot.* 3. Hdeśka; hdeśkaśka.

vt. 1. Aśamya; śamśamya: *you will spot your dress.* 2. Wa'petogtoŋ; samya: *spot the thief.*

spotless, *a.* Wosapewanin; wa'kaśoteśni.

spotted, *pa.* Hdeśka; hde'ġa. *A spotted horse,* śuŋghdeśka.

spousal, *a.* Kiciyuzapi.

spouse, *n.* Hihnaku; tawicu.

spouseless, *a.* Taŋśnauŋ.

spout, *n.* 1. Mini ohna hiyu; i: *the spout of the teakettle.* 2. Minibosdi. *vt.* 1. Hiyuya; bosdi: *the whale is spouting water.* 2. Heyayaŋka; iahaŋ. *vi.* Uya; bosdi.

sprain, *vt.* Naġuka.

sprained, *pa.* Gukahaŋ; naġuka.

sprang, *imp.* of SPRING.

sprawl, *vi.* Nasoŋsoŋ: sdohaŋ.

spray, *n.* 1. Minibozaŋ; minipo: *the spray from the falls.* 2. Caŋiŋkpa opaȟte; caŋwopamna. *vt.* Miniabozaŋ.

spread, *vt.* 1. Yumdaya; kamdaya: *spread his wings; spread the blanket.* 2. Taŋ'kaya yeya; yeya; iyayeya: *spread its branches; spread the disease.* 3. Yaotaŋiŋ; oyaka: *spread the news.* 4. Akadada; enana eȟpeya: *spread manure.* 5. Iuŋ; a'skamya: *spread butter.* 6. Akaȟpa; wi'yeya aehnaka: *spread the table.* *vi.* 1. Iyaya; taŋ'kaya iyaye: *disease spreads.* 2. Otaŋiŋ; taŋ'kaya iyaya. *n.* Waakaȟpe; wayaotaŋiŋpi: *the spread of the gospel.* — *Bedspread,* owiŋżaakaȟpe.

spread-eagle, *n.* Waŋmdikamdaȟ owapi. *a.* Waihdataŋ.

spree, *n.* Witkoiçiyapi; śkatapi.

sprig, *n.* Caŋiŋkpa; caŋteca; kośkadaŋka.

spright, *n.* Wanaġi.

sprightliness, *n.* Wooȟaŋko.

sprightly, *a.* Oȟaŋko; waciŋksapa; mdiheca.

spring, *vi.* 1. Ipsica; kaȟoiyeiçiya: *spring on the horse.* 2. Naśkopa; naśkom iyaye: *the board sprang.* 3. Hinaŋpa; waŋkan u: *the grass springs from the ground.*—*Spring at,* iyapsica. —*Spring forth,* psin hiyu.—*Spring on* (or *upon*), iyaȟpaya. *vt.* Ipsinkiya; napsinya; iyayeya.—*Spring a leak,* naoȟdoka.—*Spring the wheel,* caŋhdeśka naoȟmiŋyaŋ. — *Spring a trap,* mazaȟtakiyapi naoȟpa. *n.* 1. We'tu; wato u'ya: *next spring.* 2. Miniȟdoka; ecamni: *go to the spring for water.* 3. Woipsica; hiyuiçiyapi: *no spring in him.* 4. Ma'zainahuhuza: *the springs of a wagon.* 5. Owahinapa; ka'ġa: *the springs of joy.*

spring-balance, *n.* Tkeutapi otkehaŋ.

spring-board, *n.* Caŋmdaska oipsica.

springer, *n.* Ipsices'a; psi'psin ya.

Springfield, S. D., *n. prop.* Ti'pizizina.

springiness, *n.* 1. Oipsica. 2. Wiwina; cocona.

springing, *n.* Oipsica; oicaġe.

springlet, *n.* Miniuyena; wakpana.

springtime, *n.* We'tu aŋpetu.

spring-wheat, *n.* Aġuyapi we'tu ożupi.

springy, *a.* Świŋświŋżedaŋ: *a springy board.* 2. Wiwina; spa'ya: *springy ground.*

sprinkle, *vt.* Amnimni; akaśtaŋśtaŋ; mniakaśtaŋ: *sprinkle the clothes.* *vi.* 1. Hiŋ'haŋ; iwaśtedaŋ maġażu. 2. Śbuśbu. *n.* Maġażu; minihiŋhe.

sprinkler, *n.* Oŋ amnimnipi.

sprinkling, *n.* Akaštaŋpi; cikcistiŋna; wokitaŋyaŋ.
sprout, *vi.* Camni uye: *the seeds are sprouted.* *n.* Camni.
spruce, *n.* Wazicaŋ (ocaże). *a.* Ayuco: *a spruce young lad.*
sprucely, *adv.* Ayucoya.
sprung, *imp.* of SPRING.
spry, *a.* Oȟaŋko; huhawašte.
spun, *imp.* of SPIN.
spunk, *n.* Caŋkaġica; wocaŋtahde.
spunky, *a.* Caŋze; caŋniyaŋ.
spur, *n.* 1. Mazinażipe: *he wore golden spurs.* 2. Woiyopaštake. 3. Šake; aŋ'paohotoŋna mdoka šake; ta'ku pe'sto. 4. Ipa: *the spur of a mountain.* *vt.* Pażipa; i'yopaštake.
spurious, *a.* Wicakešni; etaŋhaŋšni; ta'wašni.
spuriously, *adv.* Wicakešniyaŋ.
spuriousness, *n.* Wowicakešni.
spurn, *vt.* Nahaiyeya; aktašni. *vi.* Waaktašni.
spurt, *vt.* Bosdi: *spurt water.* *vi.* Ni'na iyaya: *the horse spurted.* *n.* Obosdi; hiyuiçiyapi.
sputter, *vi.* 1. Naġaġa; kpa'kpa. 2. I'mniġaġa ia.
spy, *n.* Naȟmaŋ toŋweyašipi. *vt.* 1. Iwaŋyaka; naȟmaŋna iwaŋyaka: *spy out the enemy.* 2. Waŋyaka: *I spied him in a tree.* *vi.* Iwaŋyag uŋ.
spy-glass, *n.* Maziwaŋyake.
squabble, *vi.* Akinica; kiciza. *n.* Woakinica; wokicize.
squabbler, *n.* Waakinices'a.
squad, *n.* Akicita oŋġe; wicobe.
squadron, *n.* 1. Akicita suŋgakanuŋpi optaye. 2. Ozuyewata optaye.
squalid, *a.* Piyapišni; ša'pa.
squall, *vi.* Ho'taŋka ce'ya. *n.* 1. Ce'yapi ho: *the baby's squall.* 2. Ibobdu: *a snow squall.*
squaller, *n.* Ho'taŋka ce'yes'a.
squally, *a.* Ibobdus'a.
squalor, *n.* Wosape; wicaoŋšika.
squander, *vt.* Makoskan yutakunišni; yusota; yutakunišni.
squanderer, *n.* Wayutakunišni.
square, *n.* 1. To'paicaġopi; to'paomdotoŋ: *he drew a square.* 2. Mazwiyute: *a steel square.* 3. Ho'coka to'pa omdoton: *the village square.* 4. Icihduotapi: *nine is the square of three.* 5. Akicita omdotoŋ na'żiŋpi. *vt.* 1. To'pa omdotoŋ ka'ġa; kaomdotoŋ. 2. Piya ka'ġa. 3. I'ciyuota. 4. Oicazo yuštaŋ; oicazo wi'taya e'hnaka. *vi.* Kici akidecece; kipi; owotaŋna uŋ; kipi. *a.* 1. To'pa omdotoŋ; anokataŋhaŋ iakidecece: *a square timber.* 2. Owotaŋna; itaŋcaŋ: *a right angle.* 3. Omdotoŋ: *square shoulders.* 4. Iyecetu; owotaŋna: *a square trader.* 5. I'tkoŋsya yuštaŋpi; i'tkoŋzedaŋ: *his accounts were square.* 6. Taŋ'ka; okipi: *a square meal.*
squarely, *adv.* Owotaŋna.
squareness, *n.* Woowotaŋna.
squash, *n.* 1. Wamnu; *Y.* wakmu; *T.* wagmu. 2. Ta'ku kašużapi. *vt.* Kašušuża; owihaŋkeya.
squash-bug, *n.* Wamduškazizi.
squasher, *n.* Wakašušuża.
squat, *vi.* Pustagwaŋka; pustagi yotaŋka. *a.* Pustaka; pte'cedaŋ.
squatter, *n.* 1. Tu'we pustag yaŋka. 2. Makoce nahaŋȟ ikiciyutapišni akan i'yotaŋka.
squaw, *n.* Ikcewicaštawiŋyaŋ.
squeak, *vi.* Kiŋ'za; piŋ'za; oyaka. *n.* Wokiŋza; kiŋ'zapi.
squeaker, *n.* Kiŋskiŋza; oyakes'a.
squeaky, *a.* Kiŋskiŋza.
squeal, *vi.* Hotoŋ; kiŋs'hotoŋ.

squeamish, *a.* Tukte ciŋ taŋiŋśni; hitihda.
squeamishly, *adv.* Iyokipiśniyaŋ.
squeeze, *vt.* Ṭiŋsa yu'za; paskica; po'skin yuza. *vi.* Paskiniyaya; oṭiŋs'yaya. *n.* Paskicapi; poskin yu'zapi.
squeezer, *n.* Wapaskica.
squeezing, *n.* Wapaskicapi.
squelch, *vt.* Paṭa; kasni.
squib, *n.* 1. Caḣdi bopopapi. 2. Iapi pe'stona. *vi.* Caḣdi napomya; pe'stoya ia.
squint, *vi.* Iśtokśiŋkiya. *a.* Iśtakśiŋ; kśiŋ.
squinter, *n.* Iśtakśiŋkiyes'a.
squint-eyed, *a.* Iśtakśiŋ.
squire, *n.* *Same as* ESQUIRE.
squirm, *vi.* Ihdukśaŋkśaŋ.
squirrel, *n.* Taśnaheca; żica; hetkadaŋ; pśiŋca.
squirt, *vt.* Bosdi; minibosdi. *n.* Ibosdi; obosdi.
squirt-gun, *n.* Wi'bosdi.
stab, *vt.* Capa: *stab the hog.* *vi.* Wacapa.
stabber, *n.* Wacapa.
stability, *n.* 1. Wosuta; hohopicaśni: *the stability of our government.* 2. Wowaciŋtaŋka.
stable, *n.* Śuŋktaŋkatipi; wanuyaŋpi ti'pi: *no stable for my horse.* *vt.* Timahen na'żiŋkiya. *a.* 1. Suta: *a stable foundation.* 2. Caŋteṭiŋza; waciŋtaŋka; tawaciŋhaŋ'ska.
stableroom, *n.* Śuŋktaŋka owaŋka.
stack, *n.* 1. Peżipaha; paha. 2. Ocetitaŋka. *Smoke-stack,* wa'tapeta oceti.—*Stack of arms,* ma'zakaŋ akiżupi. *vt.* Pahakaġa: *stack hay.*
staff, *n.* 1. Caŋsagye; caŋ: *leaning on his staff.* 2. Sagye; wowaciŋye: *the staff of life.* 3. (*Mus.*) Ho ikicaġopi. 4. Caŋwakaŋ: *the flag-staff.* 5. Ookiye: *he was one of the general's staff.*
stag, *n.* 1. Tamdoka: *I shot a fine stag.* 2. Tataŋka taŋ'ka susu eḣpeyapi.
stag-party, *n.* Wica cee kicicopi.
stage, *n.* 1. Wohdakapi oanażiŋ. 2. Wośkate waecoŋcoŋpi. 3. Oyaŋke; oanażiŋ; ouŋ: *stage of disease.* 4. Wowapi tokśu: *who drives the stage.*
stage-coach, *n.* Wowapitokśu awakeyapi.
stage-driver, *n.* Wowapitokśu kaḣapa.
stage-play, *n.* Waecoŋpi wośkate.
stage-player, *n.* Wapazo wicaśta.
stager, *n.* 1. Tu'we te'han wapazo. 2. Śuŋktaŋka te'han wowapitokśu.
stagger, *vi.* Kacegcegmani; aptaŋptaŋ; waciŋiboś'aka: *he staggered under the weight.* *vt.* Kacegya; kahuhuza.
staggeringly, *adv.* Kacegya.
stagnant, *a.* Śkaŋśkaŋśni; miniṭa; śi'ca: *stagnant water.*
stagnate, *vi.* Śi'ca a'ya; yuhuŋkeśni.
staid, *imp.* of STAY.
staid, *a.* Oḣaŋtaŋka; śke'heśni.
staidness, *n.* Oḣaŋtaŋkapi.
stain, *vt.* Kaḣtaŋ; toya; yuśapa: *stain clothes.* *n.* Wokaḣtaŋ; wośape; samyapi; dunyapi.
stainless, *a.* Śa'peśni; wa'kaśoteśni.
stairs, *n. pl.* Caŋiyadipi. *Down-stairs,* ti'pi ku'ya.—*Up-stairs,* waŋkantipi.
staircase, *n.* Caŋiyadipiokaśke.
stairway, *n.* Caŋiyadipicaŋkuye.
stake, *n.* 1. Caŋ'ipasdate; caŋ'pasdatapi: *tied to a stake.* 2. Wayekiyapi: *held the stake.*—*At stake,* iyowaś uŋ.—*Fence-stake,* coŋ'kaśkeipasdate. *vt.* Pasdata; caŋ kipasdata: *stake the*

beans. 2. (*With* OUT) Wasaghde; wa'petogtoŋ: *stake out the road.* 3. Yekiya; iyakaśka: *he staked ten dollars.*

stake-holder, *n.* Wayekiyapi yuha.

stalactite, *n.* Iŋ'yaŋcaḣoiŋ.

stale, *a.* Ehaŋna; ḣoŋwiŋmna.

stalk, *n.* Hu; caŋhu. *vi.* Ma'ni.

stall, *n.* 1. Śuŋ'kawakaŋ onażiŋ. *A double stall,* akicaśka onażiŋ. 2. Wopetoŋ onażiŋ; caŋkukahda ma'zaehdepi. *A butcher's stall,* tado wi'yopeyapi onażiŋ. *vt.* 1. I'yaninya: *he stalled his horse.* 2. Śuŋgonażiŋ en hde. *vi.* I'yanica; okihiśni: *his oxen stalled.*

stall-fed, *n.* Wamnaheza icemyapi.

stallion, *n.* Śuŋgmdoka.

stalwart, *a.* Taŋcaŋtaŋka; ohitika.

stamina, *n.* Wowaś'ake.

stammer, *vi.* Iekaskiska; ḣinḣicahaŋ ia.

stamp, *vt.* 1. Naskica; nahaŋ; naḣtaka: *stamp the ground.* 2. Natata: *stamp the dirt off.* 3. Apuspa. *Stamp the date on,* wiyawapi apuspa. 4. Wiciteaskamya: *stamp your letter.* 5. Ma'zaska ka'ġa. 6. A'skamya; ikoyagya: *stamp the truth on your heart.* *n.* 1. Wonaḣtake: *a stamp of the foot.* 2. Wiciteaskape; i'yaskape. *Postage-stamp,* wowapikiciçupi iyaskape. 3. Wi'puspe; ma'zaipuspe: *the stamp is broken.* 4. Okaġe; oye: *he has the stamp of a drunkard on him.* 5. Wi'bopa; wi'paskice.

stampede, *vt.* Napeya; ḣamya: *the wolf stampeded the horses.* *n.* Wonażice; wonapa.

stamper, *n.* Wi'bopaŋ; wi'puspe.

stamping-machine, *n.* Oŋ wi'puspapi; oŋ wi'bopaŋpi.

stamping-mill, *n.* Oŋ iŋ'yaŋ bopaŋpi.

stanch, *vt.* Anapta; pusya: *stanch the flow of blood.* *a.* Suta; ṭiŋze; wicaka; waciŋyepica.

stanchion, *n.* Ipataŋ.

stanchness, *n.* Wosuta; waciŋyepica.

stand, *vi.* 1. Na'żiŋ: *stand still.* 2. Haŋ; waŋka: *some trees stood in the field.* 3. Ecenhaŋ; sutaya haŋ. *Come and stand,* hinażiŋ.—*Go and stand,* kinażin.—*Stand against,* pataŋ na'żiŋ; kipażiŋ.—*Stand by,* kici na'żiŋ; o'kiya.—*Stand for,* e'ekiya na'żiŋ; nakiciżiŋ.—*Stand his ground,* he'cehnana na'żiŋ; napeśni.—*Stand in hand,* iyecetuka.—*Stand it,* iyowiŋyaŋ; waciŋtaŋka.—*Stand off,* i'tehaŋ i'nażiŋ; wicadaśni.—*Stand one off,* pataŋ na'żiŋ; ḣam'ya.—*Stand on,* akan na'żin; anażiŋ.—*Stand out,* pażoya uŋ; okitaŋiŋ; wakitaŋ.—*Stand to,* napeśni; ecen ecoŋ.—*Stand up,* bosdan na'żiŋ; na'żiŋhaŋ na'żiŋ.—*Stand up for,* nakiciżiŋ; iciya. *vt.* 1. Na'żiŋkiya; e'hde: *stand the umbrella in the corner.* 2. Ki'cinażiŋ; kici ecoŋ; itokecaśni; en uŋ; iyowiŋyaŋ: *stood the enemy's fire.*—*Stand it,* iyowiŋyaŋ. — *Stand one's ground,* napeśni.—*Stand trial,* aiapi kta iyowiŋyaŋ. *n.* 1. Onażiŋ; oeyoḣpa. 2. Ta'ku ahna na'żiŋpi; wowapi aehnakapi; ahna wowapi ka'ġapidaŋ. — *Come to a stand,* waanin hinażiŋpi.

standard, *n.* 1. Wa'paha; caŋwapaha; wi'yokihedaŋ; miniḣuha opasdate. *The standard-bearer,* wa'paha yu'za. 2. Oiyute yustaŋpi; wikiyutapi otokahe. 3.

Woope hde'pi. *a.* Wahehantu; otaŋiŋ; a'taya uŋ'pi.

standing, *pa.* Na'żiŋhaŋnażiŋ; ecayuhapi; bosdan haŋ.—*A standing army,* akicita eca yuhapi. —*Standing corn,* wamnaheza yukseśŋi haŋ.—*Standing water,* mini kaduześni. *n.* 1. Na'żiŋpi; wonażiŋ: *standing wearies me.* 2. Waciŋkiyuzapi; yawapi: *a man of high standing.*

Standing Rock, *n. prop.* Iŋ'yaŋ bosdata; *T.* Iŋ'yaŋ woslata.

standing-point, *n.* Onażiŋ; woiwaŋyake.

stank, *imp.* of STINK.

stanza, *n.* Odowaŋ oehde.

staple, *a.* Itaŋcaŋ; iyotaŋ; o'hiŋni yuhapi; ni'na icaħyapi. *n.* 1. Wokaġe itaŋcaŋ; iyotaŋ ożupi. 2. Ta'ku etaŋhaŋ ka'ġapi. 3. Maziyokataŋ śuŋżoyake: *staples for wire fence.*

star, *n.* 1. Wicaŋħpi. *The morning star,* aŋ'pao wicaŋħpi. 2. Wicaŋħpikaġapi: *mark it with a star.* 3. Iyotaŋ wayupika: *the star singer.* *vt.* Wicaŋħpi koyagya; wicaŋħpikaġa.

starboard, *n.* Wa'ta etapataŋhaŋ.

starch, *n.* Miniħuha ipatiŋ. *vt.* Ipatiŋye.

starched, *pa.* Patiŋ.

stare, *vt.* Opaħta kuwa. *vi.* Iśtowaŋżidaŋ e'toŋwaŋ.

star-fish, *n.* Wicaŋħpi hoġaŋ.

star-gazer, *n.* Wicaŋħpi waŋyaka; makoskan e'toŋwaŋ.

stark, *a.* Ecaca; a'taya.

starless, *a.* Wicaŋħpi wanica.

starlight, *n.* Wicaŋħpi i'żaŋżaŋ.

starlike, *a.* Wicaŋħpi iyececa.

starred, *a.* Wicaħpi koyake.

starry, *a.* Wicaŋħpi o'ta; wicaŋħpi.

star-spangled, *a.* Wicaŋħpi żu'pi: *star-spangled banner.*

start, *vi.* Iyaya; waŋna iyaye; napa; nabaka; iyopte; ya. *Start after,* hakam iyaye; tapa. *Start to,* ekta ya.—*Start up,* bosdan iyeiçiya; naśdoġ iyaya. *vt.* Iyayeya; yuħica; tokaka'ġe; iyeya; ħamya. *n.* Woiyopte; wonaśdoka; ħamyapi; woipsica; otokahe. *Get the start,* tokaheya iyaye.

starting-point, *n.* Etaŋhaŋ ya'pi.

startle, *vt.* Yuśiŋyeya; napeca.

startling, *a.* Woyuśiŋyaŋ.

starvation, *n.* Wicaakiħaŋ; woyute wanica.

starve, *vi.* Akiħaŋ; icakiża. *Starve to death,* akiħaŋ ţa. *vt.* Akiħaŋya; kakiśya; wokuśni.

starveling, *n.* Akiħaŋţena.

state, *n.* 1. Makobaśpe: *the State of Nebraska.* 2. Ouŋ; to'ketu kiŋ: *the state of his health.* 3. Wowitaŋ wicoħaŋ. 4. Oyate; oyate omniciye: *the laws of the State; State policy.* *vt.* Oyaka: *state the number.*

stated, *pa.* Oyakapi; ka'pi; ecayuhapi: *a stated amount.*—*Stated meetings,* omniciye eca yuhapi.

statedly, *adv.* Iyehaŋyaŋ.

state-house, *n.* Makobaśpe oitaŋcaŋ ti'pi.

stateliness, *n.* Wowicataŋka.

stately, *a.* Hiŋ'skotaŋka; taŋ'kaħca; wowinihaŋ.

statement, *n.* Woyake; oyakapi.

state-prison, *n.* Makobaśpe; wokaśketipi.

stateroom, *n.* 1. Ti'piitaŋcaŋ. 2. Iśtiŋma ti'pidaŋ.

statesman, *n.* Ksapotaŋcaŋ; oyatewiwicakiciyukcaŋ.

statesmanlike, *a.* Itaŋcaŋiyececa.

statesmanship, *n.* Woitaŋcaŋouŋ.

station, *n.* Oinażiŋ; oyaŋka; onażiŋ. *Railroad station,* ħemani onażiŋ. *vt.* Na'żiŋkiya; yaŋkekiya.

station-house, *n.* Oinażiŋ ti'pi.
stationary, *a.* Owaŋżi haŋ.
stationer, *n.* Wowapiska wi'yopeya.
stationery, *n.* Wowapikaġa icuwa.
statistical, *a.* Owicawapi.
statistics, *n.* Owicawapi; owapi.
statuary, *n.* Wicaśtakaġapi.
statue, *n.* Wicaśtakaġapi.
stature, *n.* Ohaŋske.
statute, *n.* Woope; oyatetoope.
statute-book, *n.* Woope wowapi.
stave, *n.* Kokapahmihma caŋ. *vt.* Kaḣuġa; paḣdoka. *Stave off,* paḣeyata iyeya; kihnaka.
stay, *vi.* Yaŋka; owaŋżiyaŋka; akipe. *Stay away,* tokaŋ uŋ. *vt.* 1. Kaġiya: *stay the proceedings.* 2. Pataŋyuza; yu'za. *n.* 1. Ipataŋ; wi'yuze: *the stay broke.* 2. En ouŋye: *he made a long stay.*
stead, *n.* Oyaŋke: *in his stead.*
steadfast, *a.* Tawaciŋ suta; yuhohopicaśni.
steadfastly, *adv.* Waciŋtaŋkaya; hohośniyaŋ.
steadfastness, *n.* Wowaciŋtaŋka.
steadily, *adv.* Iwaśtedaŋ; he'cetuwaŋżica.
steadiness, *n.* Pa'tawaŋżina; yuśnaśni.
steady, *a.* He'cetuwaŋżica; hohośni; oḣaŋṭiŋza. *vt.* Owaŋżi yu'za.
steak, *n.* Tadoceġuġuyapi.
steal, *vt.* Manoŋ; naḣmaŋ icu: *steal apples.* *vi.* 1. Wamanoŋ: *thou shalt not steal.* 2. Naḣmaŋ iyaye: *he stole away.*
stealing, *n.* Wamanoŋpi.
stealth, *n.* Wonaḣbe.
stealthily, *adv.* Naḣmana.
stealthy, *a.* Wamanonse; naḣmaŋpi.
steam, *n.* Mini po; opo; po. *vi.* .Po; ipiġa. *vt.* .Poya; apoya; skemya; ipiḣya. *Steam one's self,* ini.
steamboat, *n.* Pe'tawata; *Y. & T.* wa'tapeta.
steam-boiler, *n.* Minioipiḣya.
steam-engine, *n.* Pe'tawata ma'zaśkaŋ.
steamer, *n.* Pe'tawata; wi'ṫawatapeta.
steampipe, *n.* Minipo ma'zaoḣdoġeca.
steam-plow, *n.* Minipo maḣiyumdu.
steamship, *n.* Miniwaŋcawatapeta.
steamvessel, *n.* Minipowata.
steam-whistle, *n.* Minipożożo.
steamy, *a.* Minipoota.
steed, *n.* Śuŋktaŋka.
steel, *n.* 1. Ma'zasuta: *a knife made of good steel.* 2. Ta'ku ma'za oŋ ka'ġapi; mi'na. 3. Maziyohdi; iyohdi. *Fire-steel,* caŋka. *vt.* Ma'zasuta ka'ġa; yusuta.
steel-trap, *n.* Ma'żaḣtakiyapi; mazihmuŋke.
steep, *a.* Maya; i'taŋwaŋbde; a'pamahde; oteḣika. *n.* Maya; ḣeuŋnaptaŋ. *vt.* Ḣpaŋyaŋ; mini ohna hde.
steeple, *n.* Ipasotka; iŋ'kpa.
steepness, *n.* Maya; wobosdata.
steer, *n.* Tataŋkadaŋ; tataŋkasusuwanica. *vt.* Iyupseyuza; yuhomni. *vi.* Hiyu.
steering-wheel, *n.* Wa'taiyuhomni.
steersman, *n.* Wasiŋteyuza.
stem, *n.* Hucaŋ; hu; suŋ'ta; pa. *Pipe-stem:* caŋduhupasuŋta. *vt.* Itkom ya.
stench, *n.* Ḣuŋwiŋmna; śicamna.
stencil, *n.* Oowa kaosmagkaġapi.
stenographer, *n.* Wowapi oḣaŋko ka'ġa.
stenography, *n.* Wowapi oḣaŋkokaġapi.
stent, *n.* Tohaŋyaŋ yuśtaŋ kte.

stentorian, *n.* Ho'tanka; hiŋ'skotaŋka.

step, *vi.* Caehde; ma'ni. *Step around,* o'kšaŋ ma'ni.—*Step aside,* icuŋom na'žiŋ.—*Step back,* he'kta na'žiŋ.—*Step forth,* cokam inažiŋ.—*Step in,* en inažiŋ.—*Step over,* acakšiŋ. *n.* 1. Caehdepi; cahdepi. 2. Siiyahe; cahdepi: *the second step.* 3. (*Mus.*) Hooiyadi. *A false step,* eciŋšni caehdepi.—*Door-step,* tiyopa siehde.—*Foot-steps in the snow,* wa kiŋ en sihaoaehde—*Known by his step,* caehde oŋ iyekiyapi.—*Only a step,* cahdepi waŋžina.—*Step by step,* cahdepi ḣaŋhi.

step-brother, *n.* Ciŋyeku tawaġaŋ.

step-child, *n.* Tawaġaŋyaŋ ciŋca.

step-father, *n.* Atkuku tawaġaŋ.

step-mother, *n.* Huŋku tawaġaŋ.

steepe, *n.* Tiŋ'ta.

stepping-stone, *n.* Iŋ'yaŋ siehdepi.

step-sister, *n.* Tawinoḣtiŋ tawaġaŋ.

step-son, *n.* Ciŋhiŋtku tawaġaŋ.

sterile, *a.* 1. Waicaġešni: *a sterile field.* 2. Ciŋca wanica: *a sterile cow.* 3. Iapi co wanica; wowiyukcaŋ ni'ca: *a sterile writer.*

sterility, *n.* Woicaġešni.

sterling, *a.* 1. Wašteḣiŋca; e'cedan: *a sterling writer.* 2. Sagdašiŋ tamazaska.

stern, *a.* Ḳeza; ksizeca; hiŋyaŋzeca: *a stern teacher.* *n.* Wahektapa.

sternly, *adv.* Ksizeya.

sternmost, *a.* Uŋzeta; ehake.

sternness, *n.* Ksizecapi.

sternum, *n.* Makuhu.

stew, *vt.* Ohaŋ; ipiḣya. *vi.* Ipiġa. *n.* 1. Ohaŋpi: *a beef stew.* 2. Mde'zecešni: *he was in a stew.*

steward, *n.* Wa'waŋyake; woyute awaŋyake.

stick, *n.* 1. Caŋ; caŋksa: *he hit me with a stick.* 2. Ohna ma'zaahdiḣpeyapi. *vt.* 1. Capa: *stick a hog.* 2. Icam e'hde; pasdata; paḣdi: *stick it in the ground.* 3. A'skamya: *stick the stamp on the letter.* 4. I'yaninya. *vi.* 1. A'skapa; o'tkapa; o'ha: *the mud sticks.* 2. Icam haŋ; paḣdi: *it stuck fast.* 3. I'yanica; okihišni: *his team stuck in the creek.*—*Stick by,* en iyaskapa; tokaŋ ye šni.—*Stick out,* pažoya waŋka; taŋiŋ.—*Stick to, stick at,* ayuštaŋšni kuwa.

sticker, *n.* Wi'yaskape; woiyaoŋpe.

stickiness, *n.* Woiyaskape.

sticking-plaster, *n.* Wi'yaskape; pežuta a'skamyapi.

stickle, *vi.* To'ketutaŋiŋšni.

stickler, *n.* Wakitaŋka; waakinices'a.

sticky, *a.* Da'pa; o'tkapa.

stiff, *a.* 1. Patiŋ; suta; tasaka: *the clothes were frozen stiff.* 2. Waš'aka: *a stiff breeze.* 3. Suta; da'pa: *stiff glue.* 4. Ḳe'za; ksizeca; botiŋ: *a stiff woman.*

stiffen, *vt.* Patiŋya; tasagya. *vi.* Patiŋ a'ya; sa'ka; da'pa.

stiffening, *n.* Oŋ patiŋyaŋpi.

stiff-necked, *n.* Tahusuta; wanaḣoŋšni.

stiffness, *n.* Wosuta; woḳeza.

stifle, *vt.* Yuniyašni; yusni. *n.* Cecuŋtoštaŋ.

stigma, *n.* Wošapa; woiyaoŋpa.

stigmatize, *vt.* .Guya; iyaoŋpa; yašica.

stile, *n.* Coŋkaške oiyadi.

stiletto, *n.* Oŋ wacapapi; wi'cape.

still, *vt.* Yuinina; yuasni; yuamdakedaŋ. *a.* 1. Inina uŋ: *a still boy.* 2. Inina: *be still.* 3. Owaŋži: *stand still.* 4. Amdakedaŋ: *a still evening.*

adv. 1. Nahaŋħiŋ : *he is still here.* 2. He'caśta : *still I shall go.* 3. Nakuŋ : *still greater.* *n.* Miniwakaŋ okaġe.
still-born, *a.* Sniyaŋ toŋ'pi ; itkotpa.
stillness, *n.* Woamdakedaŋ.
stilt, *n.* Caŋ'haŋska huyapi.
stilted, *a.* Ihduwaŋkantuya.
stimulant, *a.* Wawiyopaśtake. *n.* Woiyopaśtake ; miniwakaŋ.
stimulate, *vt.* I'yopaśtake.
stimulation, *n.* Wawiyopaśtake.
stimulus, *n.* Woiyopaśtake ; woiyutaŋye ; miniwakaŋ.
sting, *n.* Wi'cape ; woyaħtake. *vt.* Yaħtaka ; capa ; yaśipa : *a bee stung me.*
stinger, *n.* Wayażipes'a ; wayażipe.
stingily, *adv.* Wateħiŋdaya.
stinginess, *n.* Oħaŋśuŋkecapi.
stinging, *a.* Wayażipe.
stingless, *a.* Wi'capenica.
stingy, *a.* Wateħiŋda ; oħaŋśica.
stink, *a.* Śicamna ; ħwiŋ'mna. *n.* Womnaśica.
stint, *vt.* Ihukuŋ ku ; a'okpaniya ; iyawaħca ecoŋkiya.
stipend, *n.* Wokażużu ; iśi.
stipulate, *vi.* Kici yuśtaŋ.
stipulation, *n.* I'tokam yuśtaŋpi.
stir, *vt.* Yuśkaŋśkaŋ ; icahiya ; ka'ġa. *Stir the mush,* wożapi icahiya.—*Stir him up to do it,* ecoŋkta i'yopaśtaka.—*Stir up the mind,* tawaciŋ yuħica. *vi.* Śkaŋśkaŋ ; iyopte.—*Stir one's self,* ihduśkaŋśkaŋ. *n.* Wośkaŋśkaŋ ; owodutatoŋ.
stirring, *pa.* Śkaŋśkaŋuŋ ; mdiheca.
stirrup, *n.* Siinataŋ.
stitch, *vt.* Pasisa ; kaġeġe. *n.* 1. Ipasisa ; icape : *long stitches.* 2. Icamyazaŋ : *a stitch in my side.*
stitcher, *n.* Wakaġeġe.
stitching, *n.* Okaġeġe ; wakaġeġe.
stock, *n.* 1. Hucaŋ ; taŋcaŋ : *a stock without leaves.* 2. Hutkaŋ : *of the stock of Abraham.* 3. Okpahi ; ahdihe : *a large stock of goods.* 4. Ta'wayekiyapi wowapi : *railroad stock.* 5. Woyuha ; optaye : *a big stock of cattle.* 6. Huha okaśke : *put him in the stocks.*—*Live-stock,* wanuyaŋpi. *vt.* Ohnaka ; mnayaŋ ; hde. *a.* Kihnakapi ; ecayuhapi.
stockade, *n.* Caŋpasdapicoŋkaśke.
stocking, *n.* Iyahdehuŋska. *n. Y.* Huyakoŋ.
stocky, *a.* Hucaŋtaŋka.
Stoic, *n.* Caŋteṭiŋza.
stoical, *a.* Caŋteṭiŋza.
stoicism, *n.* Caŋteṭiŋzapi.
stole, *imp.* of STEAL.
stolen, *pp.* of STEAL.
stolid, *a.* Waawaciŋśni ; waciŋṭaṭake.
stolidity, *n.* Wowaciŋtoŋśni ; wowitkokoka.
stomach, *n.* Tezi ; niġe.
stone, *n.* 1. Iŋ'yaŋ : *a round stone.* 2. Su : *a plum stone.* *a.* Iŋ'yaŋ : *a stone ax.* *vt.* 1. In'yaŋ on kiŋiŋ : *stone the birds.* 2. Iŋ'yaŋ żu : *stone a well.*
stone-coal, *n.* Iŋ'yaŋcaħdi.
stone-cutter, *n.* Iŋ'yaŋkakaŋ.
stone-cutting, *n.* Iŋ'yaŋkakaŋpi.
stone-hammer, *n.* Iŋ'yaŋwiyape.
stone-hearted, *a.* Caŋteiŋyan ; waoŋśidaśni.
stone-mason, *n.* Iŋ'yaŋkaġa.
stone's-cast, *a.* Iŋ'yaŋokaħ'o.
stone's-throw, *n.* Iŋ'yaŋokaħ'o.
stonewall, *n.* Iŋ'yaŋcoŋkaśke ; in'yaŋtiobosdate.
stoneware, *n.* Makawakśica suta.
stone-work, *n.* Iŋ'yaŋkaġapi.
stony, *n.* Iŋ'yaŋ o'ta ; iŋ'yaŋ se'ca ; iŋ'yaŋ iyececa.
stood, *imp.* of STAND.
stool, *n.* Caŋ'akaŋyaŋkapimibe-

daŋ; acesdipi. *Stool of a window*, o'żaŋżaŋhdepi sicu. *n.* Akta uya.
stoop, *vi.* Patuża; patuś inażiŋ; ihduhukuya; ta'kuśniiçiya. *n.* Wopatuża; tiyopaawakeyapi.
stop, *vt.* 1. Na'żiŋkiya: *stop the man.* 2. Anapta; kaġiya: *stop the flow of water.* 3. Ayuśtaŋkiya: *he stopped the workmen.* *vi.* 1. Ayuśtaŋ; inażiŋ: *the workmen stopped; the clock stopped.* 2. Waŋ'ka; yaŋka: *the traveller stopped here.* *n.* 1. Inażiŋpi; wonażiŋ: *the train made a long stop.* 2. Woanapte; wokaġi: *put a stop to it.* 3. Oehnakedaŋ: *mark the stops.*
stoppage, *n.* Waanaptapi.
stopper, *n.* Iośtaŋ; woanapte.
stopping, *n.* Owaŋżiuŋ.
stopple, *n.* Iośtaŋ.
storage, *n.* Wakihnakapi.
store, *n.* 1. Mazopiye: *buy it at the store.* 2. Owomnaye; wakihnakapi: *stores of food.* 3. Ma'za; woyuha: *military stores.* —*In store*, wi'yeya uŋ.—*Set store by*, teħiŋda.—*Store-room*, wakihnaka ti'pi. *vt.* 1. Kihnaka: *he stored his goods.* 2. En ohnaka; ożudaŋya: *store the mind with knowledge.*
store-house, *n.* Wakihnaka ti'pi.
store-keeper, *n.* Mazopiyeyuha.
store-pay, *n.* Ma'za oŋ każużupi.
store-room, *n.* Ohna wakihnakapi.
storied, *pa.* Wi'ciwaŋkam ka'ġapi. *A four-storied house.*
stork, *n.* Hok'a (ocaże).
storm, *n.* 1. Ibomdu; icamna: *a cold storm.* 2. Wonataŋ: *taken by storm.* *vt.* Nataŋ; en iheiçiya. *vi.* Nataŋtaŋ; wohitiya śkaŋ; kiħaŋśica; ibobdu; icamna.
storminess, *n.* Woibobdu.
stormy, *a.* 1. Kiħaŋśica: *a stormy day.* 2. Kiħaŋśices'a: *a stormy country.* 3. Wohitika; wohitiya śkaŋpi: *a stormy meeting.*
story, *n.* 1. Woyake; hituŋkakaŋpi: *he wrote a story.* 2. Woitoŋśni; wowicakeśni: *the boy told a story.* 3. Ti'pi owaŋka: *in the upper story.*
story-book, *n.* Woyakapi wowapi; kakaŋpi wowapi.
story-teller, *n.* Wakakaŋs'a.
stout, *a.* Taŋ'ka; waś'aka.
stoutly, *adv.* Waś'agya; ni'na.
stove, *n.* Ma'zaoceti. *Cooking-stove*, owaśpaŋye.
stove, *imp.* of STAVE.
stow, *vt.* Ohnaka; e'hnaka; kihnaka.
straddle, *vt.* Akamdaża. *vi.* Kamdaś inażiŋ.
straggle, *vi.* Nu'ni; omdecahaŋ; icuŋom ya.
straggler, *n.* Wi'ciśni iyaye.
straight, *a.* Owotaŋna. *adv.* Waŋ'cahna; katiŋyaŋ.
straighten, *vt.* 1. Yuowotaŋna; owotaŋna ka'ġa. 2. Yukakiża; yuwaħpanica.
straightened, *pa.* Wakakiżyapi; waħpanica; yuowotaŋnapi.
straightforward, *a.* Owotaŋna; oħaŋ owotaŋna; katiŋyaŋśkaŋ.
straightly, *adv.* Katiŋyaŋ; waŋcahnana.
strain, *vt.* 1. Yuţiŋza; ţiŋsya ecoŋ: *strain the rope.* 2. To'ken okihi ecoŋ; yuţins śkaŋ: *strain every nerve.* 3. Yuġuka; naġuka; paś'aka: *strain his ankle.* 4. Yuś'agya: *strain every nerve.* 5. Puskepa: *strain milk.* *vi.* Aiçiciya; ś'agiçiya. *n.* 1. Woś'aka; ś'agiçiyapi; aiçiciyapi; woţiŋze: *the strain was very great.* 2. Odowaŋ iyokise; o'śpe; ho: *some delightful strains.*
strainer, *n.* 1. Ipuskepa: *a milk*

strainer. 2. Woyuṭiŋze ; waka-ṡ'aka.

strait, *a.* Oṭiŋza ; ci'stiŋna : *a strait gate.* *n.* 1. O'kiyute ; mniokiyute : *straits of Gibraltar.* 2. Woteḣi : *in great straits.*

straitened, *pa.* Oteḣika.

straitly, *adv.* Yaṭinsya ; a'wicakeya.

straitness, *n.* Woṭiŋze ; woteḣi.

strand, *n.* 1. O'huta ; huta : *on the ocean's strand.* 2. Kisoŋpi. *vi.* A'zi ; anica.

strange, *a.* To'keca ; to'ketutaŋiŋṡni.

strangely, *adv.* Togye ; otogye ; wowinihaŋyaŋ.

strangeness, *n.* To'keca ; okaḣniḣpicaṡni.

stranger, *n.* Wicaṡtatokeca ; wasdonyeṡni.

strangle, *vt.* Yuniyaṡni ; yuṭa. *vi.* Katka : *the babe strangled.*

strangulation, *n.* Niyaṡni.

strap, *n.* 1. Wi'kaŋmdaska ; wi'-kaŋ ; teḣmiso : *a trunk strap.* 2. Iyohdi : *a razor strap.* 3. Mdaskana : *strap-iron.* *vt.* 1. Yuskita ; aokataŋ : *strap the trunk.* 2. Iyohdiya : *strap the razor.*

strapper, *n.* Hiŋ'ṡkotaŋka.

strapping, *a.* Taŋ'ka ; otawaṭeṡica. *n.* Wi'paḣte.

strata, *n. pl.* of STRATUM.

stratagem, *n.* Oẓuye wohnaye.

strategy, *n.* Wohnaye.

stratify, *vt.* Mdaskaicaġa.

stratum, *n.* Womdaska.

straw, *n.* Aġuyapihu ; hu. *A man of straw,* wicaṡta ta'kuṡni.—*One straw,* sukaza waŋẓidaŋ.

strawberry, *n.* Waẓuṡteca.

straw-color, *n* Zi.

straw-cutter, *n.* Aġuyapi-icakpaŋ.

stray, *vi.* Nu'ni ; yukṡaŋkṡaŋ ya. *a.* Nu'ni ; to'keca.

streak, *n.* Icaġopi ; kaġopise. *A streak of lightning,* wakaŋhdi caŋkuye. *vt.* Yuhdeġa.

streaked, *pa.* Hdehdeze ; hdehdeġa.

stream, *n.* 1. Wakpa. 2. Minikaduza : *the Gulf Stream.* 3. Wokaduza ; kadushiyu : *a stream of blood.* 4. Iyoẓaŋẓaŋ : *a stream of light.* 5. O'hiŋni hiyaye : *the stream of trade.* *vi.* 1. Kaduza ; kadus hiyu ; wakaduze : *the water streams.* 2. Kaḣboke : *streaming in the wind.* *vt.* Kadusya ; kaḣbogya ; hdeḣhdeḣya icaġo.

streamer, *n.* Miniḣuha kaḣboka ; wi'yokihedaŋ.

streamlet, *n.* Wakpadaŋ.

street, *n.* Otoŋwe caŋku.

strength, *n.* 1. Wowaṡ'ake ; wosuta : *strength of body.*

strengthen, *vt.* Was'agya. *vi.* Waṡ'akaaya.

strenuous, *a.* Wakitaŋ ; wohitika.

strenuously, *adv.* Kitaŋyaŋ ; waṡ'agya.

stress, *n.* Wopataŋ ; woiyopaṡtaka. *Lay stress on,* wotaŋka yawa.—*Stress of voice,* ho ṭinsyapi.

stretch, *vt.* 1. Yutitaŋ ; yuṭiŋza : *stretch a rope.* 2. Yuzica ; yuzigzica : *stretch a skin.* 3. Nasoŋsoŋ : *stretch his legs.* 4. Akaġa : *stretch the truth.* *vi.* 1. Samya ; samyeya ; yeya ; zigzica : *the lake stretches ; the cloth stretches.* 2. Aiçiciya ; ihduzica ; du'zahaŋ. *n.* Woyutitaŋ ; woyuzica ; womdaye ; woecoŋ ; aiçiciyapi.

stretched, *a.* Yutitaŋpi ; yuzicapi. *With stretched arms,* akaġatkiya.

stretcher, *n.* 1. Caŋwiçihupa ; caŋ'-akiyuhapi : *they carried him on a stretcher.* 2. Caŋiciyakaṡka ; wi'pataŋ.

strew, *vt.* Kadaeȟpeya; kadada.
strewing, *n.* Wakadadapi.
stricken, *pa.* 1. Apapi. *The stricken dog,* śuŋ'ka apapi. 2. Caŋtiyapa; caŋtiyaȟpaya: *stricken with love.* 3. Kaŋ; ehaŋna.
strict, *a.* 1. Ecetuȟca: *strict observance.* 2. Ṭiŋza. 3. Iśtamdeza; teȟika: *a strict teacher.*
strictly, *adv.* Ecetuȟca.
strictness, *n.* Woecetu.
stricture, *n.* 1. I en iyeyapi; woiyaoŋpa. 2. (*Med.*) Natipapi.
stride, *n.* Cahdepi; ca. *vi.* Caehde.
strife, *n.* Woakinica; wokiçize; wośkiśke.
strike, *vt.* 1. Apa. *He struck me,* amapa. 2. Iyapa: *the boat struck a rock.* 3. Oŋ iyapa: *strike the blood on the wall.* 4. Iyayeya: *the tree strikes its roots deep.* 5. Kun iyeya: *struck his tent.* 6. Awaciŋya; iyaȟpeya: *strike with wonder.*—*Struck off his head,* pa kaśpa iyeya.—*Strike of the papers,* wowapi ahdiȟpeya.—*Strike out,* pażużu; kasni.—*Struck up,* ecoŋ iyeya; ecoŋ; a'ya. *vi.* 1. Waapa; apa: *he kept striking.* 2. Nataŋ; kuwa; iyaya. 3. Iyaya; a'zi: *the boat struck.* 4. Hiyaya; iyaya: *it struck through.* 5. Ayuśtaŋpi; wokażużu iwaŋkamda'pi: *the carpenters struck.* 6. Ihnuhaŋ ececa; hiyaya. *He struck a run,* iŋ'yaŋg iyaya.—*Strike for,* eciyotaŋ ya.—*Strike in,* mahen iyaya.—*Strike out,* iyaya; akan hiyu. *n.* 1. Woape; oape; apapi. 2. Woenakiye; wowaśi enakiye.
striker, *n.* Woape; wi'yape.
striking, *pa.* Wa'petokeca; okitaŋiŋ.
strikingly, *adv.* Okitaŋiŋyaŋ.
string, *n.* 1. Ikaŋ; wikaŋ; hahoŋta; ipaȟte: *tie the string.* 2. Oyaza; oboȟci; soŋ'pi: *a string of beads.* 3. Soŋ'pi: *a string of corn.* 4. Kaŋ: *the string of the tongue.* 5. I'ciyaza yeye: *what a string of people.*—*A shoestring,* haŋkpaŋ. *vt.* Yaza; kaza: *to string beads.* 2. Soŋ; kisoŋ: *string corn.* 3. Ikaŋtoŋ: *string the bow.* 4. Yuṭiŋza: *string the nerves.* 5. Kaŋ yuśdoka: *string the beans.*
string-band, *n.* Caŋ'pakiŋzapi optaye.
string-beans, *n.* Omnica yuksaohaŋpi.
stringed, *a.* Ikaŋtoŋ; kazapi.
stringency, *n.* Otehika.
stringent, *a.* Sutaya wi'yuza; teȟika.
stringently, *adv.* Sutaya; ecetuya.
stringer, *n.* 1. Ikaŋwicatoŋ. 2. Caŋhaŋska.
stringless, *a.* Ikaŋwanica.
stringy, *a.* 1. Ikaŋiyececa; kaŋ se'kse; ikaŋ ecee. 2. Da'pa; tiktica; suta.
strip, *vi.* 1. Yuśdoka: *strip him of clothes.* 2. Baġapa; yu'za: *strip the skin off.* 3. Kaȟu: *to strip bark.* 4. Ki; kanica: *stripped of his possessions.* 5. Ehakedaŋ yusdi: *strip the cow.* *vi.* Ihduśdoka. *n.* Ci'stiŋna haŋ'ska; sbu'na; mdazapi.
stripe, *n.* 1. Oicaġo; oicazo owapi: *a red stripe.* 2. Okipatapi; wi'paȟdate. 3. Oape; apapi: *punished with forty stripes.* 4. Wa'petokeca; oowa; obe: *of the same stripe.* *vt.* Yuhdeze ka'ġa.
striped, *a.* Hde'zedaŋ; zuhaŋ.
stripling, *n.* Kośkana; kośkalaka.
strippings, *n.* E'hake yusdipi.
strive, *vi.* 1. Akita; ni'na kuwa; aiçiciya. 2. Akinica; akinin kuwa; kici ecoŋ.

strode, *imp.* of STRIDE.
stroke, *imp.* of STRIKE.
stroke, *n.* 1. Oape ; apapi : *at one stroke.* 2. Wohiyahde : *the stroke of death.* 3. Icazo ; oicazo ; oicaġo. 4. Oecoŋ : *a stroke of genius.* *vt.* Kastoste : *stroke him on the head.*
stroking, *n.* Wakastopi.
stroll, *vi.* Wi'kcekce omani.
stroller, *n.* Omanisa.
strong, *a.* 1. Waś'aka : *a strong man.* 2. Suta . *a strong fort.*
stronghold, *n.* Coŋ'kaśke suta.
strongly, *adv.* Waś'aġya ; ni'na.
strop, *n.* Putiŋhiŋ icasaŋ iyohdi. *vt.* Iyohdiya.
strove, *imp.* of STRIVE.
strow, *vt.* Kadada.
struck, *imp.* of STRIKE.
structure, *n.* Okaġe ; ta'ku ka'gapi ; ti'pi.
struggle, *vi.* Ni'na śkaŋ ; ecoŋ ; kuwa ; nasoŋsoŋ. *n.* Woecoŋ ; kicicuwapi ; woakinica.
struggler, *n.* Tu'we ecoŋ ; waecoŋ.
strumpet, *n.* Witkowiŋ.
strung, *imp.* of STRING.
strut, *vi.* Wataŋkaiçida ma'ni.
strychnine, *n.* Peżutaśica ohaŋko.
stub, *n.* Hu'tena. *vt.* Iboto.
stubbed, *a.* Hu'na ; hu'tena.
stubbiness, *n.* Hu'tena ; wakahdokeśni.
stubble, *n.* Aġuyapi hupaksa.
stubborn, *a.* Wanaħoŋśni ; tahu suta ; okuwaśica.
stubbornly, *adv.* Wanaħoŋśniyaŋ ; ociŋśicaya.
stubbornness, *n.* Wowanaħoŋśni.
stubby, *a.* Hu'na.
stub-end, *n.* Hu'te.
stucco, *n.* Wi'puspa suta.
stuck, *imp.* of STICK.
stuck-up, *a.* Waħaŋiçida.
stud, *n.* 1. Caŋomdotoŋ bosdanhaŋ. 2. Taśpu yuśdoka ; ceśkikaŋ o'śtaŋpi. 3. Śuŋgmdoka ; śuŋ'kawakaŋ optaye. *vt.* Taśpu okaṭaŋ ; żu.
studded, *pa.* Żu'pi ; żu'pise.
studding, *n.* Tihuħabosdata.
student, *n.* 1. Wayawa ; wayawakośka : *a student in Santee Training School.* 2. Woawaciŋ ; waoŋspeiçiciya : *a close student.*
studhorse, *n.* Śuŋgmdoka.
studied, *pa.* 1. Iwaŋyakapi ; amdezapi : *a well studied lesson.* 2. Wi'yukcaŋ ; waoŋspeka : *a boy well studied in grammar.*
studiedly, *adv.* E'waciŋyaŋ ; ciŋ.
studio, *n.* Wokaġetipidaŋ.
studious, *a.* Waawaciŋ ; awaciŋpi.
studiously, *adv.* Awaciŋyaŋ ; mdihenya.
studiousness, *n.* Waawaciŋpi.
study, *n.* 1. Waoŋspeiçiciyapi ; waawaciŋpi : *study strengthens the mind.* 2. Woawaciŋ ; wooŋspe : *what studies are you taking.* *vt.* Awaciŋ ; oŋspeiçiciya ; aiçiciya kuwa. *vi.* Waoŋspeiçiciya ; waawaciŋ.
stuff, *n.* Ta'ku ; wi'yopuħdi ; waħpaya ; ta'kuśni. *vt.* Opuħdi ; paoṭiŋsiyeya : *stuff the ballot-box.* *vi.* Akaska.
stuffing, *n.* Iyopuħdi.
stultify, *vt.* Yuśiħtiŋ ; yuwitkotko.
stumble, *vi.* Ḣicahaŋ ; nahnayaŋ ; waħtani ; naśna. 2. Ḣinħicahaŋ ma'ni. *Stumble into,* wanu iyeya.—*Stumble over,* iboto ; oŋ ħicahaŋ. *vt.* Ḣicahaŋya. *n.* Woħicahaŋ ; wonaśna.
stumbler, *n.* Ḣicahes'a.
stumbling-block, *n.* Wonahnaye.
stumblingly, *adv.* Ḣinħicaheya.
stump, *n.* Caŋpaksa ; hu'te ; hutkaŋ. *Stump-orator,* caŋpaksa adiwohdaka.—*Take the stump,* iyaza wahokoŋwicakiya. *vt.* 1 Kahuteya : *a stumped bush.* 2 Okihiśniya ; ktedaŋ : *your ques*

tion stumps me. 3. Iwahokoŋwicakiya omani.
stumpage, *n.* Caŋpaksaiyawa kažužupi.
stumper, *n.* Wakaġiya; wohitika.
stumpy, *a.* Caŋpaksa o'ta; hu'na.
stun, *vt.* Taŋsagṭeya; kaitekpaza; yuš'iŋyeya.
stung, *imp.* of STING.
stunk, *imp.* of STINK.
stunner, *n.* Wokokipe; woyuš'iŋyaye; wowitoŋpe.
stunning, *pa.* Okokipe; woyuš'iŋyaye; wowitoŋpe.
stunt, *vt.* Yuśiḣtiŋ; yuciḳa.
stunted, *pa.* Śiḣtiŋ; ci'ḳana.
stupefaction, *n.* Wokiksuyeśni.
stupefier, *n.* Wakiksuyeśniya.
stupefy, *vt.* K ksuyeśniya; yuwitkotko.
stupendous, Wowitoŋpe; ni'na taŋ'ka.
stupid, *a.* Tawaciŋṭaṭa; waciŋksapeśni.
stupidity, *n.* Wowitkotkoka.
stupidly, *adv.* Waciŋtoŋśniyaŋ; witkotkoya.
stupor, *n.* Wokiksuyeśni.
sturdy, *a.* Waś'aka; caŋteṭiŋza.
sturgeon, *n.* Caŋhuŋ; ho'taŋka.
stutter, *vi.* Uŋ'çoŋnicaia.
stutteringly, *adv.* Uŋ'coŋninya.
sty, *n.* 1. Kukuśetipi. 2. Iśtaoḣdi.
stygian, *a.* Wakaŋśicatawa.
style, *n.* Okaġe; iapiokaġe; wi'cazo. *vt.* Cažeyata.
stylish, *a.* Wi'taŋtaŋ; oḣaŋḣaŋ.
stylishly, *adv.* Wi'taŋtaŋyaŋ.
stylishness, *n.* Wi'taŋtaŋpi; wokaġe.
styx, *n.* Wakaŋśicatawakpa.
suasion, *n.* Iyutaŋyaŋpi.
suavity, *n.* Wi'ciyokipi; woiyokipi.
sub-, *pref.* Ihukuya; ku'ya.
subagent, *n.* I'yokiheitaŋcaŋ.
subaltern, *n.* Sam'waśipi.
subaqueous, *a.* Miniihukuya.
subcommittee, *n.* *Committee* ciŋoa.
subcontract, *n.* Sameconśipi.
subdivide, *vt.* Aktakiyuṡpa.
subdivision, *n.* Aktakiyuṡpapi.
subdue, *vt.* 1. Ohiya; kte'daŋ: *subdue a nation.* 2. Kaoŋspe; yuwaśte: *subdue a horse.* 3. Kapaŋpaŋ.
subject, *a.* 1. Ihukuya uŋ; ta'waya uŋ: *subject to his master.* 2. Akipa ce'e; ececes'a: *subject to fits.* *n.* 1. Wowidake: *the subject must obey his king.* 2. Ta'ku ka'pi; ta'ku cažeyatapi; ta'ku kuwapi. 3. Tu'we ni; woawaciŋ. *vt.* Yuhukun iyeya; wowidagya.
subjection, *n.* 1. Yuhukun iyeyapi: *the subjection of the rebels.* 2. Ihukun uŋ'pi; ahopopa.
subject-matter, *n.* Iapi ka'pi.
subjoin, *vt.* Ahaŋkeya ka'ġapi.
subjugate, *vt.* Ohiya; yuhukun iyeya; ktedaŋ.
subjugation, *n.* Ohiyapi.
subjunctive, *n.* Ikoyake.
sublet, *vt.* Iyoopta ecoŋkiya.
sublime, *a.* Waŋkantuya; wowinihaŋ; taŋ'ka; owaśteka.
sublimely, *adv.* Wowinihaŋyaŋ.
sublimity, *n.* Wowinihaŋ.
sublunar, *a.* Aŋ'pawiihukuya.
submarine, *a.* Miniwaŋcakuya.
submerge, *vt.* Spa'yeya; minimahen iyeya; amnitaŋya.
submission, *n.* Ihukuniyeiçiyapi; iyowiŋyaŋpi; ihakamuŋpi.
submissive, *a.* Iyowiŋyaŋ; waanaġoptaŋ.
submissively, *adv.* Oŋ'śiya; waanaġoptaŋyaŋ.
submissiveness, *n.* Waanaġoptaŋpi.
submit, *vt.* 1. Ihukuniyeiçiya; tawaciŋ ecakicoŋ; iyowiŋyaŋ: *children submit to your teachers.*

2. Wowiyukcaŋ ku : *submit the question to the judge.*
subordinate, *a.* Ihukuya : *a subordinate officer.* *n.* Ihukuyauŋ. *vt.* Ihukuya iyeya ; wowidagya.
subordinately, *adv.* O'kiheya.
subordination, *n.* Ouŋ ku'ya.
subpena, *n.* Wa'kiiapiopeśipi.
subscribe, *vt.* 1. Caże en owa : *subscribe the contract.* 2. Kiçuŋ ; en owa. *vi.* Caże en e'içihnaka ; wicada ; he'cetueya ; wowapi yutaŋ ; wotaŋiŋwowapi icu.
subscriber, *n.* Icupi ; yuhapi.
subscription, *n.* Caże en owapi.
subsequent, *a.* Iyohakamtu.
subsequently, *adv.* Iyohakam.
subserve, *vt.* O'kiya ; idakeya. *vi.* Wawidakeya.
subservient, *a.* Waokiya.
subside, *vi.* Kun'ya ; enakiya ; sni a'ya.
subsidize, *vt.* Opetoŋ.
subsidy, *n.* Wokażużu.
subsist, *vi.* Ni ; uŋ ; iwaś'aguŋ ; wota. *vt.* Niya ; wonwicaya.
subsistence, *n.* Oŋ'nipi ; woyute.
subsoil, *n.* Makikceihukuya. *vt.* Makamahentu yuptaŋyaŋ.
substance, *n.* Ta'kuhca ; ta'ku ; woyuha ; co ; ta'ku ka'pi.
substantial, *a.* 1. Taŋtoŋ ; ta'kuhca. 2. A'wicakehaŋ ; wowicake : *a substantial house.* 4. Oiçihi ; watoŋka : *a substantial farmer.*
substantially, *adv.* A'wicakeya ; co ektakiya.
substantiate, *vt.* Yuwicaka.
substantive, *n.* Wocaże.
substitute, *vt.* E'ekiya ; e'ekiya e'hnaka. *n.* E'ekiyapi.
substitution, *n.* E'ekiyapi.
substratum, *n.* Ihukuya waŋka.
subterfuge, *n.* Wohnaye.
subterraneous, *a.* Makaihukuya ; makamahentu.
subtile, *a.* 1. Zizipedaŋ ; pe'sto ; hna'yaŋ wayupika ; ksa'pa. 2. Wicahnayeś'a ; wayupika ; ksa'pa.
subtleness, *n.* Wonahbe ; wohnaye.
subtlety, *n.* Wonahbe ; wowayupika.
sub-tonic, *n.* Ho'cikadaŋ.
subtract, *vt.* Etaŋhaŋicu.
subtraction, *n.* Etaŋhaŋicupi.
subtrahend, *n.* Icupikte.
sub-treasury, *n.* Oyatetamazaska a'kamwohnake.
suburb, *n.* Otoŋweahaŋke.
subversion, *n.* Yużużupi ; yutokecapi.
subversive, *a.* Wayużużu.
subert, *vt.* Yutokeca ; yużużu ; yuśica.
subverter, *n.* Wayuśice.
succeed, *vt.* O'kihaŋ ; ihakam uŋ ; o'śtaŋ uŋ ; to'he ohna uŋ : *he succeeded his father.* *vi.* Okihi ; waokihi ; ecen yuśtaŋ : *he succeeded in doing it.*
success, *n.* Waokihipi ; wookihi ; woekicetu.
successful, *a.* Taŋ'yaŋ ; wa'pi ; a'taya ; waokihi.
successfully, *adv.* Taŋ'yaŋ.
succession, *n.* O'kicihaŋpi ; i'ciyokiheya yeya. *In succession,* o'weciŋhaŋ.
successive, *a.* I'ciyokiheya.
successively, *adv.* I'ciyaza ; o'weciŋhaŋ.
successor, *n.* O'kihe ; tu'we i'yokihe ecoŋ.
succinct, *a.* Katiŋyaŋ ; pte'cedaŋ.
succor, *vt.* O'kiya ; e'hdaku ; niyaŋ. *n.* O'kiyapi ; woehdaku.
succorer, *n.* Waehdaku ; wanikiya.
succorless, *a.* Wanikiya wanica.
succotash, *n.* Waskuya omnica icahi.
succulent, *a.* Waśtuŋka ; mini o'ta.

succumb, *vi.* Kun′iyaye.

such, *a.* He′ca; he′ceca; ta′ku; he′e. *Such a cold day,* ta′ku aŋpetu osni.—*Such a day as this,* aŋpetu de′cece.—*Such a man has come,* wicaŝta he′e ce hi.—*Such a time as we had,* ta′ku otawateŝica unkahipapi.

suck, *vt.* Aziŋ; yazoka; yahotoŋ; yutitaŋ. *vi.* Aziŋ; yazoka. *n.* Waaziŋpi; woyazoka.

sucker, *n.* 1. Waaziŋ; wayazoka. 2. (*Icth.*) Paȟteca; hoŝiŋyaŝeca. 3. *Illinois* wicaŝta. 4. Akta uya; hutkaŋ uya.

suckle, *vt.* Aziŋkiya.

suckling, *a.* Aziŋna.

suction, *n.* Woyazoka.

sudden, *a.* Ihnuhaŋhi; oȟaŋko; yukseknagececa.

suddenly, *adv.* Ihnuhaŋna.

suddenness, *n.* Wooȟaŋko.

suds, *n. pl.* Wi′paẑaẑahaŋpi.

sue, *vt.* Woope ekta kuwa; kuwa.

suet, *n.* Ŝiŋ; pakŝiŋŝiŋ.

suffer, *vi.* Kakiẑa; icakiẑa; ŝiȟtiŋ; taŋyaŋŝni. *Suffer for,* icakiẑa. *vt.* 1. Iyowiŋkiya: *he would not suffer him to do it.* 2. Akipa; ececa: *suffer loss.*

sufferable, *a.* Iyowiŋyepica.

sufferance, *n.* Woiyowiŋkiye.

sufferer, *n.* Wakakiŝyapi; iyotaŋiyekiya.

suffering, *n.* Wokakiẑe; wakakiẑapi; icakiẑapi.

suffice, *vi.* Wi′pi; iyehaŋyaŋ uŋ. *vt.* Wi′piya. *Let it suffice,* henana kte.

sufficiency, *n.* Iyenakeca; woozudaŋ; wookihi.

sufficient, *a.* 1. Iyenakeca; iyohi; henana: *sufficient provisions.* 2. O′kihe; waokihi.

sufficiently, *adv.* Iyehaŋyaŋ.

suffix, *n.* Aehnakapi. *vt.* Aehnaka.

suffocate, *vt.* Yuniyaŝni; yusni. *vi.* Niyaŝniṭa.

suffocatingly, *adv.* Oniyaŝniya.

suffocation, *n.* Niyaŝniṭapi; oniyaŝni uŋ′pi.

suffrage, *n.* Caẑeiyoȟpeyapi.

suffuse, *vt.* Spa′yeya.

sugar, *n.* Caŋhaŋpi: *sugar is sweet.* *vt.* Sku′yeya.

sugar-cane, *n.* Caŋhaŋpi hu.

sugar-maple, *n.* Caŋhasaŋ.

sugar-mill, *n.* Caŋhaŋpiiyuŝkice.

sugar-orchard, *n.* Caŋhasaŋoẑu.

sugar-plum, *n.* Caŋhaŋpiŝaŝakaŋta.

sugar-tree, *n.* Caŋhaŋpicaŋ.

sugary, *a.* Skuskuya.

suggest, *vt.* Iwaŋyagŝi; caẑeyata; ecoŋwaŝte keciya.

suggestion, *n.* Wowiyukcaŋ; ciŋkiyapi.

suggestive, *a.* Oŋ wokaȟniġapi.

suicidal, *a.* Iciktekta; ihaŋgiciyapi.

suicide, *n.* Iciktepi; icikte.

suit, *n.* Tawaŋẑi: *a suit of clothes.* 2. Woaie; wokuwa; aiapi: *a criminal suit.* 3. Wiokiyapi. 4. Opaȟte: *a suit of cards.* *vt.* 1. Iyokipiya; canwaŝteya: *I tried to suit him.* 2. I′ciyokipi; ki′ciwaŝte: *black suits his complexion.*

suitability, *n.* Woiyokipi; i′ciyokipipi.

suitable, *a.* Iyecetu; i′ciyokipi; iyehantu.

suitably, *adv.* Iyecetuya.

suite, *n.* Obe; tawaŋẑi.

suitor, *n.* Kuwa; okiya.

sulk, *vi.* Pamahen uŋ; ihdonica.

sulks, *n. pl.* Ihdonicapi; wowicadaŝni; tawaciŋŝicapi.

sulky, *a.* Waciŋhiŋyaŋza; ociŋŝica. *n.* Caŋpahmihmahunoŋpa.

sullen, *a.* Caŋteŝinuŋ; ociŋŝica.

sullenly, *a.* Iyokipiŝniyaŋ.

sullenness, *n.* Wotawaciŋŝica.

sullied, *pa.* Yuśapapi; yuśicapi.
sully, *vt.* Śamya; aśamya.
sulpher, *n.* Caḣdizi.
sultan, *n.* *Turkey* oyate itaŋcaŋ.
sultry, *a.* Ka'ta; odidita: *a sultry day.*
sum, *n.* 1. Yuwitayapi; o'yuwitaya: *the sum of five and two is seven.* 2. Oŋġe; omnaye: *a large sum of money.* 3. Wayawapi; oecoŋ: *a sum in division.* 4. O'iŋkpa; ihaŋke: *the sum of folly.* *vt.* Yuwitaya; ptenyedaŋ oyaka.
sumach, *n.* Caŋzi.
summarily, *adv.* Katiŋyaŋ; oḣaŋkoya; ptenyedaŋ.
summary, *a.* Pte'cedaŋ; oḣaŋko. *n.* Ptenyedaŋ oyakapi.
summer, *n.* Mdoketu. *Indian summer,* ptaŋyetu śotużu. — *Last summer,* mdokehaŋ. — *Next summer,* tokata mdoketu. *vi.* Mdoketu uŋ.
summer-fallow, *vt.* Mdokecokaya yumdu.
summit, *n.* O'iŋkpa; iyotaŋwaŋkantu.
summon, *vt.* En uśi; kico.
summons, *n.* Kicopi; kicopi wowapi.
sumptuous, *a.* Ma'zaska o'ta; ni'na waśte; otaŋtoŋ.
sumptuously, *adv.* Otaŋtoŋyaŋ.
sun, *n.* Aŋpetuwi; aŋpawi; wi. *vt.* Wi en e'hnaka; amaśteya
sunbeam, *n.* Wiiyożaŋżaŋ.
sunblind, *a.* Iśtośniża.
sunbonnet, *n.* Wiŋ'yaŋwapośtaŋ haŋ'ska.
sunburnt, *a.* Maśtiśpaŋ; ġiyenauŋ.
sundance, *n.* Wi'waŋyagwacipi.
Sunday, *n.* Aŋpetuwakaŋ.
Sunday-school, *n.* Aŋpetuwakaŋ waoŋspeiçiciyapi.
sunder, *vt.* Yukinukaŋ; kiyuksa; yukinukaŋ iyeya.
sun-dial, *n.* Wiohaŋzioiyute.
sun-dog, *n.* Wipecuza; wi'aceti.
sundown, *n.* Wi'iyaye.
sundries, *n. pl.* Ta'kuocaże; takuśniśni.
sundry, *a.* O'ta; ocaże toktokeca.
sunfish, *n.* Hoġaŋmdaskana.
sunflower, *n.* Waḣcazi.
sung, *imp.* of SING.
sunk, *imp.* of SINK.
sunken, *a.* Minimahenwaŋka.
sunless, *a.* Wi'iyożaŋżaŋśni.
sunlight, *n.* Wi'iyoyaŋpa.
sunny, *a.* Wi'iyoyaŋpa; iyoyaŋpa; wiyakpa.
sunrise, *n.* Wi'hinapa.
sunset, *n.* Wi'iyaye; wi'iyoḣpaya.
sunshade, *n.* Wiŋ'yaŋtawapaha mdaska.
sunshine, *n.* Wi'iyoyaŋpa; o'maśte.
sunshiny, *n.* Wi'iyoyaŋpa.
sunstroke, *n.* Wi'awicaśpaŋpi.
sunup, *n.* Wi'hinaŋpa.
sunward, *adv.* Wi'ektakiya.
sup, *vt.* Yatkaŋ; iyoziya yatkaŋ. *vi.* Ḣtayetu wota. *n.* Oyatke.
superabound, *vi.* Ehaeś o'ta.
superabundance, *n.* I'yakam o'ta.
superabundent, *a.* To'koŋpicaśni o'ta.
superanuated, *a.* Waniyetu kapeya uŋ; wicaḣca; kaŋ.
superb, *a.* Ni'nawaśte; wowinihaŋ.
superbly, *adv.* Ni'na taŋ'yaŋ; okinihaŋyaŋ.
supercargo, *n.* Woyuha awaŋyaka.
supercilious, *a.* Waḣaŋiçida; ihduwaŋkantuya.
superexcellent, *a.* Waŋkantuyawaśte.
superficial, *a.* Akapataŋhaŋ.
superfine, *a.* Iyotaŋwaśte.
superfluity, *n.* I'yakam o'ta.
superfluous, *a.* I'yakamtu; ituya uŋ.
superhuman, *a.* Wicaśtaiwaŋkam.

superintend, *vt.* Awaŋyaka; ecoŋkiya.
superintendence, *n.* Woawaŋyake.
superintendent, *n.* Wa'waŋyake.
superior, *a.* Waŋkantu; iwaŋkam uŋ; iyotaŋ. *n.* Watokaya; itaŋcaŋ; tokapa.
superiority, *n.* Watokapapi.
superlative, *a.* Tokapa; iyotaŋ.
supernatural, *a.* Wakaŋ; maka akantuśni; wowapetokeca.
supersede, *vt.* E'ekiyauŋ; to'he yuha.
superstition, *n.* Ituyawakaŋdapi.
superstitious, *a.* Ta'kuśniśniwakaŋda; wakaŋkaŋ.
superstitiously, *adv.* Wakaŋkaŋyaŋ.
superstructure, *n.* I'akamtu; ti'pi.
supervene, *vi.* Idazapataŋhaŋ u.
supervise, *vt.* Awaŋyaka.
supervision, *n.* Woawaŋyake.
supervisor, *n.* Wa'waŋyake; wa'mdeza.
supine, *a.* Ituŋkamuŋ; kużiṭa.
supinely, *adv.* Kużiteya.
supper, *n.* Ḣtayetuwotapi.
supperless, *a.* Htayetuwoteśni.
supplant, *vt.* To'heki; yutokaŋiyeya.
supplanter, *n.* Wawicaki.
supple, *a.* Winświŋżedaŋ; paŋpaŋna.
supplement, *n.* Ihaŋkekaġapi. *vi.* E'hakedaŋ ecoŋ; e'yaśtaŋ.
supplementary, *a.* Ehake.
suppliant, *a.* Wadauŋ; oŋ'śika.
suppliantly, *adv.* Oŋ'śiya.
supplicant, *n.* Wacekiya.
supplicate, *vt.* Ce'kiya.
supplicatingly, *adv.* Oŋ'śiya; ce'kiya.
supplication, *n.* Wocekiye.
supplicator, *n.* Wacekiya.
supplicatory, *a.* Oŋ'śiḣaŋ; wada.
supply, *vt.* 1. Ahikiḣnaka; ḳu: *he supplies the beef.* 2. Iyena ḳu; ożuya: *he supplied the deficiency.* *n.* Iyogeḣnakapi; wakiḣnakapi; woyuha; woyute.
support, *vt.* 1. Pataŋ yu'za; yuha: *supports the roof.* 2. Ki'camna; wakicamna; icaḣya: *he supports a large family.* 3. O'kiya; waś'aġya; wokażużuḳu: *support the government* *n.* Ipataŋ; wi'kicihni; oŋ niiçiyapi.
supportable, *a.* Yuspica; tawaṭenyepica.
supporter, *n.* Ipataŋyuza; ookiye.
suppose, *vt.* 1. Iyaciŋ; wi'yaciŋ: *suppose this ball was the earth.* 2. Eciŋ; keciŋ: *who do you suppose did it.* 3. O'kini. 4. Oyake; etaŋhaŋ iyukcaŋ.—*Man's footprints suppose a man,* wicowe wicaśta oyaka. 5. Ito: *suppose I go.*
supposition, *n.* Wowiyukcaŋ.
suppress, *vt.* 1. Yuasni: *suppress the rebellion.* 2. Ṭiŋs'a yu'za; yuhukun yu'za. 3 Naḣmaŋ; akaḣpa: *suppress the name.* 2. Anapta: *suppress the flow of blood.*
suppression, *n.* Woanapte.
suppressor, *n.* Waanapte.
suppurate, *vi.* Toŋ'yaŋ; toŋ au.
supremacy, *n.* Woitaŋcaŋ.
supreme, *a.* Iyotaŋwaŋkantu; wakapa; iyotaŋ.
supremely, *adv.* Itaŋcaŋyaŋ; iyotaŋyaŋ.
surcharge, *vt.* Iyatahde; o'ta ohnaka.
surcingle, *n.* Makiyutitaŋ; ipiyaka.
sure, *a.* 1. Taŋ'yaŋ sdonya. *Are you sure he has come,* hi taŋ'yaŋ sdonyaya he. 3. Suta; waciŋyepica: *a sure promise.* —*As sure as,* iyecen a'wicakehaŋ.—*To be sure,* a'wicakehaŋ.

—*Make sure*, yuwicaka; yuśtaŋpi.
surely, *adv.* A'wicakehaŋ; a'wicakeya; sutaya.
surety, *n.* 1. Wowicake: *know of a surety*. 2. Oŋ yuwicakapi: *keep the watch as surety*. 3. Okihiśni kiŋhaŋ ki'cicażużukta; kici yutaŋ.
surf, *n.* Miniwaŋca ta'ża.
surface, *n.* Akapataŋhaŋ. *vt.* Mda'ya ka'ġa.
surf-boat, *n.* Ta'żawata.
surfeit, *vt.* Wi'piṭeya. *vi.* Wi'piṭa. *n.* Woṭeyapi.
surfeited, *pa.* Woṭa.
surge, *n.* Ta'zataŋka. *vi.* Hiyu.
surgeon, *n.* Peżutawicaśta.
surgery, *n.* Taŋcaŋakapataŋhaŋ kuwapi.
surlily, *adv.* Iyokipiśniyaŋ.
surly, *a.* Waciŋhiŋyaŋza; ociŋśica.
surmise, *vt.* Iyukcaŋ; keciŋ. *n.* Keciŋpi.
surmount, *vt.* Iwaŋkam iyaya; ohiya.
surmountable, *a.* Adipica; ohiyepica.
surmounted, *pa.* Akaȟpa; iwaŋkam e'hnaka.
surname, *n.* Wicowazi caże; caże inoŋpa. *vt.* Caże inom ḳu.
surpass, *vt.* Kapa; kape; kapeya.
surpassing, *pa.* Wakapeya; iyotaŋ.
surpassingly, *adv.* Iyotaŋyaŋ.
surplice, *n.* O'kdeska; saŋksanica ska.
surplus, *n.* Ta'ku iyaye; iyaye.
surprisal, *n.* Ihnuhaŋyapi.
surprise, *vt.* 1. Ihnuhaŋya. *He surprised the enemy*, to'ka ihnuhaŋwicaye. 2. Inihaŋya; yuśiŋyeya. *He surprised the people.—I am surprised*, imanihaŋ. *n.* Woinihaŋ; ihnuhaŋyapi; woiyopaśtake.
surprising, *pa.* Wowinihaŋ.
surprisingly, *adv.* Wowinihaŋyaŋ.
surrender, *vt.* Wayakaiçicu; iyowiŋyaŋ; enakiya. *n.* Enakiyapi; wayaka içicupi.
surreptitious, *a.* Naȟmaŋ ka'ġapi.
surreptitiously, *adv.* Naȟmana.
surround, *vt.* 1. Ohomni iyaya; aohomniya: *the army surrounded the city*. 2. Ohomni waŋka: *a ditch surrounds the camp*. *n.* Aohomniyapi; ptewanuyaŋpi wicayuwitayapi.
surrounding, *pa.* Ohomni waŋke.
surveillance, *n.* Woawaŋyake.
survey, *vt.* 1. Waŋyaka; amdeza. 2. Iyuta; makaiyuta: *survey a railroad*. *n.* Amdeza; iyutapi.
surveying, *n.* Makaiyutapi; makaiyutapi wooŋspe.
surveyor, *n.* Makaiyuta.
survival, *n.* Ehake ni'pi.
survive, *vt.* Ihakam ni; ehake ni.
survivor, *n.* Ehakeni.
susceptibility, *n.* Wookihi; wowa ś'ake.
susceptible, *a.* Okihi; kaȟtaŋpica. sdonyepica.
susceptibly, *adv.* Taŋiŋyaŋ.
suspect, *vt.* Keciŋ; aṭungya; iyaoŋpa; ceṭuŋhda. *I suspect John did it*, *John* ecoŋ kecaŋmi.—*I suspected the driver*, wakaȟape ciŋ aṭuŋgwaya. *vi.* Waiyaoŋpa.
suspected, *pa.* Iyaoŋpapi.
suspend, *vt.* 1. Otkeya: *suspend a ball in the air*. 2. Inaȟni e'hnaka; e'kihnaka; ayuśtaŋkiya: *he suspended work*. 3. Ikoyagya. *vi.* Enakiye; ayuśtaŋ.
suspenders, *n.* Ceśkiyutitaŋ.
suspense, *n.* To'ketutaŋiŋśni.
suspension, *n.* 1. Wotkeyapi. *A suspension bridge*, caŋkaȟoŋpapi otkeyapi. 2. E'kiynakapi; woenakiye: *during his suspension from the ministry*.

suspicion, *n.* Woiyaoŋpa; wowiyukcaŋ.
suspicious, *a.* Wakokipa; śi'ca se'ca; waceṭuŋhda.
suspiciously, *adv.* Okokipeya; śicaya se'ca; waceṭuŋhdaya.
sustain, *vt.* 1. Yuha; ipataŋ yu'za; wi'wicakihni. 2. Yuwicaka: *sustain the charge.*
sustainable, *a.* Yuwicakapica; yuhepica.
sustenance, *n.* Woyute; ta'ku waś'agye.
sutler, *n.* Akicitatawopetoŋ.
suture, *n.* Okaġeġe.
swab, *n.* Ipakiŋte. *vt.* Pakiŋta.
swaddle, *vt.* Yuskiskita.
swag, *vi.* Naśkom iwaŋke.
swagger, *vi.* Ohitiiçida śkaŋ.
swain, *n.* Kośkawożu; kośka.
swale, *n.* O'smaka. *Swale-grass,* saŋtohu.
swallow, *vt.* Napca; napcaiyeya; iocoka: *swallowed a pin.—Swallow his own words,* to'ie ikikcu. —*Swallow the story,* woyakapi wicada. *n.* 1. Wonapce: *take two swallows.* 2. Icapśiŋpśiŋcadaŋ; upiżate: *the swallows are building their nests.*
swallow-tailed, *n.* Icapśiŋpśiŋcadaŋ siŋte.
swam, *imp.* of SWIM.
swamp, *n.* Pṭega; wiwi.
swampy, *a.* Ḣdiḣdidaŋ; coco.
swan, *n.* Maġataŋka; *Y.* maġaska.
swap, *vt.* Tokiyopeya.
sward, *n.* Peżito; peżiożu.
swarm, *n.* Tuḣmaġaoptaye; optaye. *vi.* Optaye içicaġapi; kicipatitaŋ.
swarthy, *n.* Sa'peca; staŋ.
sway, *vt.* Kahuhuza; ko'za; iyutaŋyaŋ. *vi.* Huhuzahaŋ. *n.* Wokazeze; wowaś'ake; woawaŋyake.
sway-back, *n.* Caŋkahu kaś'iŋ.
swear, *vi.* Wakaŋtaŋka cażeyaŋ e'ya: *he swore to the account.* 2. Wakaŋtaŋka i'ḣad cażeyata: *swear not.*
swearer, *n.* Wakaŋtaŋka cażeyates'a.
sweat, *vi.* Temni; temni au. *n.* Temni; itemni; inipi. *vt.* Temniya; inikicaġa.
sweating-room, *n.* Initipi.
sweaty, *a.* Temni; spa'ya.
sweep, *vt.* Kahiŋta; kahin e'yaya; hiyaya. *Sweep the floor,* owaŋka kahiŋta.—*It swept by,* dus hiyaya.—*The plague swept off the children,* makośica śiceca wicakasota. *vi.* Wakahiŋtapi; ahiyaya; wawiyohiya.
sweeping, *pa.* Taŋ'kaya iyohi.
sweepings, *n.* Wokahiŋte.
sweepstakes, *n.* A'taya ohiya.
sweet, *a.* Sku'ya; waśte; śkumnaśni: *a sweet apple.—Sweet butter,* asaŋpiihdi waśte.—*A sweet face,* ite waśte.—*Sweet milk,* asaŋpi śkumnaśni.—*Sweet odors,* ecamna waśte·—*Sweet songs,* odowaŋ waśte.—*Sweet water,* mini oyatke waśte. *n.* Ta'ku sku'ya; sku'ya; waśte.
sweet-corn, *n.* Wamnahezaskuya.
sweeten, *vt.* Sku'yeya. *vi.* Sku'ya a'ya.
sweetheart, *n.* Tu'wewaśteda; tu'weokiya.
sweetish, *a.* Skuskuya.
sweetly, *adv.* Taŋ'yaŋ; oiyokipiya.
sweetmeat, *n.* Caŋhaŋpiicahi; waskuya.
sweetness, *n.* 1. Woskuye: *the cane lost its sweetness.* 2. Wowaśte; wi'ciyokipi.
sweet-potatoe, *n.* Paŋġitaŋka; mdoskuya.
sweet-scented, *a.* Waśtemna.
swell, *vi.* Po; kapo; napoġaŋ; taŋ'ka a'ya; ihdutaŋka; minitaŋ: *a swollen river.* *vt.* Yutaŋ-

ka; napoġaŋ; minitaŋya. *n.* O'cim taŋ'ka; paha; mdoya; ta'ża mdoya.

swelling, *n.* Po; kapo; paha.

swelter, *vi.* Temniṭa.

sweltry, *a.* Maŝte; odidita.

swept, *imp.* of SWEEP.

swerve, *vi.* Tokaŋ ya; yupemni; kawiŋh ya.

swift, *a.* Du'zahaŋ; oḣaŋko; wotakuniŝni oḣaŋko: *swift destruction.* *n.* 1. Upiżate. 2. (*Zool.*) Ahdeŝkadaŋ.

swiftly, *adv.* Dus; oḣaŋkoya.

swiftness, *n.* Woduzahaŋ; wooḣaŋko.

swill, *n.* Kukuŝe tawoyatke.

swim, *vi.* 1. Niwaŋ: *I can swim.* 2. O'kapota: *the log swims.*—*A swimming-gait,* niwaŋpi se iyopte.—*His head swims,* itomni; itekpaza. — *Swim in wealth,* wowiżice okaponya uŋ. *vt.* 1. Niwaŋ; aniwe: *swim the river.* 2. Niwekiya: *swim the horse.* *n.* Oniwe; niwaŋpi.

swimmer, *n.* Niwewayupika; niwes'a.

swimmingly, *adv.* Yupiya; niwaŋpise.

swindle, *vt.* Hnayaŋkiyusota; hnayaŋ. *n.* Wohnaye.

swindler, *n.* Wicahnayes'a.

swine, *n.* Kukuŝe (ni uŋ heca).

swing, *vi.* Kaozeze; kahomni; ho'tadaŋ kiçuŋ.—*The rope swings,* haḣoŋta kaozeze. — *The boat swung round,* wa'ta kiŋ kahomni. *vt.* Kaozezeya; ko'za; kaŝkaŋŝkaŋ. *John swung his hat, John* wapoŝtaŋ ko'za. *n.* 1. Ho'tadaŋ: *put the baby in the swing.* 2. Wokazeze; oyuhomni; to'ken ciŋ: *let us take a swing.*

switch, *n.* 1. Caŋsakadaŋ: *a willow switch.* 2. (*Railway*) Ḣemani ma'zaakiżate: *change the switch.* *vt.* 1. Kapsiŋsiŋta: *switch the child.* 2. A'kiżate ohna iyayeya: *switch the train.*

switch-man, *n.* A'kiżateapiya.

swivel, *n.* Ma'zaicicaḣiḣa yuhomni.

swollen, *pp.* of SWELL.

swoon, *vi.* Kiksuyeŝni; taŋsagṭa.

swoop, *vt.* Iyaḣpaya; yuwaŋkan e'yaya. *n.* Woiyaḣpaya.

sword, *n.* Ma'zasagye; *Y.* miwakaŋ.

swore, *imp* of SWEAR.

sworn, *pp.* of SWEAR.

swum, *imp.* of SWIM.

swung, *imp.* of SWING.

sycamore, *n.* Taŋpacaŋtaŋka.

sycophant, *n.* Iskuya; wicahnayes'a.

syllable, *n.* Iapiokihe.

sylvan, *a.* Caŋ; caŋowaŋca.

symbol, *n.* 1. Wi'yaciŋpi; wadiyaciŋpi: *a lion is the symbol of courage.* 2. Wosukiye: *the symbols of faith.*

symbolic, *a.* I'yaciŋpi; ka'pi.

symbolically, *adv.* I'yaciŋyaŋ.

symbolize, *vt.* I'yaciŋ.

symmetrical, *a.* Okaḣwaŋżidaŋ.

symmetry, *n.* I'ciyokipi.

sympathetic, *a.* Wawaciŋktayuza.

sympathize, *vi.* Waciŋkiyuza; waciŋyuza.

sympathizer, *n.* Waciŋkiyuza.

sympathy, *n.* Waciŋenkiciyuzapi; oŋŝikicidapi.

symptom, *n.* Wotoketu; to'keca; wowapetokeca.

synagogue, *n.* *Judah* ti'piwakaŋ.

synchronical, *a.* I'akidehantu.

syndicate, *n.* Woecoŋ okodakiciye.

synod, *n.* Omniciye ocokaya.

synonim, *n.* Iapiowaŋżidaŋ.

synonimous, *a.* I'akidececa.

synopsis, *n.* Owohdake co.

syntax, *n.* Iapiokaġe oyaka.

syphilis, *n.* Ce'ḣdipi woyazaŋ.

syringe, *n.* Wi'bosdi; minibosdi.

syrup, *n.* Caŋhaŋpitiktica; *Y.* tuȟmaga.
system, *n.* 1. Okaġe; oecoŋ: *the railroad system.* 2. Wowiyukcaŋ: *work by system.* 3. Obe; ta'ku i'cikoyake ko'ya: *the solar system.*
systematic, *a.* Wi'yukcaŋ śkaŋ.
systematize, *vt.* Obe kaȟya e'hnaka.

T

tabernable, *n.* Wakeya.
table, *n.* Wa'hnawotapi; omdaye. *vt.* Kihnaka.
table-spoon, *n.* Tukihataŋka.
tablet, *n.* Wowapiska a'skape.
taboo, *vt.* Teȟiŋda.
tabular, *a.* O'cimdaȟ owapi.
tacit, *a.* A'nini; iyowiŋyaŋ.
tack, *n.* Ma'żapepe. *vt.* Okataŋ.
tackle, *vt.* Yu'za; yuhomni. *n.* Wa'ta icuwa.
tact, *n.* Wowayupika.
tactics, *n.* Akicita wooŋspe.
tadpole, *n.* Hośuŋpeśda.
taffy, *n.* Caŋhaŋpi sagyapi.
tag, *n.* Kaŋsuikoyagyapi.
tail, *n.* Siŋte. *Bird's tail,* upi.
tailor, *n.* Wakaġeġe wicaśa.
taint, *vt.* Śicamnaya.
tainted, *a.* Ḣwiŋ'mna.
take (**took**), *vt.* 1. Icu, *take the book.* 2. Yu'za, *he took a wife.* 3. A'ya; akiyahda, *take it away.* 4. Kipi; iyohi; yusota, *how much will it take.*—*Take after,* kuwa a'ya; kinma.—*Take aim,* e'pazo.—*Take away,* tokaŋ a'ya.—*Take care,* taŋyaŋ amdeza; itoŋpa.—*Take care of,* awaŋyaka.—*Take cold,* sni yahotoŋ.—*Take effect,* iyokihi.—*Take from,* ki.—*Take hold of,* oyuspa.—*Take notice,* amdeza.—*Take off:* (*the hat*), yuśdoka; (*the foot*), baksa; (*as cattle*), tokaŋ a'ya.—*Take part,* oŋśpa ecoŋ; o'pa.—*Take sides with,* kici ti'daŋ.—*Take to, taken with,* iyokipi; waśtedaka.—*Take a walk,* omani.
take off, *n.* Uŋ'capi.
tale, *n.* Woyakapi; kakaŋpi.
talebearer, *n.* I'wakaŋ.
talent, *n.* Ma'zaska wokiŋ; woksape.
talented, *a.* Waciŋksapa.
talk, *vi.* Ia; wohdake. *To talk to,* eciya.—*To talk about* (or *of,* or *over*), iwohdaka.
talkative, *a.* Wohdakes'a.
tall, *a.* Haŋ'ska.
tallow, *n.* Wasna.
tally, *n.* Icaġo; kici iyececa.
talon, *n.* Śake.
tamarack, *n.* Śiŋta.
tame, *a.* Wa'ȟbana; wanuyaŋpi. *vt.* Yuwaȟbadaŋ.
tamper, *vi.* Yuha śkaŋ.
tan, *vt.* Kpaŋyaŋ; uka wi aśpaŋye.
tandem, *a.* I'ciyaza.
tangible, *a.* Yutaŋpica.
tangle, *vt.* Yuwi; i'cikoyake.
tap, *vt.* Apapa; yuȟdoka.
tape, *n.* Śinaapaȟdate.
taper, *vi.* O'cim ci'stina; sdi. *n.* Petiżaŋżaŋ.
tar, *n.* Wazi caŋśiŋ.
tardy, *a.* Iyehan hi śni.
target, *n.* Owiŋheca.
tariff, *n.* Oyatetokeca kici wopetonpi awamnayaŋpi.
tarnish, *vt.* Aśamya.
tarpaulin, *n.* Caŋśiŋ iuŋpi.
tarry, *vi.* Apeyaŋka.
tart, *a.* Sku'ya.
task, *n.* Woȟtani.

taskmaster, *n.* Wowaŝi itaŋcaŋ.
taste, *vt.* U'ta; ci'stiŋna yu'ta. *n.* U'tapi; wowiyukcaŋ; wocaŋtiheye.
tasteful, *a.* Oiyokipi.
tasteless, *a.* U'tapi ṭaṭake.
tatters, *n.* Oḣdeḣdeca.
tattoo, *vt.* Akito.
taught, *imp.* of TEACH.
taunt, *vt.* I'enhde.
tautology, *n.* Akihdehde e'yapi.
tavern, *n.* Owotetipi.
tawny, *a.* Ha sa'peca.
tax, *n.* Woyuha hdażużupi; wokażużu.
tea, *n.* Waḣpepeżuta; waḣpe.
teach, taught, *vt.* Oŋspekiya.
teachable, *a.* Oŋspekiyapi waŝte.
teacup, *n.* Waḣpeiyatke.
teakettle, *n.* Miniikanye.
teacher, *n.* Waoŋspekiye.
team, *n.* Ŝuŋgakicaŝka; wi'yutitaŋpi.
teamster, *n.* Wakaḣape.
teapot, *n.* Waḣpeikanye.
tear, tore, *vt.* Yuḣdeca. *n.* Woyuḣdeca; iŝtamnihaŋpe.
tearer, *n.* Wohitika.
tease, *vt.* Naġiyeya.
teaspoon, *n.* Tukiha ci'stina; *Y.* kiŋŝkaci'ḳana.
teat, *n.* Azeiŋkpa.
teem, *vi.* Ożudaŋ; o'ta.
teeter, *vi.* Kaozezeya.
teeth, *n. pl.* of TOOTH.
teething, *n.* Hi'uyapi.
teetotaler, *n.* Miniwakaŋ yatke ŝni.
telegram, *n.* Ma'zaapapiwowapi.
telegraph, *n.* Ma'zaapapi.
telephone, *n.* Ma'zahoyeya.
telescope, *n.* Maziwaŋyake haŋ'ska.
tell, told, *vt.* Oyaka; to'nakeca yawa. *Tell him,* okiyaka.—*Tell him to come,* uŝi.
tell-tale, *n.* Woyakes'a.
temper, *n.* Tawaciŋ; wosuta. *vt.* Yusuta; yuecetu.
temperance, *n.* Iyatahdeiçiyapi ŝni; mde'zeca.
temperature, *n.* Osni iŝ maŝte.
tempest, *n.* Icamna; tate.
temple, *n.* Ti'piwakaŋ; nawate.
temporal, *a.* Makaakantu.
tempt, *vt.* Iyutaŋye.
temptation, *n.* Wowawiyutaŋye.
ten, *a.* Wikcemna.
tenable, *a.* Yuhepica.
tenacious, *a.* Wi'yaskape; wakitaŋ.
tenant, *n.* Wakicaŋye.
tend, *vt.* Awaŋyake; kicaŋye. *vi.* Iyahdeya.
tendency, *n.* Ocaŋku; oaye.
tender, *a.* Waŋ'kadaŋ; waihakta. *vt.* Ḳu.
tenderly, *adv.* Iwaŝtedaŋ.
tenement, *n.* Ti'pi oḳupi.
tenet, *n.* Woope.
tenfold, *a.* Wikcemna akihde.
tenor, *n.* Ta'ku ka'pi; wicaho waŋkantu.
tense, *n.* Watohantu; hehaŋtu. *a.* Ṭiŋ'za.
tent, *n.* Wakeya. *vt.* Ticaġa.
tenth, *a.* Iwikcemna.
tepid, *a.* Iṭenyapi.
term, *n.* Iapi, *the term lawyer;* owa saghde, *a term of four years;* waciŋkiciyuzapi, *on good terms;* nażiŋŝni ecoŋpi, *a school term.* *vt.* Cażeyata; e'ya.
terminate, *vi.* Owihanke.
terrestrial, *a.* Makata.
terrible, *a.* Okokipe.
terribly, *adv.* Okokipeya.
terrific, *a.* Woitoŋpe.
terrify, *vt.* Yuŝiŋyeya.
territory, *n.* Makoce; makobaŝpe.
terror, *n.* Wokokipe.
terse, *a.* Iapi yaṭiŋzapi.
test, *vt.* Iyuta.
testament, *n.* Wokoŋze.
testify, *vt.* Wowicake oyaka.
testimony, *n.* Woyaotaŋiŋ.
tether, *vt.* Ikaŋtoŋ hde.

text, *n.* Iapi iwohdake.
text-book, *n.* Wooŋspe wowapi.
texture, *n.* Okaġe.
than, *conj.* Kici i'ciwaŋyakapi. *More than,* i'saŋpa.—*Less than,* a'okpani.
thank, *vt.* Wopida eciya. *n.* Wopida.
thankful, *a.* Pida; pidapi.
thankless, *a.* 1. Pidaṡni, *a thankless heart.* 2. Tuwedaŋ pidaṡni.
thank-offering, *n.* Wopida woṡnapi.
thanksgiving, *n.* Wopida eyapi.
thankworthy, *a.* Pidapi iyececa.
that, *a.* & *pro.* He, *that man; that is mine; that which I do ye know.* *conj.* He'oŋ; he, *he died that we might live; the day came that she should die.* *conj.* *She was that scared.*
thatch, *n.* Ṗeżiawakeyapi.
thaw, *vt.* Ṡtunya, *thaw out the frost.* *vi.* Stu'ta. *Thaw off,* skaŋ.
the, *def. art.* Kiŋ, *the day is past.*
theater, *n.* 1. Woṡkate ti'pitaŋka; ikpazotipi. 2. Oyaŋke, *the theater of war.*
theatrical, *a.* Woṡkate.
thee, *pro.* Ni'ye.
theft, *n.* Wamanoŋpi.
their, theirs, *pro.* Ta'wapi.
theism, *n.* Wakaŋtaŋka wicadapi.
them, *pro.* 1. Wica. *Kill them,* wicakte. 2. He'na, *sit by them.*
theme, *n.* Woiwohdake.
themselves, *pro.* Iyepiḣca.
then, *adv.* & *conj.* Hehan.
thence, *adv.* Hetaŋhaŋ.
thenceforth, *adv.* Hetaŋhaŋ.
theology, *n.* Wooŋspe wakaŋ.
theory, *n.* Wowiyukcaŋ.
there, *adv.* 1. Hen; he'ci, *there he is; up there.* 2. (Used indefinitely it is unexpressed.) *There arose a famine,* wicaakiḣaŋ icaġa —*There is work,* wowaṡi yukaŋ.
thereabout, *adv.* Wahehantu.
thereafter, *adv.* He iyohakam.
thereby, *adv.* Hetaŋhaŋ.
therefor, *adv.* He'oŋ.
therefore, *adv.* He'onetaŋhaŋ; he'on; he'cen.
therein, *adv.* He en.
thereof, *adv.* Hetaŋhaŋ.
thereon, *adv.* He akan; hehan.
thereupon, *adv.* Hehan.
therewith, *adv.* He kici.
thermometer, *n.* Osniiyuta.
these, *a.* & *pro.* Dena.
thesis, *n.* Woeye.
they, *pro. pl.* Iyepi; iye...pi. (Generally expressed only by the plural ending.) *They came,* hi'pi.
thick, *a.* 1. Ṡo'ka: *thick ice.* 2. Sma, *thick grass; thick hair.* 3. Akipṡapṡa, *thick grain; thick woods.* 4. Ṭiŋza; suta, *thick mush.* 5. O'ta: *thick as rabbits.*
thicken, *vt.* 1. Suta ka'ġa, *thicken the syrup.* 2. Ṡo'ka ka'ġa, *thicken the cloth.* 3. Yuota, *thicken the blows.*
thickening, *a.* O'ta a'ya; ṡo'ka a'ya. *n.* Icahiyapi.
thicket, *n.* Oteḣi.
thickhead, *n.* Ṗahu ṡo'ka.
thickly, *adv.* Ṡogya.
thickness, *n.* Ṡo'ka.
thickset, *a.* Hu'na.
thief, *n.* Wamanoŋs'a.
thieve, *vt.* Wamanoŋ.
thievery, *n.* Wamanoŋpi.
thievish, *a.* Manons'a; wamanoŋ.
thigh, *n.* Ceca. *Thigh-bone,* cecuŋte; cecaowagle.
thimble, *n.* Napoṡtaŋ.
thin, *a.* 1. Zizipedaŋ, *thin paper.* 2. Hdahaŋ; *thin mush.*
thine, *a.* Nitawa.
thing, *n.* Ta'ku; woyuha.
think, thought, *vt.* & *vi.* 1. Awa-

ciŋ; caŋteyuza, *I think of going.* 2. Kiksuya, *I cannot think what he said.* 3. Eciŋ; waciŋyuza. *He thinks well of me,* taŋ'yaŋ waciŋmakiyuza.
thinly, *adv.* Zizipayedaŋ; enana.
third, *a.* 1. Iyamni, *the third day.* 2. Ya'mni yuṡpapi, *two thirds.*
thirst, *vi.* I'puza; caŋtahde. *n.* I'puzapi; caŋtahdepi.
thirsty, *a.* I'puza.
thirteen, *a.* Akeyamni.
thirteenth, *a.* I'akeyamni.
thirty, *a.* Wikcemnayamni.
this, *a.* De, *this man. pro.* De, *whose dog is this? adv.* De'-cen. *This soon.*
thistle, *n.* Caŋḣdoḣupepe.
thither, *adv.* He'ciya; heciyotaŋ.
thong, *n.* Wi'kaŋ; ikaŋ.
thorn, *n.* Caŋpepe.
thorny, *a.* Pepe.
thorough, *a.* A'wicake; wayuṡtaŋ.
thoroughbred, *a.* Obeteḣike.
thoroughfare, *n.* Caŋkuḣca.
thoroughgoing, *a.* Wakaḣdokeca.
thoroughly, *adv.* A'wicakeya.
those, *a.* & *pro.* Hena.
thou, *pro.* Niye.
though, *conj.* 1. Eṡta, *I will go, though it rains.* 2. Tuka; ķe yaṡ, *I am well though not strong.*
thought, *v. imp.* See THINK.
thought, *n.* Woawaciŋ; wowiyukcaŋ.
thoughtful, *a.* Waawaciŋ; awaciŋ.
thoughtless, *a.* Waawaciŋṡni.
thousand, *a.* Kektopawiŋġe.
thraldom, *n.* Wayaka uŋ'pi.
thrash, *vt.* Kapaŋ; apa. *vi.* Wakapaŋ; kaḣoḣoiyeiçiya ṡkaŋ.
thrashing-machine, *n.* Wi'capaŋ; wi'nakaŋye.
thread, *n.* 1. Haḣoŋta; wi'kaŋ, *silk thread.* 2. Caŋkuye. *vt.* Haḣoŋta en iyeya.
threadbare, *a.* Yutaŋnipi.
threat, *n.* Wakokipe ki'caġapi.
threaten, *vt.* Wakokipekicaġa; iteka; eyakuwa.
three, *a.* Ya'mni.
threefold, *a.* Ya'mniakihde.
threescore, *a.* Wikcemnaṡakpe.
threshold, *n.* Tiyopaahdehe.
threw, *imp.* of THROW.
thrice, *adv.* Ya'mniakihde.
thrift, *n.* Waiçihdepi.
thriftless, *a.* Içihdeṡni.
thrifty, *a.* Içiḣdeka.
thrill, *vt.* Yuṡkaŋṡkaŋ. *vi.* Huhuzahaŋ. *n.* Woṡkaŋṡkaŋ.
thrilling, *a.* Wowinihaŋ.
thrive, *vi.* Saŋ'pa taŋ'yaŋ ya.
thriving, *pa.* Icaġa; oicihi.
throat, *n.* Dote; wi'napce.
throb, *vi.* Iyapa.
throe, *n.* Wokakiże.
throne, *n.* Itaŋcaŋ toyaŋke; itaŋcaŋ.
throng, *n.* Wicota. *vt.* Aoṭiŋsya.
throttle, *n.* Dote; ioṡtaŋ.
through, *a.* Ihuŋniyaŋye, *through trains. prep.* Iyoopta; ihuniyaŋ, *through the board; through the season.*
throughout, *adv.* Ihuŋniyaŋ.
throve, *imp.* of THRIVE.
throw, threw, *vt.* 1. Kaḣoiyeya, *throw a stone.—Throw at,* kiŋiŋ. 2. Kun'eḣpeya, *he threw his antagonist.* 3. Eḣpeya, *he threw it on the ground.* 4. Ḥiyuya, *threw up his dinner.*
thrush, *n.* Waġioġi.
thrust, *vt.* Iyayeya; iyeya; capa; capaiyeya. *n.* Wacapapi.
thud, *n.* Woiyapa.
thumb, *n.* Napahuŋka. *vt.* Yutaŋtaŋ.
thump, *vt.* Apa; iyapa.
thunder, *vi.* Wakiŋyaŋhotoŋ; bu.
thunderbolt, *n.* Wakaŋhdisu.
thunderstorm, *n.* Wakiŋyaŋicamna.
thunderstrike, *vt.* Wakiŋyaŋo; o.

Thursday, *n.* Aŋpetuitopa.
thus, *adv.* He'cen, *do it thus.*—*Thus far,* hehaŋyaŋ.
thwart, *vt.* Okihiśniya.
thy, *pro.* Nita-; nitawa.
thyself, *pro.* Niyeȟca.
tibia, *n.* Husdi.
tick, *vi.* Ko'ka. *n.* 1. Ko'ka, *I hear the tick of the clock.* 2. Taskakpa, *I see a tick on the dog's ear.* 3. Owiŋżaożuha, *fill the tick with hay.* 4. Icazo, *don't buy on tick.*
ticket, *n.* Kaŋsu.
ticking, *n.* Owiŋża miniȟuha.
tickle, *vt.* Yuś'iŋś'iŋ; iȟaya.
ticklish, *a.* Iȟawaŋ'kadaŋ; to'ketu taŋiŋśni.
tidal, *a.* Mnitaŋ.
tide, *n.* Mniwaŋca waŋkanu.
tidings, *n.* Wonaȟoŋ.
tidy, *a.* Wayuco; ska.
tie, *vt.* Iyakaśka; kaśka; paȟta; yuskiya. *n.* 1. Wokaśke, *the ties of kindred.* 2. Apaȟte, *neck-tie.* 3. I'akidenakeca, *the vote was a tie.*
tier, *n.* Oehnake.
tiger, *n.* Inmutaŋka.
tight, *a.* 1. Oṭiŋza, *a tight shoe.* 2. Kuseśni; kaȟdokeśni, *a tight barrel; air-tight.* 3. Itomni, *tight on beer.*
tighten, *vt.* Yuṭiŋza.
tile, *n.* Makaśpaŋ tiakaȟpe; makaśpaŋ oȟdoġeca.
till, *prep.* Hehaŋyaŋ, *till Sunday.* *vt.* Kicaŋyaŋ, *till the ground.* *n.* Opiye; wopiye.
tillable, *a.* Kicaŋyepica.
tiller, *n.* Wakicaŋye.
tilt, *vt.* Yuptaŋyaŋ; wahukeza ecoŋpi.
timbal, *n.* Caŋ'ceġa.
timber, *n.* Caŋ; caŋ'obdotoŋ.
timbered, *a.* Caŋ'icaȟhan.
timbrel, *n.* Caŋ'ceġa mdaskana.
time, *vt.* Wihiyayedaŋ yawa. *n.* 1. Aŋpetu, *ancient times; the times are hard.* 2. Wi'hiyaya; wi'hiyayedaŋ, *be on time; what time is it?* 3. Akihde, *how many times? Two times.* 4. Iyehantu, *there is a time for everything.*—*All the time,* o'hiŋniyaŋ.—*Another time,* ake tohan.—*At any time,* tohantu kaśta.—*A short time,* ci'stiyedaŋ.—*At this time,* dehantu.—*At the same time,* iyehan.—*Beat time,* ho wi'kiyuta.—*Between time,* i'yotahedaŋ.—*By this time,* de iyehan.—*In time,* iyehan.—*It is time,* iyehantu.—*Next time,* ake tohan.—*Time about,* uŋmaŋ itogto.
timekeeper, *n.* Wi'hiyayedaŋ.
timely, *a.* Waiyehantu.
timepiece, *n.* Wi'hiyayedaŋ.
timid, *a.* Canwaŋka.
timorous, *a.* Wakokipe.
tin, *n.* Ceȟska.
tincture, *n.* Icahikaġapi; akaȟtaŋpi.
tinder, *n.* Caŋkaġica.
tinge, *vt.* Iwaśtedaŋ iuŋ.
tinker, *vt.* Apiya.
tinkle, *vi.* Sna.
tinned, *a.* Ceȟska akaȟpa.
tint, *n.* Icaȟtakapi.
tiny, *a.* Ci'stina; -daŋ; -na.
tip, *n.* Iŋ'kpa, *the tip of his ear.* *vt.* Naptaŋyaŋ; iwaśtedaŋ apa.
tippet, *n.* Nakpiyutake.
tipple, *vi.* Cikciḳayena wayatke.
tipsy, *a.* Itomni.
tiptoe, *n.* Sipiŋkpa.
tirade, *n.* Iapiśicaota.
tire, *vt.* Watukaya. *vi.* Watuka; ecoŋkapiŋ. *n.* Ma'zacaŋhdeśka.
tired, *a.* Ḣoŋ'kita; watuka.
tireless, *a.* Ecoŋkapiŋ wanica.
tiresome, *a.* Watukawicaya.
tissue, *n.* Miniȟuhaġaŋġaŋ.
tit, *n.* Oape.

titbit, *n*. Oŋšpadaŋ.
tithe, *n*. Wikcemnakibašpapi waŋži.
title, *n*. 1. Caže, *the title of the book*. 2. Oŋ ta'wa sdonyapi, *what is his title*.
titter, *vi*. Žižiiĥa.
tittle, *n*. Wokpe.
to, *prep*. & *adv*. 1. Ekta, *go to town; wrong end to*. 2. (Sign of the infinitive.) Kta, *I want to go*.
toad, *n*. Natapeĥa.
toast, *vt*. 1. Ġuġuya; ceoŋpa. 2. Tu'we cažeyan wayatke. *n*. Aġuġuyapi.
tobacco, *n*. Caŋdi.
toboggan, *n*. Caŋmdaskaowosdohe.
to-day, *adv*. & *n*. Nakaha.
toddle, *vi*. Hokšiyopamani.
toddy, *n*. Miniwakaŋicahiyapi.
toe, *n*. Siyukaza; siiŋkpa; sipa.
together, *adv*. Wi'taya; o'koŋwaŋžina.
toil, *vi*. Ḣtani. *n*. Woĥtani.
toilet, *n*. Oihduze.
toilsome, *a*. Oteĥika.
token, *n*. Wowapetokeca.
tolerable, *a*. Ki'taŋna.
tolerance, *n*. Iyowiŋyaŋpi.
tolerant, *a*. Waciŋtaŋka.
toleration, *n*. Wawiyowiŋyaŋpi.
toll, *vt*. Wan'waŋcana apa. *n*. Caŋku wokažužu.
tomahawk, *n*. Oŋspecaŋnoŋpa.
tomato, *n*. Waskuyecašaša.
tomb, *n*. Wicahnakapi.
tomboy, *n*. Wiciŋcana hokšina se'ca.
tombstone, *n*. Wicahnakapi iŋ'yaŋ.
to-morrow, *n*. Heyakeciŋhaŋ; *Y*. & *T*. hiŋ'haŋna.
ton, *n*. Tkeutapi 2000.
tone, *n*. Ho; hooadi; wocaŋteyuza.
tongs, *n*. Pe'tawiyužipe.
tongue, *n*. Ceži; iapi.
tonic, *n*. Pežuta imdihecapi.
to-night, *n*. Haŋyetu de.
too, *adv*. 1. Ni'na; ehaeš, *too long*. 2. Nakuŋ; eya, *give him one too*.
took, *imp*. of TAKE.
tool, *n*. Wi'kicaŋye; icuwa.
toot, *vt*. Yahotoŋ; yažo.
tooth, *n*. Hi. *In the teeth of*, wi'citkokim.
toothache, *n*. Hi'wicayazaŋ.
toothbrush, *n*. Hi'ipayeze.
toothless, *a*. Hi'wanica.
toothpick, *n*. Hi'pašku; *T*. hi'yopatake.
top, *n*. 1. Iŋ'kpa, *top of the house*. 2. Caŋ'kawacipi, *whirl the top*. *a*. Waŋkantu; akaŋ; o'tokahe, *a top place*. *vt*. 1. Iŋ'kpa ka'ġa, *top the stack*. 2. Iŋ'kpa baksa, *top the corn*.
toper, *n*. Miniwakaŋ yatkesa.
topic, *n*. Ta'ku ka'pi.
topknot, *n*. Pecokaokaške.
toplofty, *a*. Waŋkantu; taŋ'kaŧçida.
topmost, *a*. Iyotaŋwaŋkantu.
topography, *n*. Oyanke oyakapi.
topple, *vi*. Pacegceg.
topsy turvy, *a*. To'kenciŋciŋ.
torch, *n*. Ikcecaŋaižaŋžaŋyapi.
tore, *imp*. of TEAR.
torment', *vt*. Kakišya.
tor'ment, *n*. Wokakiže.
torn, *imp*. of TEAR.
tornado, *n*. Tateohitika.
torpedo, *n*. Caĥdi napopapi.
torpid, *a*. Ṭa se.
torpidity, *n*. Wicahuŋkešni.
torpor, *n*. Waokihisni.
torrent, *n*. Minitaŋ.
torrid, *a*. Ni'na ka'ta.
tortoise, *n*. Ke'ya.
tortuous, *a*. Kšaŋkšaŋ.
torture, *vt*. Kakišya; yuktaŋyaŋ. *n*. Wokakiže.
toss, *vt*. Kaĥoiyeya; waŋkankaniyeya; paptaŋptaŋiyeya.

tot, *n*. Ta'kuciḳana.
total, *a*. A'taya; ocowasiŋ.
totally, *adv*. A'taya.
tote, *vt*. Ḳiŋ; a'ya.
totter, *vi*. Kacekceka.
tottering, *pa*. Hahadaŋ.
touch, *vt*. 1. Icaȟtaka, *the trees touch*. 2. Yutaŋ, *he touched his hat*. 3. Iyohi, *he could'nt touch the roof*.—*The frost touched the leaves*, iwaśtena kuwa.—*Touch the heart*, cantiyapa.—*Touch off*, iyayeya; u'ta.—*Touch up*, yuwaśte kuwa; dus iyayeya. *n*. I'cicaȟtakapi; wayutaŋpi; yuwaśtepi; wokaȟtaka; wokitaŋ.
touching, *prep*. Icaȟtagya, *touching what John said*. *pa*. Caŋteiyawicapa, *a touching tale*.
touchy, *a*. Wakaȟtakeca.
tough, *a*. Suta.
tour, *n*. Oicimani; aohomni.
tourist, *n*. Oicimani.
tournament, *n*. Akicitaśka'tapi.
tow, *vt*. Yusdohaŋ; wa'ta yusdohaŋ. *n*. Caŋȟdoȟu hiŋ.
toward, towards, *prep*. Ektakiya; a'etopteya; en'tkiya.
towel, *n*. Napipakinte; itipakiŋte.
tower, *n*. Ti'piipasotka. *vi*. Waŋkan yeya.
towhead, *n*. Pa'żi.
town, *n*. Otoŋwe.
township, *n*. Makobaspe maka iyutapi śa'kpe.
toy, *n*. Wi'napiśkaŋye. *vi*. Śka'-ta.
trace, *vt*. Owe ode; ode, *trace a thief*. 2. Icaġo; caŋku icaġo, *trace the outlines on paper*. *n*. Owe; oŋśpa ci'stiŋna.
traceable, *a*. Odepica.
trachea, *n*. Dotehbeza.
track, *n*. Owe; caŋku. *vt*. Owe atab ya, *track a fox*.
tract, *n*. 1. Oŋspa; obaśpe; makobaśpe, *a rocky tract of land*. 2. Wowahokoŋkiye wowapi ci'stiŋna, *a temperance tract*.
tractable, *a*. Okiŋyaŋwaśte.
traction, *n*. Oyusdohaŋ.
trade, *vt*. Tokiyopeya, *trade horses*. *vi*. Wopetoŋ, *trade with Indians*. *n*. Wopetoŋpi; woecoŋ.
trader, *n*. Wopetoŋ.
tradewind, *n*. Waziyata tate.
trading, *pa*. Wopetoŋ.
tradition, *n*. Ehaŋna wicoie.
traduce, *vt*. Makoskan yaśica.
traffic, *vi*. Wopetoŋ. *n*. Wopetoŋpi.
tragedy, *n*. Ta'ku wocaŋtiyapa.
tragic, *a*. Wowinihaŋ.
trail, *n*. Caŋku; owe; ta'ku yusdohaŋ. *vt*. Yusdohaŋ; sdohaŋ ya.
train, *vt*. Oŋspekiya; kihiya; yutitaŋ. *n*. Ḣemani; owosdohe; woyaza.
trainer, *n*. Waoŋspekiya.
trainman, *n*. Ḣemani kicaŋye.
trait, *n*. Oȟaŋ.
traitor, *n*. Takodaku wicahnaye.
traitorous, *a*. Wicahnayes'a.
trammel, *vt*. Huŋ'keśniya.
tramp, *vt*. Siehde; ma'ni. *n*. Siehdepi; omanipi; wadaomani.
trample, *vt*. Adi; naśuża.
trance, *n*. Ihaŋmnapi se wawaŋyaka.
tranquil, *a*. Owaŋżi uŋ.
trans-, *pref*. O'pta; akasaŋpa.
transact, *vt*. Ecoŋ.
transaction, *n*. Woecoŋ.
transcend, *vt*. Kapeya.
transcribe, *vt*. Aktaowa.
transfer, *vt*. Tokaŋaya; wicaḳu. *n*. Wicaḳupi.
transfigure, *vt*. Yutokeca.
transform, *vt*. Piyakaġa.
transgress, *vt*. Waȟtani.
transgression, *n*. Woaȟtani.
transient, *a*. Aśkayedaŋ uŋ.
transit, *n*. O'pta ye ciŋ.

transitive, *a.* Ta'kuiyaheya.
transitory, *a.* Ci'stiyedaŋ uŋ.
translate, *vt.* Ieska ka'ġa ; to'kaŋ a'ya.
translation, *n.* Ieskayapi.
translucent, *a.* Kohdi.
transmigrate, *vt.* Piyaiyotaŋke.
transmit, *vt.* Ye'ya ; ḳu.
transom, *n.* O'żaŋżaŋhdepi hdakiŋyaŋ.
transparent, *a.* Kohdi ; taŋiŋ.
transpire, *vt.* Otaŋiŋ ; yuniya.
transplant, *vt.* Piya huhde.
transport, *vt.* Tokśu ; yumdeześni. *n.* Itokśu.
transportation, *n.* Watokśupi
transpose, *vt.* Yutokaŋ.
transverse, *a.* Hdakiŋyaŋ.
trap, *n.* Ma'zaḣtakiyapi; wi'hmuŋke. *vt.* Hmuŋ'ka.
trapper, *n.* Wahmuŋkes'a.
traps, *n. pl.* Ta'ku woyuha.
trash, *n.* Ta'kuśni.
travail, *vi.* Cincatoŋkta yazaŋ.
travel, *vt.* I'cimaniya.
traveller, *n.* I'cimani.
traverse, *vt.* O'ptaya.
travesty, *n.* Wawiḣa ka'ġapi.
tray, *n.* Wakśinopahi ; śuŋ'ka caże.
treacherous, *a.* Wicahnayes'a.
treachery, *n.* Wohnaye.
tread, trod, *vi.* Siha e'hde ; amani. *Tread on,* amani.—*Tread out,* nasuya.
treadle, *n.* Siipataŋ.
treason, *n.* Wohnaye, oyate en.
treasure, *vt.* Kihnaka ; kpataŋ. *n.* Woyuha ; wakihnakapi.
treasurer, *n.* Ma'zaskaawaŋyaka.
treasury, *n.* Ma'zaska wohnake.
treat, *vt.* 1. Kuwa ; ta'ku ecakicoŋ, *he treated me well.* 2. Miniwakaŋ yatkekiya. *n.* 1. Wowiyuśkiŋ, *the music was a treat.* 2. Won'tkiyapi ; wayatkekiyapi, *a treat of beer.*
treatise, *n.* Wowapitaŋka.
treatment, *n.* Wokuwa ; okuwa.
treaty, *n.* Oyate wowapiyutaŋpi.
treble, *a.* Ya'mniakihde ; ho waŋkantu.
tree, *n.* Caŋ ; caŋ'bosdanhaŋ. *vt.* Caŋadikiya.
tremble, *vi.* Caŋcaŋ.
tremendous, *a.* Otaŋtoŋka.
tremor, *n.* Wocaŋcaŋ ; wicanaka.
tremulous, *a.* Caŋcaŋ.
trench, *n.* Makaoḳapi.
trend, *n.* Tokiyotaŋ ye.
trepidation, *n.* Wocaŋcaŋ.
trespass, *vi.* Waḣtani. *n.* Woaḣtani.
tri-, *pre.* Ya'mni ; ya'mnikiya.
trial, *n.* 1. Iyutapi, *a trial of his speed.* 2. Aiapi, *a trial for murder.* 3. Wokakiże, *trials by fire.*
triangle, *n.* Ya'mnioisetoŋ.
tribal, *a.* Oyate ta'wa.
tribe, *n.* Oyate ośpaye.
tribulation, *n.* Wokakiże.
tribunal, *n.* Waaia omniciye.
tributary, *a.* Adetka ; ookiye.
tribute, *n.* Itaŋcaŋ tawomnaye.
trice, *n.* Iśtakakpapise.
trick, *n.* Wohnaye ; woecoŋ.
tricky, *a.* Wicahnayes'a.
tried, *pa.* Iyutapi.
triennal, *a.* Waniyetu ya'mni.
trifle, *n.* Ta'ku ci'stiŋna. *vi.* Ta'kuśnikiya śkaŋ.
trifler, *a.* Waawaciŋśni.
trigger, *n.* Ma'zakaŋiyutaŋ.
trill, *n.* Hoḣnaġicahotoŋ.
trim, *vt.* 1. Basmiŋ, *trim the hair.* 2. Aopazaŋ, *trim a hat.* 3. Taŋ'yaŋ piya. *a.* Wayuco.
trinity, *n.* Ya'mni waŋżipi.
trinket, *n.* Oiŋ.
trio, *n.* Ya'mnipi.
trip, *n.* Oicimani. *vi.* Oḣaŋko ma'ni ; ḣicahaŋ ; yuśna.
tripe, *n.* Taśupe.
triple, *a.* Ya'mnikiya.
triplet, *n.* Ya'mniakicaśka.

triplicate, *a.* Ya'mni.
tripod, *n.* Hu ya'mni.
tripper, *n.* Psi'psin ma'ni.
trite, *a.* Ehaŋna; poŋpoŋ.
triumph, *n.* Ohiya. *n.* Woohiya.
triumphal, *a.* Ohiyapi.
triumphant, *a.* Ohiya.
triune, *a.* Ya'mniwaŋżina.
trivial, *a.* Ta'kuitokecaśni.
trod, *imp. of* TREAD.
troop, *n.* Akicita optaye; optaye.
trophy, *n.* Woohiye; wakipi.
tropic, *n.* Wi'ihukuya.
trot, *vi.* Nacam ya; iŋ'yaŋka.
troth, *n.* Wowicake.
trouble, *vt.* Naġiyeya; yuśkaŋśkaŋ. *n.* Wonaġiyeya; wosice.
troubled, *pa.* Iyoyaka.
troublesome, *a.* Wanaġiyeya.
troublous, *a.* Oiyokiśica.
trough, *n.* Can'kaskokpa.
trousers, *n.* Oŋzeoġe.
trout, *n.* Hoġaŋwicaśtaśni.
trowel, *n.* Upśiżaipawiŋte.
truant, *n.* Wayawanażica.
truce, *n.* Wokicize kihnakapi.
truck, *n.* Ta'kuśniśni; huha.
truckle, *vi.* Ihukuya iyeiçiya.
true, *a.* Wicaka; ecetu.
truism, *a.* Wicaka taŋiŋ.
truly, *adv.* A'wicakehaŋ.
trump, *n.* Itaŋcaŋkiyapi.
trumpery, *n.* Oŋ i'kpazopi.
trumpet, *n.* Ma'zawayaotaŋiŋ. *vt.* Yaotaŋiŋ. *vi.* Wayaotaŋiŋ.
trunk, *n.* 1. Caŋ'ohnaka; heyakeopiye, *a leather trunk.* 2. Hucaŋ; caŋkaġa, *the trunk of the tree.* 3. Pasu, *the elephant's trunk.* 4. Taŋcaŋ, *the trunk only remained.*
truss, *n.* 1. Caŋ'yuhaha, *bridge truss.* 2. Teziwiyutiŋze.
trust, *vt.* 1. Waciŋyaŋ, *trust God.* 2. Waciŋyaŋ yuhekiya, *trust your horse to his care.* 3. Wicada, *I trusted his word.* 4. Eciŋ; awaciŋ uŋ, *I trust he will come.* 5. Icazokiya, *he trusted him for ten dollars.* *n.* 1. Waawaŋyagkiyapi, *national trusts.*
trustee, *n.* Awaŋyagkiyapi.
trustful, *a.* Waciŋyaŋ.
trustless, *a.* Wowaciŋyecodaŋ; waciŋyepicaśni.
trustworthy, *a.* Waciŋyepica.
trusty, *a.* Waciŋyepica; wicaka.
truth, *n.* Wowicake; he'cetu.
truthful, *a.* Wicaka.
try, tried, *vt.* 1. Iyuta, *try your new pen.* 2. Akita; kuwa, *tried to kill me.* 3. Aia, *he was t·ied for murder.*—*Try to do,* ecoŋuta.—*Try to kill,* ktewaciŋ.—*Try the taste,* u'ta.
tub, *n.* Wi'yużażakoka; kokabaksa.
tube, *n.* Wiohdoġeca.
tuber, *n.* Hutkaŋ pśuŋkaka; pśuŋkaya po.
tubercle, *n.* Pśuŋkakana po.
tuck, *vi.* 1. Pakśiża, *tuck up the skirt.* 2. Paoskica, *tuck in the cover.*
Tuesday, *n.* Aŋpetuinoŋpa.
tuft, *n.* Wopamna, *a tuft of grass.* — *A tuft of hair,* aśke.
tug, *vt.* Yutitaŋ; śogya kuwa. *n.* Woyutitaŋ; pe'tawata wayusdohaŋ; śuŋgikaŋ woyutitaŋ.
tuition, *n.* Wooŋspe wokażużu.
tulip, *n.* Mnahcahca obe.
tumble, *vt.* 1. Paptaŋiyeya; ehpeya, *tumbled it out of the wagon.* 2. To'kenciŋciŋ ehpeya, *tumbled up the bed.* *vi.* Paptaŋptaŋ; hiŋhpaya.
tumble-bug, *n.* Uŋkcepakmikma.
tumbler, *n.* 1. Żaŋzaŋwiyatke, *broke a tumbler.* 2. Waihduptaŋptaŋ.
tumor, *n.* Po.
tumult, *n.* Owodutatoŋ.
tumultuous, *a.* Wohitiyaśkaŋpi.

tune, *n.* Odowaŋ ho. *vt.* Ho ecetuya; piya.
tuner, *n.* Ho'ecetuya.
tunic, *n.* O'kde.
tunnel, *n.* Ḣe'oḣdogyapi.
turban, *n.* Pa'iyuskite.
turbid, *a.* Ṡoṡe.
turbulent, *a.* Ṡkaŋṡkaŋ; wohitika.
turf, *n.* Peżihutkaŋ; peżito.
turkey, *n.* Żicataŋka; *T.* Waglekśuŋtaŋka.
turkey-buzzard, *n.* Heca.
turmoil, *n.* Woṡkaŋṡkaŋ.
turn, *vt.* 1. Yuhomni, *turn the wheel.* 2. Iyayeya, *turn the cattle into the pasture.* 3. E'e ka'ġa, *turn water into wine.*—*Turn the corner,* oise ayuhomni.—*Turn over,* yuptaŋyaŋ.—*Turn the stock,* ḣoŋyakoŋ yueci.—*Turn the stomach,* hitihdaya. *vi.* Kawiŋġa; namni; ihduptaŋ. *n.* Oyuktaŋ; oecoŋ. *By turns,* uŋmaŋ itogto.—*His turn,* i'ye iyehantu.
turns, *n.* Iṡnatipi.
turn-about, *adv.* Uŋmaŋitogto.
turn-coat, *n.* Titokaŋki.
turning-point, *n.* Tukten to'kecapi.
turnip, *n.* Ti'psina.
turnkey, *n.* Tiyopayuḣdoka.
turnpike, *n.* Caŋkumdoya.
turpentine, *n.* Wazihaŋpi.
turpitude, *n.* Woṡice.
turtle, *n.* Ke'ya. *Soft-shell,* kezoŋta.
turtle-dove, *n.* Tin'wakiyedaŋ.
tush, *interj.* Hoḣ.
tusk, *n.* Hiŋske.
tussle, *vi.* Kici ecoŋ.
tut, *interj.* Hiŋte.
tutelage, *n.* Wooŋspe.
tutor, *n.* Waoŋspekiya.
twaddle, *vt.* Itutuia.
twain, *a.* Noŋ'pa.
tweezers, *n.* Wi'yużipe.
twelfth, *a.* Iakenoŋpa.
twelve, *a.* Akenoŋpa.
twenty, *a.* Wikcemnanoŋpa.
'twere, *contr.* IT WERE.
twice, *a.* Noŋ'paakiḣde.
twig, *n.* Caŋiŋkpa.
twilight, *n.* Ki'taŋna aŋ'pa; owataŋiŋṡni.
twill, *vt.* Yuġopise kazoŋta.
twin, *n.* Cekpa.
twine, *n.* Haḣoŋta oŋ wapaḣtapi. *vt.* Yuwi; soŋ.
twinge, *vt.* Yażimżipa; naŋ'ka.
twinkle, *vi.* Iyeġa; *T.* ileġa.
twirl, *vt.* Yuhomni.
twist, *vt.* Pahmuŋ; yukṡa.
twit, *vt.* Oṡtehda.
twitch, *vi.* Tanapa; naŋ'ka.
twitter, *vi.* Żiżi.
'twixt, *contr.* of BETWIXT.
two, *a.* Noŋ'pa. *Only two,* nom'nana.—*Two-edged,* anogope.—*These two,* denaoza.—*Two by two,* nom'noŋpa.
twofold, *a.* Noŋ'paakihde.
Twokettles, *n. pr.* Oohenoŋpa.
tying, *pp.* of TIE.
type, *n.* Ma'zaoowa; wocaże.
typhoid, *a.* Taŋcaŋkatapi ḣaŋhi.
typhoon, *n.* Tateiyumni.
typical, *a.* Woiyaciŋ.
tyrannical, *a.* Wawakipażiŋ.
tyrannize, *vi.* Oŋ'ṡiya kuwa.
tyranny, *n.* Wicaohitikapi.
tyrant, *n.* Itaŋcaŋ suta.

U

ubiquitous, *a.* O'waŋca uŋ.
udder, *n.* Aze.
ugly, *a.* Owaŋyagṡica; ṡica.
ulcerate, *vi.* Toŋye.

ultimate, *a.* Ihaŋke.
ultimately, *adv.* Uŋ'haŋketa.
ultra, *a.* Aokaġeca.
umbrage, *n.* Wośihda.
umbrella, *n.* O'haŋzihdepi.
un-, *pref.* Śni.
unable, *a.* Okihiśni.
unanimous, *a.* Tawaciŋwaŋżidaŋ.
unanswerable, *a.* Ayuptepicaśni.
unavoidable, *a.* Yutokecapicaśni.
unawares, *a.* Tak'eciŋśni.
unbar, *vt.* Yukca.
unbelief, *n.* Waceṭuŋhdapi.
unbend, *vt.* Yuowotaŋna; yuzica.
unbid, *a.* Kicopiśni; da'piśni.
unbind, *vt.* Yukca.
unbolt, *vt.* Yuśdoka.
unbosom, *vt.* Wonaḣbe oyaka.
unbounded, *a.* Woptecaśni.
unbridle, *vt.* Iiyuwi yuśdoka.
unbuckle, *vt.* Yuśka.
unburden, *vt.* Yuḣpa.
unbutton, *vt.* Yukca.
uncertain, *a.* To'ketutaŋiŋśni.
unchain, *vt.* Ma'za yuśka.
uncle, *n.* Dekśi. *Your uncle*, nidekśi.—*His uncle*, dekśitku.—*My father's brother*, ate.
unclothed, *a.* Taŋcodaŋ.
uncoil, *vt.* Yuhda.
uncomfortable, *a.* Taŋyaŋśni.
uncommon, *a.* He'cetuśni ece; to'keca.
unconcerned, *a.* Tak'eciŋśni.
uncork, *vt.* Iośtaŋicu.
uncouth, *a.* Oŋspeśni.
uncover, *vt.* Yuzamni.
unction, *n.* Caŋtiyowicahi.
uncurl, *vt.* Kiyusto.
undeceive, *vt.* Okaḣniḣya.
undeniable, *a.* I'enhdepicaśni.
under, *prep.* Ihukuya; iyohiśni. *Under the house*, ti'pi ihukuya.—*Under weight*, tkeutapi iyohiśni.—*Under fire*, kutepi en'tu. *a.* Hukuya; imahen, *an under layer.*
underbid, *vt.* Ihukya ka.
underbrush, *n.* Oteḣi.
underclothes, *n.* Mahenuŋpi.
undergo, *vt.* Akipa.
underhanded, *a.* Naḣmaŋ śkaŋ.
undermine, *vt.* Oḣdateya ḳa.
underneath, *a.* Ihukuya.
underpin, *vt.* Tihute ka'ġa.
underrate, *vt.* Ihukuya yawa.
understand, *vt.* Okaḣniġa; eciŋ; naḣoŋ.—*Do you understand*, oyakaḣniġa he.—*Do you understand English*, Waśicuŋ iapi nayaḣoŋ he.
understanding, *n.* Wookaḣniġe.
understate, *vt.* Ihukun oyaka.
undertake, *vt.* Ecoŋiyuta.
undertaker, *n.* Wicaḣa.
undo, *vt.* Yużużu.
undone, *pp.* of UNDO.
undoubted, *a.* Ceṭuŋhdaśni.
undress, *vt.* Heyake hduśdoka.
undying, *a.* Ṭepicaśni.
unearth, *vt.* Yutaŋiŋ.
unearthly, *a.* Maka etaŋhaŋ śni; wakaŋse.
uneasy, *a.* Iyokipiśni uŋ.
unequal, *a.* Iyekicetuśni; kaociptetu.
unequivocal, *a.* Taŋiŋ ḣca.
uneven, *a.* Mda'yeśni; iyehaŋyaŋśni.
unexpected, *a.* Waktapiśni.
unfailing, *a.* Yusotepicaśni.
unfair, *a.* Owotaŋnaśni.
unfaithful, *a.* Wicakeśni.
unfasten, *a.* Yuśka.
unfavorable, *a.* Okiciwaśteśni; iyowicakipiśni.
unfeeling, *a.* Caŋtewanica.
unfit, *a.* Iyecetuśni. *vi.* Ecetuśnikiya.
unfix, *vt.* Yuecetuśni.
unfold, *vt.* Yumdaya; yutaŋiŋ.
unfortunate, *a.* Wa'piśni.
unfortunately, *adv.* Wa'piśniyaŋ; śinya.
unfounded, *a.* Yuwicakapiśni.
unfriendly, *a.* Watoghda.

unfurl, *vt.* Yuzamni.
ungainly, *a.* Oŋspeśni.
ungodly, *a.* Wakaŋtaŋka awaciŋśni.
unhappy, *a.* Caŋtewaśteśni.
unharness, *vt.* Ikaŋ yuśdoka.
unhealthy, *a.* Zaniśni.
unhitch, *vt.* Yuśka.
unhorse, *vt.* Paȟpa.
unhurt, *a.* Ksu′weyeśni.
uniform, *a.* O′waŋżidaŋ; a′kidececa. *n.* Akicita taheyake.
uniformly, *adv.* He′cetuwaŋżica.
unify, *vt.* Yuokoŋwaŋżidaŋ.
uninterrupted, *a.* Naǧiyeyeśni.
union, *n.* Yuokoŋwaŋżipi; yuwaŋżipi; wowaŋżi. *a.* Yuwitaya.
unique, *a.* Wiciśnana.
unison, *n.* O′waŋżi.
unit, *n.* Waŋżina; wayawapi oiyute.
unite, *vt.* Yuokoŋwaŋżidaŋ; i′cikoyagya.
universal, *a.* Siŋtomni.
universalist, *n.* A′taya ni′pi kta wicada.
unjointed, *a.* O′kihe papśuŋ.
unkind, *a.* Waoŋśidaśni.
unlawful, *a.* Woope ohnaśni.
unlearned, *n.* Waoŋspeśni.
unless, *conj.* Śni kiŋhaŋ.
unlike, *a.* Iyececeśni.
unlimited, *a.* Woptecaśni; tohaŋyaŋ cen.
unload, *vt.* Ḣeteżu; paȟpa.
unlock, *vt.* Yuȟdoka; yuśdoka.
unloose, *vt.* Yuśka.
unmarried, *a.* Taŋśna uŋ.
unnatural, *a.* Oȟaŋtokeca.
unnecessary, *a.* Ituya; iyececeśni.
unpack, *vt.* Yużużu; icu.
unpleasant, *a.* Oaśica.
unravel, *vt.* Yukca.
unreasonable, *a.* Tawaciŋwanica; aokaǧeca.
unripe, *a.* Sutoŋśni.
unroll, *vt.* Yumdaya.
unruly, *a.* Wanaȟoŋśni.
unsaddle, *vt.* Aḳiŋ yuśdoka.
unsafe, *a.* Okokipe.
unscrew, *vt.* Yuhbezapi yuśdoka.
unsightly, *a.* Owaŋyagśica.
unsound, *a.* Zaniśni; ecetuśni.
unspeakable, *a.* Oyagpicaśni.
unsuitable, *a.* Iyecetuśni.
untie, *vt.* Yuśka.
until, *prep.* Hehaŋyaŋ; ecen.
untiring, *a.* Ecoŋkapiŋ śni.
unto, *prep.* Hehaŋyaŋ; ekta.
untoward, *a.* E′citapeśni; ȟmiŋ.
untrue, *a.* Wicakeśni.
untried, *a.* Iyutapiśni.
untwist, *vt.* Yuhda.
unusual, *a.* He′cetuśni ecee; wa′petokeca.
unwell, *a.* Wayazaŋhda.
unwind, *vt.* Yuhda.
unwonted, *a.* Nakahaś.
unworthy, *a.* Iyecetuśni.
unyoke, *vt.* Wanapiŋ yuśka.
up, *prep.* Waŋkan; bosdan; i′taŋwaŋkaŋhde; iŋ′kpata; iyehan; a′taya. *Go up*, waŋkan ya.—*Stand up straight*, bosdan owotaŋna na′żiŋ.—*Up hill*, paha i′taŋwaŋkaŋhde.—*Up the river*, wakpa iŋ′kpata.—*He ate it all up*, a′taya owasiŋ yu′ta.—*Blow up the boiler*, minioipiȟye bomdaza.—*Burn up*, a′taya ȟuȟnaǧa.—*The time is up*, waŋna iyehantu.—*Upside down*, ahdapśiŋyaŋ.
upbraid, *vt.* Ba; iyopeya.
upheave, *vt.* Pawaŋkan iyeya.
uphold, upheld, *vt.* O′kiya; waŋkan yu′za.
upland, *n.* Mdamdata.
uplift, *vt.* Yuwaŋkan icu.
upon, *prep.* Akan; ehan. *Borders upon*, opapuŋ icaȟtaka.—*Live upon*, oŋ ni.
upper, *a.* Waŋkantu. *Upper lip*. pute.

uppermost, *a.* Iyotaŋ waŋkantu.
upright, *a.* 1. Bosdantu : *an upright post.* 2. Owotaŋna : *an upright man.*
uprising, *n.* Anaźiŋpi.
uproar, *n.* Owodutatoŋ.
uproot, *vt.* Yuźuŋ.
upset, *vt.* Yuptaŋyaŋ.
upshot, *n.* Woyuśtaŋ.
upside down, *adv.* Ahdapśiŋyaŋ.
upstairs, *n.* Waŋkantipi.
upstart, *n.* Nakahaś taŋiŋ.
upward, *adv.* Waŋkantkiya.
urban, *a.* Otoŋwekaḣya.
urbane, *a.* Oḣaŋwaśteka.
urchin, *n.* Wakaŋheźa.
urge, *vt.* I'yopaśtake ; inaḣniya.
urgent, *a.* Wakitaŋ.
urinate, *vi.* De'źa.
urn, *n.* Makaceġa.
us, *pro.* Uŋkiyepi.
usage, *n.* Woecoŋ ; wicoḣaŋ.
use, *vt.* Uŋ ; kiçun. *Use for,* e'ekiya uŋ.—*Use up,* yusota.—*Use well,* taŋ'yaŋ kuwa. *vi.* 1. Ecewakta : *he is used to work.* 2. To'hiŋni : *he used to live here.* *n.* Uŋ'pi ; ta'ku oŋ waśte. *No use,* uŋpicaśni ; -Ecoŋpicaśni.
useful, *a.* Uŋ'piwaśte ; uŋpica.
useless, *a.* Ta'ku oŋ uŋpicaśni.
usher, *n.* Tiyopa awaŋyake.
usual, *a.* Ecoŋpiecee ; to'ketu ece.
usurp, *vt.* Icu ; ta'waśniicu.
usury, *n.* Wakapeya kaźuźukiya.
Ute, *n. pr.* Sa'pawicaśta.
utensil, *n.* Wi'kicaŋye.
uterus, *n.* Tamni.
utilitarian, *n.* Wakiçuŋkteḣca.
utilize, *vt.* Ta'kuye.
utmost, *a.* Ihaŋke ; iyotaŋ.
utter, *vt.* E'napeya ; taŋiŋyaŋ e'ya. *a.* Ocowasiŋ.
utterance, *n.* Ho e'napeya.
uttermost, *a.* Ihaŋketaḣ.

V

vacancy, *n.* Oko.
vacant, *a.* Cokadaŋ haŋ ; okaŋ.
vacate, *vt.* Kiyukaŋ ; tokaŋ ya.
vacation, *n.* Oko ; oziyapi.
vaccinate, *vt.* Peźuta okaḣdogya.
vacillate, *vi.* Ake to'keca cee ; ptaŋptaŋna.
vacuum, *n.* Ta'kudaŋ en uŋ śni.
vagabond, *n.* Tu'we ituya uŋ.
vagina, *n.* Śaŋ ; wiśaŋ.
vagrant, *n.* Ituya omani.
vague, *a.* To'ketutaŋiŋśni.
vain, *a.* Wi'taŋtaŋ ; ta'kuśni oŋ itaŋ ; ta'kuśni.
vainly, *adv.* Ituya.
va'le, *interj.* Taŋyaŋ yauŋ nuŋwe.
vale, *n.* O'smaka.
valedictory, *n.* Ehake wohdaka.
valiant, *a.* Waditaka.
valid, *a.* Wicake ; he'cetu ; suta.
valise, *n.* Wizipaŋ ; wapapśuŋka.
valley, *n.* Makosmaka.
valor, *n.* Wcwaditake.
valuable, *a.* Yuhapi waśte ; teḣike ; wi'yokihi.
value, *vt.* Yawa ; teḣiŋda. *n.* Iyawa.
valueless, *a.* Ta'kudaŋ iyokihiśni.
van, *n.* Otokahe.
vane, *n.* Tate e'pazo.
vanish, *vi.* Taŋiŋśni iyaye.
vanity, *n.* Ta'kuśni
vanquish, *vt.* Ohiya.
vapor, *n.* Opo ; minipo.
variable, *a.* Aketokeca ece.
variation, *n.* Tohaŋyaŋ to'keca.
variety, *n.* Ocaźe ; toktokeca.
various, *a.* Toktokeca.
varnish, *n.* Iuŋpi wiyakpa. *vt.* Wiyakpaya iuŋ.

vary, *vt.* Togye ka'ġa ; yutokeca.
vase, *n.* Kampeska wohnake.
vast, *n.* Taŋ'ka ; woptecaśni.
vat, *n.* Kokataŋka.
vault, *n.* Mibeya awakeyapi.
vaunt, *vi.* Ihdataŋ.
veal, *n.* Pteżicedaŋ tado.
veer, *vi.* Yuktaŋ iyaye.
vegetable, *n.* Ta'kuśniśni wożupi.
vehement, *a.* Wohitika.
vehicle, *n.* Oaye ; caŋpakmiyaŋ.
veil, *n.* Iteakaȟpe ; miniȟuha ġaŋġaŋ. *vt.* Akaȟpa.
vein, *n.* We'kaŋiyapaśni ; iŋ'yaŋwaŋka.
velocity, *n.* Woduzahaŋ.
velvet, *n.* Miniȟuha hiŋ'toŋ wiyakpa.
vend, *vt.* Wi'yopeya.
venerable, *a.* Okinihaŋ.
venerate, *vt.* Yuonihaŋ.
vengeance, *n.* Watokiçoŋpi.
venison, *n.* Taȟca ta'do.
venomous, *a.* Wayuśica.
vent, *vt.* Yataŋiŋ. *n.* Woyataŋiŋ ; wohiyu.
ventilate, *vt.* Okadusya ; yutaŋiŋ.
venture, *vt.* Oṭoya ; tawaṭenya ; iyuta. *n.* Woiyute. *At a venture,* ituyaciŋ.
venturesome, *a.* Itoŋpeśni śkaŋ.
veracity, *n.* Iewicakapi.
verb, *n.* Wawoyake iapi.
verbatim, *adv.* Iapi iyohi.
verdant, *a.* To.
verdure, *n.* Wato.
verdict, *n.* Woyaco ; woyasu.
verge, *n.* Tete ; opapuŋ ; oiŋkpa.
verify, *vt.* Yuwicaka.
verily, *adv.* A'wicakehaŋ.
veritable, *a.* Wicaka.
vermilion, *n.* Waśeśa ; wase.
vermin, *n.* Wamdudaŋ ; he'ya.
vernacular, *n.* Huŋkake iapi ta'wa.
versatile, *a.* Wayupika.
verse, *n.* Oehde.
version, *n.* Ieskayapi ; oyakapi.
versus, *prep.* I'tkokim.
vertebra, *n.* Caŋȟaȟaka.
vertex. *n.* O'iŋkpa ; ipa.
vertical, *a.* Bosdata.
very, *adv.* Ni'na ; ȟiŋ ; ȟtiŋ ; ȟca ; *Y.* ȟciŋ. *Very good,* ni'na waśte ; waśteȟca.
vesper, *n.* Ḣtayetu wocekiye.
vessel, *n.* Ce'ġa ; wakśica ; wa'ta. *Blood vessel,* we kaŋ.
vest, *n.* A'okihaŋna ; *Y.* kaȟdogośtaŋpi. *vt.* Ḳu ; yuhekiya.
vestibule, *n.* Tiyopatipi.
vestige, *n.* Owe ; wowakta.
vestment, *n.* Heyake ; śina.
vestry, *n.* Wicaśtawakaŋ ookiye.
veteran, *n.* Tu'we ehaŋna. *a.* Ehaŋna.
veto, *vt.* Teȟiŋda ; anapta.
vex, *vt.* Naġiyeya.
vexation, *n.* Wonaġiyeya.
via, *prep.* Iyoopta.
vial, *n.* Żaŋżaŋna.
vibrate, *vi.* Kaozeze.
vicarious, *a.* E'ekiya.
vice, *n.* Wicoȟaŋśica ; ma'zaiyużipe.
vice-, *prep.* O'kihe. *Vice-president,* itaŋcaŋ o'kihe.
vicinity, *n.* Oakiyedaŋ.
vicious, *n.* Ociŋśica ; śi'ca.
victim, *n.* Wośnapi ; woṭeyapi.
victor, *n.* Tu'we ohiya.
victorious, *a.* Ohiya.
victory, *n.* Woohiye.
victuals, *n.* Woyute.
vide, *v.* Waŋyaka.
vie, *vi.* Econ : *vie with.*
view, *vt.* Waŋyaka ; amdeza. *n.* Wowaŋyake ; owaŋyake.
vigil, *n.* Haŋkiktapi.
vigilant, *a.* Wakta uŋ.
vigor, *n.* Wowaś'ake ; ni'na.
vigorous, *a.* Waś'aka.
vile, *a.* Śi'ca ; waȟteśni.
vilify, *vt.* Yaśica.
village, *n.* Otoŋwe ci'stiŋna.
villain, *n.* Tu'we śi'ca.

villainy, *n.* Woṡice.
vim, *n.* Woohitika.
vindicate, *vt.* Yuwicaka; ikiya.
vindictive, *a.* Watokiçoŋwaciŋ.
vine, *n.* Caŋwiyuwi.
vinegar, *n.* Miniṡkumna.
vineyard, *n.* Hastaŋhaŋka owożu.
violate, *vt.* Kicaksa; yuṡica.
violence, *n.* Woohitika; woṡice.
violent, *a.* Wohitika.
violently, *adv.* Wohitiya.
violet, *n.* Waḣca tahukṡaŋ.
viper, *n.* Wamduṡkaṡica.
virago, *n.* Wiŋ'yaŋ ohitika.
virgin, *n.* Witaŋṡna; te'ca.
virile, *a.* Wica; wicaṡta.
virtue, *n.* Wowaṡte; wowaṡ'ake.
virulent, *a.* Wayuṡica.
virus, *n.* Woṡice su.
visage, *n.* Itohnake.
vise, *n.* Mazwiyuskite.
visible, *a.* Taŋiŋ.
vision, *n.* Wowaŋyake; wi'waŋyake; wawaŋyakapi.
visionary, *a.* Wi'haŋmna se.
visit, *vt.* Titokaŋ i. *n.* Titokaŋipi.
visitor, *n.* Tu'we titokaŋ i.
vial, *a.* Oŋ ni'pi.
vitality, *n.* Ni'pi wowaṡ'ake.
vitiate, *vt.* Yuṡica.
vituperate, *vi.* I en hde.
vivacious, *a.* Wi'haha.
vivid, *a.* Taŋiŋ ḣca.
vocabulary, *n.* Ieska wowapi; iapi.
vocal, *a.* Wicaho; dowaŋpi.
vocation, *n.* Wicoḣaŋ.
vogue, *n.* Woecoŋ.
voice, *n.* Wicaho. *vt.* Yataŋiŋ.
void, *a.* Ecetuṡni; cokadaŋ.
volatile, *a.* Kohaŋ ske'pa.
volcano, *n.* Paha ide.
volition, *n.* Owaciŋyuze.
volley, *n.* Ptaya ecoŋpi.
volume, *n.* Wowapi waŋżi; o'yuwitaya.
voluntarily, *adv.* Iyeciŋka.
voluntary, *a.* Iyeciŋka ecoŋpi.
volunteer, *vi.* Iyeciŋka e'ya. *n.* I'ye ciŋ o'pa; akicita.
voluptuous, *a.* Wiciŋs'a; wacaŋtahde.
vomit, *vt.* Hde'pa. *n.* Hde'papi.
voracious, *a.* Ni'na dociŋ; ni'na wota.
vortex, *n.* Miniomni.
votary, *n.* Iḣakta.
vote, *vi.* Wowapi iyoḣpeya; kaḣniġa.
vouch, *vi.* Yuwicaka. *Vouch for*, ki'ciyuwicaka.
voucher, *n.* Wayuwicaka.
vouchsafe, *vt.* Ḳu; okihiya.
vow, *vi.* Wakaŋtaŋka ceżeyan e'ya. *n.* Woiçicoŋze.
vowel, *n.* Oowa ho'waŋżi. Oowa dena hecen iciyapi: *a, e, i, o, u.*
voyage, *n.* Watom oicimani.
vulgar, *a.* Waoŋspekeṡni; ikceka; ṡi'ca.
vulnerable, *a.* Boḣdogpica.
vulture, *n.* Heca.

W

wabble, *vi.* Paptaŋptaŋ; yuktaŋktaŋ.
wad, *n.* Iyopuḣdi.
waddle, *vi.* Maġa se ma'ni.
wade, *vt.* Copa.
wafer, *n.* Wi'puspe.
waft, *vt.* Kaḣbogya.
wag, *vt.* Yuhuhuza. *Wag the head*, po'ptaŋptaŋ.—*Wag the tail*, sicupsaŋpsaŋ. *n.* Tu'we wawiḣaḣa.
[illegible]. *vt.* Kuwa. *n.* Wi'ṡi.

wager, *vt.* Yekiya.
wages, *n.* Wokažužu ; wi'si.
waggish, *a.* Wawiȟaye.
wagon, *n.* Caŋpahmiȟma; *Y.* caŋpakmiyaŋ ; *T.* caŋpagmiyaŋ.
wagon-bow, *n.* Caŋkšaŋakeyapi.
wagon-box, *n.* Caŋpakmiyaŋ škokpa.
waif, *n.* Hokšiyopa eȟpeyapi.
wail, *vi.* Ce'ya. *Wail for,* aceya.
wainscot, *n.* Timahen hepiyaokataŋpi.
waist, *n.* Niġute ; ipiyake.
waistband, *n.* Nitoške ipiyake.
wait, *vi.* 1. Apeuŋ : *wait till he comes.*—*Wait for,* akipe ; wakta uŋ. 2. Wi'yeya na'žiŋ ; waokiya na'žiŋ : *wait on the table.* *n.* Wi'yeya un'pi. *Lie in wait,* waape. *interj.* Hiŋyaŋhaŋka.
waiter, *n.* Wayutaŋkiyapi.
waive, *vt.* Ķu ; kiyukaŋ.
wake, *vt.* Yuȟica. *vi.* Kikta. *n.* 1. Haŋkiktapi. 2. Wa'ta owe.
wakeful, *a.* Kiktasa.
waken, *vt.* Yuȟica.
walk, *vi.* Ma'ni : *does the baby walk.*—*Walk on,* amani.—*Walk around,* omani. *n.* 1. Ma'nipi : *his gait is a walk.* 2. Omanipi ; oomani : *take a walk.*
walker, *n.* Manipi ; mani.
wall, *n.* 1. Tibosdata : *a painting on the wall.* 2. Coŋ'kaške : *a stone wall.* *vt.* Acaŋkaške.
walled, *a.* Acaŋkaškapi.
wallet, *n.* Ma'zaskaožuha ; wapapšuŋka.
wallop, *vt.* Kasaksaka ; popomya ipiġa.
wallow, *vi.* Ihduptaŋptaŋ.
walnut, *n.* Hma ; kma ; gma.
walrus, *n.* Uŋkteȟi ; uŋkceȟi.
waltz, *n.* Kaicitkokim wacipi.
wampum, *n.* Wamnuhadaŋ ; waboslata.
wan, *a.* Ukaececešni.
wand, *n.* Caŋsakadaŋ.
wander, *vi.* Nu'ni ; omani.
wanderer, *n.* Omanisa.
wane, *vi.* Ci'stiŋna a'ya.
want, *vt.* 1. Ciŋ : *I want some water.* 2. Icakiža ; co'daŋ uŋ : *she wants even bread.* 3. Iyohišni : *it wants one inch.* *n.* 1. Wokakiže : *in want.* 2. Co'daŋ uŋ : *withered for the want of rain.* 3. Ta'ku ciŋ'pi : *civilization increases man's wants.*
wanting, *pa.* Wanica ; iyehaŋyaŋšni ; iyokpani.
wanton, *a.* Wanaȟoŋšni.
war, *n.* Wokicize. *Make war,* wokicize ka'ġa.—*War-club,* caŋ'ȟpi.—*War-dance,* iwakicipi.—*War-party,* ozuye. *vi.* Kiciza.
warble, *vi-* I'yasnasna dowaŋ.
war-cry, *n.* I'yakišašapi.
ward, *n.* Tu'we awaŋyakapi.
ward off, *vt.* Kakamiyeya.
warden, *n.* Waawaŋyake.
wardrobe, *n.* Heyake ; heyake woknake.
ware, *imp* of WEAR.
ware, *n.* Wi'kicaŋye : woyuha.
warehouse, *n.* Wokihnaketipi.
warfare, *n.* Wokicize.
warily, *adv.* Waktaya.
warlike, *a.* Kiswaciŋ ; ksi'zeca.
warm, *a.* 1. Ka'ta : *warm water; warm weather.* 2. Co'za : *warm clothing.* 3. Waihaktapi : *warm friends.* *vt.* Kanya ; ka'ta a'ya.
warmth, *n.* Wokata.
warn, *vt.* Iwaktaye.
warning, *n.* Iwaktayapi.
warp, *vt.* Yuškopa ; yutokeca. *n.* Haȟoŋta kazoŋtapi.
warrant, *n.* Oyuspešipi wowapi. *vt.* 1. Yuwicake : *I warrant the goods.* 2. Iyowiŋyaŋ : *it did not warrant your going.*
warrior, *n.* Ozuye wicašta.
wart, *n.* Ukaanoġe.
wary, *a.* Wakta uŋ ; ksa'pa.

was, *imp.* of BE. Uŋ.
wash, *vt.* 1. Yużaża : *wash clothes.* 2. Pakiŋta : *wash away sins.* *vi.* Wayużaża : *he washed.*
wash, *n.* Oŋ yużażapi.
wash-basin, *n.* Napożaża.
wash-board, *n.* Caŋipaskice.
wash-boiler, *n.* Heyake ipiħye.
wash-bowl, *n.* Napożaża.
wash-pan, Napożaża.
wash-stand, *n.* Ahna ihdużażapi.
washout, *n.* Miniboħya.
washtub, *n.* Wi'yużaża.
wasp, *n.* Tuħmaġa haŋ'ska.
waste, *vt.* Yutakuniśni. *a.* Ta'kuyepicaśni; makoskantu. *n.* Wotakuniśni; woihaŋke.
wasteful, *a.* Waihaŋgyes'a.
wasting, *pa.* Yutakuniśni.
watch, *vt.* 1. Awaŋyaka : *watch the cattle.* 2. Amdes uŋ ; opaħta kuwa : *watch the thief.* *vi.* Waawanyag uŋ ; amdes uŋ. *n.* 1. Waawaŋyake : *the watch stood guard.* 2. Sicaŋopiye wi'hiyayedaŋ. 3. Śuŋ'ka caże.
watchful, *a.* Waktauŋ.
watchman, *n.* Waawaŋyake.
watchword, *n.* Wowaktaiapi.
water, *n.* Mini; *Y.* mni. *n.* 1. Miniku : *water the cows.* 2. Miniapapsoŋ : *water the plants.* 3. Mini icahi : *watered the milk.* *Water-cask,* miniyaya.—*Water-elm,* peikceka. — *Water-fowl,* miniwakiŋyaŋna. —*Water-mill,* miniwokpaŋ.—*Water-tight,* kuse śni ; minioħdogyeśni.
watercloset, *n.* Taŋkantipi.
watercourse, *n.* Wakpadaŋ.
watercure, *n.* Mini oŋ kuwapi.
watered, *a.* Miniyukaŋ.
waterfall, *n.* Minihiŋhe.
waterhole, *n.* Miniośkokpa.
watermelon, *n.* Sa'kayutapi ; *Y.* śpaŋ'śniyutapi.
waterpipe, *n.* Minimazoħdoġeca.
waterpot, *n.* Miniwakiśkokpa.
waterproof, *a.* Minikaħdokeśni.
waterspout, *n.* Maħpiyahomni.
watersupply, *n.* Minioicu.
waterway, *n.* Wa'tatacaŋku.
waterwheel, *n.* Minibohomni.
waterwork, *n.* Minioicukaġapi.
watery, *a.* Mini o'ta.
wattle, *n.* Iyoħaśaśa.
wave, *n.* Ta'ża : *the waves roll.* *vt.* Ko'za ; kaħboka.
waver, *vi.* Pataka ; kitaŋśni.
wavy, *a.* Mnimiża.
wax, *n.* Caŋśiŋ ; tuħmaġacesdi. *vi.* 1. Icaġa : *wax great.* 2. A'ya ; o'cim : *wax angry.*
waxy, *a.* Caŋśiŋ o'tkapa.
way, *n.* Caŋku ; wokuwa ; woiyopte. *By the way,* tahepi ; icuŋhaŋnakeś.—*By way of,* iyaopteya.—*Half-way,* cokaya.—*In many ways,* o'takiya.—*A little way,* ci'stiyedaŋ.—*A long way,* te'han.—*Out of the way,* caŋku anawam.—*To give way,* enakiya ; ksa.—*To make way,* iyopte.—*That way,* caŋku he ; he'ciya.—*Way passenger,* caŋku ihaŋke śni na'ziŋ kta.
wayfaring, *a.* I'cimaniuŋ.
waylay, *vt.* Iyape.
wayside, *n.* Caŋkuicahda.
wayward, *a.* Wanaħoŋsni ; śke'he.
wayworn, *a.* Omaniwatuka.
we, *pro.* Uŋkiyepi ; uŋkiye.
weak, *a.* Waś'akeśni ; sutaśni ; ta'kuśni ; hahadaŋ.
weaken, *vt.* Waś'akeśniya. *vi.* Waś'akeśni.
weakly, *a.* Śiħtiŋ ; wayazaŋs'a.
weakness, *n.* Wowaśakeśni.
weal, *n.* Wozani.
wealth, *n.* Wowiżice ; woyuha.
wealthy, *a.* Żi'ca ; wi'żica.
wean, *vt.* Aziŋ ayuśtaŋkiya.
weapon, *n.* Wi'pe ; ikteka.
wear, wore, worn, *vt.* 1. In ; uŋ ; otoŋ : *wore a white dress.* 2. Patani ; payeza ; pakuka. 3.

Yutakuniśni : *worn out.* *Wear off*, yutepa.—*Wear well*, te'han taŋni śni. *n.* 1. Uŋ'pi : *worse for wear.* 2. Heyake : *summer wear.*
wearily, *adv.* Watukaya.
weariness, *n.* Wowicatuka.
wearisome, *a.* Wawicatuka.
weary, *a.* Watuka ; mdo'kiṭa ; ecoŋkap'iŋ. *vt.* Watukaya. *vi.* Watuka ; kap'iŋ.
weasel, *n.* Hituŋkasaŋ.
weather, *n.* Aŋpetu to'keca ; aŋpetu ; tate. *Warm weather*, aŋpetu maśte.—*Out in the weather*, taŋkan tate kin en. *vt.* En śkaŋ ; i'tkokipa.
weave, *vt.* Kazoŋta.
weaver, *n.* Wakazoŋta.
web, *n.* Wakazoŋtapi. *Spider's web*, uŋktomi tahokata ; wahiŋpeya.
wed, *vt.* Yu'za ; wakaŋyuza ; kici i'ciyakaśka : *he is wedded to his pipe.*
wedding, *n.* Wakaŋkiciyuzapi.
wedge, *n.* Caŋicaśdeca. *vt.* En paoṭins iyeya.
wedlock, *n.* Okiciyuze.
Wednesday, *n.* Aŋpetuiyamni.
wee, *a.* Ni'na ci'stiŋna.
weed, *n.* Caŋȟdoȟu ; wato. *vt.* Caŋȟdoȟu yużuŋ.
weedy, *a.* Caŋȟdoȟu o'ta.
week, *n.* Aŋpetuwakaŋ oko ; aŋpetu śakowiŋ.
weekly, *a.* Aŋpetuśakowiŋ ca.
weep, wept, *vi.* Ce'ya ; iśtamnihaŋpe au. *Weep for*, aceya.
weigh, *vt.* 1. Tkeuta : *weigh corn.* 2. Iyukcan : *weigh his words.* 3. Tkeya waŋka : *weighs him down.*
weight, *n.* Otkeute ; tkeutapi.
weighty, *a.* Tke ; waciŋyepica.
weird, *a.* Wakaŋse.
welcome, *vt.* Iyuśkiŋ kuwa ; ikiciyuśkiŋ : *I welcome you.* *a.* Taŋ'yaŋ hi ; waśtedapi : *a welcome guest.* *n.* Wowiyuśkiŋ ; wocaŋteyuza waśte.
weld, *vt.* Ma'zaiyaskamya.
welfare, *n.* Zaniyaŋuŋpi.
well, *adv.* Taŋ'yaŋ ; caŋpteȟ ; yupiya ; aiecetu. *a.* Taŋ'yaŋ ; zani ; waśte. *n.* 1. Mniçapi ; mnioȟdogyapi : *a deep well.* 2. Oahinape ; oicu : *wells of learning.* *excl.* Eca ; huŋ'huŋhe.
well-being, *n.* Taŋ'yaŋuŋpi.
well-known, *a.* Okitaŋiŋ.
well-off, *a.* Wayuha ; taŋ'yaŋ uŋ.
well-spring, *n.* Oahinape.
welt, *n.* Oko wi'puspe.
welter, *vi.* Kadomdopa.
wench, *n.* Wiŋ'yaŋ.
wend, *vt.* Iokawiŋȟ ya.
went, *imp.* of GO.
wept, *imp.* of WEEP.
were, *imp. pl.* of BE.
west, *a.* & *n.* Wiyoȟpeyata. *West of*, i'wiyoȟpeyata.
west-bound, *a*, Wiyoȟpeyata ya.
westerly, *adv.* Wiyoȟpeyatakiya.
western, *a.* Wiyoȟpeyata.
westward, *a.* Wiyoȟpeyatakiya.
wet, *a.* 1. Spa'ya : *wet clothes.* 2. Maġażus'a : *a wet day.* *vt.* Spa'yeya. *n.* Mini ; wospaya.
wether, *n.* Ta'ȟcaśuŋka susuwanica.
whack, *vt.* Skabyeȟ apa.
whale, *n.* Hoġaŋ iyotaŋ taŋ'ka ; uŋkteȟi. *Whale-bone*, uŋkteȟi hu.
wharf, *n.* Wa'taoihuni.
what, *pro.* 1. Ta'ku : *what do you want.* 2. To'ken : *what do they call you.* 3. To'nakeca : *what is the weight.* *a.* 1. Tukte : *what boy.* 2. Ta'ku : *what rascals.* 3. Tohantu. *What time is it*, wi'hiyaye tohantu he. 4. To'na : *he gave them what chickens he had.*
whatever, *pro.* Ta'kukaśta.

whatsoever, *pro.* Ta'kukaŝta.
wheat, *n.* Aġuyapisu.
wheedle, *vt.* Iskuyakuwa.
wheel, *n.* Caŋpaḣmiḣma hu; caŋhdeŝka; ma'zamibe. *vt.* Paḣmiḣma iyeya; aohomniya. *vi.* Ohomni ya; paḣmiḣma ya.
wheelbarrow, *n.* Huwaŋżipaḣmiḣmapi.
wheeze, *vi.* Ḣmuŋyaŋ niya.
whelp, *n.* Ŝuŋḣpadaŋ.
when, *adv.* Tohan: *when I go.*—*They stayed till dark, when they went,* o'tpaza hehaŋyaŋ en uŋ'pi, hehan kihdapi.
whence, *adv.* To'kiyataŋhaŋ; totaŋhaŋ.
whenever, *adv.* Tohaŋtukaŝta.
whensoever, *adv.* Tohaŋtukaŝta.
where, *adv.* Tukten, *where are you.* — To'kiya, *where is he going.*
whereabouts, *adv.* Tuktentu.
whereas, *conj.* Nakaeŝ; caŋkedaka.
whereat, *conj.* Tukte ekta; he'oŋ.
whereby, *adv.* Ta'ku oŋ; tukte oŋ.
wherefore, *adv.* To'keca; ta'ku oŋ.
wherein, *adv.* Tukte en.
whereinsoever, *adv.* Tukteentukaŝta.
whereinto, *adv.* Tukteentu.
whereof, *adv.* Tukte etaŋhaŋ.
whereon, *adv.* Tukte akan.
wheresoever, *adv.* Tuktentukaŝta.
whereto, *adv.* Tukte ekta.
whereupon, *adv.* Ta'ku akan; iyehan.
wherever, *adv.* Tuktentukaŝta.
wherewith, *adv.* Ta'ku oŋ.
wherwithal, *adv.* Ta'ku oŋ.
whet, *vt.* Yuman; iyohdiya.
whether, *conj.* Uŋmaŋtukte: *tell us whether you are going or not.*
whetstone, *n.* Iyohdi; *Y.* miyokdi; *T.* miyogli; izuza.
whey, *n.* Asaŋpimini.
which, *pro.* Tukte: *tell which you prefer; which boy did it.*
whichever, *pro.* Tukte waŋżi.
whiff, *vt.* Ipoḣiyeya.
while, *conj.* Icuŋhaŋ: *while you are here.* *n.* Wi'hiyayedaŋ oŋŝpa: *rest a while.* *vt.* Wi'hiyaye yusota: *while away your time.*
whilst, *conj.* Icuŋhaŋ.
whim, *n.* Inaḣni tawaciŋ.
whimper, *vi.* Iyokipiŝni ia.
whimsical, *a.* Tawaciŋŝkehe.
whine, *vi.* Ho'piŋsyaceya.
whinny, *vi.* Ŝuŋ'kawakaŋhotoŋ.
whip, *n.* Icapsiŋte. *vt.* 1. Kapsiŋpsiŋta; apa: *she whipped the boy.* 2. Oḣaŋkoya icu: *whipped out a knife.* 3. Ohiya; wicakte: *our side whipped.*
whiphandle, *n.* Icapsiŋte ihupa.
whirl, *vt.* Kahomni. *vi.* Homni.
whirlpool, *n.* Miniomni.
whirlwind, *n.* Tateiyumni.
whisk, *vt.* Kahiniyeya.
whisk-broom, *n.* Wi'cahiŋtena.
whiskers, *n.* Ikuhiŋ.
whisky, *n.* Miniwakaŋ.
whisper, *vi.* Żiżi. *Whisper to,* ażiżi. *n.* Żiżipi.
whistle, *vt.* & *vi.* Żo; żożo; ḣemani hotoŋ. *n.* Yahotoŋpi; co'yatanka.
whistler, *n.* Żo'sa.
whit, *n.* Oŋŝpadaŋ; ecaca.
white, *a.* Ska. *White man,* Waŝicuŋ.—*White paint,* wi'saŋye.
whitecap, *n.* Tażabobdu.
whiten, *vt.* Ska ka'ġa.
whiteness, *n.* Ska; woska.
whitening, *n.* Oŋ yuskapi.
whitewash, *n.* Miniwisaŋye.
whither, *adv.* To'kiya.
whitish, *a.* Saŋ.
whittle, *vt.* Pażipa; yucika.
whiz, *vi.* Ḣmuŋ.
whizzing, *a.* Ḣmuŋ'yaŋ.

who, *pro. inter.* Tu′we : *who did it. pro. rel.* 1. He. *The man who gave me the book,* wicaṡta wowapi maḳu kiŋ he. 2. Tu′we. *He who did it will be sorry,* tu′we ecoŋ kiŋ he caŋteṡice kta.
whoa, *interj.* Owaŋżinażiŋ.
whoever, *pro.* Tu′wekaṡta.
whole, *a.* 1. A′taya ; ocowasin : *I want the whole hog.* 2. Zani : *they that are whole.*
wholeness, *n.* Ecaataya.
wholesale, *a.* 1. Opiye a′taya wi′yopeyapi : *a wholesale store.* 2. Ad′ataya : *a wholesale slaughter.*
wholesome, *a.* Owicawaṡte.
wholly, *adv.* 1. A′taya : *he is wholly ignorant.* 2. Heceedaŋ : *it was not wholly ignorance.*
whom, *objective* of WHO. Tu′we ; he.
whoop, *n.* I′yaki′ṡapi.
whooping-cough, *n.* Niyaṡni hoḣpapi.
whop, *vi.* Yuptaŋyaŋ.
whopping, *a.* Hiŋ′skotaŋka.
whore, *n.* Witkowiŋ.
whortleberry, *n.* Ha′za.
whose, *pos. pro.* Tu′we ta′wa.
whosoever, *pro.* Tu′we kaṡta.
why, *adv.* & *conj.* To′keca ; to′ka.
wick, *n.* Petiżaŋżaŋhaḣoŋta.
wicked, *a.* Ṡi′ca ; wicaṡtaṡni.
wickedly, *adv.* Sicaya.
wickedness, *n.* Woṡice ; woahtani ; ta′ku ṡi′ca.
wicker, *a.* Caŋyaŋkapi.
wickiup, *n.* Caŋsakawakeya.
wide, *a.* 1. Hdakiŋyaŋtaŋka ; taŋ′ka, *a wide river.* 2 Hdakiŋyaŋ, *a foot wide. adv.* 1. Taŋ′kaya : *spread wide.* 2. I′tehaŋ : *he shot wide of the mark.*
wide-awake, *a.* Mde′za ; waktapi.
widely, *adv.* Taŋ′kaya.
widen, *vt.* Yutaŋka.
wideness, *n.* Woptecaṡni.
widow, *n.* Wiwazica.
widower, *n.* Wicawiwazica.
width, *n.* Ohdakiŋyaŋ.
wield, *vt.* Uŋ ; yuha.
wife, *n.* Tawicu. *My wife,* mitawiŋ.—*Your wife,* nitawiŋ.
wig, *n.* Wicapahakaġapi.
wiggle, *vi.* Yupsaŋpsaŋ.
wiggle-tail, *n.* Capoŋkaciŋca.
wigwam, *n.* Tiikceka.
wild, *a.* 1. Ikceuŋ : *a wild hog.* 2. Watoghda : *his horse is wild ; a wild Indian.* 3. Wohitika ; otaŋtoŋka : *a wild storm.* 4. Mde′zeṡni : *wild with delight ; wild speculation.* 5. Iwiciŋṡniyaŋ : *wild of the mark.*
wild, *n.* Makoce ikceka.
wildcat, *n.* Inmu ; inmutaŋka.
wilderness, *n.* Ḣe′makoskan ; ḣewoskan.
wildly, *adv.* Watoghdaya.
wilful, *a.* 1. Tawaciŋ suta. 2. I′ye ciŋ ecoŋ : *wilful mischief.*
wilfully, *adv.* Ṡicawaciŋ ecoŋ.
wilfulness, *n.* Ṡicawaciŋpi.
will, *n.* 1. Tawaciŋ : *thy will be done.* 2. Wocaŋteyuza : *his will is right.* 3. Ecoŋwaciŋpi : *he works with a will. vi. sign of future.* Kta : *I will go. vt.* 1. Koŋ′za ; waciŋyuza : *God willed that there should be light.* 2. Ḳu ; tohaŋ i′ye ṭe ciŋhaŋ yuha kta keya : *he willed the horse to his son.*
willing, *a.* Wicada ; iyowiŋyaŋ.
willow, *n.* Coḣwaŋżica ; waḣpopa.
wilt, *2d pers. sing.* of WILL. Kta. *vi.* Ṡe′ca a′ya : *the leaves wilt.*
wily, *a.* Wicahnayes′a.
win, won, *vt.* Ohiya.
wince, *vi.* Napa ; naṭuŋka.
wind, *n.* 1. Tate : *a cold wind.* 2. Oniya : *took his wind.* 3. Woomna ; wosdonye : *the police got wind of the thief. vt.* 1. Iyapehaŋ : *wind the thread.* 2. Yu-

homni: *wind the clock.* 3. Yukšaŋkšaŋ ya: *he winds through the woods.*
windbreak, *n.* Tatewakaġiye.
windbroken, *a.* Oniyašica.
windfall, *n.* 1. Tatekawaŋka. 2. Ta'ku aiḣpekiyapi.
winding, *a.* Kšaŋ.
windlass, *n.* Ayuhomnipi.
windmill, *n.* Tateyuhomni.
window, *n.* Owaŋyeye; *Y.* o'żaŋżaŋkdepi; *T.* o'żaŋżaŋglepi.
windpipe, *n.* Dotehbeze; *Y.* dotekbeze; *T.* glogleska.
windrow, *n.* Peżi; caŋkuyeżupi.
windward, *a.* Tatoheya.
windy, *a.* 1. Tate: *a windy day.* 2. Ta'ku ka taŋiŋ šni: *a windy talk.*
wine, *n.* Minišа.
wing, *n.* 1. Ḣupahu. 2. Ti'pi oŋšpa aka'ġapi. *vt.* Kiŋyaŋ ya.
winged, *a.* Ḣupahutoŋ.
wink, *vi.* Ištakakpaŋ. *n.* Ištakakpaŋpi.
Winnebago, *n.* Hotaŋ'ke.
winner, *n.* Tu'we ohiya.
winning, *a.* 1. Ohiya: *the winning horse.* 2. Oiyokipi: *winning ways.* *n.* Wakamnapi.
winnow, *vt.* Kaduġa.
winsome, *a.* Oḣaŋ wašte.
winter, *n.* Waniyetu: *a cold winter.* *a.*Waniyetu: *winter clothes.* *vt.* Waniyetu awaŋyaka: *I wintered ten cows.* *vi.* Waniyetu uŋ: *winter in the South.*
wintry, *a.* Waniyetu.
wipe, *vt.* Pakiŋta; apawiŋta.
wire, *n.* Ma'zapsoŋpsoŋna. *vt.* 1. Ma'za oŋ yuskiskita. 2. Mazakipe.
wiry, *a.* 1. Suta; wakišaka: *a wiry little man.* 2. Ma'zapsoŋpsoŋna se'ca: *wiry hair.*
wisdom, *n.* Woksape.
wise, *a.* 1. Ksa'pa: *a wise king.* 2. Woksape: *wise sayings,* woksape iapi. *n.* Woecoŋ: *in any wise.*
wisely, *adv.* Ksamya.
wish, *vt.* 1. Ciŋ: *I wish father would come.* 2. Uŋ'kaŋš eciŋ: *I wish it was day.* 3. Ciŋkiya: *I wish you good-night.* *n.* Ta'ku ciŋ'pi.
wishful, *a.* Caŋtiheya; ciŋ.
wishfully, *adv.* Caŋtiheyaken.
wishy-washy, *a.* Takumnašni.
wisp, *n.* Peżiopaḣte.
wist, *imp.* of WIT. Sdonya.
wistful, *a.* Sdonyewaciŋ.
wistfully, *adv.* Awaciŋken.
wit, *n.* Wowiḣa; wokaḣniġe; tawaciŋ. *To wit,* iokawiŋḣ de'cetu.
witch, *n.* Tu'we wakaŋkaŋ; wiŋ'yaŋ wicaḣmuŋġa.
witchcraft, *n.* Wicaḣmuŋġapi.
with, *prep.* 1. Kici: *eat with him.* 2. Om: *eat with them.* 3. Oŋ: *cut with a knife; silent with shame.* 4. Yuha: *a horse with horns.* 5. Iyaḣna: *his infirmities increase with his years.*— 6. Ekta: *with Indians time is of no value.*
withal, *adv.* Ko'ya.
withdraw, withdrew, *vt.* E'hdaku: *he withdrew the troops.* *vi.* Hdicu; tokaŋ iyaye: *he withdrew.*
withe, *n.* Caŋsakadaŋ; coḣwaŋżica.
wither, *vi.* Šni'za. *vt.* Yušniża.
withered, *pa.* Šni'ża; še'ca.
withers, *n.* Amdoiŋkpa
withold, *vt.* Ipida; anica.
within, *prep.* 1. Mahed: *within the house.* 2. I'tato; itahena: *within ten days.* *adv.* Mahen.
without, *prep.* 1. Taŋkan; i'taŋkan: *without the gate.* 2. Co'daŋ: *without money.*
withstand, *vt.* I'tkokipa; he'cehna uŋ.

witless, *vt.* Waciŋksapeśni.
witness, *vt.* 1. Waŋyaka : *witness a battle.* 2. Yataŋiŋ : *he witnessed against him.* *n.* Wayaataŋiŋ.
wittily, *adv.* Wowiȟaya.
wittingly, *adv.* Amdesya.
witty, *a.* Wawiȟaye.
wives, *n.* *Plural* of WIFE.
wizard, *n.* Wicaȟmuŋġa.
woe, *n.* Woiyokiśica.
wo-be-gone, *a.* A'śinya uŋ.
woful, *a.* Oiyokiśica.
woke, *imp.* of WAKE.
wolf, wolves, *n.* Śuŋktokeca; śuŋgmanitu.
wolfish, *a.* Śuŋktokecase.
woman, women, *n.* Winoȟiŋca; *Y.* & *T.* wiŋ'yaŋ. *A young woman; S.* & *Y.* Wikośka; *T.* wikośkalaka. *An old woman,* wakaŋka; *Y.* & *T.* winoȟca.
womb, *n.* Tamni; tezi.
won, *imp.* of WIN.
wonder, *vi.* 1. Inihaŋ : *I wondered at the sight.* 2. To'keca eciŋ : *do you wonder why I came.* *n.* Wowinihaŋ.
wonderful, *a.* Wowinihaŋ.
wondrous, *a.* Woyuśiŋyaŋ.
won't, *contr.* of WILL NOT.
wont, *vt.* Ecewakta. *n.* Oȟaŋ.
woo, *vt.* Okiya; wiokiya.
wood, *n.* Caŋ; coŋ'taŋka.
woodchuck, *n.* Haŋkaśa.
wooden, *a.* Caŋ; caŋ se.
woodpecker, *n.* Kaŋketaŋka.
woodwork, *n.* Caŋ oŋ ka'ġapi.
woody, *a.* Caŋ etanhaŋ.
woof, *n.* Haȟoŋta hdakiŋyaŋ.
wool, *n.* Ta'ȟcahiŋ; hiŋ'yumnimniża.
woolen, *a.* Ta'ȟcaȟiŋ.
woolly, *a.* Yumnimniża.
word, *n.* Iapi; wicoie. *vt.* Wicoie ka'ga : *he worded it well.*—*Send word to,* iwahoya.—*Word by word,* iapi iyohi.
wordy, *a.* Iapi o'ta; iapi ece.
wore, *imp.* of WEAR. Uŋ.
work, *vi.* 1. Ḣtani; wowaśi ecoŋ : *work for a living.* 2. A'ya : *the fire worked down.* 3. Śkumna a'ya; napoȟ a'ya : *the cider works.* *vt.* 1. Kuwa; kicaŋyaŋ; *work a farm.* 2. Ḣtanikiya : *work his horse.* 3. Ecoŋkiya : yuhomni; yuśkaŋśkaŋ; *work a machine.* 4. Ecoŋ : *work iniquity.* 5. Ka'ġa; icaȟya : *faith worked patience.*—*Work oneself into a passion,* caŋniyeiçiya. *n.* 1. Wicoȟaŋ; *Y.* & *T.* wowaśi; woȟtani : *he wants work.* 2. Woecoŋ; wokaġe; ta'ku ecoŋ; ta'ku ka'ġe : *the works of God.* 3. Ma'zayuhomni : *the works of a watch.*
workable, *a.* Kuwapica; kuwa okihi.
worker, *n.* Tu'we ȟtani; wowaśi.
working, *pa.* Ḣtani; wowaśi ecoŋ. *n.* 1. Woecoŋ : *the workings of the mind.* 2. Śkumna a'ye.
workman, *n.* Wicawowaśi.
workshop, *n.* Wokaġetipi.
world, *n.* 1. Maka : makamibe : *the world and all therein.* 2. Makawita : *the Old World.* 3. Makata wicaśta : *all the world knows.* 4. Wicobe : *the scientific world.* 5. Ouŋcaġe; okaġe : *the animal world.* 6. Oyate; wicaśta : *the world smiles.* 7. Oni; makata wiconi : *begin the world anew.* 8. Woptecaśni; ni'na o'ta : *a world of trouble.*
wordly, *a.* Makata.
worm, *n.* Wamdudaŋ; wamduśkadaŋ; oyuhbeza. *vt.* En ihdusdohaŋ.
wormy, *a.* Waŋmdudaŋ yukaŋ.
worn, *pa.* Patanipi; owihaŋkeyapi.
worry, *vt.* Naġiyeya; kakiśya.

vi. Icaŋteśica. *n.* Wonaġiyeya; naġiyeiçiyapi.
worse, *a.* & *adv.* Saŋ'pa si'ca.
worship, *vt.* Ce'kiya; ohoda. *vi.* Wacekiya. *n.* Wocekiye; woohoda; wacekiyapi.
worshipful, *a.* Okinihaŋ.
worst, *vt.* Kte'daŋ; ohiya; yuśica. *a.* Iyotaŋ śi'ca; iyotaŋ teḣika.
worth, *a.* 1. Iyokihi iyecetu: *the dog is worth ten dollars, but you can't get it for him.* 2. Woyuha yuha: *died worth a million.* 3. Iyececa: *worth going to see.* *n.* Iyokihi iyecetu; wowaśte yuha.
worthily, *adv.* Iyecetuya.
worthless, *a.* Ta'kudaŋ on waśteśni.
worthy, *a.* Wowaśte yuha; waśte. *Worthy of,* oŋ waśte; yuha iyececa.
would, *imp.* of WILL. 1. Kta: *he said he would go.* 2. Ciŋ: *I would know the truth.* 3. Kta tuka: *he would come if he could.* 4. Kta kitaŋ; kta ḣca: *it stormed but she would go.*
wound, *vt.* 1. O; tao: *he wounded the deer.* 2. Caŋteśinya; kiuŋniyaŋ. *n.* Oo; oyazaŋ.
wound, *imp.* of WIND. Iyapehaŋ.
wrangle, *vi.* Iaakinica.
wrangler, *n.* Waakinicas'a.
wrap, *vt.* Iyapemni; paḣta; yuwi; he'yuŋ; iyapehaŋ. *n.* Oŋ iyapeiçihaŋpi; śina; hiyete akaḣpe.
wrapper, *n.* Akaḣpe; oẓuha.
wrapping, *n.* Apaḣte.
wrath, *n.* Wocaŋniye.
wrathy, *a.* Caŋniyaŋ.
wrathful, *a.* Caŋniyeḣca.
wreak, *vt.* Ahiŋheya.
wreath, *n.* Oyuwi; teśdake.
wreathe, *vt.* Yuwi.
wreck, *vt,* Ihaŋgya; yutakuniśni. *n.* Ihaŋgyapi; ta'kuniśni.
wren, *n.* Pteġanicadaŋ.
wrench, *n.* Yuhomni iyuśdoke. *vt.* Yukśaŋ; naġuka; yukabicu.
wrest, *vt.* Yuśpa; yutokeca.
wrestle, *vi.* Kaḣo ecoŋ.
wretch, *n.* Tu'we śi'ca; waḣteśni.
wretched, *a.* 1. Oŋ'śika: *a wretched man.* 2. Oiyokiśica: *a wretched day.* 3. Śi'ca: *a wretched bed.*
wriggle, *vi.* Yukśaŋkśaŋ ya.
wring, *vt.* Yuśkica.
wringer, *n.* Wi'yuśkice.
wrinkle, *n.* Yuśiŋpi; iyupiẓa; yuśkipi. *vt.* Yuśiŋśiŋ.
wrist, *n.* Napokaśke.
wristband, *n.* Napokaśke apaḣte.
writ, *n.* Wowapi.
write, wrote, written, *vt.* Owa; ka'ġa. *vt.* Wowapi ka'ga. *Can you write,* wowapi yakaġa oyakihi he.—*I want you to write a letter for me,* wowapi miyecicaġa wacin.—*Write for,* kicicaġa.—*Write to,* ki'caġa.
writer, *n.* Ka'ġa; wowapi ka'ġa.
writhe, *vi.* Yutimtipa.
writing, *n.* Owapi; wowapi; wowapikaġapi.
writing-paper, *n.* Wowapiska.
wrong, *a.* 1. He'cetuśni: *a wrong answer.* 2. He'eśni: *the wrong road.* 3. Owotaŋa śni: *a wrong act.*—*Turn it wrong side out,* yueci. *vt.* Owotaŋna ecakicoŋśni.—*Wrong one out of,* ki. *n.* Woowotaŋnaśni. *adv.* Eciŋśniyaŋ.
wrongful, *a.* Śi'ca.
wrongfully, *adv.* Śicaya.
wrote, *imp.* of WRITE.
wrought, *vt.* Ecoŋ; kuwa.
wrung, *imp.* of WRING.
wry, *a.* Ḣmin; kśaŋ.

Y

yacht, *n*. Miniwaŋca wa'tadaŋ.
Yankee, *n. pr.* Isaŋtaŋkaȟca.
Yankton, *n. pr.* (*Indian*) Ihaŋktoŋwaŋ.
Yankton, *n. pr.* (*City*) Śadotoŋwe.
Yankton Agency, *n. pr.* Ihaŋktoŋwaŋ Owakpamni.
Yanktonais, *n. pr.* Ihaŋktoŋwaŋna; Huŋkpati.
yard, *n*. 1. No'ġeiyutayi; cahdepi; sihaiyutapi yamni: *a yard of cloth*. 2. Caŋhdakiŋyaŋ: *the yard was too short for the sail*. 3. Tiokśaŋ; ti'pi acaŋkaśkapi: *you have nice grass in your yard*. —*Barn-yard*, wanuyaŋpi acaŋkaśkapi. — *Brick-yard*, makaśpaŋ ka'ġapi owaŋka.
yardstick, *n*. Miniȟuha iyutapi.
yarn, *n*. 1. Wapaȟmuŋpi: *a ball of yarn*. 2. Ohuŋkahaŋ: *the boys were telling yarns*.
yawl, *n*. Wa'tadaŋ: *two men rowed the yawl*.
yawn, *vi*. Iyowa.
ye, *pro*. Niyepi.
yea, *adv*. Haŋ; ho.
year, *n*. Wi'akenoŋpa; waniyetu; o'maka.—*Three years*, waniyetu ya'mni.
yearling, *n*. Makicima; ecenica.
yearly, *adv*. Waniyetu iyohi.
yearn, *vi*. Caŋtokpani.
yeast, *n*. Wi'napoȟye.
yell, *vi*. Paŋ; i'yaś'a; hotoŋ.
yellow, *a*. Zi.
yelp, *vi*. Hotoŋ; paŋ.
yeoman, *n*. Wicaśta makoce yuha.
yes, *adv*. Haŋ; ho; toś.
yesterday, *adv*. Ḣtanihaŋ.
yet, *adv*. Nahaŋȟiŋ; ehake; he'caśta.—*He is sleeping yet*, nahaŋȟiŋ iśtiŋma.—*Not yet*, nahaŋȟiŋkeśni.—*Yet a little while*, ehake ci'stiŋna.—*Yet he will go*, he'caśta ye kta. *conj*. Tuka.—*Willing yet unable*, wicada tka okihiśni.
yield, *vt*. Icaġa; ḳu.—*It yielded tenfold*, wikcemna akihde icaġa. *vi*. Iyowiŋyaŋ; iciçu; kiyukaŋ.
yoke, *n*. Caŋ'wanapiŋ; woȟtani. —*A yoke of oxen*, tataŋka akicaśka. *vt*. Ikoyagya: *yoke the oxen*.
yolk, *n*. Itkazica.
yon, *a*. Ka; ka'e.
yonder, *a*. Ka; kana.—*Over yonder*, ka'kiya.
yore, *adv*. Ehaŋna.
you, *pro*. Ni'ye. *pl*. Niyepi.
young, *a*. Aśkatudaŋ; decana; te'ca. *n*. Ciŋca.
younger, *a*. Hakakta; aśkatudaŋ.
youngest, *a*. Iyotaŋ ci'stiŋna; hakaktaȟca.
youngster, *n*. Tu'we aśkatudaŋ.
your, *pro*. Nitawa; ni'ye nitawa.
yourself, *pro*. Niyeȟca.
yourselves, *pro. pl*. Niyepiȟca.
youth, *n*. Kośka; wikośka; waniyetu tonana.
youthful, *a*. Wicakośka.

Z

zeal, *n*. Wooȟitika; ni'na kuwapi.
zealot, *n*. Tu'we oȟitiya śkaŋ.
zealous, *a*. Ni'na śkaŋ.
zealously, *adv*. Mdiheṇya.
zebra, *n*. Śuŋgḣdezedan.
zenith, *n*. Maȟpiyapesdete,
zephyr, *n*. Tateowaśteca.
zero, *n*. Osniocoka; ta'kuśni.
zest, *n*. Woiyokipi.
zigzag, *adv*. Yuktaŋktaŋ.
zinc, *n*. Ma'zato.
Zion, *n. pr*. Davidtoti; Pahawakaŋ.
zone, *n*. Makaipiyake.
zoology, *n*. Wamakaśkaŋ wooŋspe.